Dimensions of Inequality in Canada..........

Equality
Security
Community

The Equality, Security, and Community (ESC) project, conducted during a
six-year period, was conceived as a multidisciplinary collaborative research
project. Its objectives were concisely described in its subtitle: "Explaining
and Improving the Distribution of Well-Being in Canada." *Explaining the
distribution of well-being* requires a concerted multidisciplinary effort that
considers the interplay among market behaviour, political and community
participation, and policy formation. *Improving the distribution* requires effective and durable policies, which, in turn, must be based on sound theoretical and empirical foundations. Using a wide range of research
methodologies, the ESC project sheds light on these complex issues, while
it advances our ability to steer public policies toward improved outcomes.

Numerous journal articles and book chapters have resulted from the
ESC project. Another major product is a unique national longitudinal survey of Canadians that covers the economic, political, cultural, and attitudinal bases of inequality. This database was analyzed by project co-investigators
and has been posted for research by others (on the website of York
University's Institute for Social Research).

Dimensions of Inequality in Canada is one of three edited volumes stemming from the ESC project. The other two volumes are:

Racing to the Bottom? Provincial Interdependence in the Canadian Federation
Edited by Kathryn Harrison

Social Capital, Diversity, and the Welfare State
Edited by Fiona Kay and Richard Johnston

All three volumes are published by UBC Press.

Dimensions of Inequality in Canada

...... Edited by David A. Green and
Jonathan R. Kesselman

UBCPress · Vancouver · Toronto

15 14 13 12 11 10 09 08 07 06   5 4 3 2 1

Printed in Canada on ancient-forest-free paper (100% post-consumer recycled) that is processed chlorine- and acid-free, with vegetable-based inks.

Library and Archives Canada Cataloguing in Publication

Dimensions of inequality in Canada / edited by David A. Green and Jonathan R. Kesselman

(Equality, security, community, ISSN 1715-8117)
Includes bibliographical references and index.
ISBN-13: 978-0-7748-1207-8
ISBN-10: 0-7748-1207-9

1. Equality – Canada. I. Kesselman, Jonathan R., 1946- II. Green, David A. (David Alan). III. Series.

HN110.Z9S6 2006   305.0971   C2006-903636-5

Canadä

UBC Press gratefully acknowledges the financial support for our publishing program of the Government of Canada through the Book Publishing Industry Development Program (BPIDP), and of the Canada Council for the Arts, and the British Columbia Arts Council.

The authors acknowledge, with thanks, the financial support of the Social Sciences and Humanities Research Council of Canada through a Major Collaborative Research Initiatives Grant (#412-97-0003).

This book has been published with the help of a grant from the Canadian Federation for the Humanities and Social Sciences, through the Aid to Scholarly Publications Programme, using funds provided by the Social Sciences and Humanities Research Council of Canada.

UBC Press
The University of British Columbia
2029 West Mall
Vancouver, BC V6T 1Z2
www.ubcpress.ca

•••• *This volume is dedicated to the memories of Ellen Gee and Jim Curtis. Ellen and Jim were leading Canadian sociologists who made substantial contributions to our understanding of inequalities in Canadian society. Fortunately for all those who read this volume, they devoted some of their considerable expertise to it. Our sadness at their parting is tempered by our gratitude for what they left behind.*

Contents

Figures and Tables

Dimensions of Inequality in Canada ....

1

Dimensions of Inequality in a Just Society

David A. Green and Jonathan R. Kesselman

Inequality in economic and social outcomes is pivotal in the politics, public policy, and justice of a society. The many dimensions of inequality in Canada are analyzed in this volume by researchers from economics, sociology, political science, and philosophy.[1] Their studies examine what is known about Canadian inequality, adding to the evidence, identifying research gaps, and suggesting policies for reducing inequality. A wide variety of conceptual, analytical, and statistical approaches are employed in the studies. Inequality is measured in income, consumption, political participation, social exclusion, income mobility, earnings, work hours, and health. Inequality is seen to vary with gender, ethnicity, skill and education level, employment status, and family status. Data deficiencies and potential biases of research methodology are identified and assessed. The studies combine to give a detailed picture of inequality in Canada, a better understanding of its causes, and insights into the impacts of policies designed to affect it. They take a large step toward establishing a sounder basis for choosing future policies to create a more just society.

Establishing the Framework: Why Study Inequality?

In any measurement exercise, one needs first to decide on the questions being asked. Only then can we choose appropriate variables to measure, how to measure them, and what statistics to build from them. In these respects, Chapter 2 by Colin Macleod and Avigail Eisenberg offers a basic foundation for the rest of the volume. The authors argue that understanding equality is important on two grounds. First, justice is fundamentally egalitarian in nature. Recent political philosophy, they say, holds that a just society is morally impartial, that is, it accords equal moral standing to all its members. Second, justice has a special status among standards for judging society's institutions.

In the well-known phrase of philosopher John Rawls, "justice is the first virtue of social institutions." Macleod and Eisenberg argue that, from an eqalitarian point of view, "fundamental equality is not a value that can be balanced against other values such as efficiency, stability, productivity, community, or even individual liberty ... Their accommodation occurs within equality itself rather than in any form of compromise between themselves and equality" (35). So equality is of central importance and deserves study on its own merits, not as an adjunct to the maximization of efficiency.

This position is the starting point for the current volume. All the chapters take inequality as their central focus. Most of them examine direct measures of inequality of outcomes, and this introductory chapter relates their findings. In a larger sense, placing the research results in light of the concepts set out by Macleod and Eisenberg, this chapter considers whether Canada could be deemed a just society, or, more manageably, whether Canada was becoming a more just society in the past two decades.

Macleod and Eisenberg go on to observe that moral impartiality need not imply complete equality of measured outcomes. The forms of equality and inequality in modern societies are complex. Economists and other social scientists are likely most familiar with notions of distributive justice associated with forms of welfarism. In this context, one can imagine moving directly from considerations of equality of welfare or opportunity for welfare to equality of income or consumption. However, Macleod and Eisenberg observe that, in the "resourcist" approaches that are at the forefront of recent political philosophy, the goal is somewhat subtler: to provide persons "with a fair share of the resources that can contribute to the formation and successful implementation of life plans. In effect, the problem of determining how resources should be distributed focuses on determining what share of resources each person is entitled to receive in pursuit of his or her conception of the good" (43). Macleod and Eisenberg recommend that we take this kind of resourcist approach rather than a traditional welfarist approach to equality.

Taking a resourcist approach has two implications for measurement. First, we are less interested in whether society has equalized the direct inputs to individual utility than in whether society has provided individuals with the resources needed to form and pursue reasonable conceptions of what is good. This could mean, for example, that equality of access to education is of paramount importance even after taking account of the added income and utility from knowledge that extra education might bring. Equality of social status and access to influencing the political decisions of society also may be of

importance over and above any direct impacts on utility. Thus, simple measures of the level of inequality are only a starting point; we need to consider
how inequality in any dimension affects abilities to make and pursue life
plans.

The second implication of the resourcist approach is that the list of resources in which we want to examine levels of inequality is potentially large.
The list includes measures of income and consumption, to be sure, but it
also includes, in Rawls's view, "liberty, opportunity, power and prerogatives
of office, the social basis of self-respect." Macleod and Eisenberg note that
even this list is too restrictive if cultural identity is crucial for accessing and
appreciating other opportunities. An attempt to encompass this broader array of resources is reflected in the many dimensions of inequality described
in the chapters of this book.

Even on an expanded list of outcomes, however, making comparisons
among notional individuals is only part of the answer. As Macleod and
Eisenberg point out, such comparisons assume that individuals have equal
abilities to use opportunities. They assume an idealized, autonomous individual making rational choices. Feminist critiques of this model argue that
women, who more often than men assume the role of caregivers, tend not to
fit the idealized mould. Whereas theory and measurement typically consider
outcomes in the public sphere, for many women the relevant interactions
and outcomes are disproportionately in the private or family sphere, where
they provide care and homemaking. One obvious implication is that women
and men should be examined separately. Another is that, by extension, we
should pay special attention to all those who do not fit the mould of the
idealized individual: dependants as well as non-commercial caregivers.
Chapter 8 addresses this issue directly by examining outcomes for children.
Chapter 11 looks explicitly at inequality outcomes for women. Furthermore,
at least some of the analysis should be based at the level of the family, rather
than the head of household, as the relevant unit operating in the public sphere.
Understanding movements in inequality at the family level requires further
investigation of individual market outcomes, how resources are distributed
within families, and how decisions are made for family formation and composition.

Similar arguments about appropriate measurement choices can be made
with respect to cultural minorities. Macleod and Eisenberg discuss a literature that argues that standard liberal theory undervalues the importance of
culture in framing and evaluating choices. They suggest that it is particularly

important to understand not only the outcomes for minority groups but also the role of culture in affecting those outcomes. Chapter 9 addresses these questions in depth.

Inequality, poverty, and social exclusion are not just issues of political philosophy but also matters of great concern for the public at large. These aspects of socioeconomic outcomes are crucial for assessing the performance of any society. The United Nations Human Development Index (2003) ranks countries' development on a wider basis than average incomes. On that index, Canada has often ranked higher than other countries with higher levels of per capita income; indeed, for the seven years prior to 2001 Canada ranked in first place among all nations. Comparisons of Canada with the United States on the basis of average incomes yield an incomplete picture of the relative well-being of large parts of the populations in the two countries. For example, in 1995 the lower half of Canadian families by income had greater purchasing power than the counterpart ranking of American families (Wolfson and Murphy 1998); the higher overall average incomes in the United States stemmed from a concentration of earnings among the wealthy in the upper part of the distribution. In recent years analysts have also developed broader measures of economic well-being than average incomes to include factors such as inequality, poverty, and insecurity (Osberg and Sharpe 2002).

Establishing the Patterns of Inequality

OVERALL PATTERNS IN INEQUALITY

To assess the justness of our society we need to understand what patterns of inequality exist and how they arose. The latter is particularly important because, as Macleod and Eisenberg state, moral impartiality does not require perfect equality in outcomes. Not all inequality is undesirable, and an understanding of the reasons for the various forms of inequality is crucial. Most studies in this volume look at the origins of the types of inequality being examined.

Our discussion of patterns of inequality begins with the most common and encompassing measure – income. In Chapter 3, Marc Frenette, David Green, and Garnett Picot use a variety of data sources to examine movements in income inequality in Canada over the last two decades, with emphasis on the most recent years. They make families their unit of analysis, converting incomes for different-sized family units to a comparable basis by using an adult-equivalent-income measure. Their findings for the 1980s support those of several earlier studies. When cyclically similar years are compared, inequality increased substantially in that decade in pre-tax, pre-transfer (or market) income (which includes paid employment earnings, self-employment earnings, and investment income). But inequality actually declined slightly in after-tax, after-transfer (or disposable) income. Thus, the tax and transfer system was effective during the 1980s in undoing market-driven increases in inequality.[2] Market income inequality rose strongly during the recession in the early years of the decade and then in the subsequent boom declined, though not to pre-recession levels. During the recession, the tax and transfer system largely offset for disposable income the increases in market income inequality.

Income inequality patterns in the 1990s appear similar to those in the 1980s if one uses the standard survey data sources employed in earlier studies. Increases in market income inequality in the depth of the early 1990s recession were offset to some extent by the tax and transfer system. Market income inequality again fell in the subsequent boom. The main difference between the decades is that the tax and transfer system during the 1990s recession actually generated *increases* in inequality, which then declined with the boom in the second half of the 1990s. However, Frenette, Green, and Picot argue that the standard survey data (in particular the Survey of Consumer Finances or SCF), while providing an accurate picture of inequality patterns in the 1980s, in the 1990s severely under-represents the level and increase in inequality both before and after taxes and transfers. Using a combination of tax and Census data, they find that the standard surveys undercount people at the bottom of the income distribution. Thus, the standard surveys represent the 1990s as a decade in which the top of the distribution witnessed strong increases in market income while the bottom of the distribution experienced more moderate increases. The tax and Census data agree with the survey data about increases in market income at the top of the distribution but, in contrast, show dramatic declines in average income at the bottom. Moreover, while the survey data show market income inequality declining in the latter half of the decade, the tax data indicate that, for those at the bottom, the decline in average income and increasing inequality continued throughout the decade. The tax and Census data agree with the survey data that, during the early 1990s recession, the tax and transfer system partly offset the market income inequality increases but, in contrast, show that the tax and transfer system actually accentuated increases in inequality in the subsequent boom. Frenette, Green, and Picot hypothesize that the perverse effect of the tax and transfer system in the latter half of the 1990s could have been related to major reforms in the unemployment insurance program and in many provincial social assistance systems.

Overall, Frenette, Green, and Picot find that income inequality among families increased substantially in the 1990s, particularly among families with children. The growth of inequality reflected strong increases in income at the top and strong decreases in income at the bottom of the distribution. It is interesting to consider these patterns in light of John Rawls's Difference Principle: inequality is acceptable to the extent that it improves outcomes for the least well-off in society. As we will discuss below, one might reasonably see the increased market incomes for top earners, and, indeed, movements in inequality in general, as reflections of a process of technological change that ultimately raises at least the average standard of living. But the absolute declines in real market incomes at the bottom of the distribution contradict the Difference Principle. Of course, societies create redistributive institutions to convert the outcomes of efficiency improvements such as technological change into outcomes that fit with their notions of justice. In the 1980s, the Canadian tax and transfer system did this by converting increases in market income inequality into declines in disposable income inequality. In the 1990s, however, changes in the tax and transfer system accentuated inequality trends, and people at the bottom of the disposable income distribution on average faced real declines. It is hard to see how Canadian institutions and changes in them in the 1990s met the basic requirements of any of the theories of justice discussed in Chapter 2.

Frenette, Green, and Picot observe how cross-sectional measures of inequality in earnings and income change over time. However, cross-sectional income inequality can misrepresent true inequality patterns in an economy and may not provide enough information in strictly economic terms to allow judgments about a society's attainment of justice. This critical view is argued cogently in Chapter 4 by Charles Beach and in Chapter 5 by Tom Crossley and Krishna Pendakur. They advance two principal objections. First, earnings and income change over the life cycle as individuals move from investing in skills to earning full returns on those skills to retiring. A given level of cross-sectional inequality would not be troubling if, for example, the low end of the income distribution consisted of younger individuals who were taking reduced earnings in order to learn skills. In such a situation, movements in cross-sectional inequality across years might merely reflect demographic shifts such as those associated with the movement of the baby boom through the age structure. Second, there may be a natural amount of "churning" in the income distribution, with individuals constantly facing temporary shocks that move them up or down the distribution. Thus, a cross-sectional distribution that includes a given level of poverty would be more acceptable if everyone took turns moving briefly through poverty than if one group was chronically poor.

In Chapter 4, Beach tackles the churning issue, measuring how people move through the Canadian earnings distribution over time. He does this by dividing taxpayers into six earnings categories and then computing the probability that over a period of time a person moves from one category to another or stays put. Of greatest interest here are the probabilities associated with the periods 1982-1990 and 1991-99, presented separately for men and women. Those measurements clearly do not support an extreme churning model in which everyone faces the risk or hope of moving just about anywhere in the distribution. For males, for example, the probability is less than 2 in 100 that someone who is in the highest earnings category (earnings over 200 percent above the median) in 1982 will be found in the lowest category (earning less than 25 percent of the median) in 1990. At the other extreme, the probability is only 6 in 100 that a male in the lowest category in 1982 will be found in the highest category in 1990. Overall, Beach finds a high degree of immobility, that is, most people stay put in their original earning category. As Beach argues, this finding is directly relevant to discussions of equality of opportunity in Canadian society. Immobility suggests that we are not performing well in terms of providing everyone with the resources needed for an equal chance to pursue their notion of the good. It also relates to theories of justice that emphasize equal dignity for all members of society. You are more likely to regard someone as an equal if you know there is a good chance you could have an income as high – or as low – as theirs in a few years. But what about choice of lifestyle? Perhaps one's income level simply reflects the value one places on what money can buy? In that case, even a highly immobile population, as represented by Beach's estimates, may reflect a just society if people's material preferences diverge sharply. But it takes very little observation of Canadian society to conclude that free choice is not the source of the immobility represented here.

Differences in earnings mobility between men and women cast an interesting light on the earlier discussion of justice. Beach found that women are generally less mobile than men and when mobile more likely to move down the distribution. This may imply that women have fewer opportunities. Beach hypothesizes that women's greater downward mobility may involve moving to part-time work while taking care of children. If true, this ties in with the discussion of feminist notions of justice by Macleod and Eisenberg. If this pattern represented a rational choice by individual women in circumstances similar to those of men, it would not represent an injustice. But if it reflects a society that talks the language of equal opportunity while undervaluing resources and choices available for bearing and raising children, the difference in mobility would indeed be unfair.

Clearly some interpretation is involved in drawing conclusions about fairness from estimates of earnings mobility. However, Beach argues, when it comes to well-being, it is possible to make statements about whether changes in earnings mobility over time represent improvements.[3] For males, the 1991-99 mobility pattern is unlike that for 1982-90. The probability of staying in the same income category increased in the 1990s for almost all categories. For people in the second and third lowest categories, the probability of moving down in the distribution increased. For people in the second and third highest categories, the probability of moving up also increased. At the same time, the probability of people moving down at least two categories increased. Overall, everyone in the distribution had a greater chance of ending up in the bottom categories, while chances of escaping from the bottom categories went down. And yet, the chances of staying at the top of the distribution, for those who got there, increased. Overall, these changes seem to be the opposite of those implied by social goals, which suggest that people should share equally in chances to move up or down but that, once at the bottom, chances of moving up are particularly high. These findings also provide interesting insight into the increased inequality found by Frenette, Green, and Picot in cross-sectional measures using tax data from the 1980s to the 1990s. Beach shows that the increased inequality reflected a polarization in income distribution, with people at the top of the distribution tending to move up and those at the bottom tending to move down.

A large part of Beach's discussion is dedicated to making these types of judgments more precise. He presents measures for translating changes in earnings mobility into statements about changes in societal well-being.[4] Perhaps not surprisingly, those measures indicate that the changes in male earnings mobility from the 1980s to the 1990s represent a clear decline in well-being among men. For women, however, the pattern is not quite as clear. While the probabilities of staying in the bottom categories again rise, the probabilities of staying in the top two categories decline. The second lowest category again experiences an increased probability of having an earnings decline, but this is not true for the third lowest category. In instances like this, attempts to quantify the impact on societal well-being are particularly useful. Beach shows that we can make an unequivocal statement that the 1990s represent a deterioration relative to the 1980s if we are willing to impose stronger pro-equality restrictions in our calculations, such as placing greater weight on changes at the bottom of the distribution.

In Chapter 5, Crossley and Pendakur examine the measurement of inequality in terms of consumption. There are at least two reasons to believe that measurement using consumption data would be preferable to measurement using income data. The first is that consumption is a step closer to notions of individual well-being. In general, we assume that people value income for the consumption it can fund rather than as an end in itself. The second is that people tend to try to smooth their consumption over their lifetime and across fluctuations in their income. Some part of measured cross-sectional income inequality will reflect temporary income drops caused by factors such as illness or intermittent layoffs. These temporary fluctuations will be cushioned by borrowing against income in better times. Household actions to smooth levels of consumption imply that family well-being fluctuates less than income. In this respect, consumption levels provide a better measure of true inequality. This smoothing effect applies not only to short-term, typically unexpected, fluctuations in income but also to longer-term, predictable changes in earnings over a lifetime. If households smoothed their consumption perfectly to keep it constant over their lifetimes, then consumption inequality in a given period would perfectly reflect differences in lifetime inequality. In that case, using consumption data would address the fact, mentioned earlier, that we do not want to count lower incomes of younger families as a problem if they are part of a standard life-cycle pattern.

Unfortunately, as Crossley and Pendakur observe, only in a world with peculiar preferences, constant interest rates, and no variations in risk could households smooth consumption so well that cross-sectional measures of consumption inequality would perfectly capture differences in household lifetime well-being. Since our world is not like that, consumption data provide an alternative measure of inequality that may have advantages over cross-sectional income measures but is still far from perfect as a measure of lifetime well-being. Indeed, consumption profiles have a humped shape that is reminiscent of earnings profiles over the life cycle, which suggests that cross-sectional comparisons with consumption data face life-cycle concerns similar to those of income data.

With these reservations in mind, Crossley and Pendakur show that consumption inequality as measured by the Atkinson index declined from the late 1960s to the mid-1990s and then took a small upturn in the last half of the 1990s.[5] It is worth noting, though, that these trends are not strong; if we use a Gini index as our measure, consumption inequality is virtually unchanged over time. Furthermore, the decline in inequality captured in the Atkinson index is almost entirely confined to cohorts born before 1933. More recent cohorts show little variation in consumption inequality over time. Cross-cohort comparisons reveal that successive cohorts have higher levels of consumption, though this pattern has stalled for cohorts born after 1954.

The consumption inequality patterns match up in an interesting way with income inequality. As discussed by Frenette, Green, and Picot, disposable income inequality is essentially flat over the 1980s and 1990s if measured using standard survey data. This is the general pattern seen in the consumption data as well. However, Frenette, Green, and Picot find that inequality has actually increased strongly in the 1990s when measured using more representative samples, and it would be useful to know whether sampling problems at the bottom of the distribution in the Survey of Consumer Finances (SCF) also arise in the Family Expenditure Survey (FES), which is the source of consumption data. Given that the response rate of 75 percent in the FES is slightly below that in the SCF, this seems possible. It is also notable that the consumption-based measures indicate an increase in inequality after 1996, a period when taxes and transfers were less effective in combatting income inequality.

Even if we had good observational data on consumption and if consumption qualified as a good measure of inequality, Lars Osberg argues in Chapter 6 that consumption would still be incomplete as a measure of individual well-being. Some people may choose time in preference to material goods – essentially buying leisure rather than goods with their potential income. In that situation neither actual income nor consumption provides a complete picture, and we would want to adjust for changes in hours of work over time or across countries in making inequality comparisons. Osberg finds that hours of work are generally higher at higher deciles of the income distribution for Canada and a set of other Western economies. One might conclude from this that measures of inequality based only on income overstate true inequality in utilities because those at the low end of the distribution are choosing leisure rather than income and the consumption goods that go with it. To put it another way, if those in the low deciles of the income distribution worked as much as those at the top their incomes would increase, thereby reducing overall inequality.

However, Osberg's results suggest a different interpretation. He begins with the standard leisure-consumption choice model from labour economics. In this model, hours of work and leisure are chosen by individuals to maximize utility conditional on their wage rates and non-labour income. The important assumption is that hours of work are a choice, at least within certain constraints posed by workplace practices. Osberg uses this model to explain why Americans work longer hours and have more income inequality than Canadians and, especially, Europeans.

To see how different preferences could create more inequality, consider the following hypothetical situation. Suppose that American workers have a very high taste for market goods regardless of whether their wages are low or high, and suppose that European workers in contrast tend to "spend" more of any higher wages by purchasing more leisure, thereby working less and reducing their incomes and purchases of market goods. Suppose also that the two continents offered the same distribution of market wages and opportunities to earn income. The inequality of earned incomes would be greater among American workers than among European workers, because time off reduces higher wages more than it reduces lower wages. Therefore, the difference in measured incomes between low-wage and high-wage workers in Europe, smaller than the difference among American workers, tends to understate the true European differential in well-being, since the high-wage workers would also be enjoying more leisure time.

To evaluate this explanation of the effect of preferences on inequality, Osberg conducts a counterfactual exercise of assigning workers in other countries the same employment rate as Canadian workers. Thus, Europeans get both the higher employment rates of North America and the benefits of the more equal wage structure and tax and transfer systems of Europe. This exercise results in reductions in poverty and inequality in Europe, which are already lower than they are in North America, thus increasing the differences in inequality and poverty rates between continents. Since Europeans' working more would increase the difference in inequality between Europe and North America, Osberg argues that the existing difference cannot be explained by their working less. He concludes that simple leisure-consumption trade-offs cannot explain the differences in inequality across the United States, Canada, and European countries.

What can we learn from this exercise to help us in thinking about inequality and justice in Canadian society? A principal insight is that, while there may be elements of choice in differences in hours worked across countries and across the income distribution within a country, much of the difference seems related to an inability to find employment among the less well-off. In other words, the rise in hours with income in the Canadian data likely does not reflect a simple choice by some people to have less income and more leisure but, rather, a difficulty in finding employment among those with the most limited skills. This is hardly a surprising conclusion, but it is important in thinking about measures of inequality. Income inequality measures may overstate inequality of utility since those with less income tend to have more time to enjoy leisure than those with high income. Yet that overstatement may be mild, since the extra hours of leisure among low-income individuals is often involuntary unemployment and thus carries little utility.

Osberg's results also raise complex questions about the interactions in a society of preferences, earnings structures, tax and transfer systems, and employment rates. In the counterfactual exercise, giving Canadian employment rates to non-employed Europeans improves the European situation relative to Canada because the newly employed Europeans get European earnings, which are better at the low end of the distribution than those in Canada. But if these better low-end earnings are partly supported by an equilibrium in which a good transfer system allows individuals to turn down low-paying jobs, choosing non-employment with benefits instead, then we do not face a simple situation of redistributing hours of work in order to improve inequality outcomes. Instead, we end up back in complex considerations raised in theories of justice.

Systems that redistribute income extensively but are accompanied by lower employment rates may or may not yield more just societies. Even if we accept that equal consideration is the sovereign virtue, allowing for different preferences means that equality does not necessarily imply equality of income or even of hours-adjusted income. If what we ultimately want is equal dignity for all, then we have to consider how issues such as individual responsibility and a feeling of full citizenship in a country interact with material equality. Part of the difficulty is deciding how we measure true equality (say, in terms of dignity) instead of just equality of income or even of consumption and leisure.

Inequalities of Participation

Rather than measures of individual or family well-being, we can examine measures of equality of participation in society.[6] Being an equal and full member of society means not only sharing most of the material advantages enjoyed by one's fellow citizens but also being an equal participant in the community and political life of one's society. Measures of the equality of such participation are presented by James Curtis, Edward Grabb, and Thomas Perks in Chapter 7. They ask whether participation varies with socioeconomic status and with ascribed statuses such as race and gender. The answer to this question helps to assess the justness of a society. If people of low socioeconomic status or with particular ascribed statuses, such as visible minorities, are less involved in political activity, we have to consider what that means. It might indicate a voluntary withdrawal from key forms of participation in the belief that the system does not serve them and that they suffer an unequal status in key decision-making institutions of society. Or it might mean they are being involuntarily "frozen out" of key institutions by other groups.

Curtis, Grabb, and Perks base their inquiry on the World Values Survey and present results on political participation and political interest. Their main conclusion is that participation and interest differ. Active participation in politics among Canadians as a whole is very limited, with only 8 percent of the sample belonging to a political party. At the same time, a majority of Canadians express interest in politics, claim to discuss it, and vote in elections. While there is clear evidence that individuals with higher socioeconomic status are more likely to take part in all forms of political expression, there are substantial levels of interest and discussion in all socioeconomic status groups. It seems that some inequality exists in political participation, but not enough to make those with lower status give up on the political system. Of course, recent, well-known declines in voter turn-out at elections may suggest that this situation is deteriorating.

Curtis, Grabb, and Perks also provide evidence on participation in both formal and informal community networks. The results for the formal organizations, such as volunteer groups, are much the same as for political participation: there is relatively widespread participation, with higher participation levels among those with higher socioeconomic status. This positive relationship holds even for hours of volunteering in formal organizations. However, higher socioeconomic status is negatively correlated with participation in informal networks. What these patterns imply about the justness of Canadian society is far from clear. On one hand, participation is widespread, with the highest levels of participation in some organizations for the relatively disadvantaged. This may suggest that individuals from all walks of life are given equal consideration in key community networks. On the other hand, it may suggest that higher-status individuals focus their efforts on controlling organizations that have more power in society, leaving participation in less organized networks to those of lower status. In that case, widespread participation would reflect heterogeneity in power rather than a high degree of equality. As the authors note, the evidence is not sufficient to allow us to differentiate between these interpretations.

Curtis, Grabb, and Perks also examine how attained and ascribed statuses are correlated with political participation. A wide variety of these status measures show significant simple correlations with levels of participation. However, their main interest is in marginal effects, that is, in finding which factors make the most difference. In this light one factor stands out as particularly important – education. Differences by ascribed status such as race and differences across income levels become weaker (and perhaps even nonexistent) once the authors control for education, whereas the impact of education differentials remains after controlling for other factors. This finding has several noteworthy implications. First, if income level does not drive participation, then there is less concern that the rising income inequality described in Chapter 3 will lead to increased inequality in political and community participation. The translation from income inequality to inequality in political rights is not direct. Second, differences in ascribed status do not appear to lead to inequality in political and community participation. Ascribed status may be associated with discrimination in the political and justice systems – a basic failure of moral impartiality – but there are means of expression for persons of every status. Third, education should hold a central place in discussions of equality in a society. Education appears to be an important key to unlocking equal access to political and community organizations. As we shall see in Chapter 10, education also plays a key role in earnings inequality levels and trends.

BRIEF RECAPITULATION

In summary, Chapters 3 to 7 paint a complex picture of overall inequality in Canadian society. The "economic" measures of well-being in the cross-section (market income, disposable income, consumption, and hours of leisure) reveal considerable inequality. Furthermore, movements within the earnings distribution follow a pattern in which the rich tend to stay rich and the poor tend to stay poor. Depending on the data source used, inequality also seems to have been growing, especially in the late 1990s. While consumption and income data from standard survey sources indicate stability in inequality across the 1980s and 1990s, measuring income inequality with more reliable tax and Census data leads to the conclusion that Canada experienced a period of rapidly increasing inequality in the 1990s. This is consistent with results on mobility within the earnings distribution, which point to the conclusion that workers were more likely to fall into and less likely to escape from the bottom of the earnings distribution in the 1990s than in the 1980s. Moreover, a tax and transfer system that worked to offset increases in market income inequality in the 1980s failed to fulfill that role in the 1990s.

Not all is doom and gloom, however. Inequality in some of the measures may be ethically acceptable. For example, mobility within the income distribution, though perhaps not as high as we would like, is far from zero. One needs to know more about who benefits and who loses in a given distribution, such as the degree to which inequality is age-related and therefore shared across lifetimes. One also needs to know whether the processes that generate distributional change are themselves accepted as morally impartial. Moreover, when education is accounted for, there appears to be very limited impact of income on inequality in political and community participation, which suggests that equality in key public arenas has not been completely compromised by economic inequality. Finally, the existence of a political will to move towards equality and justice may be seen in earlier patterns of taxes and transfers offsetting market income inequality. Though the redistributive weakening of the tax and transfer system in the late 1990s might represent a lapse of this political will, it might simply have been the result of mistaken attempts to "reform" the system or from the transitory impacts of budgetary deficit pressures. Subsequent policy changes following from budgetary surpluses in the new millennium, such as repeated enrichment of the National Child Benefit System, should have acted to reduce inequality.

Inequalities among Groups in Society

A key conclusion by Macleod and Eisenberg is that the typical focus of liberal theory on fully autonomous individuals distorts our views on justice in a society that includes many who do not have such autonomy. The largest group without autonomy in Canadian society is children. Of course, there are good reasons that they do not have full autonomy, but those reasons make it even

more incumbent on adults to be keenly aware of issues of justice for children. If justice is a sovereign virtue, then fairness toward those who do not
have the means to defend, or even define, their own interests must surely be
a marker of a just society. In this light, Chapter 8 is of particular interest.
Shelley Phipps and Lynn Lethbridge provide measures of inequality among
children in Canada and show where children fit into the overall income distribution. The income measure they use for each child is the household's
total income converted into adult-equivalent amounts. The main result is
that children fall in the lower part of the Canadian income distribution. Approximately 62 percent of children have associated incomes that put them
below the median income for the population as a whole in 1997. Children
in single-parent families fall even lower in the overall distribution, with about
35 percent of these children having associated incomes that place them in
the bottom decile.

While children fare relatively poorly in terms of income, Phipps and
Lethbridge find that there has at least not been a significant worsening either
of inequality among children or of their position within the overall income
distribution. Substantial increases in market income inequality have been
completely offset by the tax and transfer system. Furthermore, the percentage
of children with associated incomes below the median for the overall population in 1997 was 62 percent, the same as in 1973, despite growing market
income inequality.

However, there are reasons to question this conclusion. First, as Frenette,
Green, and Picot argue, the SCF data used by virtually all analysts, including Phipps and Lethbridge, greatly understates the increase in income inequality in the 1990s. If their results carry over to children, then inequality
among children almost certainly increased in this period, despite the SCF
data. But there remain uncertainties about the position of children in the
overall distribution. To the extent that children tend to be in lower-income
families and that those families are under-counted in the SCF, the problems outlined by Phipps and Lethbridge may be larger than their estimates
suggest and may be getting worse. Moreover, Phipps and Lethbridge observe that the relative position of children held steady over the 1980s and
1990s in spite of some changes that might have been expected to lead to
improvements in the relative position of children – increased ages of mothers
and increased numbers of two-earner families. Though these potential improvements have been offset by increases in the number of single-parent

families, the overall implication is that if these demographic changes had not occurred then children would have been worse off than they are. Hence, the trends hide a pattern that may become apparent once the demographic changes abate.

As Phipps and Lethbridge point out, the low position of children in the income distribution might be dismissed as almost definitional. Children tend to be in families in which the adults are young, that is, at an age at which they have relatively low incomes. Furthermore, in using adult-equivalence scales (the simplest of which consists of dividing family income by the square root of the number of people in the family), members of families with children seem automatically to have low adult-equivalent incomes since market incomes are subdivided among more members. However, comparisons across countries can be useful in interpreting this matter. Phipps and Lethbridge show that children in Norway tend to fall in the middle of the overall income distribution rather than in the lower end as in Canada and many other countries. So it is not inevitable or definitional that children fall in the bottom of the distribution. We need to think carefully about how children fit in and whether outcomes for children satisfy our notions of justice. Access to material resources in childhood can also affect individuals' opportunities for developing their full personal and educational potential and thus can have lifelong consequences for well-being.

Our definitions of a just society also need to be broad enough to encompass the outcomes for different ethnic groups. Canadian society has historically been very strongly segregated along ethnic lines, a result highlighted in John Porter's 1965 study, *The Vertical Mosaic*. In Chapter 9, Ellen Gee, Karen Kobayashi, and Steven Prus revisit that claim using both an examination of the existing literature and their own investigation with Census and health outcome data. They find that there are still clear differentials along ethnic lines in terms of economic outcomes such as income, occupation, and employment rates. Visible minorities, and especially recent immigrants who do not speak either official language, fare worse than European-origin, native-born Canadians in virtually all economic outcome categories. Results for Aboriginal Canadians appear even worse, with dramatic economic and health deficits below those of the rest of the population. Many of these differences, though, are dwarfed by gender differences, and the authors note that the interrelation of ethnic and gender dimensions is an important area for future research. All these differences underline Macleod and Eisenberg's argument that we need to be concerned about deficits in access to cultural capital. Any measurement of such deficiencies would surely combine with the outcome deficits presented here to paint an even worse picture of ethnic inequality.

In spite of unsatisfactory results in terms of ethnic differences in Canada, there are some more hopeful points. Older studies reviewed by Gee, Kobayashi, and Prus found economic and health differences among European-origin groups that have essentially disappeared. Canadians of various European origins appear relatively equal in well-being. Perhaps, over time, greater equality will emerge for other groups in Canadian society. Also, there is no clear health deficit for many visible minority groups, with the notable exception of Aboriginal Canadians. Still, the differences for new immigrants and Aboriginal Canadians suggest that Canadian society has considerable work to do in becoming fully just in the sense that all its members, regardless of their ethnic origins, are treated with equal dignity and given equal opportunities.

Explaining Movements in Inequality

In order to evaluate the levels and movements in inequality described above, we need to understand the causes of that inequality. As we have already discussed, the temporary inequality arising from life-cycle developments experienced by all members of a society is of less concern than permanent inequality in overall lifetime well-being. But even if we set aside life-cycle considerations, we may find some inequality acceptable and even desirable. Rawls's Difference Principle, in which inequality is accepted if it improves the well-being of the least well-off in society, is a strong statement along these lines. Similarly, other resourcist theories of justice appear willing to entertain inequality that arises from personal choices, in order to preserve incentives for individual responsibility and autonomy.

Thus, we would like to know more about the origins of the observed increases in family income inequality in the 1990s. Several studies in this volume provide building blocks that contribute to that understanding. Chapter 10 examines movements in underlying returns to education and experience, which have often been observed to play an important role in inequality trends. Chapter 11 provides more complete gender breakdowns and an analysis of how results for individual earnings are combined into results for family income inequality. Chapter 12 then examines how the tax and transfer system interacts with family incomes to generate disposable income inequality.[7]

In Chapter 10, Brahim Boudarbat, Thomas Lemieux, and Craig Riddell provide updated evidence on the evolution of earnings differentials with respect to education and experience for Canada. Using Census data for the period 1980 to 2000, they demonstrate the substantial differences in earnings across education levels. Like earlier investigators, they find that differences in weekly earnings between education groups were relatively stable for both men and women before 1995. However, this overall stability hides considerable differences across age groups for men, with younger workers experiencing substantial increases in returns to education while older workers experienced declines. Boudarbat, Lemieux, and Riddell provide new evidence on wage patterns after 1995. Using the Census, which they argue provides much more reliable estimates than other survey data, they find a strong increase in returns to education for men and some increases for women between 1995 and 2000.[8] Notably, a pattern of increasing differences in wages between older and younger workers continued from 1980 to 1995 and then, after 1995, reversed for men and stalled for women. As a result, overall inequality between age and education groups did not change dramatically after 1995. This means that the increases in earnings inequality in the 1990s observed by Frenette, Green, and Picot arise among people of similar age and education.

In Chapter 11, Nicole Fortin and Tammy Schirle extend the analysis by adding a more complete gender dimension. Using SCF data, they show that inequality in weekly earnings increased more for men than for women during the 1980s and 1990s. Male inequality grew because of increases at the top of the distribution as well as declines at the bottom, while female inequality grew mainly because of declines at the bottom. Underlying the movements in female earnings are dramatic increases in participation rates, in levels of experience and education, and in the presence of female single-parent families.

Fortin and Schirle offer an insightful analysis of movements in overall family earnings inequality between 1982 and 1997. They examine changes in the returns to education and experience, the substantial increases in female participation rates, increases in assortative mating of men and women (the tendency to marry a spouse with similar education and attainment, as measured by their earnings), changes in family composition (dominated by the increasing incidence of single-parent families), and changes in productive characteristics such as education and experience levels. Their results indicate that the changes in returns to education and experience discussed by Boudarbat, Lemieux, and Riddell for subsequent years probably increased inequality in family earnings. The changes in returns to these characteristics accounted for about twice as much of the increased spread in the lower half of the family distribution for women as for men.[9] The substantial increase in female participation acted to reduce overall inequality but was surprisingly less influential than other factors. For example, if the changes in female labour force participation had not occurred, the change in the 50-10 differential[10] in family earnings between 1982 and 1997 would have been only 1.6 percent larger, whereas, if the changes in family composition had not occurred, the change in the 50-10 differential would have been 56 percent smaller. Changes in family composition were the most important factor in explaining declines in the lower levels of the family earnings distribution, something the authors attribute to increased single parenthood. Assortative mating has increased substantially over the period of investigation and accounts for a further 32 percent of the increase in the 50-10 differential. Finally, increases in both education and experience levels between 1982 and 1997 acted to reduce family earnings inequality. The authors conclude that these changes implied improvements for families at the upper end of the earnings distribution but significant erosion for those in the middle, leading to the substantial increases in market income inequality described here and in some of the other chapters.

The changes in family income inequality over the last twenty years have been greatly affected by the tax and transfer system, whose redistributive impacts are thoroughly discussed by Jonathan Kesselman and Ron Cheung in Chapter 12. Their data on taxes paid and transfers received across the income distribution for the period 1971 to 2000 indicate that the redistributive tilt of both cash transfers and personal taxes has increased over the period. Rates of receipt of transfers have increased most at the bottom of the distribution, and average tax rates have increased most at the top of the distribution. It is noteworthy, though, that the last five-year period examined (1996-2000) shows disturbing breaks from this trend: transfers as a proportion of income decline sharply for unattached individuals in the lower quintiles of the distribution, and average tax rates increase much more at the bottom than the top. This finding matches the observation by Frenette, Green, and Picot that the role of the tax and transfer system in reducing inequality changed at the end of the 1990s. Nonetheless, Kesselman and Cheung conclude that the tax and transfer system remains strongly progressive and that most of the redistributive "work" is done by transfers rather than taxes at the lowest two quintiles of the distribution.

Kesselman and Cheung also provide an important warning about studies of the impact of the tax and transfer system on income distribution. A full explanation of this impact must take into account a wider range of taxes than is typically done in studies like that by Frenette, Green, and Picot. Furthermore, tax incidence issues raise serious questions about whether measures commonly used in the research literature overstate the impact of taxes on redistribution. A review of the relevant literature leads Kesselman and Cheung to conclude that a significant part of the burden of personal income tax may fall on firms, and thus on their customers through higher product prices, rather than on the individuals who nominally pay the tax. This effect is strongest at the top end of the distribution, where labour mobility, particularly across subnational jurisdictions, may force employers to compete for workers on a net-of-tax basis rather than on gross wages. By raising market wages to compensate for tax levels, this process can effectively undo the tax progressivity of the provinces. Moreover, to the extent that market wage levels reflect tax levels, the measured inequality of gross earnings is itself in part the result of the tax system.

Interpreting the Component Patterns
In analyzing the extent to which Canada is moving toward or away from the goal of becoming a just society, Chapters 10 to 12 strikingly suggest that something big changed in the latter half of the 1990s. Boudarbat, Lemieux, and Riddell show that the later 1990s saw dramatic increases in returns to education accompanied by reductions in earnings differentials between older and younger workers. Kesselman and Cheung show that the later 1990s saw a reversal in the long-term redistributive trends in transfers and taxes. Fortin and Schirle observe that, starting in the mid-1990s, the only group of women to experience increased labour force participation were single mothers, a trend consistent with changes in social assistance policies affecting mainly single parents. Thus, in the late 1990s, a sharp change in the wage structure was accompanied by reductions in the redistributive role of taxes and transfers. Together, these contributed to the increases in overall income inequality observed by Frenette, Green, and Picot.

On the surface, these changes, and many other longer-term changes depicted in these studies, indicate a society moving away from equality. Whether that also implies a movement toward a less just society depends on the nature of the forces driving the increased inequality. For example, the increased education differentials described by Boudarbat, Lemieux, and Riddell might be viewed as less problematic if they reflect a process of technical change that will ultimately benefit all members of society, and their study provides some evidence for evaluating this possibility.

A standard explanation of rising education differentials is that new information-based technologies make more intense use of skills and thus increase wage differentials between more and less skilled workers. Such a vision of increased productivity and earnings for those with education seems hopeful. It would mean that the increased inequality may be part of a tide lifting all boats. In this vision, the natural policy response is to increase education and training for the less skilled. This would give access to the benefits of the technological change to more people, eventually reducing education-wage differentials by increasing competition for more skilled workers and reducing competition for less skilled workers.

Murphy et al. (1998) apply this theory to Canada, arguing that the overall educational differential did not rise in Canada in the 1980s because of offsetting supply movements associated with more educated baby-boomers moving into the labour market. However, the evidence in Boudarbat, Lemieux, and Riddell does not support this interpretation because the group that would be most affected by the supply movements (the youngest workers) was the group that experienced the largest increases in the returns to education. Nor does the theory explain the large increase in the differentials in the late 1990s observed by Boudarbat, Lemieux, and Riddell. Furthermore, an explanation that stresses a tendency of new technologies to enhance the productivity of the most skilled does not help in understanding what happens to the least skilled. Something more is needed to explain the results of Fortin and Schirle, which show that much of the increase in inequality for men and especially for women occurs because of declines for those at the bottom of the distribution and not because of increases at the top.

This does not mean, though, that technological change has not played a substantial role in the rise in inequality. Beaudry and Green (2003) present a model in which firms choose between a newer, skilled-labour-intensive technology and an older, unskilled-labour-intensive technology. Increased education levels lead to firms preferring the newer technology since its main input is now relatively more abundant and cheaper. The shift toward the newer technology effectively takes capital out of the hands of unskilled workers employed in the older technology, resulting in lower wages for them and increased wage differentials between the skilled and the unskilled. Beaudry and Green (1998) argue that this model fits the Canadian wage patterns in the 1980s. Whether it is consistent with the sharp rise in the education differential in the late 1990s would depend on relative movements in physical and human capital. To the extent that it does fit, the model implies that the generation and distribution of physical capital is crucial for explaining the distribution of labour income. As Kesselman and Cheung observe, this has potential implications for the tax structure. Shifting the tax mix toward consumption bases, and away from income bases, will increase saving and thus raise capital accumulation. In the Beaudry and Green model, this raises real wages for both skilled and unskilled workers and lowers wage differentials. On the other hand, within this framework, increasing education levels does not, by itself, solve rising inequality. To the contrary, it can lead to further expansion of the skill-intensive sector, shifting more capital out of the hands of the less skilled and leaving them further behind.

Fortin and Schirle, following earlier work by Fortin and Lemieux (1997), offer an alternative explanation for increases in market income inequality. That is, institutional changes, including declining union power and changes in the minimum wage, may have shifted families who were formerly in the middle of the distribution to the bottom. The effect of institutional changes ties in interestingly with Kesselman and Cheung's point that changes in taxes and transfers (and, by extension, regulations) can affect the distribution of market wage rates for various types of work. Institutional changes may also include a reduction in the political will to support or use policy tools that promote income equality at a time of technological change, as described by Beaudry and Green. Such an outcome would be a disturbing shift away from equality since it reflects a move away from redistributive policies precisely at a time when technological change is generating increased inequality and declining real incomes for the less skilled.

Other results reported by Fortin and Schirle are also potentially worrisome – in particular, their finding that increased assortative mating has played a substantial role in growing family income inequality. If people have increasingly been marrying within their own income levels, this could imply greater stratification of Canadian society. However, caution is needed when measuring assortative mating, as Fortin and Schirle do, by proximity of spouses in the earnings distribution. This measure could increase over time even without any changes in who marries whom simply because some wives have become more likely to enter the labour market. Alternatively, suppose that the increased correlation of husbands' and wives' incomes reflects a growing tendency for people from high socioeconomic status to marry others from a similar background. This hypothesis could be investigated by examining the correlation in the socioeconomic status of partners' fathers. If this were confirmed, it would imply a relative concentration of wealth in a smaller subgroup of the population. It could also imply that we are facing greater social stratification, with people from different backgrounds being less likely to meet and, hence, understand each other. If the basis for redistribution ultimately stems from empathy, tendencies toward greater stratification in marriage represent a challenge to building a just society.

Fortin and Schirle further find that changes occurring in family composition are important for social equality. An increasing proportion of families are headed by a single parent, and our society treats this group particularly unequally. This point recalls Macleod and Eisenberg's arguments that liberal social structures can work to the disadvantage of women within family units in ways that carry over to their position after a marital dissolution.

Policy Responses in Broad Perspective

The changing patterns explored in the empirical and analytical chapters of the volume relate closely to what Keith Banting in Chapter 13 calls the 1990s paradigm shift in Canadian social policy. For decades, Banting argues, we operated on a security-based paradigm in which Canadians were asked to accept exposure to the vagaries of a free market economy while being assured that there were public transfer programs in place to reduce the risks they faced. But in the later 1990s, this traditional view was losing ground to a belief that the forces of technological change and globalization had made the economic risks in the global market too large for a traditional social safety net to continue to handle. Moreover, technological change requires an economy and a labour force flexible enough not to be left behind in the race for innovation. The result, says Banting, has been the emergence of a new paradigm in which citizens are expected to create their own security by investing in their human capital with better traditional education and lifelong learning.

The new paradigm has a ring of plausibility, but Banting observes that this new Emperor, if not naked, has been dressed too hurriedly and in something less than a full suit. Banting argues that there are two main problems with the shift to the new paradigm. The first is what he refers to as a cardinal sin of policy implementation – impatience. Governments at all levels in Canada, spurred partly by budgetary pressures and partly by ideological shifts, have worked quickly and assiduously to dismantle the old, "passive" transfer systems but have not replaced them with effective human-capital investment policies. There has been lip service to the new ideal but not enough in the way of new funding. But even with more than lip service, a human-capital investment policy will take at least one generation, and quite likely several, to implement fully and to get right. Banting argues that shifting paradigms effectively would entail a double fiscal burden since we need to continue to offer security to unskilled workers in the current generation, for whom complete adjustment to such investment is not possible, while expanding investments in younger generations and those who are able to access them in the current generation. Instead, by rushing to tear down the old system, we are exposing the unskilled to great insecurity during a transition that will take a long time to complete.

The second problem with the recent paradigm shift, Banting argues, is that human capital policy alone is being asked to carry too much of a burden. Citing a substantial body of research on socioeconomic gradients in access to education, he asserts that one cannot simply spend on education and training programs and hope to create true equality of security. Despite considerable advances in overall educational attainment in Western economies, children from disadvantaged backgrounds continue to be left behind in their educational attainment. Addressing this inequality requires both educational opportunities and a complex web of programs for dealing with social and economic exclusion. Moreover, many problems relating to economic and social justice cannot be addressed through education policies.

The shift in paradigms described by Banting may provide the explanation for what has been depicted by Frenette, Green, and Picot and by Kesselman and Cheung as a sea change in the impact of tax and transfer policies on inequality in the last half of the 1990s. In this period, both the provincial and federal governments altered programs such as social assistance and unemployment insurance, making them more difficult to access and placing greater emphasis on making recipients "job ready." These constraints on public spending for income transfers occurred during a period when governments at all levels faced intense pressures from mounting deficits as well as from public resistance to further tax increases. It appears, just as Banting predicts, that the dismantling of these programs left those at the bottom of the distribution in a particularly disadvantaged position. Given Kesselman and Cheung's argument that the transfer part of the tax and transfer system does the work of redistribution at the lower end, this outcome should perhaps not be surprising.

This sea change in policy has been occurring precisely at a time of high structural change in the economy. The extent of these economic changes has been observed in the sharp increases in the returns to education found by Boudarbat, Lemieux, and Riddell, the reduction in mobility shown by Beach, and the changes in family composition and female participation discussed by Fortin and Schirle. We saw earlier that one potential explanation for these phenomena is provided by a model of technological change in which firms are gradually making a transition from an older, unskilled-labour-intensive technology to a newer, skill-intensive technology. We also saw that, if enough new physical capital was not created during the transition phase, unskilled workers were likely to be particularly disadvantaged because the transition process effectively transferred capital out of their hands and into those of the more skilled. Thus, we may be removing transfer-system support from the least skilled just when changes in a market economy are exposing them to job loss and lower wages.

In the Beaudry and Green technology-shift model, the rush to educate more of the work force will improve the performance of the overall economy and benefit those who get the increased education but leave even further behind those who remain unskilled. If, as Banting argues of the shift in policy paradigms, the shift in technological paradigms is to the long-run benefit of society as a whole, it has imposed the burden of change on the one group least able to handle it. At a time when technological change is creating a group that most needs access to traditional income-transfer policies, we are busy diluting those very policies. This lends strong resonance to Banting's conclusion that our main challenge is "to design a redistributive complement to a human-capital strategy, one that makes meaningful the promise of education as an instrument of economic security and compensates for its limitations" (445). Unfortunately, he also concludes, Canada has thus far ignored this challenge.

Even these arguments, though, may not go far enough in critiquing the role played by education in the current policy discourse. Banting's second criticism might reasonably be expanded to say that education policy itself has been viewed in too narrow a light. The findings of Curtis, Grabb, and Perks indicate that education plays a central role in determining participation in political and community organizations. Thus, unequal access to education impairs not only economic security but also equality of citizenship. This is disturbing, in part, because even with complete equality of access to education, we will not attain complete equality of educational attainment –

nor would we expect to. Heterogeneity in education within the population is likely to persist for economic and other reasons. Many tasks in an economy can be performed by workers with less than a post-secondary education, sometimes much less. Even with completely equal access to education, differences in educational requirements and productivity across tasks will generate a set of wages that imply that it is not in some workers' interests to go on to higher education. Indeed, forcing them to do so through government mandates would be inefficient for the economy as a whole. Differences in individuals' innate abilities mean that many would not benefit much from pursuing advanced education, and these benefits would be swamped by the costs of the education and the forgone earnings while studying. Nevertheless, differing levels of education could create undesirable inequalities in political participation and perhaps political power, thus excluding less skilled workers from true equality in the citizenship sense.

How, then, do we reconcile the requirement to avoid inefficiencies with the power of education to open the doors of effective participation in society? The answer must be in altering the education system such that it provides resources for full participation to those who do not go on to post-secondary education or even complete high school. That is, public education must be enhanced as an institution of citizenship and social capital and not operated solely as a human-capital-generating institution (Green 2003). This point was anticipated in Adam Smith's discussion of education in *The Wealth of Nations*. Smith argued that specialization of labour is a strong force for productive efficiency but is also a force that cripples the human intellect:

> The man whose life is spent in performing a few simple operations ... has no occasion to exert his understanding, or to exercise his invention in finding out expedients for removing difficulties which never occur. He naturally loses, therefore, the habit of such exertion, and generally becomes as stupid and ignorant as it is possible for a human creature to become. The torpor of his mind renders him, not only incapable of relishing or bearing a part in any rational conversation, but of conceiving any generous, noble, or tender sentiment, and consequently of forming any just judgement concerning many even of the ordinary duties of private life. Of the great and extensive interests of his country he is altogether incapable of judging. (Smith 1937, 734-35)

The antidote to this, according to Smith is public education, not to teach potential workers how to be more productive but to help citizens take a larger view of their society.

The period since 2000 has witnessed most governments in Canada getting their public finances under control and in many cases allowing tax cuts. This improved fiscal environment has also created an opportunity to redress some of the policy mis-steps of the 1990s that Banting describes. While tax progressivity at the upper income levels may not be critical to inequality and issues of insecurity for less-skilled workers, as suggested by Kesselman and Cheung, collecting sufficient revenues to finance suitable public programs is crucial to the well-being of the less-skilled and disadvantaged.[11] This point can be combined with insights from Beaudry and Green's technology-shift framework to suggest new directions for public policy aimed at long-run gains for equality and justice. In the Beaudry-Green model, increasing access to higher education increases inequality because it diverts tangible capital away from sectors of the economy that employ less-educated workers. In order for Canada to reduce inequality while also raising wages for all workers, total investment must be increased. One strategy that could sustain or, if desired, increase overall tax revenues while also encouraging saving, investment, and capital accumulation would be to reorient the federal and provincial tax systems away from income and toward consumption, as envisaged by Kesselman (2004). This strategy could be implemented in ways that avoid sharp losses in tax progressivity, thus minimizing the sacrifice of equality in the short-run. The long-run benefits of this approach would be to raise real living standards for all workers, reducing inequality while simultaneously generating the revenues for more adequate programs of income support, in-kind benefits, and human capital investments. Coincidentally, this approach would also align the tax system more closely with consumption, which was identified earlier as a better proxy than income for the well-being of individuals.

Conclusion

We conclude by returning to our original questions about Canada as a just society. Do the levels and characteristics of inequality we find in Canada suggest that we are a particularly just society? Have changes in recent decades moved us toward or away from that goal? The studies in this volume paint a picture of considerable inequality in Canada in many dimensions of economic outcomes and political and community involvement. While this is not a novel finding, these studies have considerably deepened our understanding. However, a just society is not necessarily one with complete equality of outcomes. One might define it as one in which all members regard one another with equal dignity and respect. In this light, findings of unequal outcomes and participation for groups delineated by ethnicity and gender suggest departures from the conditions defining a just society. Findings of declining individual earnings mobility, of growing inequalities of family incomes, of increasing assortative mating, and of rising single-parent families with low incomes all paint a worrisome landscape. In short, inequality of income and earnings increased significantly in the 1990s and particularly in the last half of that decade, a period that also displayed reduced buffering of inequalities in market incomes by the tax and transfer system.

The studies in this volume have also provided insights into the causes of inequality and thereby suggest useful directions for future policy. Education is found to be a crucial element for advancing community and political participation, and hence its potential for improving social justice extends beyond the equalization of market earnings. Public transfer programs play a critical role in protecting incomes of the most vulnerable and disadvantaged, and this role must continue even as overall policy shifts more toward enhancing individual labour market skills. Both the level and structure of the tax system also have an important role in generating sufficient revenues to finance programs of income support and human capital investment and in inducing greater accumulation of tangible capital to raise worker productivity and earnings, particularly for the least skilled. The decade of the 1990s, and especially the latter part of that decade, witnessed many public policies adverse to those developments: restrained funding for public and advanced education; significant cuts to transfer programs; higher taxes with the revenues applied to deficit reduction rather than social investments; and heavier tax burdens on savings and investment.

Beginning in 2000, many of these policies have been reversed: partial restoration of public support for training and education; expanded transfers such as enriched National Child Benefits; the use of growing public revenues for new social investments; and tax cuts and reforms targeted at reducing the burden on savings, capital, and investment income. Most of the studies in this volume go no further than the year 2000 because of lags in data availability, research, and publication. One can hope that subsequent policy developments will show a reversal in Canada's declining inequality and social justice once the data and research have caught up, although, of course, ongoing changes in the market economy may have continued the deteriorating trend.

What we can conclude definitively from the studies in this volume is that, at least until the turn of the century, Canada experienced deteriorating inequality and social justice in many dimensions. Processes in the market economy that were leaving the worst-off further behind have been accentuated by shifts in public policy that actually reduced their support and compelled them to bear the brunt of economic changes. The one hopeful point in this scenario is that the policy changes were carried out with the stated purpose of generating better outcomes across society in the longer run. Time will tell whether those policy changes, and those that have followed in the early years of this century, do produce significant economic gains not only on average or for those well-placed in the labour market and society but particularly for individuals at the bottom of the distribution. In the short run, though, the impact of the combination of changes in the economy and in public policy at least through 2000 has been to increase inequality markedly. It is hard to escape the conclusion that these developments have also made Canada a less just society.

NOTES

1 Most of the authors have been associated with the ESC project (Equality, Security, and Community: Explaining and Improving the Distribution of Well-Being in Canada), of which this book is an outcome. The project was conducted from 1998 to 2004 with the support of a Major Collaborative Research Initiatives grant from the Social Sciences and Humanities Research Council.

2 However, one needs to keep in mind the point raised by Kesselman and Cheung (Chapter 12) that simply adding taxes and transfers onto market incomes ignores issues of behavioural responses to the incentives in the tax and transfer system and, therefore, the ultimate incidence of taxes and transfers.

3 This assumes, again, that most people in society want higher earnings and are not seeking a lifestyle with lower earnings and more leisure-oriented pursuits. See Osberg (Chapter 6) for further discussion of the role of leisure time variations in measuring inequality.

4 The measure of societal well-being is a function of individual utilities and thus fits most closely with the welfarist approaches described by Macleod and Eisenberg. However, by defining these functions with a large weight on whether initial levels of income were above some threshold, one could make the overall measure closer in spirit to a resourcist approach.

5   The Atkinson, Gini, Theil, and other inequality indices used throughout this vol-
    ume are described and compared in Kesselman and Cheung (Chapter 12).
6   For additional studies on inequalities of social participation and social capital,
    see Kay and Johnston (2006), a companion product of the ESC project.
7   One important topic not included in this volume is the distributional impact of
    in-kind benefit programs, such as health care and education. For two such studies
    that also discuss the methodological difficulties of assigning in-kind benefits, see
    Gillespie (1980) and Ruggeri et al. (1996).
8   Still, it is worth noting that this late 1990s increase for young men is similar to the
    increase they experienced in the early 1980s.
9   Note that the Fortin and Schirle analysis ends with data for 1997, before the ma-
    jor changes in returns to education documented by Boudarbat, Lemieux, and
    Riddell, which would have accentuated the results of Fortin and Schirle.
10 The 50-10 differential is defined as the difference between an individual at the
    50th percentile of the distribution (the median) and an individual at the 10th
    percentile from the bottom.
11 The impact of constrained public spending at the provincial level on less-skilled
    workers and the disadvantaged has been apparent; see for example the BC situa-
    tion in Kesselman (2002).

REFERENCES

Beaudry, Paul, and David A. Green. 1998. "What Is Driving U.S. and Canadian Wages:
    Endogenous Technical Change or Endogenous Choice of Technique?" Working
    Paper No. 6853. Cambridge, MA: National Bureau of Economic Research.
—. 2003. "Wages and Employment in the United States and Germany: What Explains
    the Differences?" *American Economic Review* 93(3): 573-602.
Fortin, Nicole M., and Thomas Lemieux. 1997. "Institutional Changes and Rising Wage
    Inequality: Is There a Linkage?" *Journal of Economic Perspectives* 11(2): 75-96.
Gillespie, W. Irwin. 1980. *The Redistribution of Income in Canada*. Agincourt, ON: Gage
    Publishing and Institute of Canadian Studies, Carleton University.
Green, A.J. 2003. "The Equal Opportunity Society: Determining the Role of Government."
    Research Paper No. 34. Toronto: Ontario Panel on the Role of Government.
Kay, Fiona, and Richard Johnston, eds. 2006. *Social Capital, Diversity, and the Welfare
    State*. Vancouver: UBC Press.
Kesselman, Jonathan R. 2002. "Fixing BC's Structural Deficit: What, Why, When, How?
    And for Whom?" *Canadian Tax Journal* 50(3): 884-932.
—. 2004. "Tax Design for a Northern Tiger." *Choices* 10(1). Montreal: Institute for Re-
    search on Public Policy.
Murphy, Kevin M., W. Craig Riddell, and Paul M. Romer. 1998. "Wages, Skills, and
    Technology in the United States and Canada." In Elhanan Helpman, ed., *General
    Purpose Technologies and Economic Growth*, 289-309. Cambridge, MA: MIT Press.

Osberg, Lars, and Andrew Sharpe. 2002. "An Index of Economic Well-Being." *Indicators: The Journal of Social Health* 1(2) 24-62.

Porter, John. 1965. *The Vertical Mosaic: An Analysis of Social Class and Power in Canada.* Toronto: University of Toronto Press.

Ruggeri, G.C., D. Van Wart, and R. Howard. 1996. *The Government as Robin Hood: Exploring the Myth.* Kingston, ON: School of Policy Studies, Queen's University; Ottawa: Caledon Institute of Social Policy.

Smith, Adam. 1937. *An Inquiry into the Nature and Cause of the Wealth of Nations.* New York: Modern Library.

United Nations Development Programme. 2003. *Human Development Report 2003.* New York: Oxford University Press.

Wolfson, Michael C., and Brian B. Murphy. 1998. "New Views on Inequality Trends in Canada and the United States." Cat. 11F0019MPE, No. 124. Ottawa: Statistics Canada.

2
Normative Dimensions of Equality

Colin M. Macleod and Avigail Eisenberg

This chapter provides an overview of some recent work in egalitarian political philosophy. Three broad areas are explored: (1) the general status of equality as a fundamental value, (2) the interpretation of equality in the context of economic justice, and (3) the interpretation of equality in the context of feminism and the political accommodation of minorities. These domains of inquiry are not analytically distinct because considerations of economic equality bear upon dimensions of gender and cultural equality and vice versa. However, for the purposes of exposition, the chapter will focus less on the overlaps among these areas than on aspects that can be explored separately. The recent literature on equality in political theory is vast and complex. Accordingly, the analysis developed here does not purport to be comprehensive. Rather it will identify central themes, problems, and theoretical trends that have emerged and that are important to the assessment of forms of inequality generated or sustained by existing institutional arrangements and public policy. Many of the theoretical issues discussed here are explored empirically in subsequent chapters of this volume.

Impartiality, Justice, and Equality

In contemporary political discourse, equality is a popular but elusive ideal. On the one hand, an egalitarian consensus has emerged according to which all citizens of a political community, irrespective of race, sex, ethnicity, or religion, are to be regarded as entitled to equal social and political standing. Invidious forms of racial and sexual discrimination are now recognized as gross and illegitimate denials of equality. On the other hand, there are often heated controversies about how best to interpret and give effect to the equal standing of citizens. For instance, programs of affirmative action are both defended and criticized by appeals to equality. Similarly, proposals to extend special protections to linguistic, cultural, or religious minorities are both applauded as appropriate expressions of egalitarian concern and assailed as betrayals of equality. Equality, it seems, is a sovereign yet deeply contested political ideal.

One useful way of framing debates about the meaning of equality is to distinguish an abstract but fundamental concept of equality from particular conceptions of equality that provide practical interpretations of the abstract ideal. This approach can capture the way in which an egalitarian consensus co-exists with disagreement about the particular demands of equality (Dworkin 1977, xv). The underlying premise shared by the different conceptions of equality considered here is an abstract but substantive concept of moral impartiality that accords equal moral standing to all persons. At this abstract level, all persons are "self-originating sources of valid claims" (Rawls 1980, 543). The task for any normative political theory that accepts moral impartiality as fundamental is to determine what the basic interests of persons are, what an impartial consideration of these interests entails, and how the resulting legitimate claims of all can be accommodated by social and political institutions. The process of theory construction can be seen as proceeding from a general concept of abstract equality or impartiality toward articulating a developed conception of what it is to treat persons as equals. The different theories canvassed in this chapter reflect different and to some degree competing conceptions of the fundamental ideal of impartiality.[1] With respect to economic issues, the basic problem is to determine the norms that should govern the distribution of benefits and burdens that are the upshot of human co-operation if persons are to be treated as equals. With respect to gender and cultural matters, the basic problem is to determine what forms of political, institutional, and social recognition of the distinct and diverse dimensions of persons' cultural, national, sexual, and religious identities best give effect to the demand that we treat persons as equals.

The claim of fundamentality for an abstract concept of equality is closely allied with two less familiar but important claims about justice as a political ideal. The first is that justice is fundamentally egalitarian in being predicated upon a notion of moral impartiality that reflects the equal standing of all persons. Racist institutional arrangements such as slavery or apartheid are deeply unjust precisely because of their profound assault to the equal dignity of persons. The second idea is that justice has special status as a standard for the regulation of basic social institutions. John Rawls's formulation of this idea has been particularly important. He holds that "justice is the first virtue of social institutions" and consequently that "laws and institutions no matter how efficient and well-arranged must be reformed or abolished if they are unjust" (Rawls 1971, 3). If there are conflicts between justice and other values that seem relevant to the design of social and political institutions, other values must give way to justice. Ronald Dworkin expresses essentially the same claims about the importance of justice and its connection to equality when he states that "equal concern is the sovereign virtue of political community – without it government is only tyranny" (Dworkin 2000, 1). On this view, fundamental equality is not a value that can be balanced against other values such as efficiency, stability, productivity, community, or even individual liberty. Such other values may merit recognition from an egalitarian point of view, but their accommodation occurs within equality itself rather than in any form of compromise between themselves and equality.

It is important to note that the ideal of fundamental equality that animates egalitarian theories of justice is different from a conception of equality that requires equal treatment. Equal consideration of basic interests does not necessarily entail that all persons, in all contexts, are to be accorded identical treatment. In some settings, treating persons as equals requires that persons be treated differently. For instance, although providing special accommodation for persons with disabilities in employment settings involves treating disabled persons differently from persons without disabilities, it need not constitute a violation of the principle of equal consideration. Treating persons as equals does not preclude different treatment.

Interpreting Equality: Method, Scope, and Ingredients

METHOD

A fully comprehensive theory of justice as impartiality will have many facets. It will include a theory of distributive equality, an account of democratic institutions, and appropriate constitutional structures including the nature and importance of the basic civil and political liberties of citizens. In a more theoretical vein, it typically involves distinctive methodological commitments about the processes through which an interpretation of impartiality is best developed. In recent literature, an influential methodological strategy is John Rawls's sophisticated form of contractarianism. Rawls argues that we can determine the content of justice by asking what principles rational agents would agree to in a special imaginary setting known as the original position. A different strategy, also pioneered by Rawls, involves testing theories by the degree to which they cohere with reflective moral intuitions about justice and fairness.[2] This is known as the method of reflective equilibrium. Other related approaches employ elaborate thought experiments or devices such as hypothetical insurance markets to illuminate dimensions of justice in an effort to articulate and clarify fundamental convictions of justice and their implications (Dworkin 2000).

Ultimately, it is impossible to treat the substantive normative elements of a theory as analytically distinct from the methodological strategies that are employed in the justification of normative commitments. Methodological strictures concerning justification can affect the substantive normative principles a theory accepts. To some degree, the divergent theories of distributive equality canvassed below reflect divergent positions on complex justificatory issues. We will not broach the various justificatory issues here, but we note them since they represent an important source of philosophical controversy concerning the interpretation of equality.

SCOPE

Recent debates about the nature of justice have addressed the appropriate scope of application of a conception of distributive equality. Do norms of distributive equality apply only or primarily within states or do they apply globally? Much work on distributive equality has followed Rawls's lead in assuming that principles of justice concern the basic structure of society conceived of as a "cooperative venture for mutual advantage" (Rawls 1971, 126). On this "political" approach (Nagel 2005), distributive ideals are appropriately used to assess the distribution of income, wealth, and opportunity within existing political societies such as Canada. A motivation for this approach is the idea that justice is closely linked to reciprocity. Persons who share common social, political, and economic institutions and cooperate within these structures to generate valuable resources stand in a special relation of reciprocity to one another – the possibility of achieving and sustaining mutual beneficial social cooperation depends crucially on their mutual respect for one another. The scope of distributive norms might thus seem to coincide with areas of reciprocal interaction.

However, from the perspective of impartiality, this construal of the scope of distributive norms can be criticized as unduly narrow. After all, the conception of moral impartiality arguably requires us to give equal consideration to the interests of all persons and not just to fellow citizens. Although distinct political communities exist with distinct economic and political institutions, why should distributive norms only apply within and not also across particular societies or states? Thus defenders of a "cosmopolitan" approach to justice argue that distributive norms should have global scope and our judgments about the degree to which egalitarian distributive ideals are realized should be sensitive to how income, wealth, and opportunity are distributed globally. Given the huge global divide between rich and poor, the practical implications of adopting a cosmopolitan rather than political approach to justice are far-reaching. However, one does not need to accept a cosmopolitan conception of justice in order to think that the scale of global inequality and extreme deprivation constitute a grave injustice.[3]

Ingredients

What are the ingredients of a successful conception of distributive equality? What are the normatively significant considerations to which a sound conception of distribution should be responsive? How are different considerations to be weighed? As we shall see below, competing conceptions of distributive equality reflect different interpretations of the nature and importance of different candidate norms. Nonetheless, five ingredients seem important to a conception of distributive equality. First, distributive norms should be sensitive to considerations of individual well-being. Treating persons as equals involves showing concern for how well their lives go, and, in general, it is a factor in favour of a distributive scheme that it improves the well-being of persons.[4] Second, autonomy needs to be facilitated and respected. Human beings have distinctive moral capacities that have special significance, and the capacity for autonomy needs to be recognized and respected and not merely as a facet of well-being. Acknowledging the importance of autonomy involves consideration both of the way in which the distribution of resources can affect the development of autonomy (e.g., how the provision of basic educational resources affects the development of autonomy in children) and of the way in which the distribution of resources should be sensitive to the exercise of autonomy (e.g., how people choose to use resources in the pursuit of their chosen life projects). Third, individual responsibility needs to be considered. This is closely linked with viewing persons as autonomous. To some degree, individuals must assume responsibility for the consequences of their actions. In distributive contexts, the share of resources to which individuals are entitled seems appropriately influenced, though perhaps not wholly determined, by their choices concerning the production and consumption of resources. So, other things being equal, a person who elects to work longer hours than another similarly situated person is entitled to a larger income than the person who works fewer hours. Fourth, a conception of distributive equality should be sensitive to considerations of dignity. A conception of equality that stigmatizes some persons (e.g., disabled persons) as inherently defective or that legitimizes humiliating tests of a person's worthiness to receive social assistance would be problematic. All persons should be adequately furnished with both the material and social resources (including symbolic markers) necessary to ensure that dignity is respected. Fifth, arbitrary sources of disadvantage that significantly affect the life prospects of persons should be recognized and mitigated or eliminated. For example, a person's family background should not place them at a substantial disadvantage vis-à-vis others with respect to access to economic or educational resources. In general, a person's genetic endowment – such as their raw talents – should not, insofar as possible, be a major determinant of the share of resources to which they have access. The mere fact that a person is lucky enough to be born with rare and valuable talents does not generate an entitlement to a share of resources greater than those with less valuable talents or, indeed, others with inherited disabilities.

Conceptions of Distributive Equality

These ingredients of distributive equality can pull in different directions. For instance, should some dimensions of well-being (e.g., physical health) be promoted by limiting individual autonomy? There are ways of holding persons responsible for the consequences of their choices that are an affront to their dignity. And efforts aimed at eliminating arbitrary sources of disadvantage can be very costly and thus can reduce aggregate well-being in troubling ways. The challenge is to articulate a conception of distributive equality that adequately accommodates these different considerations.

In what follows, we shall outline some of the influential contributions to this project and identify some objections to them. We have grouped the theories loosely according to the normative considerations they emphasize. Each approach is recognizably egalitarian in the sense that it offers an account of what must be equalized if individuals are to be treated as equals. The main categories of theories considered below are welfarist approaches, the capabilities approach, resourcist approaches, and democratic equality and theories that address gender and cultural inequality; finer distinctions are made for some of the categories.

Welfarist Approaches

UTILITARIANISM

Utilitarianism is a comprehensive moral theory according to which moral rightness consists in the maximization of overall utility, where utility is understood as human welfare (variously construed as happiness or preference satisfaction). Utilitarian theory has been developed in various complex ways, and what it means for distributing social benefits and burdens varies to a degree between interpretations of its constitutive elements.

Utilitarianism assigns priority to the maximization of welfare. Distributive equality (e.g., of income or wealth) is favoured only to the extent that equal distributions maximize aggregate welfare. Nonetheless, there are two respects in which utilitarianism can be represented as offering a theory of distributive equality. First, utilitarianism is impartial in giving equal weight to the interests of all persons. In utilitarian calculations, each person's welfare is considered on an equal basis. Second, with respect to the distribution of resources (e.g., income and wealth), utilitarianism has a strongly egalitarian tendency. Because of the diminishing marginal utility of income (and resources generally) and because of the similarity of individuals' utility functions (the way in which a person derives welfare from resources), an equal distribution of resources will tend to generate maximum aggregate utility.

An important caveat to this claim is that the utilitarian criterion is sensitive to considerations that affect the total amount of resources available for distribution. If, for instance, total resource productivity is bolstered by a form of economic organization that distributes resources unequally and the productivity gains contribute significantly to an increase in total welfare, then utilitarianism will judge inequalities in income and wealth to be justified. Indeed, though it is empirically unlikely, the utilitarian criterion is, in principle, compatible with enormous distributive inequality. Aggregate utility might be maximized in a world in which most are wealthy but a minority group is desperately poor.

Despite its concern to factor in the welfare of all persons equally, utilitarianism is often faulted on the grounds that the criterion of utility maximization is not sufficiently sensitive to the importance of ensuring that every person be secured a reasonable level of welfare. Utilitarianism can legitimize sacrificing the interests of the poor in the name of promoting total welfare. This result arbitrarily discounts the interests of those disadvantaged by utility-maximizing distributions of resources.

EQUALITY OF WELFARE

A seemingly simple way to remedy this insensitivity in utilitarianism is to retain the focus on welfare promotion but to replace the maximizing criterion with an equalizing function. Perhaps the best way to treat people as equals in a distributive scheme is to distribute resources so that the level of welfare enjoyed by everyone is equalized. Doing so would recognize the equal moral importance of each person's life, and it would probably not imply a strictly egalitarian distribution of income and wealth. Some persons, such as the disabled, might require more resources than others to achieve a level of welfare equal to that of everyone else. However, if most persons have roughly the same ability to transform economic resources into welfare, this approach will tend to produce a broadly equal distribution of economic resources.

The sensitivity of this approach to the welfare deficits faced by some individuals makes it seem initially an attractive way of eliminating arbitrary disadvantages. However, the theory is beset with a variety of difficulties (Dworkin 2000, 11-64). A principal flaw is its insensitivity to considerations of individual responsibility affecting entitlement to resources. Consider the problem of "expensive tastes." Suppose we begin with an equal distribution of resources that also happens to result in the equalization of welfare. Assume that A and B both initially derive their welfare from drinking beer and eating pizza. A then decides to cultivate a taste for champagne and caviar. Now an equal distribution of resources will no longer equalize the welfare of A and B. In order to equalize welfare, it will be necessary to devote more resources to A so that he can satisfy his newly formed expensive tastes. But it seems manifestly unfair to require B to subsidize A's deliberately cultivated taste for champagne and caviar. A's new welfare deficit, compared to others, is traceable to choices that A made, so it seems reasonable to hold A, and not B, responsible for the welfare consequences of his choice.

EQUALITY OF OPPORTUNITY FOR WELFARE

The degree to which individuals are responsible for their choices is controversial and, even when their responsibility is acknowledged, there is disagreement about the degree to which they can reasonably be held accountable for the consequences of their choices. (For example, is it reasonable for a person's whole life to be ruined by one very poor decision made early in life?) Nonetheless, a promising approach to dealing with issues of individual responsibility while retaining a concern for the promotion of welfare is to focus on opportunities for welfare. Equality of opportunity for welfare requires that each person has the same opportunity as everyone else to achieve an equal level of welfare (Arneson 1989). This approach allows individuals to be compensated for unchosen welfare deficits but also permits inequalities in the actual welfare experienced by different individuals. Welfare differences attributable to choices are just, provided that the choices are made against a background in which, over the course of a life, every person has the same chance to achieve equally good welfare outcomes.[5]

The practical implications of this choice-sensitive welfarist approach are unclear. The theory supposes that we can identify and compare the opportunity sets for individuals. This is a daunting challenge because there are various ways in which opportunity sets could be deemed equal, and it is difficult to determine which theoretical construal best tracks the sense in which a person's welfare should be linked to personal choice. For instance, are opportunities for welfare equal for A and B if each can achieve the same level of welfare by making a choice but where A can pursue the choice much more easily than can B? Or must the available choices be equally easy for A and B to pursue? Must A and B have the same number of choices (or possible routes) to achieve equal welfare in order for the opportunity to achieve welfare to be equal? Or is it compatible with the ideal if A has many routes to achieve a given level of welfare while B only has one route available to her? Even if such theoretical measurement puzzles can be answered, the practical measurement problems are arguably insurmountable (Rakowski 1993, 49).

A different sort of objection to this theory is that its implementation could be unreasonably demanding in light of the severe welfare deficits faced by some persons. Ensuring that persons with severe and painful disabilities have a genuinely equal opportunity for welfare is probably impossible since, in the worst cases, no transfer of resources could fully eliminate the unchosen welfare deficit. But even an approximation of the ideal might require huge transfers of resources that would lead to massive limitations on the opportunities for welfare enjoyed by others. Rakowski claims that "it seems wrong to require that resources be transferred to those with limited opportunities where the costs to others are very high and the marginal gains to recipients are negligible" (1993, 43).

A more general reservation about this approach concerns the focus on welfare. Preference satisfaction, as a standard of well-being, may not adequately represent the importance of "non-utility information" (Sen 1982, 322). For instance, the satisfaction of certain needs – to basic food, shelter, clothing, etc. – often seems more urgent than satisfaction of a person's preferences

(Scanlon 1975). From the point of view of distributive justice, welfarist approaches arguably have too narrow a conception of the interests that matter.

The Capabilities Approach

One way of addressing this apparent "informational" defect of welfarism is to assess the quality of persons' lives in terms of a broader conception of valuable activities to which they have access. An influential approach to the interpretation of equality that emphasizes the plurality of sources of value in human life is the capabilities approach pioneered by Amartya Sen (1992, 1999) and Martha Nussbaum (2000). On this complex theory, we begin by identifying basic and valuable "functionings" of human beings – that is, general human activities and achievements that characteristically contribute value to a human life. The list of functionings is somewhat open-ended but often includes life, health, bodily integrity, exercise of cognitive powers of reason, imagination, and emotion. Capabilities are then defined in terms of access to functionings. Consuming a diet that meets a human being's nutritional needs is a valuable functioning. A person has the capability of achieving this functioning if they have reliable access to clean drinking water and nutritious food. On the capabilities approach, the demands of equality are met to the degree that persons enjoy equal capabilities, that is, that they have equal access to valuable functionings.[6]

The capabilities approach has been influential in discussions of global justice, especially in evaluating measures aimed at the reduction of extreme forms of poverty and deprivation. The theory does not aim at guaranteeing the equal basic functioning of human beings. Rather it aims at securing the conditions under which persons have equal access to basic human goods. It provides a useful and sophisticated way of highlighting the importance of ensuring that all persons have access to the prerequisites of a decent human life. By contrast, measures of economic development that focus on aggregate economic indicators such as GDP can be insensitive to the ways in which individuals suffer deprivation. For instance, a country with a high GDP may have many people who lack enough to eat.

The capabilities approach offers a more nuanced interpretation than welfarist approaches of the way different human interests are relevant to problems of distributive justice. Its principal limitation is that it offers little guidance concerning matters of justice that arise above the threshold of basic human functioning. But it involves explicit identification of the elements of a good human life, and it tries to respect the way in which individuals have a measure of responsibility for how their lives go. The capabilities approach, as a non-welfarist conception of human interests that acknowledges the diversity of human capacities and plans, somewhat resembles resourcist approaches, to which we now turn.[7]

Resourcist Approaches

The common thread running through welfarist theories of equality is the idea of determining the impact of the distribution of resources on the achievement of different levels of welfare. Resourcist theories adopt a different strategy for giving content to the interests of individuals. Rather than locating interests in welfare directly, resourcists analyze interests in terms of each person's capacity to form and pursue a conception of a worthwhile or meaningful life plan. So rather than aiming at securing some level of welfare or the chance of securing it, resourcist theories focus on providing persons with a fair share of the resources that can contribute to the formation and successful implementation of life plans. In effect, the problem of determining how resources should be distributed focuses on determining what share of resources each person is entitled to receive in pursuit of his or her conception of the good.

An important dimension of the resourcist approach is the idea that persons have the responsibility to form their life plans in light of their fair share of resources, and any person's claim to resources is independent of the content of their preferences. Resourcists hold that "equality should enter into the very formation of our preferences" (Kymlicka 2002, 42). Welfarist theories, by contrast, treat the content of a person's preferences as at least partly determinative of their claim to resources. For instance, if C has preferences that are easily satisfied with little income and D has preferences that are more expensive to satisfy, then equalizing the welfare of C and D will involve providing D with more resources than C. The resourcist denies that such preference-dependent differences in utility functions are relevant to the fair assignment of resources. Other things being equal, C and D can lay claim to equal shares of income, even if this means that C will be happier than D.

The resourcist approach obviates the need to make interpersonal comparisons of welfare. This represents an important practical advantage over welfarist approaches. Instead of assessing the justice of resource distribution by trying to assess its impact on welfare, the resourcist can assess the justice of resource distribution through a more direct assessment of patterns of resource distribution.

Primary Goods and the Difference Principle

In his celebrated and enormously influential work *A Theory of Justice*, John Rawls provides a sophisticated resourcist theory. A key element of Rawls's theory is the idea of social primary goods. Social primary goods are goods such as "liberty, opportunity, the powers and prerogatives of office, the social basis of self-respect, income and wealth" (Rawls 1971, 62). Social primary goods are goods that can contribute to the pursuit of one's conception of the good, irrespective of the particular content of that conception. (For example, Christians, Jews, and atheists all have different conceptions of the good and, in virtue of these different conceptions, they value different projects. Nonetheless, social primary goods are valuable to them all because they provide the means through which their different projects can be effectively pursued.) The distribution of these goods to individuals can be directly affected by the design of social institutions. For Rawls, the basic problem faced by a theory of justice is that of determining the principles for structuring social and political institutions that should govern the distribution of social primary goods.

In the context of developing an answer to this problem, Rawls deploys his famous social contract argument. We can determine what share of social primary goods persons are entitled to in a just society by asking what principles for the distribution of these goods rational persons would agree to in a hypothetical scene of negotiation called the "original position." In the original position, the contracting parties are behind a "veil of ignorance" in which: "no one knows his place in society, his class position or social status, nor does any one know his fortune in the distribution of natural assets and abilities, his intelligence, strength and the like. I shall even assume that the parties do not know their conception of the good or their special psychological properties" (Rawls 1971, 12).

The original position is an imaginative way of modelling the basic equal standing of persons, and it provides a device through which a resourcist theory of distributive equality can be articulated. Rawls's contract argument is complex and nuanced, but the overall conception is strongly egalitarian. Rawls holds that parties in the original position would attach special priority to the provision and protection of equal basic civil and political liberties. He thinks that opportunities to attain "offices and positions" must be open to all under "conditions of fair equality of opportunity" (Rawls 1971, 302). Moreover, the distribution of economic resources is governed by the "difference principle," according to which "social and economic inequalities are to be arranged so that they are ... to the greatest benefit of the least advantaged" (Rawls 1971, 302-3).

The degree to which the difference principle permits actual economic inequality depends on the degree to which economic inequality is a necessary condition of improving the economic standing of the worst off. Interpreting the practical implications of the difference principle turns crucially on questions about the degree to which economic productivity depends on a system of economic incentives that offers inducements to individuals to engage in beneficial economic activity. It is important to observe here that measures of overall economic productivity, such as Gross National Product or average annual income, are not sufficient to determine the degree to which a distribution satisfies the difference principle. The crucial issue is whether economic inequalities work to the advantage of the worst off.

The difference principle has many attractions. It provides a way of extinguishing some of the arbitrary sources of inequality while permitting beneficial inequality. On the difference principle, a person's access to resources with which to pursue a conception of the good is not determined by arbitrary factors such as gender or economic class. Similarly, a person's access to economic resources is not a function of the degree to which they were lucky in the natural lottery of talents and skills. (Wayne Gretzky's natural hockey talent does not entitle him to a greater than equal share of income.) In this way, the theory seems admirably "endowment-insensitive." Yet the difference principle also treats individuals as capable of assuming responsibility for their own lives. The share of income to which persons are entitled does not guarantee them a level of welfare. Instead, persons assume responsibility for the directions of their lives. Everyone can allocate their fair share of resources among their own projects as they see fit.

EQUALITY OF RESOURCES

In some respects, Rawls's theory seems neither sufficiently "endowment-insensitive" nor sufficiently "responsibility-sensitive." Although the difference principle reasonably extinguishes the arbitrary impact of some kinds of brute luck, it does not address the endowment disadvantage of persons who, through no fault of their own, face diminished life prospects because of disabilities. The difference principle provides no basis for providing persons with disabilities with the various resources they may need in order to enjoy life prospects that are reasonably equal to those of persons who face no such disadvantages. In some cases, of course, no amount of economic compensation can fully eliminate the diminished life prospects attributable to severe disabilities. However, we do not treat otherwise similarly situated persons as equals in a scheme of distribution simply by giving them each an equal share of income if one of them is significantly disabled. Such an approach leaves a significant and arbitrary source of disadvantage untouched.

The difference principle is insufficiently sensitive to responsibility because it does not allow that considered choice can give rise to differential entitlements to resources. Persons who prefer surfing to gainful employment are as much entitled to an equal share of income under the difference principle as persons who diligently pursue economic opportunities and work hard. This overlooks an individual's responsibility to choose carefully in light of the consequences.

Ronald Dworkin's innovative equality of resources theory can be seen as a way of developing a resourcist theory that addresses these difficulties in Rawls's theory (Dworkin 2000). Like Rawls's theory, Dworkin's theory of equality is comprehensive, complex, and multifaceted. Like Rawls, Dworkin articulates a theory of distributive equality that is systematically linked to accounts of liberty, democracy, community, and neutrality. However, whereas Rawls uses the original position to articulate his theory of justice, Dworkin uses the idea of a market to articulate his brand of egalitarianism. According to Dworkin, we can harness the price system of a perfectly competitive market in order to model an initially equal distribution of resources. As a first approximation, we are to imagine how immigrants to a desert island should distribute the island's resources among themselves. Dworkin claims that an equal distribution is defined by the outcome of an imaginary auction that is perfectly competitive and in which all participants have equal purchasing power. The auction is complete when an "envy test" is satisfied – no person prefers the bundle of resources she has acquired to the bundle anyone else has acquired.

The price system of such a market provides a measure of the value of resources in a way that gives content to the idea that a person's claim to a fair share of resources should reflect the impact of the claim on other members of the community. The operation of a perfect market from such a position of initial equality will, according to Dworkin, also preserve equality through time as persons engage in production and exchange of resources. Because differences in the economic rewards that accrue to ongoing market activity reflect different choices individuals make about the lives they wish to lead, a perfectly competitive market-determined distribution of resources links individual responsibility to entitlement. A person who chooses more leisure over work will, other things being equal, have a lower income than the person who chooses more work over leisure. But since the resulting income inequality is traceable to choice against a background of initial resource equality, the difference is just. If Dworkin is right, there is a surprising affinity, at least in theory, between the market and distributive equality.

Of course, even the fictional perfectly competitive market will not ensure equality over time if the participants in the market have significantly different natural endowments. Two persons who make the same choices will fare differently in the market if one is lucky enough to have valued skills that the other lacks. Similarly, unadjusted market outcomes, even those generated from a position of initial equality, will not address the arbitrary disadvantages in life prospects faced by those with disabilities. To handle these problems, Dworkin introduces a complex scheme of hypothetical insurance markets that are designed to indicate: (1) the sort of compensation to which persons with disabilities are entitled, and (2) the ways in which actual market outcomes should be adjusted (e.g., through a system of redistributive taxation) in order to mitigate the impact on income distribution of arbitrary differences in natural talent. To simplify Dworkin's argument greatly, we can determine how much compensation is owed to persons with disabilities by asking how much insurance persons would buy against being disabled if the insurance decision were made from a position in which each person has equal purchasing power and does not know whether they will become disabled. The hypothetical insurance market scheme for dealing with the problem of unequal talents has a similar structure but operates under some different conditions. Roughly, we can determine appropriate rates for redistributive taxation by speculating about the insurance decisions individuals would make if they knew their talents but not their economic value.

Dworkin's articulation of the requirements that a just distribution of resources be endowment-insensitive and choice-sensitive is extremely important. It captures the way in which individuals must assume responsibility for the consequences of their decisions about how to conduct their lives while also acknowledging that a person's life prospects should not be adversely affected by arbitrary aspects of natural endowment.

Yet it is far from clear that the idealized markets used in Dworkin's theory successfully track these crucial requirements. There are reasons to doubt that, even in ideal settings, market-determined distributions accurately represent considerations of individual responsibility. Market-determined distributions of income can, in theory and practice, generate inequalities that are grossly disproportional to the differences in the choices of individuals. For instance, in some circumstances, prudent and sensible choices can expose individuals to unfair disadvantage while handsomely rewarding the reckless gambles of others (Macleod 1998, Chapters 2 and 3). The hypothetical insurance mechanisms invoked by Dworkin rest on controversial claims about the possibility of making counterfactual judgments in ways that invest them with normative significance. It is enormously difficult to speculate about what insurance decisions individuals would make under the complicated epistemic conditions imposed by Dworkin. Even when it is possible to speculate meaningfully about the likely implications of various kinds of hypothetical insurance decisions, it is doubtful that the resulting theory adequately distinguishes between justified and unjustified economic and social inequalities. For instance, on Dworkin's scheme, the provision of resources to the disabled falls well short of mitigating the obstacles they face (Macleod 1998, Chapter 4). Similarly, as Dworkin interprets his income insurance scheme, justice requires only modest redistribution of market-derived income. This means that potentially vast and arbitrary inequalities between the talented rich and less talented poor will remain largely untouched (Macleod 1998, Chapter 5). Dworkin's articulation of the abstract demands of egalitarian justice is better worked out than is his description of how market forces will represent those demands.

Democratic Equality

Dworkin's work succeeded in drawing attention to the apparent significance of different forms of inequalities. Unchosen inequalities in life prospects seem more worthy of remedy than inequalities attributable to the choices of responsible individuals. So a responsibility-sensitive theory of equality seeks ways of distinguishing unchosen inequalities, which should be eliminated, from chosen inequalities, which should be allowed. Some theorists have recently argued, however, that the effort to distinguish these forms of inequality can be misguided and indeed antithetical to fundamental egalitarian concerns. Elizabeth Anderson claims that "luck egalitarianism" – the form of egalitarianism championed by Dworkin and others, which views the basic egalitarian impulse as a desire to extinguish the ill-effects of bad luck – leads to theoretical commitments that are insensitive to respect for the equal dignity of all persons. For instance, the effort to devise schemes of compensation for disabled persons carries with it the demeaning suggestion that disabled persons are somehow defective as persons. Similarly, the attempt to distinguish between chosen and unchosen inequalities may lead to the endorsement of invidious requirements for individuals seeking assistance to prove their worthiness – i.e., to prove that their plight was unchosen. And those deemed to be responsible for their impoverished status are not entitled to assistance even if their poverty denies them status as self-respecting members of a community of mutual concern.

Anderson favours a construal of equality as centrally concerned with ensuring that all persons are treated with dignity and self-respect. In her view, in order to achieve "democratic equality," it is not necessary to develop a theory of distributive shares that is sensitive to endowment and responsibility. Instead, there should be relatively unconditional access to the basic prerequisites of dignity and self-respect because a person does not forfeit this entitlement through poor choices. Anderson is also less concerned with eliminating arbitrary differences in income. The fact that some are richer than others, even where this is attributable to luck in the natural lottery, should not be an object of egalitarian concern. Huge differences in wealth and income are significant to the degree that they affect the capacity of citizens to participate as equals in the public realm of democratic self-governance. What matters is not income inequality itself but the pernicious effects that such inequality can have on the achievement of democratic equality. Whether or not Anderson is right about the potentially pernicious effects of luck egalitarianism, she is right to note that equality concerns not only the distribution of transferable resources. The way in which institutions recognize and respond to persons on the basis of their identities is also crucial. So we now turn to some issues less expressly concerned with distributive matters.

Gender and Cultural Inequality

The most significant critical responses to liberal theories of distributive justice argue that the primary goods and resources upon which distribution conventionally focuses are too narrow and express implicit biases based on the culture and gender of individual actors. For the most part, these criticisms do not challenge the premise of moral impartiality. Rather, the critics either claim that the abstract conceptions or the institutions derived from them are biased. Feminist analysis contends that liberal theories of equality fail to take account of the unpaid labour done primarily by women in the family, including child-rearing and other caregiving, and this failure distorts liberal assessments of equality and equal opportunity. Any assessment of equality, including equality of opportunity, welfare, or resources, is incomplete without considering the division of labour in the domestic sphere and how it affects opportunities and choices. Those who focus on cultural inequality and minority rights argue that individuals may be treated unjustly, as less worthy members of society or second-class citizens, on the basis of the ethnic, racial, or national group to which they belong – even in societies where income is distributed equitably. A concern of "multiculturalists" is that approaches to equality that focus only on the distribution of a narrow set of alienable resources, such as income, fail to address the structural bias built into various institutions and modes of distribution that give rise to cultural inequality. Some of these critics argue that, for fairness, distributive schemes must factor in the distribution of "cultural resources." Others argue that we need to look beyond the "logic of distribution" for solutions to cultural inequality. Will Kymlicka's "multicultural citizenship" (1995) and Iris Young's "politics of difference" (1990) both attempt to address cultural- or identity-related gaps in distributive theories.

LABOUR AND GENDER INEQUALITY

Most societies, including liberal societies, have historically tolerated overtly sexist rules that have barred women from fully participating in public life – as voters, political leaders, judges, and jurors – from owning property independently, and from gaining access to jobs and professions that would allow them to assume positions of status and power. While overt restrictions of these sorts have been lifted, at least in Western societies, women's inequality relative to men remains. On average, women in Canada are more likely than men to be poor. They are far more likely to be employed in part-time, low-paying jobs and to lack the skills, education, and independence required to gain better jobs. Single mothers are especially prone to finding themselves poor and lacking good employment. These factors point to one of the main obstacles to women's equality both historically and currently, namely, the unequal division of domestic labour. Worldwide, women are the primary caregivers of children and the elderly. The demands that caregiving imposes on them accounts for the main explanations of women's poverty, unemployment, and lagging skill set. Amartya Sen has linked the absence of women in the work force in the developing economies of Asia, Africa, and Latin America to human rights abuses against women and to women's higher rate of mortality after the age of thirty (Sen 1990). In light of these social ills and their

suspected causes, addressing the domestic division of labour is a crucial component of an adequate understanding of equality and inequality.

The feminist critique of liberal equality goes beyond the failure of these
theories to factor in domestic labour. It critiques the ways in which liberal
political and economic theories characterize the abstract individual and the
individual's capacity for autonomous choice. It further finds fault with how
these theories treat the market as a level playing field without gender bias.
Feminist analysis highlights three standard criticisms of liberalism.

First, the abstract individual who enters the market and whose welfare
and choices drive most approaches to equality is not a gender-neutral being
in any historical or social sense (Pateman 1988). Rather, he has values and a
lifestyle that are typical of some men but not typical of women. Liberal theory
has traditionally assumed that the main actor in society has a household, is
capable of making decisions for his household, and uses property and the
rules of the market to advance his interests and those of his household.
Although both men and women are capable of heading households, this
self-interested, utility-maximizing, autonomous person has values associated
with social roles that are more characteristic of men than of women.

The second criticism is that theories of equality usually only apply to
relations and distributions within the public sphere while ignoring the profound inequality that often characterizes relations in the private and especially the domestic sphere. So the circumstances of those within households,
including those who are physically dependent, such as children, and those
who are financially dependent, such as the caregivers who nurture children,
are simply beyond what theorists of equality have conventionally considered relevant to their concerns.[8]

The third criticism, the one that we focus on here, is that liberal theories
tend to view individuals as "choosers" and thereby as beings that possess the
autonomy to choose goods or sets of goods based on their interests, needs,
and desires. This focus on the autonomous individual is pervasive in liberal
theory, including the theories of Rawls and Dworkin explored above. In fact,
it is key to liberal political and economic theory and usually permeates the
public policy and political debates of liberal societies. For these reasons, it is
worth exploring in some depth.

Theories of equality take individual choice seriously in at least two
senses. First, these theories are premised on ensuring that individual choosers have equal opportunities to choose how they will lead their lives and
participate in the market. Second, most theories of equality strive to be

responsibility-sensitive in the sense that the individual chooser has to take responsibility for the choices she makes or, at least, for those choices that are not imposed by good or bad luck. For example, those who choose to be negligent or lazy are not entitled to the same income or status as those who choose to be careful and hardworking.

Feminists tend to agree with liberals that individual autonomy is important to leading a good life. The problem with liberalism, they argue, is that it ignores the factors that structure individual choice and especially women's choices. A good example of a theory that ignores factors that structure choice is the human capital approach to gender inequality employed by Gary Becker and other neoclassical economists. Like seventeenth-century liberal theories, the human capital approach assumes that individuals are voluntary choosers, and it frames explanations for why particular choices are made in terms of this assumption. Thus, according to this theory, the reason women tend to occupy lower-paid, part-time jobs is that they choose these sorts of jobs in light of the needs of their families (Becker 1981; see Okin 1989, 147). This explanation fails to consider the power imbalances in family life that guide women to choose to assume most of the responsibility for domestic work and child-rearing.

Most liberal approaches recognize that some people choose under conditions that are not altogether fair, which raises problems related to equality of opportunity and individual responsibility. With respect to equality of opportunity, one favoured solution to unequal conditions is affirmative action. The hope is that weighting selection processes in favour of women (or other groups) will compensate for the implicit or historical discrimination that women have suffered. As a method of compensation, affirmative action helps to sustain the basic model of equality, premised on individual autonomy, equal opportunity, and responsibility for the choices we make.

Feminists tend to be critical of such solutions on the ground that they amount to nothing more than "add women and stir." Affirmative action programs generally fail to bring about equality because they aim only to compensate for biases in the opportunity structures open to women and other disadvantaged groups. They thus leave untouched the actual biases that characterize this opportunity structure. In short, affirmative action does not restructure jobs and specifically fails to address the fact that the structure of paid labour is incompatible with child-rearing (Mackinnon 1987). However they are hired, women with jobs in fields dominated by men will usually be forced to choose either not to have children or to assume the double duty of domestic labour and paid labour. Men are usually not confronted with these choices because the child-rearing duties and domestic responsibilities typically expected of and assumed by men are compatible with their paid employment.

Another strategy, favoured in some liberal theories of equality, for addressing the tension between the structure of paid labour and child-rearing is to reaffirm the individual as responsible for the choices she makes by treating children as expensive tastes that require no compensation (Rakowski 1993, 109; see Anderson 1999, 297). Like the human capital approach, the expensive tastes approach levels down the factors that structure individual choice. It suggests that having children should be treated as a choice like any other choice, which comes with its benefits and burdens. If some people choose to get married, raise children, or otherwise engage in relations that typically involve unremunerated caregiving, they should not expect society to compensate them for these choices. Child-rearing, after all, is personally fulfilling in many ways (more so than much paid employment), and this reward is enough to make it rational to choose to have children even with all the disadvantages. Some people choose to have children, while others forgo this pleasure to devote their attention to writing or art. This approach suggests that society should not be obliged to sustain those who choose to have children – any more than it should compensate those who work part time in order to be poets. In this view, a theory of equality remains responsibility-sensitive by recognizing that children are expensive tastes whose associated costs should be paid by the bearer, not by society.

Public policy in Canada contains some good examples of the expensive tastes approach. For instance, in *Symes v. Canada* ([1993] 4 SCR 695), Symes sought to deduct child care costs as a business expense against the income she earned as a partner in a small law firm. Revenue Canada did not allow the deduction. Two questions were put to the Supreme Court in this case. First, can child care count as a business expense rather than a personal expense? Second, will a restrictive interpretation of what counts as a business expense discriminate against women? The Supreme Court answered "no" to each question, and its decision used the expensive taste approach to circumvent the structural biases that contribute to gender inequality. The court first reaffirmed the division between the domestic sphere (i.e., personal expenses) and the public sphere (i.e., business expenses). It noted that the unequal domestic burden that women bear was mandated by society, not by the law. The court was only willing to scrutinize the legal burdens created by financial responsibilities, and since no evidence was presented to suggest that women are disproportionally responsible for financing child care expenses, the tax burden was not discriminatory. It then based its outlook on the fact that women choose to have children. As Justice Major stated: "Isn't that a matter of their choice, knowing that having a child is going to bear some costs in time and money?" (quoted in Johnson 2000, 208; also see Young 1994). Major's comments reflect the idea that children are expensive tastes and as such come with costs that those who choose to have children must absorb. The argument that women are made financially and socially vulnerable by these choices, thus deserving public compensation, was rejected by the court.

As with the court's decision in *Symes*, the expensive tastes solution circumvents but does not resolve the difficulties created for theories of equality by the domestic division of labour. One problem is that, though men and women share the "taste" of having families and raising children, women assume most of the burdens for this taste and, unlike men, are rendered vulnerable to poverty and exploitation as a result. Another problem is that raising children and taking care of domestic work is, in many respects, socially necessary labour. If mothers (or in some cases fathers) were unwilling to perform this labour, they would have to pay someone to perform it for them. And if parents did not assume responsibility one way or another for raising their children, then society would have to organize and pay for alternative means. In this view, the choice of whether or not to be a parent is a red herring in the discussion. The crucial fact is that all individuals rely, at different times in their lives, on the caregiving of others. Therefore, which person chooses to be a parent or caregiver is irrelevant to the broader need, namely the social necessity of child-rearing and caregiving services on which all societies depend (Anderson 1999).

Whereas the expensive tastes solution is sometimes cited by liberal theorists of equality as a means of resolving the tension between the structure of paid labour and child-rearing, feminists favour solutions that restructure paid labour so that it is compatible with the raising of children and the sharing of domestic responsibilities. In this respect, Susan Okin's path-breaking work of 1989, *Justice, Gender and the Family*, remains among the most comprehensive attempts to adopt this approach. Okin's proposals include conventional suggestions such as paid maternity and parental leave, four-day work weeks with flexible work hours/days so that parents can spend time with their children, especially in the early years, and high-quality, on-site daycare that is subsidized for low-income earning families. She also argues that the demands of high-status jobs must be restructured (e.g., tenure, making partner, promotion) so that professional demands do not coincide with the peak period of child-rearing (Okin 1989, 176). Her less conventional suggestions include teaching children about the "present inequalities, ambiguities, and uncertainties of marriage, the facts of workplace discrimination and segregation, and the likely consequences of making life choices based on assumptions about gender; including home economics courses that teach girls and boys how to combine working and parenting" (ibid., 177). Perhaps her most provocative suggestion is that domestic labour ought to be treated as paid work that should be remunerated by a pay cheque. Those who stay home to take care of the children ought to be "legally entitled to earnings coming into the household" (ibid., 180-81). This could be done, she suggests, by requiring that the income earned by one spouse's job be split by employers into two paycheques, made payable to each spouse.

Interestingly, Okin suggests that her proposals will not merely get rid of gender inequality; they will get rid of gender. Gender (as opposed to sex), she argues, is code for social power; once we get rid of the framework by which social power is distributed, in particular the way that the public sphere (including the market) has been divided from the private sphere (including the domestic), we undermine one of the main ways in which gender has been associated with social power. Once these markers of social power are gone, then gender will be gone, according to Okin, because, among other things, it will no longer structure the division of labour. Moreover, even if the division of labour continues to be structured in part along gender lines and thereby places one partner mostly in the home and the other in the paid workplace, this arrangement will not cause the economic dependence of one partner on the other.

MULTICULTURALISM AND CULTURAL INEQUALITY

Theories of cultural inequality arise from the observation that, even where income is distributed equally, individuals may be treated as less worthy members of society because of the ethnic, racial, or national minority to which they belong. Cultural and economic inequalities are often related (see Fraser 1997, Chapter 1), but the inequality associated with culture is not fully accounted for by the presence of economic inequality.[9] Until recently, theories of distributive equality have ignored the problem of cultural inequality and instead presumed that racial and other social inequalities matter primarily in terms of their relation to economic inequality.

As with gender, the neglect of cultural inequality is not easily remedied because distributive approaches tend to obscure our understanding of cultural inequality in at least two ways. The first obstacle relates to what counts as a resource. Theorists of equality who focus on the effects of cultural and linguistic diversity argue that culture is a kind of resource and that equal access to a cultural structure ought to figure into distributive theories as a primary good (Kymlicka 1989). Cultural identity is valuable because only within the context provided by a rich cultural structure does the array of opportunities available to individuals, and the choices they make in relation to these opportunities, have meaning for them. According to Kymlicka, how we understand our culture, its history, traditions, and conventions "is a precondition of making intelligent judgments about how to lead our lives" (Kymlicka 1995, 83).

The need for access to a rich cultural structure gives rise to potential inequality between mainstream and minority cultures. Cultural minorities have limited access to their own cultural structures because they live amidst a majority whose cultural structure dominates the public sphere. Minorities often speak a different language, and their cultural narrative does not define public life, is not taught in the schools, and does not inform the practices, conventions, and traditions of public institutions. The cultural cues written into the literature, history, and art that they study in public schools are the cues for another culture with a different history. In this sense, in comparison with the majority, cultural minorities have ready access to fewer cultural resources in making meaningful choices about their lives.

Since it is impossible to strip the public sphere of all cultural and linguistic values, the public sphere will inevitably be biased, lending itself to easier access for some than for others. For instance, a nation-state will give an advantage to those fluent in the language in which public life is conducted. Language is a significant means by which the public sphere is biased in favour of some groups over others. Many liberal states also recognize a state religion, adopt religious symbolism, and structure public life, if only through the timing of public holidays, according to the values of one set of religious traditions. The institutions of all liberal states, while purportedly serving citizens of different cultural backgrounds equally, promote particular interpretations of history and particular national values that are based on myths and stories about the nation and its accomplishments. These inevitably speak to the experiences and historical memories of some dominant groups, and less so to others. Therefore, members of the majority will have ready access to their cultural structure when they participate in the public sphere, while members of minorities will not have ready access.

Since it is often impossible to remove these biases entirely, as in the case of language, or undesirable to neutralize them, as in the case of teaching or celebrating national history and symbols, societies committed to equality must devise a different way to address them. Unequal access to the rich cultural structure found in the public sphere can foreclose minority members' access to many opportunities, including job opportunities. It can also impose on the minority extra costs for participating in the public sphere. The example of language is again instructive. Minority language speakers must either expend considerable resources to learn the dominant group's language or accept a much narrower set of employment and other opportunities.

In addition to skewing the public sphere in favour of the majority, cultural inequality can lead to forms of devaluation that undermine the political and social status of minority groups. For instance, the dominance of a particular ethnic group in positions of status and power and the absence of members of other groups may not only indicate but also add to the devaluation of the absent groups. Cultural inequality can be reflected and fostered in patterns of communication that privilege the ways in which some groups present and defend their interests and devalue others. It can also be reflected and fostered in patterns of access to public resources such as health care and in the relative vulnerability of minority groups to societal violence. Insofar as opportunities available to individuals are affected by factors such as shared cultural values, communication and language skills, access to public resources, and vulnerability to violence or illness, these considerations are resources to be factored into distributional schemes.

Theorists like Kymlicka advocate amending the liberal theory of equality by expanding the concept of a resource to include "cultural resources." Others argue that cultural inequality cannot be corrected through redistribution. According to Iris Young, the logic of distribution focuses our attention on taking resources away from some individuals who have power and giving them to others who have less power in order to ensure that everyone gets an equal share. This logic, she claims, is based on two faulty assumptions. First, power is assumed to be an alienable resource that can be traded, exchanged, and equalized. Alienable resources can be taken from us or given to us. But many sources of cultural and other forms of inequality are not about "stuff" that can be redistributed. For example, how can a cultural structure be redistributed? Some groups have ready access to cultural resources because they are the majority and their culture dominates the public sphere. Other groups, such as recent immigrants and small ethnic communities, have neither sufficient resources nor a population able to sustain societal institutions. So paying attention to the distribution of resources is not enough. Resources are not themselves powerful unless sustained by structures and relations, such as culture, and these give more meaning and power to some resources than to others.

A second problem with the distributive approach is its focus on the particular people or agents who have power and those who do not rather than on the systems that sustain inequality. Focusing on discrete agents within power relationships – such as "the ruler and the subject," "the husband and the wife," or "the judge and the prisoner" – as models for the distribution of power do (Young 1990, 31), largely ignores the many relations that sustain the power of some agents and the powerlessness of others. In order to address cultural inequality, Young claims our focus ought to be on the system in which distribution takes place rather than on the precise division of goods among particular people. As with gender, the problem of cultural inequality is not usually a matter of explicit discrimination. Rather, cultural oppression tends to be the result of people simply doing their jobs in, sometimes, perfectly well-intentioned ways. The point is that the institutions through which people act also sustain relations in which, for instance, some groups are viewed as the standard to which others are compared and found wanting. To get at these sorts of biases, Young argues for a "politics of difference," which entails looking at inequality in terms of systems that sustain the marginalization, exploitation, powerlessness, cultural imperialism, and violence suffered by some groups and not by others (Young 1990, Chapter 2). It requires examining the structures, actions, and relations within society, whether or not they intentionally lead to the domination of some groups by others.

MEASURES TO ADDRESS CULTURAL INEQUALITY
The measures to address cultural inequality vary from those aimed at radically reworking all institutions of society to those that require consciously scrutinizing and reforming institutions to ensure that they do not limit the access of one group to the cultural structures sustained by mainstream society. In Canada, two categories of measures are usually the focus of critical attention.

The first category is group rights, which are rights that extend the means of limited self-government to national minorities, such as French Canadians in Quebec and Aboriginal peoples. Group rights help to address cultural inequality by providing a way to ensure that groups have a chance to create and enjoy their own societal cultures, through their own institutions, while enjoying some protection from the overwhelming influence and impact of the majority.

As a means of addressing cultural inequality, group rights potentially have three drawbacks. First, they can fragment society and undermine its ability to engage in cooperative projects, including projects that could advance social justice for all members. Large-scale social projects, such as public health care and public pension plans, redistribute resources and require a high degree of social cohesion and cooperation. Some critics worry that these projects are weakened by the sort of cleavages in social organization that characterize multinational states (Miller 1995, Chapter 5; see also Banting and Kymlicka forthcoming).

Second, the social cohesion that is jeopardized by fragmenting the state is precisely what is needed in order to motivate reluctant but wealthy majorities to devote resources to the well-being of powerless minorities (see Barry 2001; in relation to Aboriginal peoples in Canada, see Cairns 2001). The flaw of self-government as a solution to inequality is that it cuts off fragile minorities from the resources they need to build their own institutions and to ensure their economic well-being. Rather than addressing inequality, self-government might worsen it because self-governing groups will not have the resources needed to build the rich cultural context they need.

A third criticism of group rights is that they potentially create additional categories of oppression within the group. While group rights protect a group from external influences, they may also protect the group from changes urged by their own members. Dissenting members of the group find that rights that protect their group from the influence of the external majority greatly increase the group's resistance to internal change (Shachar 2001). In an effort to equalize opportunities between groups, some group rights policies end up rendering vulnerable those individuals who are already disadvantaged within groups.

After group rights, a second category of measures used to address cultural inequality can be labelled "measures of multicultural integration." Kymlicka argues that group rights might be appropriate for colonized groups, particularly Aboriginal peoples, who have suffered from profound cultural inequality and insecurity due to continuous attempts by settler societies to coercively assimilate them. But he argues that immigrants who voluntarily uproot themselves to gain the prospective advantages in new countries "relinquish the rights that go along with their original national membership" (Kymlicka 1995, 96) and forgo the benefit of enjoying the cultural security of being members of a majority or protected minority. These groups primarily require the means to integrate successfully into the mainstream culture and thereby to gain access to the rich array of resources found in the public sphere. They need social services and educational programs that will help them learn the language and culture of their new country. They also need policies and programs that fight prejudice and discrimination against them.

One way to respond to these needs is to "fix" the cultural marketplace by giving minorities extra resources so they have a better chance of gaining access to the rich cultural structure of the majority. In Canada, funding devoted to language programs, specifically English and French as a Second Language, is an example of the sort of extra resources devoted to encouraging immigrants to integrate into the cultural and linguistic mainstream. Even if, in light of these programs, some groups enjoy extra educational resources (e.g., publicly subsidized language instruction), these additional resources are intended to equalize access of cultural minorities to the rich cultural structure of the majority.

Another way of addressing the problem is through policies to ensure that members of cultural minorities can enter public life feeling comfortable about the ethnic background they bring to it. Multiculturalism "has made the possession of an ethnic identity an acceptable, even normal, part of life in mainstream society" (Kymlicka 1998, 44). Policies that aim at this result include extending to some groups exemptions from particular laws that interfere with their core practices or deeply held beliefs, including those related to religious dress or dietary rules. Similarly, policies that fund minority cultural associations, such as ethnic community centres, clubs, and events, are seen through the multiculturalist lens, not as policies that favour cultural minorities but, rather, as policies that help restructure the public sphere to encourage cultural minorities to enter and become fully integrated.

As with policies that provide group rights, measures of multicultural integration have been criticized for fragmenting society in ways that jeopardize social solidarity and cohesion. For instance, Brian Barry argues that rather than helping citizens belong to a single society and share a common fate, "the whole point of the 'politics of difference' is to assert that the right answer is for each cultural group to have public policies tailored to meet its specific demands" (Barry 2001, 300). Although little empirical evidence exists one way or another, the indicators available seem to point to the opposite conclusion. Survey studies confirm that multiculturalism policy in Canada has eased the transition of immigrants, who then become devoted to Canada and eager to identify with the political community and the government of that community (Harles 1997, 734-35). Compared to other countries, Canada experiences relatively low levels of segregation in housing and education, only moderate ethnic inequality in income and earnings, and broadly equal cultural participation rates across the labour market and in unions (Kurthen 1997, 261; also see Kymlicka 1998, 21-22). Kymlicka has argued that, with respect to naturalization, political participation, and official language acquisition, immigrants are more integrated today than they were before multiculturalism was instituted (1998, 18), and mainstream society is more tolerant of ethnic diversity. This tolerance and integration are signs that cultural minorities are gaining access to the cultural structure of mainstream society and that cultural inequality is thereby being addressed.

Conclusion

Consideration of the nature of equality as a fundamental social value raises numerous philosophical issues. Our discussion has focused on three main themes: the general status and importance of equality as a normative ideal, the interpretation of equality in the context of distributive justice, and the interpretation of equality in the context of feminism and cultural diversity. We have not attempted to forge direct links between the philosophical literature and the empirical data examined in the other chapters of this volume. But we hope to have provided a useful perspective for assessing the normative significance of the empirical findings. At least we may have revealed the enormous complexity and variability of the issues currently considered central to equality.

NOTES

1 This conception of justice as impartiality is often contrasted with an approach that views justice in terms of mutual advantage. In this approach, justice is not an inherently egalitarian standard. Instead, principles of justice are those that rational, self-interested agents have reason to adopt in order to achieve and facilitate mutually advantageous cooperation. Thus, equal consideration of the interests

of persons is at best a contingent condition of advantageous forms of social co-operation. Where the achievement of mutual advantage does not depend on treating persons as equals, justice does not require it. The most influential recent exponent of justice as mutual advantage is David Gauthier (1986).

2　We cannot avoid appeals to intuition. We must, of course, try to ensure that the intuitions we employ in reasoning about justice are reasonable. Some intuitions may reflect or be the product of forms of socialization in ways that diminish their authority. But as Nagel notes: "To trust our intuitions, particularly those that tell us something is wrong even though we don't know exactly what would be right, we need only believe that our moral understanding extends farther than our capacity to spell out the principles that underlie it. Intuition can be corrupted by custom, self-interest, or commitment to a theory, but it need not be, and a person's intuitions will provide him with evidence that the arrangements he has been brought up to find natural are really unjust. Intuitive dissatisfaction is an essential resource in political theory" (Nagel 1991, 7).

3　For recent discussion about debate between "political" and "cosmopolitan" construals of the scope of justice, see Nagel (2005) and Tan (2004).

4　The nature of well-being is itself a topic of debate. Does it consist in pleasure? Or desire satisfaction? Or the development of distinctive human capacities? (Griffin 1986).

5　What counts as an equally good welfare outcome will depend on the conception of welfare that is embraced. The main proponent of equality of opportunity for welfare, Richard Arneson, proposes that welfare should be interpreted as consisting in the satisfaction of considered, self-interested preferences.

6　The existence of equal capabilities does not necessarily imply equal functioning. Two persons who have the same access to nutritious food may respond differently to the option. For instance, a hunger striker may refuse food that another person eats. The former, unlike the latter, will not achieve the functioning of consuming a nutritious diet but both can be equal in capabilities.

7　Usually, the capabilities approach is characterized as falling somewhere between welfarist theories and resourcist theories. However, some theorists question whether the differences between resourcist and capabilities approaches are theoretically significant. See Pogge (2002).

8　Much empirical work nicely challenges these sorts of divisions while illustrating the vulnerability of those within the domestic sphere. For an analysis of women's wage equality see Fortin and Schirle (Chapter 11). For a discussion of children's economic equality see Phipps and Lethbridge (Chapter 8). For a philosophical discussion of issues related to children's equality see Archard and Macleod (2002).

9　For empirical analysis of the impacts of ethnicity, national origin or immigrant status, and native language on economic, health, and social capital outcomes, see Curtis, Grabb, and Perks (Chapter 7) and Gee, Kobayashi, and Prus (Chapter 9).

REFERENCES

Anderson, Elizabeth. 1999. "What's the Point of Equality?" *Ethics* 99(2): 287-337.

Archard, David, and Colin Macleod, eds. 2002. *The Moral and Political Status of Children*. Oxford: Oxford University Press.

Arneson, Richard. 1989. "Equality and Equal Opportunity for Welfare." *Philosophical Studies* 56: 77-93.

Banting, Keith, and Will Kymlicka, eds. Forthcoming. *Is Multiculturalism Bad for the Welfare State?* Oxford UK: Oxford University Press.

Barry, Brian. 2001. *Culture and Equality*. Cambridge, UK: Polity.

Becker, Gary. 1981. *A Treatise on the Family*. Cambridge, MA: Harvard University Press.

Cairns, Alan C. 2001. *Citizens Plus: Aboriginal Peoples and the Canadian State*. Vancouver: UBC Press.

Dworkin, Ronald. 1977. *Taking Rights Seriously*. London: Duckworth.

—. 2000. *Sovereign Virtue: The Theory and Practice of Equality*. Cambridge, MA: Harvard University Press.

Eisenberg, Avigail. 2006. "Equality, Trust and Multiculturalism." In Richard Johnston and Fiona Kay, eds., *Social Capital, Diversity, and the Welfare State*. Vancouver: UBC Press.

Fraser, Nancy. 1997. *Justice Interruptus*. New York: Routledge.

Gauthier, David. 1986. *Morals by Agreement*. Oxford: Oxford University Press.

Griffin, James. 1986. *Well-Being: Its Meaning, Measurement, and Moral Importance*. Oxford: Oxford University Press.

Harles, John C. 1997. "Integration before Assimilation: Immigration, Multiculturalism and the Canadian Polity." *Canadian Journal of Political Science* 30: 711-36.

Johnson, Rebecca. 2000. "If Choice Is the Answer, What Is the Question? Spelunking in *Symes v. Canada*." In Dorothy E. Chunn and Dany Lancombe, eds., *Law as a Gendering Practice*. Don Mills, ON: Oxford.

Kurthen, Hermann. 1997. "The Canadian Experience with Multiculturalism and Employment Equity: Lessons for Europe." *New Community* 23: 249-70.

Kymlicka, Will. 1989. *Liberalism, Community and Culture*. Oxford: Oxford University Press.

—. 1995. *Multicultural Citizenship*. Oxford: Oxford University Press.

—. 1998. *Finding Our Way*. Toronto: Oxford University Press.

—. 2002. *Contemporary Political Philosophy*. Oxford: Oxford University Press.

Macleod, Colin. 1998. *Liberalism, Justice and Markets: A Critique of Liberal Equality*. Oxford: Oxford University Press.

Mackinnon, Catharine. 1987. *Feminism Unmodified: Discourses on Life and Law*. Cambridge, MA: Harvard University Press.

Miller, David. 1995. *On Nationality*. Oxford: Oxford University Press.

Nagel, Thomas. 1991. *Equality and Partiality*. Oxford: Oxford University Press.

—. 2005. "The Problem of Global Justice." *Philosophy and Public Affairs* 33(2): 113-47.

Nussbaum, Martha. 2000. *Women and Human Development: The Capabilities Approach.* Cambridge, NY: Cambridge University Press.

Okin, Susan Moller. 1989. *Justice, Gender and the Family.* New York: Basic Books.

Pateman, Carol. 1988. *The Sexual Contract.* Stanford, CA: Stanford University Press.

Pogge, Thomas. 2002. "Can the Capability Approach Be Justified?" In Martha Nussbaum and Chad Flanders, eds., *Global Inequalities.* Special issue of *Philosophical Topics* 30(2): 167-228.

Rakowski, Eric. 1993. *Equal Justice.* Oxford: Oxford University Press.

Rawls, John. 1971. *A Theory of Justice.* London: Oxford University Press.

—. 1980. "Kantian Constructivism and Moral Theory." *Journal of Philosophy* 77(9): 515-72.

Scanlon, Thomas. 1975. "Preference and Urgency." *Journal of Philosophy* 72: 655-69.

Sen, Amartya. 1982. *Choice, Welfare, and Measurement.* Oxford: Basil Blackwell.

—. 1990. "More than 100 Million Women are Missing." *New York Review of Books*, 20 December, 61-65.

—. 1992. *Inequality Reexamined.* Cambridge, MA: Harvard University Press.

—. 1999. *Development as Freedom.* New York: Knopf.

Shachar, Ayelet. 2001. *Multicultural Jurisdictions: Cultural Differences and Women's Rights.* Cambridge: Cambridge University Press.

Tan, Kok-Chor. 2004. *Justice without Borders: Cosmopolitanism, Nationalism, and Patriotism.* Cambridge: Cambridge University Press.

Taylor, Charles. 1992. "The Politics of Recognition." In Amy Gutmann, ed., *Multiculturalism and the Politics of Recognition.* Princeton, NJ: Princeton University Press.

Young, Claire F.L. 1994. "Child Care: A Taxing Issue." *McGill Law Journal* 39(3): 539-67.

Young, Iris Marion. 1990. *Justice and the Politics of Difference.* Princeton, NJ: Princeton University Press.

3
Rising Income Inequality in the 1990s: An Exploration of Three Data Sources

Marc Frenette, David A. Green, and Garnett Picot

The levels and trends in inequality in income are key inputs into any discussions of equity in a society, of how that society's economy functions, and of how both of these have been changing over time. It is particularly useful to compare inequality in raw pre-tax, pre-transfer income with that in after-tax, after-transfer income to assess the role of government redistribution in economic well-being. For this reason, our study distinguishes between "market income," which consists of gross income from earnings and investments, and "disposable income," which is the net income after accounting for taxes paid and transfers received.

In Canada's case, several authors document that while earnings inequality rose throughout the 1980s and early 1990s in Canada, family disposable income inequality changed very little (e.g., Beach and Slotsve 1994; Morissette et al. 1994; Jäntti 1997; Rashid 1998; and Wolfson and Murphy 1998). Canada's tax and transfer system thus played a strong role in offsetting market-driven inequality increases. Less is known about the patterns in the 1990s. The goal of this chapter is to expand our knowledge of inequality patterns in the 1990s and compare them with the better-known patterns of the 1980s.

Beginning in the mid-1990s, the Canadian tax and transfer system underwent substantial change, including an overhaul of the Unemployment Insurance system (now the Employment Insurance system), substantial reforms to provincial social assistance programs (such as declining benefits and tighter eligibility rules), the introduction of the Child Tax Benefit, and the (modest) beginning of a round of tax cuts at the end of the 1990s. The late 1990s also saw a very strong economic recovery, with prime-aged unemployment and employment rates reaching levels by 2000 not observed since at least 1981. These changes raise several questions. Did earnings inequality fall significantly during the later part of the cycle, given the very strong economic growth, and as witnessed late in the cycle in the United States (e.g., Llg and Haugen 2000)? This would have tended to reduce family income inequality. Or was the earnings growth primarily concentrated at the top of the earnings distribution, tending to increase inequality? To the extent that earnings inequality increased, did the tax and transfer system continue to offset the inequality increases, as it did through the 1980s?

Though not the case with similar analyses for earlier periods, the comparability of data over time is a major issue for the 1990s. Ensuring that the data are appropriate for the analysis is a major component of the research for the decade. Hence, to answer these and related questions, we use three different data sources. We start with survey data covering the period 1980 to 2000, using a combination of the Survey of Consumer Finances (SCF) up to 1996 and then the Survey of Labour and Income Dynamics (SLID) (which replaced the SCF as Statistics Canada's main survey) beginning in 1996. We complement our findings with results from taxation data (the T1 Family Files, or T1FF). The T1FF provides a consistent series of income estimates from 1992 to 2000 (thus covering the "seam" created by the transition from the SCF to SLID) and, given its large size, does not suffer from the variability of estimates often associated with survey data. Another advantage of the T1FF is its relatively high coverage rate. Finally, we use Census data for the years 1980, 1985, 1990, 1995, and 2000. In particular, we focus on 1980, 1990, and 2000, years that are in roughly comparable positions in the business cycle. This provides another consistent source that covers the last two business cycles. Coverage at the bottom levels of the distribution may be better in the Census than in the surveys because reporting is compulsory and response rates tend to be much higher than in the income surveys. The disadvantage of the Census is that it lacks information on income taxes paid and can thus only provide post-transfer, pre-tax data. As a result, effects of changes in the tax system on family income inequality are missed.

From this description, one can see there is no perfect data source for the 1990s. The survey data have a discontinuity in 1996, the taxation data do not cover the complete 1990s cycle, let alone allowing comparisons with the 1980s cycle, and the Census data are pre-tax and only occur every five years. We use all three sources to develop a picture of trends in family income inequality during the 1990s. Unfortunately, the survey and tax data provide quite different pictures of the level and trends in family income inequality. The survey data suggest a far more equal income distribution than do other data sources and point to an increase in family market income inequality generated from larger increases in incomes at the top than at the bottom of the distribution. According to that same source, the tax and transfer system largely, though not completely, offset the increase in market income inequality, resulting in a small rise in disposable income inequality over the 1990s. Interestingly, the offsetting effects from the tax and transfer system appear to occur entirely in the first half of the decade; adding in tax and transfer effects actually leads to *increases* in inequality over the second half of the 1990s.

In contrast, the tax data point to much larger increases in market income inequality, driven both by rises in market income at the top of the distribution and a lack of improvement among families at the bottom. Further, the inequality-increasing effects of the tax and transfer system in the second half of the decade are just as strong as those observed in the survey data. Thus, according to the tax data, and in contrast to the survey data, the 1990s witnessed very substantial increases in disposable income inequality. Moreover, the level of inequality is much higher in the tax data than the survey data in each year, due mainly to much lower earnings at the bottom of the distribution.

Given the very different inequality patterns observed in the two types of data, it is important to consider the strengths and weaknesses of each source. To do so, we turn to the Census data, which have coverage rates comparable to those of the tax data but a survey methodology closer to that of the Survey of Consumer Finances. While the Census market income inequality levels more closely resemble those observed in the tax data, the trends diverge substantially from those observed in both the survey and tax data.

The Census and survey data both point to a similar increase in income inequality over the 1990s, although the pathways are very different. The survey data suggest that inequality rose moderately in both the first and second halves of the decade. In the first half, this was largely due to a moderate decline in income at the bottom of the distribution, while in the second half it was mainly due to a large improvement at the top of the distribution (incomes improved moderately at the bottom at this time). According to the Census data, inequality rose substantially in the early 1990s, due mainly to a large decline in the bottom of the distribution. In the latter half of the decade, inequality remained fairly stable, since there were substantial improvements at the top and bottom of the distribution. In essence, the main difference between the Census and survey data lies in what both sources suggest happened at the bottom of the distribution. According to the survey data, incomes fell moderately in the early 1990s and then rose moderately in the latter half of the decade. The Census data also suggest a decline followed by an increase, but the fluctuations were much larger. It is possible, though not certain, that the difference between the survey and Census data is the result of the inherent difficulty in capturing the bottom end of the distribution in non-mandatory surveys. So the tax data might be regarded as somewhat more reliable, though we later discuss other shortcomings of the tax data.

The income distributions appear to be more alike in the Census and tax data, although the trends at the bottom diverge just as much as they do when we look at the Census and survey data. In the late 1990s (the only period in which we can compare Census and tax data), both sources point to a large increase at the top (as do the survey data), but the tax data indicate a moderate decline at the bottom. Recall that the Census data show a substantial improvement at the bottom. As a result, in the late 1990s income inequality rose considerably according to the tax data, yet remained fairly stable according to the Census data.

In summary, while all three data sources point to an increase in income inequality over the 1990s, there are substantial differences in the levels of inequality, as well as in the extent and timing of the trends. The main objective of this chapter is to document these differences, which point to the importance of establishing the true levels and trends in future research.

The chapter has six sections. The next section provides details on the SCF/SLID and tax data used for the majority of the analysis. The third section describes our approach to measuring changes in inequality. The fourth section discusses cyclical elements in the economy that may affect the analysis. The fifth section constitutes most of the chapter and presents our results. The sixth section presents our conclusions.

Details of the Data

Income inequality studies generally rely on survey data, and the traditional source has been the Survey of Consumer Finances (SCF), which is available up to 1997.[1] The SCF was an annual cross-sectional survey that targeted all households in Canada, excepting persons living in the territories, in institutions, or on native reserves. The exceptions accounted for less than 3 percent of the Canadian population. The SCF sample of roughly 35,000 households was selected as a supplement to the April Labour Force Survey (LFS). The primary objective of the SCF was to provide income estimates by detailed sources, and responses by proxy were allowed (i.e., one person in the household could answer questions about other members).

The SCF was Statistics Canada's official source of income estimates until 1996, when the Survey of Labour and Income Dynamics (SLID) began to be used for this purpose. The SCF and SLID share many features. Both are annual household surveys that use the LFS as a sampling frame and have the same target population. Although SLID can be (and is) used for cross-sectional estimates, it is also designed for longitudinal analysis. Panels are interviewed for up to six years, with new (and overlapping) panels introduced every three years. New panels were introduced in 1993, 1996, and 1999. Each year, a panel is interviewed in January (mainly to collect labour information) and in May (to collect income information). For the income interview, respondents have the option of allowing Statistics Canada to link to their T1 tax files (if possible) in order to collect their income information, thus eliminating the need for an income questionnaire. More than 80 percent of respondents give Statistics Canada permission to attempt this match, and the income of about 70 percent of all respondents is obtained from the tax files in this way. Another difference between the two surveys relates to the formation of families. In the SCF, families were derived with respect to the "head" of the family, which gives priority to the husband. In SLID, it is with respect to the "major income recipient." Sample surveys must of course deal with sampling error (by which a selected sample does not exactly mirror a population) and non-sampling error, including potential non-response bias.

Response rates in the SCF generally hover around 80 percent, while in SLID it is slightly higher (80 to 85 percent). The cross-sectional sample weights in SCF and SLID are adjusted for non-response to ensure accurate population counts for different province-age-sex groups, as well as by household and family size. The weights are *not* adjusted for income-related response bias, that is, for potentially differential response rates at different levels of the income distribution. If important changes are occurring at the top or bottom of the income distribution, the data being used to track changes in inequality must have a good coverage rate in these parts of the distribution, yet these are typically the segments that present the most difficulties with response rates and coverage.

Official income estimates used the SCF up to and including 1995; since then, SLID has become the official Statistics Canada source. Since two data sources are used to create one time-series, there is the potential for the "seam" problem: a discontinuity in the series that is related to the change in data sources. In particular, the (partial) use of tax data in SLID may help reduce response errors (relative to SCF).

Coverage of particular income components is also an issue in surveys. Generally speaking, coverage of the earnings income component has been good, but that of transfer components such as employment insurance benefits and social assistance receipts less so (Kapsalis 2001). Changes in these coverage rates can influence the outcomes of analyses such as the one conducted here, particularly for the bottom end of the distribution. In particular, the movement toward partial tax data in SLID (compared to full survey data in SCF) may have changed the coverage of transfer income.

We complement our survey findings with taxation data. The Canada Customs and Revenue Agency (CCRA) collects personal income tax forms (T1) from all tax filers in Canada. From the T1 file, Statistics Canada creates the T1FF (the T1 Family File), which attempts to reconstruct Census families by imputing the presence of non-filing children and spouses. The T1FF is a census of all individuals who file taxes or whose social insurance number (SIN) appears on another family member's tax file. Non-filing children (and those with a SIN that does not appear on another family member's tax file) are imputed. Unlike survey data, T1FF may contain records of people living in the territories, in institutions, or on native reserves. At best, we can only identify people living in the territories with a reasonable amount of certainty; to be as consistent as possible, we have deleted those records.

The T1FF has been particularly well-suited for estimates of income at the lower end of the distribution since 1992 because of the large number of incentives for lower-income families to file tax returns.[2] On the other hand, the creation of those incentives implies that tax data are unlikely to be based on a consistent sample of observations before versus after 1992. Indeed, given changes from the Child Tax Credit to the Child Tax Benefit in 1993, the 1992 data may also not be comparable to data for subsequent years.[3] This discrepancy plus the fact that transfer income was not reported at all before 1989 and not reported consistently before 1992, implies that we cannot use tax data before 1992 or, possibly, 1993. We present results including both 1992 and 1993 tax data but emphasize 1993 as a starting point in establishing trends.

Tax data offer three distinct advantages over SCF/SLID. First, the population coverage rate has been over 95 percent since 1992 in T1FF, which is better than with survey data (generally around 80 percent). Second, T1FF gives us a consistent time-series over the SCF/SLID seam (including fairly consistent estimates of transfer income). Finally, sampling error is minimized in tax data given the much larger sample sizes. Its main potential drawback is that sample composition may change over time in response to sometimes subtle incentive changes for filing and reporting. These may be the source of some of the differences in trends between the tax data and the Census and SCF data. Our investigation so far has not produced a simple explanation for the differences, such as incentive changes associated with a particular tax policy change, but this feature of the tax data needs to be kept in mind.

One drawback of using tax data is the lack of consistent income estimates prior to 1992, especially at the bottom of the distribution. Another issue is that the tax data create census families rather than the more commonly used economic families. A census family is defined as a now-married couple (with or without children), a common-law couple (same), or a single parent with a child under the age of 25 who does not have his or her own spouse or child living in the household. In our analysis, unattached individuals are also considered census families so that the complete population is covered. An economic family is defined as a group of two or more persons who live in the same dwelling and are related to each other by blood, marriage, common-law, or adoption. Once again, this analysis includes unattached individuals when the economic family concept is employed. By definition, all persons who are members of a census family are also members of an economic family.[4] Economic families are generally the preferred family unit of analysis for studies of economic well-being. However, to facilitate comparisons between survey and tax data, we often turn to the census family concept. The move from economic to census families has virtually no effect on our results; the same general conclusions hold no matter which concept is used.

Approach

In this study, the focus is on disposable, or after-tax family income (except with the census data, which do not have information on taxes paid). This is total income (including transfers) minus taxes paid.[5] Total income consists of market income plus transfer income. Market income is composed of employment earnings plus other (non-transfer) income (such as investment and pension income). Finally, employment earnings consist of paid earnings plus net self-employment income and other employment income. The following equations summarize these definitions:

$$\text{disposable income} = \text{total income} - \text{income taxes}$$

$$\text{total income} = \text{market income} + \text{transfer income}$$

$$\text{market income} = \text{employment earnings} + \text{other market income}$$

$$\text{employment earnings} = \text{paid earnings} + \text{net self-employment income} + \text{other employment earnings}$$

$$\text{other market income} = \text{actual dividends} + \text{interest income} + \text{net rental income} + \text{pension income} + \text{alimony received}$$

Other market income does not include capital gains. In the SCF, net partnership income is included as part of net self-employment income, while in SLID and T1FF, it is included as part of investment income. Note that, starting in 1997, new alimony arrangements were no longer tax-deductible (for payments made) nor taxable (for payments received).[6] Thus, there may be a discontinuity in the measurement of other income in tax data (T1FF and to a lesser extent SLID). Since only new arrangements are affected, however, the break should be minimal. This was confirmed by re-running all estimates without alimony received. It had no significant effect on the findings.

To measure inequality and its evolution through time, we rely on a series of indices that are sensitive to changes at various points of the income distribution. The Gini coefficient, G, is perhaps the most commonly used inequality index.[7] The Gini coefficient is sensitive to changes in the middle of the distribution, which renders it less than ideal in detecting changes over time when these are driven by events at the top and/or bottom. To provide a more complete picture, we also look at the exponential measure, Exp,[8] which is bottom-sensitive, and the coefficient of variation squared, CV^2, which is top-sensitive. The formula for each appears below:

$$\text{Exp} = \sum_{i=1}^{n} p_i \exp(-y_i / \overline{y}). \tag{1}$$

$$G = 2\sigma_{y,F(y)} / \overline{y}. \tag{2}$$

$$CV^2 = \left(\sigma_y / \overline{y} \right)^2. \tag{3}$$

Note that p_i denotes the share of the size of family (i) in the sample of n families, y denotes income, σ_y denotes the standard deviation of income, and $\sigma_{y,F(y)}$ denotes the covariance between income and its cumulative distribution $F(y)$. The Exp and CV^2 measures may be heavily influenced by outlier incomes, which may be relatively more prominent in smaller data sets such as SCF and SLID. To reduce this undesirable impact, we have dropped the top and bottom 0.1 percent of the income distribution in each year for all calculations (about sixty families a year).[9]

For significance tests, we rely on the work of Kovacevic and Binder (1997), who used the 1991 SCF to study variance in the estimation of earnings inequality measures. After accounting for the complex survey design (clustered sampling), they conclude that the coefficients of variation of the exponential, the Gini, and the CV^2 are 0.0026, 0.0066, and 0.0564, respectively. Assuming homoscedastic variances and equal population sizes over time, significant results (at 1 percent) are achieved with minimum movements of 0.005 (Exp), 0.01 (G), and 0.16 (CV^2) in absolute terms. We apply these thresholds throughout the chapter. We also apply the same statistical significance criteria in the tax data as we do in the survey data, although one could relax the criteria substantially, given the much larger sample sizes.

If the Exp, G, and CV^2 move in the same direction, then it is likely that the old and new Lorenz curves do not cross, which indicates an unambiguous change in inequality (based on the Lorenz ordering). However, if the three measures do not agree in the trends over time, then the Lorenz curves definitely cross, resulting in an ambiguous change in inequality.[10] These three inequality measures (Exp, G, and CV^2) provide a fairly robust set of summary inequality measures but, to acquire a better sense of what part of the income distribution changes over time, we also turn to an analysis of changes in mean income by vingtiles (ordered groups of 5 percent) and related top/bottom ratios.

We use the SCF/SLID series in a manner intended to account for the seam, or break in the series. In particular, rather than calculating change over the seam (1995 to 1996) using data from two different and possibly not comparable surveys, SCF and SLID, we sum the *changes* from each of the two data sources to minimize the impact of the seam. For example, the total change between 1989 and 2000 would be the change in the SCF measure between 1989 and 1996, plus the change in the SLID measure between 1996 and 2000. This is possible because two sets of income data are available for 1996. Of course, the SCF and SLID numbers may be different not just in terms of levels but also in terms of change over time. The incremental approach suggested here only accounts for the difference in levels, which is likely the more prominent discontinuity.

Income Inequality in Context: The Role of the Economic Cycle

When inequality measures are compared over time, it is vital to place the results within context of the economic cycle. A longstanding line of research in economics investigates whether hourly wages move pro- or counter-cyclically. Much of that investigation focuses on accounting for sample selection effects generated from the fact that layoffs do not occur randomly within the wage distribution. Wages may appear to rise in a recession when in reality we are simply observing the effects of the lower-wage workers being laid off first. We do not face this type of composition effect because we keep all sample observations, including those with zero market income, throughout our period. Our market income measure will still reflect the cycle, though, because spells of unemployment will generate substantial reductions in annual earnings. Furthermore, if returns to assets of various types fall during recessions, this will also cause drops in annual market income. We view the fact that our measure will capture all of these types of effects as a good feature since movements in annual income generated from moving in and out of the labour market definitely affect individual well-being.

The first of these effects (the layoff effect) will likely cause inequality to increase during recessions since we expect layoffs to fall disproportionally on the lower part of the market income distribution. During periods of expansion, this pattern should reverse itself and lead to larger increases in earnings at the bottom than at the top of the distribution. On the other hand, we expect the second effect (the reduction in returns to assets) to reduce inequality in a recession, especially if we focus on non-retired individuals. On balance, we expect the first effect to be stronger and so predict that we will observe a counter-cyclical movement in market income inequality. Since the tax and transfer system may partially or fully cushion these fluctuations, disposable income inequality should be much less variable over a business cycle and, generally speaking, over time.

The Canadian economy saw two full business cycles between 1980 and 2000 (Figure 3.1). The economy was essentially at a business cycle peak in 1980 or 1981 (with a prime-aged male unemployment rate of around 5.1 percent), 1989 (6.3 percent), and 2000 (5.7 percent). Cyclical troughs were observed in 1983 (9.9 percent), and 1992/1993 (10.7 and 10.6 percent, respectively).

In our analysis, we focus on two "peak-to-peak" year comparisons: 1980 and 1989, and 1989 and 2000. When we turn to tax data, only the years 1992 to 2000 are suitable for income estimates, and 1993 to 2000 are best

FIGURE 3.1

Annual national unemployment rate: males 25-54, 1976-2002

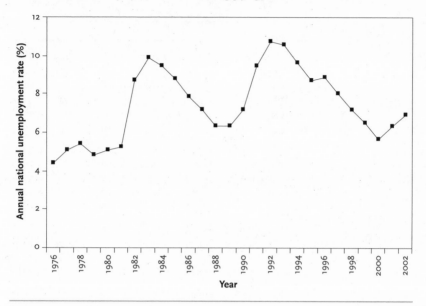

suited for this purpose. Since this period does not cover a full business cycle, we cannot compare similar years in the cycle. Consequently, we place the tax results in context of the economic recovery during this period. When using the census data, we focus on changes between 1980 and 1990, and 1990 to 2000. These years are at (or very near) business cycle peaks.

Results

EVIDENCE FROM SURVEY DATA

In Table 3.1, three measures of income inequality are shown for the SCF (1980 to 1996) and the SLID (1996 to 2000): a bottom-sensitive (the exponential measure, Exp), a middle-sensitive (the Gini coefficient, G), and a top-sensitive (the coefficient of variation squared, CV^2) measure. Market and disposable incomes are measured at the economic family level, but the unit of analysis is the individual. Thus, the results relate to income inequality among all individuals, based on their economic family income. The income data are "adult equivalent adjusted" to account for economies of scale in larger families.[11]

Table 3.1

Market and disposable income inequality, SCF/SLID: economic families

Data source	Year	Market income			Disposable income		
		Exp	G	CV²	Exp	G	CV²
SCF	1980	0.4446	0.3687	0.4690	0.4141	0.2849	0.2855
	1981	0.4443	0.3684	0.4658	0.4134	0.2837	0.2801
	1982	0.4514	0.3867	0.5199	0.4143	0.2864	0.2889
	1983	0.4573	0.4015	0.5735	0.4168	0.2944	0.3128
	1984	0.4575	0.4010	0.5756	0.4164	0.2923	0.3131
	1985	0.4544	0.3936	0.5537	0.4151	0.2884	0.3062
	1986	0.4542	0.3932	0.5531	0.4147	0.2874	0.3012
	1987	0.4536	0.3921	0.5404	0.4139	0.2856	0.2910
	1988	0.4532	0.3907	0.5315	0.4125	0.2811	0.2779
	1989	0.4508	0.3849	0.5318	0.4118	0.2783	0.2779
	1990	0.4545	0.3945	0.5443	0.4124	0.2806	0.2752
	1991	0.4619	0.4123	0.6241	0.4146	0.2873	0.3022
	1992	0.4626	0.4140	0.5958	0.4131	0.2832	0.2807
	1993	0.4659	0.4213	0.6254	0.4139	0.2858	0.2899
	1994	0.4653	0.4200	0.6248	0.4132	0.2834	0.2837
	1995	0.4654	0.4204	0.6414	0.4147	0.2878	0.2997
	1996	0.4656	0.4211	0.6392	0.4158	0.2914	0.3053
SLID	1996	0.4679	0.4263	0.6786	0.4174	0.2962	0.3195
	1997	0.4681	0.4269	0.6957	0.4189	0.3003	0.3377
	1998	0.4672	0.4247	0.7097	0.4189	0.2998	0.3439
	1999	0.4635	0.4163	0.6730	0.4182	0.2978	0.3322
	2000	0.4625	0.4140	0.6802	0.4192	0.3009	0.3467

Absolute growth in inequality

		Exp	G	CV²	Exp	G	CV²
Peak of the cycle	1980-1989	0.0062	0.0162	0.0629	−0.0023	−0.0065	−0.0076
comparisons	1989-2000	0.0094	0.0239	0.1090	0.0059	0.0178	0.0546
The 1989-2000	1989-1993	0.0151	0.0365	0.0936	0.0021	0.0074	0.0120
period in detail	1993-1996	−0.0002	−0.0002	0.0138	0.0019	0.0056	0.0155
	1996-2000	−0.0054	−0.0124	0.0016	0.0018	0.0048	0.0272

NOTE: Income is measured at the economic family level, but the unit of analysis is the individual. Income is divided by the number of "adult equivalents" in the family (see text for more details). To partially account for the introduction of SLID in 1996, the absolute growth in inequality is the sum of the absolute growth in SCF up to 1996, plus the absolute growth in SLID from 1996 onwards. Significance tests were performed on the growth in the Exp, G, and CV² measures that appear in Tables 3.1 and 3.2. Shaded cells denote results significant at the 1% level.

Our thresholds for statistically significant changes are: 0.005 for the exponential, 0.01 for the Gini, and 0.16 for the CV^2. Given the differences in these thresholds, one must be careful in comparing the magnitude of the changes over time among inequality measures.

Not surprisingly, the level of market income inequality is higher than that of disposable income inequality, as the tax and transfer system offsets market income inequality to some extent (Figure 3.2).

Our results are consistent with the well-known fact that earnings inequality rose during the 1980s and early 1990s, even though our focus is different in several ways. First, we examine total market income (which includes income from sources such as investment and pensions) rather than earnings alone. Our analysis is also at the family level, whereas earnings studies are normally conducted on individuals. Finally, in earnings studies, the sample is normally limited to employed individuals, but we include all families in our analysis (including those with no earnings). These measures were taken since we want to compare inequality before and after accounting for the tax and transfer system, which can potentially affect all families.

FIGURE 3.2

Gini coefficient, SCF/SLID: economic families, 1980-2000

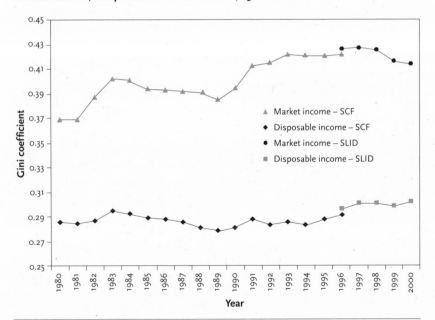

Between 1980 and 1989 (peak-to-peak), market income inequality rose by 0.0162 based on the Gini coefficient, and by 0.0062 based on the Exp measure, both of which are well above the significance threshold. The CV^2 also rises substantially over this period (in fact, more so in percentage terms than the other two measures) but fails to exceed the 1 percent significance threshold. Thus, it is difficult to be sure from these measures whether the inequality increases are being disproportionally driven by one part of the distribution. To investigate this issue more carefully, in Figure 3.3 we present the 10th, 50th, and 90th percentiles of the real market income distribution from the SCF/SLID (relative to their 1980 value). This chart implies that in the 1980s, the main driving force in rising inequality was declining real incomes for families at the bottom of the distribution. However, Saez and Veall (2003), using tax data, show that the income share going to the top 1 percent of tax filers increased substantially in the 1980s and 1990s, while the income share even of those between the 95th and 99th percentiles was unchanged.

FIGURE 3.3

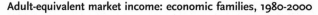

Adult-equivalent market income: economic families, 1980-2000

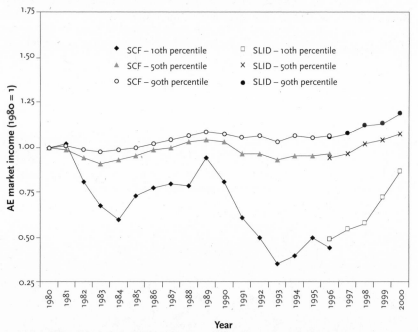

Thus, rising inequality appears to have come from declines in real incomes in the bottom portion of the distribution and increases at the very top.[12]

Over this same period (1980 to 1989), disposable income inequality appears to have declined very moderately by all measures, although the changes are not statistically significant. In essence, as market income inequality was rising in the 1980s, the tax and transfer system offset this trend. This is not surprising, as the transfer system was becoming increasingly generous at the time. For example, social assistance benefits were rising during that period, especially in Ontario (National Council of Welfare 1997). A glance at Figure 3.2 indicates that, at the same time, the tax and transfer system also acted to dampen cyclical fluctuations in inequality.

In the 1990s, market income inequality continued to rise as a result of the recession in the early part of the decade and the "weak recovery" that followed. The largest increases were registered between 1989 and 1993, a transition from the peak of the cycle to the trough of the recession. Once again, all three indices show strong increases, but we are unable to make clear statistical statements based on the CV^2. The tax and transfer system reduced the magnitude of the inequality increase but did not fully offset it, as disposable income inequality also rises in the heart of the recession. However, the same was true of the recession of the early 1980s: the tax and transfer system did not fully offset market income inequality increases then either. For example, the Gini for market income rose by 0.033 from 1980 to 1983 while the after tax and transfer income Gini rose by 0.010, changes very similar to those recorded for the 1989-93 period at the bottom of Table 3.1. None of the changes in disposable income inequality in either period is statistically significant at the 1 percent level.

Between 1993 and 1996, family market income inequality was relatively stable, with changes that were both economically insubstantial and statistically insignificant. The same is true of the disposable income inequality, though the indices all register slightly higher increases in inequality for this measure than for market income. The lack of a clear trend is perhaps not surprising in a period that is a mixed bag in terms of labour market trends and, as described below, changes in the tax and transfer system.

The late 1990s witnessed a fall in market income inequality, though not by nearly enough to offset the increases during the previous recession. The same ratcheting-up of inequality occurred in the 1980s business cycle. Indeed, the recessionary increases and expansionary declines in the inequality indices were very similar in the 1980s and 1990s.[13] However, the economic expansions in the two decades were dramatically different in terms of the roles played by the tax and transfer system. In the 1980s expansion, the inequality indices for disposable income fell by almost exactly the same amount as the indices for market income. In contrast, in the late 1990s expansion, declines in market income inequality were observed, but disposable income inequality rose marginally. The increases in the inequality indices for disposable income in the 1996-2000 period are not statistically significant in their own right, although the differences between the increases in the disposable income indices and the declines in the corresponding market income inequality indices are statistically significant for both the Exp and the Gini.

Do these trends match what we would expect to see over the business cycle? During recessionary periods, people at the bottom levels of the earnings distribution are normally the ones who are hardest hit. Young workers who were recently hired may be the first to experience a layoff, while potential new entrants to the labour market may find it difficult to land a job. As a result, one would expect earnings to fall at the bottom end. In other words, market income inequality is expected to rise. In expansionary periods, firms need to hire more workers to meet demand. Improvements are thus expected to occur mainly at the bottom end of the distribution, so that market income inequality is expected to fall during economic recoveries. The tax and transfer system generally plays a mitigating role in this respect: laid-off individuals are often eligible for employment insurance benefits and, failing that, social assistance benefits; income taxes may also smooth out increases registered at the top.[14] This should imply that as market income inequality falls, disposable income inequality moves much less.

The outcome of this discussion is that we would expect market income and disposable income inequality indices to move relative to one another in roughly the manner they did in the 1980s. The only difference between what happened in the 1980s and our description of the expected scenario is that disposable income inequality declined as much as market income inequality in the 1980s expansion. Similarly, the various indices moved in the predicted manner in the recession of the early 1990s. However, in the late 1990s, the marginal increase in disposable income inequality that accompanied the decline in market income inequality may be related to changes in the transfer system in the last half of the 1990s. This issue is being addressed more fully in a subsequent study.

To summarize, survey data suggest that family market income inequality rose in the 1980s, but disposable income inequality remained relatively stable.

In the 1990s, these data suggest that family market income inequality rose more than it did in the 1980s. Disposable income inequality also rose marginally. It appears that the tax and transfer system offset only part of the rise in family market increase inequality over the 1990s. This is in contrast with the 1980s cycle, when the tax and transfer system more than offset the rise in market inequality. In all cases, the Exp and the Gini show significant changes, while the CV² does not (although its change is in the same direction).

Evidence from Tax Data

The taxation data provide an alternative source for examining income inequality trends. We focus on the years 1993 to 2000 since this period yields the most reliable and consistent source of income estimates in the tax data, particularly for low-income families. We also show results for 1992 onwards, but it is clear from the tables that follow that the data improved in 1993 with the introduction of the Child Tax Benefit and a sudden increase in lower-income filers. Only census families are formed in the tax data, as opposed to economic families. In Table 3.2, we show estimates from our three inequality measures (Exp, G, and CV²) for both survey and tax data, all measured on a census family basis. We also present results for the Gini in Figure 3.4. Note that to reduce processing time, a 2 percent random sample of the tax data was used in these calculations.

The broad inequality trends in the survey data are virtually identical whether we use census or economic families between 1992 and 2000 (compare the census family results from survey data in Table 3.2 to economic family results from survey data in Table 3.1). The change in the family concept associated with the move to tax data should thus have no substantial impact on the results. As in our discussions based on economic families, the survey data grouped by census family shows no substantial movements in market income inequality between 1993 and 1996 but does show declines in inequality in the 1996-2000 period. The declines in the latter period are statistically significant for both the exponential and Gini indices. Also, as in the earlier discussion, although family market income inequality declines during the expansion, disposable income inequality increases over the same period. The difference in the trends in inequality based on the two income measures is again statistically significant for the Exp and the Gini.

The trends in market income inequality using tax data are substantially different from those observed in the survey data. In particular, in the tax data, there is evidence of a substantial (though not quite statistically significant)

TABLE 3.2

Market and disposable income inequality, SCF/SLID and T1FF: census families

		Survey data						Tax data					
		Market income			Disposable income			Market income			Disposable income		
DATA SOURCE	Year	Exp	G	CV²	Exp	G	CV²	Exp	G	CV²	Exp	G	CV²
Survey data: SCF	1992	0.4671	0.4242	0.6264	0.4157	0.2912	0.2971	0.4837	0.4627	0.8508	0.4267	0.3228	0.4024
Tax data: T1FF	1993	0.4703	0.4313	0.6521	0.4163	0.2934	0.3057	0.4905	0.4770	0.9194	0.4314	0.3357	0.4360
	1994	0.4695	0.4296	0.6551	0.4154	0.2904	0.2998	0.4920	0.4798	0.9290	0.4323	0.3385	0.4401
	1995	0.4695	0.4298	0.6708	0.4170	0.2950	0.3157	0.4923	0.4807	0.9420	0.4339	0.3428	0.4562
	1996	0.4700	0.4310	0.6710	0.4181	0.2985	0.3214						
Survey data: SLID	1996	0.4755	0.4435	0.7407	0.4211	0.3070	0.3475	0.4951	0.4865	1.0185	0.4363	0.3490	0.4873
Tax data: T1FF	1997	0.4763	0.4451	0.7621	0.4229	0.3120	0.3694	0.4950	0.4865	1.0152	0.4373	0.3518	0.4950
	1998	0.4752	0.4426	0.7734	0.4229	0.3117	0.3756	0.4963	0.4893	1.0912	0.4386	0.3548	0.5317
	1999	0.4712	0.4338	0.7307	0.4220	0.3090	0.3610	0.4954	0.4875	1.0846	0.4400	0.3585	0.5426
	2000	0.4706	0.4326	0.7496	0.4233	0.3129	0.3803	0.4965	0.4898	1.1433	0.4427	0.3653	0.5835

ABSOLUTE GROWTH IN INEQUALITY

		Survey data						Tax data					
		Market income			Disposable income			Market income			Disposable income		
		Exp	G	CV²	Exp	G	CV²	Exp	G	CV²	Exp	G	CV²
The 1993-2000	1993-2000	−0.0052	−0.0112	0.0279	0.0040	0.0109	0.0485	0.0060	0.0129	0.2239	0.0113	0.0295	0.1476
recovery	1993-1996	−0.0003	−0.0003	0.0189	0.0018	0.0050	0.0157	0.0046	0.0096	0.0992	0.0049	0.0133	0.0513
	1996-2000	−0.0050	−0.0110	0.0089	0.0023	0.0059	0.0327	0.0014	0.0033	0.1248	0.0064	0.0162	0.0963

NOTE: Income is measured at the census family level. For details see note to Table 3.1.

FIGURE 3.4

Gini coefficient, disposable income: census families, 1992-2000

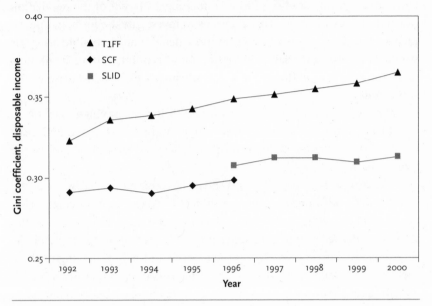

increase in market income inequality even during 1993-96. Furthermore, in contrast to the survey data, the expansion period witnessed additional increases in market income inequality. The sum of the effects for the two sub-periods is substantial and statistically significant. As in the survey data, the tax and transfer system increased inequality in disposable income relative to market income. Indeed, the net result is very large and often statistically significant increases in disposable income inequality within both sub-periods and for the 1993-2000 period as a whole. In the end, the tax data point to much stronger increases in inequality and no mediating role for the tax and transfer system in the period following 1993. In fact, changes in taxes paid and transfer benefits received tended to increase (not reduce) inequality over this period.

It is important to keep in mind that the significance thresholds applied to the tax data are based on the work of Kovacevic and Binder (1997), which used SCF data. The samples we use in the tax data are much larger and would thus yield smaller significance thresholds (if such work were carried out). In other words, our significance tests on the tax data understate the true level of significance.

RESULTS BY VINGTILE

We turn now to examining the distribution of income using mean incomes by vingtile (groups of observations containing 5 percent of the population ordered by income level). This allows us to investigate the form and movements of the income distributions in more detail than is possible using the summary measures we have employed up to this point. Further, it will help us shed more light on the differences in inequality movements between the survey and tax data.

Mean market income and mean disposable income by vingtile are shown in Tables 3.3 and 3.4, respectively, for survey and tax data, based on census families. The values are in 2000 constant dollars and are adjusted for family size as before.

The survey data suggest that disposable income rose across all of the distribution, with gains ranging from 10 to 14 percent for most vingtiles between 1993 and 2000 (Table 3.4). The ratio of the mean incomes in the top to bottom deciles rose by 13.3 percent over the period. In the top vingtile, disposable income rose by 20.9 percent, while in the bottom vingtile there was a much smaller increase of 3.1 percent. This implies that the rising inequality detected over this period was the consequence of above-average gains at the top and a lack of relative improvement at the bottom.

The tax data paint a somewhat different picture. As with the survey data, the rising inequality seems to have resulted in part from an improvement in the top vingtile. Indeed, the tax and survey data register quite similar increases in average incomes over about the top 40 percent of the distribution. In contrast with the survey data, however, we find a sharp decline in disposable income at the bottom. In the bottom vingtile, disposable income declined by 29.2 percent between 1993 and 2000. As a result of the large gains at the top and the very large declines at the bottom, the ratio of the mean incomes in the top and bottom deciles rose by more than 40 percent between 1993 and 2000. This is a direct reflection of the trends in market income portrayed in Table 3.3. While the survey data show increases in mean market income across most of the distribution, suggesting that almost everyone benefited from the 1990s expansion (though to varying degrees), the tax data on market income indicate that people in the bottom 20 percent of the distribution saw no real improvement.

In addition to the differences in trends in income between the two data sources, especially at the bottom of the income distribution, there are also large differences in the levels of income, once again especially at the bottom

TABLE 3.3

Mean adult-equivalent market income by vingtile: census families

DATA SOURCE	Year	Bottom	2nd	3rd	4th...	...8th...	...10th...	...12th...	...17th...	18th	19th	Top
							Vingtile					
SCF	1992	−93	456	3,418	6,823	19,036	24,273	29,573	47,130	53,409	62,250	88,834
	1993	−13	219	2,710	6,058	18,036	23,409	28,794	45,823	51,893	60,621	87,762
	1994	−20	263	2,978	6,374	18,685	23,950	29,296	46,902	53,092	62,041	90,019
	1995	−26	432	3,311	6,652	18,802	23,992	29,403	46,605	52,753	62,118	93,616
	1996	−9	314	3,175	6,752	18,852	24,179	29,470	47,455	53,395	62,926	93,882
SLID	1996	−67	226	2,701	5,848	17,341	23,134	28,566	46,121	52,154	60,812	94,035
	1997	−71	217	2,677	5,986	17,883	23,564	29,141	47,090	53,278	62,656	98,076
	1998	−144	325	3,141	6,599	19,018	24,752	30,352	49,206	55,583	64,841	103,544
	1999	−49	709	3,888	7,290	19,705	25,486	31,163	49,783	56,204	65,913	103,901
	2000	−97	958	4,471	7,892	20,554	26,418	32,190	51,253	57,909	68,433	110,245
TIFF	1992	−251	309	2,634	5,324	16,020	21,523	27,054	45,473	51,812	61,678	98,768
	1993	−182	38	1,550	4,300	15,073	20,630	26,264	44,754	51,159	61,151	99,524
	1994	−209	3	1,262	4,101	15,122	20,823	26,616	45,408	52,017	62,109	100,716
	1995	−197	13	1,382	4,110	15,296	20,933	26,779	45,772	52,444	62,765	102,774
	1996	−201	10	1,287	4,022	15,226	20,980	26,779	46,083	52,789	63,349	107,513
	1997	−187	14	1,411	4,175	15,486	21,288	27,221	46,818	53,797	64,641	109,801
	1998	−163	28	1,561	4,443	16,089	21,918	27,991	48,364	55,526	66,841	117,913
	1999	−148	33	1,718	4,779	16,665	22,660	28,830	49,555	56,992	68,741	121,520
	2000	−118	46	1,770	4,915	17,110	23,173	29,495	51,083	58,684	70,807	127,182
ABSOLUTE GROWTH (1993-2000)												
SCF/SLID		−25	827	2,235	2,739	4,029	4,054	4,301	6,764	7,258	9,926	22,330
Tax data		64	8	219	614	2,037	2,543	3,231	6,329	7,525	9,656	27,658

NOTE: In 2000 dollars. Income is measured at the census family level. The percentage growth is the absolute growth divided by the base (or earlier) year of analysis, expressed in percentage terms. For details see note to Table 3.1.

TABLE 3.4

Mean adult-equivalent disposable income by vingtile: census families

| Data source | Year | Vingtile | | | | | | | | | | | Top decile/bottom decile |
		Bottom	2nd	3rd	4th...	...8th...	...10th...	...12th...	...17th...	18th	19th	Top	
SCF	1992	5,065	9,648	12,008	13,941	20,278	23,312	26,682	38,317	42,478	48,545	65,257	7.7
	1993	5,229	9,500	11,709	13,497	19,495	22,618	26,017	37,400	41,303	47,456	64,802	7.6
	1994	5,354	9,599	11,935	13,888	19,998	23,096	26,211	37,779	41,827	47,917	65,231	7.6
	1995	5,253	9,463	11,834	13,717	19,784	22,847	26,275	37,681	41,740	47,896	67,354	7.8
	1996	4,981	9,113	11,576	13,630	19,740	22,851	26,168	37,994	41,944	48,256	67,262	8.2
SLID	1996	4,221	8,795	11,010	12,944	19,032	22,320	25,773	37,414	41,421	47,166	67,368	8.8
	1997	4,058	8,835	11,168	13,137	19,271	22,618	26,176	38,107	42,355	48,578	70,913	9.3
	1998	4,299	9,263	11,734	13,637	19,991	23,393	26,920	39,392	43,638	50,327	74,046	9.2
	1999	4,351	9,292	11,979	14,006	20,624	24,000	27,666	40,313	44,715	51,278	74,237	9.2
	2000	4,632	9,589	12,303	14,264	21,030	24,560	28,257	41,471	45,904	52,890	78,476	9.2
TIFF	1992	3,520	8,199	10,423	12,361	18,701	21,814	25,192	37,501	41,878	48,560	71,728	10.3
	1993	2,088	7,352	9,655	11,561	17,998	21,192	24,632	36,834	41,204	47,958	71,747	12.7
	1994	1,913	7,225	9,684	11,531	18,069	21,391	24,881	37,342	41,825	48,710	72,359	13.2
	1995	1,866	7,028	9,439	11,362	17,998	21,284	24,834	37,432	41,968	48,958	73,616	13.8
	1996	1,780	6,820	9,230	11,094	17,883	21,260	24,841	37,661	42,271	49,420	75,827	14.6
	1997	1,825	6,694	9,130	11,079	17,957	21,340	24,954	38,028	42,798	50,090	77,023	14.9
	1998	1,964	7,029	9,552	11,647	18,381	21,879	25,664	39,382	44,252	51,878	82,456	14.9
	1999	1,692	6,914	9,621	11,826	18,841	22,421	26,301	40,417	45,533	53,545	85,315	16.1
	2000	1,479	6,629	9,469	11,788	19,167	22,905	26,921	41,622	46,897	55,108	89,039	17.8

ABSOLUTE GROWTH (1993-2000)

SCF/SLID	163	408	1,159	1,454	2,243	2,473	2,635	4,651	5,124	6,524	13,569	1.0
Tax data	-609	-723	-185	227	1,169	1,714	2,289	4,788	5,693	7,150	17,292	5.1

PERCENTAGE GROWTH (1993-2000)

SCF/SLID	3.1%	4.3%	9.9%	10.8%	11.5%	10.9%	10.1%	12.4%	12.4%	13.7%	20.9%	13.3%
Tax data	-29.2%	-9.8%	-1.9%	2.0%	6.5%	8.1%	9.3%	13.0%	13.8%	14.9%	24.1%	40.2%

NOTE: In 2000 dollars. Income is measured at the census family level. The percentage growth is the absolute growth divided by the base (or earlier) year of analysis, expressed in percentage terms. For details see note to Table 3.1.

end. In a very broad sense, the distribution of income generated from survey and tax data might differ for two reasons: either the respondents/tax filers report different levels of income, or the population covered is different. It is of course likely that income from some sources is not reported in tax data. It is also conceivable that people at the bottom of the income distribution under-report to a greater extent, at least expressed as a proportion of their income. However, survey respondents may also not include income from some sources. The gap in the bottom vingtile between tax and survey data (SCF, a file without any tax information) is generally about $3,000 in adult-equivalent 2000 dollars. For a family of four, this difference is about $6,000 in unadjusted 2000 dollars. This represents a difference in the order of 200 percent of the incomes reported in the tax data. The move from the SCF survey data to (mainly) tax data in the SLID series did not result in a signifi-cant narrowing of this gap. This suggests that the difference may lie more in coverage than in differential reporting between survey and tax data. Whether survey data (both SCF and SLID) cover a different population than tax data is a very difficult question to answer, and is beyond the scope of this study.[15]

In the next section, we discuss how the Census can be used to provide a third portrait of inequality trends and assess whether they more closely re-semble the tax or the survey data results.

Evidence from Census Data

If the gap between survey and tax data is indeed caused by a difference in the way income is reported, we would expect the gap to remain even if the cover-age were as high in the survey data as in the tax data. Alternatively, if the difference in coverage is at the heart of this gap, we would expect the gap to disappear if the coverages matched.

One way of shedding light on this issue is to turn to Census data. The Census is a survey aimed at collecting information from the entire popula-tion and is conducted every five years shortly after the tax season (sometime in May in recent years). By law, response is mandatory, and every fifth house-hold has to fill out the "long form," which includes detailed questions on the amounts of various income sources from the previous year. Thus, the Census provides a convenient vehicle for examining the importance of the extent of coverage: it is a survey like the SCF, but it has coverage rates that are closer to those in the tax data. One drawback of the Census is that it does not contain information on taxes paid. We could impute taxes, but instead we focus on differences in total income (the sum of market and transfer income before taxes). This still provides a good basis for comparison among the data sets, especially at the bottom of the distribution, where taxes are less important.

The distribution of total income of census families in adult-equivalent 2000 dollars is shown below in Table 3.5 for SCF, Census, and T1FF. We focus on a comparison in 1995 to maximize the comparability between the survey and Census data. If we were to focus on 2000, our "survey" data would come from SLID, in which most of the income data actually comes from tax files.

Based on total income, the bottom of the distribution in Census data looks more like the tax data. In 1995, mean total adult-equivalent income in the bottom vingtile was around $2,300 in the Census and $2,000 in T1FF, compared to $5,300 in SCF. In the second vingtile, Census and T1FF are only about $500 apart, while Census and SCF are about $2,000 apart; in relative terms, the gap between SCF and Census is non-negligible.

At the bottom of the table, the mean incomes by vingtile in the SCF and T1FF data are compared to the Census numbers in the same vingtile. The SCF data exhibit much larger differences from the Census data, particularly at the bottom of the distribution. In the bottom vingtile, the SCF value is 2.3 times the Census value. This is followed by the second vingtile in SCF, which is 1.3 times the Census value. The difference between the SCF and Census becomes smaller and smaller at successive vingtiles until the tenth vingtile where it disappears, and after the twelfth vingtile it increases moderately in the other direction until, by the twentieth vingtile, the SCF value is 93 percent of the Census value. In contrast, the values taken from tax data tend to be a relatively even proportion below those from the Census, with no discernible pattern across vingtiles.

Although it is quite possible that income is under-reported in T1FF relative to surveys (SCF), this does not appear to be the major cause of the difference between tax data and SCF at the bottom of the income distribution. If reporting of income components were the major cause of the difference, this should be detected when moving from purely survey (SCF) to largely tax (SLID) reporting, given that these two data sources have the same coverage issues; however, very little change is observed. Given the similarities between tax and Census results (which differ in the method of income reporting but not very much in coverage), a likely explanation for the discrepancy between the SCF and the other data sources is relative under-coverage at the very bottom of the income distribution in SCF (and SLID). However, further analysis would be required to reach a more definitive conclusion in this regard, since

TABLE 3.5

Mean adult-equivalent total income by vingtile, SCF, Census, and T1FF: census families

Data source	Year	Bottom	2nd	3rd	4th...	...8th...	...10th...	...12th...	...17th...	18th	19th	Top	Top decile/bottom decile
SCF	1980	4,441	9,259	11,833	14,397	23,705	27,672	31,791	46,191	51,497	59,749	84,383	10.5
	1985	4,833	9,095	11,822	14,050	22,685	26,893	31,166	46,563	51,793	59,700	86,674	10.5
	1990	5,556	10,129	12,902	15,340	24,598	29,196	33,874	49,991	55,569	64,302	93,656	10.1
	1995	5,279	9,589	12,185	14,417	22,919	27,355	32,210	48,506	54,407	63,574	95,041	10.7
	1996	5,051	9,231	11,906	14,338	23,010	27,490	32,252	49,206	55,107	64,415	95,204	11.2
SLID	1996	4,332	8,911	11,274	13,540	21,848	26,493	31,370	47,956	53,701	62,262	95,542	11.9
	2000	4,814	9,742	12,670	14,943	24,238	29,200	34,526	52,708	59,140	69,394	111,212	12.4
Census	1980	2,588	8,389	11,408	13,884	22,982	27,127	31,447	46,858	52,417	61,236	93,229	14.1
	1985	2,373	7,871	11,019	13,463	22,297	26,560	30,959	46,828	52,585	61,675	94,301	15.2
	1990	3,005	8,979	12,315	14,900	24,464	29,016	33,812	51,118	57,393	67,378	104,864	14.4
	1995	2,262	7,586	10,800	13,398	22,639	27,353	32,240	49,449	55,684	65,542	102,365	17.0
	2000	3,104	8,757	12,480	15,227	24,939	29,970	35,356	54,574	61,663	73,157	121,260	16.4
T1FF	1995	1,972	7,123	9,593	11,670	20,273	25,003	30,102	47,867	54,279	64,371	104,274	18.5
	2000	1,734	6,784	9,654	12,146	21,587	26,862	32,459	52,909	60,325	72,212	128,590	23.6
1995 COMPARISONS													
SCF/Census		2.33	1.26	1.13	1.08	1.01	1.00	1.00	0.98	0.98	0.97	0.93	0.63
T1FF/Census		0.87	0.94	0.89	0.87	0.90	0.91	0.93	0.97	0.97	0.98	1.02	1.09

PERCENTAGE GROWTH

1980-1990												
SCF	25.1%	9.4%	9.0%	6.6%	3.8%	5.5%	6.6%	8.2%	7.9%	7.6%	11.0%	-4.3%
Census	16.1%	7.0%	7.9%	7.3%	6.4%	7.0%	7.5%	9.1%	9.5%	10.0%	12.5%	2.1%
1990-2000												
SCF/SLID	-0.4%	-0.7%	3.1%	2.6%	3.3%	3.4%	4.5%	7.9%	9.0%	11.3%	18.4%	15.9%
Census	3.3%	-2.5%	1.3%	2.2%	1.9%	3.3%	4.6%	6.8%	7.4%	8.6%	15.6%	14.0%
1995-2000												
SCF/SLID	4.8%	4.9%	9.2%	9.2%	10.8%	10.4%	9.9%	11.2%	11.3%	12.5%	16.7%	9.4%
Census	37.2%	15.4%	15.6%	13.6%	10.2%	9.6%	9.7%	10.4%	10.7%	11.6%	18.5%	-3.9%
TIFF	-12.1%	-4.8%	0.6%	4.1%	6.5%	7.4%	7.8%	10.5%	11.1%	12.2%	23.3%	27.1%

NOTE: In 2000 dollars. Income is measured at the census family level. The percentage growth is the absolute growth divided by the base (or earlier) year of analysis, expressed in percentage terms. For details see note to Table 3.1.

the less than 100 percent use of tax data in SLID leaves open the possibility that the discrepancy is due to reporting differences.

While Census and T1FF yield similar distributions in 1995, this is not the case in 2000. Specifically, improvements at the bottom of the distribution in the Census simply don't register in T1FF, although income levels in the Census are still quite far from those registered in SLID. It is unclear why the Census and T1FF do not yield similar stories at the bottom of the distribution in the late 1990s. In particular, the dichotomy does not seem to be generated by a difference in any one particular income component. The Census shows improvements across a broad range of components, while no changes or slight declines are registered in T1FF. It is not clear why this dichotomy exists, but it is worth noting that in tax data, census families must be imputed, and some evidence suggests that important differences in family type exist at the bottom of the income distribution. For example, the number of couples with less than $10,000 in total income is 46 percent greater in tax data than in the Census, despite the fact that there is virtually no difference in the number of couples across the entire income distribution.[16] Furthermore, average family size is markedly higher in the bottom of the T1FF distribution, particularly in 2000. In 1995, average family size in the bottom vingtile is 7 percent higher in T1FF. By 2000, this gap had risen to 12 percent. More work would be needed to determine the cause of these differences in family structure at the bottom of the income distribution, and whether it can explain why income trends are so different in the late 1990s.

Let us now look at the trends in income in the 1980s and 1990s with survey data and Census, the two data sources available for such an analysis. Although Census data cannot be used to study trends in disposable income inequality (because income taxes paid are not recorded), one can nevertheless compare total (pre-tax) income inequality trends between the Census and SCF/SLID data. In the 1980s, inequality remained fairly stable over the entire period according to both data sources, although a slight increase is observed in the early 1980s in the Census data (but not in the SCF). In the 1990s, both data sources suggest that inequality rose. In the SCF/SLID data, the top/bottom decile ratio rose by 15.9 percent, compared to a 14 percent increase in the Census data. When one separates the early and late 1990s, however, the data sources tend to disagree. According to SCF/SLID, inequality rose moderately in the early 1990s because of a moderate decline at the bottom and no change at the top. In the late 1990s, SCF/SLID suggests that inequality continued to rise moderately, although this was the result of a substantial rise at the top outweighing a moderate improvement at the bottom. Census data paint a very different picture. In the early 1990s, inequality increased substantially because of a large decline at the bottom and no change at the top. In the late 1990s, inequality actually remained fairly stable, since income rose substantially at both the top and the bottom. In essence, the two data sources disagree on the extent to which the bottom of the income distribution was affected by the recession of the early 1990s and the recovery in the latter half of the decade. This is consistent with the notion that the Census has a greater tendency to accurately represent families in the bottom of the income distribution, and it is this segment of the population that saw the largest fluctuations in income over the 1990s. Of course, additional investigation is needed to ensure that this is indeed the case. Whether this is true or not doesn't affect the main story that can be drawn from both data sources: income inequality rose in the 1990s as the result of large improvements at the top of the income distribution and no change at the bottom.

Conclusion

This study examines trends in disposable family income inequality over the 1980s and 1990s, a period covering two full economic cycles. We began our investigation with survey data (SCF and SLID) but quickly turned to tax data (T1FF) for three reasons. First, survey data have a break in the series in 1996. Second, the response rate in survey data is generally around 80 to 85 percent, and no adjustments are made to make the samples representative of the Canadian population in various income groups. Tax data are less likely to suffer from income-related response bias since the coverage rate is above 95 percent (since 1992). Finally, given the larger sample sizes in tax data, their inequality estimates are less susceptible to sampling error.

Using survey data, we confirm the findings of others for the 1980s: family market income inequality rose over the decade,[17] but the tax and transfer system offset this trend, resulting in no significant change in disposable income inequality.

Survey data suggest a small statistically significant increase in disposable income inequality in the 1990s (1989 to 2000). Over the whole decade, this again reflects an increase in market income inequality offset by the actions of the tax and transfer system. However, on closer examination, the inequality-reducing effects of the tax and transfer system occur entirely in the recessionary period before 1993. In the expansionary period following 1996, market income inequality falls but inequality in disposable income rises. It is possible that this reflects changes in the tax and transfer systems that begin in the middle of the decade, including reduced social assistance benefits and changes in unemployment insurance. However, this chapter does not try to establish the effects of program changes on inequality.

The tax data point to much larger increases in market income inequality driven both by rises at the top of the distribution and very substantial falls at the bottom. According to the tax data, and in contrast to the survey data, significant increases in disposable income inequality were witnessed in the 1990s. Moreover, the level of inequality is much higher in the tax data than the survey data in each year, due mainly to much lower earnings at the bottom of the distribution.

In essence, the survey and tax data differ in their estimates of the extent to which inequality rose during the recovery of the 1990s. This difference was largely due to the fact that in the tax data disposable income at the bottom of the distribution fell substantially, while in survey data it simply failed to increase at the same pace as at the top of the distribution.

Aside from differences in trends, the level of income received by families at the bottom of the income distribution is considerably higher in survey data than in tax data. We put forth two hypotheses that could explain the difference. First, survey respondents may be more likely to report certain (small) income amounts than tax filers. These small income amounts might be more prominent at the bottom of the distribution. However, the move from pure survey data (in SCF) toward partial tax data (in SLID) does not result in any substantial decline in income at the bottom of the distribution, suggesting this is not likely the primary explanation.

A second hypothesis relates to the possible under-coverage of low-income individuals in the survey data. If the gap between survey and tax data is indeed caused by a difference in the way income is reported, we would expect the gap to still be present even if somehow the coverage in survey data were as high as that in tax data. Alternatively, if the difference in coverage is at the heart of this gap, we would expect the gap to disappear if the coverage in survey data were to match that of tax data.

To shed some light on this issue, we compare the pre-tax income distribution from survey and tax data with that of Census data. The Census collects income data in much the same was as the SCF did, yet the coverage rate is much higher (as in the tax data).

We find that the bottom end of the income distribution in Census data more closely resembles the tax data than the survey data. Income at the bottom end of the distribution is always higher in survey data than in Census and tax data. However, the trend in income inequality suggested by tax data is much different than what we observe in Census. In the late 1990s, tax data point to a large increase in income inequality as the result of a large rise in income at the top and no change at the bottom. Census data also point to a large increase at the top, but this is counterbalanced by an equally large rise at the bottom (in relative terms). Although it is not clear what is driving this difference, we note that tax data tend to have substantially more couples with very low incomes compared to Census data, despite the fact that the overall number of couples is virtually identical.

If we focus on survey and Census data, we find very little difference in the trends over the 1980s. Essentially, both data sources suggest that inequality remained stable. Over the entire period covered by the 1990s, we also get similar results in both data sources, although this time, income inequality rose substantially. This agreement in the trends for the 1990s masks important differences observed in the experiences of families in the bottom of the distribution over different parts of the decade. Specifically, the SCF/SLID data suggest that these families saw moderate declines during the recession of the early 1990s and moderate improvements during the recovery of the late 1990s. Census data suggest that they were harder hit by the recession, but that greater gains were registered later in the decade.

APPENDIX

We have described trends in market income inequality by referring to earnings (the main component of market income). To confirm our approach, the appendix table divides the sample in the tax data by vingtile of market income and looks at the mean of the three components of market income: paid earnings, net self-employment income, and other market income. Clearly, the overall trend in market income inequality is being driven by paid earnings.

ACKNOWLEDGMENTS

This chapter represents the views of the authors and does not necessarily reflect the opinions of Statistics Canada. An earlier version of the chapter was released as Statistics Canada, Analytical Studies, Research Paper 219. The authors would like to thank Phil Giles, Jon Kesselman, and Michael Wolfson for useful comments. All remaining errors are the responsibility of the authors.

TABLE 3.A

Mean adult-equivalent paid earnings, net self-employment income, and other market income by vingtile of market income: census families, tax data (T1FF)

							Vingtile					
INCOME TYPE	Year	Bottom	2nd	3rd	4th	...8th...	...10th...	...12th...	...17th	18th	19th	Top
Paid earnings	1992	191	162	1,381	2,832	11,839	17,363	23,003	40,427	45,982	53,952	70,531
	1993	130	25	786	2,219	10,842	16,619	22,105	40,003	45,386	53,266	71,310
	1994	135	2	652	2,162	10,734	16,423	22,448	40,096	46,067	54,093	72,591
	1995	125	10	680	2,067	11,033	16,371	22,541	40,169	46,227	53,955	72,807
	1996	153	3	627	2,011	10,937	16,493	22,122	40,383	45,803	54,044	74,733
	1997	148	9	697	2,120	10,951	16,750	22,540	41,077	47,132	55,396	76,887
	1998	115	24	754	2,304	11,605	17,205	23,378	42,220	48,742	57,641	82,713
	1999	105	16	851	2,542	12,154	17,772	23,873	43,411	49,816	58,828	85,111
	2000	84	19	884	2,609	12,529	18,339	24,435	44,557	51,292	60,894	90,412
Net self-employment income	1992	-406	-60	26	343	934	960	948	1,271	1,636	2,350	13,360
	1993	-287	-14	-22	202	962	980	1,074	1,332	1,640	2,790	13,914
	1994	-305	-2	-51	175	1,045	1,166	1,143	1,596	1,711	2,592	14,367
	1995	-334	-11	-70	226	989	1,160	1,122	1,567	1,774	2,789	15,012
	1996	-395	-5	-39	229	1,037	1,207	1,276	1,448	1,958	2,808	16,570

1997	-323	-11	-27	260	1,228	1,117	1,334	1,740	1,959	3,279	17,116
1998	-284	-11	-4	305	1,103	1,260	1,245	1,815	2,041	3,279	17,888
1999	-271	-8	-3	361	1,140	1,260	1,349	1,817	2,071	3,474	19,134
2000	-235	-13	-19	373	1,130	1,230	1,277	2,007	2,205	3,339	19,362

Other market income											
1992	-36	206	1,227	2,150	3,247	3,200	3,103	3,774	4,194	5,376	14,877
1993	-25	27	787	1,879	3,270	3,030	3,086	3,419	4,133	5,096	14,299
1994	-39	4	661	1,764	3,343	3,235	3,026	3,716	4,239	5,424	13,757
1995	12	14	772	1,818	3,273	3,402	3,116	4,037	4,443	6,021	14,955
1996	40	12	699	1,782	3,253	3,281	3,382	4,253	5,028	6,497	16,211
1997	-12	15	741	1,795	3,307	3,421	3,348	4,001	4,706	5,966	15,797
1998	6	15	811	1,834	3,381	3,453	3,367	4,329	4,743	5,921	17,313
1999	18	26	870	1,875	3,372	3,628	3,608	4,327	5,106	6,440	17,276
2000	33	40	905	1,933	3,452	3,605	3,783	4,519	5,187	6,574	17,409

NOTE: In 2000 dollars. Income is measured at the census family level, but the the unit of analysis is the individual. Income is divided by the number of adult equivalents in the family (see text for details).

NOTES

1   The following information on the SCF and SLID draws heavily from Statistics Canada (2002).

2   The Child Tax Credit, available prior to 1993 as a non-refundable tax credit for families with children, did nothing for families with earnings below the taxable threshold. The Child Tax Credit was replaced by the Child Tax Benefit in 1993, and this provided an incentive for families with children to file taxes even if they had no earnings. Finally, tax filers could apply for the Goods and Services Tax (GST) Credit beginning in 1989, although no payments were made until December 1990.

3   The overall population coverage rate in T1FF (relative to the Census) went from 95.12 percent in 1992 to 96.15 percent in 1993, possibly because the Child Tax Benefit gave some families an incentive to file taxes. Its coverage rate generally hovered around 96 percent in subsequent years, with no sudden substantial changes.

4   Examples of the broader concept of economic family include the following: two co-resident census families who are related to one another are considered one economic family, and two co-resident siblings who are not members of a census family are considered an economic family.

5   Note that taxes paid include only the personal income tax (federal and provincial) and not EI or CPP/QPP premiums.

6   Alimony paid is not available in SLID and the Census and thus could not be included in our definition of after-tax income. The results were not sensitive to this limitation, however, as we generated similar numbers from T1FF when alimony paid was subtracted from after-tax income.

7   The Gini is based on the Lorenz curve, which is a mapping of the functional relationship between the cumulative percentage of income held by the population and the cumulative percentage of the population. Perfect equality is achieved if the Lorenz curve is a straight line – each member of the population holds an equal share of the total income in the economy. The Gini measures the ratio of the area between the line of perfect equality and the Lorenz curve to the area between line of perfect equality and the segment of lines under perfect inequality (all income is held by one member of the economy).

8   Unlike other bottom-sensitive measures (e.g., Theil-Entropy or Theil-Bernoulli), the exponential measure is well defined for zero or negative incomes. Since we include business and self-employment income, we expect to have some negative incomes.

9   Although dropping the top and bottom 0.1 percent of the income distribution in each year is really only necessary in survey data to control the effects of large outliers, to be consistent, we applied this measure to tax data as well.

10 See Cowell (1977) or Wolfson (1986) for more details.

11 Specifically, family income is divided by the square root of the family size (the number of members in the family) – in essence, the needs of each additional member in the family can be met at lower cost due to economies of scale.

12 Note that the SCF does not detect larger increases in the 1980s at 95th and 99th percentiles than at the 90th percentiles. Since the response rate is about 80 percent in the SCF, it may be that individuals at the very top are not represented as well as they are in the tax data used by Saez and Veall (2003).

13 For example, the market income Gini increased by 0.033 from 1980 to 1983, and by 0.036 from 1989 to 1993. It then declined by 0.017 in the expansions from 1983 to 1989 and by 0.012 from 1996 to 2000.

14 See Beach and Slotsve (1994) for more discussion on the cyclical aspects of the earnings distribution.

15 Note that the coverage rate in T1FF is about 96 to 97 percent for the period of study. The response rate is between 80 and 85 percent in SLID, and slightly lower in SCF. As mentioned in the data section, the weights in the survey data are adjusted to make the sample more representative of various province-age-sex groups, as well as household and family sizes. However, no specific adjustments are made to correct the non-representativeness of the sample by income level that may be introduced by non-responses. In particular, it would be difficult to automatically dismiss the possibility that lower-income families are under-represented in survey data. For example, we do know that estimates of the immigrant population are considerably lower in survey data, and immigrants are more concentrated at the bottom end of the income distribution (Hou and Picot 2003). Of course, other possibilities would also be difficult to dismiss. (In 1996, immigrants account for 21.5 percent of individuals fifteen years or older in the Census, compared to 19.2 percent in SLID, by our calculation.)

16 These numbers were produced by the Small Area and Administrative Data Division at Statistics Canada, where the T1FF file and other files derived from it are housed.

17 Our calculations differ from those typically reported for the 1980s in that we include people with zero earnings in the sample; most studies focus on individuals with positive earnings.

REFERENCES

Beach, C.M., and G.A. Slotsve. 1994. "Polarization of Earnings in the Canadian Labour Market." Bell Canada Paper on Economic and Public Policy.

Cowell, F.A. 1977. *Measuring Inequality.* Oxford: Phillip Allan Publishers.

Frenette, M., and G. Picot. 2003. "Life after Welfare: The Economic Well-Being of Welfare Leavers in Canada during the 1990s." Statistics Canada, Analytical Studies Research Paper Series no. 192. Catalogue No. 11F0019MIE2003192.

Hou, F., and G. Picot. 2003. "The Rise in Low-Income Rates among Immigrants in Canada." Statistics Canada, Analytical Studies Research Paper Series No. 198. Catalogue No. 11F0019MIE2003198.

Jäntti, M. 1997. "Inequality in Five Countries in the 1980s: The Role of Demographic Shifts, Markets and Government." *Economica* 64(255): 415-40.

Kapsalis, C. 2001. "An Assessment of EI and SA Reporting in SLID." Statistics Canada, Analytical Studies Research Paper Series No. 166. Catalogue No. 11F0019MIE 2001166.

Kovacevic, M.S., and D.A. Binder. 1997. "Variance Estimation for Measures of Income Inequality and Polarization: The Estimating Equations Approach." *Journal of Official Statistics* 13(1): 41-58.

Llg, R.E., and S.E. Haugen. 2000. "Earnings and Employment Trends in the 1990s." *Monthly Labor Review*, March: 21-33.

Morissette, R., J. Myles, and G. Picot. 1994. "Earnings Inequality and the Distribution of Working Time in Canada." *Canadian Business Economics* 2(3): 3-16.

National Council of Welfare. 1997. *Another Look at Welfare Reform.* Minister of Public Works and Government Services, Canada.

Rashid, A. 1998. "Family Income Inequality, 1970-1995." *Perspectives on Labour and Income* 10(4): 11-17.

Saez, E., and M.R. Veall. 2003. "The Evolution of High Incomes in Canada, 1920-2000." NBER Working Paper 9607.

Sargent, T.C. 1998. "The BU Ratio: Prospect and Retrospect." Economic and Fiscal Policy Branch, Department of Finance, Working paper 98-09.

Statistics Canada. 2002. *Income in Canada 2000.* Statistics Canada Catalogue No. 75-202-XIE.

Wolfson, M. 1986. "Stasis amid Change: Income Inequality in Canada, 1965-1983." *Review of Income and Wealth* 32(4): 337-69.

—. 1997. "Divergent Inequalities: Theory and Empirical Results." *Review of Income and Wealth* 43(4): 401-21.

Wolfson, M., and B. Murphy. 1998. "New Views on Inequality Trends in Canada and the United States." *Monthly Labor Review*, April: 3-23.

4
How Has Earnings Mobility in Canada Changed?

Charles M. Beach

For a long time in Canada, income distribution studies have focused on the inequality of income as measured from annual cross-sections of data (such as the Census and Surveys of Consumer Finance). But the social value or concern that one attaches to such inequality measures depends in part on how static or changing are individuals' incomes within the distribution. If the observed degree of inequality corresponds to the same people remaining at the bottom or top of the income distribution year after year, one would be more concerned than if that degree of inequality corresponds to, say, everyone passing through and spending the same amount of time in all regions of the distribution (Shorrocks 1978a). Standard economic theory such as the human capital literature predicts that a person will shift through different regions of the income distribution over a life-cycle and working career, and simple observation reveals that a person can experience different luck with respect to health, employment, and advancement patterns over time.

Understanding the role and contribution of mobility to income inequality helps one to better interpret observed inequality changes and to better evaluate alternative hypotheses of what may be driving these changes (Katz and Autor 1999, 1493). Mobility is the dynamic complement of inequality. It is also an aspect of economic opportunity that is of particular concern to Macleod and Eisenberg (Chapter 2). So, empirically, what is the pattern of income mobility affecting the distribution of income in Canada? This chapter presents basic evidence on how workers' earnings change on average over time and then examines whether the degree of mobility has changed between the 1980s and 1990s in Canada.

Several recent studies (e.g., Beach and Finnie 1998, 2004) have examined data and patterns on earnings mobility in Canada. Not surprisingly, some groups have moved up in the distribution while others have moved

down. Some regions of the distribution have seen a reduction in their earnings mobility, while other regions have experienced an enhanced degree of
upward or downward earnings change. In line with a resourcist approach to
inequality, one might also express a greater concern about what has been
happening to low-earnings workers than to those at the top end of the distribution. In general, from a complex mix of distributional changes over time,
what can one infer about the economic well-being of workers as a whole?
This chapter examines how one might make such a normative evaluation. In
the case of inequality, a considerable literature has developed about drawing
inferences about distributional change from what economists call social welfare functions (Atkinson 1970). This chapter applies the same reasoning to
the concept of income mobility, to consider how a set of mobility changes
affects social welfare.

This study thus has two main objectives. First, it shows how conventional techniques derived from the literature of income inequality can be
used to evaluate how income mobility patterns affect economic well-being.
A relatively little known, but recently expanding, theoretical literature used
by researchers in the area can help clarify the linkage between the concepts of
(static) income inequality and (dynamic) income mobility. The ranking of
distributions on the basis of social welfare is largely expressed in terms of
"stochastic dominance," and this chapter shows how the techniques of stochastic dominance can be applied to rank overall income mobility patterns.
Second, in doing so the techniques are applied to Canadian data on earnings
mobility over the period 1982 to 1999 – a time of economic and labour
market change in Canada – to discover whether there were changes that would
represent a gain or a loss in the economic well-being of Canadian workers.

Approaches to Income Mobility

Sociologists have a long tradition of analyzing generational and occupational
mobility (e.g., occupational status of sons compared to fathers). The practice
of examining intergenerational mobility is now appearing in economics studies as well (e.g., Corak and Heisz 1995, 2000, for Canada; Solon 1992, 1999,
for the United States; and more generally, Corak 2004).

Within economics, one can identify several approaches to measuring
and evaluating income mobility over the past two decades. First are a number of summary or aggregative descriptive statistics of income mobility, such
as the proportion of people who change their income group from one period

to the next. Such mobility measures are called aggregative because they are single statistics that summarize mobility information across the whole distribution. Such measures are called descriptive (as opposed to normative) in that they describe some aspect of income change over time without implying any judgment of whether the measured degree of mobility is good or bad. A convenient summary of such measures can be found, for example, in Conlisk (1990) or Atkinson et al. (1992); an early application for Canada is Kennedy (1989). A second approach to the analysis of income mobility derives the summary measures of mobility from a set of axiomatic criteria (Shorrocks 1978a; Maasoumi 1998). That is, in choosing among a set of alternative mobility measures, one may wish to focus on a class of measures (or possibly a single measure) that can be shown to satisfy certain desirable statistical or normative properties. This is an advance over the first approach in that, under certain conditions, one is better able to infer whether a measured mobility change represents an increase or decrease in economic well-being.

But any summary mobility index combines or averages out different, possibly conflicting, mobility patterns. A more informative approach would allow the display of different mobility patterns over different regions of the income distribution. The natural way of implementing this is by means of an income transition matrix (explained below), which shows how people change income classes during a given period. This approach has been initially examined by Shorrocks (1978b), who imposed various desirable criteria or properties on possible transition matrices. A third approach to measuring and evaluating mobility changes uses the disaggregated transition-matrix approach to compare and rank the different sets of changes in terms of social welfare functions or other criteria. Thus one can say (under certain conditions) whether one set of income class changes (a transition matrix calculated, say, over the 1990s) leads to an increase or reduction in social welfare compared to another set of income class changes (a transition matrix computed over the 1980s). Contributions in this area include Atkinson (1983), Markandya (1984), Conlisk (1989), Dardanoni (1993), and Maasoumi (1998). Just as Atkinson (1970) showed how one can base inequality rankings on social welfare criteria, these authors extend the same principles of social welfare ranking to transition matrices (Atkinson and Bourguignon 2000).

This chapter focuses on the third approach. More specifically, it illustrates how the social welfare approaches of Atkinson (1983) and Dardanoni (1993) can be implemented with longitudinal earnings data for Canada covering the period 1982 to 1999 in order to evaluate how earnings mobility (expressed separately for women and men) has changed over this period in terms of social welfare criteria. The data used came from longitudinal tax files for Canada.

The next section of this chapter introduces transition matrices and sets out the theoretical conditions for ranking transition matrices in terms of social welfare. The theoretical literature is expressed in terms of stochastic dominance criteria. The data source used is also explained. The third section begins the empirical work by looking at how mobility increases with length of the period in terms of a leading summary measure of mobility. The fourth section applies the approaches of Atkinson (1983) and Dardanoni (1993) to evaluate whether earnings mobility changed for the better or worse between 1982 and 1999 in Canada. Summary remarks conclude the chapter.

A Social Welfare Approach to Evaluating Income Mobility

We should care about income mobility because it is connected with income inequality. Income change over time is basic in the modern economic theory of earnings determination, which is generally dynamic and tested with longitudinal microdata. Atkinson et al. (1992) describe the importance of earnings mobility as both intrinsic and instrumental. Intrinsically, mobility of earnings is viewed as an indicator of equality of opportunity in the labour market, particularly in a life-cycle career framework where young workers may start off with relatively low earnings and, through talent, hard work, and experience, move up through the earnings distribution over much of their career. The restrictions of a segmented or dual labour market could inhibit such career progression, and imperfect capital markets could limit investment in education and training of workers and flatten earnings trajectories – either of which would reduce earnings mobility (or conversely, increase the stratification of earnings), potential consumption, and hence economic well-being. If all workers systematically progress along a given age-earnings trajectory over their careers, there is less social concern about any degree of earnings inequality in the economy. But if workers are largely stratified within lower, middle, and upper regions of the distribution throughout their careers, the degree of earnings inequality carries a much greater degree of social concern (Friedman 1962, 171). In this sense, a measure of earnings mobility is a useful complement to conventional indices of earnings inequality. Mobility and opportunity or flexibility in the labour market may also increase efficiency in the economy by providing incentives for advancement and penalties for not keeping up.

Earnings mobility also has an instrumental importance in that it affects other matters of concern. As we've seen, it contributes to the reduction of lifetime inequality. But it may also be relevant to social policy. Are observed cross-sectional poverty rates due to a large number of persons passing through a low-income phase very temporarily or to particular groups facing very lengthy persistent periods in poverty? Social insurance schemes (such as employment insurance) would seem a more appropriate policy response in the former case, while appropriately targeted employment, pension, and training schemes would seem better suited to the latter case. Access and entitlement to current government programs such as employment insurance, pensions, and income-averaging tax options depend on some aspect of income mobility.

THE LAD DATA SOURCE AND TRANSITION MATRIX ESTIMATES

The LAD (for Longitudinal Administrative Datafile) data set used in this chapter is a 10 percent representative sample of all Canadian tax-filers assembled by Statistics Canada from income tax data from 1982 on. It is thus very large. In order to focus on a relatively homogeneous source of income that is very widely received, we look at total employment income (henceforth "earnings") rather than total income from all sources (including, for example, government transfers and investment income). Quite different demographic and structural factors underlie different sources of income. A great deal of research in the last decade and a half has highlighted various changes in the labour market (e.g., increased globalization and use of technology) as the principal driving factors in the observed widening of inequality and growing polarization of incomes in most developed economies such as Canada. Hence we will concentrate attention on mobility of earnings in this chapter. Earnings here consist of all wage and salary income and net self-employment income.

The analysis sample for this study consists of one in ten of all earners aged twenty to sixty-four who were not full-time students in the income year and who received at least $1,000 in earnings (in constant 1999 dollars) as reported on the T1 Canadian income tax forms. The intention is to approximate Statistics Canada's concept of "All Earners" while excluding those who have only a limited attachment to the labour market.[1] Full-time post-secondary students were excluded on the grounds that they have only a secondary attachment to the labour market and their earnings do not accurately reflect their labour market opportunities. The time period covered in this study is 1982-99. The resulting final analysis sample used in this study varies from

1.035 million observations (608,000 men and 427,000 women) in 1982 to 1.176 million observations (643,000 men and 533,000 women) in 1991 and up to 1.270 million observations (679,000 men and 591,000 women) in 1999. More complete details of the analysis sample are found in Beach and Finnie (2004).

To construct transition matrices, one divides the range of earnings in the distribution into a set of ordered earnings categories separated by a set of earnings cut-offs. Following the convention in the polarization literature, the cut-offs are expressed in terms of the median annual earnings level. Also, in order to address issues of where various individuals lie in the overall distribution of earnings, or how well women and men are doing in the overall earnings distribution, all cut-offs are computed from a common median earnings level for the earnings distribution as a whole each year. The following cut-off levels are used in this study:

Below 25 percent of median ("Very low")
25-50 percent of median ("Low")
50-100 percent of median ("Low middle")
100-150 percent of median ("High middle")
150-200 percent of median ("High")
Above 200 percent of median ("Very high")

These cut-off levels thus vary year to year with changes in the median real earnings level. However, the median actually changed relatively little during 1982-99. Its lowest value was $25,600 in 1994 and its highest values were $27,500 in 1998 and $27,700 in 1999; excepting these values, the range of the median over the period covered was only $25,900 (in 1986) to $27,200 (in 1989). All figures are in constant 1999 dollars.

The transition matrix is a two-dimensional array of earnings groups for an initial year down the left-hand side and for a subsequent year along the top, and whose ijth elements indicate the probabilities (expressed in percentages) of moving from earnings group i in the initial year to earnings group j in the subsequent year. If these probabilities sum to 100 percent across each row, it is referred to as a conditional transition matrix or just a transition matrix for short. By convention, the earnings groups are ordered from lowest to highest. The estimation sample underlying any transition matrix consists of those workers in the analysis sample who appear in at least the beginning and end years of the transition period (what Beach and Finnie refer to as their Broad Estimation Sample).

Eight-year earnings transition matrices are illustrated to provide concrete examples in Tables 4.1 (1982-1990) and 4.2 (1991-99). This split provides equal-length transition intervals that do not overlap and that cover approximately the same phases of their respective business cycles. Separate transition matrices are presented for women and men because the earnings experiences of the two are quite different on average. The earnings categories VL, L, ..., VH stand for very low, low, low middle, high middle, high and very high as defined above. Corresponding one-year transition matrices are presented in Table 4.3 (for 1998-99, essentially the peak of an economic business cycle) and Table 4.4 (for 1991-92, a trough of the cycle). In these tables, the numbers (in bold) on the principal diagonal running from north-west to south-east corners are the staying probabilities (multiplied by 100). Numbers above the principal diagonal represent probabilities of *moving up* one or more earnings groups. Numbers below this diagonal indicate probabilities of *moving down* one or more earnings groups. Therefore, in the top row of Table 4.1, the figures indicate that 15.0 percent of men who were in the very low or bottom earnings category in 1982 remained in that earnings group in 1990, while 27.9 percent of lowest-earning men moved up to the lower middle

TABLE 4.1

Eight-year transition matrices, 1982-90

1982/90		VL	L	LM	HM	H	VH
Men	VL	**15.04**	19.16	27.93	21.52	10.60	5.75
	L	10.75	**19.02**	29.31	22.84	11.76	6.31
	LM	5.89	11.65	**30.19**	29.40	14.58	8.29
	HM	3.28	5.25	14.62	**37.78**	26.45	12.62
	H	2.18	3.04	7.50	17.72	**38.12**	31.44
	VH	1.85	2.22	4.54	6.41	13.06	**71.91**
Women	VL	**22.95**	24.46	32.21	14.56	4.41	1.39
	L	15.24	**25.39**	37.05	16.09	4.56	1.68
	LM	8.56	13.03	**40.53**	28.45	6.92	2.52
	HM	5.10	5.99	17.74	**45.08**	19.91	6.17
	H	3.14	3.53	9.09	18.15	**41.58**	24.50
	VH	2.43	2.52	5.15	7.77	16.89	**65.24**

SOURCE: LAD data as discussed in text.

TABLE 4.2

Eight-year transition matrices, 1991-99

1991/99		VL	L	LM	HM	H	VH
Men	VL	**17.48**	20.12	29.56	18.89	8.69	5.26
	L	11.96	**21.22**	32.67	20.52	8.39	5.24
	LM	6.37	11.43	**34.59**	28.97	11.75	6.89
	HM	3.32	5.03	16.01	**40.34**	22.78	12.52
	H	2.44	3.03	7.28	17.39	**37.61**	32.24
	VH	2.69	2.35	4.44	5.85	12.18	**72.48**
Women	VL	**25.41**	26.62	30.81	12.14	3.60	1.43
	L	16.24	**28.03**	37.51	13.43	3.39	1.40
	LM	8.41	13.55	**44.41**	25.45	5.76	2.42
	HM	4.31	5.56	18.90	**46.70**	18.06	6.48
	H	3.25	3.25	8.40	19.65	**40.25**	25.21
	VH	3.02	2.75	5.24	7.82	16.48	**64.69**

SOURCE: LAD data as discussed in text.

region of the distribution. In the lower panel, 45.1 percent of women who were in the higher middle earnings category in 1982 remained there eight years later, while 28.8 percent (sum of 5.10, 5.99 and 17.74) of that group fell one or more earnings categories over this period.

Several features of these transition matrices are evident. First, there is a greater degree of earnings mobility, particularly with respect to the probability of moving up, over the longer interval. This will be examined in more detail below. Second, since the probability of staying in the same earnings category is higher for women than for men (except at the top end of the distribution), the degree of earnings mobility is generally higher for men. This is consistent with men's age-earnings profiles typically being steeper, more continuous, and more concave than women's. The probabilities of moving up the distribution are generally higher for men, while the probabilities of moving down one or more earnings categories are higher for women, who are more likely to move into part-time work during periods of child-raising or to change to a broader range of jobs to accommodate a husband's new job in a different location. This is consistent with Macleod and Eisenberg's argument in Chapter 2 that women generally face lower earnings opportunities than men. Third, the probability of remaining in the same earnings group from one period to the next generally rises with the level of earnings. That is, workers with high earnings levels are more likely to continue with high earnings from one period to the next (as higher skill levels generally reduce employment risk), whereas workers who find themselves with low earnings (possibly because of part-time work or simply bad luck) one year are less likely to stay with low earnings year after year. Mobility

TABLE 4.3

One-year transition matrices, 1998-99 (peak of cycle)

1998/99		VL	L	LM	HM	H	VH
Men	VL	**43.56**	30.82	20.34	3.96	0.86	0.46
	L	15.24	**43.22**	33.43	6.29	1.22	0.61
	LM	4.25	10.51	**61.13**	20.32	2.81	0.99
	HM	1.28	2.11	12.11	**66.18**	15.70	2.61
	H	0.63	0.90	2.96	13.37	**65.03**	17.10
	VH	0.33	0.47	1.07	2.29	8.72	**87.12**
Women	VL	**52.34**	32.34	13.36	1.61	0.24	0.11
	L	16.22	**50.73**	29.42	3.15	0.35	0.14
	LM	4.02	10.49	**69.12**	14.72	1.31	0.35
	HM	1.10	2.07	12.83	**71.78**	10.85	1.38
	H	0.56	0.82	3.63	14.39	**68.11**	12.49
	VH	0.33	0.49	1.52	3.48	10.98	**83.20**

SOURCE: LAD data as discussed in text.

TABLE 4.4

One-year transition matrices, 1991-92 (trough of cycle)

1991/92		VL	L	LM	HM	H	VH
Men	VL	**46.27**	29.49	19.03	3.97	0.83	0.40
	L	19.71	**42.51**	29.81	6.18	1.29	0.49
	LM	7.11	14.11	**56.46**	18.53	2.86	0.94
	HM	2.16	3.47	14.26	**62.05**	15.95	2.12
	H	0.86	1.35	4.11	13.17	**65.35**	15.16
	VH	0.41	0.62	1.66	2.86	8.94	**85.51**
Women	VL	**55.86**	29.24	12.93	1.66	0.22	0.08
	L	20.28	**49.73**	26.19	3.32	0.37	0.11
	LM	5.67	12.17	**65.54**	14.95	1.36	0.31
	HM	1.42	2.67	13.27	**71.04**	10.51	1.09
	H	0.61	0.98	4.45	12.83	**67.10**	14.02
	VH	0.34	0.54	1.68	3.56	9.90	**83.99**

SOURCE: LAD data as discussed in text.

is evidently much greater toward the bottom end of the earnings distribution than at the top end. Again, this may reflect greater vicissitudes of employment luck, steeper age-earnings profiles among young workers (who typically have relatively low earnings levels), greater year-to-year changes in labour market opportunities among young workers, and more shifting between full-time and part-time work among young and older workers than among mid-career prime-age workers in the labour market. Fourth, the probabilities of moving up the distribution are generally higher in periods of economic prosperity (around the peak of an economic expansion), while the probabilities of moving down are more marked in periods of strong labour market recession.

ATKINSON'S APPROACH TO EVALUATING MOBILITY CHANGES

We now review the approach proposed by Atkinson (1983) for evaluating and comparing the degree of income mobility between two transition matrices. The comparison is on the basis of social welfare. At this stage we need some analytical notation. Let Y_1 and Y_2 be random variables representing individuals' incomes in an initial and subsequent period respectively, and let them have a joint density function $f(y_1,y_2)$ over a finite range $0 \leq Y_i \leq a_i$. Then a social welfare function,

$$W = \int_0^{a_i} \int_0^{a_2} U(y_1,y_2)f(y_1,y_2)dy_2 dy_1, \tag{1}$$

is a weighted average (with weights given by the joint density) of "social utilities" attached to alternative joint values of Y_1 and Y_2. Here the $U(\cdot,\cdot)$ function can be viewed as the way in which society values alternative combinations of Y_1 and Y_2 (Atkinson and Bourguignon 2000, 42). If two different income distributions, $f(y_1,y_2)$ and $f^*(y_1,y_2)$, are being compared, their difference can be expressed as

$$\Delta f(y_1,y_2) = f(y_1,y_2) - f^*(y_1,y_2)$$

and their difference in social welfare as

$$\Delta W = \int_0^{a_1} \int_0^{a_2} U(y_1,y_2) \Delta f(y_1,y_2)dy_2 dy_1.$$

In empirical applications, however, it is convenient to represent income discretely as falling within a set of K income groups or categories (in our examples, $K = 6$ in Tables 4.1-4.4). Correspondingly, let the distribution of income in period i be represented by the K-element (row) vector

$$m_i = (m_i^l, ..., m_i^K), i = 1, 2,$$

where m_i^k is the proportion of income recipients in the (marginal) distribution i with incomes in category k. Also, let $P = [p_{ij}]$ be the K×K income transition matrix linking the two marginal distributions

$$m_2 = m_1 P. \tag{2}$$

Inequality in period i is a function of m_i and mean incomes in each category. Mobility is represented by the transition matrix P, where $\Sigma_{j=1}^{K} p_{ij} = 1$. In discrete terms, then, the social welfare evaluation criterion becomes

$$W = \Sigma_{j=1}^{K} \Sigma_{k=1}^{K} U(y_1^j, y_2^k) m_1^j m_2^k \tag{3}$$

where $m_2^k = \Sigma_{j=1}^{K} p_{jk} m_1^j$.

Given initial-period data on m_1 and the transition matrix P, how one evaluates degree of income mobility depends on the properties of the social evaluation function U. For example, if U were additively separable,

$$U(y_1, y_2) = u_1(y_1) + u_2(y_2),$$

where $u_i' > 0$ and $u_i'' < 0$, the cross-product terms in (3) fall out, the degree of mobility does not influence the level of social welfare, and $\Delta W = 0$ (Atkinson 1983, 65). When the cross-derivative

$$\frac{\partial^2 U}{\partial y_1 \partial y_2} = U_{12}$$

is not zero, W now depends on the degree of income mobility between periods. When the cross-derivative is negative, social welfare is judged lower the more highly correlated are Y_1 and Y_2 (i.e., the greater the stratification of incomes over time).

One distribution is said to stochastically dominate another for our purposes if social welfare is at least as high for all U functions that satisfy certain properties.[2] Atkinson (1983) derives two stochastic dominance conditions for tests that are each sufficient for ranking distributions. They are not necessary and thus do not provide complete rankings. But they do allow one to rank distributions and hence disaggregate mobility, where applicable, without having to know the exact functional form of either $f(\cdot,\cdot)$ or $U(\cdot,\cdot)$. Just as univariate stochastic dominance has been used to help rank inequality of income distributions at any given time, so bivariate stochastic dominance principles can be applied to help rank the mobility of income distributions between two time periods. Technical derivations of the two tests can be found in Atkinson (1983). The tests can be expressed in practical form as follows.

In the case of the first test, for all social evaluation functions $U(\cdot,\cdot)$ with positive first derivatives, non-positive second derivatives, and $U_{12} \leq 0$, the income mobility represented by transition matrix P has a higher level of social welfare than that of another transition matrix P^* if

$$\alpha(D_1 P) - \alpha(D^*_1 P^*) \tag{4}$$

has at least one negative element and no positive elements, where $\alpha(D_1 P)$ and $\alpha(D^*_1 P^*)$ are the cumulative joint density matrices of $D_1 P$ and $D^*_1 P^*$, respectively, and D_1 and D^*_1 are diagonal matrices with the elements of m_1 and m^*_1 arrayed along their principal diagonals, respectively. To calculate the α test criterion matrices, consider first the rescaled transition matrix

$$\underset{K x K}{D_1 P} = \begin{bmatrix} m_1^1 & & 0 \\ & \ddots & \\ 0 & & m_1^K \end{bmatrix} \begin{bmatrix} p_{11} & \cdots & p_{1K} \\ \vdots & & \vdots \\ p_{K1} & \cdots & p_{KK} \end{bmatrix} = \begin{bmatrix} m_1^1 p_{11} & m_1^1 p_{12} & \cdots & m_1^1 p_{1K} \\ m_1^2 p_{21} & m_1^2 p_{22} & \cdots & m_1^2 p_{2K} \\ \vdots & \vdots & \ddots & \vdots \\ m_1^K p_{K1} & m_1^K p_{K2} & \cdots & m_1^K p_{KK} \end{bmatrix}. \tag{5}$$

The $\alpha(D_1 P)$ is the cumulative joint density matrix whose ijth element is obtained by forming a rectangular box of all elements in $D_1 P$ subtended by the ijth element, and adding all the elements of (5) in this box. That is

$$\underset{K x K}{\alpha(D_1 P)} = \begin{bmatrix} m_1^1 p_{11} & m_1^1 p_{11} + m_1^1 p_{12} & \cdots & \cdots & \sum_k^K m_1^1 p_{1k} \\ m_1^1 p_{11} + m_1^2 p_{21} & m_1^1 p_{11} + m_1^2 p_{21} + m_1^1 p_{12} + m_1^2 p_{22} & \cdots & \cdots & \sum_1^K m_1^1 p_{1k} + \sum_1^K m_1^2 p_{2k} \\ \vdots & \vdots & & & \\ \sum_j^K m_1^j p_{j1} & \sum_1^K m_1^j p_{j1} + \sum_1^K m_1^j p_{j2} & \cdots & \cdots & \sum_j^K \sum_k^K m_1^j p_{jk} \end{bmatrix}. \tag{6}$$

$\alpha(D^{\cdot}_1P^{\cdot})$ is calculated analogously. The double-sum bottom right-hand (i.e., KKth) element in both is unity. This first test corresponds to first-order stochastic dominance.

As already noted, the first test provides only a partial ranking of transition matrices with relatively weak or minimal restrictions imposed on the U function. If stronger restrictions are imposed, then more orderings of transition matrices could be obtained in general. Atkinson's second test does this by imposing the further restrictions of strict inequality on $U_{12} < 0$ along with third- and fourth-order derivative requirements that $U_{112}, U_{122} \geq 0$ and $U_{1122} \leq 0$. In this case, for social evaluation functions with this stronger set of restrictions, income mobility for transition matrix P and cumulative joint density matrix $\alpha(D_1P) = \alpha$ has a higher level of social welfare than that of another transition matrix P^*, and joint density matrix $\alpha(D^{\cdot}_1P^{\cdot}) \equiv \alpha^{\cdot}$, provided the matrix

$$\beta(D_1P) - \beta(D^{\cdot}_1P^*) \tag{7}$$

has at least one negative element and no positive elements, where

$$\beta_{kl} \equiv \beta(D_1P)_{kl} = \Sigma^k_{i=1}\Sigma^l_{j=1}\alpha_{ij}, \text{ and}$$
$$\beta^{\cdot}_{kl} \equiv \beta(D^{\cdot}_1P^{\cdot})_{kl} = \Sigma^k_{i=1}\Sigma^l_{j=1}\alpha^{\cdot}_{ij} \tag{8}$$

(i.e., $\beta_{kl} \leq \beta^{\cdot}_{kl}$ for all k,l). This second test provides more weight or social concern to a greater degree on mobility at lower income levels than at higher levels of income. This second test corresponds to second-order stochastic dominance. If the first test holds, the second test should hold *a fortiori*. But it is quite possible for the second test to imply a ranking where the first test could not.

Dardanoni's Approach to Evaluating Mobility Changes

We turn next to the approach proposed by Dardanoni (1993) for comparing income mobility between transition matrices. In this case, more restrictions are incorporated on the structure of the transition matrices themselves. He interprets transition matrices within a Markov chain framework where P is regular (i.e., strictly positive elements for our purposes), in which the elements across a row sum to unity and for which there exists a strictly positive equilibrium probability vector $m(1xK)$ that is the unique solution to

$m = mP$. He then evaluates mobility in terms of expected lifetime discounted utility, which, for an infinite lifetime, may be expressed as

$$\underset{(K\times 1)}{V} = (1 - \rho)[I -\rho P]^{-1}u = P(\rho)u, \qquad (9)$$

where ρ is a scalar time discount factor and u is a non-decreasing Kx1 vector of instantaneous utilities representing the utility value of income in the various income categories. The element $P(\rho)_{ij}$ of $P(\rho)$ is interpreted as the average probability (discounted over a lifetime) of moving from the initial state i to state j (Dardanoni 1993, 375).

The inequality literature makes a distinction between the degree of pure inequality or equity concerns (as represented, say, by a Lorenz curve) in a distribution and the mean level of incomes (as representing efficiency concerns) as jointly affecting social welfare. The mobility literature similarly distinguishes between mobility that affects social welfare by changing the available income categories in a distribution (so-called structural mobility) and mobility that affects the intertemporal movement of individuals across income categories for a given equilibrium distribution of individuals across categories (i.e., given vector m), which is called exchange or pure mobility. Dardanoni's tests abstract from the former in order to focus on the latter pure mobility effects embodied in income transition matrices by considering the situation in which the two distributions being compared (with transition matrices P and P^*) have the same distribution vector m. So his tests are, in effect, tests of pure mobility.[3]

Dardanoni also assumes that transition matrices are monotone, that is, each row stochastically dominates the row above it. Empirically, this means that, if one calculates a cumulative transition matrix (which has the cumulative transition probabilities within each row), then the cumulative probabilities should increase as one moves from the bottom element to the top element within a column of the cumulative matrix. A monotone transition matrix is one in which a person ending up in income category (column) j is more advantaged by having originated in the higher income category $j+1$ than in category j in the sense that those originating in income category $j+1$ had less prospect of moving (down) to income category j or lower by the end of the transition period than had those originating in income category j. All transition matrices in Tables 4.1-4.4 are indeed monotone or almost so.

With this additional structure on transition matrices, Dardanoni (1993) considers social welfare functions that are linear (and hence additively separable) in V, but asymmetric in weighting the income categories, so that greater weights are applied to lower initial income categories:

$$W = \Sigma_{i=1}^{K} w_i m^i V_i, \tag{10}$$

where m^i and V_i are respective elements of vectors m and V (ordered from lowest to highest income categories) and $w_l \geq w_2 \geq \ldots \geq w_K \geq 0$. Thus mobility within the lower portion of the distribution counts for more of a change in social welfare than mobility in the upper region of the distribution.

Dardanoni (1993) presents two tests for ranking income transition matrices. Indeed, he provides both necessary and sufficient conditions for social welfare rankings of transition matrices. It is convenient to define the KxK upper-triangular matrix

$$T = \begin{bmatrix} 1 & 1 & \cdots & 1 \\ 0 & 1 & \cdots & 1 \\ \vdots & \vdots & \ddots & \vdots \\ 0 & 0 & \cdots & 1 \end{bmatrix}.$$

Then post-multiplying a matrix, P, by T yields

$$PT = \begin{bmatrix} p_{11} & p_{11} + p_{12} & \cdots & \Sigma_{j=1}^{K} p_{1j} \\ p_{21} & p_{21} + p_{22} & \cdots & \Sigma_{j=1}^{K} p_{2j} \\ \vdots & \vdots & & \vdots \\ p_{K1} & p_{K1} + p_{K2} & \cdots & \Sigma_{j=1}^{K} p_{Kj} \end{bmatrix},$$

so that T is often called a summation or cumulation matrix. Similarly, pre-multiplying a diagonal matrix, D, with elements of m along its principal diagonal by T' yields

$$T'D = \begin{bmatrix} m^1 & 0 & \cdots & 0 & 0 \\ m^1 & m^2 & \cdots & 0 & 0 \\ \vdots & \vdots & \ddots & \vdots & \vdots \\ m^1 & m^2 & \cdots & m^{K-1} & \\ m^1 & m^2 & \cdots & m^{K-1} & m^K \end{bmatrix}.$$

Finally, a reverse monotone transition matrix P is a regular transition matrix with $D^{-1}P'D$ being monotone, a condition that Dardanoni argues is also likely to be satisfied by typical empirical transition matrices.

Let us now pull these results together. Suppose one wants to rank two transition matrices, P and P^*. In the case of Dardanoni's first test, let P and P^* both be regular monotone transition matrices with common equilibrium vector m and with P^* additionally reverse monotone. Then social welfare as specified in (10) will be at least no lower for P than for P^* for all $0 \le \rho < 1$ if and only if

$$T'D(P - P^*)T \le 0. \tag{11}$$

Proofs can be found in Dardanoni (1993, 378-81). That is, under the above conditions, all social welfare functions of the form (10) will rank the mobility in transition matrix P as preferable to that in P^*. This test requirement corresponds to a first-order stochastic dominance condition.

An interesting property, Dardanoni notes, follows from this test condition. The mobility ordering ranks the identity matrix (where no changes between income categories occur) as having the least degree of mobility, while a transition matrix having identical rows with vector m in each row is ranked as having maximal mobility as it corresponds to the same transition opportunities for each initial income category. So the ordering corresponds to simple intuition of ranking extreme degrees of income mobility.

The second test proposed by Dardanoni (1993) further restricts the class of social welfare functions in (10) by incorporating a requirement of transfer sensitivity (Shorrocks and Foster 1987) on the intensity with which mobility's effects on social welfare change across income categories. This is the joint condition that, first, the greater weight in the social welfare function given to mobility occurring at the lower end of the income distribution (the w_i's) declines at an increasing rate as one moves to higher income categories and, second, the elements in the instantaneous utility vector u in (9) increase at a decreasing rate. Under this additional requirement of transfer sensitivity, transition matrix P will have at least as high a level of social welfare as P^* if and only if

$$T'^2D(P - P^*)T^2 \le 0. \tag{12}$$

This stronger test requirement corresponds to a second-order stochastic dominance condition.

Mobility Increases with Time Frame

A way to illustrate typical scalar or aggregate measures of mobility is to examine how the degree of mobility changes the longer is the time window over which the mobility is calculated. For example, Tables 4.3 and 4.4 present transition matrices calculated over a one-year time frame, whereas Tables 4.1 and 4.2 refer to an eight-year time frame. It is clear simply by inspection that the probabilities of staying in the same earnings categories are lower (i.e., mobility in some sense is higher) over an eight-year time frame than over just one year.

There are a number of alternative ways tò capture the idea of mobility in a scalar measure. Beach and Finnie (1998) measure earnings mobility as

$$\text{Avg. mobility} = 1 - \text{avg. } Pr(S)$$

where "avg." indicates average and $Pr(S)$ is the empirical probability of staying. Thus, avg. $Pr(S)$ is the simple average of the K elements along the principal diagonal of a transition matrix. This can be alternatively written as

$$\text{Avg. mobility} = 1 - \frac{tr(P)}{K} = \frac{K - tr(P)}{K} \text{ ,}$$

where $tr(P)$ is the trace of the transition matrix P. If minimal mobility is indicated by an identity matrix, $tr(I) = K$, and average mobility is zero, as one would wish. However, if maximal mobility corresponds to P having the same probability vector in each row, then $tr(P) = 1$ and average mobility has an upper value of $K\text{-}1/K$. It would thus be more convenient to rescale the mobility measure to an index,

$$M = \frac{K - tr(P)}{K - 1} \text{ ,} \tag{13}$$

which has an upper value of one, so that now $0 \leq M \leq 1$. This is in fact the mobility index originally suggested by Prais (1955). It is perhaps the most widely used mobility measure, and Shorrocks (1978b) shows that it satisfies a number of intuitively desirable properties.

For progressively longer time frames, the values of M are computed as follows. Over a time frame of zero, there is no mobility of earnings, the transition matrix is the identity matrix, and M takes its minimal value. For a one-year time frame, M is calculated from the average of the transition matrices in Tables 4.3 and 4.4. Similarly, for the eight-year time frame, M is averaged

TABLE 4.5

Estimates of M by length of time frame

Length of time frame (years)	Men	Women
0	0	0
1	0.476	0.411
8	0.764	0.710
17	0.865	0.827

from Tables 4.1 and 4.2. The calculation of M for a time frame of seventeen years is based on the transition matrix for the full 1982-99 time frame. The first thing to notice from the estimates of M shown in Table 4.5 is that, as expected, the estimated mobility of earnings does indeed increase quite markedly with the length of the adjustment period. The longer the time frame, the more people's earnings change. Second, summary earnings mobility is everywhere lower for women than for men, again consistent with women generally having lower and flatter age-earnings profiles than men.

Evaluating Earnings Mobility Changes in Terms of Social Welfare

This section examines the question of whether earnings mobility in Canada has changed for the better or the worse between the 1980s and 1990s in terms of the social welfare test criteria described earlier. The last two decades have seen two severe economic recessions followed by lengthy periods of sustained economic growth. The Canada-US Free Trade Agreement followed by NAFTA have occasioned marked structural change in the Canadian economy as trade patterns shifted more north-south from east-west. Concerns about burgeoning deficits resulted in significant government cutbacks in expenditure and employment levels, and the provisions of a number of social programs were tightened up. Over much of this period, unemployment rates were high relative to those in the United States. It is thus reasonable to ask whether labour market income mobility changed over this period as well.

The LAD data used in this chapter are available from 1982 to 1999 and can be divided into two non-overlapping eight-year intervals, 1982-90 and 1991-99. Earnings transition matrices for the two periods have already been presented in Tables 4.1 and 4.2. Since men and women have had somewhat different earnings experiences over the last two decades, the transition matrices appear separately for women and men. Using the Prais M scalar measure of mobility, we compute the following:

	Men	Women
1982-90	0.776	0.718
1991-99	0.753	0.701

One can see that for both groups earnings mobility so measured decreased between these two periods, though by only 2.4-3.0 percent or about 2 percentage points. But, as has been noted, different scalar measures can potentially yield somewhat different mobility results. A more disaggregated flexible approach may provide more convincing and meaningful conclusions.

RESULTS BASED ON ATKINSON'S APPROACH

We first apply the test criteria of Atkinson (1983) to the transition matrices in Tables 4.1 and 4.2. The formulas in equations (4), (6), (7) and (8) allow for different initial-year earnings distributions – the m_1 and m_1^* vectors. This means that differences in social welfare over the two periods may be due to differences in initial distributions as well as differences in mobility as captured in the transition matrices. In order to net out the former effect and concentrate on just exchange or pure mobility, we calculate the simple average of the two initial-year distributions, m_1 and m_1^* and use this average vector m when

TABLE 4.6

Percentage distribution of earners by earnings category: men and women, selected years

		Very low	Low	Low middle	High middle	High	Very high
1982	Men	7.50	9.65	19.73	23.06	19.97	20.09
	Women	16.80	18.68	33.21	20.59	7.54	3.18
1990	Men	7.64	10.27	20.07	22.54	18.33	21.15
	Women	15.91	17.89	30.94	21.39	9.05	4.82
1991	Men	8.91	10.81	19.55	20.92	17.71	22.10
	Women	16.15	17.54	29.26	21.70	9.52	5.83
1999	Men	8.19	10.69	21.26	21.53	16.07	22.26
	Women	14.58	17.14	29.61	21.49	9.91	7.27
Avg. '82–'91	Men	8.205	10.230	19.640	21.990	18.840	21.095
	Women	16.475	18.110	31.235	21.145	8.530	4.505
Avg. 4 years	Men	8.060	10.355	20.153	22.012	18.020	21.400
	Women	15.860	17.813	30.755	21.292	9.005	5.275

SOURCE: Beach and Finnie (2004).

applying the above formulas. Values for m_1, m_1', and m are reported in Table 4.6 in the first, third, and fifth panels, respectively.

Calculating the test matrix $\alpha(D_1P) - \alpha(D_1'P')$ for men yields the following results. (The m vector values were expressed as decimal proportions between 0 and 1, while the transition matrix elements were expressed as percentages with maximal value of 100.)

$$
\begin{bmatrix}
0.200 & 0.279 & 0.413 & 0.197 & 0.040 & -0.000 \\
0.324 & 0.628 & 1.105 & 0.652 & 0.151 & 0.001 \\
0.418 & 0.679 & 2.021 & 1.483 & 0.426 & 0.001 \\
0.427 & 0.639 & 2.287 & 2.312 & 0.448 & 0.001 \\
0.476 & 0.686 & 2.292 & 2.256 & 0.295 & -0.001 \\
0.653 & 0.891 & 2.476 & 2.321 & 0.175 & -0.001
\end{bmatrix} \tag{14}
$$

As can be seen, all but three elements in the computed matrix are positive. The three negative values, however, are the result of differences between five or six digit numbers (e.g., the second-to-last negative value arises from 78.9032-78.9038), so are well within rounding error given that one started with input of three- and four-digit numbers in m and P. So the evidence strongly favours the conclusion that men experienced a social welfare loss between these two periods, a loss associated with a decline in their earnings mobility.

If one imposes the stronger conditions of second-order stochastic dominance, one makes use of Atkinson's test criterion (7). As the formulas in (8) make clear, the large positive elements earlier in the matrix in (14) completely swamp the few small negative elements, so that it is massively the case that the observed reduction in men's earnings mobility indeed corresponds to a decline in their social welfare based on second-order stochastic dominance.

The first test criterion for women yields the following results.

$$
\begin{bmatrix}
0.405 & 0.761 & 0.530 & 0.132 & -0.002 & 0.005 \\
0.586 & 1.420 & 1.273 & 0.393 & 0.047 & 0.003 \\
0.540 & 1.536 & 2.601 & 0.783 & 0.075 & 0.000 \\
0.373 & 1.278 & 2.588 & 1.113 & 0.014 & 0.004 \\
0.382 & 1.263 & 2.514 & 1.168 & \underline{-0.045} & 0.006 \\
0.409 & 1.300 & 2.556 & 1.211 & \underline{-0.020} & 0.006
\end{bmatrix} \tag{15}
$$

Again there are three negative values. But, in this case, the two underlined negative elements are large enough not to be rounding errors. Consequently, Atkinson's first criterion does not allow us to unambiguously evaluate the observed scalar decline in women's earnings mobility. Calculation of Atkinson's second criterion, however, does result in a test matrix of completely positive elements. So, on the basis of second-order stochastic dominance, one can indeed infer a decline in women's social welfare associated with a decrease in earnings mobility.

Results Based on Dardanoni's Approach

Dardanoni (1993) provides two alternative tests of change in mobility based on an alternative specification of social welfare along with stronger conditions on the structure of transition matrices. As it turns out, the two tests in (11) and (12) are easier to program and calculate than are the tests in the previous section. Each element in the Atkinson test matrices involves computing a double sum, whereas each element in the Dardanoni test matrices can be calculated by a simple sum $((P - P^*)T)$ and by a partial inner product $(T'D \cdot (P - P^*)T)$. Since the difference $P - P^*$ is calculated from the raw data rather than from results of the double-sum calculations $(\alpha - \alpha^*)$, rounding error is much less likely to be a problem as well. The Dardanoni tests are also based on a long-run equilibrium distribution vector m assumed to be the same between the two situations being compared, again to focus on differences in exchange or pure mobility. We implement this by averaging the distribution vectors of the initial and terminal years of each transition period and then averaging these two estimates between the two time periods being compared (see the bottom panel in Table 4.6).

For men, the results of the first test matrix are as follows.

$$
\begin{bmatrix}
0.197 & 0.274 & 0.405 & 0.193 & 0.040 & 0 \\
0.322 & 0.627 & 1.106 & 0.654 & 0.151 & 0 \\
0.419 & 0.680 & 2.046 & 1.507 & 0.434 & 0 \\
0.428 & 0.640 & 2.312 & 2.337 & 0.456 & 0 \\
0.474 & 0.685 & 2.317 & 2.283 & 0.310 & 0 \\
0.654 & 0.893 & 2.504 & 2.349 & 0.188 & 0
\end{bmatrix}
\tag{16}
$$

The elements in the last column are zero because the matrix T cumulates the $P - P^*$ probability differences across each row, and the sum of the probabilities in each row of P and P^* is one. As is evident, all elements in the criterion matrix are non-negative, so Dardanoni's first test clearly implies that the reduction in men's earnings mobility over the period corresponds to a reduction in their social welfare. Since this is a first-order stochastic dominance test, Dardanoni's second test (based on second-order stochastic dominance) would imply the same result *a fortiori*. This is evident from the computation perspective. Since the first test matrix $T'D(P - P^*)T$ has positive elements everywhere, post-multiplying this by T simply cumulates these numbers (horizontally) to yield even larger positive numbers. So the two Dardanoni tests provide consistent but crisper results than the Atkinson tests.

The first Dardanoni test criterion matrix for women yields the following results.

$$
\begin{bmatrix}
0.390 & 0.733 & 0.511 & 0.127 & -0.002 & 0 \\
0.568 & 1.381 & 1.241 & 0.383 & 0.047 & 0 \\
0.522 & 1.495 & 2.548 & 0.768 & 0.074 & 0 \\
0.354 & 1.235 & 2.535 & 1.100 & 0.012 & 0 \\
0.364 & 1.220 & 2.458 & 1.158 & \underline{-0.050} & 0 \\
0.395 & 1.263 & 2.506 & 1.208 & \underline{-0.021} & 0
\end{bmatrix}
\tag{17}
$$

As with Atkinson's first test, three elements here turn out negative. The top one might be rounding error, but the two underlined elements cannot be. So, as with Atkinson's first test, we cannot infer that the observed decline in women's earnings mobility made them worse off based on the informational input of the test.

However, if one builds in the stronger assumption of transfer sensitivity, the second Dardanoni test, as specified in (12), does yield (strictly) positive elements everywhere in the criterion matrix. This can be seen immediately from (17) where post-multiplying by T cumulates the elements across a row, so that the (relatively) larger elements to the left of the negatives in each row of (17) swamp the negative values and leave a matrix of only positive elements, which pre-multiplication by T' then takes weighted averages of these elements. Thus, again, as with Atkinson's second test, the stronger built-in egalitarian assumptions of the second-order test allow one to infer for women as well that the observed decline in scalar earnings mobility has reduced women's social welfare as well as men's.

Conclusion

This chapter has examined whether changes in earnings mobility in Canada between the 1980s and the 1990s have left workers better or worse off over this period. Mobility is represented separately for women and men in a general and flexible fashion in terms of earnings transition matrices. The basis for evaluating mobility change is a social welfare criterion. Two approaches are set out for evaluating differences in transition matrices based on social welfare. Atkinson (1983) proposes two tests that make use of assumed derivative properties of non-additively separable social welfare functions. Dardanoni (1993) offers an alternative set of two tests that assume asymmetrically weighted, additively separable social welfare functions but make use of stronger properties of the transition matrices themselves. Both sets of tests are empirically implemented with the Canadian LAD longitudinal data on workers' earnings over the period 1982-99.

Earnings mobility is found to be generally higher for men than for women, as women typically have lower and flatter age-earnings profiles over their working careers. Probabilities of moving up the distribution are generally higher for men, while probabilities of moving down one or more earnings categories are more usual for women. These characteristics are consistent with women generally facing lower earnings opportunities than men. Mobility is also much greater toward the bottom end of the earnings distribution than at the top end where high-skill workers enjoy much more stable earnings patterns.

Mobility generally rises the longer the time frame over which earnings changes can occur. Earnings mobility, a dimension of economic opportunity, has also been found to have declined on average for both men and women between the two periods of 1982-90 and 1991-99, though the average decline is only about 2 percent to 3 percent.

The social welfare-based tests are implemented empirically to evaluate the observed mobility declines. The two sets of tests show similar results. For men, the decline in earnings mobility over this period is associated with a reduction in men's social welfare based on both first- and second-order stochastic dominance tests. For women, both first-order tests of Atkinson and Dardanoni are not able to draw any welfare inferences from the results. But under the stronger assumptions built into their second-order tests, both Atkinson's and Dardanoni's second-order tests confirm a reduction in women's social welfare as well. So both men's and women's welfare have been inferred to have declined in this regard, though the conclusion is more broadly based on a weaker set of assumptions for men than for women.

While the two sets of tests – of Atkinson and Dardanoni –examined in this study both lead to similar results, those of Dardanoni appear slightly preferable to applied practitioners. Their basic intuition – both analytic and computational – seems more evident, they are easier and slightly more reliable to compute, and they use more fully general information about the typical structure of empirical transition matrices.

Over most of the 1980s and 1990s, earnings inequality generally increased in Canada, as in many other developed western economies. An analysis of inequality change based on social welfare criteria indicates a resulting reduction in social welfare (Beach and Slotsve 1994). The present analysis extends this conclusion by examining how individual workers move around in the earnings distribution over time. Greater mobility for a given level of inequality of earnings is viewed as corresponding to greater labour market opportunity and potential for enhanced equity and efficiency. The finding of a welfare-reducing decline in earnings mobility complements the earlier results for inequality and should raise concern for what has been happening in Canadian labour markets over the eighties and nineties. More broadly, the finding that earnings mobility has declined while, at the same time, earnings inequality or differences have substantially widened should also raise concerns about the possibly growing stratification of Canadian society.

ACKNOWLEDGMENTS

I would like to thank David Green and Jonathan Kesselman for providing the initiative for this study, Roger Sceviour and Ross Finnie for providing the data, and David Gray and David Green for very helpful comments on an earlier draft of this chapter. All errors and infelicities, of course, are solely mine.

NOTES

1　It could be argued that the sample should be narrowed to those under age fifty-five in order to remove people whose later earnings may reflect part-time work while retired. A declining retirement age of men over this period could change the age distribution mix between the two sub-periods of interest. This would be worth further investigation. But as the first empirical application of social welfare criteria to evaluate earnings mobility change, this study seeks to maintain consistency with Statistics Canada's concept of "All Earners" and to have as broad coverage as reasonable in light of a social welfare criterion. More generally, though, since young workers typically have steeper age-earnings gradients than older workers, changes in the age demographics of the population could affect transition matrix probabilities. So one might wish to extend the current approaches of comparing transition matrices to net out (in some sense) such underlying population dynamics.

2   More specifically, if we view the social welfare function as a representation of *expected* utility where $U(\cdot,\cdot)$ is interpreted as a utility function and $f(\cdot,\cdot)$ as the probability weights, then one income distribution is said to stochastically dominate another if the level of expected utility in the former is at least as high as in the latter for all $U(\cdot,\cdot)$ functions belonging to a specified class of utility functions (Atkinson 1983, 66).

3   Dardanoni's first test has recently been extended by Formby et al. (2003) to allow for income growth (and hence a changing *m* vector) as well.

REFERENCES

Atkinson, Anthony B. 1970. "On the Measurement of Inequality." *Journal of Economic Theory* 2: 244-63.

—. 1983. "The Measurement of Economic Mobility." Republished in Anthony B. Atkinson, *Social Justice and Public Policy*. Cambridge, MA: MIT Press.

Atkinson, Anthony B., and François Bourguignon, eds., 2000. *Handbook of Income Distribution*. Vol. 1. Amsterdam: Elsevier Science.

Atkinson, Anthony B., François Bourguignon, and C. Morrisson. 1992. "Empirical Studies of Earnings Mobility." *Fundamentals of Pure and Applied Economics*. Vol. 52. Reading, UK: Harwood Academic.

Beach, Charles M., and George A. Slotsve. 1994. "Recession and Recovery: Men's Earnings through the 1990s." *Journal of Income Distribution* 4: 121-46.

Beach, Charles M., and Ross Finnie. 1998. "Earnings Mobility 1982-1994: Women Gaining Ground and Low-Paid Males Slipping." *Canadian Business Economics* 6: 3-25.

—. 2004. "A Longitudinal Analysis of Earnings Change in Canada." *Canadian Journal of Economics* 37: 219-40.

Conlisk, John. 1989. "Ranking Mobility Matrices." *Economics Letters* 29: 231-35.

—. 1990. "Monotone Mobility Matrices." *Journal of Mathematical Sociology* 15: 173-91.

Corak, Miles, ed. 2004. *Generational Income Mobility in North America and Europe*. Cambridge, UK: Cambridge University Press.

Corak, Miles, and Andrew Heisz. 1995. "The Intergenerational Income Mobility of Canadian Men." *Canadian Business Economics* 14: 59-69.

—. 2000. "The Intergenerational Earnings and Income Mobility of Canadian Men: Evidence from Longitudinal Income Tax Data." *Journal of Human Resources* 34: 504-33.

Dardanoni, Valentino. 1993. "Measuring Social Mobility." *Journal of Economic Theory* 61: 372-94.

Formby, John P., W. James Smith, and Buhong Zheng. 2003. "Economic Growth, Welfare and the Measurement of Social Mobility." *Inequality, Welfare and Poverty: Theory and Measurement* 9: 105-11.

Friedman, Milton. 1962. *Capitalism and Freedom.* Chicago: University of Chicago Press.

Katz, Lawrence F., and David H. Autor. 1999. "Changes in the Wage Structure and Earnings Inequality." In Orley C. Ashenfelter and David Card, eds., *Handbook of Labor Economics* 3A: Chap. 26. Amsterdam: North-Holland Elsevier.

Kennedy, Bruce. 1989. "Mobility and Instability in Canadian Earnings." *Canadian Journal of Economics* 22: 383-94.

Maasoumi, Esfandiar. 1998. "On Mobility." In Aman Ullah and David E.A. Giles, eds., *Handbook of Applied Economic Statistics:* Chap. 5. New York: Marcel Dekker Inc.

Markandya, A. 1984. "The Welfare Measurement of Changes in Economic Mobility." *Economica* 51: 457-71.

Prais, S.J. 1955. "Measuring Social Mobility." *Journal of the Royal Statistical Society* Series A. 118: 56-66.

Shorrocks, Anthony F. 1978a. "Income Inequality and Income Mobility." *Journal of Economic Theory* 19: 376-93.

—. 1978b. "The Measurement of Mobility." *Econometrica* 46: 1013-24.

Shorrocks, Anthony F., and James Foster. 1987. "Transfer Sensitive Inequality Measures." *Review of Economic Studies* 54: 485-97.

Solon, Gary. 1992. "Intergenerational Income Mobility in the United States." *American Economic Review* 82: 393-408.

—. 1999. "Intergenerational Mobility in the Labor Market." In Orley C. Ashenfelter and David Card, eds., *Handbook of Labor Economics* 3A: Chap. 29. Amsterdam: North-Holland Elsevier.

5
Consumption Inequality in Canada

Thomas F. Crossley and Krishna Pendakur

Many studies of inequality, including other chapters in this volume, investigate inequality in earnings and household income. It is natural, at least for economists, to think of the material well-being of individuals as being determined by the goods and services that they actually consume in any period. Of course, wages, earnings, and income are important determinants of this. We can think of a chain of variables as follows:

Wages → Earnings → Income → Consumption → Material Well-being

Bourdarbat, Lemieux, and Riddell in Chapter 10 examine wage inequality. The link between wage rates and earnings is mediated by labour supply responses. The link between earnings and income is in turn mediated by the tax and transfer system and by savings decisions made in the past. Frenette, Green, and Picot in Chapter 3 examine income inequality in Canada. The link between income and consumption is mediated by saving and borrowing decisions, which are determined by past and future needs, risks, and credit market conditions. Finally, the link between consumption and material well-being is mediated by many poorly understood psychological factors. Certainly, though, well-being also depends on hours of work and leisure, as emphasized by Osberg in Chapter 6.

In this chapter we make the case that measures of consumption inequality are useful in addition to, or possibly instead of, measures of income inequality. We then outline the steps that are necessary to measure consumption inequality, focusing especially on issues relating to the use of Canadian expenditure data. Finally, we apply these ideas to Canadian family expenditure data to measure consumption inequality in Canada by birth-year cohort over the period 1969 to 1999.

An old line of macroeconomic research, pioneered by Friedman (1957), argues that aggregate personal income ought to fluctuate more than aggregate personal consumption due to the fact that people can save in good times and borrow in bad times.[1] Recently, this argument has been brought to the forefront of the microeconomic literature on inequality. Applied researchers in Canada (Pendakur 1998, 2001a), the United States (Cutler and Katz 1992; Slesnick 1998, 2001), the United Kingdom (Blundell and Preston 1995, 1998), Europe (Zaidi and de Vos 2001) and Australia (Barrett et al. 2000a, 2000b) have outlined the following basic argument. At the micro level, families[2] choose consumption for any period (say, a year) based on their past history of income and needs, their future income and needs, and credit market conditions, such as interest rates, which determine how valuable saving is for future consumption.

Realistic models of how families allocate their resources through time are complex, but several features stand out. If a family faces a lot of random income fluctuation, but knows something about the frequency and severity of this fluctuation, then it will try to save when incomes are high, when needs are low, or when interest rates (the return to saving) are high, and it will try to borrow when incomes are low, when needs are high, or when interest rates (the cost of borrowing) are low. There is also an implied negative correlation between consumption and future risk because prudent families save in the face of risk.

The relevance of all this to the measurement of inequality is fourfold. First, at the level of the family, within-period consumption may provide a better measure of material well-being than within-period income. Deaton (1998, 45) summarized this view: "It is not necessary to subscribe to the permanent income or life-cycle hypothesis to believe that consumption, rather than income, is the better indicator of household living standards, or to recognize that households take steps to smooth consumption over time."[3] Second, since we know consumption must vary with needs, comparisons of families with different needs must take account of this. Third, since we know that different birth cohorts face different interest rate histories, the most trustworthy and easy way to interpret inequality measurement must be within birth cohorts. Fourth, the connection between consumption inequality and inequality in well-being may depend on how consumption responds to risk and how well-being is affected by risk.[4]

Several papers have estimated consumption inequality at the birth-cohort level. Blundell and Preston (1998) found substantial differences in growth in inequality over the 1980s across birth cohorts in the United Kingdom. Barrett et al. (2000b) found somewhat smaller differences across cohorts in Australia over the 1970s and 1980s. Although there has been much interest in cohort-level income inequality (for example, Beaudry and Green 2000), there has been no research on cohort-level consumption inequality in Canada.

Canada has appropriate data for the examination of consumption inequality. The next section describes these data. The third section reviews the methodological and measurement issues that arise in measuring consumption inequality. The fourth section presents estimates of consumption inequality in Canada by birth-year cohort over the period 1969 to 1999. The fifth section considers the last link in the chain presented above: when is consumption inequality equivalent to inequality in economic resources or in well-being? A final section presents conclusions.

Household Consumption Data in Canada

The data used in this chapter come from the following public use sources: (1) the Family Expenditure Surveys 1969, 1978, 1982, 1986, 1992, and 1996; (2) the Surveys of Household Spending 1997, 1998, and 1999; and (3) Browning and Thomas's "Prices for the Famex 1969 to 1996" (1999), with updates and extensions to rental prices from Pendakur (2001b).

The Family Expenditure Surveys (FAMEX) were conducted at irregular intervals between 1969 and 1996. In 1997, the Survey of Household Spending (SHS) replaced the FAMEX and has been conducted annually since. Both are cross-sectional household surveys. The data are intended to be representative of all persons living in private households in the ten provinces of Canada.[5] A principal use of national, cross-sectional expenditure surveys is the construction of goods baskets for price indices, such as the Consumer Price Index. However, the microdata are useful for many other purposes, including the one highlighted by this chapter.[6]

In contrast to many national cross-sectional expenditure surveys, the FAMEX is not a diary survey.[7] Instead, face-to-face interviews are conducted in the first quarter of a year to collect expenditure and income information for the entire previous year. For example, the 1996 data are collected in January, February, and March of 1997. Compared to diary procedures (which typically collect expenditures on non-durable items over short periods such as two weeks), this procedure may suffer from greater recall error (Battistin 2002). On the other hand, short diaries suffer from problems of purchase infrequency that are not experienced by the FAMEX and SHS. Statistics Canada expends considerable effort to ensure that the data collected are of high quality. Households are often asked to consult bills and receipts; income is carefully reconciled with expenditures and savings; and multiple visits to a household are sometimes used. Various checks on the data are undertaken by Statistics Canada.

The FAMEX and SHS are multi-stage stratified samples. The sampling frame for these surveys is the Labour Force Survey Sampling Frame, a feature they share with the Surveys of Consumer Finances, which is discussed by Frenette, Green, and Picot in Chapter 3. Low-population regions (such as the Atlantic provinces) are oversampled. Sample weights, but not cluster information, are included in the public use files. The omission of cluster information means that standard errors are typically underestimated.

The FAMEX and SHS data are generally thought to be of good quality. Statistics Canada has reported that the overall response rate is about 75 percent. However, because the FAMEX and SHS are based on the same Labour Force Sampling Frame as the Survey of Consumer Finances, they may suffer from the same problem of undersampling of the poor that Frenette, Green, and Picot documented for that survey. With respect to item non-response, total income is imputed in about 1 percent of cases, and some imputation of expenditures is required in about 12 percent of cases (excepting some components of clothing expenditure). Unfortunately, there is no flagging of imputation in the public use files.

Certain compromises are necessary to ensure that the pooled data represent a consistent sample through time. The most important issue is that in several years (1974, 1984, and 1990) a limited FAMEX was conducted in only fifteen major urban centres, so those years have been dropped from our analysis.

Only regional analysis is possible in the FAMEX prior to 1992. Provincial identifiers are available in the 1992 and 1996 FAMEX and in the SHS. This is important because the estimation of a demand system (discussed below) requires price variation, and geographic variation is one source of price variation.

The unit of analysis for social welfare measurement is typically the individual. However, consumption decisions are usually made by groups of individuals. Such groups might be households, families, or "spending units." The grouping of individuals is typically constrained by the data, and, in Canadian expenditure data, spending unit consumption data is available to

1992 and "household consumption" data thereafter (the "household" and the "spending unit" are slightly different concepts). However, by restricting our attention to families that were spending units alone in their households prior to 1992 and households consisting of single families in 1992 and after, we can construct a consistent series. (Note that in both cases a family might consist of a single individual.) For consistency we must also restrict attention to "whole year" households (in which all the members were present for the full year). These restrictions never exclude more than 10 percent of spending units or households, and in most years exclude somewhat less than 10 percent.

It remains to define birth cohorts for the analysis. Unfortunately, although birth-cohort is an individual-level concept, Canadian expenditure data do not provide individual-level age information; rather, they provide the age of the household head and spouse (when present), usually bounded by top- and bottom-coding.[8] Thus, we attribute an age to each household. A common way to do this is to use the age of the household head. However, Statistics Canada's definition of a household head has changed through time. In order to have a consistent series, we take the woman as the head of all married couple families (regardless of whether Statistics Canada labels her the head or spouse). We then create ten-year birth cohorts beginning in 1884.

How Do We Measure Consumption Inequality?

The measurement of consumption inequality requires four important measurement choices. Researchers must choose: (1) the consumption measure; (2) an equivalence scale to adjust for different needs; (3) a price index to adjust for differences in commodity prices across regions and time periods; and (4) an inequality measure.

The Consumption Measure

The definition of the consumption measure is complex. Canadian expenditure data cover annual expenditures, but which expenditures should make up annual consumption? Ideally, the consumption measure should capture all consumption flows used during the year and should not include any forms of savings or deferred consumption. Consumption flows must include all nondurable expenditures plus the consumption flows from durables. Savings and deferred consumption must include direct savings and also indirect savings such as life insurance premiums, lumpy durable expenditures, and so forth.

Unfortunately, we are usually unable to perfectly separate durables from non-durables and to perfectly estimate the consumption flow from durables. In this research, we focus on non-durable consumption plus the imputed consumption flow from accommodation. Even with this narrow basket of consumption flows, we can't get at all non-durable consumption. Because we need price data to compute price indices (see below), we must restrict our attention to those commodities for which price data are available. Thus, in this chapter, we use the following eight elements of non-durable consumption: (1) food purchased from stores, (2) restaurant food, (3) household operation (including child care), (4) household furnishings and equipment,[9] (5) clothing, (6) private transportation operation,[10] (7) public transportation, and (8) personal care.

We also add the imputed consumption flow from accommodation. For rental tenure families, the accommodation consumption flow may be known, but for owner-occupier families, the accommodation consumption flow is not known, because for these families the flow of spending includes an investment component. Since many poor families – especially the elderly – own their accommodation, it is important to account for this. Further, since in some urban areas as many as 15 percent of rental tenure families live in subsidized or cooperatively owned housing (CMHC 1997), families may get a larger flow of consumption than their rental expenditures indicate. So we impute the consumption flow from accommodation for all families.

As noted in Smeeding et al. (1993) and Katz (1983), imputed consumption flows may be based on either the market value of the good or the opportunity cost of the capital embodied in the good (see Diewert 1974 or Yates 1994). In the former case, the researcher assigns the market value of housing, conditional on dwelling characteristics, to the family as its flow of imputed rent. In the latter case, the researcher assigns the opportunity cost, or alternative capital market return, of the capital implicitly invested in housing to the family as its flow of imputed rent. Smeeding et al. (1993) impute consumption flows from owned accommodation based on the opportunity cost of home equity. Unfortunately, Canadian expenditure data lack information on home equity after 1996. However, local housing costs can always be estimated by looking at what renters pay for accommodation. Thus, we use the market value approach.

We estimate the market value of accommodation as the average rent for accommodation in the same year and region (forty-five region-years) with the same number of rooms (1 to 11+ rooms).[11] We then assign the imputed market value of accommodation to each household instead of actual shelter expenditure.

EQUIVALENCE SCALES AND PRICE INDICES

We adjust family expenditure for differences in prices with a price deflator and for differences in family size with an equivalence scale. Price deflators and equivalence scales are recovered from estimation of a consumer demand system. A consumer demand system is the micro-level relationship between expenditure shares on commodities, total expenditure, the prices of commodities, and the demographic characteristics of families. For example, an estimated consumer demand system would give the magnitudes for statements saying how fast the food share of total expenditure declines with expenditure (since food is a necessity), rises with the price of food (since it is not substitutable), and rises with the size of the household (since food is not very shareable). This information can illuminate how an increase in the price of food would affect each household in the population. A family that spends a bigger share of its money on food is hurt more by an increase in the price of food than a family that devotes a smaller share to food.

We adjust family consumption for differences in the prices faced by families in different years and regions by dividing family consumption by a "price deflator." A price deflator gives the ratio of expenditure needs between a base price situation (in this case, that facing residents of Ontario in 1982) and an alternative price situation. Intuitively, the effect of a price change – for example, the increase in the relative price of shelter in Ontario between 1982 and 1992 – on how much expenditure a household needs to maintain the level of well-being of its members depends on the share of expenditure commanded by that commodity. Since the share of expenditure on shelter – a necessity which is shareable – declines as total expenditure and household size rise, an increase in the price of shelter hurts poor families more than rich families and small families more than large families. Thus, the price deflator must depend on prices, the total expenditure of the family, and the size of the family.

Since consumer demand systems specify how expenditures are allocated across commodities, estimation of a consumer demand system reveals everything one needs to compute price indices. We use the demand system and price indices estimated in Pendakur (2001b), which are computed for the price situations in each of five regions in each data year, and which also depend on total expenditure and family size.

An equivalence scale gives the ratio of expenditure needs across household types. For example, if, in some given year and region of residence, a couple with two children needs twice as much expenditure as a childless single adult to be equally well off, then we say the equivalence scale for the couple with two children is equal to two. An equivalence scale may also be revealed through the estimation of a consumer demand system, but, unfortunately, consumer demand estimation does not provide all the information necessary to construct an equivalence scale (for details see Donaldson and Pendakur 2004). If equivalence scales are allowed to vary arbitrarily with expenditure, they cannot be identified from demand estimation alone. However, if equivalence scales are assumed to be the same for families at all expenditure levels, then they may be identified via consumer demand estimation (Blackorby and Donaldson 1993; Pendakur 1999). We use the equivalence scale estimated under this assumption in Pendakur (2001b). For families in Ontario in 1982, it is equal to family size raised to the power 0.46, or just a little less than the square root of family size.

The assumption that equivalence scales are the same for families at all expenditure levels is commonly used and has the virtue of transparency. However, it almost surely is false. To see why, consider two households, one with children and one without. The former household will purchase some children's goods that the latter does not. For the equivalence scale to be independent of the level of expenditure, the budget share of children's goods bought by the first household must also be independent of the level of expenditure. That is, all children's goods must be neither luxuries nor necessities. More recent research has developed ways to estimate equivalence scales that vary with expenditure and are thus different for rich and poor households, but the empirical implementation of these methods is beyond the scope of this chapter.[12]

Inequality Indices

For each individual in each family, we compute equivalent consumption as family consumption divided by the equivalence scale. We then compute real equivalent consumption as equivalent consumption divided by the price index. These individual-level observations of real equivalent consumption are the basis for our measurement of consumption inequality. Each individual in each family is assigned the family weight (which corrects for unequal sampling probabilities across regions and family sizes) and is assigned the real equivalent consumption for the family.

It is important to note that at the stage of inequality measurement, the unit of analysis is the individual. It is mathematically (though not conceptually) equivalent to treat the unit of analysis for inequality measurement as the family, with all the weights multiplied by the number of family members. (In fact, this is how we actually implement our analysis of individuals). Most welfare analysis in economics – such as utilitarian social evaluation – takes the aggregation of well-being across individuals as the object of interest. This is because we believe individuals have well-being but families and other groups don't. Thus, our object of interest is inequality among individuals, even though our data come in the form of family consumption.

Many researchers use the family as the unit of analysis for inequality measurement. In continental Europe (especially Germany), many researchers use the family as the unit of analysis with the weights multiplied by the equivalence scale. In the United States, many researchers use the family as the unit of analysis without multiplying the weights by anything. We believe that both of these approaches are wrong and that the mistake stems from their failure to recognize that inequality measurement motivated from social evaluation has as its object of interest the distribution of well-being among individuals.[13]

In this chapter we use an Atkinson index of inequality and the Gini coefficient of inequality, each computed over the equivalent real consumption of all individuals.[14] The Atkinson index is the proportional deviation of the average of consumption raised to a power from the average of consumption itself. The power chosen determines the sensitivity of the measure to inequality at the bottom of the distribution, and we use a power of −2. The Gini coefficient is twice the area between the Lorenz curve for the actual population and the Lorenz curve for a population with perfectly equal consumption. The Lorenz curve is the graph of cumulative consumption shares versus cumulative population shares. The Gini coefficient is the most commonly used inequality index, and the Atkinson with parameter −2 generates broadly similar levels of inequality.

One desirable feature of these measures is that they are easy to explain to a wide audience. The Gini and Atkinson indices are members of the Atkinson-Kolm-Sen (AKS) inequality index family. They can be interpreted as the percentage of average (or total) consumption that a society with this degree of inequality-aversion would be willing to forgo to eliminate all inequality. The thought experiment is: if everyone were to have the same real equivalent consumption level, how much total consumption would give us the same level of social well-being? The percentage difference between this amount of consumption and the actual amount of consumption in society is the value of the inequality index. Some researchers refer to this amount as the consumption that is "wasted" by inequality.

Note that the Atkinson and Gini indices differ in their sensitivity to transfers in different parts of the distribution. In particular, the Gini coefficient weights transfers according to the rank order of individuals involved. In contrast, the Atkinson index weights transfers according to the ratio of the income shares of the individuals involved. This tends to make the Atkinson index more sensitive to the bottom of the distribution.

A second desirable feature of the Atkinson and Gini indices is that both have well-known asymptotic properties for the computation of standard errors and confidence bands (for the Atkinson indices, see Barrett and Doiron 1996; for the Gini coefficient and related indices, see Barrett and Pendakur 1995).

Consumption Inequality in Canada, 1969 to 1999

Table 5.1 gives the number of observations of families in each birth cohort in each year. Most cohort-year cells have one to three thousand observations, which is enough to support the measurement of inequality within cells. The bottom row, labelled "All cohorts," and the final column, labelled "All Years," provide information on the number of observations available in the entire sample for each year and cohort respectively. We note that the eldest cohorts (top cells in each column) often have fewer observations, frustrating inequality comparisons as cohorts become elderly.

Table 5.2 gives the average real equivalent consumption for individuals in each birth cohort-year cell. Figure 5.1 shows this information graphically. It is clear from Figure 5.1 that, for most birth cohorts, average consumption rose between 1969 and 1986 and then stayed static or fell between 1986 and 1999. The eldest birth cohorts show a slightly different pattern, with falling or static consumption over the entire period. These patterns confound time and age effects, a point to which we return below. Nevertheless, these patterns for Canadian data are quite different from those found by Blundell and Preston (1998) in the British data. They conclude that once demographic effects are controlled for with equivalence scales (as they are in this chapter), within-cohort consumption growth is essentially nil.

We also note that some birth cohorts consume consistently more than other birth cohorts. People born in the earliest birth cohorts consume least

TABLE 5.1

Number of observations by birth cohort and year

Birth cohort	Year									All years
	1969	1978	1982	1986	1992	1996	1997	1998	1999	
1884 to 1893	659									659
1894 to 1903	1,246	451								1,697
1904 to 1913	1,979	863	1,086	748			204	210		5,090
1914 to 1923	2,590	1,207	1,278	1,138	1,221	798	1,254	907	1,205	11,598
1924 to 1933	2,947	1,352	1,431	1,331	1,162	1,191	1,746	1,492	1,561	14,213
1934 to 1943	3,318	1,521	1,576	1,391	1,219	1,277	2,013	1,698	1,897	15,910
1944 to 1953	1,866	2,331	2,566	2,225	1,846	1,988	3,065	2,504	2,838	21,229
1954 to 1963		944	2,033	2,392	2,333	2,413	3,968	3,273	3,705	21,061
1964 to 1973				319	1,103	1,809	3,200	2,447	2,844	11,722
All cohorts	14,605	8,669	9,970	9,544	8,884	9,476	15,450	12,531	14,050	

SOURCE: Authors' calculations using Family Expenditure Survey and Survey of Household Spending public use microdata files from Statistics Canada (explained in text).

TABLE 5.2

Average consumption by birth cohort and year

Birth cohort	Year									All years
	1969	1978	1982	1986	1992	1996	1997	1998	1999	
1884 to 1893	5,873									5,873
1894 to 1903	6,664	6,847								6,713
1904 to 1913	8,020	7,950	7,513	7,603			7,541	7,398		7,794
1914 to 1923	8,596	9,729	9,008	9,269	8,253	8,203	8,539	8,564	8,441	8,737
1924 to 1933	8,149	10,499	10,332	10,568	9,794	9,447	9,556	9,100	9,412	9,473
1934 to 1943	7,838	10,304	10,592	11,681	11,205	10,626	10,426	10,195	10,438	10,053
1944 to 1953	8,050	9,772	9,588	10,537	10,909	11,312	10,633	10,958	11,099	10,363
1954 to 1963		9,843	9,329	9,766	9,858	10,090	9,756	9,766	10,258	9,859
1964 to 1973				9,187	9,471	9,650	9,186	9,480	9,735	9,479
All cohorts	8,006	9,859	9,676	10,311	10,135	10,215	9,832	9,878	10,173	

NOTE: Ontario 1982 dollars
SOURCE: Same as Table 5.1.

FIGURE 5.1

Consumption by birth cohort and year

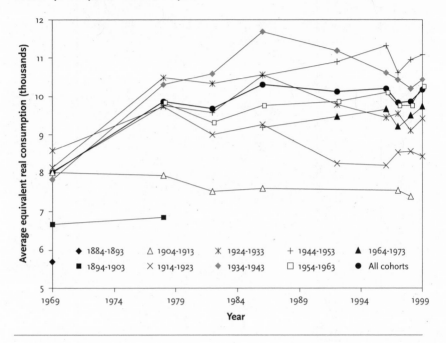

in all years. Families whose heads were born between 1934 and 1953 seem to consume more than all others, especially in the later years. Again, these patterns may confound at least two different effects. They may be cohort differences, or they may include age effects (as over the time span of the data, we observe different cohorts over different age spans).

Table 5.3 and Figure 5.2 give the estimated Atkinson index value (with $r = -2$) for real equivalent consumption for each cohort in each year. The estimated standard errors (not reported) range from 0.002 to 0.004 for cohorts with more than 1,000 observations.

The thick black line in Figure 5.2 shows the path of real equivalent consumption inequality for all individuals taken together over 1969 to 1999. Inequality declined over the 1970s, rose to 1986, and then declined in the 1990s. There is also some evidence of increasing inequality in the late 1990s, where the level of inequality rose from 0.128 in 1997 to 0.135 in 1999. This increase is statistically significant (with a t-value of 8), but is small relative to

TABLE 5.3

Inequality of consumption by birth cohort and year

Birth cohort	1969	1978	1982	1986	Year 1992	1996	1997	1998	1999
1884 to 1893	0.177								
1894 to 1903	0.156	0.101							
1904 to 1913	0.170	0.112	0.106	0.086			0.074	0.088	
1914 to 1923	0.145	0.142	0.119	0.110	0.089	0.088	0.096	0.090	0.106
1924 to 1933	0.134	0.140	0.130	0.143	0.115	0.095	0.087	0.090	0.100
1934 to 1943	0.123	0.145	0.127	0.162	0.135	0.126	0.135	0.123	0.132
1944 to 1953	0.139	0.127	0.129	0.136	0.131	0.135	0.120	0.136	0.130
1954 to 1963		0.130	0.143	0.141	0.121	0.129	0.125	0.128	0.129
1964 to 1973				0.149	0.127	0.148	0.135	0.130	0.138
All Atkinson	0.146	0.143	0.137	0.148	0.130	0.136	0.128	0.131	0.135
All Gini	0.176	0.180	0.175	0.185	0.173	0.176	0.169	0.173	0.175
All Atkinson (1992 = 100)	112	109	105	114	100	105	98	100	104
All Gini (1992 = 100)	102	104	101	107	100	101	98	100	101

NOTE: Atkinson index value ($r = -2$)
SOURCE: Same as Table 5.1.

FIGURE 5.2

Inequality of consumption by birth cohort and year

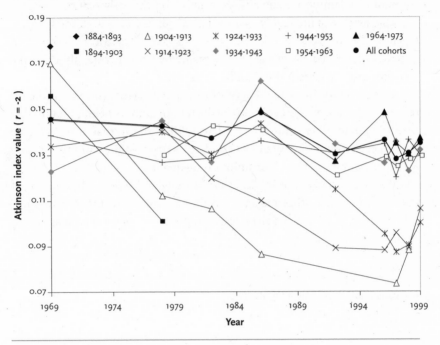

earlier movements and is potentially contaminated by the (minor) changes in survey design between the FAMEX and SHS.

Recall that one can interpret the Atkinson and Gini indices as the percentage of average consumption that a society with the corresponding degree of inequality aversion would be willing to give up to eliminate all inequality. Thus the results at the bottom of Table 5.3 indicate that in Canada in 1999, if we (as a society) thought that Atkinson ($r = -2$) was the correct inequality index, we would have been willing to reduce average consumption by 13.5 percent in order to eliminate all inequality. If our inequality aversion was properly captured by the Gini index, we would have been prepared to reduce average consumption by more – by 17.5 percent – to eliminate all inequality.

Looking at the results for different cohorts, we see that pooling together all the cohorts masks some differences between them. In particular, consumption inequality is quite strongly declining over time for the eldest three birth cohorts. In contrast, for the youngest five cohorts, inequality seems much more stable over time. Given that confidence bands are approximately one percentage point wide, the youngest five birth cohorts seem to have relatively constant consumption inequality, especially over the early years.

The increase in inequality over the late 1990s, seen for all cohorts pooled together, does not seem to hide differences across cohorts. Most cohorts seem to have experienced an increase in inequality over this period, although the increases are not statistically significant in many cases.

One can also compare the levels of inequality across cohorts (more on this below). The youngest cohort (to which both authors belong) has higher inequality than other cohorts in the late 1990s. Prior to that, it seems to be the two cohorts born between 1934 and 1953 (the wealthy cohorts in Figure 5.1) that exhibit the most consumption inequality.

We can rearrange the information in Tables 5.2 and 5.3 by looking at age-consumption profiles and age-consumption inequality for different birth cohorts. Figures 5.3 and 5.4 show the average consumption at each age (with

FIGURE 5.3

Age-consumption profiles by birth cohort

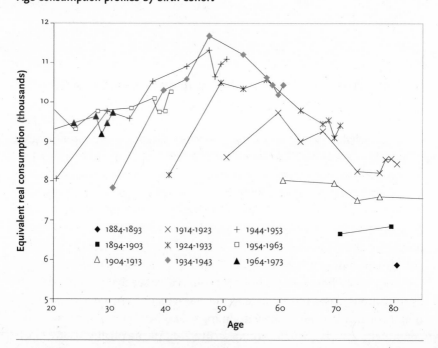

ages being the mid-points of the appropriate ranges) and the level of consumption inequality at each age for each birth cohort.

In Figure 5.3, one can see that the hump-shaped profile associated with earnings over age reproduces itself with consumption over age. This is somewhat surprising given that families are presumed to dislike fluctuation in their consumption. However, it's important to note that what life-cycle theory predicts is that households smooth marginal utility, not consumption. It is possible that marginal utility is constant over age if the observed movements in consumption are offset by changes in labour supply, by demographic effects that are not captured by our equivalence scale, or by other factors. For example, Browning and Ejrnaes (2002) show that the hump shape in British consumption data is removed by more detailed adjustments for needs (particularly, taking account of not just household size but also the number and ages of children present). For a detailed discussion of possible interpretations of the age profile of consumption levels, see Browning and Crossley (2001).

Turning to cross-cohort comparisons, we see again that the eldest cohorts consume less at all ages. The life-cycle theory interpretation of these cohort effects is that they reflect productivity growth. Younger cohorts are wealthier in a lifetime sense. If this interpretation is correct, then the smaller cohort effects to the left-hand side of the figure would be consistent with a slowdown in productivity growth at the end of the twentieth century.

The pattern of higher consumption seen in Figure 5.2 for those born between 1934 and 1953 is somewhat attenuated in this view of the data. These cohorts have somewhat higher consumption conditional on age, but much of the difference seen in Figure 5.2 is driven by the hump shape of the consumption-age profile. There is some evidence in Figure 5.3 that the younger two cohorts have slower consumption growth over age than the high-consumption cohorts. However, the overall impact of this is diminished by the fact that these younger cohorts also have higher consumption at the start of their lives.

Turning to the age-inequality profile, Figure 5.4 puts a new light on the patterns of inequality across cohorts. Inequality seems to decline with age after about fifty years old for all cohorts. This pattern is difficult to interpret. As noted by Deaton and Paxson (1994), if households experience uninsurable shocks, then differences in lifetime resources should accumulate through time and, for a given cohort, inequality should increase with age.[15] If households are fully insured, then inequality should be constant.[16]

FIGURE 5.4

Age-inequality profiles by birth cohort

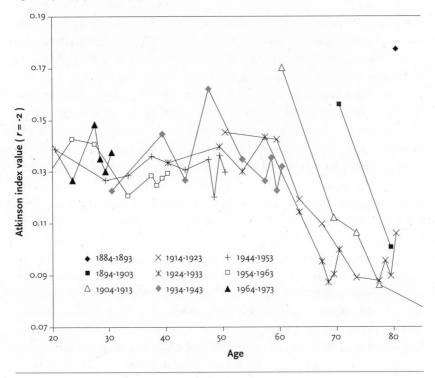

The observed pattern may reflect a data problem. One possibility is that it is generated by differential mortality. There is a well-known association between socioeconomic status and measures of health, including mortality. It may be that as each cohort ages, the bottom of the distribution experiences greater mortality, so that our repeated cross sections exhibit the decreasing inequality of survivors. A second possible explanation is that our consumption bundle (comprising seven goods and imputed services from housing) represents a different approximation to total consumption of goods and services at different ages.

As with the levels, the observed pattern may suggest that our adjustments for differences in needs are inadequate. As each cohort ages, the variance of household size decreases, so that if our equivalence scale does not properly adjust for differences in needs across different household sizes, this could generate a spurious decline in consumption inequality.

Turning to cross-cohort comparisons, the eldest three cohorts seem to have the highest levels of inequality for their age. Comparisons across birth cohorts, however, are interesting only if we believe that the distribution of material well-being relates to the distribution of consumption in the same way in both cohorts. The reasonableness of this assumption is one of the issues we consider in the next section.

When Is Consumption Inequality Revealing of Economic Inequality?

Finally, we consider the last link in the chain we presented in the introduction: the link between consumption inequality and the object of ultimate interest, which is economic inequality or inequality in material well-being. Two issues arise here. First is the link between the consumption measure, based on household spending on a limited range of goods, and total individual consumption of goods and services. Second is the link between individual consumption in a given period and a person's level of material well-being.

In this study, we have examined components of non-durable consumption, as well as imputed consumption flows from accommodation. As noted above, this is only a proxy for total consumption. The latter should include all non-durable consumption and flows from all durables. Moreover, individuals certainly derive well-being from the consumption of public goods and services, and access to such goods and services is probably not equally distributed. Thus, public goods and services provide another wedge between consumption inequality, as we measure it with expenditure data, and inequality in total consumption.

Throughout this chapter, we have assumed that family consumption and allocation decisions are made for the equal benefit of all family members. Of course, this may not be the case, and there is increasing empirical evidence that it is not the case (see, for example, Browning et al. 1994 and Lundberg et al. 1997). Thus inequality of individual consumption likely arises as a consequence of both inequality between households and inequality within households. The latter is extremely difficult to assess, because with household-level expenditure data it is very difficult to attribute observed expenditures to the consumption of particular individuals. Haddad and Kanbur (1990) provide one analysis of intra-household inequality, with data on individual food consumption from a developing country.

Beyond these issues, we can ask: if we perfectly observed the total consumption of individuals in a period, would that reveal inequality in well-being? Blundell and Preston (1998) investigate the conditions under which the consumption of a family – suitably adjusted for differences in needs and prices across families – provides an ordinal measure of material well-being for that family. They show in a model with certainty and perfect credit markets – where people face no risk and so have perfect information about their future incomes, needs, and interest rates, and where they are able to borrow and save as they see fit – the consumption profile over the life-cycle will be sometimes high and sometimes low. Consumption will be high when needs are high or when interest rates are low; consumption will be low when needs are low or when interest rates are high. This means that consumption cannot be used as a measure of well-being comparable across age because the optimal consumption profile over age might be tilted. Neither can it be comparable across birth cohorts because interest rate histories are different. Even in a world of certainty, consumption could only be used as an ordinal measure of well-being within age groups and birth cohorts.

However, taking consumption as an ordinal measure of well-being within age groups and birth cohorts doesn't necessarily mean that inequality of consumption captures inequality of something we care about. Pendakur (1998) shows that, given certainty and perfect credit markets, if families exhibit constant relative risk aversion (CRRA), then the value of an inequality index computed over consumption is equal to the value of that same inequality index computed over unobservable lifetime wealth. This is because, if families exhibit CRRA, any increase in lifetime wealth results in a proportional increase in consumption over the entire lifetime consumption profile. Since relative inequality indices – a class that includes all commonly used inequality indices like the Gini and the Atkinson – are insensitive to proportional increases in consumption, this implies that consumption inequality is lifetime wealth inequality.

CRRA is a strong restriction. It requires that rich and poor families have the same distaste for proportional fluctuations in consumption. Browning and Crossley (2001) argue that since rich families buy luxuries and poor families buy necessities, a 10 percent loss in consumption must hurt poor families more than rich families, so the CRRA cannot be true – the distaste for proportional fluctuations should be lower for rich families. However, CRRA is testable in this context. Assuming certainty and perfect credit markets, CRRA also implies that consumption inequality must be constant over time within birth cohorts. The results presented in Figure 5.2 suggest that CRRA might be true for the younger six cohorts, but not for the eldest cohorts.

In an uncertain world – where people face risk and so do not have perfect knowledge about the future paths of their income, their needs, or interest rates – inequality measurement is considerably more complicated. Even comparisons within age groups and birth cohorts are frustrated by the fact that people face different risks and thus will have different savings behaviour. Within a birth cohort and age group, having high consumption could be due to having low risk or high wealth. Of course, low risk and high wealth are both good things. Blundell and Preston (1998) investigate conditions under which consumption increases due to increased wealth are associated with the same utility difference as consumption increases due to decreased risk. They find that this is the case if, and only if, families exhibit constant absolute risk aversion (CARA). If families exhibit CARA, then any family with a given consumption level is exactly as well-off in a lifetime sense as any other family with the same consumption level, regardless of whether that consumption choice is driven by risk or by wealth. Unfortunately, CARA is a very strong restriction, since it requires that rich and poor families have the same distaste for fixed-dollar fluctuations in consumption. Thus, Blundell and Preston conclude that uncertainty makes comparison of material well-being using consumption measures impossible, even within age groups and birth cohorts.

Measures of consumption inequality are a useful complement or even alternative to income or earnings inequality. Because households do take some steps to smooth consumption (see Browning and Crossley 2001 for evidence on this point), consumption inequality is probably the better measure of inequality in well-being or economic resources. The discussion above highlights the fact that consumption inequality is not a *perfect* measure of inequality in well-being and indicates that comparisons of consumption inequality (including comparisons across ages, cohorts, or risk levels) should be taken with some care. However, similar considerations apply to comparisons of inequality in income or earnings.[17]

Conclusion

Income and earnings inequality are important factors driving inequality in material well-being. However, because households can, and to some extent do, borrow and save to move resources between periods, inequality in consumption (that is, in the resources that households actually expend) may be a better proxy for inequality in material well-being. Of course, even the connection between consumption and well-being is complicated, and the role of responses to interest rates and uncertainty must be kept in mind. Nevertheless, measures of consumption inequality are an important complement to studies of income and earnings inequality, helping to fill out our picture of what might be broadly termed "economic inequality."

Canada has suitable data for the study of consumption inequality: the Family Expenditure Surveys and their descendants, the Surveys of Household Spending. As with analyses of income or earnings, it is necessary when studying consumption inequality to make adjustments for the different prices that households face (with a price index) and for differences in needs that arise from their differences in size and composition (with an equivalence scale). Expenditure data can be used to help determine reasonable price indices and equivalence scales.

Using these data and methods, we have examined the age pattern of average consumption levels, and consumption inequality, for different birth cohorts of Canadians. Within cohorts, we observe a pattern of fairly constant inequality until retirement, and then substantial decreases in inequality; the explanation of this is a topic of ongoing research. Our principal finding is that consumption inequality has fallen slightly over the last thirty years. There seems to be an increase in the late 1990s, though this change is similar in size to earlier survey-to-survey movements. It remains to be seen whether this recent upturn develops into a trend, but both researchers and policy makers will undoubtedly wish to closely follow future developments in consumption inequality.

ACKNOWLEDGMENTS
We have benefited from many conversations with our friends and colleagues – Martin Browning, Richard Blundell, Ian Preston, Garry Barrett, Federico Perali – and with conference participants at the University of British Columbia and seminar participants at the Institute for Social and Economic Change, Bangalore, India.

NOTES
1   Note that this prediction only follows if income is mean-reverting. See Deaton (1992).
2   The unit of analysis can be the family, the individual, the household, or some other grouping of individuals. We will use the word "family" to indicate any individual or group of individuals who live together in a household and who are related by blood, adoption, marriage, or common-law marriage. Of course, once the family is taken as the relevant unit, the question of how decisions are made

arises. For the purposes of this chapter, we assume that family consumption and allocation decisions are made for the equal benefit of all family members.

3   Another argument for measuring resources by consumption rather than income is that the former is better measured. This is often true in developing countries but less so in developed countries (except perhaps for the self-employed). See Deaton (1997) for further discussion.

4   Some readers will be uncomfortable with inequality in "welfare," "well-being," or "material welfare" as the object of interest. An alternative is to take inequality in lifetime wealth as the object of interest. If banks were smart enough not to issue bad debts and families were not interested in bequeathing resources, then families would make plans that equate their consumption in all periods with their lifetime income and wealth. Thus, if we had information on lifetime consumption or lifetime income, they would add up to the same thing: lifetime wealth. However, typical data are within-period rather than lifetime, giving information on consumption or income for, say, a month or a year. The same arguments about household smoothing of income fluctuations suggest that within-period consumption is likely a better indicator of lifetime wealth than within-period income.

5   Data are collected in the Territories but are not included in all the public use files.

6   These microdata have been used by many researchers for demand analysis and for analysis of specific policies, such as assessing the impact of the GST (sales tax) on families in Canada (Curtis and Kingston-Riechers 2002).

7   A well-known example of a diary survey is the British Family Expenditure Survey. The American Consumer Expenditure Survey has both diary and interview components.

8   If the ages of all members of the family were available, we could then impute equivalent consumption (defined below) to every member of the family, and then follow individual birth cohorts through time.

9   Household furnishings and equipment includes an important durable component. However, we believe that these durables have a sufficiently high depreciation rate to merit inclusion in the consumption flow.

10 Private transportation operation excludes all capital expenditures, such as car purchases.

11 Pendakur (2001b) imputes separately for families living in cities with 30,000 or more residents and families living outside such cities. In the current chapter, families in the same region-year with the same number of rooms are assigned the same imputed rent regardless of their city size.

12 Interestingly, while the assumption that equivalence scales are independent of expenditure level cannot be confirmed by the data, it does have implications that can be tested. These implications are usually rejected. Some of these rejections might be attributed to the parametric assumptions used in the studies. In a semiparametric analysis, Pendakur (1999) does not reject the expenditure level

independence of equivalence scales between childless families of different sizes, or between families of different sizes with children. He does, however, reject the independence of expenditure level assumption for equivalence scales between families with and without children.

Donaldson and Pendakur (2004) show that if equivalence scales are assumed to be log-linear (iso-elastic) in expenditure, they may be identified from behaviour alone. Donaldson and Pendakur (1999) also develop a framework for equivalence scales that are the same for rich and poor households except for a fixed cost varying across household types. In these environments, equivalence scales vary with the level of expenditure (and thus material well-being), and childrens' goods may be luxuries or necessities.

13   We further note that, although inequality among families (as in the United States literature) may have some descriptive interest, it is hard to see what is interesting about inequality among "equivalence-scale weighted" families (as in the German literature).

14   The Atkinson Index, I, with parameter r is given by

$$ I = 1 - \frac{N}{\sum y_j} \left(\frac{1}{N} \sum (y_j)^r \right)^{1/r} $$

where $y_j = 1, ..., N$ is the real equivalent consumption of individual j in a population of size N. For further discussion of the Atkinson and Gini indices, see Kesselman and Cheung (Chapter 12).

15   For example, in a simple permanent income model, consumption follows a random walk so that the variance grows with age.

16   This assumes that preferences over consumption at different ages are homothetic (for example, additive with a CRRA within-period utility function).

17   In considering the limits to interpreting consumption inequality as inequality in well-being, Blundell and Preston (1995, 43) note that "none of these arguments offers reasons to prefer income, against which equally pertinent points could be made."

REFERENCES

Apps, Patricia, and Elizabeth Savage. 1989. "Labour Supply, Welfare Rankings and the Measurement of Inequality." *Journal of Public Economics* 39(3): 335-64.

Banks, James, Richard Blundell, and Arthur Lewbel. 1997. "Quadratic Engel Curves and Consumer Demand." *Review of Economics and Statistics* 79(4): 527-39.

Barrett, Garry, Thomas Crossley, and Chris Worswick. 2000a. "Consumption and Income Inequality in Australia." *Economic Record* 76(233): 116-38.

—. 2000b. "Demographic Trends and Consumption Inequality in Australia between 1975 and 1993." *Review of Income and Wealth* 46(4): 437-56.

Barrett, Garry F., and Denise J. Doiron. 1996. "Inequality in Male and Female Earnings: The Role of Hours and Wages." *Review of Economics and Statistics* 78(3): 410-20.

Barrett, Garry, and Krishna Pendakur. 1995. "Asymptotic Distributions for the Generalised Gini Inequality Indices." *Canadian Journal of Economics* 28(4b): 1042-55.

Battistin, Erich. 2002. "Errors in Survey Reports of Consumption Expenditures." Institute of Fiscal Studies Working Paper. London: IFS.

Beaudry, Paul, and David Green. 2000. "Cohort Patterns in Canadian Earnings: Assessing the Role of Skill Premia in Inequality Trends." *Canadian Journal of Economics* 33(4): 907-36.

Blackorby, Charles, and David Donaldson. 1993. "Adult Equivalence Scales and the Economic Implementation of Interpersonal Comparisons of Well-Being." *Social Choice and Welfare* 10: 335-61.

Blundell, Richard, Alan Duncan, and Krishna Pendakur. 1998. "Semiparametric Estimation of Consumer Demand." *Journal of Applied Econometrics* 13(5): 435-61.

Blundell, Richard, and Ian Preston. 1995. "Income, Expenditure and the Living Standards of UK Households." *Fiscal Studies* 16(3): 40-54.

—. 1998. "Consumption Inequality and Income Uncertainty." *Quarterly Journal of Economics* 113(2): 603-40.

Browning, Martin, Francois Bourguignon, Pierre-Andre Chiappori, and Valerie Lechene. 1994. "Income and Outcomes: A Structural Model of Intrahousehold Allocation." *Journal of Political Economy* 102(6): 1067-96.

Browning, Martin, and Thomas Crossley. 2001. "The Life-Cycle Model of Consumption and Saving." *Journal of Economic Perspectives* 15(3): 3-22.

Browning, Martin, and Mette Ejrnaes. 2002. "Consumption and Children." Unpublished working paper. Centre for Applied Microeconomics, University of Copenhagen.

Browning, Martin, and Irene Thomas. 1998. "Reconciled Famex Codebook." Unpublished working paper. Department of Economics, McMaster University.

—. 1999. "Prices for the Famex: Methods and Sources." Unpublished working paper. Department of Economics, McMaster University.

Buhmann, Brigitte, Lee Rainwater, Guenther Schmaus, and Timothy M. Smeeding. 1988. "Equivalence Scales, Well-Being, Inequality, and Poverty: Sensitivity Estimates across Ten Countries Using the Luxembourg Income Study (LIS) Database." *Review of Income and Wealth* 34(2): 115-42.

CANSIM. 2000. "Consumer Price Indices." Matrices 09941-50. Ottawa: Statistics Canada.

CENSUS. 1996. "Public Use Microdata – Economic Families." Ottawa: Statistics Canada.

CMHC Canada Mortgage and Housing Corporation. 1997. "Housing Conditions Monthly." Ottawa: Government of Canada.

Curtis, Lori, and JoAnn Kingston-Riechers. 2002. "Implications of the Goods and Services Tax for Families in Canada." Paper presented at the Canadian Economic

Association Meetings, University of Calgary, May 31-June 2, Calgary; unpublished working paper, Dalhousie University, Department of Community Health and Epidemiology.

Cutler, David M.., and Lawrence F. Katz. 1992. "Rising Inequality?" *American Economic Review* 82(2): 546-51.

De Nardi, Mariacristina, Liqian Ren, and Chao Wei. 2000. "On the Distribution of Income in Five Countries." LIS Working Paper #227. Maxwell School of Citizenship and Public Affairs, Syracuse University, Syracuse, NY.

Deaton, Angus. 1992. *Understanding Consumption*. London: Oxford University Press.

—. 1997. *The Analysis of Household Surveys*. Baltimore, MD: Johns Hopkins University Press.

—. 1998. "Getting Prices Right: What Should Be Done?" *Journal of Economic Perspectives* 12(1): 37-46.

Deaton, Angus, and Christina Paxson. 1994. "Intertemporal Choice and Inequality." *Journal of Political Economy* 102(3): 437-67.

Diewert, W. Erwin. 1974. "Intertemporal Consumer Theory and the Demand for Durables." *Econometrica* 42(3): 497-516.

—. 1993. "Index Numbers." In W. Erwin Diewert and Alice O. Nakamura, eds., *Essays in Index Number Theory. Volume 1*. Amsterdam: Elsevier Science.

Donaldson, David. 1992. "The Aggregation of Money Measures of Well-Being in Applied Welfare Economics." *Journal of Agricultural and Resource Economics* 17(1): 88-102.

Donaldson, David, and Krishna Pendakur. 1999. "Equivalent Expenditure Functions and Expenditure-Dependent Equivalence Scales." Longer unpublished working paper version, Department of Economics, Simon Fraser University, http://www.sfu.ca/~pendakur.

—. 2004. "Equivalent Expenditure Functions and Expenditure-Dependent Equivalence Scales." *Journal of Public Economics* 88(1-2): 175-208.

Friedman, Milton. 1957. *A Theory of the Consumption Function*. Princeton: Princeton University Press.

Gouveia, Miguel, and Jose Tavares. 1995. "The Distribution of Household Income and Expenditure in Portugal." *Review of Income and Wealth* 41(1): 1-17.

Haddad, Lawrence, and Ravi Kanbur. 1990. "How Serious Is the Neglect of Intra-Household Inequality?" *Economic Journal* 100(402): 866-81.

Idson, Todd, and Cynthia Miller. 1999. "Calculating a Price Index for Families with Children: Implications for Measuring Trends in Child Poverty Rates." *Review of Income and Wealth* 45(2): 217-33.

Katz, Arnold. 1983. "Valuing the Services of Consumer Durables." *Review of Income and Wealth* 29(4): 405-27.

King, Mervyn A. 1983. "Welfare Analysis of Tax Reforms Using Household Data." *Journal of Public Economics* 21: 183-214.

Lancaster, Geoffrey, Ranjan Ray, and Maria R. Valenzuela. 1999. "A Cross-Country Study of Equivalence Scales and Expenditure Inequality on Unit Record Household Budget Data." *Review of Income and Wealth* 45(4): 455-82.

Lundberg, Shelly, J., Robert A. Pollak, and Terence J. Wales. 1997. "Do Husbands and Wives Pool Their Resources? Evidence from the United Kingdom Child Benefit." *Journal of Human Resources* 32(3): 463-80.

Osberg, Lars. 1997. "Economic Growth, Income Distribution and Economic Welfare in Canada 1975-94." *North American Journal of Economics and Finance* 8(2): 153-66.

Pashardes, Panos. 1995. "Equivalence Scales in a Rank-3 Demand System." *Journal of Public Economics* 58: 143-58.

Pendakur, Krishna. 1998. "Family Income and Consumption Inequality in Canada over 1978-1992." *Review of Income and Wealth* 44(2): 259-83.

—. 1999. "Semiparametric Estimates and Tests of Base-Independent Equivalence Scales." *Journal of Econometrics* 88(1): 1-40.

—. 2001a. "Consumption Poverty in Canada, 1969 to 1998." *Canadian Public Policy* 27(2): 125-49

—. 2001b. "Taking Prices Seriously in the Measurement of Inequality." *Journal of Public Economics* 86(1): 47-69.

—. 2001c. "Integrability and the Semiparametric Estimation of Consumer Demand." Unpublished working paper, Department of Economics, Simon Fraser University.

—. 2005. "Semiparametric Estimation of Lifetime Equivalence Scales." *Journal of Applied Econometrics* 20(4): 487-504.

Phipps, Shelley. 1993. "Measuring Poverty among Canadian Households." *Journal of Human Resources* 28(1): 162-84.

Pollak, Robert A., and Terence J. Wales. 1979. "Welfare Comparisons and Equivalence Scales." *American Economic Review* 69(2): 216-21.

Slesnick, Daniel. 1998. "Empirical Approaches to the Measurement of Welfare." *Journal of Economic Literature* 36(4): 2108-65.

—. 2001. *Consumption and Social Welfare.* Cambridge MA: Harvard University Press.

Smeeding, Timothy, Peter Saunders, John Coder, Stephen Jenkins, Johan Fritzell, Aldi J.M. Hagenaars, Richard Hauser, and Michael Wolfson. 1993. "Poverty, Inequality, and Family Living Standards Impacts across Seven Nations: The Effect of Noncash Subsidies for Health, Education and Housing." *Review of Income and Wealth* 39(3): 229-56.

Yates, Judith. 1994. "Imputed Rent and Income Distribution." *Review of Income and Wealth* 40(1): 43-66.

Zaidi, M. Asghar, and Klaas de Vos. 2001. "Trends in Consumption-Based Poverty and Inequality in the European Union during the 1980s." *Journal of Population Economics* 14: 367-90.

6
How Much Does Employment Matter for Inequality in Canada and Elsewhere?

Lars Osberg

This chapter compares income inequality in Canada with inequality in a selection of other advanced capitalist countries in the mid-1990s and examines how much of the differences in income distribution stem from inter-country differences in employment. Most studies in this volume focus on Canadian inequality and analyze trends over time within Canada; this chapter offers international comparisons as a complementary way of viewing our current level of inequality. It also emphasizes the importance of differences in the probability of paid employment and in working time, a dimension missing from almost all of the voluminous research on inequality.[1] Although we are interested in the distribution of money income primarily because it is thought to be a good guide to the distribution of economic well-being, most people care about both money income and the amount of time they have to work to earn that income. If money income differences are heavily influenced by differences in working time, and if well-being depends on both time and money, comparisons of inequality based solely on differences in the distribution of money income may be misleading.

The working time issue is likely to be important for cross-country comparisons because differences across countries are now large, and Europe and the United States seem to be following different paths. For example, data from the International Labour Organization (2000) indicate that from 1980 to 2000, average actual working time per adult (ages fifteen to sixty-four) rose in the United States by 234 hours to 1,476 while falling in Germany by 170 hours to 973. In 1980, Canada, France, Germany, Sweden, the United Kingdom, and the United States all had average actual hours of paid work per adult that clustered in a fairly narrow range, but by 2000 dramatic differences had arisen among them (see Figure 6.1). When working hours change to this degree, it is reasonable to ask whether inequality might also be affected.

The measurement of working hours, however, is not unambiguous,[2] and the correspondence between differences in working hours and differences in well-being depends crucially on preferences – that is, whether working hours are voluntarily chosen and whether tastes change over time or across countries. In comparing inequality across countries, it is also important to unpack the effects of differences in common entitlements to holiday and vacation time, differences in labour force participation, and differences in individual hours of paid labour supply, conditional on participation. Differences between countries in average working hours per adult are determined both by differences in labour force participation (sometimes called the "extensive margin" of labour supply) and by the distribution of hours among those with some employment (the "intensive margin" of labour supply). Because families in which nobody has a job are completely outside the paid labour market, the correlation between household members in probability of employment is also particularly important for social exclusion – a dimension of inequality that increases the importance of examining international differences in household paid labour supply driven by differences in labour force participation.

The next section therefore begins with a discussion of the problems created by consideration of working time in comparing relative levels of inequality. It argues that differences between countries in the probability of employment are responsible for much of the inter-country differences in average usual hours of work that have emerged in recent years. These differences are particularly marked for women, and there is some evidence that they are consistent with differing attitudes across countries toward the relative importance of paid work, child care, and unpaid household production. The third section therefore proposes a methodology for assessing the extent to which differences in workforce participation may help to explain cross-country comparisons of inequality. The fourth section compares the actual distribution across individuals of disposable (after-tax, after-transfer) household money income, adjusted for family size, with the results of two simulations. In one simulation, other nations' female workforce participation rates are held at the Canadian level, and, in the other, their aggregate participation rates are fixed at the Canadian level. A final section offers concluding thoughts.

Inequality in Well-Being, Work, and Money Income

In Figure 6.1, the countries plotted seem to group themselves into three broad types, with Canada, Sweden, and the United Kingdom having very similar

FIGURE 6.1

Annual number of hours worked per person

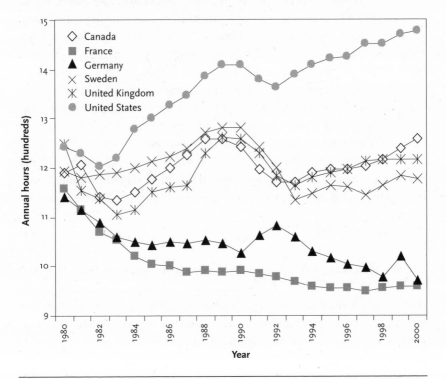

NOTE: Average hours worked per employed person aged 15 to 64. Extrapolations are used for Canada and France 1999, 2000, and United Kingdom and United States 2000.
SOURCE: Hours of work from International Labor Organization (2002); population and employment data from OECD (1998).

trends, intermediate between those observed in the United States and France/ Germany. However, the trends in working time observed in Figure 6.1 do not indicate simply that European labour markets were unable to generate as many jobs as does the United States. If one adds to actual work hours the total number of unemployment hours (assuming that the desired weekly hours of the unemployed equal the actual weekly hours of the employed) the differences narrow somewhat, but the same basic picture emerges.

Because Figure 6.1 focuses on relative hours of work, differences in employment rates matter more than differences in unemployment rates. When the unemployment rate is 10 percent, one could equally well say that 90 percent of the labour force is employed. Even though the unemployment rate in the United States (4 percent) in 2000 was less than half that in France (10 percent), the difference in employment rates (96 percent of the labour force employed compared to 90 percent) is proportionally much smaller. Hence, adjusting Figure 6.1 for unemployment does not change the basic picture. Adding together hours of actual work for pay and desired work (unemployment), one still gets the result that cross-country differences are large – about nine hours per week more for the average adult aged fifteen to sixty-four in the United States compared to the average adult in France or Germany. What model might explain these differences?

In thinking about the relationship between time and money income, neoclassical labour supply theory often starts, in a one-period model, with each individual maximizing a utility function, as in the following equation:

$$U = u(C, L),\tag{1}$$

where C represents consumption and L represents non-work time. The wage rate available in the paid labour market (w), the amount of non-labour income (V), and the total time (T) available (which has to be divided between hours of paid work (H) and non-work time) are the fundamentals driving the time and money income constraints, as per the equations:[3]

$$H + L = T\tag{2}$$
$$C = wH + V\tag{3}$$

In this model, individuals are seen as choosing hours of work H to maximize utility U. If it were true that individuals could always obtain as many hours of work as they desired, at a constant real wage, then one could think of "full income" ($wT + V$) as the potential consumption available to each person. An individual's money income would, in this view, reflect that person's choice to consume part of their potential income in the form of material goods rather than as leisure time.

The labour/leisure choice model has many deficiencies, but it can be used to assist a discussion of why working time might affect the measurement of inequality. Figure 6.2 is constructed to represent the possible impact on observed inequality of differing leisure preferences (i.e., a different "income effect" on leisure demand). Imagine that two societies (labelled A

Figure 6.2

Differences in tastes and money income inequality

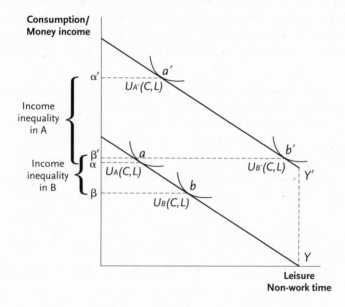

and B) are exactly alike in the hourly wage that they present to the rich and the poor – as represented by the budget lines Y and Y' in Figure 6.2.[4] Imagine also that society A has more materialistic preferences, so that rich people in A maximize their utility at point a' (implying money income α') and poor people in A maximize their utility at point a (implying money income α). In less materialistic country B, which has different preferences but exactly the same choice set, rich people maximize utility at b' (hence have money income β') and poor people maximize utility at b (with money income β). It is clear that money income inequality is greater in A than in B [$\alpha' - \alpha > \beta' - \beta$]. However, labour market opportunities are the same and the distribution of wealth is the same, because people in A prefer to take more of any given level of potential income in the form of money income rather than in leisure. Graphically, the expansion path of consumption with greater non-labour income has a steeper slope for residents in A than in B.

If this were a reasonable picture of the world, and if one were to assume that the United States is a more materialistic society than other nations, then this model might help to explain the greater inequality of money income – and the longer average hours of work and higher average money incomes – in the United States than in Europe. It would also fit with the general observation (in inequality and working time as in much else) that Canada is "in between" France/Germany and the United States. This model also predicts a lower variance of hours worked in the United States than in Europe, which is also true for the population as a whole. It implies that correcting for differences in tastes would narrow measured cross-country differences in inequality of money incomes.

However, can this model explain the trends in average actual hours of work per person of working age outlined in Figure 6.1? These trends mingle the effects of: (1) common entitlements to leisure (e.g. paid public holidays and statutory paid vacations), (2) individual participation in the paid work force, and (3) actual hours of work of workers. It is not reasonable to expect that trends in all three components will be driven by the same processes or have the same impacts on inequality.

Common entitlements are determined by collective action, through the political process or in collective bargaining. By their nature, common entitlements tend to be an equalizing element in the distribution of economic well-being, but although differences in such entitlements across nations can be significant,[5] their determinants are not well understood. The number of paid public holidays, for example, is determined by a set of political processes quite different from the determinants of individual decisions to enter the workforce and to work specific hours. It is clear from employment legislation that the number of public holidays differs across countries, but the standard economics model does not explain why.[6] Individuals in some countries choose more or less of a *common* entitlement via collective decision making, as opposed to choosing *individually* optimal hours of work and leisure.

The model depicted in Figure 6.2 is one of *individual* choice, of workers' decisions about labour supply. Hence, it is best suited to analysis of inequality *among workers* and is less well-suited to an examination of the influence of labour supply differences on inequality among the whole population. However, an important source of inter-country differences in labour supply is differences in the proportion of adults with zero paid employment.

Additionally, the simple labour/leisure choice model of equation (1) assumes the absence of involuntary unemployment. Over time, total working hours within a country can change quite quickly as the macro economy moves from boom to bust or vice versa. Variation in the quantity of labour demanded can impose involuntary changes in the amount of working time obtained by workers, and it is clear that constraints on available hours of work are most acutely experienced by the lower paid.[7] Since inequality in access to employment often interacts with inequality in hourly wages, measuring inequality solely in terms of a "full income / hourly wage" (which is not actually available to the involuntarily unemployed) seems likely to be misleading.

Osberg (2003a) has argued that the distribution of usual hours of work of workers is very similar for Germany and the United States, particularly for prime age males, except for the extreme lower tail of the distribution. Differences between these two countries in usual hours of work in the 1990s appear to be dominated by differences at the extensive margin of labour supply, especially among women and older men.

However, within Canada and the United States, the argument has also been made that the trend over time to greater inequality in household income is partly driven by the correlation of potential earnings of husbands and wives and the workforce entry of well-educated women. In general, well-educated women tend to marry well-educated (potentially high-income) men. If well-educated wives in the 1950s tended to stay home but in the 1990s tended to get paid jobs, then rising female employment might disproportionally swell the household income of upper-income groups, thereby increasing measured inequality in household money income. Applying this explanation to cross-country differences in measured inequality, one might think that if workforce participation elsewhere were to increase to North American levels, measured inequality in household money income in other countries would also rise. Hence, comparing inequality in the actual distribution of household money income might overstate international differences in inequality.

Average actual working hours per adult can differ across countries because countries differ in both the probability of working at all and in average working hours per worker. Table 6.1 therefore decomposes the difference in average actual hours of work across countries due to differences in employment rates and hours per worker.[8] If we compare, for example, Canada and Germany, the difference of 212 hours of work per working age person per year can be decomposed into 118 hours attributable to the difference in employment rates and 94 hours per year due to differences in working hours per employee.

TABLE 6.1

International differences in average actual hours worked: Canada and other countries, 1996-97

	Average actual hours per employee	Monthly average employment rate		Average actual hours per working age person	Difference in actual hours per person	Employment rate difference	Hours/ employee difference
		Male	Female				
Canada, 1996	1,732	66.3	53.2	1,024	–	–	–
United States, 1997	1,966	71.3	56.8	1,254	–230	–92	–138
United Kingdom, 1997	1,731	64.5	49.3	1,013	11	10	1
Germany, 1997	1,574	63.8	42.3	812	212	118	94
France, 1997	1,656	57.5	41.2	808	216	171	45
Sweden, 1997	1,552	61.0	54.3	883	141	34	107

NOTE: The working age population in the data for the United States, the United Kingdom, and Sweden is 16 and over, for Canada and France 15 and older, and for Germany 14 and older.

SOURCE: Hours from International Labour Organization (2002); employment rates from United States Bureau of Labour Statistics (2005).

In the Canada-Germany and Canada-France comparisons, differences in the proportion of the working age population who have any employment make up the larger part of the total hours differential, while the Canada-Sweden and Canada-US comparisons are dominated by differences in average working hours per employee. The Canada-UK overall differential is relatively small. Evidently, although differences in employment probability are often very important, sometimes such differences are small. Hence no single explanation of cross-country differences in working time per adult is likely to apply to all cases.

Nevertheless, Freeman and Schettkat (2002) have suggested that differences in the "marketization" of production explains the US/Europe employment gap. They argue that the European Union "produces relatively more goods and services through household production and less through the market than the US" (ibid., 2). Although they suggest this has implications for relative employment levels in the low-skill service sector, and argue generally for the efficiency advantages of greater female labour force participation, they do not explain how or why such a large difference in marketization might have occurred. They avoid judgment as to whether inter-country differences in work hours are explained mainly by differences in preferences or by differences in the incentives that individuals face, leaving open the question of whether higher tax rates or differences in lifestyle tastes are more significant.

By contrast, Garhammer (1999) does not hesitate to assert that nations can be characterized in terms of a specific "time culture," in which social institutions (such as the non-working weekend or the Christmas and New Year's holiday period) and other social norms for time use are expressed in laws (such as working hour regulations, legal holidays, and shop opening hours), collective agreements, and national customs (e.g., siestas). He argues that there is a distinctive European model of time culture in which the social enjoyment of time is highly prized and both "time prosperity" and material wealth are valued. He notes, for example, that "the majority of middle-aged Germans define the quality of life to which they personally aspire as "not being rushed" (ibid., 69).

Typically, economists have been reluctant to appeal to differences in preferences to explain international differences in outcomes and have preferred to emphasize differences in incentives. Sociologists such as Garhammer, on the other hand, have seen the description of national differences in values as entirely legitimate – indeed, some would say, central to their discipline.

These contrasting methodological approaches are quite important for the empirical analysis of the connection between working time and inequality. If one wants to compare the extent of economic inequality across countries and "standardize" the distribution of money income for differences in the probability of working, it might well be asked: "What thought experiment should be performed?"

If preferences are similar across countries, and if actual working time differences reflect primarily differences in incentive structure, then one could not have a change in hours of work without a change in incentives. In this case, one should run the thought experiment of a change in incentives and examine its impact on both money incomes and time worked, because the structure of income distribution processes (i.e., the net income obtainable from work, after taxes and after any impact of earnings on transfer payments) would have to change if working hours were to change. In this case, for example, one should model the impact of a similar income tax regime on both net earned income and working time.

However, if the sociologists are correct in asserting that differences in social values can be significant,[9] then it is plausible to ask how the distribution of income would change if preferences were similar, but the structure of incentives were unchanged. One might, for example, examine what the German distribution of income would look like if Germans had the same preferences for material goods and non-work time as Canadians but continued to face unchanged incentives in the labour market.

These contrasting methodological models are particularly relevant for analysis of the differences between countries in the extent of non-employment by women. If there are differences between countries in such social norms as the proper locus of care for young children and the relative importance of paid work and family life in the definition of personal identity, then these cultural differences may be the primary determinants of differences in female workforce participation. Hakim (2000) is one of the sociologists who have tried to explain the evolution of female attitudes to "home-centred" and "work-centred" models of identity. If national societies evolve differently in these dimensions, so that differences in preferences arise, then one can ask (without necessarily having to model differences in the income tax and social policy regimes) the question: "What would the German distribution of income look like if German women had similar attitudes to workforce participation as North American women, but faced the same labour market incentives as they now do?"[10]

Many readers may already have some opinions on national differences in social attitudes, but one does not have to rely solely on casual observation. The World Values Survey (WVS) and the International Social Survey Program (ISSP) have, in repeated random samples, asked a comparable set of questions on social attitudes in advanced capitalist countries. Table 6.2 summarizes the results of some questions asked in the 1990-91 WVS and 1998 ISSP survey rounds, which were intended to probe social attitudes to "home-centred" and "work-centred" models of female identity.

In thinking about whether to enter the workforce, women must compare the positive attractions of pay and of possible greater intrinsic satisfactions of work for pay, compared to work in the home, with a possible negative – a potential cost in relationships, particularly with children. To the extent that families make joint decisions on these issues, male attitudes on these issues also matter. To track perceptions of these issues, the WVS asked respondents whether they agreed that "a working mother can establish just as warm and secure a relationship with her children as a mother who does not work" and the ISSP asked whether respondents disagreed that "family life suffers when the woman has a full-time job." Although there is some evidence that younger Canadian women have more "non-traditional" attitudes than young American women, the similarity in Canadian and American responses is otherwise fairly high. There is evidence in Table 6.2 of generational effects, and there are also strong national differences, even among the relatively young. For example, the difference between younger German and North American women in the 1990-91 WVS was very large (25 percentage points), but by 1998 there was less, albeit still significant, difference between Germany and the United States in attitudes to whether "family life suffers when the woman has a full-time job."

Moreover, it is notable that on the straightforward role differentiation question "do you agree, disagree ... A husband's job is to earn the money, a wife's job is to look after the home and family," the percentage of younger Germans and North Americans who "disagree" or "strongly disagree" in 1998 differed by 16 percentage points for women and 26 percentage points for men. Evidently, there continue to be substantial differences between countries in how people answer questions that are designed to elicit the extent of support for a more traditional "home centred" model of female identity. These differences may also help to explain differing definitions in Europe and North America of what it means to be a "feminist" and differing desired reforms to patriarchal institutions.

The responses summarized in Table 6.2 do not always conform to the stereotype of "more liberated American women." In 1998, for example, the percentage of American women under thirty-five who disagreed with role

TABLE 6.2

Attitudes toward traditional gender roles across countries: males and females, all ages and those under 35 years

	International Social Survey Program, 1998				World Values Survey, 1990-91	
	V 12 – How much do you agree, disagree ... A husband's job is to earn the money, a wife's job is to look after the home and family.		V 13 – How much do you agree, disagree ... All and all, family life suffers when the woman has a full-time job.		V 98 – Do you agree strongly, agree, disagree ... A working mother can establish just as warm and secure a relationship with her children as a mother who does not work.	
	% DISAGREE		% DISAGREE		% AGREE	
	Male	Female	Male	Female	Male	Female
ALL AGES						
US	56.0	56.7	43.0	51.3	65.6	79.9
Canada	56.6	68.9	43.0	56.6	63.8	75.4
UK	50.6	61.5	43.3	48.4	66.5	72.8
Germany	35.2	41.6	34.0	40.0	41.8	50.0
France	39.4	59.8	23.6	34.0	73.0	73.4
Sweden	57.6	74.6	48.1	57.3	64.6	81.7
< 35 YEARS						
US	66.9	66.2	52.5	56.0	73.6	83.3
Canada	66.6	72.9	53.3	62.9	71.3	83.3
UK	71.4	77.1	65.4	61.5	78.5	78.3
Germany	40.0	50.7	39.5	47.1	48.1	58.6
France	60.8	73.4	36.2	44.7	81.8	72.4
Sweden	65.3	84.3	54.6	67.7	62.2	80.9

NOTE: "Disagree" includes "strongly disagree" and "disagree"; "agree" includes "strongly agree" and "agree."

SOURCE: Author's calculations from microdata from International Social Survey Program: Religion II, 1998, Köln, Germany (Ann Arbor: Inter-University Consortium for Political and Social Research, 2001); Ronald Inglehart et al., "World Values Surveys and European Values Surveys 1981-84, 1990-93, 1995-97" (Ann Arbor: Inter-University Consortium for Political and Social Research, 2000).

differentiation was appreciably less than in Canada, the United Kingdom, Sweden, or France. Male and female attitudes to gender roles also clearly differ; the 20 percentage point gap between under-thirty-five Swedish males and females in attitudes to husband and wife roles is especially notable. However, attitudinal survey evidence is consistent with the hypothesis of international differences in attitudes toward female participation in the paid workforce. Moreover, the differences between "all ages" and "under 35" attitudes might be broadly taken as evidence of converging attitudes (although it might also show how attitudes change with age). If so, then the thought experiment of "changing values" may not be entirely fanciful.

Statistical Issues

The United States is the largest nation in our sample, with the longest average working hours and the highest average money incomes, and it is often used as the basis for comparisons. However, for Canadians the most interesting thought experiment is to apply Canadian probabilities of paid employment to other countries, given the reward structures already in place there. To understand the impact of differing probabilities of employment on economic inequality, this study models the impact of a change (from the current country determinants to a Canadian model) in the probability of any employment in a year and, conditional on being employed at some point in the year, the expected net income associated with employment for a person or household of given characteristics. The analysis proceeds in two stages, first examining the implications of changed workforce participation by women and then considering men and women together.

The analysis considers separately the employment outcomes of single individuals and of multi-person households. A probit model of the probability of employment at some point in the year in Canada is estimated for single workers, with the results presented in Appendix Table 6.A. There is a long tradition in labour economics (see, for example, Killingsworth 1983) that recognizes the interdependence of husbands' and wives' labour supply decisions. Accordingly, I estimate a multinomial logit model of household labour market decisions in Canada, conditional on the characteristics of both partners. For each household, four possible states are identified: (1) both husband and wife are employed at some point in the year; (2) husband is employed but wife is never employed; (3) wife is employed but husband is never employed; (4) neither husband nor wife is employed at any point in the year. The results for married persons are presented in Appendix Table 6.B.

The coefficients from these estimated equations are then used to answer the question: "What would the probability of employment at some point in the year be, for a person of given characteristics, if it was determined by the same probability process as in Canada?" For a single person, it is their own characteristics, plus the structural parameters summarized in Table 6.A, which determine an expected probability of some employment. For a married person, the probability of being employed at some point in the year is the sum of the associated probabilities of household behaviour implied by Table 6.B. For example, a married woman's probability of employment is the sum of the expected probability that a household whose members have the same characteristics as her household will have both husband and wife employed plus the expected probability that a household whose members have the same characteristics as hers will be a "wife employed but husband not employed" household.

In these regressions, the influence of education on probability of employment is captured by a relative education variable calculated as the mean educational rank of a person of given educational credentials in their ten-year birth cohort. Countries differ significantly in the educational credentials they report, and equivalencies between credentials in different countries are sometimes problematic, but relative intra-cohort educational rank is a concept that can be directly compared across countries. Individuals are classified as employed if they report any earnings or any weeks of work during the survey year.

To simulate the income distribution that could be expected in European countries if the workforce expanded to a Canadian level of participation, the expected probability of employment is calculated for each person, and those outside the workforce are ranked by that probability. Table 6.3 reports the results obtained from a simulation of (1) changed behaviour by women and (2) both male and female workforce participation being at Canadian levels. Assuming that a change (to Canadian values) in the probability of employment would most affect those at the margin of labour market participation, this study simulates the change in outcomes by adding to the workforce of the United Kingdom, Germany, France, and Sweden the non-employed who have the greatest relative probability of employment. Table 6.3 assumes that those individuals who already have some employment would continue in employment and that, if workforce participation were to rise to Canadian levels, it would be the jobless individuals with highest expected probability of employment who would join the workforce.

TABLE 6.3

Income inequality in Canada, UK, US, Germany, France, and Sweden, 1994-97: working age households (actual and simulated as if at Canadian levels of work force participation)

	Median (Can 2000 $)	Mean (Can 2000 $)	Gini	Theil	% <.5 median	% >1.5 median	90/10 ratio	90/50 ratio	50/10 ratio	Poverty intensity*
Canada 97 (actual)	25,576	27,982	0.293	0.144	13.5	20.0	8.0	2.5	3.2	8.2
US 97 (actual)	27,480	33,127	0.371	0.252	16.9	24.5	13.5	3.6	3.7	11.0
Female simulation	27,423	33,096	0.371	0.252	16.9	24.6	13.5	3.7	3.7	11.0
Female + male sim.	27,210	32,860	0.374	0.255	17.3	24.7	13.7	3.7	3.7	11.2
UK 97 (actual)	17,938	21,144	0.344	0.212	15.6	23.8	10.1	3.3	3.1	8.4
Female simulation	19,032	21,515	0.321	0.184	14.0	20.2	8.4	2.9	2.8	7.0
Female + male sim.	20,286	22,626	0.291	0.154	10.6	18.0	6.5	2.8	2.3	4.0
Germany 94 (actual)	18,983	21,027	0.269	0.139	8.4	17.4	6.3	2.6	2.5	4.7
Female simulation	19,560	21,319	0.257	0.129	7.6	15.2	5.8	2.5	2.4	4.1
Female + male sim.	19,910	21,553	0.252	0.125	7.2	14.3	5.6	2.4	2.3	3.8
Sweden 95 (actual)	16,504	17,230	0.223	0.093	7.6	11.5	5.7	2.0	2.8	6.6
Female simulation	16,664	17,268	0.216	0.088	7.3	10.4	5.4	2.0	2.7	6.2
Female + male sim.	16,647	17,216	0.210	0.082	6.6	10.0	4.9	1.9	2.5	5.3
France 94 (actual)	17,629	20,395	0.289	0.154	7.9	19.7	6.6	2.9	2.3	3.6
Female simulation	18,308	20,637	0.272	0.137	7.4	17.9	5.9	2.7	2.2	3.2
Female + male sim.	18,498	20,743	0.264	0.129	6.4	17.5	5.5	2.6	2.1	2.6

NOTE: After-tax equivalent household disposable income per person; population is all persons in households with working age head (18-64); equivalence scale is square root of number in household.

*SST INDEX: Poverty line = ½ median equivalent disposable income, calculated separately for actual and simulated income distributions

SOURCE: Luxembourg Income Study microdata, calculations by author.

In the United States, the probability of employment in 1997 was quite close to, but a bit higher than, Canadian levels. This implies that in simulating the income distribution corresponding to Canadian patterns of employment one has to *subtract* from the work force those individuals at the margin of employment (i.e., those employed persons with the *lowest* estimated probability of employment). However, because the difference between Canadian and American employment probabilities is not large, the simulated income distribution is in practice not much different from the actual American income distribution, albeit with somewhat more inequality and poverty.

The impact on the household distribution of disposable income caused by individuals joining the workforce will depend on the size of their additional individual earnings, the size of any associated change in the earnings of other household members, the impact of changed joint earnings on transfer payments, and the change in taxes paid by both partners. To estimate the net income that would be received by the households containing additional workers, country-specific OLS regressions are used to estimate net disposable income as a function of age, age squared, relative education, family status, disability status, immigrant and labour market participation status, and so on.

These regressions are used to generate predicted values to be applied in the simulations. They can be viewed as a reduced form of the structural equations system that might predict the expected working hours of a person (or household) of given characteristics with specific expected wage(s), the earnings that those work hours would imply, and the net income that a household with those earnings would receive after income tax is deducted and transfer payments are added. Both the structure of the tax/transfer system and the functional form of the labour supply function may be rather complex; hence their linear functional form should be seen as a first-order approximation.[11]

In the simulated income distributions for each country reported in Table 6.3, this imputed net disposable income of the households with simulated additions to the workforce is added to the income of the other households whose labour market status is unchanged, and household equivalent income distribution statistics are calculated for the population as a whole. Note that this methodology will impose on all countries the Canadian pattern of correlation across spouses in employment, but it leaves the country-specific income determination process of workers unchanged, under the maintained hypothesis that those households with unchanged workforce status do not change their net income.

The important issue for the accuracy of the simulations reported in Table 6.3 is whether the conditional expectation of disposable household income of workforce entrants (as calculated using the combination of their personal characteristics and the additional income associated with those characteristics) is systematically biased to a degree that affects the summary statistics on income distribution reported in Table 6.3. Since there is always an element of judgment in the specification of the net income function (e.g., in choice of functional form or selection of right-hand-side variables), one way to check is to use an alternative plausible specification. The alternatives tried to date do not make very much difference.

Data Issues

This chapter uses Luxembourg Income Study (LIS) microdata to present point estimates[12] of income distribution for the following economies: Canada (1997), France (1994), Germany (1994), Sweden (1995), United Kingdom (1995), and United States (1997). The focus is on "standardizing" the distribution of equivalent income among individuals to account for the impact of different national probabilities of employment, but the statistical starting point is the LIS definition of total household money income after tax and including transfers (disposable household income)[13] as the basis for calculation of the "equivalent income" of all working age individuals (and dependent children). All summary statistics refer to the distribution of equivalent disposable income among all national residents living in households with a head aged sixty-four or less, excluding only those economic families or unattached individuals who reported a zero or negative before-tax money income. In all cases, where money figures are provided, local currency figures for income have been converted to year 2000 Canadian dollars using the relevant country price deflator for consumer expenditure and OECD estimates of purchasing power parity for consumption by households.

Estimates of the economic well-being of individuals within households depend heavily upon the assumptions made about the degree and pattern of economic sharing within households.[14] Estimates of the total well-being of the household also depend upon the equivalence scale used to estimate the economies of scale in household consumption.[15] This chapter uses the so-called LIS equivalence scale[16] in which the number of equivalent adults in each household is calculated as the square root of N. The LIS equivalence scale implies fairly large economies of scale in household consumption: the second person in a household counts as 0.41, the third person receives a weight of 0.32, and a four-person household is thought of as having the same relative level of consumption needs as two unattached individuals. This study assumes equal sharing among all household members and calculates the equivalent income of each household member as equal to the total money income of the household, divided by the number of equivalent adults in the household. This equivalent income is attributed to all household members, and the distribution of equivalent income across individuals is then calculated.

The most popular summary statistic of inequality is undoubtedly the Gini index, which is most sensitive to changes in the mid-range of the distribution. The Theil index is more sensitive to the bottom end and also has the advantage of being additively decomposable (for further discussion see Jenkins 1991).[17] As an indicator of the extremes of the income distribution, we present also the "90/10 ratio" – the ratio between the average income of the top 10 percent of persons and the average income of the bottom 10 percent. However, none of these measures reveals directly which part of the income distribution is changing – whether inequality is widening because the top end is pulling away from the middle or because the poor are falling behind those at the middle. Since these issues are often of interest, Table 6.3 also presents the 90/50 and 50/10 ratios. The percentages of the population with equivalent income greater than 150 percent, and less than 50 percent, of the median are also reported, as these statistics have also often been used as a guide to the degree of "polarization" in living standards.

In international comparisons, a frequently used relativistic conception of poverty draws the poverty line at one half the median national standard of living (Hagenaars 1986, 1991). Since this study calculates the equivalent income of each individual in each year, it defines the poverty line as one-half the median equivalent income of all individuals in that year.[18] Two measures of poverty are presented: the poverty rate (percentage below half the median equivalent income) and the Sen-Shorrocks-Thon (SST) index of poverty intensity. Although the poverty rate is undoubtedly the most commonly used measure of poverty, it does not reflect the average "poverty gap" (the percentage shortfall by which the incomes of the poor, on average, fall below the poverty line), and it ignores the degree of inequality among the poor.

As Osberg and Xu (2000) note, the SST index of poverty intensity is preferable on axiomatic grounds and can be decomposed into:

$$SST = (RATE)\,(GAP)\,(1+G(X)), \tag{4}$$

where *RATE* is the poverty rate, *GAP* is the average poverty gap ratio (the average percentage shortfall) among the poor, and $G(X)$ is the Gini index of poverty gap ratios among all people. Since $(1 + G(X))$ is in practice nearly constant over time and across countries, the SST index has the appealing property of being roughly proportional to the expected poverty gap of a randomly selected individual (the crude probability of poverty multiplied by the expectation of the percentage gap between the poverty line and actual income, conditional on being poor).

Empirical Results

Table 6.3 presents the actual median and mean equivalent disposable income and the above set of income distribution summary statistics for Canada, the United States, the United Kingdom, Germany, Sweden, and France. For the latter five countries it also presents the results of simulating a Canadian-level employment probability of women and of men and women combined. In these simulations, the impact on household disposable income of a change in the probability of workforce participation is simulated. The simulations calculate the net benefit to household incomes of greater workforce participation after subtracting direct taxes and after any associated reduction in transfer payments.

In thinking about how changes in workforce participation would affect the level and distribution of economic well-being, one must recognize that household disposable income is only part of the picture. Typically, the impacts of greater workforce participation on GDP per capita exceed its impacts on average disposable personal earnings, because rising employment levels would partially benefit the budgetary balance of governments. This would enable greater consumption of public services, with likely equalizing impacts, even if tax rates were held constant. However, the focus of the current study is narrower – the distribution of households' command over private resources (of time and money). Hence, this study emphasizes the change in equivalent disposable household income.

It is no surprise that in all countries the results indicate that if additional workers entered the paid labour force, the average and median equivalent income would rise. The effect is particularly marked in the United Kingdom when additional workforce participation by both men and women is considered; the simulations indicate that median equivalent disposable income might be expected to rise by about 13 percent and average income by 7 percent. As a number of authors have noted,[19] although the UK employment rate in aggregate is fairly high, that employment is concentrated. The percentage of working age households with zero employment income is particularly high in UK data, so the impacts on average and median income of moving to Canadian workforce participation levels would be particularly large in the United Kingdom. Furthermore, since households without earnings are the poorest of the poor, bringing more households into the workforce would have large impacts on poverty.

The biggest changes in UK data therefore occur at the bottom of the income distribution. Bringing male and female workforce participation to Canadian levels could be expected to cut poverty intensity from 8.4 to 4.0, and the poverty rate would fall from 15.6 to 10.6 percent. Polarization (as measured by the 90/10 ratio) would decline from a 10:1 ratio to about a 6.5:1 ratio, mostly because of a compression at the bottom, since the 50/10 ratio shrinks by more than the 90/50 ratio. All these improvements in the money income of the less affluent would reduce measured inequality, and, since the Theil index is more low-end sensitive than the Gini, the fall in inequality as measured by the Theil (from 0.212 to 0.154) is proportionally much larger than the fall in the Gini (from 0.344 to 0.291). In general, bringing female workforce participation to Canadian levels produces about half the total change of bringing both male and female participation to Canadian levels.

Where there are smaller differences in workforce participation to begin with, the impacts on average and median incomes of changing to Canadian participation levels are correspondingly smaller. In the United States, for example, median income changes by only $57 (about 0.2 percent) if the female workforce participation rate falls to the Canadian level, and by $270 (about 1 percent) if male and female employment levels are standardized. There is some change in poverty rate (an increase from 16.9 percent to 17.3 percent) when the impact of lower Canadian male workforce participation is simulated, but the impacts of simulated participation changes on the American income distribution are otherwise notably small – or non-existent. The broad conclusion is that very little of the United States-Canada difference in income inequality can be explained by differences in workforce participation.

In Table 6.3 the Swedish results project a very small change in median and average equivalent income and a tendency for income changes to be somewhat concentrated in the lower part of the income distribution. When both male and female participation are modelled at Canadian levels, poverty intensity falls significantly (from 6.6 to 5.3) and the bottom tail of the distribution compresses by considerably more than the top; the 90/50 hardly changes (shrinking from 2.0 to 1.9), while the 50/10 ratio declines from 2.8 to 2.5. Actual Canadian inequality starts from a considerably higher level than actual Swedish inequality, by any measure one can choose, but the difference would be even larger if Canada and Sweden had similar patterns of workforce participation.

In the United Kingdom, and to a lesser extent in Sweden, the simulated changes in workforce participation reduce inequality most at the low end of the income distribution. In Germany and France, however, changes in family income from an increase in workforce participation to Canadian levels would be spread more evenly throughout the distribution. If Germans had the same probability of employment as Canadians, the German income distribution would be compressed, especially at the top end – the drop in the German population percentage with incomes above 150 percent of median income is considerably larger (3.1 percentage points) than the decline in the poverty rate (1.2 percentage points). In both Germany and France, the simulated income distribution is more compressed than the actual income distribution; the simulated decline in the 50/10 ratio and the drop in the 90/50 ratio are of roughly the same size. Poverty intensity starts from a lower base in both countries than it does in Canada, and, although it falls in both (from 4.7 to 3.8 in Germany and from 3.6 to 2.6 in France), the decline is not nearly as dramatic as in the United Kingdom.

The continental European countries have an initial income distribution that is substantially more equal than that in the United States, the United Kingdom, or Canada. Their actual poverty rates (among working age households) are in the 8 percent range, well below the poverty rates in Canada (13.5 percent), the United Kingdom (15.6 percent), and the United States (16.9 percent). Poverty intensity and the 50/10 ratio are similarly much lower in Germany, Sweden, and France than in the Anglo-American countries, even before one considers the impact of added workforce participation. In continental Europe, one can therefore argue that the income, poverty, and employment dimensions of social exclusion are, to begin with, much less closely aligned than in the Anglo-American countries. Hence, the simulations of rising workforce participation tend to show, for France and Germany, a compression of the distribution of income *as a whole* rather than an effect that is concentrated in the lower tail.

Simulations of the impact of changing workforce participation on income distribution can be a useful way of analyzing particular welfare state regimes. As Table 6.3 shows, if Germans had the same probability of employment as Canadians, their Gini index would fall from 0.269 to 0.252 and the poverty rate in Germany would decrease from 8.4 percent to 7.2 percent. If French men and women had Canadian employment rates, the Gini index of inequality in France would decline from 0.289 to 0.264, and the French poverty rate would shrink from 7.9 percent to 6.4 percent. Similar impacts are observed in the United Kingdom and Sweden. Table 6.3 therefore yields two very general conclusions: (1) in Europe, a higher employment rate would mean more equality of income distribution and less poverty; and (2) in the mid-1990s the differences between Canada and continental European countries in inequality and poverty would have *increased* if other countries had Canadian levels of employment.

As Table 6.4 shows, annual employment rates in Canada and the United States are significantly higher than are those prevalent in Europe. The argument suggested by Figure 6.2 was that standardizing for labour-leisure preferences should have narrowed differences in measured inequality of income. Similarly, if the workforce entry of well-educated women married to high-income men in the 1980s and 1990s were responsible for increasing measured inequality in household money income,[20] then an increase in other countries' workforce participation to Canadian levels should raise their measured inequality in household money incomes. If either hypothesis were true, comparing inequality in the actual distribution of household money income

TABLE 6.4

Annual employment rates, ages 18-64, 1994-97

	Males and females	Females
United States, 1997	83.4	76.2
United Kingdom, 1995	67.1	59.7
Canada, 1997	81.7	75.0
Germany, 1994	74.7	64.9
Sweden, 1995	66.2	65.1
France, 1994	72.6	63.1

NOTE: Based on those who had positive employee hours or weeks in the past twelve months or who were self-employed.
SOURCE: Same as Table 6.3.

would overstate international differences in inequality. However, the present simulations find emphatically that neither is the case. In every country, increased workforce participation would reduce inequality and poverty. If continental European countries had Canadian-style determinants and levels of employment, differences in money income inequality and poverty would be larger, not smaller, than they are in actual data.

Figure 6.3, which examines working hours per household adult at different points in the distribution of income in 1994-95, may help explain the simulation results. In Figure 6.3, individuals are ordered in each country by their equivalent individual disposable money income (after direct taxes and after transfers), and the average labour supply per household adult is calculated for each income decile. The upper panel of the figure presents the average hours total. In the lower panel each country's decile average of working hours per household adult is expressed as a proportion of the corresponding Canadian decile. With the exception of the top income decile in the United Kingdom (which has the least work effort of the top decile of all countries examined),[21] there is a clear tendency for work hours to be higher in higher deciles of the income distribution, both absolutely and relative to Canada. At all points in the income distribution, Americans work more hours. Yet, although the American incentive system has its greatest differentials in hourly rewards at the top of the income distribution, the differential in hours of work is significantly *smaller* at the top of the income distribution than it is at the bottom.

If non-work time has utility, these data indicate that comparisons of money income inequality between the United States and other countries will underestimate differences in the inequality of utility. In the United States, the relatively poor work significantly harder for their greater relative poverty than they do in other countries. Cross-country comparisons of inequality in money alone understate inequality differences in time and money.

Implications and Conclusion

The concepts of "quality of life" and "economic well-being" are hard to define precisely, but most people would agree that they are influenced by both an individual's money income level and the discretionary time they have available in which to enjoy it. Hence, if leisure time varies substantially, money income alone will be a misleading indicator of economic well-being. This implies that international comparisons of money income inequality are potentially misleading indicators of the inequality of well-being.

FIGURE 6.3

Average working hours in Canada compared to other countries, 1994-95

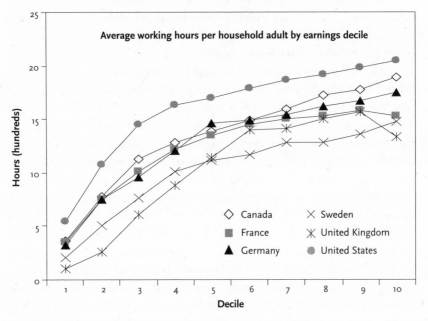

Average working hours per household adult by earnings decile

Canada   X Sweden
France   X United Kingdom
Germany   ● United States

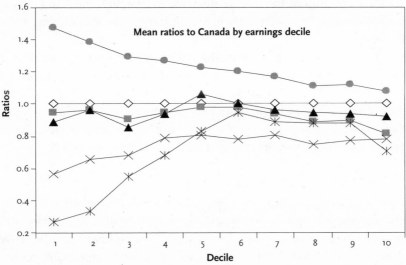

Mean ratios to Canada by earnings decile

NOTE: Deciles by after-tax equivalent household income, where the equivalent scale is the square root of the total number in the household.
SOURCE: Author's calculations using the Luxembourg Income Study microdata.

Trends in average actual working time are driven by collective decisions on common leisure entitlements, individual probabilities of having any employment, and the average working hours of workers. The United States and continental Europe (particularly France and Germany) have diverged sharply in these trends in recent years, while Canada is an intermediate case. This chapter has examined how far differences in employment probability can explain international differences in income inequality. The basic conclusion is that international comparisons of the level of money income inequality likely *understate* the degree of differences in the inequality of economic well-being. In the United States, the relatively poor have to work quite a lot harder and still end up with less income than do their counterparts in European countries. In both working time inequality and money income inequality, Canada is an intermediate case between Europe and the United States. Comparisons of inequality in money income have long indicated that Canadian inequality is greater than inequality in European nations.[22] It is clearly worse to be poor in both leisure time and money income than to be poor in money income alone. Therefore, this chapter concludes that, compared to Europe, particularly Sweden and the United Kingdom, the distribution of economic well-being among Canadians is even more unequal than money income comparisons alone would indicate.

APPENDIX: MEASUREMENT ISSUES

How many hours do people work in a given year? What methodology provides the best estimates? To some extent, the answer depends on why one wants to know. Economists who are concerned with the study of factor productivity are interested in how many hours are worked, in total, at work sites and are uninterested in how those hours are distributed among particular workers. For this purpose, establishment-based surveys may be appropriate, even if such surveys cannot reveal whether the same worker has a number of simultaneous part-time jobs or how working hours are combined within households.

This study, however, is concerned with hours worked as part of the distribution of economic well-being. Consequently, the aggregation of an individual's jobs into total hours and the correlation of hours within households is crucial. Household-based surveys are thus the appropriate instrument, but, as the OECD notes (Organization for Economic Cooperation and Development 2001, 6), such surveys do not align exactly with administrative records in their aggregate totals.

As the OECD also notes (ibid., 5): "There are six main concepts of hours of work that are retained in different sources of labour statistics: actual hours, usual hours, contractual hours, legal hours, paid hours, hours offered (by employers)." The first two concepts come closest to the labour supply concept used in economics. The "actual" hours of work concept highlighted in Figure 6.1 differs from "usual" hours of work since it allows for time not worked due to public holidays, paid vacation, illness, and other factors.[23] Using "actual" hours of work for a given respondent in a given week in a microdata survey exposes the data to both individual sampling variability in such events as vacations and illnesses and full sample variability in such events as the survey's being run during a week with a public holiday. As a consequence, the "usual hours" concept is commonly used in empirical work in labour economics. Still, one must be aware that international differences in average actual hours substantially exceed international differences in average usual hours (partly because countries differ in the number of paid public holidays and in mandatory vacation time entitlements).

TABLE 6.A

Probability of employment in the past twelve months in Canada, 1997, probit regression: single males and females aged 18-64, head or spouse

	Males		Females	
Intercept	−0.681**	(0.271)	−2.427*	(0.220)
Age	0.109*	(0.014)	0.181*	(0.012)
Age squared	−0.002*	(0.0001)	−0.002*	(0.001)
Relative education	0.007*	(0.001)	0.014*	(0.001)
Dummy = 1 if children < 18 in household	0.490**	(0.221)	−0.293*	(0.082)
Number of children	−0.247**	(0.123)	−0.231*	(0.041)
Dummy = 1 if immigrant	−0.217*	(0.062)	−0.278*	(0.055)
Dummy = 1 if disabled	−2.382*	(0.116)	−2.329*	(0.121)
Observations	4,002		5,243	
−2 log likelihood	3,203.5		4,575.9	

NOTE: Employed means respondent had positive employee hours or weeks in the past twelve months or was self-employed. Individuals are put into percentiles based on education level within each age cohort. Since education is reported differently across countries (e.g., the United States reports the highest level attained while the United Kingdom reports years of education), a relative measure of education is used. The population is divided into five age groups (18-24, 25-34, 35-44, 45-54, and 55-64) and ordered by education within each age cohort. Each individual is then assigned the average percentile for their education level.
* Significant with 99% confidence; ** significant with 95% confidence; standard errors are reported in parentheses.

Table 6.b

Probability of employment in the past twelve months in Canada, 1997, multinomial logit: married males and females

	Both not working vs. both working		Wife working, husband not working vs. both working		Husband working, wife not working vs. both working	
Intercept	8.420*	(0.653)	2.245*	(0.794)	2.871*	(0.372)
Age of the wife	−0.401*	(0.050)	0.085	(0.060)	−0.308*	(0.027)
Age of the wife squared	0.005*	(0.001)	−0.001***	(0.001)	0.004*	(0.0003)
Relative education of wife	−0.021*	(0.002)	0.002	(0.002)	−0.017*	(0.001)
Wife is an immigrant	0.455*	(0.164)	0.328**	(0.165)	−0.036	(0.081)
Wife is disabled	3.008*	(0.292)	−1.389	(1.003)	3.376*	(0.230)
Age of the husband	−0.255*	(0.053)	−0.439*	(0.058)	0.038	(0.029)
Age of the husband squared	0.004*	(0.001)	0.006*	(0.001)	−0.0004	(0.0003)
Relative education of husband	−0.005*	(0.002)	−0.004**	(0.002)	0.001	(0.0009)
Husband is an immigrant	−0.042	(0.165)	0.151	(0.163)	0.321*	(0.079)
Husband is disabled	4.589*	(0.217)	5.274*	(0.211)	−0.173	(0.394)
Dummy = 1 if children < 18	−0.394**	(0.182)	−0.521*	(0.197)	0.155***	(0.080)
Number of children	0.416*	(0.078)	0.235*	(0.091)	0.356*	(0.031)
Observations	17,074					
Likelihood ratio	19,143					

NOTES: There are four categories: (1) husband and wife have no employment; (2) the wife has employment but the husband has no employment; (3) the husband has employment but the wife does not; and (4) both are employed. Employed means employee hours > 0 or weeks in past twelve months > 0 or self-employed. For education, see note to Table 6.A.
* Significant with 99% confidence; ** significant with 95% confidence; *** significant with 90% confidence; standard errors are reported in parentheses.

Both usual and actual hours measures are assessed by the direct questioning of the respondents to household surveys (such as the Current Population Survey in the United States or the Labour Force Survey in Canada). It is this sort of data that the LIS data base records and that this chapter uses. This methodology relies on the underlying assumption that the individual respondents to household surveys can provide unbiased estimates of their working time, subject to some ambiguity about the actual reporting of unpaid interruptions in working time (e.g. lunch or coffee breaks), an unavoidable amount of random reporting error, and a tendency to "spiking" at standard working hour norms (such as thirty-five or forty hours per week).

In the "time-use" field, Zick (2002) is one of those who have attacked this assumption, arguing that "time diaries provide the most cost effective way of gathering valid and reliable time-use information." In time diary surveys, respondents are asked to record sequentially how they spend their time; ideally at least two twenty-four-hour periods (one from a weekday and another from a weekend) are recorded for each respondent. Because interviews must also be spaced over the year in order to capture any possible seasonal variations in time use, a time diary survey is a very expensive and time-intensive proposition, so time diary data have been infrequently gathered. Gershuny (2000, 249-53) has noted that when respondents fill in a time use diary, their answers to the question "What did you do yesterday?" are a narrative which follows the time line through the day (e.g. "got up at 7, left the house at 8, got to work at 9, etc."). This method is the natural way people keep track of time, and it necessarily imposes consistency in aggregate time use, but it is then up to the researcher to calculate aggregate "work" or "leisure" hours by summing across similar uses of time. Nevertheless, Gershuny argues that this is likely to be more accurate than the implicit process of categorization and aggregation demanded when respondents are asked to add up in their heads the amount of time they spent "working for pay"[24] last week. The riposte, by defenders of the summary question methodology, is that time use diaries are typically constructed for one or two days, which imposes a sampling of days within the working week (or month) and introduces errors of its own.

How much might reporting error in paid labour supply matter? Zick (2002, 440) comments: "the few time-use reporting error studies that have been done to date suggest that data taken from stylized questions may be systematically less accurate than time-diary data and this reporting error may be related to individual and/or household characteristics that are often used as covariates in time use analyses." However, whether time diaries are more accurate, the core problem for researchers is the scarcity of data on working hours drawn from time use diaries and the lack of linkage with comparable international data on the distribution of money income. Hence, this chapter depends on the "stylized survey question" methodology.

ACKNOWLEDGMENTS

This chapter is based on a paper first presented at the International Workshop on "Income Distribution and Welfare" organized for the Bocconi University Centennial, 30 May – 1 June 2002, in Milan. I thank Lynn Lethbridge for her exemplary work on this project and the Social Sciences and Humanities Research Council for financial support. Thanks also to the co-editors and referees for very useful comments and to the Institute for Social and Economic Research at the University of Essex for their hospitality during a productive sabbatical.

NOTES

1 Exceptions include: Johnson and Kuhn (2004), Jenkins and O'Leary (1996), Lee (2001), Doiron and Barrett (1996), and Burtless (1993).

2 The distinction between "actual" and "usual" hours of work is particularly important for comparative analysis. The OECD Growth Project (see Organization for Economic Cooperation and Development 2001) and the University of Groningen GGDC Total Economy Database 2002 (available at http://www.eco.rug.nl/ggdc) provide somewhat different estimates of actual hours of work per employee than the ILO. The Groningen estimates and the OECD numbers, together with the employment/population ratio data available from the Bureau of Labor Statistics, can be used to compute the same concept of "average actual working hours per working age adult" as reported in Figure 6.1. There are differences in detail but the same basic picture emerges of widening differences in average actual work hours between the United States and France/Germany, with Canada, Sweden, and the United Kingdom as intermediate cases. See the Appendix for a fuller discussion of data issues.

3 Clearly, this formulation assumes that work hours are available without quantity constraint at a constant real wage and without progressive taxation. Non-labour income (from capital or transfer payments) is assumed to be V, and any complications of human capital investment through on-the-job training are ignored.

4 Implicitly, Figure 6.2 portrays a world where rich and poor differ in assets held (and therefore in non-labour income V), but not in human capital; hence the hourly wages implicit in both budget constraints are identical. Inequality in both human and financial capital is more realistic, but the same basic point applies.

5 Using data from 1990, Bell and Freeman (1994, 4) argue that "differences in weeks of vacation and holiday time translate into a 17 percent reduction in working time in Germany compared to a 9 percent reduction of work time in the United States, and therefore contribute .08 ln points to the annual hours gap between the two countries."

6 See, however, Jenkins and Osberg (2005) for a model stressing the importance of coordination of leisure time; public holidays are all about *simultaneous* leisure time.

7 Using the Labour Market Activity Survey of Statistics Canada, Osberg and Phipps (1993, 283) estimated that the Atkinson index of inequality (with inequality aversion parameter = -0.5) of earned income in Canada would have fallen by about 30 percent if all Canadian workers had been able to obtain their desired weeks of work in 1986/87. (See Chapter 12 for the definition of the Atkinson index.) In the interpretation of unemployment, Jahoda (1979), Kelvin and Jarrett (1985), and

others have also stressed that involuntary joblessness carries significant social and psychological costs.

8 Define: annual hours per person = H, hours per worker = h, employment/population ratio = E, and subscripts (c, o) denote Canada and other countries. Then annual hours per person equals the product of hours per worker and the employment/population ratio:

$H_c = h_c E_c$ and $H_o = h_o E_o$

Hence,

$H_c - H_o = h_c E_c - h_o E_o$
$\quad = h_c E_c + h_o E_c - h_o E_c - h_o E_o$
$\quad = h_o (E_c - E_o) + E_c (h_c - h_o),$

which are the two right-hand columns in Table 6.1.

9 Scott et al. (1996) examine the evolution of gender-role attitudes in the United Kingdom, Germany, and the United States. The difference in levels of support for what they call "pro-feminist" attitudes is striking.

10 However, if Germans had different attitudes as workers, they might also have different attitudes as voters, and changes in social policy and labour market incentives might result. German tax/transfer incentives strongly favour the "traditional" model of the family and child care by stay-at-home mothers; substantial financial incentives, for up to two years, are provided for women to remain at home and care for their children (Phipps 1994, 1998). By contrast, American social policy has provided no such support for mothers to stay at home. Indeed welfare policy has shifted strongly to encouraging or requiring the labour force participation of welfare beneficiaries. This chapter is, therefore, best thought of as an other-things-equal approximation in which labour market attitudes change but voting behaviour does not. As well, if labour supply shifted, the wage rate observed in labour markets would likely change, to a degree that would depend on the wage elasticity of labour demand. This chapter, however, holds constant both the current tax and transfer regimes and the wage payment structures in each country.

11 These regression results are available on request from the author and can be downloaded from an earlier version of this chapter available on the author's web site (http://myweb.dal.ca/osberg). The paper is "How Much Does Work Matter for Inequality: Time, Money, and Inequality in International Perspective," which is also available as LIS Working Paper 326.

12 Although estimates of the confidence intervals surrounding these point estimates are not presented here, interested readers can find such estimates (for the population as a whole), calculated using a bootstrap methodology, in Osberg and Xu (2000).

13 Disposable income consists of the sum of gross wages and salaries, farm self-employment income, non-farm self-employment income, cash property income,

sick pay, disability pay, social retirement benefits, child or family allowances, unemployment compensation, maternity pay, military/veteran/war benefits, other social insurance, means-tested cash benefits, near cash benefits, private pensions, public sector pensions, alimony or child support, other regular private income, and other cash benefits; minus mandatory contributions for self employed, mandatory employee contribution, and income tax.

14 Phipps and Burton (1995, 194) have demonstrated the potential importance of inequality within the family: the same Canadian family income data are consistent with a child poverty rate (for two-parent families) of as little as 5.9 percent if resources are equally shared or as much as 52.1 percent if resource sharing is minimal. However, this chapter does not address these issues.

15 Phipps and Garner (1994, 13) argue that if one uses the same methodology for estimating equivalence scales, American and Canadian results are statistically and practically indistinguishable. Burkhauser, Smeeding, and Merz (1996) emphasize the differences in incidence and patterns of poverty implied by alternative equivalence scale methodologies in official use in Germany and the United States and provide estimates of the sensitivity of the poverty rate in those countries to alternative scale elasticities. See also Buhmann et al. (1988); Coulter et al. (1992).

16 Figini (1998, 2) notes that "OECD and other two-parameter equivalence scales empirically used show a similarity of results [in measurement of inequality] to one parameter equivalence scales with elasticity around 0.5."

17 Kesselman and Cheung in Chapter 12 give a basic description of the attributes of the various inequality measures used in this study.

18 Measures of aggregate inequality (such as the Gini index) are dominated by the income distribution of the non-poor (the great majority of the population). Hence, defining the poverty line in this way does not necessarily imply that poverty and aggregate inequality are closely related; see Osberg and Xu (2000).

19 Osberg (2002) notes that 20.4 percent of households of working age in the United Kingdom in 1995 LIS data have no reported employment, well above the rate in other countries. See also Gregg et al. (1999).

20 For evidence about the role of assortative mating in changes in Canadian family income inequality, see Fortin and Schirle in Chapter 11.

21 Given the rhetoric surrounding "incentives" and "initiative" during the Thatcher era, this is an intriguing finding.

22 See, for example, Osberg (2003) or Förster and d'Ercole (2005)

23 The LIS data contain both actual and usual weekly hours and give as possible reasons for any discrepancy: "Person has worked more than usual due to: 1. variable hours (e.g., flexible working hours) 2. other reasons; person has worked less than usual due to: 3. bad weather 4. slack work for technical or economic reasons 5. labour dispute 6. education or training 7. variable hours (e.g., flexible working hours) 8. own illness, injury or temporary disability 9. maternity leave 10. special

leave for personal or family reasons 11. annual holidays 12. bank holidays 13. start of/change in job during reference week 14. end of job without taking up a new one during reference week 15. other reasons" (see page 4 at http://www. lisproject.org/les/varvalue.pdf).

24   As a check, the reader might want to think how to respond to the question: "What is the usual number of hours per week you spend working for pay?"

REFERENCES

Bell, Linda, and Richard Freeman. 1994. "Why Do Americans and Germans Work Different Hours?" NBER Working Paper No. 4808. Cambridge, MA: National Bureau of Economic Research.

—. 2000. "The Incentive for Working Hard: Explaining Hours Worked Differences in the U.S. and Germany." NBER Working Paper No. 8051. Cambridge, MA: National Bureau of Economic Research.

—. 2001. "The Incentive for Working Hard: Explaining Hours Worked Differences in the US and Germany." Labour Economics 8(2): 181-202.

Buhmann, Brigitte, Lee Rainwater, Gunter Schmaus, and Tim Smeeding. 1988. "Equivalence Scales, Well-Being, Inequality and Poverty: Sensitivity Estimates across Ten Countries Using the Luxembourg Income Study (LIS) Database." Review of Income and Wealth 34(2): 115-42.

Burkhauser, Richard V., Tim Smeeding, and Joachim Merz. 1996. "Relative Inequality and Poverty in Germany and the United States Using Alternative Equivalence Scales." Review of Income and Wealth 42(4): 381-400.

Burtless, Gary. 1993. "The Contribution of Employment and Hours Changes to Family Income Inequality." American Economic Review 83(2): 131-35.

Coulter, Fiona A.E., Frank A. Cowell, and Stephen P. Jenkins. 1992. "Equivalence Scale Relativities and the Extent of Inequality and Poverty." Economic Journal 102(414): 1067-82.

Doiron, Denise J., and Garry F. Barrett. 1996. "Inequality in Male and Female Earnings: The Role of Hours and Wages." Review of Economics and Statistics 78(3): 410-20.

Figini, Paolo. 1998. "Inequality Measures, Equivalence Scales and Adjustment for Household Size and Composition." Paper presented at the General Conference of the International Association for Research in Income and Wealth, Cambridge, UK.

Förster, Michael, and Marco Mira d'Ercole. 2005. "Income Distribution and Poverty in OECD Countries in the Second Half of the 1990s." OECD Social, Employment and Migration Working Papers No. 22. Paris: OECD.

Freeman, Richard B., and Ronald Schettkat. 2002. "Marketization of Production and the US-Europe Employment Gap." NBER Working Paper No. 8797. Cambridge, MA: National Bureau of Economic Research.

Garhammer, Manfred. 1999. "Time Structures in the European Union: A Comparison of West Germany, UK, Spain and Sweden." In Joachim Merz and Manfred Ehling, eds., *Time Use: Research, Data and Policy*. Baden-Baden: NOMOS Verlagsgesellschaft.

Gershuny, Jonathan. 2000. *Changing Times: Work and Leisure in Postindustrial Society*. Oxford: Oxford University Press.

Gregg, P., K. Hansen, and J. Wadsworth. 1999. "The Rise of the Workless Household." In Paul Gregg and Jonathan Wadsworth, eds., *The State of Working Britain*. Manchester: Manchester University Press.

Hagenaars, Aldi J.M. 1986. *The Perception of Poverty*. Amsterdam: North Holland.

—. 1991. "The Definition and Measurement of Poverty." In Lars Osberg, ed., *Economic Inequality and Poverty: International Perspective*. Armonk, NY: M.E. Sharpe.

Hakim, Catherine. 2000. *Work-Lifestyle Choices in the 21st Century: Preference Theory*. Oxford: Oxford University Press.

International Labour Organization. 2002. "KILM Hours of Work." *Key Indicators of the Labour Market*. Available at http://www.ilo.org/public/english/employment/strat/kilm.

Jahoda, Marie. 1979. "The Psychological Meanings of Unemployment." *New Society* (6 September): 422-25.

Jenkins, Stephen. 1991. "The Measurement of Income Inequality." In Lars Osberg, ed., *Economic Inequality and Poverty: International Perspectives*. Armonk, NY: M.E. Sharpe.

Jenkins, Stephen, and Nigel C. O'Leary. 1996. "Household Income Plus Household Production: The Distribution of Extended Income in the UK." *Review of Income and Wealth* 42(4): 401-19.

Jenkins, Stephen, and Lars Osberg. 2005. "Nobody to Play With? The Implications of Leisure Co-ordination." In D.S. Hamermesh and G.A. Pfann, eds., *The Economics of Time Use*. Amsterdam: Elsevier B.V.

Johnson, Susan, and Peter Kuhn. 2004. "Increasing Male Earnings Inequality in Canada and the United States, 1981-1997: The Role of Hours Changes versus Wage Changes." *Canadian Public Policy* 30(2): 155-76.

Kelvin, Peter, and Joanna Jarrett. 1985. *Unemployment: Its Social Psychological Effects*. Cambridge: Cambridge University Press.

Killingsworth, Mark. 1983. *Labor Supply*. Cambridge Surveys of Economic Literature. Cambridge: Cambridge University Press.

Lee, Chulhee. 2001. "Changes in Employment and Hours, and Family Income Inequality in the U.S., 1969-1989." *International Economic Journal* 15(2): 27-49.

Luxembourg Income Study. Available at http://www.lisproject.org.

Merz, Joachim, and Manfred Ehling, eds., 1999. *Time Use: Research, Data and Policy*. Baden-Baden: Nomos Verlaggesellschaft.

Organization for Economic Cooperation and Development. 1998. *OECD Health Data: A Comparative Analysis of 29 Countries*. CD-ROM. Paris: OECD.

–. 2001. "Activities of the Working Party on Employment and Unemployment Statistics: Estimates of Hours Actually Worked in OECD Countries." Working Party on Statistics,_DSTI/EAS/IND/SWP(2001)16. Paris: OECD.

Osberg, Lars. 2001. "Labour Supply and Inequality Trends in the U.S.A. & Elsewhere." Paper presented at CSLS/IRPP conference, "Linkages between Economic Growth and Inequality," Ottawa, 26 January 2001, and at Canadian Economics Association, McGill University, Montreal, 2 June 2001.

—. 2002. "Trends in Poverty: The UK in International Perspective: How Rates Mislead and Intensity Matters." Working Papers of the Institute for Social and Economic Research, 2006-10. University of Essex, Colchester.

—. 2003a. "Understanding Growth and Inequality Trends: The Role of Labour Supply in the U.S.A. and Germany." *Canadian Public Policy* 29(Supplement): S163-84.

—. 2003b. "Long Run Trends in Income Inequality in the US, UK, Sweden, Germany and Canada: A Birth Cohort View." *Eastern Economic Journal* 29(1): 121-42.

Osberg, Lars, and Shelley Phipps. 1993. "Labour Supply with Quantity Constraints: Results from a Large Sample of Canadian Workers." *Oxford Economic Papers* 45(2): 269-91.

Osberg, Lars, and Kuan Xu. 2000. "International Comparisons of Poverty Intensity: Index Decomposition and Bootstrap Inference." *Journal of Human Resources* 35(1): 51-81.

Phipps, Shelley. 1994. "Maternity and Parental Leaves and Allowances: An International Comparison." Report to Human Resources Development Canada. Department of Economics, Dalhousie University.

—. 1998. "Maternity and Parental Benefits: An International Comparison." Department of Economics, Dalhousie University.

Phipps, Shelley, and Peter Burton. 1995. "Sharing within Families: Implications for the Measurement of Poverty among Individuals in Canada." *Canadian Journal of Economics* 28(1): 177-204.

Phipps, Shelley, and Thesia I. Garner. 1994. "Are Equivalence Scales the Same for the United States and Canada?" *Review of Income and Wealth* 40(1): 1-18.

Scott, Jacqueline, Duane F. Alwin, and Michael Braun. 1996. "Generational Changes in Gender-Role Attitudes: Britain in a Cross-National Perspective." *Sociology* 30(3): 471-92.

United States Bureau of Labor Statistics. 2005. *Comparative Civilian Labour Force Statistics, Ten Countries, 1960-2004.* Available at ftp://ftp.bls.gov/pub/special.requests/ForeignLabor/flslforc.txt.

Zick, Cathleen. 2002. "Clocking the Progress in Time Use Research." *Review of Income and Wealth* 48(3): 435-42.

7
Inequalities in Political and Community Participation

James Curtis, Edward Grabb, and Thomas Perks

The Thesis of Equal Participation

Canada is widely thought to be a comparatively free and democratic society in which all citizens have the same right to influence political decisions and to engage in collective action and community activities. This image of the nation gives rise to what might be called "the thesis of equal participation": that Canadians of different social statuses and economic backgrounds should demonstrate similar levels of involvement in the formal political process and in the "parapolitical" activities among local community interest groups. If this thesis is accurate, the evidence should reveal that Canadians, irrespective of their backgrounds, tend to participate to about the same degree in such activities as voting, discussing politics, working for political groups, joining community associations, and making public protests. Similarly, being involved in primary groups in the community (e.g., interacting with friends, neighbours, or family members outside the home) and volunteering time to help other people should occur at roughly the same rate for individuals from all walks of life.

However, observers have questioned whether there really is such a broad base to political and community participation in Canada. As with the economic and other inequalities discussed in this volume, inequalities in participation have been shown to occur. Studies have revealed that individuals who rank relatively low on various economic and social-status dimensions also have lower participation levels in political and community affairs. This finding has important implications for inequality in Canada. The ability to influence others in the pursuit of both personal and collective interests is normally seen as fundamental to basic human rights; it also affects political processes and policy outcomes that impinge directly on economic inequalities.

This chapter tests the accuracy of the thesis of equal participation by analyzing recent national survey data. We use three surveys, each involving large samples of Canadian adults. The respondents were asked about their involvement in various forms of political and community participation and also about their economic and social-status backgrounds. The surveys did not ask about the same types of community and political activities; they vary considerably in this respect. But the differences among the surveys have certain advantages, because taken together the data cover a broad range of political and community activities and so allow for a comprehensive test of the equality thesis. The surveys also vary somewhat in the economic and social-status measures they apply, again providing a larger and more diverse set of economic and social-status predictors. Included in the surveys are background factors such as educational status, employment status, occupational status, and income (personal and household), which are commonly understood to be the core dimensions of "achieved" socioeconomic status in Canada (see, e.g., Curtis et al. 2004a). The major dimensions of "ascribed" social status are also measured, including race/ethnicity or "visible minority" status, language group, nativity (country of birth), age, gender, and region of residence.

The surveys overlapped somewhat in their measures of political and social participation. Where such overlaps occurred, we chose one indicator from one survey for discussion, typically the most detailed measure. Analyses for comparable measures in the other surveys were also conducted to confirm that the results were largely similar to those presented here, though the additional results are not presented.

The sources of survey data are the first wave of the Equality, Security, and Community Survey (ESCS) completed in 2000; the Canadian wave of the World Values Survey (WVS) conducted in 2000; and the National Survey of Giving, Volunteering, and Participating (NSGVP) from 1997 (for details on the procedures of the three studies, see, respectively, Northrup 2002, Inglehart et al. 2004, and Hall et al. 1998).

In considering the results from each of the data sources, we ask three broad questions: (1) For any particular type of political or community activity, how large is the portion of the adult population involved? (2) Are some economic and social categories of adults more participatory and, if so, which ones? (3) What are the relative effects upon participation of different economic and social statuses?

Before turning to the survey results, we briefly consider two traditions of social theory that tell us to expect results opposite to the thesis of equality of participation. The two approaches to be considered are "relative centrality theory" and "social capital theory." Both these perspectives suggest that we should expect substantial inequality in the political and community participation of Canadians from different economic and social groupings.

Theories of the Effects of Relative Centrality and Social Capital

Research in Canada and other societies, including extensive work in the United States, has frequently shown that there are positive relationships between achieved and ascribed social statuses, on the one hand, and levels of involvement in both politics and community organizations, on the other hand (see, e.g., Curtis 1971; Smith 1975; Curtis and Lambert 1976; Milbrath and Goel 1977; McPherson and Lockwood 1980; Palisi and Palisi 1984; Knoke 1986; Kay et al. 1987; Curtis et al. 1989; Chui et al. 1991; Curtis et al. 1992; Curtis et al. 2001; Curtis and Grabb 2002; Curtis et al. 2004b). These studies have found, for example, that persons with higher education, occupational status, and income are more likely than other people to join and participate in voluntary organizations of various kinds. Some studies also indicate that disadvantaged racial and ethnic groups, such as Canadian visible minorities or American blacks, are less likely to be involved in voluntary associations than are groups higher in the ethnic or racial stratification system. However, other research also suggests that these ethnic or racial differences may be partially the result of socioeconomic inequalities, rather than being due to the effects of racial or ethnic differences themselves (e.g., Smith 1975; Grabb and Curtis 1992; Lin 2000). Along similar lines, other research indicates that males are more likely to participate in voluntary organizations than are females, and middle-aged people are more likely to do so than are older and younger people (e.g., Curtis 1971; Smith 1975; Cutler 1976; McPherson and Lockwood 1980; Edwards et al. 1984; Palisi and Palisi 1984; Knoke 1986; Curtis et al. 1992; Curtis et al. 2001; Curtis et al. 2004b). Similar patterns have been shown for participation in formal politics, such as voting, political party membership, political interest, and so on (e.g., Curtis and Lambert 1976; Milbrath and Goel 1977; Curtis et al. 2004b).

These differences have been explained in a variety of ways. One well-known explanation is that these patterns are largely accounted for by the "relative centrality" of different groups in society (see, e.g., Milbrath and Goel 1977; Curtis et al. 2004b). According to this perspective, some people are more centrally located in resource-rich social networks. Persons from the higher socioeconomic strata and from the more privileged or established racial, ethnic, gender, and age groupings are perhaps the best examples. These individuals generally have more power and resources at their disposal than do their less privileged counterparts. The resources include, for example, greater knowledge, information, and awareness about how various organizations operate in the community and elsewhere. For these reasons, it is argued, people of higher economic or social status are more likely to be active participants in the political processes that help to shape their society.

More recently, some social scientists have used notions of "social capital" as an organizing concept for understanding the ways in which opportunities for political and community participation are unequally distributed in society (e.g., Becker [1964]1993; Bourdieu 1980; Lin 1982, 2000; Coleman 1988; Burt 1992; Putnam 1993, 2000; Portes 1998). The theories that emphasize the concept of social capital have some passing affinity with classical Marxism, most notably the idea that capital is something that is largely invested and accrued by the bourgeoisie. However, social capital theorists typically go beyond the basic Marxist argument, which emphasizes the importance of economic capital, to consider the explanatory import of social capital. This form of capital is viewed as a resource that is usable in the pursuit of valued goals, including access to community and political participation. For most theorists working in this area, social capital is conceptualized as the quantity or the quality of resources that an actor can access or use through different social networks or social relations. The investment of these resources may have planned or expected "returns" for the individual or group that invests them, although it is also possible for the returns or consequences to be unanticipated (e.g., Portes 1998; Lin 2000). Social capital is said to account for differential success in achieving a host of valued outcomes, ranging from participation in democratic institutions to attainment of economic status (e.g., Coleman 1988; Putnam 1993, 2000; Portes and Sensenbrenner 1993; Lin et al. 1981; Burt 1997; Curtis et al. 2003).

Relative centrality theory somewhat predated social capital theory in the literature, but the two perspectives are very similar. Social capital theory places greater emphasis on the resources that are accumulated. This perspective is especially concerned with what these resources are and how they are utilized (e.g., the ways that having greater contact with others who participate in politics will increase participation opportunities). Less attention is given to the economic and social groupings that tend to control more of these resources. In contrast, the relative centrality perspective gives more attention to the types of social and economic backgrounds that are correlated with higher levels of resources and with community and political participation. Notwithstanding these differences, proponents of the two perspectives have come to quite similar conclusions.

Interaction in Informal Social Networks, Association Memberships, and Voting Behaviour

DATA SOURCE AND PROCEDURES, ESCS

We begin with the data on political and social participation available from the first of two waves of the ESCS. This telephone survey was conducted in 2000 as part of the overall ESC project that also generated the present volume. In the ESCS, a representative sample of Canadians aged eighteen and older were interviewed, with over-sampling in metropolitan areas (to increase the representation of visible minorities). From the total sample of 5,152, we selected the subsample of respondents aged twenty and over, which comprised 4,754 cases. Younger respondents, aged eighteen to twenty, were excluded from the analyses because many were still in school and may not have been able to give as much time to political activities as older people.

Our data analysis procedures involved ANOVA with Multiple Classification Analysis (MCA). ANOVA/MCA assesses the effects of a particular predictor variable on a dependent variable both before controls and while controlling for the effects of other factors. The procedure yields mean scores for the dependent variable for each category of the predictor variable, with adjustments for the effects of the control factors and statistical interactions, and provides an F-test for statistical significance. The procedure also generates eta measures for the relationships before controls and beta coefficients, or partial correlation ratios, for the relationship for each predictor in the controlled analysis. These coefficients, when squared, roughly indicate the proportion of the total variance in the dependent variable accounted for by each predictor when partialing out the effects of the other predictors.

Measures of Community and Political Involvement

The ESCS featured questions on household structures, income, and attitudes about various topics. There were also questions on informal social networks, or interaction with family members, friends, and neighbours. As well, questions were asked about voting in the last provincial and federal elections.

Finally, the ESCS contained some questions on voluntary association affilia-
tions. We have used the data from the latter three sets of questions. These
were the only activity measures in either the first or the second wave of the
ESCS. Our activity measures, then, were: (1) an index of interaction in informal networks of family, friends, and neighbours; (2) voting in the last provincial and federal elections; and (3) number of voluntary association
memberships. (Appendix A gives more details on the questions asked and
our procedures for coding the responses.)

Measures of Economic and Social Statuses

In regard to economic and social status factors, the ESCS provided measures
of each respondent's achieved socioeconomic statuses, i.e., education level,
employment status, occupation, and personal income. Questions were also
asked about the following ascribed statuses: age, gender, language group,
nativity, and visible minority status. The latter measure was especially important because it allowed us to consider Aboriginal peoples as a distinct
group. See Table 7.1 for the categories for each measure.

RESULTS FROM THE ESCS

Overall Involvement Levels

We begin with the overall levels of activity reported in the ESCS. The questionnaire asked about the frequency of involvement with family members
living outside the home, with close friends, and with neighbours. The respondents were asked to respond, for each of these types of involvement, on
a seven-point scale ranging from "every day" to "several times per year" and
"less often." There were reasonably high levels of involvement, particularly
in the case of friends. For all three types of involvement, the most frequent
response was "at least once per week" (26.9 percent for family, 31.7 percent
for friends, and 23.6 percent for neighbours). The "every day" responses were
13.9 percent for family members, 18.1 percent for close friends, and 21.8
percent for neighbours. Only a small minority saw family members (10.0
percent), friends (4.0 percent), and neighbours (14.0 percent) less than several times per year. For the analyses for Tables 7.1 and 7.2, responses for all
three types of contact with others were summed together for an Index of
Interaction in Informal Social Networks, which had a range from 7 (for low
activity) to 21 (for high activity). (See Appendix A for more details.)

Turning to voting activity, we see that 73.6 percent reported voting in
the last provincial election and 76.8 percent said that they voted in the last

federal election. When the two elections were considered together, 80.9 percent voted in at least one of the elections, and 69.7 percent voted in both of them; 19.1 percent reported that they had not voted in either election.

Respondents were asked whether they belonged to or volunteered with each of six types of voluntary associations, plus any "others." The overall result was that 28.7 percent reported having no memberships, 17.7 percent indicated that they had only one membership, and 53.6 percent stated that they had multiple memberships.

Thus, these three measures suggest that sizable proportions (though by no means all) of the adult population were involved in community and political activities. Fully three-quarters of respondents reported that they engaged in the (not very time-consuming) activity of voting in provincial or federal elections. Also, about three-quarters had at least one association affiliation (although there is no measure of their level of activity in these memberships). And 85 percent or more had contact with family members, friends, and neighbours at least a few times per year.

Assessing Equality-Inequality

In Table 7.1, we turn to the key question: are levels of involvement in the three forms of community and political activity related to the economic and social status variables? For the measure of involvement in informal networks, the higher socioeconomic status categories, particularly for education and income, were *least* involved. We also found the following: retired people and homemakers were higher in involvement than were the employed or the unemployed; there was no difference between males and females; older people were more involved than younger people; the English were more involved than the French or other language groups; visible minorities were less involved than others; the native-born were more involved than the foreign-born; and people living in the provinces east of Quebec were more involved than people residing in other provinces.

The effects of socioeconomic status on voting behaviour over the two elections and on voluntary association membership were positive; that is, the higher the respondent's socioeconomic status, the greater was his or her involvement in these two types of activity. There was curvilinearity in the relationship between age and association involvement, although not for voting, and there were no gender differences. Aboriginal people, other ethnic or visible minorities, and the foreign-born were considerably less involved than other respondents in each of these two measures. The very low voting rate

Table 7.1

Economic and social status categories and mean involvement levels in informal networks, voting, and community organization memberships (ESCS national sample, 2000)

Economic/social status categories	N	Involvement in informal networks	Voting over two elections	Voluntary association memberships
Total sample/grand means	4,754	11.93	1.51	2.28
Educational level attained				
Elementary school or less	201	12.25	1.53	1.18
Some secondary school	598	12.48	1.55	1.60
Completed secondary school	1,111	12.20	1.48	1.98
Some tech./comm. college	305	11.68	1.48	2.21
Completed tech./comm. college	852	11.94	1.53	2.27
Some university	363	11.76	1.50	2.59
Bachelor's degree	897	11.51	1.51	2.85
Graduate degree	331	11.38	1.53	3.28
eta significance		(.12)***	(.03)*	(.23)***
Employment status				
Retired/student/homemaker	1,457	12.29	1.54	2.22
Unemployed/looking for work	261	11.88	1.21	1.71
Employed	3,017	11.76	1.52	2.36
eta significance		(.08)***	(.09)***	(.07)***
Occupational status				
Self-employed professionals	38	11.35	1.42	2.67
Employed professionals	508	11.63	1.72	3.02
High-level managers	130	12.07	1.73	3.26
Semi-professionals	457	11.82	1.55	2.55
Technicians	99	11.61	1.54	1.73
Mid-managers	271	12.20	1.58	2.85
Supervisors	101	12.22	1.69	2.42
Foremen/women	65	12.35	1.63	2.10
Skilled clerical/sales	310	11.71	1.62	2.23
Skilled crafts	272	12.10	1.55	2.01
Farmers	68	13.31	1.72	2.78
Semi-skilled clerical/sales	478	11.69	1.45	1.91
Semi-skilled manual	265	12.02	1.46	1.66
Unskilled clerical/sales	294	11.97	1.57	2.44
Unskilled manual	416	12.51	1.35	1.54
Farm labourers	52	11.97	1.66	2.00
All others	930	11.84	1.31	2.16
eta significance		(.11)***	(.18)***	(.20)***

▶

◀ TABLE 7.1

Economic/social status categories	N	Involvement in informal networks	Voting over two elections	Voluntary association memberships
Personal income level				
No income	1,256	12.12	1.50	2.03
< $5,000	290	12.17	1.35	2.16
$5,000 to 9,999	220	11.51	1.40	2.18
$10,000 to 14,999	335	11.75	1.33	2.05
$15,000 to 19,999	288	12.05	1.40	2.01
$20,000 to 29,999	597	12.00	1.51	2.16
$30,000 to 39,999	590	11.83	1.55	2.35
$40,000 to 49,999	353	12.03	1.66	2.65
$50,000 to 59,999	298	11.80	1.66	2.80
$60,000 to 69,000	200	11.60	1.65	2.50
>$70,000	207	11.64	1.65	3.03
eta significance		(.07)***	(.13)***	(.14)***
Age				
20-29	881	11.60	1.06	2.11
30-39	1,158	11.78	1.41	2.32
40-49	1,158	11.76	1.61	2.42
50-59	686	11.99	1.74	2.38
60-69	431	12.52	1.78	2.20
70+	440	12.81	1.79	2.08
eta significance		(.13)***	(.32)***	(.06)**
Gender				
Male	2,199	12.00	1.50	2.23
Female	2,555	11.87	1.52	2.32
eta significance		(.02) n.s.	(.01) n.s.	(.02) n.s.
Language group				
English	3,344	12.23	1.54	2.47
French	857	11.30	1.68	1.66
Other	514	11.05	1.00	1.78
eta significance		(.16)***	(.24)***	(.13)***
Visible minority status				
Not visible minority	4,002	12.07	1.58	2.36
Aboriginal	106	12.16	1.33	1.99
Other visible minority	479	10.67	0.97	1.67
eta significance		(.15)***	(.24)***	(.10)*
Nativity				
Foreign-born	1,012	11.01	1.09	1.92
Born in Canada	3,701	12.17	1.62	2.38
eta significance		(.16)***	(.27)***	(.08)***

▶

◀ TABLE 7.1

Economic/social status categories	N	Involvement in informal networks	Voting over two elections	Voluntary association memberships
Province				
NF	187	13.55	1.63	2.10
PE	184	13.08	1.74	2.68
NS	196	12.98	1.64	2.55
NB	187	12.71	1.71	2.63
QC	982	11.16	1.60	2.78
ON	1,174	11.80	1.40	2.10
MB	369	12.45	1.58	2.60
SK	377	12.18	1.65	2.88
AB	376	11.80	1.49	2.85
BC	722	11.63	1.29	2.28
eta significance		(.22)**	(.17)***	(.16)***

NOTE: The number of cases, N, varied depending on non-response to the questions on social and political participation and the predictor variables. These Ns are the largest numbers of cases for the status category for any of the analyses presented in the table.
*** Refers to statistically significant at the $p < .001$ level; ** = at the $p < .01$ level; * = at the $p < .05$ level; n.s. = not statistically significant.

among minorities (other than Aboriginals) is probably partly due to the recent arrival of some minority group members in Canada and their consequent ineligibility to vote.

In Table 7.2 we see the same relationships expressed in a different way, as betas, and with controls for the effects of other variables. The betas show the relative impact of each status dimension on the three dependent measures, net of the effects of the other status dimensions. Most but not all of the statistically significant relationships that were found before controls and shown in Table 7.1 remained significant in Table 7.2. Involvement in informal networks was least affected by the social status dimensions, judging from the lower R^2 of 0.101. Education and occupation were the only significant predictors among the four socioeconomic status characteristics, and they continued to show inverse relationships with involvement in informal networks, i.e., the higher the status, the lower the involvement. Age and nativity were the strongest social status predictors of voting, with the other factors each accounting for less than 1 percent of the variance (and with no significant effects for gender and language group). Education, occupational status, and province of residence were the strongest predictors for association

TABLE 7. 2

Relative effects (betas) for economic and social status factors in controlled analyses of the ESCS 2000 data

Economic/ social status indicators	Dependent measures		
	Interaction with informal networks	Voting over two elections	Number of voluntary association memberships
Educational level	.06 *	.07 **	.22 ***
Employment status	.04 n.s.	.05 *	.03 n.s.
Occupational status	.08 *	.08 *	.11 ***
Personal income level	.05 n.s.	.06 *	.08 **
Age group	.09 ***	.31 ***	.05 n.s.
Gender	.03 n.s.	.01 n.s.	.02 n.s.
Language group	.06 *	.04 n.s.	.03 n.s.
Visible minority status	.07 ***	.06 ***	.07 ***
Nativity	.12 ***	.20 ***	.05 *
Province	.16 ***	.09 ***	.15 ***
(R^2)	(0.101)	(0.217)	(0.121)

*** Refers to statistically significant at the $p < .001$ level; ** = at the $p < .01$ level; * = at the $p < .05$ level; n.s. = not statistically significant.

membership, with three ascribed characteristics (age, gender, and language) and employment status having no significant effects. The variance explained for voting reached 21.7 percent, while for number of association memberships, it was 12.1 percent.

Four Types of Political Involvement

DATA SOURCE AND PROCEDURES, WVS

Our second set of results comes from a national sample survey of adult Canadians in 2000. The data were collected as part of the larger set of World Values Surveys collected in 1999-2001. These were international surveys of more than fifty countries conducted by Ronald Inglehart and associates (for details, see Inglehart et al. 2004). The present analyses are limited to the Canadian respondents aged twenty-one and older ($n = 1,497$). Some younger respondents were excluded from the analyses for the same reasons that were applied in the case of the ESCS.

Our procedures for the analysis of the WVS data were identical to those used for the ESCS. We begin by describing the overall distribution of responses for the activity measures we selected, and then we look at how the activities are related to economic and social statuses. The assessment of these results is followed by a consideration of the relative effects of the social background factors on voluntary activity. Again, the analyses involve ANOVA/MCA.

Measures of Political and Public Protest Activities
Four measures of political activities from the WVS were employed here. (It should be noted that the WVS data also had measures of voting and voluntary association membership and that, in analyses not reported here, the patterns we found for these measures were similar to those reported above for voting and association involvement using the ESCS.) The measures we chose from the WVS were: discussing politics, interest in politics, political group activity, and public protest activity. The measure of public protest activity was based on responses to a series of questions having to do with: signing a petition, joining a boycott, attending lawful demonstrations, joining strikes, or occupying buildings or factories. The responses for each of these activities, which were arrayed on a three-point scale ("have done," "might do," or "would do"), were summed for each respondent to give her or him an overall measure of participation in public protest activity. This measure ranged from 5 (low protest activity) to 15 (high protest activity). (Appendix B gives further details on the measures.)

Economic and Social Status Measures
Nine different measures of economic and social status were available from the WVS, and these were examined for their possible relationships to political activity. The economic status measures were: education, employment status, occupational status, and household income. The social status measures were: age, gender, language group, race, and region. Table 7.3 provides details on the categories used for each of these variables.

RESULTS FROM THE WVS

Overall Levels of Involvement
In the WVS, nearly half of the respondents said that they were either "very" interested (11.9 percent) or "somewhat" interested (37.3 percent) in politics. Only 12.1 percent discussed politics "often," but another 52.2 percent did so

TABLE 7.3

Economic and social status categories and mean levels for interest in politics, discussing politics, political group activity, and public protest actions (WVS national sample, 2000)

Economic/social status categories	N	Interest in politics	How often discuss politics	Political group activity	Public protest actions
Total sample/grand mean	1,497	2.44	1.78	.10	9.07
Education level attained					
Some primary	37	2.14	1.50	.04	7.10
Primary completion	49	2.27	1.59	.01	7.93
Some secondary	243	2.34	1.64	.07	8.32
Secondary completion	342	2.26	1.67	.06	8.63
Some college	105	2.26	1.74	.09	9.30
College completion	271	2.37	1.73	.04	9.29
Some university	137	2.67	2.00	.12	9.70
University completion	314	2.80	2.03	.23	9.99
eta significance		(.22)***	(.25)***	(.19)***	(.32)***
Employment status					
Full-time	779	2.47	1.82	.11	9.37
Part-time	134	2.17	1.65	.10	9.41
Other	584	2.46	1.76	.09	8.58
eta significance		(.09)*	(.07)*	(.03) n.s.	(.17)***
Occupation status					
Managerial	108	2.49	1.89	.06	8.88
Professional	267	2.83	2.03	.17	10.04
Supervisors	91	2.65	1.85	.14	9.13
Foreman etc.	93	2.51	1.84	.09	8.83
Skilled clerical/sales	304	2.46	1.78	.13	8.87
Skilled manual	344	2.22	1.66	.09	8.95
Semi-skilled manual	166	2.31	1.63	.04	9.05
Unskilled	123	2.08	1.58	.02	8.11
eta significance		(.24)***	(.23)***	(.13)**	(.23)***
Household income level					
<$12,500	89	2.26	1.64	.01	8.11
$12,501-$20,000	156	2.27	1.60	.08	8.08
$20,001-$27,500	194	2.10	1.64	.09	8.77
$27,501-$35,000	183	2.27	1.69	.04	8.85
$35,001-$42,500	165	2.42	1.77	.07	8.96
$42,501-$50,000	132	2.61	1.81	.11	9.20
$50,001-$62,500	163	2.62	1.89	.12	9.56
$62,501-$75,000	155	2.49	1.87	.15	9.16

▶

◄ TABLE 7.3

Economic/social status categories	N	Interest in politics	How often discuss politics	Political group activity	Public protest actions
$75,001-$100,000	144	2.80	1.97	.10	10.00
> $100,000	116	2.74	1.98	.25	9.87
eta significance		(.23)***	(.20)***	(.15)**	(.26)***
Age					
21-24	116	2.21	1.67	.10	9.43
25-34	318	2.23	1.69	.04	9.27
35-44	375	2.44	1.78	.10	9.31
45-54	283	2.52	1.87	.10	9.32
55-64	191	2.64	1.84	.02	9.24
65-97	214	2.61	1.82	.09	7.68
eta significance		(.16)**	(.11)*	(.11)*	(.26)***
Gender					
Male	794	2.54	1.87	.13	9.20
Female	703	2.33	1.68	.07	8.92
eta significance		(.11)**	(.14)**	(.09)**	(.06) n.s.
Language group					
English	1,031	2.56	1.80	.11	9.23
French	382	2.16	1.69	.07	8.84
Other	83	2.25	1.87	.07	8.07
eta significance		(.18)**	(.08)*	(.06) n.s.	(.13)**
Race					
White	1,349	2.44	1.77	.10	9.12
Black	35	2.42	1.84	.01	9.31
Native	15	2.12	1.88	.01	8.54
Other	97	2.46	1.52	.06	8.12
eta significance		(.03) n.s.	(.06)*	(.06) n.s.	(.11)**
Region					
Atlantic	119	2.45	1.66	.11	9.25
Quebec	390	2.14	1.70	.07	8.85
Ontario	560	2.57	1.80	.09	9.16
Prairies	251	2.56	1.86	.14	9.06
BC	176	2.55	1.86	.15	9.08
eta significance		(.19)**	(.11)*	(.08)*	(.05) n.s.

NOTE: The number of cases, N, varied depending on non-response to the questions on social and political participation and the predictor variables. These Ns are the largest numbers of cases for the status category for any of the analyses presented in the table.
*** Refers to statistically significant at the $p < .001$ level; ** = at the $p < .01$ level; * = at the $p < .05$ level; n.s. = not statistically significant.

"occasionally." Also, only about 6.7 percent reported membership in what the respondent identified as "political parties or groups," with 4.1 percent saying that they were simply a member of such a group, and another 2.6 percent indicating that they did volunteer work for the group. If we look at the other end of the continuum and consider those who were completely uninvolved in political parties or groups , we see considerably higher rates of non-participation: about half of the respondents were "not very" interested (29.2 percent) or "not at all" interested (21.5 percent) in politics, while 35.9 percent never discussed politics with others, and fully 93.3 percent were not involved in political groups in any way.

The WVS also measured levels of involvement in the five types of public . protest. Here we found, once more, that participation levels were generally low, with the exception of signing petitions; 73.7 percent of respondents reported signing a petition, while another 18.1 percent thought that they might do so sometime in the future, and only 8.2 percent said that they would never do so. However, only about one-fifth (20.9 percent) had ever joined a boycott, and 37.4 percent said that they would never do so. With respect to attending demonstrations, 19.7 percent indicated that they had done so, while 39.9 percent indicated that they would never do so. The rates of involvement were even lower for "joining a lawful strike," with only 7.2 percent having done this, and 67.4 percent saying that they would never do it. Finally, only 3.0 percent had occupied facilities, and 79.9 percent said that they would never engage in such behaviour. When the responses were summed across these items, to create an index of public protest activities, the sample had an average score of 9.07 out of a possible 15.

Assessing Equality-Inequality in Involvement
We now ask how economic and social statuses are related to levels of involvement in the four political activities. In other words, do all categories of Canadians get involved more or less equally, despite the low overall levels of involvement, or do people from more advantaged groups get involved more than others?

Table 7.3 provides data on the relationship between the four forms of political participation and the nine different measures of economic and social status. Based on the relative centrality perspective, we would expect the following groups to be higher in political involvement than their less advantaged or less "central" counterparts: the more highly educated, those with higher incomes, those with higher occupational status, English-speakers, whites, the native-born, males, the middle-aged, and those living in the more economically powerful regions of the country, especially Ontario.

Overall, the findings confirm many, though not all, of these expectations. As predicted, education, occupational status, and income have statistically significant relationships with all four measures of political participation, and in the expected direction (although the relationships with employment status were less clear). That is, the more highly educated respondents and those with higher occupational status and incomes were more likely than other people to show interest in politics, to discuss politics with others, to be involved in political groups, and to engage in public protests.

Age and region were significantly related to all four of the political activity measures. As expected, the middle-aged expressed greater political interest and discussed politics more than did younger people and (particularly) older people. The younger age group (21-24) was comparatively high on political group involvement and protest activity. As for region, residents of the more powerful or more prosperous areas, especially Ontario and the Western provinces, tended to be higher on political interest and discussing politics. Respondents from the Western region also showed higher levels of political group involvement.

Moving on to other ascribed statuses in Table 7.3, we see that language group is related to political interest and discussing politics, with English-speakers higher than French-speakers, as predicted by the relative centrality hypothesis. Race appeared to be related to only two of the measures of political activity: discussing politics and public protest. Whites were not higher in involvement than Blacks, and they were lower than Blacks in discussing politics and protest activity.

We also conducted multivariate analyses, using ANOVA/MCA, to study the relationship between each of the status variables and the activity measures, while simultaneously controlling for the effects of all the other status variables. The results shown in Table 7.4 were largely the same as those seen in Table 7.3. The patterns did not change in direction, even with the inclusion of controls, although some of the relationships were no longer statistically significant after controls. In Table 7.4 we see that, with controls, one of the effects of occupational status (for political discussion) was no longer significant. The effect before controls may have been largely due to the strong joint effect of educational status on both occupation and the political

Table 7.4

Relative effects (betas) for economic and social status effects in controlled analyses of the WVS 2000 data

Economic/ social status indicators	Dependent measures			
	Interest in politics	How often discuss politics	Political group activity	Public protest actions
Educational level	.14 **	.18 ***	.19 ***	.25 ***
Employment status	.04 n.s.	.01 n.s.	.03 n.s.	.05 n.s.
Occupational status	.14 ***	.11 n.s.	.12 *	.11 **
Household income level	.13 **	.09 n.s.	.11 *	.12 *
Age group	.17 ***	.13 ***	.15 ***	.21 ***
Gender	.11 ***	.14 ***	.09 **	.04 n.s.
Language group	.06 n.s.	.03 n.s.	.04 n.s.	.12 **
Race	.05 n.s.	.05 n.s.	.03 n.s.	.14 ***
Region	.14 n.s.	.08 n.s.	.07 n.s.	.08 n.s.
(R^2)	(0.160)	(0.125)	(0.086)	(0.210)

*** Refers to statistically significant at the $p < .001$ level; ** = at the $p < .01$ level; * = at the $p < .05$ level; n.s. = not statistically significant.

discussion measure. The same change occurred for the effect of income on political discussion. This outcome also appears to have resulted mainly from the effects of educational status differences. In addition, three effects of race (on interest, discussion, and group activity), three effects of language group (on interest, discussion, and group activity), and the effects of region on all four dependent variables were not statistically significant after controlling for education, occupation, and income. These changes from the patterns found in Table 7.3 suggest that it was mainly differences resulting from the three socioeconomic characteristics that made for the apparent bivariate differences by race, language, and region in regard to the political involvement measures.

The R^2 statistic showed that the economic and status dimensions best explained variance in public protest actions ($R^2 = 0.210$), followed by interest in politics (0.160), and discussing politics (0.125). For each type of activity, education status and age were comparatively strong predictors, surpassing the effects of the other achieved and ascribed statuses.

Volunteering Time to Others and Giving to Charities

Data Source and Procedures, NSGVP

The data for our final set of analyses come from the 1997 National Survey of Giving, Volunteering, and Participating (NSGVP). This survey was conducted by Statistics Canada through telephone interviews with a representative sample of Canadians aged fifteen and over. The content focus of the interviews was the three areas cited in the survey's title: giving to charities, volunteering time in the aid of organizations and individuals, and association participation. Each of these topics received several minutes of attention in the interviews, which averaged thirty-five minutes in length. We shall draw on measures for the first two topics here. (This survey also provided data on voting, association memberships, and socializing with family members, friends, and neighbours, which showed patterns similar to the results for the ESCS as reported above; see Hall et al. 1998.)

We chose as a working sub-sample from the NSGVP data file only respondents aged twenty-five and over (n = 15,912). The Statistics Canada coding for the NSGVP data placed all respondents under age twenty-four together in the same ten-year category (aged fifteen to twenty-four), at least for the coding in the public-use data file. Therefore, respondents in their teens could not be separated from respondents in their early twenties. The age restriction of twenty-five and older for our working sample was chosen to assure that virtually all the respondents included in our analyses had completed their schooling and had started their adult lives, so that their volunteering and giving would not be school-related. The statistical procedures we employed were the same as those used above for the data from the ESCS and WVS.

We chose four alternative measures of adult community participation, each of which refers to the last twelve-month period: total number of hours spent volunteering for organizations, total number of organizations volunteered with, total number of donations to organizations, and total amount of dollars donated. (See Appendix C for more details.)

The measures for socioeconomic background characteristics were: level of education completed, current employment status, and personal income (persons with incomes above $80,000 per year were not included in the public-use sample to preserve respondent anonymity). The other social status measures were: gender, age group, language group, nativity, and region. Measures of race and ethnicity were not made available in the public-use data.

RESULTS FROM THE NSGVP

Overall Participation Levels

As Table 7.5 shows, in the grand means for the overall sample, respondents averaged ninety-three hours of volunteering over the past year and averaged a little more than one organization assisted per respondent. The average amount of donations given in the year was $285, with a mean number of between four and five donations for the year.

Assessing Equality-Inequality

Each socioeconomic status characteristic was positively related to all four forms of involvement. This is perhaps not surprising in the instances of dollars given and number of donations, because those with higher economic status have more money. However, the positive effect of socioeconomic status also extends to the amount of time given to volunteering and to the number of organizational memberships. This is surprising in the sense that people with higher education and occupation often work more hours per week than do other individuals. Yet volunteering may be easier for those who are more highly educated and have higher status occupations, since their work time is more flexible, in most instances, than is the case for people with lower education and lower-status jobs. With respect to the ascribed characteristics of age, language, nativity, and region, we found that young people, Francophones, the foreign-born, and those residing in Quebec were the least participatory.

Table 7.6 shows the same relationships, but now with multivariate controls. Education was the most consistent predictor, always having a positive relationship with the dependent measures, followed by age and region, both of which had the same relationships to involvement as they did before controls. As we might expect, income remained positively related to dollars donated and to number of donations; interestingly, income had no significant effect on time volunteered, after controls. Number of donations ($R^2 = 0.163$) was most closely associated with the economic and social status dimensions, and volunteer hours ($R^2 = 0.023$) was only weakly predicted by these factors.

Interpretations of the Results

We have presented representative survey evidence on patterns of political and community participation in Canada across economic and social status categories. Our main purpose has been to assess what we have called "the thesis of equal participation," the idea that, in a free and democratic nation

Table 7. 5

Economic and social status categories and mean levels of volunteering (hours to organization) and donations (amounts and number) (NSGVP national sample, 1997)

Economic/social status categories	N	Total hours volunteering	Total number of volunteer organizations	Total amount of donations given ($)	Total number of donations given
Total sample/grand means	15,912	93	1.12	285	4.42
Educational status					
Less than high school	4,164	61	0.68	187	3.42
High school diploma	2,707	92	1.04	233	4.28
Some post-secondary	1,240	115	1.18	251	4.37
Post-secondary diploma	5,229	96	1.21	293	4.72
University degree	2,572	104	1.70	488	5.58
eta significance		(.11)***	(.25)***	(.14)***	(.19)***
Employment status					
Full-time	7,659	86	1.18	289	4.56
Part-time	1,734	114	1.46	231	4.90
Not working	6,519	95	0.96	267	4.12
eta significance		(.04)**	(.12)***	(.03)*	(.07)***
Personal income level					
< $20,000	7,647	87	0.98	192	3.75
$20,000 to 39,999	4,884	92	1.15	290	4.59
$40,000 to 59,999	2,362	107	1.35	392	5.49
$60,000 to 79,999	1,019	110	1.49	683	6.03
eta significance		(.04)**	(.12)***	(.18)***	(.20)***
Gender					
Male	6,823	95	1.05	290	4.04
Female	9,089	92	1.17	281	4.70
eta significance		(.01) n.s.	(.05)***	(.01) n.s.	(.09)***
Age					
25-34	3,636	75	1.01	163	3.49
35-44	4,280	94	1.31	256	4.51
45-54	2,883	104	1.24	324	4.84
55-64	2,109	98	1.08	342	4.89
65 +	3,004	99	0.89	396	4.68
eta significance		(.05)***	(.12)***	(.12)***	(.14)***
Language of interview					
English	12,880	96	1.20	332	4.68
French	3,032	79	0.77	124	3.32
eta significance		(.03)**	(.13)***	(.11)***	(.15)***

▶

◄ TABLE 7.5

Economic/social status categories	N	Total hours volunteering	Total number of volunteer organizations	Total amount of donations given ($)	Total number of donations given
Nativity					
Foreign-born	1,810	93	0.99	331	3.52
Born in Canada	13,869	93	1.14	279	4.49
eta significance		(.01) n.s.	(.03)**	(.02) n.s.	(.05)***
Region					
Atlantic	3,198	95	1.20	263	5.38
Quebec	2,858	77	0.74	128	3.19
Ontario	4,809	98	1.07	333	4.57
Prairies	3,659	99	1.40	365	4.56
BC	1,388	111	1.17	297	3.81
eta significance		(.05)**	(.16)***	(.12)***	(.19)***

NOTE: The number of cases, N, varied depending on non-response to the questions on social and political participation and the predictor variables. These Ns are the largest numbers of cases for the status category for any of the analyses presented in the table. *** Refers to statistically significant at the $p < .001$ level; ** = at the $p < .01$ level; * = at the $p < .05$ level; n.s. = not statistically significant.

such as Canada, levels of activity in politics and community life should be roughly the same for all citizens, regardless of their social background or position in the general system of social inequality. We counter-posed this thesis with both relative centrality theory and social capital theory, each of which argues that, on the contrary, inequalities in social and economic background are clearly correlated with public participation in political and community activities.

Previous research and theory on the subject suggests that the latter two theories are more accurate than is the equal participation thesis. Social groupings that enjoy more relative centrality in our society (e.g., those with higher education and higher socioeconomic status, English speakers, whites or non-visible minorities, the Canadian-born, males, and the middle-aged) tend to be more highly involved in various forms of political and community activity. Social capital theory leads to the same predictions, which are based on the slightly different premise that the groups that are more active in political and community life are able to capitalize on their accumulated advantages in the form of social contacts, interpersonal experiences, and other social resources.

Table 7. 6

Relative effects (betas) for economic and social status factors in controlled analyses of the NSGVP 1997 data

Economic/ social status indicators	Dependent measures			
	Volunteer hours	Number of volunteering organizations	Amount of dollars donated	Number of donations
Education	.13 ***	.23 ***	.12 ***	.17 ***
Employment status	.07 ***	.07 ***	.04 ***	.06 ***
Personal income level	.02 n.s.	.07 ***	.17 ***	.22 ***
Age group	.07 ***	.09 ***	.16 ***	.22 ***
Gender	.02 *	.06 ***	.03 ***	.15 ***
Language of interview	.01 n.s.	.03 n.s.	.06 *	.06 ***
Nativity	.01 *	.05 ***	.07 n.s.	.07 ***
Region	.05 ***	.13 ***	.17 ***	.17 ***
(R^2)	(0.023)	(0.105)	(0.078)	(0.163)

*** Refers to statistically significant at the $p < .001$ level; ** = at the $p < .01$ level; * = at the $p < .05$ level; n.s. = not statistically significant.

Predictions based on the relative centrality and social capital perspectives received partial but not complete support in the results from our analyses of three Canadian national surveys. The strongest and most consistent support across the different types of involvement was found for educational status, occupational status, income, and age. For some types of activity, the two perspectives also receive support with respect to the effects of gender and language group. The patterns of results for race, visible minority status, and nativity were much less consistent with, and sometimes even contradicted, the relative centrality or social capital argument. Moreover, controlled analyses showed that some of the effects of race and nativity that obtained without controls occurred because of differences in education, occupation, and income across these two characteristics. However, these findings may not so much call into question the relative centrality or social capital arguments as to suggest a specification of them. Namely, the results may demonstrate that power and resource differences that are rooted in achieved statuses such as occupation, income, and education (particularly the latter) are the key explanations for why such ascribed statuses as race, visible minority status, and nativity are correlated with political and community activity.

Still, the findings appear to cast doubt on any comprehensive claims that political and community participation is easily understood or explained as simply the consequence of the relative centrality or social capital accumulation deriving from all the various forms of social status. Instead, a more complex set of processes seems to be at work in making some individuals more likely than others to join and participate in various political and community activities. Also, the R^2 statistics, which indicate only very modest levels of explained variance for most of our dependent measures, show that political and community involvements were not accounted for primarily by processes associated with economic and social status. The latter factors were of some importance as predictors of activity but by no means accounted for most of it. Much variance is left unexplained after taking the effects of the various economic and social status categories into account. Therefore, there is much more at issue in explaining political and community participation. Also, as we have seen, formal memberships in community organizations and voting are better predicted by economic and social status than are interactions in informal networks and volunteer hours assisting others. Furthermore, the effects of educational status and the other socioeconomic status measures are in the reverse direction for involvement in informal networks. In this instance, the higher the status, the lower the involvement in such activities.

The patterns for regions were also rather complex and do not lend themselves to easy generalizations with respect to our competing hypotheses. Perhaps our finding of higher involvement in some political activities among Ontarians or people from the Western provinces can be traced to relatively greater socioeconomic advantages in these regions, in which case there may be some support here for the relative centrality or social capital explanations. (Note, though, that we found a different pattern for involvement in informal networks.) Just as people of lower socioeconomic status were, if anything, more likely to be involved in informal social networks, so too were people in the less advantaged provinces of Eastern Canada more likely to have high levels of participation in informal networks.

Also consistent with this interpretation of economic effects are the results showing that respondents from Quebec, a somewhat disadvantaged province by some economic indicators, were lower than other respondents on both volunteering and giving. (These activities were also comparatively low for French-speaking respondents, as were voluntary association memberships.) An alternative interpretation of these results for Quebec is that they denote a more collective or social democratic model of how people who are in need should be helped. Quebeckers may be more likely than people from other provinces to see assisting others as the responsibility of the state and not of individual citizens (e.g., Grabb and Curtis 1992, 2005, Chapters 8, 11).

What should we make of those relationships that appear to counter the relative centrality and social capital arguments? One interpretation would be that those who are low in social status do what they can. If opportunities for formal community involvement and political participation are limited, or if necessary resources and skills are scarce, people of lower social status may engage in more of what is available and easy to achieve, i.e., informal social networking. It may also be that higher-status individuals have less free time, at the appropriate instances, for interacting with family, friends, and neighbours, and they may also be more geographically mobile, so that they tend to move farther away from family and friends than do other people. As a result, higher-status groups may also stay in the same neighbourhood for less time, on average, than do lower-status people. Each of these is a possible partial explanation of the results. These interpretations also remind us that the usual arguments of relative centrality theory and social capital theory may have less applicability to informal network involvement.

The two theories may well be more helpful in explaining involvement in *formal* modes of community and political action. Political activities, in par- ticular, may require less intimate contact and also may appear to be more imposing, less comfortable, and occupy a less penetrable terrain for those without a great deal of experience with them. Research consistent with this line of reasoning has shown that, for any age sub-group of either gender, people with early experience in voluntary community activities are the most likely to be currently involved in such activities (Curtis and Perks 2006; cf. Jones 2000).

In general, we have found that, apart from voting in elections and a few other exceptions, it is rare for the majority of Canadians to become involved in most types of community action or political activity. Perhaps the low level of involvement in behaviours such as public protests is an indication that most Canadians are relatively happy about the way things are in their coun- try and so feel no strong need to participate in political life. Nevertheless, just as political activities are partially structured by economic and social sta- tus, it is also true that those who are higher in status tend to be the most involved in protest actions. Because we would assume that these individuals should be happier about the status quo than those who are lower in social status, this pattern may seem surprising. One possibility is that such actions on the part of those in advantaged situations are mainly directed toward helping and promoting the interests of others less fortunate than themselves. An alternative interpretation for the greater involvement of more privileged groups is that they feel a greater need to protect their own interests through such activities and also possess the material and other resources necessary for participation.

Another possibility to consider is that relative centrality or social capital may explain some kinds of political and organizational involvement better than others. To some theorists, the existence of a wide range of voluntary political and community activities, as well as broad involvement by less powerful groups, may be indicative of a democratic and "pluralist" power structure in society (e.g., Dahl 1982). A different view, however, must also be considered: it may be that people with more centrality or social capital are simply being strategic and selective when deciding which activities they choose to pursue and which organizations they choose to join. Some writers argue that voluntary organizations serve as the representatives of competing or conflicting interest groups, some of which have a much greater capacity than others to ensure that their particular policy preferences are implemented (e.g., Hayes 1978, 1983). From this perspective, we would expect that people with higher social status – those with more relative centrality or more social capital – would concentrate on truly influential organizations and activities, rather than participating in the whole range, as the best way to maintain their greater power or privilege (see Curtis et al. 2004b).

Evidence from other research suggests that such a pattern may be at work. For example, individuals with higher social status are significantly more likely than other people to run for political office. Moreover, previous studies have found that such people are even more likely to be successful in being elected to parliament, and more likely still to serve as senior ministers in government (see, e.g., Forcese and de Vries 1977; Guppy et al. 1988). Those with higher social statuses are also far more likely to occupy powerful positions in Canada's system of elites, both in public or government organizations and in the private economic and social spheres (e.g., Porter 1965; Clement 1975, 1977; Olsen 1980; Nakhaie 1997; see also Curtis et al. 2004a). Thus, while the present analysis gives some indication of a relatively broad base to political and community group involvement in Canada, the findings clearly do not support the conclusion that those with privileged social statuses are rivalled by less advantaged groups in the overall power structure.

APPENDIX A: ACTIVITY MEASURES USED WITH THE DATA FROM
THE EQUALITY, SECURITY, AND COMMUNITY SURVEY, 2000

INVOLVEMENT IN INFORMAL NETWORKS

These three questions were asked: (1) How often do you see family members who do not live with you? (2) How often do you see close friends – not your husband or wife or partner or family member, but people you feel fairly close to? and (3) How often do you talk with your neighbours?

The response options for each question were: Would you say every day, several times a week, at least once a week, at least once a month, several times a year, or less often? And no family (no friends, no neighbours). The seven response options were given scores of 7 to 1, and then we summed across the three questions to create an Index of Involvement in Informal Networks with a range of 7 (very low involvement) to 21 (very high involvement).

MEMBERSHIP IN COMMUNITY VOLUNTARY ORGANIZATIONS

Seven questions were asked:

1   How many service clubs, such as Lions or Meals on Wheels, do you belong to?
2   How many recreational groups, such as sports leagues or clubs, music or hobby clubs, or exercise classes are you involved in?
3   How many organizations active on political issues, such as the environment or taxpayers' rights, do you belong to?
4   Sometimes people give time to various types of organizations. For instance, how many youth-oriented groups, such as Girl Guides or Minor Hockey, have you given time to in the last twelve months?
5   How about organizations providing cultural services to the public, such as a museum or music festival. How many of these have you given time to in the last twelve months?
6   How about organizations that help people, such as the Cancer Society or a food bank? How many of these have you volunteered time to in the last twelve months?
7   Do you belong to or volunteer for any other groups or organizations that we have not asked about? How many of these other groups do you volunteer for or belong to?

The number of types of organizations cited was established by summing across the seven responses for a measure with a range of 0 to 7.

VOTING IN RECENT ELECTIONS

The following two questions were asked, and the responses summed, for a measure ranging from 0 to 2:

1   Did you vote in the last federal election in 1997?
2   Did you vote in the last provincial election in [year of provincial election]?

APPENDIX B: ACTIVITY MEASURES USED WITH THE DATA FROM THE WORLD VALUES SURVEY, 2000

DISCUSSING POLITICS

"When you get together with your friends, would you say you discuss politics frequently, occasionally, or never?" These three response categories were given scores of 3, 2, 1, respectively.

INTEREST IN POLITICS

"How interested would you say you are in politics: very interested, somewhat interested, not very interested, or not at all interested?" The four response categories were given scores of 4, 3, 2, 1 respectively.

POLITICAL GROUP ACTIVITY

"Please look carefully at the following list of voluntary organizations and activities and say which, if any, do you belong to, and which if any are you currently doing unpaid voluntary work for." The responses for political parties or groups were coded as: no membership = 0, nominal membership = 1, and working membership = 2.

PUBLIC PROTEST ACTIVITIES

A measure of public protest activity was based on responses to the following questions: "Now I would like you to look at this card. I am going to read out some different forms of political action that people can take, and I would like you to tell me, for each one, whether you have actually done any of these things, whether you might do it, or would never, under any circumstances, do it: signing a petition, joining a boycott, attending lawful demonstrations, joining strikes, or occupying buildings or factories."

The responses for these activities were given scores as follows: have actually done = 3, might do it = 2, would never do it = 1. The scores were then summed for each respondent. This measure ranged from 5 (low protest activity) to 15 (high protest activity).

APPENDIX C: ACTIVITY MEASURES USED WITH THE DATA FROM THE NATIONAL SURVEY OF GIVING, VOLUNTEERING, AND PARTICIPATING, 1997

Volunteering for Organizations

Respondents were asked whether they had volunteered in any one or more of the following ways through an organization in the past twelve months: canvassing, campaigning, or fundraising; as a member of a board or committee; helping educate, influence public opinion, or lobby others; consulting, executive, office or administrative work; teach or coach; provide care or support; provide health care; as a member of a self-help group; collect, serve, or deliver food or other goods; maintain, repair, or build facilities; help with first-aid, fire fighting, or search and rescue; activities aimed at protecting the environment or wildlife; in any other way not mentioned yet.

Hours of Volunteering

Respondents were also asked the number of yearly hours given over to each activity, and the responses were summed.

Number of Volunteer Organizations

The question was: For how many organizations did you volunteer in the past twelve months?

Number of Donations

This measure was based on responses to a set of questions that determined the number of donations given over the past year in each of the following ways: responding to a request through the mail; to attend a charity event; using payroll deductions; sponsoring someone in an event; made in memoriam; when asked by someone at work; someone doing door-to-door canvassing; someone canvassing for a charitable donation at a shopping centre or street corner; responding to a telephone request; through collection at a place of worship; responding to a television or radio request; approaching a nonprofit or charitable organization on your own; made in any other ways. The measure provided the sum across all these forms of donation.

Amount of Donations

This was the sum of the amounts of money reported as given in the past twelve months in conjunction with the above questions on donations.

ACKNOWLEDGMENTS

We thank Ronald Inglehart and colleagues and the Inter-University Consortium for Political and Social Reasearch, University of Michigan, for making the 2000 World

Values Survey data available; Statistics Canada for making available the 1997 National Survey of Giving, Volunteering, and Participating data; and Jon Kesselman and colleagues for making available the 2000 Equality, Security, and Community Survey data. In all cases, only the authors are responsible for the analyses and interpretations presented here.

REFERENCES

Becker, Gary S. 1993. *Human Capital*. 3rd ed. Chicago: University of Chicago Press.

Bourdieu, Pierre. 1980. "Le capital social: Notes provisoires." *Actes de la Recherche en Sciences Sociales* 3: 2-3.

Burt, Ronald S. 1992. *Structural Holes: The Social Structure of Competition*. Cambridge, MA: Harvard University Press.

—. 1997. "The Contingent Value of Social Capital." *Administrative Science Quarterly* 42: 339-65.

Carroll, William, ed. 1992. *Organizing Dissent: Contemporary Social Movements in Theory and Practice*. Toronto: Garamond.

Chui, Tina, James Curtis, and Edward Grabb. 1993. "Who Participates in Community Organizations and Politics?" In James Curtis, Edward Grabb, and Neil Guppy, eds., *Social Inequality in Canada: Patterns, Problems and Policies*. 2nd ed. Scarborough: Prentice-Hall.

Chui, Tina, James Curtis, and Ronald Lambert. 1991. "Immigrant Background and Political Participation: Examining Generational Patterns." *Canadian Journal of Sociology* 16(4): 375-96.

Clement, Wallace. 1975. *The Canadian Corporate Elite*. Toronto: McClelland and Stewart.

—. 1977. *Continental Corporate Power*. Toronto: McClelland and Stewart.

Coleman, James S. 1988. "Social Capital in the Creation of Human Capital." *American Journal of Sociology* 94 (Supplement): S95-S120.

Curtis, James. 1971. "Voluntary Associations Joining: A Cross-National Comparative Note." *American Sociological Review* 36(5): 872-80.

Curtis, James, Douglas Baer, and Edward Grabb. 2001. "Nations of Joiners: Explaining Voluntary Association Membership in Democratic Societies." *American Sociological Review* 66(6): 783-805.

Curtis, James, and Edward Grabb. 2002. "Involvement in the Organizational Base of New Social Movements in English Canada and French Canada." In Douglas Baer, ed., *Political Sociology: Canadian Perspectives*. Don Mills, ON: Oxford University Press.

Curtis, James, Edward Grabb, and Douglas Baer. 1992. "Voluntary Association Membership in Fifteen Developed Countries: A Comparative Analysis." *American Sociological Review* 57(2): 139-52.

Curtis, James, Edward Grabb, and Neil Guppy, eds. 2004a. *Social Inequality in Canada: Patterns, Problems, Policies*. 4th ed. Scarborough, ON: Pearson Education Canada.

Curtis, James, Edward Grabb, Thomas Perks, and Tina Chui. 2004b. "Political Involvement, Civic Engagement, and Social Inequality." In Curtis, Grabb, and Guppy, eds.,
Social Inequality in Canada. 4th ed.

Curtis, James, and Ronald Lambert. 1976. "Voting, Political Interest, and Age: National
Survey Findings for French and English Canadians." *Canadian Journal of Political
Science* 9: 293-307.

Curtis, James, Ronald Lambert, Steven Brown, and Barry Kay. 1989. "Affiliating with
Voluntary Associations: Canadian-American Comparisons." *Canadian Journal of
Sociology* 14(2): 143-61.

Curtis, James, William McTeer, and Philip White. 2003. "Do High School Athletes Earn
More Pay? Youth Sport Participation and Earnings as an Adult." *Sociology of Sport
Journal* 20(1): 60-76.

Curtis, James, and Thomas Perks. 2006. "Gender, Early Experiences with Voluntary
Community Activities, and Adult Community Involvement." In Fiona Kay and
Richard Johnston, eds., *Social Capital, Diversity, and the Welfare State.* Vancouver:
UBC Press.

Cutler, Steven T. 1976. "Age Differences in Voluntary Association Membership." *Social
Forces* 55(1): 43-58.

Dahl, Robert. 1982. *Dilemmas of a Pluralist Democracy.* New York: Oxford University
Press.

Edwards, Patricia K., John N. Edwards, and Alan DeWitt Watts. 1984. "Women, Work,
and Social Participation." *Journal of Voluntary Action Research* 13(1): 7-22.

Elections Canada. 1993. *Official Voting Results: 35th General Election.* Ottawa: Elections
Canada.

Forcese, Dennis, and John de Vries. 1977. "Occupational and Electoral Success in Canada:
The 1974 Federal Election." *Canadian Review of Sociology and Anthropology* 14(3):
331-40.

Gordon, C. Wayne, and Nicholas Babchuk. 1959. "A Typology of Voluntary Associations." *American Sociological Review* 24: 22-9.

Grabb, Edward, and James Curtis. 1992. "Voluntary Association Activity in English
Canada, French Canada and the United States: Multivariate Analyses." *Canadian
Journal of Sociology* 17(4): 371-88.

—. 2005. *Regions Apart: The Four Societies of Canada and the United States.* Don Mills:
Oxford University Press.

Guppy, Neil, Sabrina Freeman, and Shari Buchan. 1988. "Economic Background and
Political Representation." In James Curtis, Edward Grabb, Neil Guppy, and Sid
Gilbert, eds., *Social Inequality in Canada: Patterns, Problems, Policies.* 1st ed.
Scarborough, ON: Prentice-Hall Canada.

Hall, M., T. Knighton, P. Reed, P. Bussiere, D. McRae, and P. Bowen. 1998. *Caring Canadians, Involved Canadians: Highlights from the 1997 National Survey of Giving, Volunteering, and Participating.* Ottawa: Statistics Canada.

Hayes, Michael T. 1978. "The Semi-Sovereign Pressure Groups: A Critique of Current Theory and an Alternative Typology." *Journal of Politics* 40: 134-61.

—. 1983. "Interest Groups: Pluralism or Mass Society?" In Allan J. Cigler and Burdett A. Loomis, eds., *Interest Group Politics*. Washington, DC: CQ Press.

Inglehart, Ronald et al. 2004. *World Values Surveys and European Values Surveys, 1999-2001.* Ann Arbor, MI: Inter-University Consortium for Political and Social Research [computer file].

Jones, Frank. 2000. "Community Involvement: The Influence of Early Experience." *Canadian Social Trends* (Summer): 15-19.

Kay, Barry, Ronald Lambert, Steven Brown, and James Curtis. 1987. "Gender and Political Activity in Canada: 1965-84." *Canadian Journal of Political Science* 20(4): 851-63.

Knoke, David. 1986. "Associations and Interest Groups." *Annual Review of Sociology* 12: 1-21.

Larana, Enrique, Hank Johnston, and Joseph Gusfield, eds. 1994. *New Social Movements: From Ideology to Identity.* Philadelphia: Temple University Press.

Lin, Nan. 1982. "Social Resources and Instrumental Action." In Peter V. Marsden and Nan Lin, eds., *Social Structure and Network Analysis*. Beverly Hills, CA: Sage.

—. 2000. "Inequality in Social Capital." *Contemporary Sociology* 29(6): 785-95.

Lin, Nan, Walter M. Ensel, and John C. Vaughn. 1981. "Social Resources and Strength of Ties: Structural Factors in Occupational Status Attainment." *American Sociological Review* 46(4): 393-405.

McPherson, J. Miller, and William G. Lockwood. 1980. "The Longitudinal Study of Voluntary Association Memberships: A Multivariate Analysis." *Journal of Voluntary Action Research* 9(1-4): 74-84.

Milbrath, Lester. 1968. *Political Participation.* Chicago: Rand McNally.

Milbrath, Lester, and M. Lal Goel. 1977. *Political Participation.* 2nd ed. Chicago: Rand McNally.

Nakhaie, M. Reza. 1997. "Vertical Mosaic among the Elites: The New Imagery Revisited." *Canadian Review of Sociology and Anthropology* 34(1): 1-24.

Northrup, David. 2002. *Equality, Security, and Community (ESC), Data Collection Technical Documentation.* Toronto: Institute for Social Research, York University.

Olsen, Dennis. 1980. *The State Elite.* Toronto: McClelland and Stewart.

Olson, Mancur, Jr. 1965. *The Logic of Collective Action: Public Goods and the Theory of Groups.* Cambridge, MA: Harvard University Press.

Palisi, Bartolomeo J., and Rosalie J. Palisi. 1984. "Status and Voluntary Associations: A Cross-Cultural Study of Males in Three Metropolitan Areas." *Journal of Voluntary Action Research* 13(3): 32-43.

Porter, John. 1965. *The Vertical Mosaic.* Toronto: University of Toronto Press.

Portes, Alejandro. 1998. "Social Capital: Its Origins and Applications in Modern Sociology." *Annual Review of Sociology* 24: 1-24.

Portes, Alejandro, and Julia Sensenbrenner. 1993. "Embeddedness and Immigration: Notes on the Social Determinants of Economic Action." *American Journal of Sociology* 98(6): 1320-50.

Putnam, Robert D. 1993. "The Prosperous Community: Social Capital and Public Life." *The American Prospect* 13: 35-42.

—. 2000. *Bowling Alone: The Collapse and Revival of American Community*. New York: Simon and Schuster.

Smith, David H. 1975. "Voluntary Action and Voluntary Groups." *Annual Review of Sociology* 1: 247-70.

8
Fitting Kids In: Children and Inequality in Canada

Shelley Phipps and Lynn Lethbridge

This chapter examines children's experiences of inequality in Canada – a dimension of inequality that has received relatively little attention. There is a large literature describing children's experiences of poverty in Canada over time and in comparison with other countries (see, for example, Crossley and Curtis 2003, or Picot et al. 1998; Bradbury and Jäntti 2000; Rainwater and Smeeding 2003). However, as emphasized by Smeeding and Rainwater (2002), we might care about "equality of opportunity" for children or about children having "a fair chance in life" as well as about children living in poverty. Inequality among children is an important issue from the perspective of equity. For example, do some children start life with substantially less than their peers? Do children have significantly lower material standards of living than most adults in society? We might also care about health inequality among children, given research findings that health status is strongly influenced not only by the family's level of income but also by its position within an income distribution (Wilkinson 1996; Lynch et al. 2000).

Smeeding and Rainwater (2002) measure "equality of opportunity" as the ratio of income at the ninetieth percentile to income at the tenth percentile of a country's income distribution (the 90:10 ratio). The income concept used is family disposable income (after-tax and after-transfer) adjusted for differences in need by families of different sizes, using a household equivalence scale; this is called "household equivalent income." By the 90:10 ratio measure, Canadian performance is "middle of the road" (3.55 versus 2.29 in Norway and 5.11 in the United States). Smeeding and Rainwater measure "a fair chance in life," using a 50:10 ratio. Canadian performance is again middle-of-the-road by this measure of inequality among children (children in the bottom decile have average incomes that are 44 percent of those in the fifth decile versus 35 percent for children living in the United States and 55 percent for Norway).

Oxley et al. (2001) provide a second international comparison of inequality among children. They calculate aggregate measures of inequality, including the Gini coefficient, mean logarithmic deviation, and squared coefficient of variation for children in OECD countries as well as changes in these inequality indicators for the period 1984-94. (Kesselman and Cheung in Chapter 12 offer a description of the various inequality indices.) In general, they find evidence of growing inequality in children's equivalent disposable incomes. Canada is an exception, with inequality among children falling very slightly over their study period. Oxley et al. again find that inequality among Canadian children, in 1994, is middle of the road in comparison with the inequality of children in other affluent countries: the Gini for Canadian children is computed to be 0.265 versus 0.337 for the United States and 0.180 for Denmark. In every country, as Oxley et al. find, aggregate indicators show that inequality is less among children than among the full population.

This chapter adds to the literature on children and inequality a more detailed descriptive analysis of changes in children's experiences of inequality in Canada across time (1973 to 1997) and further comparisons of the inequality experiences of Canadian children with those of children in five other affluent countries . Like Smeeding and Rainwater, we focus on inequality of disposable income adjusted for family size, or "equivalent income." We have chosen to compare Canada with three countries with relatively similar social programs (the United States, the United Kingdom, and Australia are all from what Esping-Andersen (1990) labels the "liberal" cluster) as well as with two countries with rather different social programs (Germany is classified as a "conservative corporatist" state while Norway is "social democratic"). We focus on how changes across time and differences across countries in the family settings of children are related to their experiences of inequality.

To examine where children fit in the Canadian income distribution and how this may have changed over time as family structure, family size, age of parents, and labour-force participation of parents have changed, we use microdata from the Survey of Consumer Finances (1973 to 1997). The position of children in the Canadian income distribution in the late 1990s is also compared to that of children in other affluent countries using micro-data from the Luxembourg Income Study with links made to differences across the countries in terms of family structure and size, for example.

The remainder of the chapter is organized as follows. The next section outlines key trends in family settings, such as household structure, family size, and parental labour-force participation, experienced by Canadian children. The third section presents summary measures of inequality among Canadian children and illustrates how children fit into the Canadian income distribution, overall and for specific groups (e.g., children in single-parent families, children in one-earner versus two-earner families). The fourth section compares Canadian children's experience of inequality with that of children living in other affluent countries. A final section offers conclusions.

Overview of Key Trends

We use cross-sectional microdata drawn from the public use samples of the Survey of Consumer Finances (SCF) from 1973 through 1997 (with 1974, 1978, and 1980 missing). The analysis stops with 1997 because this was the last year of the SCF, which has now been replaced entirely by the Survey of Labour and Income Dynamics (SLID). While there are public use versions of more recent SLID cross-sectional files, they do not report the number of children under eighteen in a family. For the analysis of trends in Canada over time, we use the "economic family" files, but since our focus is on children, each child is counted as an individual observation assigned the appropriate characteristics of the household and that household's sample weight. "Children" are defined to be less than eighteen years of age.

As described below, some very significant changes in family life and organization have occurred in the twenty-five years from 1973 through 1997, and these might be expected to affect how children fit into the country's income distribution. First, there has been a steady reduction in the average size of families with children – from 5.3 in 1973 to 4.2 in 1997. Most noticeably, the proportion of children living in families with six or more members has fallen continuously from 36.5 percent in 1973 to 11.7 percent in 1997. Correspondingly, the proportion of children living in families with three or four members has climbed (from 11.0 percent to 19.7 percent for three-person families and from 27.8 percent to 40.3 percent for four-person families). For families with children, smaller family sizes will on average increase the equivalent incomes[1] of children and might be expected to "move children up" the distribution, other things being equal.

Another important point is the steady decline between 1973 until 1997 in the proportion of the Canadian population aged less than eighteen years (from 34.4 percent to 23.6 percent). Correspondingly, the proportion of households with any children present has fallen continuously from 53.7

percent in 1973 to 38.8 percent in 1997. Overall, the population has been steadily increasing while the number of children has remained fairly steady.

Significant trends in the age distribution of mothers are also apparent between 1973 and 1997.[2] There has been a clear increase in the percentage of mothers aged thirty-five to forty-four (from 39.1 in 1973 to 50.1 percent in 1997) and a corresponding reduction in the percentage of mothers aged twenty-five to thirty-four (from 35.7 to 32.7). The percentage of mothers aged less than twenty-five has fallen (from 6.0 to 3.8) as has the percentage of mothers in the oldest age category (greater than forty-five years). At least three key factors are at work in explaining these changes: (1) as women have fewer children, they are less likely to have additional births in their late thirties or early forties, (2) women are more likely to have first children at older ages, and (3) "baby boom" mothers have moved into higher age categories through this period. To the extent that earnings increase with age, children with older parents would be expected, other things being equal, to be higher in the income distribution.

While the majority of children live in two-parent families, there has been a steady and substantial increase in the percentage of children living in single-parent families (from 9.3 in 1973 to 17.7 in 1997). And, while there has also been an increase in the number of single fathers, the vast majority of single parents are still mothers (only 2.8 percent of children lived with single fathers in 1997). An increase in the number of single-mother families would be expected to push children down the income distribution.

Finally, it is important to note trends in the labour-force participation of parents. For children living with two parents, there has been a dramatic increase in the percentage of two-earner families (from 40.0 percent in 1973 to 72.8 percent in 1997) and a corresponding decline in the percentage of one-earner families (from 57.5 percent in 1973 to 23.9 percent in 1997). It is not obvious, a priori, how this change is likely to have affected inequality among children. If mothers in lower-income families have entered the labour market in an attempt to support family incomes, the trend would have an equalizing impact. If, on the other hand, the trend primarily represents growth in "yuppie" households (two well-paid individuals who marry and start a family), then the growth in two-earner families would be dis-equalizing. (Fortin and Schirle in Chapter 11 discuss implications for family earnings inequality of women's increased labour-force participation and assortative mating.)

It remains relatively rare for a child living with both parents to have neither in the labour force. For children living with a single parent, rates of labour force participation have generally increased, if slowly, over the sample period (from 56.1 in 1973 to 65.9 in 1997). While rates of labour-force participation for single fathers are higher than for single mothers, the upward trend is particularly evident for single mothers.

Children in the Canadian Income Distribution

INEQUALITY AMONG CANADIAN CHILDREN

Following Smeeding and Rainwater (2002), we begin our analysis of inequality among Canadian children by calculating a measure of "equality of opportunity," which we operationalize as the ratio of mean equivalent income for children in the top and bottom deciles of the income distribution. We also present a variant of Smeeding and Rainwater's measure of "fair chance in life" – the ratio of mean equivalent income for children in the fifth and bottom deciles of the distribution. As is evident in Figure 8.1, the 90:10 ratio for children in Canada has dropped from 8.8 to 7.6 (i.e., children in the top

FIGURE 8.1

Mean disposable household equivalent income: ratios of top to bottom decile, fifth to bottom decile, Canada, 1973-97

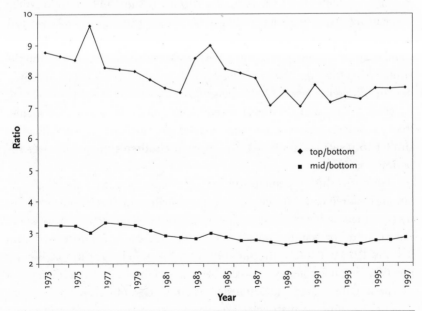

income decile have equivalent disposable incomes 7.6 times those of children in the bottom). The 50:10 ratio has remained remarkably stable over the period (varying from a high of 3.3 in 1977 to a low of 2.6 in 1993).

Similar patterns are apparent in aggregate measures of income inequality such as the Gini coefficient.[3] We have calculated trends in the Gini coefficient using equivalent income for all Canadian children and, for comparative purposes, for all Canadians and for all working age Canadians (defined as adults aged twenty-five to fifty-four years). We restrict attention for the "working age" sample to adults most likely to be finished with education but not yet retired. Like Frenette, Green, and Picot in Chapter 3, we find that the inequality of equivalent income among all Canadians remained fairly constant over the 1973 to 1997 period, though Frenette et al. argue convincingly that the survey data we use here likely understate the level of inequality in Canada because lower-income households are under-represented. In our SCF data, inequality for adults aged twenty-five to fifty-four was consistently lower than for the full population until the early 1990s, but became slightly higher between 1990 and 1997. Like Oxley et al. (2001), we find consistently less inequality among children than among all individuals or among all adults aged twenty-five to fifty-four for the full period from 1973 through 1997.[4]

A second point is that among children there was a small reduction in overall inequality of equivalent income from 1973 to 1997[5] (from 0.288 to 0.276 using a Gini coefficient).[6] To assess how big a change this was, we note that the difference in Gini coefficients (for the full populations) between Canada and the United States (in 1994) was 0.076; between Canada and the United Kingdom, the difference was 0.057; and between Canada and Sweden, the difference was 0.220 (Osberg 1999). Since the reduction in inequality among Canadian children between 1973 and 1997 was much smaller than the difference in inequality between Canada and the two countries most similar to it, we conclude that the drop in children's inequality over the period was small.

However, this very small reduction in equivalent income inequality among children contrasts with significant growth in market income inequality (i.e., income before transfers are added or taxes are deducted) over the same period. For example, the market income Gini coefficient increased from 0.314 in 1973 to 0.392 in the mid-1990s – a *change* in inequality that is twice the *difference* in inequality between Canada and the United States. Through this period, the Canadian tax/transfer system successfully managed to counteract these quite dramatic increases in market income inequality to keep increases in inequality among children rather small. (Mainly the transfers, because taxes have been relatively unimportant in offsetting increases in market income inequality, as argued by Kesselman and Cheung in Chapter 12.) However, since the late 1990s (after our study period), as Frenette, Green, and Picot indicate in Chapter 3, inequality has increased in the Canadian population overall, and taxes and transfers no longer play as strong a redistributive role.

FITTING CHILDREN INTO THE CANADIAN INCOME DISTRIBUTION

A small body of research assesses the contribution of changes in household structure, labour market participation, and family size to overall inequality in the population, though most studies do not refer specifically to inequality among children. A common conclusion in this literature is that these demographic changes account for very little of the change in overall inequality (see, for example, Fortin and Schirle in Chapter 11, Jenkins 1995, Rainwater and Smeeding 1997, Brandolini and D'Alessio 2001).

But even if overall inequality of equivalent income has changed very little, and even if others have found that changes in demographic/family characteristics have contributed relatively little to overall changes in inequality, it is worth considering how children's places *within* the population income distribution have changed as important family characteristics have changed. This section attempts to fit children into the Canadian equivalent income distribution by calculating the percentage of children who live in families in each of the population-level equivalent income deciles. That is, we computed cut points for each decile of the equivalent income distribution for *all* Canadians in each year. We then asked how many children lived in families with equivalent incomes in the bottom decile, the second decile, and so forth.

Our preferred comparison group is always all Canadians – that is, we are interested in the question of how children, as an important demographic subgroup, compare with everyone else in society. However, children typically live with adults who are younger than the average for the population. Since earnings increase with age but at different rates for different people so that inequality in earnings grows over time, it would not be surprising to find that children live in households with lower-than-average and less dispersed earnings. Thus, we have repeated all of our analyses comparing children with prime-aged adults, defined as those aged twenty-five to fifty-four.[7]

Figure 8.2 illustrates that children are much more likely to be located in the bottom half of the equivalent income distribution and that this did not

FIGURE 8.2

Distribution of children by equivalent income deciles: all children, Canada, 1973, 1985, 1997

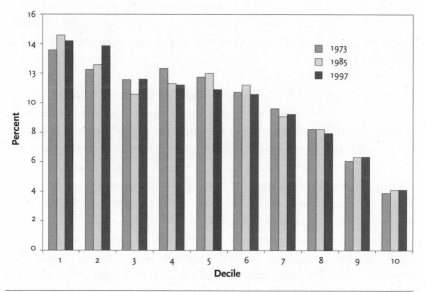

change much over the time period studied. For example, 61.5 percent of children had equivalent incomes in the bottom half of the distribution in 1973, 61.1 percent in 1985, 61.8 percent in 1997.[8] (Since the socio-demographic changes noted above were, by and large, fairly continuous over the period, we illustrate the distributional information only for three years at the beginning, middle, and end of the period – 1973, 1985, and 1997.[9]) Only 4.1 percent of children were located in the top decile in 1997 (4.1 percent in 1985, 3.9 percent in 1973). On the other hand, 14.2 percent of children were located in the bottom decile in 1997 (14.6 in 1985, 14.0 in 1973). Thus, at any point in the study period, children were approximately 3.5 times more likely to be in the bottom than in the top decile.

As noted earlier, the position of children in the country's income distribution may be the result of parents' life-cycle stage (e.g., young parents are developing careers, many mothers with pre-school children withdraw from the labour market to care for their children, temporarily depressing household income).[10] This does not mean that it is unimportant whether children are located at the bottom of the income distribution now – indeed, evidence suggests that both level of income and position within the income distribution regardless of level are important determinants of health status (Wilkinson 1996). However, when we follow an analogous procedure to that described above, except that children are fit into the equivalent income distribution for prime-age adults,[11] children are even more noticeably located toward the bottom of the income distribution of working age adults. The exclusion of elderly Canadians removes many individuals living on low pension incomes toward the bottom of the full Canadian income distribution.[12]

Figures 8.3 and 8.4 consider how children from two-parent families of different size fit into the Canadian equivalent income distribution and how this has changed over time. The results are almost mirror images. Only children (those with no siblings) living with two parents are, on average, relatively affluent, whereas children living with two parents and two siblings are relatively poor. For example, in 1997, 58.3 percent of only children have equivalent family incomes in the top half of the distribution versus 30.4 percent of children with two siblings. This basic pattern remained much the same from 1973 through 1997 (recall, though, that the number of larger families has fallen and the number of smaller families has grown).

Figure 8.3

Distribution of children by equivalent income deciles: two parents, one child familes, Canada, 1973, 1985, 1997

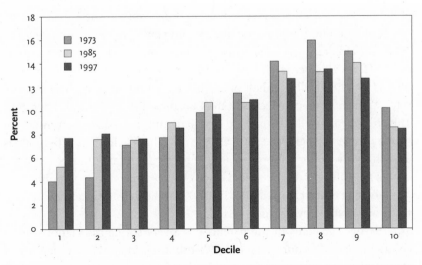

FIGURE 8.4

Distribution of children by equivalent income deciles: two parents, three children families, Canada, 1973, 1985, 1997

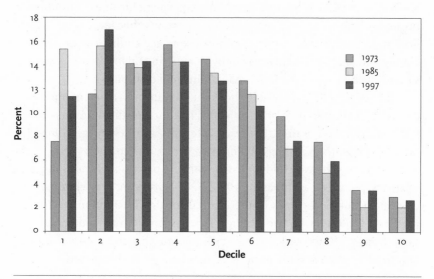

Figure 8.5 illustrates the implications of mother's age for child's position in the Canadian income distribution. In all years, the child is likely to be at the bottom of the income distribution if the mother is less than twenty-five years old. But, it is also true that the probability of being in the bottom decile for children with young mothers increased markedly over the study period (from 13.4 percent in 1973 to 29.4 percent in 1985 to 39.0 percent in 1997). By 1997, well over half of all children with young mothers were located in the bottom two deciles of the Canadian distribution (61.9 percent). This change may well be explained by deteriorating market opportunities for young people through the 1990s. On the other hand, children with mothers aged thirty-five to forty-four are found in relatively equal numbers across the deciles (e.g., there is no more than a two or three percentage point difference from the first to the eighth deciles in 1997), and this feature has held consistently across the 25-year study period.

The marital status of the parents has a very strong association with a child's place in the country's income distribution. In all years, a majority of children living in single-mother families have equivalent incomes that place

FIGURE 8.5

Distribution of children by equivalent income deciles: families with mothers under age 25, Canada, 1973, 1985, 1997

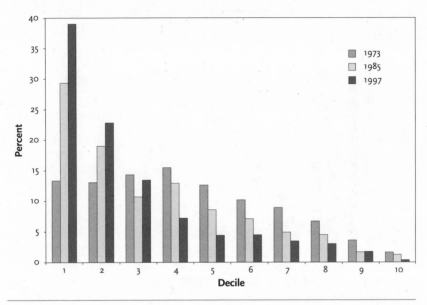

them in the bottom two deciles of the income distribution (see Figure 8.6). Given this pattern, however, there has at least been some movement up the income distribution. In 1973, 64.2 percent of children in single-mother families had incomes in the bottom two deciles of the population income distribution, but by 1997 this figure had declined to 55.8 percent. Thus, while children living in single-mother households continue to be some of the poorest of Canadians, there has at least been some improvement in their relative financial standing, possibly because of increases in the labour-force participation of single mothers or enhanced transfers for lower-income families with children.

Figures 8.7 and 8.8 illustrate the relative positions in the Canadian income distribution held by children in two-parent families when one or both parents are in the labour force (and, as noted previously, the proportion of two-earner families has grown dramatically over the sample period). Not surprisingly, children living in families in which both parents work are much more affluent than children with one parent not working. Middle incomes are particularly likely with two earners (50.0 percent of children in two-earner

SHELLEY PHIPPS AND LYNN LETHBRIDGE

FIGURE 8.6

Distribution of children by equivalent income deciles: single-mother families, Canada, 1973, 1985, 1997

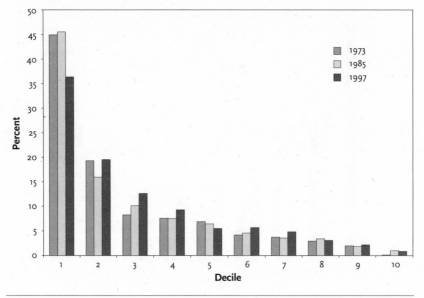

couples had incomes in the fourth, fifth, sixth, or seventh deciles in 1997). However, from 1973 through 1997 there was no noticeable change in the positions held by children in two-parent families in the full Canadian income distribution.

Children in two-parent, one-earner families are concentrated in the bottom half of the income distribution, and, as such families became less common over the study period, the children in them appeared lower in the income distribution. Thus, for example, in 1973, 26.0 percent of children in two-parent, one-earner couples were located in the bottom two deciles of the income distribution while, in 1997, 43.4 percent were located there. Similarly, in 1973, 46.2 percent of children in two-parent, one-earner families had incomes in the middle of the distribution in 1973 (in the fourth to seventh deciles) while, in 1997, 33.9 percent were in the middle. Of course, it is important to keep in mind that families with one parent at home have more time to engage in household production activities and so have a higher standard of living than a two-earner family with the same income.

FIGURE 8.7

Distribution of children by equivalent income deciles: two parents, one-earner families, Canada, 1973, 1985, 1997

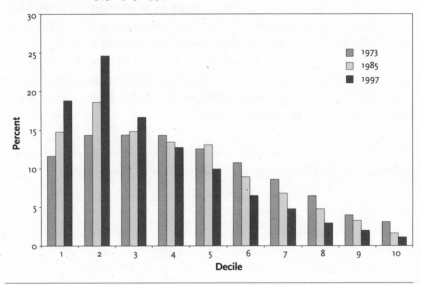

FIGURE 8.8

Distribution of children by equivalent income deciles: two parents, two-earner families, Canada, 1973, 1985, 1997

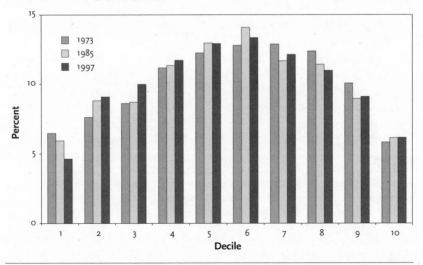

STATISTICAL ANALYSIS

To obtain more systematic insights into the results of the preceding section, we have estimated very simple ordinary least squares models in which the dependent variables are two aggregate measures of inequality (the Gini and the mean logarithmic deviation[13]) as calculated for each year of SCF data we had available. Explanatory variables included: percentages of mothers in different age categories (under twenty-five, twenty-five to thirty-four, forty-five and over), average family size, percentages of single-mother families, and percentages of two-parent families with two earners (versus no earner or one earner). The results are reported in Table 8.1.

TABLE 8.1

Ordinary Least Squares estimates of inequality measures, Canada, 1973-97

Variable	Gini coefficient		Mean log deviation	
	All individuals	Children < 18	All individuals	Children < 18
Intercept	0.691 *	0.748**	0.680**	0.675***
	(0.216)	(0.301)	(0.263)	(0.330)
Percentage of mothers under 25	0.156	−0.029	0.136	−0.093
	(0.464)	(0.647)	(0.564)	(0.708)
Percentage of mothers aged 25-34	−0.257*	−0.324*	−0.364*	−0.359*
	(0.078)	(0.108)	(0.095)	(0.119)
Percentage of mothers aged 45 and over	−0.400**	−0.542**	−0.369**	−0.416***
	(0.136)	(0.189)	(0.165)	(0.207)
Average number of persons in households	−0.029	−0.029	−0.041	−0.037
	(0.026)	(0.036)	(0.031)	(0.039)
Percentage of married couple households with no earner	0.018	−0.005	−0.261	−0.301
	(0.242)	(0.338)	(0.294)	(0.370)
Percentage of married couple households with two earners	−0.184***	−0.194	−0.234**	−0.227
	(0.088)	(0.122)	(0.107)	(0.134)
Percentage of households headed by single mothers	−0.059	−0.165	−0.030	−0.153
	(0.140)	(0.195)	(0.170)	(0.213)
Adjusted R^2	0.647	0.310	0.744	0.556

NOTE: Mothers with children under 18 in the household. If no mother is present, then father's age is used. Households are those with children under 18.
 * statistically significant with 99% confidence
 ** statistically significant with 95% confidence
 *** statistically significant with 90% confidence
Standard errors are reported in parentheses.

In explaining aggregate inequality among children, whether measured using a Gini or a mean log deviation index, changes in the age distribution of mothers appear to have the largest association with inequality (both overall in the population and among children). Higher percentages of older mothers are associated with lower values for the inequality indices. The only other variable found to be statistically significant is the percentage of two-parent, two-earner families. Higher percentages of two-earner families are associated with lower levels of inequality, suggesting that adding second incomes to families operated more to boost low family incomes toward the middle than to increase family incomes already high in the distribution. The proportion of single-parent families does not appear to have had a significant association with aggregate measures of inequality in Canada over time, perhaps because as the number of single mothers has increased, their relative economic status has also improved slightly (perhaps partly as a result of increased labour force participation). Reductions in family size are similarly insignificant.

International Comparisons

This chapter has thus far focused upon how changes in children's experiences of inequality in Canada have changed over time as household characteristics have changed. This section switches to a cross-sectional comparison of how children's place in the income distribution varies across countries with differences in key household characteristics, although the material presented here is less comprehensive than what we have provided for Canada across time. To fully understand the links between household structure and children's inequality cross-nationally would require further examination of differences in tax-transfer policies, labour markets, and wage and education distributions.

International Comparison of Socio-Demographic Characteristics

To conduct the international comparisons, we use microdata from the Luxembourg Income Study (LIS), a collection of microdata sets contributed to the project by member countries and then recoded to enhance comparability across countries (e.g., of total transfers received or total taxes paid). These data are housed in Luxembourg but can be accessed via the internet. We compare Canada with five other similarly affluent countries: the United States, the United Kingdom, Australia, Germany, and Norway. Comparisons are all made in the mid- to late 1990s, though years do not always match when data are missing. The data set included in LIS for the United States is the 1997 Current Population Survey, with a full sample size of 50,320 observations; the UK data set is the Family Expenditure Survey for 1995, with 6,797 observations; Australia's is the 1994 Survey of Income and Housing Costs, with 7,441 observations; Germany's is the German Socio Economic Panel for 1994, with 6,045 observations; and Norway's is the Income Distribution Survey for 1995, with 10,127 observations. The Canadian data set included in the LIS is the 1997 Survey of Consumer Finances, Household file, which has 33,843 observations. Note that, when analyzing the time trends for Canada in the previous section, we utilized the Survey of Consumer Finances, Economic Family file, which differs slightly from the Household file.

We begin by using the LIS data to compare the family settings of children in the six LIS countries. Note, first, that there are important differences across the six countries in the percentage of the population composed of children (aged under eighteen). The United States has the largest child population (27.3 percent), while Germany has the smallest (21.0 percent). Canada (23.7 percent children) most resembles Norway (23.2 percent children). The mean household size for families with children is 4.5 persons in the United States and Australia, 4.2 persons in the United Kingdom and Canada, and 4.1 persons in Germany and Norway.

In all countries, children are most likely to live in four-person families, although this family configuration is most likely in Germany (43.6 percent) and least likely in the United States (35.5 percent). While German and Norwegian children have, on average, the same family sizes, the distributions are somewhat different. For example, more Norwegian than German children live in five-person families (26.7 versus 18.9 percent), but more German than Norwegian children live in six-or-more person families (10.2 versus 8.0 percent). Finally, American and Australian families with children have the same average household size, although Australians are much less likely to live in two-person households (2.4 percent versus 4.1 percent in the United States) and more likely to be very large households (43.8 percent of Australian children are in households with five or more persons compared with 41.9 percent of American children).

Some striking differences exist across the countries in terms of the marital structure of parents. Single parents are much more common in the United States (25.5 percent) and the United Kingdom (22.6 percent) than in Germany (11.8 percent) or Australia (12.3 percent). Single fathers are not very common in any of the countries studied – at 4.0 percent or less in all countries.

Differences also exist across the countries in the paid work patterns of parents. For children living with two parents, the two-earner family is most common in Canada (72.8 percent), the United States (68.8 percent), and Norway (68.7 percent). While still the majority case in Germany (52.1 percent) and Australia (52.7 percent), two-earner couples are noticeably less common in these countries. In the United Kingdom, on the other hand, two-parent, one-earner families are slightly more common (38.8 percent) than two-earner families (38.4 percent). In general, few children live with two parents of whom neither works, but, as with the two-parent, one-earner family, this situation is most common in the United Kingdom (22.8 percent), where worries about social exclusion from the labour market have arisen (Atkinson and Hills 1998).

Labour force participation rates for single parents also vary considerably across the countries, from a high of 74 percent in the United States to a low of 32 percent in the United Kingdom. The Canadian rate (65.9 percent) is thus in the middle and not dissimilar from the German rate (61.6 percent).

INEQUALITY AMONG CHILDREN IN LIS COUNTRIES

Table 8.2 provides aggregate measures of inequality in disposable equivalent income (Gini and mean log deviation) for each of the six countries included in our sample. These measures are calculated first for all individuals in the country and then for all children in the country. Several results are evident in the figures. There is less inequality among children than in the population overall. Canadian children (Gini 0.275) are more equal than children living in the United States (0.373) or the United Kingdom (0.335), are about as equal as children living in Germany (0.263) or Australia (0.281), and are less equal than children living in Norway (0.208). The same pattern is evident with the mean log deviation index.

Full population measures of inequality can also be ranked in the same way. One implication of the differences in inequality across the countries studied is that we will be fitting children into income distributions that are quite different from one another (in contrast with the study of Canada across time, where inequality remained fairly constant). And, as Smeeding and Rainwater (2001) point out, children in the same positions of their country's income distributions can have quite different real standards of living. For example, they demonstrate that children living in the United States in the top decile of the American income distribution are richer than children living anywhere else in the world; on the other hand, children in the bottom

TABLE 8.2

Inequality measures Canada (1997), US (1997), UK(1995), Germany (1994), Norway (1995), and Australia (1994): all individuals and children

	Gini coefficient		Mean log deviation	
	All individuals	Children < 18	All individuals	Children < 18
Canada, 1997	0.291	0.275	0.159	0.146
United States, 1997	0.380	0.373	0.269	0.261
United Kingdom, 1995	0.341	0.335	0.214	0.216
Germany, 1994	0.270	0.263	0.131	0.133
Norway, 1995	0.232	0.208	0.103	0.089
Australia, 1994	0.307	0.281	0.184	0.143

NOTE: The income concept used is equivalent income; OECD equivalence scales are used.

decile of the American income distribution are among the poorest children living in affluent countries.

WHERE CHILDREN FIT IN OTHER COUNTRIES' INCOME DISTRIBUTIONS
Figures 8.9 through 8.11 show the percentage of all children under eighteen found in each decile of the distribution of equivalent income for the full population for each country. Comparing Canada and the United States, Figure 8.9 shows a reasonably similar pattern of declining probability of children's presence as we move up the income distribution. In Canada, 62.2 percent of Canadian children have incomes in the bottom half of the distribution in 1997; in the United States, 63.3 percent of children are located in the bottom half of the income distribution. In Canada, 41.9 percent of children have incomes in the middle four deciles, close to the 40.8 percent for American children. Finally, children are more likely to be located in the bottom decile of the US distribution (15.8 percent versus 14.9 percent in Canada).

Figure 8.10 shows that children in the United Kingdom are even more likely than those in North America to be located in the bottom decile (17.7 percent versus 14.9 percent in Canada) and slightly more likely to be in the bottom half of the income distribution (62.5 percent) than Canadian children (61.8 percent). However, having a "middle income" is somewhat less common in the United Kingdom than in Canada (38.7 versus 41.9 percent).

The position of children in the Australian equivalent income distribution, also shown in Figure 8.10, looks rather different from that of children in Britain or North America in that a higher proportion have middle incomes.

FIGURE 8.9

Distribution of children by equivalent income deciles: all children, Canada and US, 1997

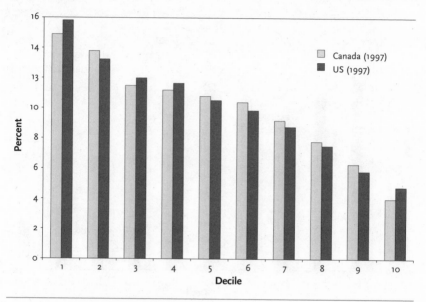

In Australia, 46.2 percent of children have incomes in the middle four deciles versus 41.9 percent in Canada. Roughly the same proportion of children are located in the bottom decile (14.4 percent in Australia versus 14.9 percent in Canada), which is lower than for either the United States (15.8 percent) or especially the United Kingdom (17.7 percent).

The position of children within the German equivalent income distribution is similar to Canada and the US. Again, children are most likely to be located at the bottom of the income distribution (15.7 percent in the bottom decile) and least likely to be located at the top (4.5 percent in the top decile). In fact, 67.1 percent of German children are located in the bottom half of the distribution (compared to 62.2 percent of Canadian children). Having a "middle income" is less likely in Germany (39.2 percent) than in Australia, for example, where 46.2 percent of children have equivalent incomes in the middle four deciles.

Finally, the Norwegian situation is the most different from the other countries studied (see Figure 8.11). In Norway, children are particularly likely to be found in the middle of the income distribution (47.3 percent), and,

FIGURE 8.10

Distribution of children by equivalent income deciles: all children, UK (1995) and Australia (1994)

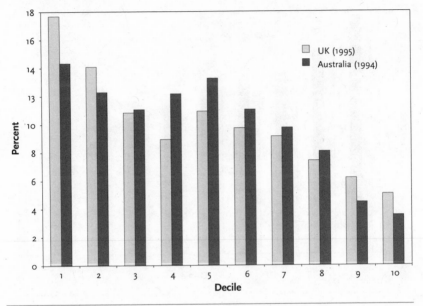

while they are more likely to be found at the bottom (10.9 percent) than the top (4.5 percent) of the distribution, the difference is not so extreme as it is in the other countries. In Canada, children are 3.5 times more likely to be in the bottom than the top decile; in the United States they are 3.3 times more likely; in Norway, they are only 2.4 times more likely. Since the same issues of parents' life-cycle stage apply to Norwegian as to Canadian children, these results are helpful in pointing out that children are not inevitably found at the bottom of the income distribution.

Consider next the association between children's experience of inequality in a country and the characteristics of the families in which they live. We focus on two family characteristics that differ significantly across the six countries studied: labour force participation of parents and single-parent status.[14]

First, when we contrast the positions in the income distribution of children in two-parent families as between one and two earners, it is clear that children living with one earner are more likely to be found toward the bottom half of the income distribution in countries where one-earner families are less common (Canada, Norway, and the United States). In the UK, how-

FIGURE 8.11

Distribution of children by equivalent income deciles: all children, Germany (1994) and Norway (1995)

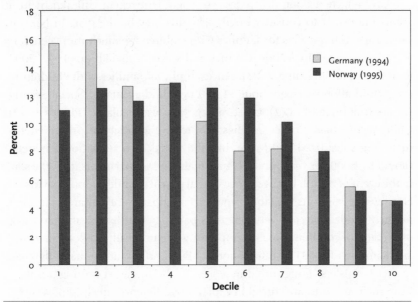

ever, where one-earner families are more common than two-earner families, children from one-earner families are distributed fairly evenly throughout the income distribution.

Second, while single-mother families tend to be less affluent in all countries studied, there are marked differences across the countries in the degree to which this is true. For example, over 45 percent of children in single-mother families are located in the bottom decile of the German income distribution, whereas only about 20 percent of children in Norwegian single-mother families are in the bottom decile. In fact, in Norway, more children from single-mother families are found in the second than in the bottom decile. Children in single-mother families in Canada and the United States fit into their respective country income distributions in much the same way – over 35 percent are located in the bottom decile in both cases.

The results for Norway stand out from those of the other countries studied here. Overall levels of inequality are lower, and children are much more likely to be located toward the middle of the Norwegian income distribution than are children in Canada and the United States, who are more likely to be found toward the bottom. Even children in single-mother Norwegian households are located much higher up the income distribution in Norway than is the case in Canada or the United States.

Given such striking differences in where Norwegian children fit in, it seems important to consider briefly *why* this may be the case. In Norway, universal social transfers for families with children are much more generous (e.g., Curtis and Phipps 2004; Gornick and Meyers 2003; Phipps 1999, 2003; Rainwater and Smeeding 2003). For example, *all* families with children receive child allowances of about $1,500 per child annually (Social Security Administration 2005, 172); tax advantages are also available (Phipps 1999). Children in single-mother families also receive a variety of other benefits, including subsidized child care, income-tested cash transitional benefits (about $14,000 per year), and advance maintenance payments from the state in the event of default by the non-custodial parent in child support payments. Norway also supports the labour-market participation of all parents through publicly funded daycare, very generous paid parental leaves, and paid days off to care for children who are temporarily or chronically ill. Both Smeeding and Rainwater (2003) and Bradbury and Jäntti (2000) argue that differences in social transfers, along with differences in labour market earnings resulting from such supports, are crucial in explaining differences in child poverty between Scandinavian and North American countries. Further research examining links between children's experiences of inequality and cross-country differences in policies and institutions would be worth pursuing.

Conclusion

While much is known about children's experiences of poverty in Canada and in comparison with other countries, less attention has been paid to children's experiences of inequality. Yet, this seems important, both as an issue of equity and as a determinant of children's well-being. This chapter analyzes changes in Canadian children's experiences of inequality across time (1973 to 1997) and in comparison with the experiences of children living in five other affluent countries (the United States, the United Kingdom, Australia, Germany, and Norway). The study examines how changes across time and differences across countries in the family settings of children relate to their experiences of inequality.

Our results indicate that there is less inequality in disposable household equivalent income among Canadian children than in the Canadian population overall. Inequality of market income increased significantly for Canadian children over the study period (1973-97). But the Canadian tax and transfer system managed to counteract increased market inequality so that inequality of disposable income among Canadian children actually fell very slightly. Note that the magnitude of the reduction in aggregate inequality among children observed between 1973 and 1997 appears small in comparison with the sometimes quite dramatic changes in the characteristics of the families in which they lived (such as increases in single-parent families, increases in two-earner families, reductions in family sizes, changes in the ages of mothers). Research by Frenette, Green, and Picot (Chapter 3) suggests that in the late 1990s, after our study period, inequality increased in Canada, and our tax and transfer system began to play a diminished redistributive role. Thus, our findings on inequality among Canadian children deserve to be updated for this new policy environment.

However, it is important to go beyond summary measures of inequality to study where children fit within the country income distribution. In Canada, children tend to be located toward the bottom of the country income distribution (although the same is not true for all countries). Moreover, changes in family characteristics have shuffled children's positions within the income distribution. For example, children in single-parent families or in families with one parent not working for pay are now lower in the distribution.

A comparison of Canada with five other affluent countries indicates that Canadian children experience a middling level of inequality, less than children living in the United States or the United Kingdom but more than children living in Norway. The international comparison also indicates that particular family circumstances are not always associated with the same position in the income distribution. For example, Canadian children living with single parents are almost always located at the very bottom of the income distribution, but that is not true in Norway. Comparative research on child poverty and social policy (Curtis and Phipps 2004; Gornick and Meyers 2003; Phipps 1999, 2001; Rainwater and Smeeding 2003) suggests that both labour market supports (e.g., maternity/parental benefits, leave to care for sick children, child care) and cash transfers (e.g., universal child benefits, special cash transfers for single-parent families, advance maintenance payments) are important explanations for Norway's lower levels of child poverty. Additional research could usefully examine the extent to which those factors play a role in reducing inequality among children.

SHELLEY PHIPPS AND LYNN LETHBRIDGE

ACKNOWLEDGMENTS

We thank Peter Burton, Lori Curtis, and Jon Kesselman for very helpful suggestions and the Social Sciences and Humanities Research Council for financial support.

NOTES

1 Throughout most of the chapter, we use an after-tax, after-transfer measure of household equivalent income. Obviously, larger families require larger incomes in order to have the same material standard of living as smaller families, but, given possibilities for sharing (e.g., housing and heating) within families, two people do not require twice the income of a single individual living alone. We use the equivalence scale recommended by the OECD, which assigns the first person in the household a value of one and adds 0.7 for each additional adult and 0.5 for each child. Thus, the equivalence scale for a two-parent plus one-child family would be $1.0 + 0.7 + 0.5 = 2.2$.

2 We use age of mother whenever a mother is present. For the relatively small number of single-father households, we use age of father. Although it would, perhaps, be preferable to use "age of mother at birth of first child," we do not have this information, since the public use versions of the SCF report only the number of children in a set of age categories.

3 We have separately conducted all the analyses reported here using a mean logarithmic deviation measure of inequality and have found the same story.

4 Some individuals with very low incomes may choose not to have children because they are unable to support them, and some individuals with very high incomes may choose not to have children because it interferes with their capacity to earn.

5 There was, however, an increase in inequality among children in the early 1980s, presumably reflecting increases in unemployment as a result of recession.

6 These points are consistent with Oxley et al. (2001).

7 Recall that we are studying all children from age 0 to 17. Most parents are thus members of the group aged twenty-five to fifty-four. In addition, we carried out our analyses for adults aged twenty-five to forty-four, a tighter age band. Ginis for the two groups of adults were extremely similar, and, again, general conclusions were not sensitive to the choice of comparison group.

8 Since children are always members of multi-person households, adjusting for family size will automatically move children down the income distribution. For example, while 61.8 percent of children had disposable *equivalent* incomes in the bottom half of the income distribution in 1997, if we do not adjust for family size, only 44.4 percent are located in the bottom half of the distribution. Using equivalent disposable income, only 4.1 percent of children were located in the top decile while using unadjusted disposable income, 9.5 percent are found in the top decile.

However, failing to adjust for family size would suggest that "two can live as cheaply as one," which is surely an exaggeration. Equivalent income comes much closer to measuring the standard of living actually experienced by the children themselves.

9   Unemployment rates were 5.6 in 1973, 10.6 in 1985, and 9.1 in 1997.

10 These points are, of course, much less important for parents with teenagers.

11 Again, we also replicated this analysis by fitting children into the distribution for the smaller set of adults aged twenty-five to forty-four. The results were essentially indistinguishable from those for the adults only.

12 We also calculated where children fit in the distribution of market income (pre-tax and pre-transfer). In the case of the full population distribution, adding transfers to household income results in a relative shift down in children's place in the distribution (in 1997, 14.1 percent are in the bottom decile of the disposable income distribution versus only 8.5 percent who are in the bottom decile of the market income distribution, presumably because elderly households receive much more in the way of transfers). If, on the other hand, we fit children into the distribution of working age adults, the tax-transfer system has little impact on where children are located (e.g., in 1997, 13.7 percent are in the bottom decile of market income versus the 14.6 percent who are in the bottom decile of post-transfer pretax income versus the 14.9 percent who are in the bottom decile of disposable income).

13 We also ran regressions using the 90:10 ratio and the 50:10 ratio, but the results added little to what is discussed here.

14 In the interests of space, we do not present all results in the figures, only general trends. More detailed results are available from the authors.

REFERENCES

Atkinson, A.B., and John Hills. 1998. "Exclusion, Employment and Opportunity." Centre for Analysis of Social Exclusion, CASE Paper CASE/4. London: London School of Economics.

Bradbury, Bruce, and Markus Jäntti. 2000. "Child Poverty across the Industrialized Countries: Evidence from the Luxembourg Income Study." In Koen Vleminckx and Timothy M. Smeeding, eds., Child Well-Being, Child Poverty and Child Policy in Modern Nations: What Do We Know? 7-32. Bristol, UK: Policy Press.

Brandolini, Andrea, and Giovanni D'Alessio. 2001. "Household Structure and Income Inequality." Luxembourg Income Study Working Paper No. 254. Syracuse, NY: Syracuse University. Available at http://www.lisproject.org/liswps254.pdf.

Crossley, Thomas F., and Lori J. Curtis. 2003. "Child Poverty in Canada." Working paper 2003-06. Department of Economics, McMaster University. Available at http://socserv.mcmaster.ca/econ/rsrch/papers/archive/2003-06.pdf.

Curtis, Lori, and Shelley Phipps. 2004. "Social Transfers and the Health Status of Mothers in Norway and Canada." *Social Science and Medicine* 58(12): 2499-507.

Esping-Andersen, Gøsta. 1990. *The Three Worlds of Welfare Capitalism.* Princeton, NJ: Princeton University Press.

Gornick, Janet, and Marcia Meyers. 2003. *Families That Work: Policies for Reconciling Parenthood and Employment.* New York: Russell Sage Foundation.

Jenkins, Stephen. 1995. "Accounting for Inequality Trends: Decomposition Analyses for the UK, 1971-86." *Economica* 62(245): 29-64.

Lynch, John W., George Davey Smith, George A. Kaplan, and James S. House. 2000. "Income Inequality and Mortality: Importance to Health of Individual Income, Psychosocial Environment, or Material Conditions." *British Medical Journal* 320: 1200-4.

Osberg, Lars. 2003. "Long-Run Trends in Economic Inequality in the USA, UK, Sweden, Germany, and Canada: A Birth Cohort View." *Eastern Economic Journal* 29(1): 121-42.

Oxley, Howard, Thai-Thanh Dang, Michael F. Forster, and Michele Pellizzari. 2001. "Income Inequalities and Poverty among Children and Households with Children in Selected OECD Countries." In Koen Vleminckx and Timothy M. Smeeding, eds., *Child Well-Being, Child Poverty and Child Policy in Modern Nations: What Do We Know?* 371-405. Bristol, UK: Policy Press.

Phipps, Shelley. 1999. *An International Comparison of Policies and Outcomes for Young Children.* Canadian Policy Research Network Study No. F/05. Ottawa: Renouf Publishing Company, Ltd.

—. 2001. "Values, Policies, and the Well-Being of Young Children in Canada, Norway, and the United States." In K. Vleminckx and T. Smeeding, eds., *Child Well-Being in Modern Nations,* 79-98. Bristol, UK: Policy Press.

Picot, Garnett, John Myles, and Wendy Pyper. 1998. "Markets, Families and Social Transfers: Trends in Low-Income among the Young and Old, 1973-95." In Miles Corak, ed., *Labour Markets, Social Institutions and the Future of Canada's Children.* Ottawa: Statistics Canada, Catalogue No. 89-553-XPB: 11-30.

Rainwater, Lee, and Timothy M. Smeeding. 1997. "Demography or Income Packaging: What Explains the Income Distribution of The Netherlands?" Luxembourg Income Study Working Paper No. 169. Syracuse, NY: Syracuse University. Available at http://www.lisproject.org/publications/liswps/169.pdf.

—. 2003. *Poor Kids in a Rich Country: America's Children in Comparative Perspective.* New York: Russell Sage Foundation.

Smeeding, Timothy M., and Lee Rainwater. 2002. "Comparing Living Standards across Nations: Real Incomes at the Top, the Bottom, and the Middle." Social Policy Research Centre, University of New South Wales. Discussion Paper 120. Available at http://www.sprc.unsw.edu.au/dp.

Social Security Administration. 2005. *Social Security Programs throughout the World: Europe, 2004*. SSA Publication No. 13-11801. Office of Policy, Office of Research, Evaluation, and Statistics. Available at http://www.ssa.gov/policy/docs/progdesc/ssptw/ 2004-2005/europe.

Wilkinson, Russell. 1996. *Unhealthy Societies: The Afflictions of Inequality*. London: Routledge Press.

9
Ethnic Inequality in Canada: Economic and Health Dimensions

Ellen M. Gee, Karen M. Kobayashi, and Steven G. Prus

Canada has a long history of ethnic exclusion, discrimination, and stratification. This chapter examines ethnic inequalities in contemporary Canada, focusing on economic and health inequalities. We draw on research findings from the literature supplemented by our own quantitative analysis. If a given subtopic has been well researched, we summarize and synthesize the findings. For subtopics about which less is known, we present relevant data, undertake analysis, and describe the context. We limit ourselves to Canadian literature for the most part. While there is substantial research on ethnic inequality in the United States, its applicability to Canada is tenuous because of the different histories of the two countries, especially regarding race. Before presenting our substantive analysis and findings, we briefly review the historical background for Canada's treatment of various ethnic groups.

Historical Background

Since the time of European settlement, Canadian society has been structured along ethnic and racial lines. The racial/ethnic dimension of inequality in Canada was first systemically studied and highlighted in John Porter's (1965) now-classic study, *The Vertical Mosaic*. Analyzing national data for the period 1931-61, Porter found evidence of an ethnically ranked system in terms of occupations, income, "ethnic prestige," and entry into the Canadian elite. Canadians of British origins came out on top; French Canadians were second; persons of other European origins followed – with western and northern European origins ranking higher than southern and eastern European origins; and Blacks and Aboriginals – very small groups numerically – were at the bottom of the hierarchy. What Porter captured, for the most part, was an ethnically stratified white Canada, its "whiteness" virtually guaranteed by the immigration policies of the day.

Very few people of Asian origins lived in Canada as a result of the Oriental Exclusion Act in place from 1923 to 1947. Also, South Asians were excluded from Canadian society through an order-in-council in 1908.[1] The few Asians who had settled in Canada prior to these discriminatory immigration practices faced a number of occupational prohibitions: for example, the Chinese could not work in certain occupations (e.g., coal mining, hand-logging, law, and pharmacy), and they were not able to hire white women to work for them in, for example, restaurants and laundries (Li 1979). The overtly racist elements of Canadian immigration policy, with its characterization of "preferred" and "non-preferred" immigrants based on ethnicity/race,[2] were not eliminated, or at least softened, until 1962.[3] Even in 1971, persons of European origins made up more than 96 percent of the Canadian population (Kalbach 2000).

While Canadian immigration policy operated to exclude certain people from Canadian shores, racist policies and laws regarding Aboriginals were also in place. The Indian Act of 1876, followed by the residential school system commencing in the late nineteenth century, and the denial of the right of indigenous people to vote in federal elections (rescinded in 1960) and provincial elections (eliminated during the 1950s and 1960s, with Quebec finally allowing Aboriginals to vote in 1969) were all based on racist assumptions (Satzewich 1998).[4] Among other consequences, these practices made First Nations peoples invisible (both spatially and politically) to mainstream society. Even within the social sciences, Aboriginal Canadians were virtually ignored, except by a few anthropologists (e.g., Hawthorn et al. 1958).

Thus, Canadian history is marked by racism toward persons of non-White/non-European origins. As noted by Simmons (1998, 93), Canadian leaders and most Canadian citizens historically viewed Canada as "a new European and Christian nation in the Americas." As such, it recreated European hierarchies vis-à-vis European ethnic groups and excluded, as much as possible, non-Europeans. Porter's (1965) work, then, must be placed in its historical context – near the end of a period in which Canada was almost entirely "white."

We are no longer in the past, but the long arm of history can reach to the present. Many significant events and policy changes have occurred since the time covered by Porter's research. Important among these have been continued non-racist improvements in Canadian immigration policy, the establishment of the Canadian Charter of Rights and Freedoms, the institutionalization of multiculturalism as a federal policy, the civil rights and women's movements, the Employment Equity Act (which targets women, visible minorities,[5] Aboriginals, and persons with disabilities), increasing awareness and acknowledgement of the injustices wrought on Aboriginal Canadians and nascent developments aimed at meeting their needs (Frideres 2000), and, last but not least, research revealing that race and racial difference have no basis in biology. The last of these creates a dilemma for social scientists: while we recognize the socially constructed nature of "race," we observe the realities of racism (Fleras and Elliott 1995). However, others argue that our continued use of the term "race" as an analytical concept legitimizes it as a valid way to categorize human beings and groups (e.g., Goldberg 1990).

These changes bode well for a Canadian society in which ethnicity is less significant as a principle of social organization and as a determinant of individual life chances. However, other changes have an opposite effect. Chief among these is the rapid change in the ethnic origins of immigrants. In the 1960s, approximately 90 percent of immigrants to Canada came from Europe and the United States; now, about 80 percent are members of visible minorities (Ley and Smith 1997). The ten leading source countries of immigrants are now China (including Hong Kong), India, Pakistan, the Philippines, Korea, Iran, Romania, and Sri Lanka – as well as the United States and the United Kingdom, whose combined total is about one-quarter the number of immigrants from China alone (Citizenship and Immigration Canada 2002).[6]

Also, economic conditions have changed significantly since the 1960s. Canada has entered the global economy and has experienced considerable corporate restructuring and downsizing and increased economic inequality and uncertainty over this period (Baker and Solon 2003; Johnson and Kuhn 2004; Morissette 1995; Myles and Street 1995; Picot et al. 1990). Against this economic backdrop, ethnic inequalities are more likely to surface (Li 1995; Waters and Eschbach 1995), especially in countries with a historical legacy of racist attitudes and practices. Thus, changing demographics and an uncertain economic environment can counteract the forces aimed at eliminating discrimination based on ethnic origin.

Data and Methods

DATA

The data used for the original analyses presented here are from the 1996 Canadian Census and the 1996-97 National Population Health Survey (NPHS). Census data are used to analyze the relationship between ethnicity and economic inequality, given the detailed information provided on the demographic, social, cultural, and economic characteristics of both permanent residents (Canadian-born citizens, naturalized citizens, landed immigrants) and non-permanent residents (e.g., refugee claimants) who are the target population. The data used here are based on a 5 percent random sample of the public-use microdata individual file of the Census, with observations having missing data excluded from the analyses.

The public-use microdata health file from the 1996-97 NPHS is used to measure ethnic differences relating to issues of health status and health care utilization. Based on a multi-stage stratified probability sampling design, the data in this survey reflect comprehensive information on health, use of health services, and socio-demographic characteristics of individuals. The target population of the NPHS includes household residents in all Canadian provinces, except for people residing in First Nations reserves, on Canadian Forces bases, and in institutions. Sample weights, which were adjusted to sum to sample size, are used in all NPHS data analyses here to account for unequal probabilities of selection as a result of the multi-stage sampling design.

MEASURES

This section details the ethnocultural independent variables and the economic and health dependent variables used in the analyses of Census and NPHS data. In terms of the independent variables, the Census data file contains information on three main indicators of the ethnocultural characteristics of Canadians – ethnic origin, mother tongue, and immigrant status.

Ethnic origin refers to the ethnic or cultural group(s) to which the respondent's ancestors belonged. We collapse this variable into eleven groups: (1) British (including persons with British and other ethnic origins); (2) French (including persons with French and other ethnic origins); (3) North or West [NW] Europe; (4) South or East [SE] Europe; (5) Chinese; (6) Indo (e.g., Bangladeshi, East Indian, Pakistani); (7) Other Asian (e.g., Filipino, Vietnamese, Indonesian, Japanese); (8) African (African and Caribbean origins); (9) Aboriginal (Inuit, Métis, North American Indian); (10) Canadian[7];

and (11) Other (e.g., Latin American, South American, non-British, non-French, and non-Canadian multiple origins).

Our categorization of ethnic origin, like any based on recent Canadian Census data, contains a degree of arbitrariness and guessing. The most difficult problem concerns the categorization of persons who report multiple ethnic origins (up to six ethnic origins per person are possible in the 1996 Census). Limiting our analysis to persons with single origins is not feasible, since 38 percent of Canadians reported multiple origins in the 1996 Census (Pendakur and Mata 2000). On the other hand, a classification including multiple origins has to be workable in terms of the number of categories. We have therefore erred on the side of caution with regard to assessing ethnic inequality in that persons with another origin (or origins) along with British or French are placed in the British/French categories.

Given the inter-relatedness of ethnocultural variables (e.g., recent immigrants are likely to be of non-European ethnic origins and to have mother tongues that are neither English nor French), we combine mother tongue (i.e., first language learned in childhood and still understood) and immigrant status into the following nine categories: (1) English, Canadian-born [CB]; (2) English, immigrated more than ten years ago [> 10] (i.e., 1985 or earlier); (3) English, immigrated ten years ago or 1ess [≦ 10] (i.e., 1986 or later); (4) French, Canadian-born; (5) French, immigrated more than ten years ago; (6) French, immigrated ten years ago or 1ess; (7) Other, Canadian-born; (8) Other, immigrated more than ten years ago; and (9) Other, immigrated ten years ago or 1ess. This categorization is based on the assumptions that an official language mother tongue (or not) and place of birth (and year of immigration if foreign-born) are important dimensions of ethnocultural background.

The ethnocultural measures in the NPHS public-use microdata file – used for the analysis of health inequalities – are less refined than in the Census; there are both fewer variables and larger aggregations of responses. There is no ethnic origin variable in this datafile. We measure ethnic origin in terms of country of birth, immigrant status, and language (i.e., language(s) in which a respondent can conduct a conversation).

Country of birth is coded as Canada, Europe (including Australia), Asia, and Other countries. To examine the "healthy immigrant effect" (immigrants, and particularly recent immigrants, are healthier than Canadian-born persons), variables for the country of birth and the length of time since immigration are combined to create the following categories: (1) Canada; (2) Europe, immigrated more than ten years ago; (3) Europe, immigrated ten years ago or less; (4) Asia, immigrated more than ten years ago; (5) Asia, immigrated ten years ago or less; (6) Other, immigrated more than ten years ago; and (7) Other, immigrated ten years ago or less. Language is coded as (1) English only, (2) French only, (3) English and French only, and (4) Other.

A multi-dimensional approach is also used to measure the economic and health dependent variables. We use three indicators of economic well-being available in the Census. While these indicators are related, each provides a unique perspective on economic well-being and inequality. The first indicator, "major source of income," is the income component that constitutes the largest proportion of the total income of a family for the calendar year 1995. The major sources of income are collapsed into two categories: (1) private sources (i.e., wages/salaries, self-employment income, investment income, private pension, and other income) and (2) public sources (i.e., government transfer payments) or no income (n = 19,860 for the size of the sample responding to the question either way). This variable also gives the public-private split for major income sources as a relevant measure of economic well-being because reliance on public sources is often associated with lower economic well-being and higher economic instability and alienation, especially during the traditional working years. These are issues that are not always captured by comparing average income in dollars between groups.

The second economic indicator, employment status, refers to the labour market activity of respondents in the week prior to Census day. Persons are classified as either employed or non-employed (those who are either unemployed or not in the labour force) (n = 24,015). The third indicator, home ownership, refers to whether the respondent or some member of the household owns (partly or fully, with or without mortgage) the dwelling in which household resides, as opposed to renting it (n = 28,281).[8] Since we feel that adults are the appropriate unit of analysis, especially for economic inequality, our analyses in this chapter are confined to the adult Canadian population. The data for major source of income and employment status refer to persons aged twenty to sixty-four, and the home ownership data pertain to those aged twenty and over.

For health status, we ascertain whether respondents have a chronic health condition, that is, a health problem (e.g., asthma, arthritis, high blood pressure, migraine headaches, diabetes, heart disease) that has lasted or is expected to last six months or more and has been diagnosed by a health professional. Categories are "yes" (at least one condition) and "no" chronic condition (n = 65,473). We also examine health care access and utilization: whether a respondent had a physical check-up during the twelve months prior to the NPHS interview (n = 63,630) and whether a respondent had a mammogram during the past twelve months (n = 24,253). The categories are yes/no. The health data apply to persons aged twenty and over, except the mammogram data, which pertain only to women aged thirty-five and over. Overall, these indicators provide various insights (both unique and complementary) into ethnoculturally based inequalities in health and health-related behaviours.

Data Analysis

Logistic regression analysis is used to examine the relationship between ethnicity and economic inequality (Census data) and between ethnicity and health inequality (NPHS data). Two regression models are computed for each economic and health dependent variable. The first model includes ethnocultural variables only. The second model introduces control variables to estimate the extent to which the findings in the first model are influenced by these variables. The control variables are gender, age (twenty to thirty-four, thirty-five to fifty-four, and fifty-five and over), marital status (coded in the Census as married, divorced/separated, widowed, never married; coded in the NPHS as married, single, widowed/separated/divorced), education (coded in the Census as total years of school; coded in the NPHS as less than high school graduate, high school graduate, college graduate, university graduate), and household income (for the health/NPHS analysis only, coded as low, low-middle, middle, upper-middle, and high income). Significant findings in the second model may suggest the effects of discrimination.

Results

Overview

Table 9.1 provides an overview of the Canadian population aged twenty and over, in terms of ethnic origin(s), mother tongue, place of birth, and time since immigration. The Census sample data used in this table have been weighted to represent the entire Canadian population aged twenty and over in 1996. Nearly 15 percent of Canadians were members of visible minority groups including Aboriginals – a substantial increase from 1971 when, as mentioned earlier, fewer than 4 percent of Canadians were of non-European origins. As of 1996, more than 5 percent of adult Canadians had a mother

TABLE 9.1

Percentage distribution of ethnic groups by mother tongue and immigrant status, Canadian population aged twenty and over

| | Mother tongue and immigrant status | | | | | | | | | Total | |
| | English | | | French | | | Other | | | | |
Ethnicity	CB	>10	≤10	CB	>10	≤10	CB	>10	≤10	%	Number
British	27.5	3.6	0.4	0.5	<0.1	<0.1	0.1	0.1	<0.1	32.2	(6,638,760)
French	5.9	0.2	<0.1	12.6	0.2	0.1	0.1	0.1	<0.1	19.1	(3,941,208)
NW European	2.7	0.2	<0.1	0.1	<0.1	0.1	0.9	1.9	0.2	6.2	(1,274,004)
SE European	2.3	0.3	<0.1	0.1	0.1	<0.1	1.8	3.6	0.8	9.0	(1,855,872)
Chinese	0.1	0.1	<0.1	<0.1	<0.1	<0.1	0.2	1.1	1.4	2.9	(595,332)
Indo	0.1	0.2	0.2	<0.1	<0.1	<0.1	0.1	0.6	0.7	1.9	(390,312)
Other Asian	0.2	0.1	0.1	<0.1	<0.1	<0.1	0.2	0.9	1.2	2.6	(540,756)
African	0.2	0.5	0.2	<0.1	<0.1	<0.1	<0.1	0.1	0.2	1.4	(297,576)
Aboriginal	0.6	<0.1	<0.1	0.1	—	—	0.6	<0.1	<0.1	1.3	(267,120)
Canadian	8.6	0.1	<0.1	9.9	<0.1	<0.1	0.2	0.1	<0.1	18.9	(3,904,632)
Other	2.0	0.3	0.1	0.2	<0.1	<0.1	0.4	0.7	0.5	4.4	(904,500)
Total	50.2	5.6	1.1	23.6	0.5	0.1	4.6	9.2	5.2	100	(20,610,072)
	(10,342,188)	(1,151,352)	(218,088)	(4,855,716)	(97,596)	(30,636)	(949,284)	(1,903,716)	(1,061,496)		

NOTE: CB = Canadian-born; >10 = Foreign-born, immigrated more than 10 years ago; ≤10 = Foreign-born, immigrated 10 years ago or less.
SOURCE: 1996 Census of Canada, public-use microdata individual file (weighted to population).

tongue other than English or French and had resided in Canada for ten years or less. Another 9 percent had an "other" mother tongue but were immigrants of longer duration of residence. Of course, the majority of Canadians – approximately 73 percent – were of European origin and Canadian-born. Another 5 percent were Canadian-born, but of non-European immigrant origins.

Economic Inequalities

A considerable amount of research exists on ethnic-based economic inequalities. The most intensively researched area is income differences, for which we provide a summary of recent studies. Occupational inequality is another area that has attracted much research, which we also summarize. Less well-studied topics include sources of income, employment status, and home ownership; for these items, we provide original analysis based on 1996 Census data.

Income

Recent studies on the ethnic dimensions of income inequalities, using different data and employing somewhat differing ethnicity categorizations and sets of control variables, converge on one main finding – that visible minorities and Aboriginals earn less income than European-origin Canadians.[9] Further, ethnic variations in income between Canadians of European origin have virtually disappeared, though there is evidence that persons of southern European backgrounds earn less than their British-origin counterparts, while French-Canadians fare better, in a reversal of Porter's data regarding the two "charter groups." Although all groups of Aboriginals are disadvantaged in wages and salaries, status Indians earn the least, followed by Inuit, then Métis, and, finally, non-status Indians.

However, Hum and Simpson (1999) find that, except among black men, visible minority men who are Canadian-born do not experience a significant wage disadvantage. Language does not explain the immigrant status difference, but this finding may be related, in part, to other assimilation and acculturation indicators such as adherence to diverse value systems and sensitivity to and understanding of North American work culture. Specifically, in comparison to their Canadian-born counterparts, foreign-born visible minority men may continue to adhere strongly to traditional (country of birth) value systems around work and the family that may clash with Canadian norms, values, and beliefs. Such incongruence may give rise to conflict in the workplace, leading to employer-imposed limitations on wage opportunities.

Further insights into the salience of these indicators, which are more complex than the single variables of non-Canadian and Canadian work experience examined in Hum and Simpson's study, can be gained through the use of qualitative research methods (such as face-to-face interviews with employers and employees) in various labour market contexts.

Smith and Jackson (2002) also report that recent immigrants fare much worse in incomes than did immigrants who arrived in Canada in the 1980s – which cannot be explained by lower levels of educational attainment. In fact, recent immigrants most negatively affected in income are the well educated who were selected on the basis of their skills and language ability (Thompson 2002). Smith and Jackson (2002) attribute the economic difficulties of recent immigrants, at least in part, to increased racial discrimination, as do recent immigrants themselves (Kunz et al. 2000). Others such as Thompson (2002) see the major cause in macroeconomic conditions, while still others argue that an important policy challenge is to ensure the recognition of foreign credentials as equivalent to Canadian credentials when that is the case. More research is needed in this area, but one lesson learned is that visible minorities are a diverse group with regard to eventual incomes.

Indeed, Gee and Prus (2000) examine income inequalities within ethnic categories and find large inequalities for visible-minority men – the Gini index is 0.41 among visible-minority men compared to a Gini of about 0.34 for non-visible-minority men. Gee and Prus also find that within-Aboriginal-group income dispersion is significant, and Maxim et al. (2001) find that among Aboriginals the Inuit have the highest level of income polarization and the Métis the lowest level. Overall, these findings mean that even in disadvantaged groups, some people earn a lot of money. Gee and Prus argue that some visible minorities must "make it" in the Canadian labour force in order to entrench existing ascribed-based systems; if some minorities did not excel, the discrepancy would be too great to allow Canadians to maintain their ideology of equal opportunities. That is, the status quo depends on the existence of some "exceptions."

Most of the quantitative research on ethnicity and income does not examine the interrelationships among gender, ethnicity, and immigration status. Either gender is used as a control variable, or women are compared with women and men with men. Regarding the latter, we have seen that ethnic factors figure more strongly in men's incomes than in women's incomes. However, it has also been shown that gender differences in income are greater for members of visible minority groups than for those of European origin

(Harvey et al. 1999). This makes it is easy to overlook the fact that income is highly gendered. The disadvantaged economic fate of immigrant women can also be overlooked. Hum and Simpson (1999) find that immigrant women have very low income levels, whether or not they are members of visible minorities. They suggest that policy measures should focus more on immigrant assistance and perhaps less on traditional employment equity legislation.

Overall, it can be concluded that gender, ethnic origin, and place of birth interrelate in complex ways to affect income levels (Beach and Worswick 1993). Research in Canada is only beginning to tease out these interconnections. It is too early to conclude that race is today the fundamental basis of income differences among Canadians (Lian and Matthews 1998). Men's incomes are affected by ethnicity, but the large income gap between men and women suggests that gender is a still more influential determinant of income, even for visible minority groups. That said, however, there is much to be learned about how ethnicity and gender operate together in determining income outcomes in the Canadian context.

Occupation

The ethnic dimension of occupations was one of Porter's (1965) foci and continues to be researched in Canada, albeit considerably less than income inequality. Indeed, Nakhaie (1997) finds that those of British descent continue to dominate the Canadian "elite," although persons of non-British origins have made some inroads over the years.

As pointed out by Lautard and Guppy (1999), the relationship between ethnicity and occupation can be examined in two different ways. One approach centres on the ethnic division of labour, that is, on whether ethnic groups are concentrated in certain occupations. The other approach examines the place of "ethnic" groups in the occupational prestige hierarchy.

Looking at the first dimension, for men only, it has been reported that Aboriginals are disproportionally represented in the construction industry (more than double the Canadian male average) – and under-represented in managerial and administrative occupations. For Chinese, there is over-representation in the natural sciences, engineering, and mathematics occupations (13 percent vs. 6 percent) and in service occupations (19 percent vs. 10 percent); South Asian (Indo-Canadian) men are more likely to be in clerical occupations (11 percent vs. 7 percent) as are Black men (12 percent); the latter two groups are under-represented in managerial and administrative jobs (8 percent for both vs. 14 percent). Among women, Aboriginals are concentrated in service jobs (27 percent vs. 16 percent), but visible minority women (that is, Chinese, South Asian, and Black) do not have occupational distributions strikingly different from the average for all Canadian women (Lautard and Guppy 1999). It should be noted that the data on ethnic occupational concentration do not compare with the degree of gender occupational concentration. For example, nearly one-half of Canadian women are in clerical and service occupations, compared to 17 percent of the male labour force. Clearly, Canada has a more gendered labour force than an ethnically-differentiated one.

Turning to occupational prestige, for men, ethnic groups with high levels include the Jewish, British, and Chinese; low levels of occupational prestige are found for – in ascending order – Blacks, Greeks, Aboriginals, and Portuguese. For women, a very similar picture emerges, except that Chinese women fall below average (Lautard and Guppy 1999). For occupational prestige, ethnicity outweighs gender as a predictor, but these findings do not mean that high-prestige occupations are closed off entirely to members of visible minority groups (Satzewich 2000). As with income, the diversity of visible minorities with regard to occupational distribution is substantial. Nonetheless, as pointed out by Hou and Balakrishnan (1996), visible minorities face more hurdles in attaining equality in incomes than in occupations.

Income Source, Employment, and Home Ownership

This section expands on the literature described above by examining other dimensions of economic well-being using 1996 Census data. Table 9.2 shows the estimated odds ratios of (1) having private income (as opposed to public or no income) as the major source of family income, (2) being employed (as opposed to being unemployed or not in the labour force), and (3) owning a home (as opposed to renting) across ethnocultural groups. The odds ratios are shown separately before ("unadjusted") and after ("adjusted") controlling for gender, age, marital status, and education. The reference group for ethnicity is British origin and for mother tongue and immigration status it is English, Canadian-born.

Overall, these findings show that, as with research on income and occupation, there is inequality between visible and non-visible minority groups as well as among visible minorities. Persons of Asian, especially Chinese, origin generally fare the best on these measures of economic well-being, followed by those of European-origin (with only moderate differences among British, French, and NW/SE-European groups), while persons of African and

Aboriginal origin tend to be the most disadvantaged among the ethnocultural groups observed here. Our analysis also concurs with findings in the literature that foreign-born persons (especially recent immigrants) with a non-English mother tongue are economically disadvantaged. However, these advantages and disadvantages can be partly accounted for by differences in gender, age, marital status, and education. The advantage of persons of Asian

TABLE 9.2

Economic events: odds ratios in relation to ethnocultural factors, before (unadjusted) and after (adjusted) controlling for gender, age, marital status, and education

Ethnocultural groups	Main income: private		Employed		Own home	
	(unadjusted)	(adjusted)	(unadjusted)	(adjusted)	(unadjusted)	(adjusted)
Ethnicity						
British (ref)						
French	1.099	0.977	1.210**	1.032	0.894*	0.961
NW European	1.116	1.144	1.219**	1.334**	1.214**	1.193*
SE European	1.137	1.231*	1.290**	1.293**	1.404**	1.555**
Chinese	2.499**	2.315**	1.363**	0.872	2.684**	3.185**
Indo	1.526**	1.118	1.252*	0.793*	0.961	0.992
Other Asian	1.382*	0.862	1.696**	0.990	0.635**	0.716**
African	0.568**	0.449**	1.170	0.819	0.303**	0.408**
Aboriginal	0.265**	0.334**	0.443**	0.399**	0.126**	0.185**
Canadian	0.893*	0.829**	1. 116*	0.963	0.861**	0.965
Other	1.568**	1.159	1.521**	1.035	0.773**	0.833*
Mother tongue, immigration						
English, CB (ref)						
English, > 10	0.955	0.986	0.783**	0.943	1.107	0.907
English, ≤ 10	1.216	1.011	0.875	0.728*	0.456**	0.397**
French, CB	0.719**	1.038	0.696**	0.889*	0.896**	0.943
French, > 10	0.843	1.093	0.760	1.062	0.873	0.655*
French, ≤ 10	0.556**	0.333**	0.896	0.511 *	0.405**	0.330**
Other, CB	0.721**	0.863	0.658**	0.831*	0.936	0.906
Other, > 10	0.516**	0.914	0.500**	0.893	1.239**	0.937
Other, ≤ 10	0.424**	0.365**	0.514**	0.458**	0.281**	0.208**
Nagelkerke R^2	0.024	0.261	0.017	0.354	0.062	0.196
N	19,860		24,015		28,281	

* $p < .05$, ** $p < .01$.
SOURCE: 1996 Census of Canada, 5 percent random sample of the public-use microdata individual file.

origin in private income and employment status, for instance, is considerably reduced after introducing these control variables, while the economic disadvantage of Canadian-born Francophones and Allophones compared to their Anglophone counterparts almost entirely disappears.

HEALTH INEQUALITIES

Research into the health of Canadians has grown considerably over the past few decades. The study of ethnocultural differences in health, by contrast, has received very little attention. An overview of the literature that does exist is provided here, and we add to it by examining both health status and health care access and utilization using 1996-97 NPHS data.

Research finds that immigrants have better health than their Canadian-born counterparts (e.g., Ali 2002; Chen et al. 1996; Kopec et al. 2001; Perez 2002) and that this "healthy immigrant effect" may explain some of the variance in health across different cultural and ethnic groups. The health of immigrants, however, varies with length of time since immigration, with the most recent immigrants experiencing better health than long-term immigrants, whose health-related behaviours and thus health status are more like those of the Canadian-born population.

Using a more specific measure of ethnicity and health, Sheth and his colleagues (1999) conclude that there are significant differences in the rates of death from ischemic heart disease and cancer among Canadians of European, South Asian, and Chinese origin. In particular, European immigrants have high death rates from heart disease and cancer, South Asian immigrants have high death rates from diabetes and heart disease but low cancer mortality, and Chinese immigrants have low rates of death from heart disease and intermediate cancer mortality. The researchers note that the "relative risk of death for all other immigrants to Canada (excluding South Asians and Chinese) was similar to that for people of European origin" (ibid., 137). This suggests that the "healthy immigrant" effect has only a modest influence on the findings.

Another examination of the association between ethnicity and chronic disease is Wang and colleagues' (2000) study on arthritis prevalence and place of birth, using data from the 1994-95 NPHS. After adjusting for age, gender, socioeconomic variables, and body mass index, the findings indicate that the risk for arthritis is significantly lower among Asian immigrants than among North American-born Canadians. Thus, both immigrant status and ethnic origin are factors influencing the self-reported prevalence of arthritis in the Canadian population. Relatedly, Acharya (1998) finds differences in mental health status and its predictors by country of birth of Canadian immigrants, while Wu et al. (2003) find East and Southeast Asian, Chinese, South Asian, and Black populations experience the lowest rates of depression in Canada.

A study of social inequality, population health, and housing in British Columbia by Dunn and Hayes (2000) investigates the ways in which housing-related factors, in conjunction with other socio-demographic factors like ethnicity, affect health. With regard to culture, their findings indicate that ethnic origin, simultaneously with housing factors, is an important indicator of self-rated health. In particular, respondents were more likely to report good health if they were of non-Western ethnic origin (e.g., Chinese, Filipino, Vietnamese, East Indian) and felt that they could satisfy their needs for traditional foods, medicines, and other goods in their own neighbourhoods.

Health Status: Chronic Conditions

Data from the 1996-97 NPHS reveals differences between Canadians on the basis of country of birth/language and health status/care. Table 9.3 shows our estimated odds ratios of having (1) a chronic condition (as opposed to not having one), (2) a physical check-up during the past twelve months (as opposed to not having one), and (3) a mammogram during the past twelve months (as opposed to not having one) across ethnocultural groups. Again, results are shown separately on an unadjusted basis and after adjusting for the effects of gender, age, marital status, education, and income. The reference group for country of birth/immigration status is Canadian-born, and, for language, it is English-only.

The data indicate that the likelihood of having a chronic condition, which is often considered a broad measure of health, is lowest for recent immigrants, especially Asian-born. This finding continues to hold after socioeconomic and demographic factors are taken into account. This "healthy immigrant effect" may be due to a number of factors, such as healthier individuals self-selecting into the immigration process and health requirements in the Immigration Act tending to disqualify people with serious medical conditions from entering Canada (Oxman-Martinez et al. 2000). The likelihood of having a chronic health problem is also lower for non-English-speaking Canadians (odds ratio of 0.835 for French only and 0.840 for Other, $p < .01$). Although Canadians living in First Nations communities are not included in

TABLE 9.3

Health events: odds ratios in relation to ethnocultural factors, before (unadjusted) and after (adjusted) controlling for gender (for chronic condition and physical check-up models only), age, marital status, education, and income

Ethnocultural groups	Have chronic condition (unadjusted)	(adjusted)	Had physical check-up (unadjusted)	(adjusted)	Had mammogram (unadjusted)	(adjusted)
Country of birth, immigration						
CB (ref)						
Europe, > 10	1.346**	1.029	1.328**	1.136**	1.339**	1.229**
Europe, ≤ 10	0.586**	0.695**	0.772**	0.842*	1.160	1.379*
Asia, > 10	0.960	0.944	1.235**	1.217**	0.768**	0.826
Asia, ≤ 10	0.393**	0.412**	0.824**	0.896	0.334**	0.377**
Other, > 10	0.947	0.926	1.352**	1.385**	1.134	1.334*
Other, ≤ 10	0.485**	0.548**	0.854	0.926	0.667*	0.920
Language						
English only (ref)						
French only	0.835**	0.710**	0.621**	0.611**	0.774**	0.797**
English and French	1.003	1.078**	0.862**	0.907**	0.998	1.048
Other	0.840**	0.865**	1.091**	1.137**	1.109*	1.129*
Nagelkerke R^2	0.016	0.106	0.016	0.053	0.012	0.064
N	65,473		63,630		24,253	

$* p < .05, ** p < .01.$

SOURCE: 1996-97 National Population Health Survey, public-use microdata health file (weighted for sampling design).

this sample, research shows that the prevalence of all self-reported major chronic diseases is significantly higher among Aboriginal people than in the general population, and it appears to be increasing (Young et al. 1999).

Health Care Access and Utilization: Physical Check-Up and Mammogram
Table 9.3 also presents data on the last time a respondent had a mammogram or physical examination. A notable finding is the strong relationship between rates of breast cancer screening and country of birth. Asian-born female immigrants have a significantly decreased likelihood of having had a mammogram in the last year compared to Canadian-born women, which is consistent with the research results of Hislop et al. (2000) on breast and cervical cancer screening for Chinese-Canadian women in British Columbia.

This finding is striking, given that early detection of breast cancer by mammograms has been shown to reduce mortality among middle-aged and older women (Federal/Provincial/Territorial Advisory Committee 1999).

Why do Asian-born women, the majority of whom are long-term immigrants, not have screening mammograms? First, in some traditional Asian cultures (such as Chinese and Vietnamese) where medical assistance is sought only when an individual is feeling ill, the concept of preventive medicine may be unfamiliar (Dinh et al. 1990; Lai and Yue 1990). Second, if, in addition to cultural incongruence, a language barrier exists between physician and patient, an older woman will be even less likely to go to a diagnostic clinic for screening. Third, there may be ethnocultural differences in a fear of clinics, labs, and hospitals due to negative attitudes and behaviours of family physicians in some communities.

The likelihood of having a mammogram for French-only-speaking women and of having a physical check-up in the last year for all French-only-speaking persons is also significantly lower than for their English-speaking counterparts. Yet, the opposite occurs for non-English-speaking or non-French-speaking adults. These findings are notable because we would expect differences in health care utilization between English-speakers and Canadians who speak another language to operate in the reverse direction, and for insignificant differences to exist between the two charter language groups. The fact that French-speaking adults are less likely to have had a mammogram or physical exam in the last year may be related to differences in health status between the two groups.

Conclusion

Our findings are consistent with existing literature on ethnic inequalities in Canada. We find that persons with non-English mother tongues are at an economic disadvantage. This is especially the case for recent immigrants with mother tongues other than English or French, who are shown by our data to be among the most disadvantaged in Canadian society. We also find that certain visible-minority and Aboriginal groups tend to be economically disadvantaged, while others are economically advantaged (e.g., those of Chinese origin are the most financially secure of the groups measured here) compared to persons of European origin, even when gender, age, marital status, and education differences are taken into account. Clearly, visible minorities are a diverse group with regard to economic outcomes. By comparison, variation in average economic well-being among European groups

(British, French, and NW and SE European) is relatively minor. Overall, these findings support the argument that the economic disparities faced by ethnic groups are partly attributable to racial discrimination in Canadian society.

We also find significant differences in health status and health care utilization according to country of birth, immigrant status, and language. However, recent immigrants (especially from Asia) are advantaged in health outcomes compared to Canadian-born persons. This advantage disappears with time; recent immigrants experience fewer chronic health conditions than their long-term counterparts. Paradoxically, they are less likely to report having a physical check-up and, for older women (especially Asian-born women), a mammogram within the last year compared to Canadian-born older women. These patterns are observed for those who speak French only as their mother tongue.

In interpreting the health inequality findings, the key emergent issue is the clash between the ethnocultural values and beliefs of foreign-born and perhaps French-speaking Canadians and the health care system. Although it is difficult to provide insights into this relationship, given the paucity of research in this area, our findings indicate that cultural characteristics, regardless of socio-structural and demographic factors, are salient predictors of health.

Our findings also support Macleod and Eisenberg's suggestion in Chapter 2 that a cultural framework is needed in order to fully understand the outcomes of social inequality in Canadian society. Indeed, the cultural variables of ethnicity, immigrant status, and mother tongue are related to economic well-being, health status, and health care utilization in Canada. Specifically, Aboriginals, visible minorities, and immigrants who speak neither English nor French experience deficits in cultural capital (i.e., skills, qualifications, group memberships), which, in turn, have implications for SES and health outcomes..

Finally, an interesting and important finding from the study is that much of the economic inequality according to type of occupation (occupational concentration) can be attributed to gender rather than ethnicity; that is, the Canadian labour force continues to be more gender-differentiated than ethnicity-differentiated. Evidence of this gendered division in the labour force is presented by Fortin and Schirle in Chapter 11. Given the significance of both gender and ethnicity as predictors of economic well-being, future research should examine the intersection between the two identity markers and their relationship to social inequality.

NOTES

1 This order-in-council subjected South Asians to the "continuous journey" rule, which required immigrants to enter Canada only by one continuous trip from their home countries and with their tickets purchased in those countries. South Asians could only make a continuous journey to Canada through the Canadian Pacific Railway steamship company, which was prohibited by the Canadian government from selling tickets to South Asians (Bolaria and Li 1985).

2 Race/ethnicity was not the only basis for immigrant selection or for inclusion in or exclusion from Canadian society. As pointed out by Avery (1995), other bases included gender, sexual orientation, health status, and political beliefs.

3 Simmons (1998) argues that contemporary Canadian immigration policy is no longer blatantly racist; it is non-racist but not anti-racist. Non-racist policies can display neo-racist features, that is, systemic elements that can have racist influences and outcomes.

4 Sexism was also implicated in Aboriginal policy. For example, for many years, Aboriginal women who out-married would lose their status, whereas out-marrying men would retain theirs.

5 We use the term "visible minority/ies" in this chapter. Though this term offends some people, alternatives such as "persons of colour" are disagreeable to others. The federal government considers eleven groups to constitute visible minorities: Chinese, South Asians [Indo-Canadians], Blacks, Arabs, Central/West Asians, Filipinos, Southeast Asians, Latin Americans, Japanese, Koreans, and Pacific Islanders.

6 Moreover, some of the immigrants from the United States and, particularly, the United Kingdom are members of visible minority groups.

7 A challenge with the 1996 Census data on ethnic origin is the large number of "Canadian/Canadien" responses. Between the 1991 and 1996 Censuses, the Canadian response increased dramatically, so that is it now the largest ethnic origin group (Boyd 1999). Part of this increase is due to a change in the format of the ethnicity question in the 1996 Census – from checked boxes to open-ended – and the fact that "Canadian" was added to the list of examples on the Census form. Analyses show that most persons reporting "Canadian/Canadien" are Canadian-born of English and French origins (Boyd 1999; Pendakur and Mata 2000). Within Quebec, nearly one-half of persons reported a "Canadien" origin in 1996, which Boyd (1999) attributes to the symbolic meaning of "Canadien" as a term French-Canadians favour to distinguish themselves from the French and from the (British) Canadian elite (as well as the absence of "French-Canadian" and "Québécois" as examples on the Census form). While this change in the distribution of ethnic origins is problematic for research that assesses trends in the ethnicity of the Canadian population, it poses less difficulty for us. We make "Canadian" a separate

category, recognizing that it is largely a European-origin (and Canadian-born) group.

8 Shelter occupancy on reserves (i.e., band housing) is included in the "rent" category. The band owns a high proportion of houses on reserves. The occupants, who make "mortgage payments" to the band until the mortgage is paid off, are considered by the band to be renters and not owners.

9 See, for example, DeSilva (1999); Gee and Prus (2000); George and Kuhn (1994); George et al. (1996); Geschwender and Guppy (1995); Li (1998); Lian and Matthews (1998); Maxim et al. (2001); Pendakur and Pendakur (1998).

REFERENCES

Acharya, M. 1998. "Chronic Social Stress and Emotional Well-Being: An Analysis of Mental Health of Immigrants in Alberta." *Canadian Studies in Population* 25: 1-27.

Ali, J. 2002. "Mental Health of Canada's Immigrants." *Health Reports* 13: 1-11.

Avery, D. 1995. *Reluctant Host: Canada's Response to Immigrant Workers.* Toronto: McClelland and Stewart.

Baker, M., and G. Solon. 2003. "Earnings Dynamics and Inequality among Canadian Men, 1976-1992: Evidence from Longitudinal Income Tax Records." *Journal of Labor Economics* 21: 289-321.

Beach, C.M., and C. Worswick. 1993. "Is There a Double-Negative Effect on the Earnings of Immigrant Women?" *Canadian Public Policy* 19: 36-53.

Bolaria, B.S., and P. Li. 1985. *Racial Oppression in Canada.* Toronto: Garamond Press.

Boyd, M. 1999. "Canadian, eh? Ethnic Origin Shifts in the Canadian Census." *Canadian Ethnic Studies* 31:1-19.

Chen, J., E. Ng, and R. Wilkins. 1996. "The Health of Canada's Immigrants in 1994-95." *Health Reports* 7 (4):33-45.

Citizenship and Immigration Canada. 2002. *News Release: More Than 250,000 New Permanent Residents in 2001.* Ottawa: Citizenship and Immigration Canada, February.

DeSilva, A. 1999. "Wage Discrimination against Natives." *Canadian Public Policy* 25: 65-85.

Dinh, D., S. Ganesan, and N. Waxler-Morrison. 1990. "The Vietnamese." In N. Waxler-Morrison, J. Anderson, and E. Richardson, eds., *Cross-Cultural Caring: A Handbook for Professionals in Western Canada*, 81-213. Vancouver: UBC Press.

Dunn, J.R., and M. Hayes. 2000. "Social Inequality, Population Health, and Housing: A Study of Two Vancouver Neighborhoods." *Social Science and Medicine* 51: 563-87.

Federal/Provincial/Territorial Advisory Committee on Population Health. 1999. *Towards a Health Future. Second Report on the Health of Canadians.* Ottawa: Health Canada. Cat. No. H39-468/1999E.

Finnie, R., and R. Meng. 2002. "Minorities, Cognitive Skills, and Incomes of Canadians." *Canadian Public Policy* 28: 257-73.

Fleras, A., and J.L. Elliot. 1995. *Unequal Relations: An Introduction to Race, Ethnic and Aboriginal Dynamics in Canada.* Toronto: Prentice-Hall.

Frideres, J.S. 2000. "Revelation and Revolution: Fault Lines in Aboriginal-White Relations." In M.A. Kalbach and W.E. Kalbach, eds., *Perspectives on Ethnicity in Canada*, 207-37. Toronto: Harcourt.

Gee, E.M., and S.G. Prus. 2000. "Income Inequality in Canada: A 'Racial Divide.'" In M.A. Kalbach and W.E. Kalbach, eds., *Perspectives on Ethnicity in Canada*, 238-56. Toronto: Harcourt.

George, P., and P. Kuhn. 1994. "The Size Structure of Native-White Wage Differentials in Canada." *Canadian Journal of Economics* 27: 20-42.

George, P., P. Kuhn, and A. Sweetman. 1996. "Patterns of Employment, Unemployment and Poverty: A Comparative Analysis of Several Aspects of the Employment Experience of Aboriginal and Non-Aboriginal Canadians Using 1991 PUMP." *Royal Commission on Aboriginal People: People to People, Nation to Nation.* Ottawa: Minister of Supply and Services.

Geschwender, J., and N. Guppy. 1995. "Ethnicity, Educational Attainment, and Earned Income among Canadian-Born Men and Women." *Canadian Ethnic Studies* 27: 67-83.

Goldberg, D. 1990. *Anatomy of Racism.* Minneapolis: University of Minnesota Press.

Harvey, E., B. Siu, K. Reil, and J. Blakely. 1999. "Socioeconomic Status of Immigrant Men and Women in Selected Ethnocultural Groups in Canada." Paper presented at the Third National Metropolis Conference, Vancouver, January.

Hawthorn, H.B., C.S. Belshaw, and S. Jamieson. 1958. *The Indians of British Columbia: A Study of Contemporary Social Adjustment.* Toronto: University of Toronto Press.

Hislop, T.G., C.Z. The, A. Lai, T. Labo, and V. Taylor. 2000. "Cervical Cancer Screening in BC Chinese Women." *British Columbia Medical Journal* 42: 456-60.

Hou, F., and T.R. Balakrishnan. 1996. "The Integration of Visible Minorities in Contemporary Canadian Society." *Canadian Journal of Sociology* 21: 307-26.

Hum, D., and W. Simpson. 1999. "Wage Opportunities for Visible Minorities in Canada." *Canadian Public Policy* 25: 379-91.

Humphries, K.H., and E. van Doorslaer. 2000. "Income-Related Health Inequality in Canada." *Social Science and Medicine* 50: 663-71.

Johnson, S., and P. Kuhn. 2004. "Increasing Male Earnings Inequality in Canada and the United States, 1981-1997: The Role of Hours Changes versus Wage Changes." *Canadian Public Policy* 30: 155-75.

Kalbach, W.E. 2000. "Ethnic Diversity: Canada's Changing Cultural Mosaic." In M.A. Kalbach and W.E. Kalbach, eds., *Perspectives on Ethnicity in Canada*, 59-72. Toronto: Harcourt.

Kopec, J.A., J.I. Williams, T. To, and P.C. Austin. 2001. "Cross-Cultural Comparisons of Health Status in Canada Using the Health Utilities Index." *Ethnicity and Health* 6(1): 41-50.

Kunz, J.L., A. Milan, and S. Schetagne. 2000. *Unequal Access: A Canadian Profile of Racial Differences in Education, Employment and Income.* Toronto: Canadian Race Relations Foundation.

Lai, M.C., and K.K. Yue. 1990. "The Chinese." In N. Waxler-Morrison, J. Anderson, and E. Richardson, eds., *Cross-Cultural Caring: A Handbook for Professionals in Western Canada,* 68-90. Vancouver: UBC Press.

Lautard, H., and N. Guppy. 1999. "Revisiting the Vertical Mosaic: Occupational Stratification among Canadian Ethnic Groups." In P.S. Li, ed., *Race and Ethnic Relations in Canada.* 2nd ed., 219-52. Toronto: Oxford University Press.

Ley, D., and H. Smith. 1997. "Immigration and Poverty in Canadian Cities, 1971-1991." *Canadian Journal of Regional Science* 20: 29-48.

Li, P.S. 1979. "A Historical Approach to Ethnic Stratification: The Case of the Chinese in Canada." *Canadian Review of Sociology and Anthropology* 16: 320-32.

—. 1995. "Racial Supremacism under Social Democracy." *Canadian Ethnic Studies* 27: 1-18.

—. 1998. "The Market Value and Social Value of Race." In V. Satzewich, ed., *Racism and Social Inequality in Canada: Concepts, Controversies, and Strategies of Resistance,* 115-30. Toronto: Thompson Educational Publishing.

—. 2000. "Earning Disparities between Immigrants and Native-Born Canadians." *Canadian Review of Sociology and Anthropology* 37: 289-311.

Lian, J.Z., and D.R. Matthews. 1998. "Does the Vertical Mosaic Still Exist? Ethnicity and Income in Canada, 1991." *Canadian Review of Sociology and Anthropology* 35: 461-81.

Maxim, P.S., J.P. White, D. Beavon, and P.C. Whitehead. 2001. "Dispersion and Polarization among Aboriginal and Non-Aboriginal Canadians." *Canadian Review of Sociology and Anthropology* 38: 465-76.

Morissette, R. 1995. "Why Has Inequality in Weekly Earnings Increased in Canada?" Research Paper No. 80. Ottawa: Statistics Canada, Analytical Studies Branch.

Myles, J., and D. Street. 1995. "Should the Economic Life Course Be Redesigned? Old Age Security in a Time of Transition." *Canadian Journal on Aging* 14: 336-60.

Nakhaie, M.R. 1997. "Vertical Mosaic among the Elites: The New Imagery Revisited." *Canadian Review of Sociology and Anthropology* 34: 2-24.

O'Loughlin, J. 1999. "Understanding the Role of Ethnicity in Chronic Disease: A Challenge for the New Millennium." *Canadian Medical Association Journal* 161(2): 152-53.

Oxman-Martinez, J., S. Abdool, and M. Loiselle-Leonard. 2000. "Immigration, Women, and Health in Canada." *Canadian Journal of Public Health* 91: 394-95.

Pendakur, R., and F. Mata. 2000. "Patterns of Ethnic Identification and the 'Canadian' Response." In M.A. Kalbach and W.E. Kalbach, eds., *Perspectives on Ethnicity in Canada,* 73-87. Toronto: Harcourt.

Pendakur, K., and R. Pendakur. 1998. "The Colour of Money: Earnings Differentials among Ethnic Groups in Canada." *Canadian Journal of Economics* 31: 518-48.

Perez, C.E. 2002. "Health Status and Health Behaviour among Immigrants." *Health Reports* 13: 1-12.

Picot, G., J. Myles, and T. Wannell. 1990. "Good Jobs/Bad Jobs and the Declining Middle: 1967-1986." Research Paper no. 28. Ottawa: Statistics Canada, Analytical Studies Branch.

Porter, J. 1995. *The Vertical Mosaic.* Toronto: University of Toronto Press.

Satzewich, V. 1998. "Introduction." In V. Satzewich, ed., *Racism and Social Inequality in Canada: Concepts, Controversies and Strategies of Resistance,* 11-24. Toronto: Thompson Educational Publishing.

—. 2000. "Social Stratification: Class and Racial Inequality." In B.S. Bolaria, ed., *Social Issues and Contradictions in Canadian Society,* 165-94. Toronto: Harcourt Brace.

Sheth, T., C. Nair, M. Nargundkar, S. Anand, and S. Yusuf. 1999. "Cardiovascular and Cancer Mortality among Canadians of European, South Asian and Chinese Origin from 1979 to 1993: An Analysis of 1.2 Million Deaths." *Canadian Medical Association Journal* 161(2): 132-38.

Simmons, A. 1998. "Racism and Immigration Policy." In V. Satzewich, ed., *Racism and Social Inequality in Canada: Concepts, Controversies and Strategies of Resistance,* 87-114. Toronto: Thompson Educational Publishing.

Smith, E., and A. Jackson. 2002. *Does a Rising Tide Lift All Boats? The Labour Market Experiences and Incomes of Recent Immigrants, 1995-1998.* Ottawa: Canadian Council on Social Development.

Thompson, E. 2002. "The 1990s Have Been Difficult for Recent Immigrants in the Canadian Labour Market." *Quarterly Labour Market and Income Review* 3(1): 21-25 (Ottawa: Human Resources Development Canada).

Wang, P., R. Elsbett-Koeppen, G. Geng, and E. Badley. 2000. "Arthritis Prevalence and Place of Birth: Findings from the 1994 Canadian National Population Health Survey." *American Journal of Epidemiology* 152: 442-45.

Waters, M.C., and K. Eschbach. 1995. "Immigration and Ethnic and Racial Inequality in the United States." *Annual Review of Sociology* 21: 419-46.

Wu, Z., S. Noh, and V. Kaspar. 2003. "Race, Ethnicity, and Depression in Canadian Society." *Journal of Health and Social Behavior* 44: 426-41.

Young, T., J. O'Neill, and B. Elias. 1999. "Chronic Diseases." *First Nations and Inuit Regional Health Survey.* Ottawa: First Nations and Inuit Regional Health Survey National Steering Committee.

10
Recent Trends in Wage Inequality and the Wage Structure in Canada

Brahim Boudarbat, Thomas Lemieux, and W. Craig Riddell

After a lengthy period of relative stability, the decades of the 1980s and 1990s brought pressures toward growing inequality in Canada and several other countries. Such pressures raised concerns that Canadian society may increasingly become characterized by "haves" and "have-nots." These developments raised a number of important issues, some related to the nature of the phenomenon, including: Are the earnings of individuals indeed becoming more unequally distributed? If so, is this a general phenomenon or one concentrated on particular groups? Do changes in the earnings of individuals imply similar changes in family income? How does the tax and transfer system affect the distribution of disposable (after-tax-and-transfer) family income? Other questions are related to the causes and consequences of these developments, and many of them are addressed in the chapters in this volume.

This chapter addresses the first two questions noted above – whether individual earnings are becoming more unequally distributed, and which groups in society are affected. More specifically, this chapter examines recent Canadian trends in wage inequality and in the "wage structure," that is, the systematic variation of wages with characteristics such as education, age, and gender. While a number of studies have documented the evolution of wage inequality and the wage structure during the 1980s and early 1990s, little is known about more recent trends during the strong economic recovery of the late 1990s and the (mild) recession of 2001.

The principal contribution of the chapter is to update these trends using newly available data from the 2001 Census. An important finding is that the wage differential between more-educated and less-educated workers increased sharply during the second half of the 1990s. We also find a similar result using two other data sets, the Survey of Labour and Income Dynamics (SLID) and the Labour Force Survey (LFS). Another interesting development is that, after fifteen years of sustained expansion, the wage differential between younger and older workers declined substantially between 1995 and 2000.

Our analysis complements that provided in several other chapters. Whereas Fortin and Schirle in Chapter 11 examine gender differences in earnings, we focus mainly on wage differences by age and education, though we report results separately for males and females because the trends for the two groups are so different. Moreover, we consider the wages of individual workers, leaving the analysis of family income to Frenette, Green, and Picot in Chapter 3.

The plan of the study is as follows. We begin by surveying the existing literature on the evolution of wage inequality and the wage structure in Canada and highlight the key knowledge gaps in the area. Then we describe the various data sets available and argue that the Census is best suited to our purpose. The main Census results are presented, followed by a close examination of changes in the university-high school wage gap among subgroups of the population. We then show that our main Census findings are robust to the choice of alternative wage measures and alternative data sets. A final section summarizes our conclusions.

Literature Survey

A number of studies have examined the evolution of wage inequality and the wage structure in Canada since the early 1980s. Unlike studies of the United States, that show an unmistakable increase in wage inequality during this period, studies of Canada are more ambiguous. On the one hand, studies of inequality in hourly wage rates using special supplements to the LFS generally find little change in overall measures of wage inequality, such as the variance of log wages.[1] On the other hand, studies of inequality in weekly or annual earnings using the Survey of Consumer Finances (SCF), the Canadian Census, or administrative tax data tend to find steady growth in earnings inequality.[2]

Why these different data sources yield different trends in wage inequality remains an open issue. A possible answer is that the growth in earnings inequality is being driven by growing inequality in hours of work instead of growing inequality in hourly wages (Morissette et al. 1993; Doiron and Barrett 1996; Osberg, Chapter 6 in this volume). Another possible answer is that some of the growth in observed wage dispersion is due to increasing measurement error in wage and earnings measures (Lemieux 2003).

Despite these differences, however, a number of key trends in the wage structure appear to be robust to the choice of data source. In particular, a number of studies on the wage structure in Canada have documented a steep growth in the wage gap between older and younger workers, especially during the first half of the 1980s (e.g. Beaudry and Green 1998, 2000; Picot 1998a, 1998b). It is also widely accepted that in Canada, unlike in the United States, the wage gap between more-educated and less-educated workers remained stable throughout the 1980s and early 1990s (Freeman and Needels 1993; Murphy et al. 1998).

Overall inequality can be decomposed into two components. The "within-group" portion refers to the amount of inequality within a particular age-education-gender group, while the "between-group" component refers to the amount of inequality that arises from earnings differences across age-education-gender groups. Since the trends in wage differentials between age and education groups appear to be robust to the choice of data, within-group inequality must be the source of discrepancy across data sources in trends in overall wage inequality. Indeed, studies that use direct measures of hourly wages, such as Card et al. (1999) find no growth of within-group inequality. By contrast, studies that use the SCF, such as Morissette et al. (1993), document substantial growth of within-group inequality. This contrast is consistent with Lemieux (2003), who finds that, in the United States, within-group wage inequality grows much more in the March Current Population Survey (CPS), where earnings reports are collected on an annual retrospective basis (as in the Canadian SCF), than in the May and outgoing rotation group supplements of the CPS, where earnings reports for most workers are collected on an hourly and contemporaneous basis. In light of these measurement problems, we will focus our analysis on the evolution of the wage structure and only briefly mention trends in overall and within-group wage inequality.

The fact that returns to education appear to be relatively stable in Canada is surprising in light of the dramatic growth in returns to education south of the border. The standard explanation for this apparent paradox is that the relative supply of highly educated workers increased faster in Canada than in the United States after the early 1980s (Freeman and Needels 1993; Murphy et al. 1998). In the United States, the consensus is that returns to education increased because the relative demand for more-educated workers grew faster than the relative supply (Katz and Murphy 1992). The faster growth in relative supply in Canada may have been just enough to keep returns to education stable.

In both Canada and the United States, however, the fact that returns to education appear to have remained stable in the 1990s is puzzling. The 1990s are viewed by many as a period of unprecedented technological change that should have resulted in a large increase in the demand for highly skilled workers. In fact, Card and DiNardo (2002) view the stability in American returns to education in the 1990s as a major challenge to the view that recent changes in the wage structure are primarily driven by skill-biased technical change.

Unfortunately, the trends in the wage structure since the mid-1990s have not been as well documented in Canada as in the United States. The major challenge is the lack of consistent data sources throughout the 1990s. Until recently, most studies used the Survey of Consumer Finances (SCF), which was discontinued in 1997.[3]

An exception is Burbidge et al. (2002), who document recent changes in returns to schooling by combining data from the SCF up to 1997 with data for more recent years from the SLID and the LFS. They conclude that the return to schooling – the wage gap between university-educated and other workers – remained stable overall throughout the period 1981-2000. More surprisingly, they also find that the return to schooling remained stable even for young men over the last two decades. This finding appears to contradict studies by Bar-Or et al. (1995), Beaudry and Green (1998), and Card and Lemieux (2001), all of whom found that the return to schooling grew substantially for young men during the 1980s and early 1990s.

This chapter updates the analysis of trends in wage inequality using data from the 1981 to 2001 Census. We turn now to describe the data used in the study and explain why we think that the Census is the best data source for documenting trends in the wage structure and wage inequality in Canada.

Data

Census of Canada
Every five years from 1981 to 2001, the Census of Canada collected consistent information on educational attainment, earnings, and work experience during the previous year (annual earnings from different sources, weeks worked, and full-time employment status) and other socioeconomic characteristics of individuals. The information on educational attainment is unusually rich. The Census provides detailed information on years of schooling and degrees and diplomas obtained. We combine these variables to classify workers into seven education groups: up to eight years of elementary schooling, some high school, high school diploma, some post-secondary educa-

tion, post-secondary degree or diploma below a university bachelor's degree (including trade certificates), university bachelor's degree, and post-graduate degree (Masters, PhD, and professional degrees).

Another advantage of the Census for studying the evolution of the wage structure is the large sample size. In the Census, basic questions about demographics and educational attainment are asked of all individuals in the population. Twenty percent of individuals are also asked an additional set of questions (the "long form") about earnings and labour market activities. Over the years, Statistics Canada has made available public use samples, which are random samples of 10 to 15 percent (depending on the years) of individuals who completed the "long form." These represent large samples of 2 to 3 percent of all individuals in the country. Following the existing literature, we focus our analysis on "adults" age sixteen to sixty-five at the time of the Census (June).[4] The sizes of the available samples of workers range from 235,606 in 1981 to 418,209 in 1991.[5]

One difficulty in studying recent trends in the wage structure is that public use samples of the 2001 Census are not yet available. Fortunately, as part of this project, Garnett Picot, Andrew Heisz, and Logan MacLeod of Statistics Canada kindly provided us with special tabulations from the "master files" of the 2001 Census. These tabulations are based on the full 20 percent sample of individuals who answered the "long form" in the 2001 Census (3,041,619 workers).

One drawback of the Census for studying the evolution of the wage structure is that it only provides limited information on annual hours of work. It is, therefore, not possible to construct a direct measure of average hourly wages by dividing annual earnings by annual hours of work.[6] Following Card and Lemieux (2001) and many American studies such as Katz and Murphy (1992), we use weekly earnings of full-time workers as our main measure of wages. The existing evidence suggests that trends in the wage structure (wage dispersion between age or education groups) are relatively robust to the choice of wage measure. By contrast, trends in within-group, or residual, wage inequality should be interpreted with caution, as they appear to be sensitive to the choice of wage measure. In light of this, we focus on measures of wage dispersion between age and education groups, for both men and women.

Following most of the literature, we only use wage and salary earnings for computing weekly earnings of full-time workers. Another common practice that we do not follow here is to limit the sample to "full-year" workers who worked at least forty-nine or fifty weeks during the previous year.[7] For the sake of completeness, however, we report some results using all earnings (both wage and salary and self-employment earnings) and some results using the sample limited to full-year workers.

In the public use files of the Census, earnings are top-coded for a small fraction (less than 1 percent) of individuals with very high earnings. Statistics Canada adjusts the top-code over time to keep it more or less constant in real terms.[8] For the sake of consistency, we also top-code earnings in the 2001 Census at the same value in real terms as the $200,000 top-code in the 1996 Census ($217,850). Finally, we trim all wage observations with weekly earnings below $75 (in 2000 dollars) since they yield implausibly low values for hourly wages.[9]

OTHER DATA SETS

We think that the Census is the best data source for studying the evolution of wage inequality and the wage structure because it provides a consistent measure of educational attainment over the 1980-2000 period. As mentioned earlier, the evolution of wage differences across educational groups is a central issue in the literature on wage inequality in Canada, the United States, and other countries. It is thus essential to have a data source like the Census, which provides information on the evolution of the returns to education in a consistent fashion over a sufficiently long period of time, including recent years.

Several other microdata sets also contain information on education and earnings in Canada. In particular, most previous studies on wage inequality have relied on the Survey of Consumer Finances (SCF), which was conducted annually (or bi-annually) until 1998 (earnings year 1997). The earnings and work experience variables in the SCF are very similar to those in the Census. In principle, it is thus possible to construct the same wage measure – weekly wage and salary earnings of full-time workers – in the SCF as in the Census. The major disadvantage of the SCF is that education is not measured in a consistent fashion over time. In particular, between 1989 and 1990, there was an important change in the way educational achievement was measured in the SCF.[10] For instance, prior to 1990, the LFS questions limited post-secondary education to the type of education that normally requires high school completion. After 1990, any education that could be counted toward a community college diploma, a trade certificate, or a university degree is treated as post-secondary. As a result, the number of individuals classified as having completed post-secondary education increased very substantially in 1990, while the number of individuals with some secondary school decreased sub-stantially. Furthermore, prior to 1990, it is not possible to separate individu-als with a university bachelor's degree from those with a post-graduate degree. Prior to 1990, it is thus not possible to compute the standard wage difference between individuals with exactly a bachelor's degree and individuals with exactly a high school diploma.

The other obvious disadvantage of the SCF for measuring recent trends in the wage structure is that it was discontinued in 1998 (earnings year 1997). Since then, Statistics Canada has been releasing cross-sectional files from the SLID that are intended as a replacement for the SCF. Unfortunately, several key variables are collected very differently in the SLID than in the SCF. In particular, earnings of respondents are self-reported in the SCF, while admin-istrative tax records are used for most respondents in the SLID. Furthermore, as in all panel surveys, some of the respondents in the SLID cannot be fol-lowed over time. Relative to a pure cross-section like the SCF or the Census, this attrition bias may affect sample composition in ways that are difficult to take into account.

Because of these various measurement problems, we strongly believe that the Census is superior to the SCF/SLID for measuring the evolution of the wage structure in Canada since the early 1980s. We, nonetheless, report some results for the SCF and the SLID for the sake of completeness and com-parability with previous studies.

The last data source we use is the LFS, which has collected information about hourly wages on a monthly basis since January 1997. The key advan-tage of the LFS over the SCF and the Census is that it collects information about the hourly wage rate of workers on their main job. The LFS can thus be used to examine how using weekly earnings of full-time workers – a measure that can also be computed in the LFS – instead of using hourly wages affects the results. It also provides an additional source of information on recent trends in the Canadian wage structure.

Finally, in the SLID, unlike the SCF or the Census, it is possible to con-struct a measure of hourly wage rates from detailed information on all jobs held by individuals in the previous year. We thus report results using both this wage measure and the more traditional measure – weekly earnings of full-time workers – that can be constructed from the information about total earnings and weeks of work in the previous year. We also process the SLID, SCF, and LFS data to make the samples and wage measures as comparable as possible to those used in the Census. In particular, we trim low wage values, only use wage and salary earnings, and only retain individuals aged sixteen to sixty-five.

Main Results from the Census

In this section, we present wage differences among groups with different levels of education, age, and experience. Because the patterns often differ by gender, the wage gaps are presented separately for men and women. For ease of interpretation, we show the wage differentials over the 1980 to 2000 period graphically, so that differences at each point in time as well as trends over time are evident. We also summarize key features of the earnings data in tables.

We begin by showing wage differences by education, age, and experience without controlling for other factors. Although such unadjusted wage differences are reported in many studies, they are, by themselves, of limited value because they do not take into account other influences on wages. We then report regression-adjusted wage differentials that control for education and experience, two major influences on wages. Adjusting for experience is more appropriate than adjusting for age because individuals with the same age may have different amounts of work experience. For example, at any age, university graduates typically have about four years less experience than high school graduates.

Figures 10.1 to 10.4 show both unadjusted and regression-adjusted wage differentials among the different education groups. The wage differentials reported are all defined relative to workers with a high school diploma (but without any post-secondary education, including trade certificates). Unadjusted wage differentials are simply the difference between the mean log wage of workers in a given education group and the mean log wage of high school graduates.[11] The regression-adjusted estimates are obtained by estimating a standard regression of log wages on a set of six education dummies (high school is the base case) and a quartic in potential experience. We use the standard procedure to compute years of potential experience, defined as age minus years of schooling minus six. The Census asks detailed questions about years of schooling completed, and we use this information to compute potential experience.

Since we do not have access to the microdata from the 2001 Census, we cannot directly estimate a wage regression on individual-level data. We instead use a two-step approach. In the first step, we compute average log wages for each age-education group (or cell). We have fifty age groups (age sixteen to sixty-five) and seven education groups, for a total of 350 age-education cells. The number of cells is reduced to 332 by eliminating eighteen cells of individuals who are too young to have completed a given level of education (negative potential experience).[12] In the second step, we estimate a weighted earnings regression for mean cell wages. The weights used in the regression are the number of people in each cell. When all the variables in the regression can be written as a function of age and education, the two-step estimates are numerically equivalent to the estimates obtained by running directly the same regression on the microdata.

The two approaches do not yield identical results in our case because potential experience is constructed using the years-of-schooling variable, which is not simply a function of the seven education categories. The problem is that this variable takes on different values for individuals in the same education group. For instance, some people with exactly a bachelor's degree report sixteen years of schooling completed, while others report seventeen years of schooling. In the cell-level regressions, we use mean years of schooling within each cell to compute years of potential experience in that cell. In other words, we impute the same level of potential experience to all workers in the same age-education cell. This is different from estimating a regression model at the individual level where individual-specific potential experience is used instead. Fortunately, using average potential experience (in the cell) instead of the individual specific potential experience has little impact on the estimated wage differentials.[13]

RETURNS TO EDUCATION

Figure 10.1 presents the raw education-wage differential for men. To simplify discussion of the results, we will refer to workers with exactly a bachelor's degree as "BA" graduates, although this group also includes individuals with other types of bachelor's degrees like a B.Sc. We also interpret differences in log wages as percentage point differences for presentation purposes.[14]

The main result in Figure 10.1 is that the high school-BA wage differential increased sharply between 1995 and 2000.[15] Between 1980 and 1995, the high school-BA differential was relatively stable at around 30 to 35 percentage points. It then jumped to 40 percent in 2000. Similarly, the wage differential between university post-graduates and high school graduates expanded sharply after 1995. By contrast, the wage differentials between other education groups and high school graduates are smaller and relatively stable over time. In fact, wage differentials are close to zero for all the remaining

Figure 10.1

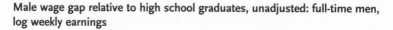

Male wage gap relative to high school graduates, unadjusted: full-time men, log weekly earnings

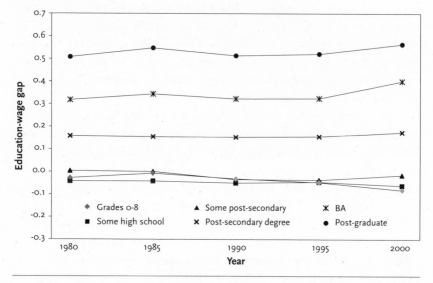

education groups except workers with a post-secondary degree below a BA (includes university certificates below a BA, community college or CEGEP diplomas, and trade certificates). Taken at face value, Figure 10.1 suggests that, for men, returns to high school completion relative to returns for elementary or some secondary schooling are very small.

However, Figure 10.2 shows that adjusting for differences in years of potential experience has important consequences for the pattern of education differentials. The regression-adjusted wage differentials are systematically larger (in absolute value) than the unadjusted wage differentials. For example, the adjusted wage gap between high school graduates and workers with only elementary schooling (zero to eight years) is 20 percent in Figure 10.2, compared to almost zero in Figure 10.1. High school dropouts make about 10 percent less than high school graduates in Figure 10.2, while workers with some post-secondary education earn 5 to 10 percent more.

The discrepancy between the adjusted and unadjusted differentials is due to the fact that the workforce has become increasingly educated over time. For instance, most of the workers with only elementary schooling are

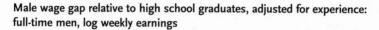

FIGURE 10.2

Male wage gap relative to high school graduates, adjusted for experience: full-time men, log weekly earnings

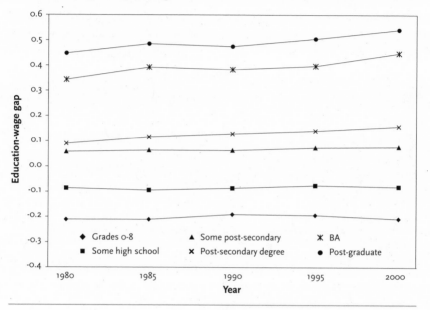

older and more experienced. This explains why the relative earnings of this group decline substantially when experience is held constant. In other words, secular growth in educational attainment generates a negative correlation between schooling and experience. As a result, returns to education are biased down when experience is not controlled for.

Unlike the unadjusted wage gap, which is stable over time, the adjusted wage gap between workers with a post-secondary diploma and a high school diploma grows steadily from 9 percent in 1980 to 16 percent in 2000. Interestingly, the adjusted wage gap between high school and university graduates increases more steadily than does the unadjusted gap in Figure 10.1. For example, the adjusted high school-BA gap increases from 34 percent in 1980 to 40 percent in 1995, while the unadjusted gap remains relatively unchanged (around 32 percent) over the same period. Most of the rise in the adjusted wage gaps took place in the early 1980s and late 1990s. For all university graduates (bachelor's degree or more), both the adjusted and unadjusted wage gaps relative to high school graduates increase sharply after 1995.

Figure 10.3

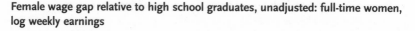

Female wage gap relative to high school graduates, unadjusted: full-time women, log weekly earnings

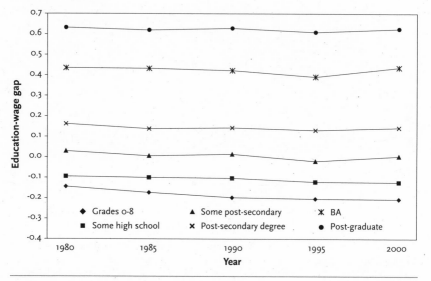

Figures 10.1 and 10.2 show clear evidence that returns to education have been increasing for Canadian men between 1980 and 2000. But while the growth in unadjusted wage differentials is limited to university graduates between 1995 and 2000, the growth in adjusted wage gaps is more evenly spread out among time periods and education groups.

The results for women reported in Figures 10.3 and 10.4 are quite different from those for men. First, returns to education are systematically larger than they are for men.[16] For instance, the adjusted high school-BA gap for women in 1980 (48 percent) is much larger than the corresponding wage gap for men (34 percent). Second, most education-wage differentials among women have increased only moderately over time. The only exception is the return to high school completion which has remained stable – as was the case for men. Overall, there has been some convergence between the returns to education of men and women between 1980 and 2000. However, returns to education remain larger for women than men in 2000.

The differences between unadjusted and adjusted differentials high-light the importance of controlling for other factors (in this case, experi-

FIGURE 10.4

Female wage gap relative to high school graduates, adjusted for experience: full-time women, log weekly earnings

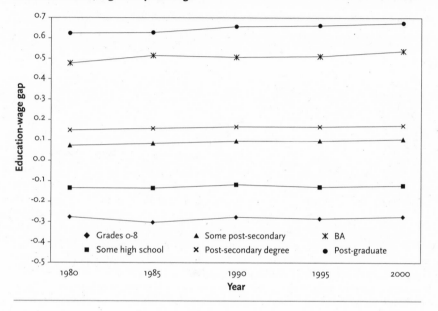

ence) when making wage comparisons among education groups and across time. Accordingly, in the remainder of the chapter we focus on the adjusted differentials.[17]

RETURNS TO AGE/EXPERIENCE

Figure 10.5 reports the adjusted wage differentials between men aged forty-six to fifty-five and men of other age groups.[18] These wage gaps are computed from a regression of log wages on a set of age dummies that also control for education (using dummies for the seven education categories). Men aged forty-six to fifty-five are used as the base group since they tend to have the highest earnings of all age groups. Figure 10.5 shows a large and steady expansion in the wage gap between younger workers (aged sixteen to twenty-five or twenty-six to thirty-five) and older workers between 1980 and 1995. This finding is consistent with other studies such as Beaudry and Green (2000) and Picot (1998a, 1998b). Our Census results for 1980-95 thus confirm the well-known fact that returns to experience grew significantly while returns to education remained relatively stable over this period.

Figure 10.5

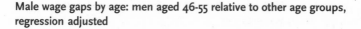

Male wage gaps by age: men aged 46-55 relative to other age groups, regression adjusted

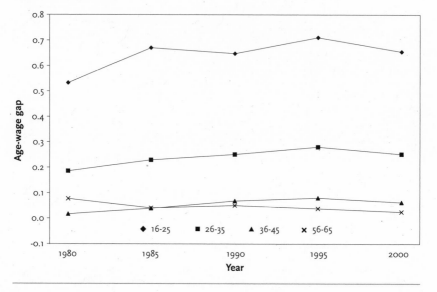

Figure 10.5 also shows, however, that after 1995 relative wages of younger workers started improving. This reversal in earlier trends is sufficiently marked that by 2000 the wage gap between younger and older workers is back to its mid-1980s level. Clearly, young workers did relatively well in terms of earnings during the economic expansion of the late 1990s.

When unadjusted wage gaps (not shown) are used instead of adjusted wage gaps, there is substantially greater growth in the age wage gaps between 1980 and 1995. For instance, the wage gap between the older base group of workers and younger workers aged twenty-six to thirty-five in 1995, both adjusted and unadjusted, was about 28 percent. The fact that controlling for education had no impact on the wage gap means that these two groups had similar levels of education. By contrast, in 1980 the unadjusted gap (12 percent) was substantially smaller than the adjusted gap (19 percent), suggesting that younger workers were more educated than older workers. This pattern of results is consistent with Card and Lemieux (2001), who show that, in both Canada and the United States, there has been stagnation in educational attainment of men born after 1950 (aged thirty in 1980). This explains why

FIGURE 10.6

Female wage gaps by age: women aged 46-55 relative to other age groups, regression adjusted

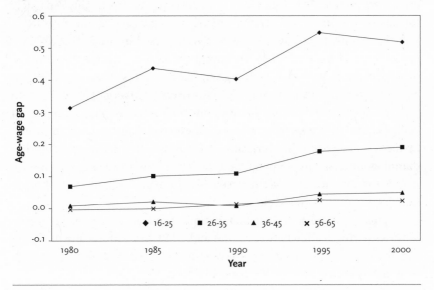

the unadjusted wage gap grew almost twice as fast as the adjusted gap between 1980 and 1995, a conclusion also reached by Morissette et al. (1999).

Figure 10.6 shows that adjusted age-wage differentials increase substantially more for women than for men over the period 1980-95. The decline in age-wage differentials after 1995 is also smaller for women than for men; indeed, for some age groups the differentials simply remain stable after 1995. Unlike educational wage differentials, age-wage differentials are also substantially lower for women than men. This is consistent with the well-known fact that returns to age, or potential experience, are lower for women because they tend to accumulate less actual experience than do men over the life cycle. The growth in age-wage differentials for women may thus simply reflect the fact that younger cohorts of women are increasingly attached to the labour market.

OVERALL WAGE INEQUALITY

We now examine trends in overall wage inequality. This analysis complements the previous examination of wage differentials by education, age, and experience. It also allows us to assess the extent to which the observed change in inequality is due to wage differences between education and experience groups and how much is due to changes in inequality within education and experience groups. As before, we examine overall wage inequality separately for men and women. We use the variance of log wages as our measure of wage inequality. In addition to being a widely used measure of inequality, the variance of log wages has the advantage of being readily decomposed into "between group" and "within group" components.

We next decompose the growth in the overall variance of log wages into between-group and within-group components. The within-group component is the variance of wages within education-experience groups. It is measured by the residuals from the regression of log wages on a set of six education dummies and a quartic in potential experience. The between-group component is the variance of wages between education and experience and is the explained part of the regression.

Figures 10.7 and 10.8 show that for both men and women the inequality of wages grows steadily between 1980 and 2000. Most of the growth in the variance is due to the within-group component. The between-group component mostly grows between 1980 and 1985 because of the large expansion in age-wage differentials during this period. The between-group inequality remains relatively stable after 1985 as the growth in education-wage differentials is offset by the decline in age-wage differentials. To illustrate this point, consider the case of men. Between 1980 and 1985, 0.016 of the 0.020 growth in the between-group variance is due to the growth in age differentials. The remaining change (0.004) is due to changes in education-wage differentials. By contrast, age-wage differentials account for a 0.003 decline in the between-group variance between 1995 and 2005, which is offset by a 0.006 growth in the between-group variance due to growing education-wage differentials.

As mentioned earlier, however, the finding that within-group inequality grows steadily over the 1980-2000 period should be interpreted with some caution. In particular, existing studies for both Canada and the United States suggest that this aspect of wage inequality is sensitive to the choice of data.

The High School-University Wage Gap by Age and Experience

As shown earlier in Figure 10.2, the wage gap between high-school-educated and university-educated men, having remained relatively constant before 1995, increased steeply between 1995 and 2000. Card and Lemieux (2001) show, however, that the stability prior to 1995 hides important differences

FIGURE 10.7

Male income inequality between and within education-experience groups: full-time men, variance of log weekly earnings

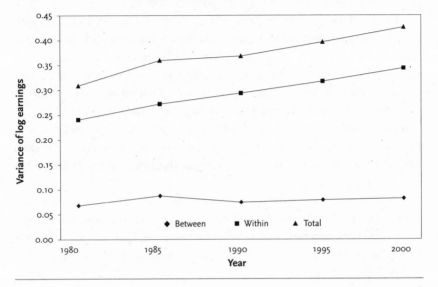

FIGURE 10.8

Female income inequality between and within education-experience groups: full-time women, variance of log weekly earnings

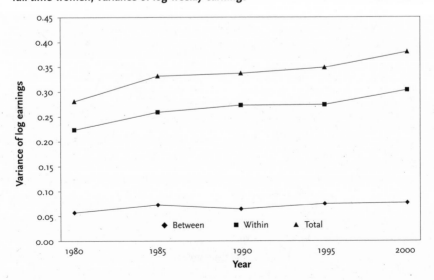

across age groups. They show that the wage gap increased for younger men but decreased for older men. Using data from the SCF, Beaudry and Green (1998) and Bar-Or et al. (1995) also find that the return to a university degree among younger men increased during the 1980s.[19]

Figure 10.9 shows the evolution in the wage gap between workers with exactly a high school diploma and workers with exactly a bachelor's degree for different age groups.[20] Consistent with the aforementioned studies, Figure 10.9 shows that the high school-BA wage gap increased by 5 to 10 percentage points for workers aged twenty-five to twenty-nine and thirty to thirty-four between 1980 and 1995. During the same period, the wage gap remained stable for workers aged thirty-five to forty-nine and declined by 5 to 10 percentage points for older workers. A consequence of these offsetting trends is that the high school-BA wage gap remained relatively stable between 1980 and 1995.

As in 1980-95, the growth in the high school-BA wage gap is more pronounced for younger workers between 1995 and 2000. The magnitude of the 1995-2000 change is much more dramatic, however, than it is for the 1980-1995 change. For example, the wage gap for men aged twenty-six to thirty almost *doubles* from 15 percent in 1995 to 28 percent in 2000. The wage gap

FIGURE 10.9

Male wage gap between high school graduates and BA graduates by age group

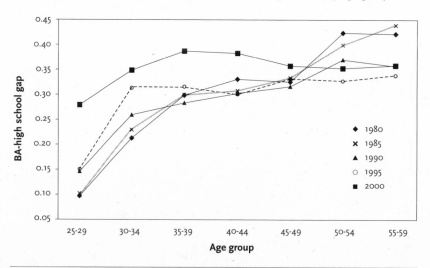

starts growing for middle-age men (aged thirty-six to fifty) by 2 to 8 percentage points. Relative to 1995, the wage gap also increases for older men although, in 2000, it remains lower than it was in the 1980s.

Figure 10.10 shows that the wage gaps for women, compared to men, are not growing over time. One exception is the wage gap for the youngest age group (aged twenty-five to twenty-nine), which is significantly higher in 2000 than in other years. For all other age groups, the high school-BA wage gap declines between 1980 and 2000, though not significantly so in most cases.

Figures 10.9 and 10.10 show wage differences between high school graduates and university BA graduates by age group. However, such comparisons do not control for labour market experience because those who enter the work force after completing secondary school have approximately four years more work experience than those with the same age who enter after graduation from university. Figures 10.11 and 10.12 therefore report the high school-BA gaps by (potential) experience groups instead of by age groups. For young workers, the high school-BA gap between individuals of the same age tends to be relatively small. The wage gain from attending university is offset by the fact that, at any given age, high-school-educated workers have more labour market experience than university-educated workers. Comparing BA

FIGURE 10.10

Female wage gap between high school graduates and BA graduates by age group

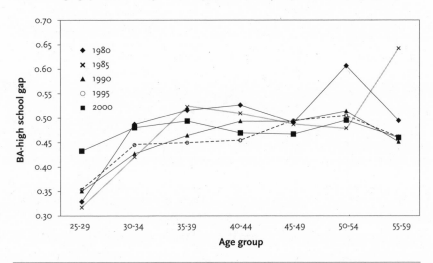

FIGURE 10.11

Male wage gap between high school graduates and BA graduates by experience group

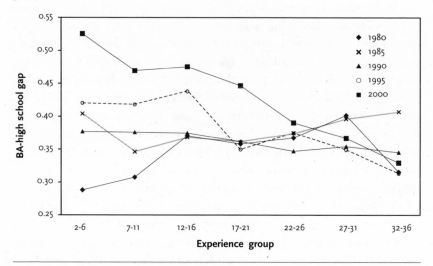

FIGURE 10.12

Female wage gap between high school graduates and BA graduates by experience group

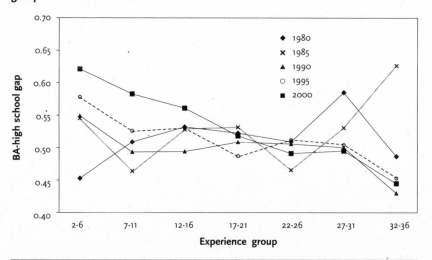

and high-school graduates with the same level of potential experience controls for this source of discrepancy. Thus the education-wage differentials among experience groups are larger than the corresponding differentials among age groups, especially at younger ages. In particular, Figure 10.11 shows that the high school-BA wage gap for inexperienced male workers is much larger than the corresponding gap for the young age groups in Figure 10.9.

The results reported in Figure 10.12 for women are qualitatively similar to those for men. The wage gap for less-experienced women increases substantially over time. By 2000, the high school-BA wage gap is substantially larger for less-experienced than for more-experienced female workers. On average, the high school-BA wage gap is higher in 2000 than it was in 1980 since the decline in the wage gap for more-experienced women is more than offset by the growth in the wage gap for less-experienced women.[21]

The high school-BA wage gaps shown in Figures 10.9 to 10.12 are reproduced in Tables 10.1 and 10.2 along with their standard errors. The wage gaps are precisely estimated for most groups and very precisely estimated in 2000, where we use the full 20 percent sample of the 2001 Census. Panel A of Table 10.1 shows that the increase in the wage gap for young men (aged thirty-four and younger) and the decrease in the wage gap for older men (aged fifty and older) are large relative to the standard errors. Formal tests indicate that these changes are statistically significant at the usual 95 percent confidence level. The last column of Table 10.1 also shows that the average wage gap for all age groups did not change significantly between 1980 and 1995.

The High School-University Wage Gap: Robustness Checks

All the results presented up to this point are based on weekly wage and salary earnings of full-time workers from the 1981 to 2001 Census. One important finding is that the wage differential between university-educated and high-school-educated workers increased significantly for men between 1995 and 2000. We now show that this key finding is robust across wage measures in the Census. We also document recent trends in the university-high school wage gap in other data sets.

ALTERNATIVE WAGE MEASURES FROM THE CENSUS

Figures 10.13 and 10.14 show the evolution of the high school-BA wage gap using four different wage measures from the Census. In addition to the benchmark wage gap used up to this point (based on weekly earnings of all wage

TABLE 10.1

High school-BA wage gap by age groups, all full-time workers

	25-29	30-34	35-39	40-44	45-49	50-54	55-59	60-64	Average
A. MEN									
1980	0.097	0.213	0.299	0.331	0.326	0.424	0.422	0.268	0.297
	(0.012)	(0.014)	(0.017)	(0.024)	(0.028)	(0.029)	(0.036)	(0.061)	(0.011)
1985	0.102	0.230	0.300	0.308	0.334	0.400	0.439	0.401	0.314
	(0.014)	(0.014)	(0.016)	(0.020)	(0.026)	(0.029)	(0.034)	(0.052)	(0.010)
1990	0.146	0.260	0.283	0.303	0.316	0.370	0.357	0.453	0.311
	(0.011)	(0.011)	(0.012)	(0.013)	(0.018)	(0.022)	(0.031)	(0.048)	(0.008)
1995	0.151	0.313	0.316	0.301	0.332	0.328	0.339	0.345	0.303
	(0.013)	(0.012)	(0.013)	(0.013)	(0.015)	(0.020)	(0.033)	(0.056)	(0.009)
2000	0.279	0.349	0.387	0.383	0.358	0.353	0.359	0.395	0.358
	(0.005)	(0.005)	(0.005)	(0.005)	(0.005)	(0.006)	(0.011)	(0.018)	(0.003)
B. WOMEN									
1980	0.329	0.487	0.516	0.526	0.491	0.607	0.495	0.665	0.514
	(0.014)	(0.019)	(0.029)	(0.034)	(0.039)	(0.040)	(0.055)	(0.112)	(0.018)
1985	0.317	0.420	0.523	0.510	0.487	0.479	0.642	0.383	0.470
	(0.014)	(0.017)	(0.020)	(0.025)	(0.036)	(0.042)	(0.051)	(0.072)	(0.014)
1990	0.350	0.427	0.464	0.493	0.493	0.514	0.451	0.477	0.459
	(0.011)	(0.012)	(0.013)	(0.014)	(0.018)	(0.026)	(0.036)	(0.058)	(0.010)
1995	0.353	0.445	0.449	0.454	0.495	0.505	0.462	0.361	0.440
	(0.014)	(0.013)	(0.014)	(0.014)	(0.015)	(0.020)	(0.035)	(0.072)	(0.011)
2000	0.433	0.480	0.494	0.469	0.467	0.495	0.460	0.353	0.456
	(0.006)	(0.006)	(0.005)	(0.005)	(0.005)	(0.006)	(0.011)	(0.025)	(0.004)

NOTE: All wage gap estimates are the difference between the mean log wage of university BA graduates and the mean log wage of high school graduates. Standard errors in parentheses

TABLE 10.2

High school-BA wage gap by experience groups, all full-time workers

	2-6	7-11	12-16	17-21	22-26	27-31	32-36	37-41	Average
A. MEN									
1980	0.288	0.308	0.370	0.358	0.367	0.402	0.315	0.292	0.338
	(0.012)	(0.013)	(0.016)	(0.022)	(0.027)	(0.028)	(0.034)	(0.057)	(0.010)
1985	0.404	0.346	0.368	0.361	0.375	0.396	0.407	0.337	0.374
	(0.014)	(0.014)	(0.015)	(0.019)	(0.024)	(0.028)	(0.032)	(0.048)	(0.009)
1990	0.377	0.376	0.375	0.362	0.347	0.354	0.345	0.384	0.365
	(0.012)	(0.011)	(0.012)	(0.012)	(0.016)	(0.020)	(0.029)	(0.043)	(0.008)
1995	0.420	0.418	0.438	0.350	0.374	0.349	0.313	0.236	0.362
	(0.014)	(0.013)	(0.013)	(0.013)	(0.014)	(0.018)	(0.030)	(0.050)	(0.008)
2000	0.525	0.469	0.475	0.447	0.390	0.367	0.329	0.298	0.413
	(0.005)	(0.005)	(0.005)	(0.005)	(0.005)	(0.006)	(0.009)	(0.016)	(0.003)
B. WOMEN									
1980	0.453	0.509	0.532	0.523	0.509	0.585	0.487	0.677	0.534
	(0.013)	(0.018)	(0.027)	(0.033)	(0.038)	(0.039)	(0.055)	(0.107)	(0.018)
1985	0.545	0.464	0.528	0.532	0.466	0.531	0.627	0.364	0.507
	(0.014)	(0.016)	(0.019)	(0.023)	(0.034)	(0.042)	(0.048)	(0.070)	(0.013)
1990	0.549	0.493	0.494	0.509	0.506	0.500	0.430	0.475	0.495
	(0.012)	(0.013)	(0.013)	(0.014)	(0.017)	(0.024)	(0.035)	(0.053)	(0.009)
1995	0.578	0.526	0.530	0.487	0.512	0.504	0.453	0.359	0.494
	(0.015)	(0.015)	(0.014)	(0.014)	(0.014)	(0.018)	(0.032)	(0.068)	(0.010)
2000	0.621	0.583	0.561	0.518	0.491	0.495	0.445	0.332	0.506
	(0.006)	(0.006)	(0.006)	(0.005)	(0.005)	(0.006)	(0.010)	(0.023)	(0.004)

NOTE: See note to Table 10.1.

and salary workers), we first show the wage gap obtained using all earnings (defined as wage and salary earnings plus self-employment earnings). The two other wage gaps are obtained using the same two wage measures on the sub-sample of individuals working more than forty-nine weeks a year (full-year workers). Thus full-time full-year (FTFY) workers consist of full-time (FT) workers who work more than forty-nine weeks per year. As explained previously, full-time workers are those who work at least thirty hours per week.

The four alternative measures of the experience-adjusted high school-BA wage gap for men are reported in Figure 10.13. The figure shows that both using all earnings and limiting the sample to full-year workers tend to increase the wage gap. For example, the wage gap obtained using all earnings for full-year workers is 3 to 6 percentage points higher than the benchmark wage gap (wage and salary earnings for all workers). The trends in all four wage gaps are broadly similar, however. They all show significant growth in the high school-BA wage gap between 1980 and 1985, modest or no growth between 1985 and 1995, followed by a steep increase in the wage gap between 1995 and 2000. All four alternative measures of the high school-BA wage gap show an increase of about 10 percentage points over the period 1980-2000.

FIGURE 10.13

Alternative measures of the high school-BA wage gap: men, adjusted for experience

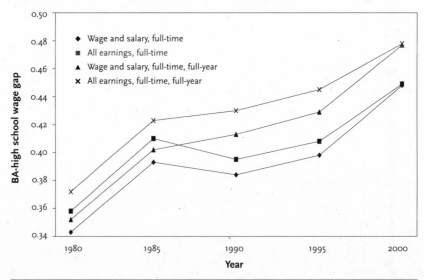

FIGURE 10.14

Alternative measures of the high school-BA wage gap: women, adjusted for experience

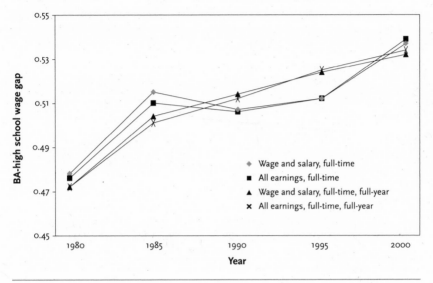

The same basic pattern of results holds for women. Figure 10.14 shows that both the average levels and the trends in the wage gap are robust across wage measures. The figure also confirms the earlier result, that the high school-BA wage gap does not increase as much for women as for men. Nonetheless, the adjusted wage gap grows by about 6 percentage points between 1980 and 2000.

ALTERNATIVE DATA SOURCES
Figures 10.15 and 10.16 compare the Census-derived high school-BA wage gap for 1990 to 2000 to the wage gaps obtained using other data sets. In all cases, the wage measure used is weekly wage and salary earnings of full-time workers. The first comparison data set is the SCF, which provides measures of the high school-BA wage gap for the period 1989-97. The second comparison data set is the SLID for 1996-2000. The third comparison data set is the LFS for 1997-2001.

Figure 10.15 shows that the adjusted high school-BA wage gap for men follows relatively similar trends in all data sets. As in the Census, the high school-BA wage gap in the SCF is relatively stable until 1995. The Census

FIGURE 10.15

Male high school-BA wage gap in four data sets: weekly earnings of full-time men, adjusted for experience

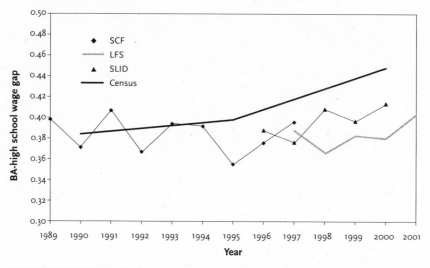

data suggest a small increase in the wage differential between 1990 and 1995, while the SCF data suggest a modest decrease. The SCF wage gap then increases between 1995 and 1997, the last year for which the SCF data were collected. Both the SLID and the LFS also exhibit upward trends during 1996-2000 and 1997-2001, respectively, although compared to the Census the growth in the differential appears to be more modest in the LFS and SLID. Similarly, the adjusted wage gaps reported in Figure 10.16 increase for all data sets over the period 1995-2001. Note, however, that the wage gaps from the LFS, the SLID, or the SCF are systematically lower than the corresponding gaps in the Census in 1995 and 2000. This mirrors the finding of Frenette, Green, and Picot in Chapter 3 that the SCF and SLID data tend to understate earnings dispersion relative to Census or tax data.

Figure 10.16 reports the same estimates for women. As for men, the three alternative data sources indicate growth in the high school-BA wage gap after 1995. In the LFS, the growth in the wage gap is smaller than in the Census, while the SCF indicates growth similar to that in the Census. In the SLID, the growth in the wage gap is larger than in the Census. On balance, the results

FIGURE 10.16

Female high school-BA wage gap in four data sets: weekly earnings of full-time women, adjusted for experience

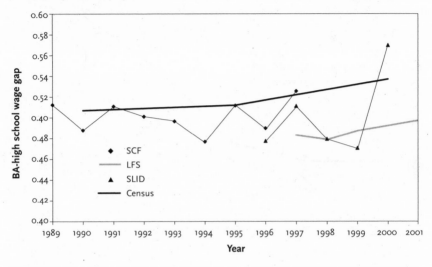

reported in Figures 10.15 and 10.16 confirm the basic finding from the Census that the wage differential between university- and high school-educated workers increased after the mid-1990s.

The main weakness of the Census is that it does not provide detailed information on average weekly hours of work. As a result, it is not possible to compute a direct measure of average hourly earnings. In both the SLID and the LFS, however, it is possible to compare the wage gap obtained using average hourly earnings to the "Census-type" wage gap based on weekly earnings of full-time workers. Figures 10.17 and 10.18 compare these two alternative measures of the adjusted high school-BA wage gap for both the LFS and the SCF.

For both men (Figure 10.17) and women (Figure 10.18), the 1997-2001 growth in the high school-BA wage differential is very similar for the two wage measures in the LFS. In the SLID, the wage gap for men based on hourly wage rates grows more than the wage gap based on weekly earnings, while the opposite is true for women. Overall, these figures suggest that using weekly earnings of full-time workers does not systematically bias the wage gap estimates in one direction or another.

Figure 10.17

Male high school-BA wage gap comparing hourly wage rates and weekly earnings: full-time men, adjusted for experience

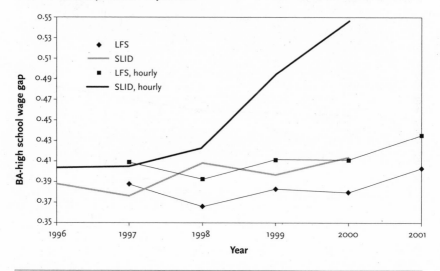

Figure 10.18

Female high school-BA wage gap comparing hourly wage rates and weekly earnings: full-time women, adjusted for experience

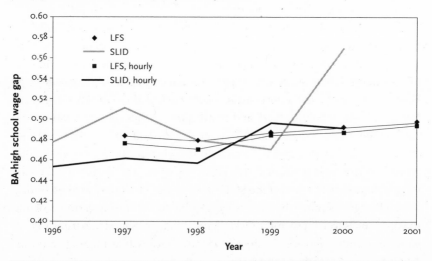

Conclusion

This chapter examines trends in the wage structure and wage inequality in Canada over the last two decades. Particular attention is devoted to wage differentials by age (or experience) and education, two major sources of earnings differences among workers. Most of our analysis is based on the Census because, unlike other data sets, it provides consistent information on earnings and educational attainment for large samples of workers between 1980 and 2000. The Census data allow us to make two innovative contributions. First, we examine behaviour during the latter half of the 1990s, a period of strong economic growth that has received little attention in previous studies of earnings inequality. Second, we provide a clearer picture of the evolution of the Canadian wage structure over the past two decades than has been possible with other data sources.

Our investigation with Census data yields several conclusions. For men and women, education-wage differentials (adjusted for experience) have increased substantially over the period 1980-2000. For men, the high school-university BA wage gap increased from approximately 35 percent in 1980 to about 45 percent in 2000, with the most dramatic rises occurring in the early 1980s and the late 1990s. There was a similar increase from about 45 to 55 percent in the gap between high school graduates and university postgraduates. For other (non-university) post-secondary programs, increased returns to education were also evident, but more modest in size. Only in the case of high school completion was there no evidence of rising returns to education. The gap between high school dropouts and high school graduates remained relatively stable, as did that between those with elementary school and high school graduates.

Returns to education also rose during this period for Canadian women, but the magnitudes of the increases were more modest. For example, the high school-university BA gap increased from 48 to 54 percent over these two decades, and the gap between university post-graduates high school graduates rose from 63 to 68 percent. As other studies have documented, the returns to education are much larger for females than for males, but the greater growth in male education differentials implies that some convergence in the male and female returns to education occurred over the sample period. Among women, there were also modest increases in the returns to non-university post-secondary education and no clear changes in the differentials between high school graduates and those with less than high school education.

Our main finding, therefore, is that the wage inequality between more-educated and less-educated workers increased substantially over the past two decades, with particularly steep growth for men between 1995 and 2000. For example, the raw wage gap between men with exactly a bachelor's degree and men with only a high school diploma increased from 32 percent to 40 percent during this period. The equivalent increase for the experience-adjusted wage gap was from 40 percent to 45 percent. For both men and women, the increase in the high school-BA wage gap was particularly large for young workers.

After fifteen years of sustained expansion, the wage gap between younger and older men declined substantially between 1995 and 2000. Indeed, by 2000, the wage gap between younger and older men had returned to its mid-1980s level. Wage gaps between younger and older women also declined, although not as dramatically as was the case for men.

Despite the recent decline in wage inequality among age groups, overall wage inequality increased steadily over the 1980-2000 period. One explanation for the increase is that the growth in education wage inequality between 1980 and 2000, together with the large increase in inequality among age groups that occurred between 1980 and 1995, more than offset the inequality-reducing effects of the decline in wage inequality among age groups from 1995 to 2000. Another explanation is that residual, or within-group, wage inequality grew very substantially over the 1980 to 2000 period. Why residual inequality grew so much remains an unresolved issue to be clarified in future research.

ACKNOWLEDGMENTS
We thank the referees and David Green for their comments. Special thanks to Garnett Picot, Andrew Heisz, and Logan MacLeod from Statistics Canada who provided us with special tabulations from the master file of the 2001 Census of Canada as part of the Equality, Security, and Community (ESC) project.

NOTES
1   See Morissette et al. (1994), Card et al. (1999), DiNardo and Lemieux (1997), Doiron and Barrett (1996), and Card et al. (2004). The data sets that include direct information on hourly wage rates are the 1981 Survey of Work History, the 1984 Survey of Union Membership, the 1986-90 Labour Market Activity Survey, the 1991 and 1995 Surveys of Work Arrangements, and the monthly LFS from January 1997 on.

2   For studies based on the SCF, see Morissette et al. (1993); for studies based on the Census, see Statistics Canada (2003); for studies based on tax data, see Baker and Solon (2003) and Saez and Veall (2003).

3   The SCF was collected as a supplement to the April LFS. The last SCF was conducted in April 1998. It contains detailed information on earnings in 1997 (the previous year).

4   The information on weeks worked and annual wage and salary earnings refer to the previous year. Thus the individuals in our samples were aged fifteen to sixty-four during the period to which our wage measures apply.

5   Samples sizes in 1986 and 1996 are 247,611 and 390,055, respectively.

6   The census asks about weeks of work and part-time/full-time status during the previous year, as well as actual weekly hours of work during the census week (in June). Since weekly hours of work vary considerably over time for many individuals, hours of work in the survey week is a poor proxy for average weekly hours of work during the previous year. In particular, many individuals who did not work during the Census week did work during the previous year.

7   Prior to 1981, it was not possible to compute average weekly earnings since the Census reported annual weeks of work in only a few intervals. The US Census and Annual Demographic Supplement of the March Current Population Survey also used to follow that practice. Given these data limitations, focusing on "full-time/full-year" workers used to be the most sensible way of obtaining a reasonable proxy for hourly wages of workers. Since the Census has been providing information on weeks of work since 1981, there is no longer a compelling reason for looking at full-year workers only.

8   The top codes in nominal dollars are $100,000 in 1980, $140,000 in 1985, and $200,000 in both 1990 and 1995. When expressed in constant dollars of 1995, these top-codes translate to $202,099 in 1980, $197,680 in 1985, and $227,010 in 1990.

9   Since full-time workers work at least thirty hours a week, a full-time worker earning $75 a week makes at most $2.50 an hour. This represents less than half of the minimum wage in any province in 2000.

10 The SCF is a supplement to the (April) Labour Force Survey (LFS). The information about educational achievement in the SCF is collected as part of the LFS. See Lavoie (1992) and Burbidge et al. (2002) for more discussion of the comparability problems in the SCF/LFS educational categories following the introduction of the new education question in the 1990 LFS.

11 The difference in log wages provides a close approximation to the percentage difference in wages.

12 We eliminate the following cells: aged sixteen with a high school diploma or more, aged seventeen with more than high school, aged eighteen to twenty-one with a

bachelor's degree or more, and aged twenty-two with a post-graduate university degree.

13   We can directly compare the results from individual-level regression with either measure of potential experience for the years where we have access to the microdata (1980 to 1995). When we do so we find that the resulting education-wage differentials are almost identical using the two approaches.

14   For example, we call a 0.10 difference in log wages a "10 percent difference."

15   A similar increase occurred in the early 1980s but was reversed during 1985 to 1995.

16   Other Canadian studies, such as Ferrer and Riddell (2002), also find that returns to education are much higher for women.

17   Our working paper (Boudarbat et al. 2003) reports both unadjusted and adjusted differentials.

18   We employ age categories, such as forty-six to fifty-five years, as of the survey date, so that the ages of the respondents during the time period when wages are measured correspond to the standard age groupings used by Statistics Canada (in this case ages forty-five to fifty-four).

19   As noted previously, an exception is a study by Burbidge et al. (2002), which concludes that the university-high school wage premium for young men was relatively stable over this period. The reason for this contradictory finding is unclear.

20   Because the education-wage differentials are shown separately for each age group, they control for age and thus are conceptually equivalent to the adjusted series reported previously.

21   Figure 10.12 shows that, controlling for experience, the BA-high school wage gap is increasing (for women). By contrast, Figure 10.10 shows that this wage gap is decreasing when age is controlled for instead of experience. This apparent puzzle is due to the fact that returns to experience have been increasing for women over this period. This reduces the BA-high school wage gap at a given age since the extra experience of high school graduates is now more valuable than it used to be.

REFERENCES

Baker, Michael, and Gary Solon. 2003. "Earnings Dynamics and Inequality among Canadian Men, 1976-1992: Evidence from Longitudinal Income Tax Records." *Journal of Labor Economics* 21: 289-322.

Bar-Or, Yuval, John Burbidge, Lonnie Magee, and A. Leslie Robb. 1995. "The Wage Premium to a University Education in Canada: 1971-1991." *Journal of Labor Economics* 13: 762-94.

Beach, Charles M., and George A. Slotsve. 1996. *Are We Becoming Two Societies?* Toronto: C.D. Howe Institute.

Beaudry, Paul, and David Green. 1998. "What Is Driving US and Canadian Wages: Exogenous Technical Change or Endogenous Choice of Technique?" NBER Working Paper No. 6853. Cambridge, MA: National Bureau of Economic Research.

—. 2000. "Cohort Patterns in Canadian Earnings: Assessing the Role of Skill Premia in Inequality Trends." *Canadian Journal of Economics* 33: 907-36.

Boudarbat, Brahim, Thomas Lemieux, and W. Craig Riddell. 2003. "Recent Trends in Wage Inequality and the Wage Structure in Canada." TARGET Working Paper 006. University of British Columbia, Department of Economics.

Burbidge, J.B., L. Magee, and A.L. Robb. 2002. "The Education Premium in Canada and the United States." *Canadian Public Policy* 28: 203-17.

Card, David, and John E. DiNardo. 2002. "Skill-Biased Technological Change and Rising Wage Inequality: Some Problems and Puzzles." *Journal of Labor Economics* 20: 733-83.

Card, David, Francis Kramarz, and Thomas Lemieux. 1999. "Changes in the Relative Structure of Wages and Employment: A Comparison of the United States, Canada, and France." *Canadian Journal of Economics* 32: 843-77.

Card, David, and Thomas Lemieux. 2001. "Can Falling Supply Explain the Rising Return to College for Younger Men? A Cohort-Based Analysis." *Quarterly Journal of Economics* 116: 705-46.

Card, David, Thomas Lemieux, and W. Craig Riddell. 2004. "Unions and Wage Inequality." *Journal of Labor Research* 25: 519-62.

DiNardo, John, and Thomas Lemieux. 1997. "Changes in Wage Inequality in Canada and the United States: Do Institutions Explain the Difference?" *Industrial and Labor Relations Review* 50: 629-51.

Doiron, Denise, and Garry F. Barrett. 1996. "Inequality in Male and Female Earnings: The Role of Hours and Wages." *Review of Economics and Statistics* 78: 410-20.

Ferrer, Ana, and W. Craig Riddell. 2002. "The Role of Credentials in the Canadian Labour Market." *Canadian Journal of Economics* 35: 879-905.

Freeman, Richard B., and Karen Needels. 1993. "Skill Differentials in Canada in an Era of Rising Labor Market Inequality." In David Card and Richard Freeman, eds., *Small Differences that Matter: Labor Markets and Income Maintenance in Canada and the United States*. Chicago: University of Chicago Press for NBER.

Katz, Lawrence, and Kevin Murphy. 1992. "Changes in Relative Wages, 1963-1987: Supply and Demand Factors." *Quarterly Journal of Economics* 107: 35-78.

Lavoie, Helene. 1992. "Changes to Educational Attainment Questions." *The Labour Force*. Ottawa: Statistics Canada, C3-C7.

Lemieux, Thomas. 2003. "Residual Wage Inequality: A Re-examination." TARGET Working Paper No. 2. University of British Columbia, Department of Economics.

Morissette, R., J. Myles, and G. Picot. 1993. "What Is Happening to Earnings Inequality in Canada?" Working Paper 60. Statistics Canada, Analytical Studies Branch.

—. 1994. "Earnings Inequality and the Distribution of Working Time in Canada." *Canadian Business Economics* 2: 3-16.

Morissette, R., G. Picot, and C. Kapsalis. 1999. "The Returns to Education and the Increasing Wage Gap between Younger and Older Workers." Working Paper 131. Statistics Canada, Analytical Studies Branch.

Murphy, Kevin M., W. Craig Riddell, and Paul M. Romer. 1998. "Wages, Skills and Technology in the United States and Canada." In Elhanan Helpman, ed., *General Purpose Technologies and Economic Growth*, 283-309. Cambridge MA: MIT Press.

Picot, Garnett. 1998a. "What is Happening to Earnings Inequality in the 1990s?" *Canadian Economic Observer.* Ottawa: Statistics Canada. Cat. No. 11-010-XPB.

—. 1998b. "What Is Happening to Earnings, Inequality and Youth Wages in the 1990s?" Statistics Canada, Analytical Studies Branch. Research Paper 116.

Richardson, David H. 1997. "Changes in the Distribution of Wages in Canada, 1981-1992." *Canadian Journal of Economics* 30: 622-43.

Saez, Emmanuel, with Michael Veall. 2003. "The Evolution of High Incomes in Canada, 1920-2000." NBER Working Paper 9607. Cambridge, MA: National Bureau of Economic Research.

Statistics Canada. 2003. Census Release on Education. *The Daily.* 11 March 2003.

11
Gender Dimensions of Changes in Earnings Inequality in Canada

Nicole M. Fortin and Tammy Schirle

Changes in the labour market outcomes of women have been among the most favourable developments characterizing the Canadian labour market over the last twenty-five years. During the 1980s, female labour force participation, which had climbed from below 30 percent in 1960 to 57 percent in 1980, continued to increase and appeared to reach a plateau in the early to mid-1990s at around 68 percent.[1] During the 1990s, women's real earnings made strong gains, increasing by more than 10 percent, while men's earnings were either stagnant or declining.[2] As a result, the female/male average earnings ratio continued to climb in the early-1990s, going from 68 percent among full-time full-year workers in 1990 to 73 percent in 1996, when it seemed to stabilize.[3] This chapter documents the economic progress of women and evaluates the implications of that progress for family earnings inequality.

We first document the changes in women's own earnings levels and dispersion, as well as their position relative to men. Like Heisz et al. (2002), we find that, over the last two decades, male earnings inequality increased more than female earnings inequality. Our numbers indicate that, although the Canadian experience is quantitatively different from the American experience in these dimensions, it is not qualitatively different. On the other hand, we find that family earnings inequality in Canada, after a sharp increase in the early 1980s, declined in the later part of the 1980s, but increased again in the early 1990s.[4] This is different from the experience of the United States, where there was no such decline in family earnings inequality in the mid to late 1980s (Daly and Valletta 2000). We next focus our analysis on the impact of women's labour market gains on family market earnings inequality. Our focus on family earnings rather than family income is justified by findings of Frenette, Green, and Picot (Chapter 3). There, the main source of after-tax family income inequality is found to be market-based inequality. Our aim is to offer an assessment of whether the favourable changes in women's labour market outcomes actually translated into substantial changes in the welfare of women and their families, in the context of other socioeconomic and labour market changes.

In the wake of increases in family dissolution (and decreases in family formation), have women's increased earnings merely compensated for their enhanced financial responsibilities in support of the family or have they contributed to increased family income inequality? An earlier Canadian family income inequality study (Henderson and Rowley 1977) pointed to changes in family size as one of the major reasons for increases in inequality over the 1965-73 period. Henderson and Rowley argued that the decline in families with at least one male earner was an important contributing factor. As pointed out by Phipps and Lethbridge in Chapter 8, an increase in the proportion of single-parent families has clear implications not only for the welfare of women but also for that of their children. Beach (1989) also classifies changing family composition as the dominant supply-side effect.

In addition, it has been suggested that increases in assortative mating (the tendency for members of a couple to have similar education and earnings) in the context of lower fertility rates could exacerbate family earnings polarization. For the United States, Juhn and Murphy's (1997) findings cast doubt on the notion that married women have increased their labour supply in recent decades to compensate for the disappointing earnings growth of their husbands. Instead, Hyslop (2001) finds that the positive correlation between the labour market outcomes of working couples is due to permanent factors, such as the convergence in educational attainment, rather than wage shocks. Burtless (1999) estimates that 13 percent of the 1979-96 increase in family-equivalent income inequality in the United States can be attributed to increases in assortative mating. Alternatively, family earnings inequality may still be largely driven by changes in male earnings inequality, as Daly and Valletta (2000) and Machin and Waldfogel (1994) have found for the United States and the United Kingdom, respectively.

On the demand side, changes in the wage structure (the relationship between individual attributes and wages) stemming from skill-biased technological change remain the leading explanation for the important changes in American wage inequality (Autor et al. 1998; Katz and Autor 1999). In Canada, these changes in the wage structure, in particular in the returns to education, are not as clearly identified and remain the subject of some controversy (Bar-Or et al. 1995; Beach and Slotsve 1994; Beaudry and Green 2000; Burbidge et al. 2002; Kapsalis et al. 1999). At best, they appear to be a phenomenon of the late 1990s and early 2000s, subsequent to our period of study, as shown by Boudarbat, Lemieux, and Riddell in Chapter 10.

To provide a more complete picture of changes in family-earnings inequality, we investigate the effects of changes in the following factors: the structure of male earnings, female labour force participation, the structure of female earnings, assortative mating, family composition and living arrangements, and family characteristics, including the human capital variables. Our analysis does not consider the impact of institutional changes, such as the decline in union density and changes in the minimum wage, which were also found to be important by Fortin and Lemieux (2000).

We use the "distribution decomposition" methodology pioneered by DiNardo, Fortin, and Lemieux (1996), known as the DFL methodology, which was further expanded by Lemieux (2002) to allow for the separation of changes in the wage structure from changes in the productive characteristics of individuals. Our study thus parallels that of Daly and Valletta (2000), which also uses the DFL methodology to look at the impact of a set of factors (such as changes in male earnings, female labour force participation, family structure, and family characteristics) on family-income inequality in the United States from 1968 to 1999. Daly and Valletta conclude that, while changes in male earnings are the dominant factor in increasing family income inequality, changes in family structure and rising female labour force participation also have substantial effects. One innovation in the present study is the ability to distinguish changes in the male and female wage structure from changes in the human capital variables. This enables us to better compare the impacts of demand-driven and supply-driven factors.

The chapter is organized as follows. We begin by discussing some conceptual and practical issues in the measurement of individual earnings and family market earnings in Canada. Next, we describe trends in women's labour market outcomes and compare them to men's. We also document the changes in men's and women's individual earnings inequality and in family-earnings inequality across different family types. Then, we analyze how the various explanatory factors have affected family-earnings inequality. A final section summarizes our main findings.

Data and Measurement Issues

Like most Canadian studies of individual and family earnings, this one uses Statistics Canada's Survey of Consumer Finances (SCF), the official source for income estimates prior to 1996, when much of the rise in women's labour force participation and labour earnings took place.[5] The publicly available "Individuals Aged 15 and Over" data files, used for the years 1981, 1982, and from 1984 to 1997, provide us with detailed information on individuals' characteristics, earnings, and labour market activity but have no information on their union status. The publicly available "Census Families" data files, used for the years 1982, 1984, and from 1986 to 1997, provide information on the characteristics and earnings of the family unit and of the head and spouse in each family. The weights attached to each record in the files, created by Statistics Canada to reflect the non-random sampling design of the survey, are used throughout this study.[6]

We are concerned with the impact of changes in labour market outcomes, particularly those of women, on inequality in labour market earnings. Thus to characterize the labour market as accurately as possible, we restrict the samples used throughout this chapter to individuals aged sixteen to sixty-four, excluding the self-employed and those with unreliably reported labour force status.[7] These individuals' annual earnings are measured as income earned as wages and salaries from employment, expressed in 1992 dollars.[8] We note that Statistics Canada does not provide allocation flags to identify individuals whose wages have been imputed. If the percentage of workers with allocated wages was important, this would bias downwards our measure of earnings inequality to the extent that there has been an increase in residual wage inequality over time (Baker and Solon 2003). Comparisons with tax data used in Chapter 3 suggest that the SCF survey data under-represents the bottom end of the income distribution. This caveat must be kept in mind when considering our Canada-US comparisons.

To facilitate comparison with other studies (e.g., Morissette et al. 1994; Burbidge et al. 1997; Heisz et al. 2002), we first present trends in individuals' annual earnings using samples of full-time, full-year workers. This sample selection was common in earlier studies when surveys did not collect information on the number of weeks worked a year and on the number of hours worked. Given the sensitivity of inequality measures to outliers, we trim the sample of full-time, full-year workers by eliminating observations reporting extremely low or high earnings, keeping individuals with annual earnings between $3,000 and $200,000.[9]

An important problem in using full-time, full-year samples for gender comparisons is that, among full-time workers, women's average number of hours worked per week are lower than men's. Thus comparing the earnings of full-time, full-year women and men confound labour supply issues with wage determination issues. To consider the latter issues, it is preferable to present trends in hourly wages. In the SCF, the usual hours of work are reported as the average hours worked in the three weeks prior to the individual's interview, which takes place in the year following the year for which income is reported. By selecting individuals with at least one year of job tenure, we minimize the possibility of a job mismatch between earnings and hours of work. We construct an individual's hourly wage by dividing their annual earnings by annual hours (the product of reported weeks worked in a year and the usual hours worked per week). We also trim this sample to exclude individuals with hourly wages lower than $1.50 or above $100 in 1992 dollars, a procedure commonly performed in American studies to eliminate outliers (Gao 2003).[10] We can then present trends in hourly wages by using the sample of workers with at least one year of job tenure.

The trends in inequality and earnings presented below depend to some extent on the sample selection made. Our trimmed samples show less erratic changes in inequality measures, but also less amplitude, especially in the early 1980s.[11] The trends presented appear to be robust to various age restrictions we investigated, although using a sample of men aged twenty-five to fifty-four indicates larger increases in inequality among men in the 1990s than the broader sample used here.

Our principal focus is the distribution of family market earnings, where we use the SCF concept of family.[12] We restrict our sample to families whose heads are both aged sixteen to sixty-four, excluding families with self-employed family heads or family heads who are permanently unable to work.[13] Because families are of different sizes, we need to appeal to the concept of equivalent family earnings. A family's earnings are simply the sum of all family members' income earned as wages and salaries from employment, as reported in the SCF. Recognizing that economies of scale may be achieved in larger households, we adjust family earnings to compare families of different sizes. We follow Daly and Valletta (2000) in adjusting a family's earnings for the number of individuals in the economic family according to the following formula:

$$EFE = \frac{E}{F^{\sigma}}, \tag{1}$$

where EFE is equivalent family earnings, E is the total family earnings, F is the number of individuals in the economic family, and σ is set at 0.5.[14]

Although this adjustment is widely used in the literature (Karoly 1993; Karoly and Burtless 1995), there is no general consensus on which equivalence scale should be preferred when adjusting family earnings. Here, we simply adjust family income for household size, thus abstracting from the fact that different types of families may have different needs.[15] Our emphasis on the comparison of living standards for different types of families follows the more recent literature (Ebert and Moyes 2003; Donaldson and Pendakur 2004).[16]

We generally consider four family types: (1) married with kids, (2) married without kids, (3) other families with kids, and (4) other families without kids. Married with kids includes families with a head and spouse, married or living common-law, who report the presence of children under the age of eighteen in the census family. Married without kids are similar to type 1 but do not report the presence of children. Other families with kids include those who are never-married, separated, divorced, or widowed, who report the presence of children under the age of eighteen. Other families without kids include all other single individuals, never married, separated, divorced or widowed, who do not report the presence of children under the age of eighteen. In Table 11.1, we report the relative shares of five different types of families from 1982 to 1997. Because of the importance of never-married mothers (87 percent of never-married parents) for policy purposes, we separate never-married parents from the other types of unmarried parents in this table.

The most dramatic change in family composition is the large 6 percentage point drop in the proportion of families consisting of married couples with children and a sizable increase of 4 percentage points in the number of

TABLE 11.1

Proportion of families in indicated categories

Year	Married, with kids	Married, without kids	Never married, with kids	Others, with kids	Others, without kids
1982	0.357	0.249	0.012	0.056	0.326
1986	0.336	0.252	0.015	0.050	0.347
1988	0.329	0.258	0.019	0.049	0.345
1991	0.311	0.256	0.022	0.051	0.360
1994	0.302	0.260	0.026	0.052	0.360
1997	0.293	0.257	0.031	0.051	0.368

NOTE: Calculated using the SCF (Census Families). Sample restricted to families whose head and spouse are aged 16-64, not self-employed. See text for definitions of family types.

single individuals without children. Also significant, the proportion of families composed of never-married parents has more than doubled over the 1980s and 1990s to reach 3 percent in 1997. Despite the fact that they represent only a small proportion of families, these families are more likely to have lower equivalent family earnings than married couples; hence an increase in this type of family places more families in the lower end of the earnings distribution.[17] Indeed, Blackburn and Bloom (1993) partly attribute the United States' larger increase in family-income equality over the 1980s, as compared to Canada's, to the fact that female-headed families with children are relatively more prevalent south of the border. Given these large changes across the different family types, changes in inequality among all families will likely depend on the proportion of each family type in the total population of families.

Trends in Women's Labour Market Outcomes and Family Earnings Inequality

Over the 1980s and 1990s, women in Canada experienced significant changes in their labour market outcomes. A striking feature of this change is the fact that women's labour force participation rates increased substantially throughout the 1980s, although they remained roughly constant at around 65 percent in the 1990s, as can be seen in Table 11.2. Beaudry and Lemieux (1999) analyze both the rise and the relative stagnation of female labour force participation from 1976 to 1994 in terms of macroeconomic effects, age effects, and cohort (generational) effects and find that the latter explain most of the phenomenon. While participation rates for men actually fell over this period, the change for men is not nearly as dramatic as for women. Between 1982 and 1997, women aged sixteen to sixty-four saw a 12 percentage point increase in participation rates, while the comparable sample of men experienced a 2 percentage point decrease in participation rates.

The observed increase in female labour force participation was largely of more educated, married women. As shown in Table 11.2, in the 1980s, the labour force participation rates of women with high school and university degrees increased by 5 percentage points. In the 1990s, while the participation rates for women with university degrees remained constant at around 82 percent, women with high school or less actually experienced declines in participation. Over the entire period, the most remarkable increase was the 20 percentage point increase in the participation rates of married women with children. Participation rates of married women without children have

TABLE 11.2

Male and female labour force participation and the proportion of women working part-time

Year	1982	1986	1988	1991	1994	1997
Male labour force participation						
Age 16-64	0.83	0.84	0.84	0.80	0.81	0.81
Age 25-54	0.93	0.93	0.93	0.90	0.91	0.92
Female labour force participation						
Age 16-64	0.55	0.62	0.65	0.65	0.65	0.67
Age 25-54	0.61	0.68	0.72	0.73	0.74	0.76
University Degree	0.78	0.82	0.83	0.82	0.83	0.82
High School	0.60	0.65	0.68	0.66	0.64	0.64
Dropouts	0.38	0.39	0.42	0.37	0.36	0.39
Married, with kids	0.50	0.61	0.65	0.68	0.69	0.70
Married, no kids	0.55	0.57	0.61	0.62	0.65	0.65
Single, with kids	0.54	0.58	0.60	0.54	0.56	0.65
Single, no kids	0.63	0.67	0.68	0.67	0.64	0.65
Proportion of participating women working part-time (aged 16-64)						
Married, with kids	0.33	0.31	0.29	0.29	0.28	0.31
Married, no kids	0.20	0.19	0.19	0.21	0.20	0.25
Single, with kids	0.15	0.16	0.18	0.21	0.20	0.26
Single, no kids	0.25	0.29	0.29	0.31	0.35	0.37

NOTE: Calculated using the SCF (individuals aged 15 and over). Sample excludes the self-employed. Dropouts are those individuals reporting less than Grade 10 completed. High school includes individuals with Grade 11-13 completed. Individuals classified as having a university degree do not include those with other post-secondary education. See text for definitions of family types. A woman is working part-time if she reports working mostly part-time in the year.

also increased, in line with the full sample of women. In contrast, participation rates of single women have remained fairly constant. However, single women with children are the only group of women who experienced a significant increase in participation in the 1990s, following a sharp drop in the late 1980s. The increases in participation among single women with children may be related to the significant changes in social assistance programs of the mid-1990s. In all provinces, single parents experienced real reductions in social assistance entitlements in the mid-1990s, and some provinces introduced work requirements.[18]

Despite the remarkable growth in women's labour force participation rates, the potential impact of this higher participation on family earnings is reduced by an accompanying increase in the proportion of women working part-time. The proportion of women working part-time increased by an average of 6 percentage points from 1982 to 1997 and now stands at 30 percent, as shown in Table 11.2. However, the proportion of married women with children working part-time has actually decreased slightly, while increases were most significant for single individuals, including single-parent families.

In the 1980s and 1990s, women made strong gains in earnings and wages relative to a general stagnation in men's earnings. Figure 11.1 illustrates women's relative wage gains by comparing the distributions (in the form of kernel density estimates) of log earnings for men and women in 1982 (solid lines) and 1997 (dashed lines). There is a clear rightward shift in the distribution of women's log earnings. In comparison, the distribution of men's log earnings shows movement from the middle to the lower end of the distribution, with a substantial widening of the distribution. The distribution of log hourly wages, a different measure of earnings, for men (not shown) exhibits a clearer shift of mass around the mode of the 1982 distribution to the

FIGURE 11.1

Densities of log earnings

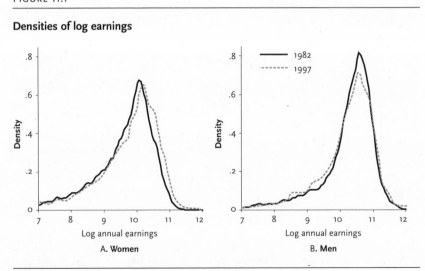

A. Women

B. Men

NOTE: Densities (smoothed histograms) are obtained using the SCF (individuals aged 15 and over). Sample is restricted to paid workers aged 16-64.

mid-lower tail of the distribution in 1997. That kind of shift has been identified in Fortin and Lemieux (2000) as the result of the decline in unionization over that period.

As a result of women's relative earnings gains, women's median earnings
and wages have been steadily catching up to men's. Figure 11.2 indicates that
the ratio of median female earnings to median male earnings has increased
steadily over the 1980s and 1990s. As expected, the female/male hourly wage
ratio for the sample of workers with one year or more of job tenure is consistently higher (reaching the 75 to 80 percent range in the late 1990s) than the
annual earnings ratio for the sample of full-time, full-year workers, which
reaches the 70 to 75 percent range. A similar differential between the female/
male hourly wage ratio and the weekly earnings ratio, of about 5 to 6 percentage points, is reported by O'Neill (2003) using American data. This is
due to the fact that even when women work full-time they work fewer hours
than men.[19]

FIGURE 11.2

Female/male ratio of median earnings

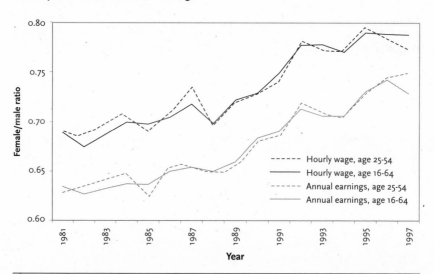

NOTE: Calculated using the SCF (individuals aged 15 and over) 1981-82 and 1984-97. The data
point presented for 1983 is an average of 1982 and 1984. Sample selection is described in text.

FIGURE 11.3

Summary measures for male log earnings (1982 = 100)

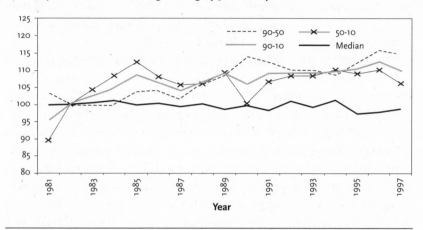

Year

NOTE: Calculated using the SCF (individuals aged 15 and over) 1981-82 and 1984-97. The data point presented for 1983 is an average of 1982 and 1984. Sample is restricted to male paid workers aged 16-64 with annual earnings between $3,000 and $200,000.

Interestingly, the substantial earning gains of women relative to men have not been achieved at the expense of increasing inequality among women. Figures 11.3 and 11.4 display the trends in log annual earnings and log hourly wage inequality among men and women separately from 1981 to 1997, plotting three different measures of inequality, which highlight changes in different parts of the earnings distribution.[20]

Among men employed full-time and full-year, earnings inequality, displayed in Figure 11.3, increased most substantially in the early 1980s, with more moderate increases in inequality for the rest of the sample period. For example, the 90-10 differential in log annual earnings increased by 16 log points between 1981 and 1989, representing an annualized 1.8 percent change. Between 1981 and 1989, the Gini index went from 0.242 to 0.267, an increase of 10 percent that represents an annualized 1.3 percent change. These results are consistent with the results in Morissette et al. (1995), which also reports a rise in the Gini index of 10 percent between 1981 and 1989 for men employed full-time, full-year. The Canadian trends in the 1980s, while not as large as those in the United States, are consistent with American trends. Katz and Autor (1999) report increases of 20 log points in the 90-10 differential in log weekly wages of full-time, full-year American male workers from 1979 to 1987, which represents an annualized 2 percent change and an annualized increase of 1.6 percent in the Gini coefficient.[21]

In the 1990s, the increases in inequality among full-time, full-year men in Canada were more moderate, and inequality continued to grow more slowly than in the United States. Between 1990 and 1997, the Gini increased by only 3 percent to 0.277, representing an annualized 0.5 percent increase, while the increase in the 90-10 log earnings differential shows an annualized 0.5 percent change. Picot (1998) finds similar annualized increases of 0.6 percent in the Gini coefficient computed for male paid employees from 1990 to 1995. For the United States, Katz and Autor (1999) report increases in inequality over the 1990s representing an annualized 1.2 percent increase in the Gini index and annualized increases of 0.6 percent in the 90-10 differential for male full-time full-year workers.[22]

We also investigated the trends in inequality among men, adjusting for hours of work. For our sample of men with at least one-year of job tenure, log hourly wage inequality increased substantially in the early 1980s, dropping for the last half of the decade and then increasing significantly through the 1990s. For the 1990s, the 90-10 differential in log hourly wages and the Gini index showed an annualized 1 percent change. Again, this is similar to trends in the United States, where Katz and Autor (1999) report an annualized change of 1.7 percent in the 90-10 hourly log wage differential over the 1980s.[23] Inequality among American men increased moderately throughout the 1990s, as the 90-10 differential shows an annualized 0.7 percent change, and the Gini coefficient increased by an annualized 0.6 percent.

Some of the differences between the Canadian trends in hourly wage and annual earnings inequality among men can be accounted for by increased polarization in hours of work, as argued in Morissette et al. (1994). For example, in the mid-1980s, average weekly hours of more-educated and less-educated men began to diverge.[24] Although inequality in men's annual earnings stagnates after this time, there were reductions in the hourly wages of more-educated men; but because their hours of work increased, this resulted in very little change in the distribution of annual earnings. Consistent with these facts, Morissette et al. (1994) find that the distribution of weekly hours among men had widened through the 1980s.[25]

Figure 11.4

Summary measures for female log earnings (1982 = 100)

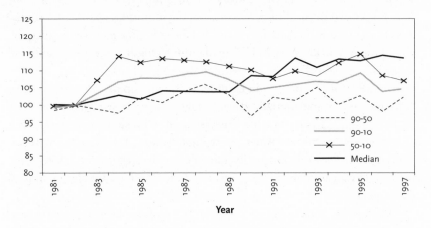

NOTE: Calculated using the SCF (individuals aged 15 and over), 1981-82 and 1984-97. The data point presented for 1983 is an average of 1982 and 1984. Sample is restricted to female paid workers aged 16-64 with annual earnings between $3,000 and $200,000.

Trends in earnings inequality among women, displayed in Figure 11.4, are substantially different from those of comparable men, as noted by others (e.g., Picot 1997, 1998). For men, the widening of the earnings distribution occurs both at the bottom and top of the distribution. The time trends in 90-50 and 50-10 differentials follow the trend in the 90-10 differentials. For women, inequality increases more at the bottom of the distribution, with the 50-10 differential trending up while the 90-50 mostly declines. The result is a more stable 90-10 differential over the entire period. As illustrated in Figure 11.1, the upper half of women's log earnings distribution experiences a rightward shift while the bottom remains pinned down.

Through the 1980s, inequality in annual earnings among women working full-time, full-year increased moderately. For this group of women, the 90-10 differential showed an annualized change of 1 percent, and the Gini increased by an annualized 0.9 percent, notably less than inequality increased among their male counterparts. Over this period, American women experienced much larger increases in inequality than their Canadian counterparts and American men. Katz and Autor (1999) report increases in inequality among women working full-time, full-year representing an annualized 3 percent change in the 90-10 differential of log weekly wages and an annualized 2 percent increase in the Gini index over the 1980s.[26] DiNardo et al. (1996) have implicated the declining real value of the minimum wage in the United States as a powerful explanatory factor for the very large increases in inequality among American women. In Canada, the 1990s also saw much different trends in inequality for men and women working full-time, full-year. Women experienced a slight increase in earnings inequality up to 1995, followed by a decline, so that the annualized percentage change from 1990 to 1997 was basically nil at 0.1 percent, while changes in the Gini stood at an annualized -0.07 percent. In contrast, American women working full-time, full-year saw continued increases in inequality into the 1990s, as the 90-10 differential increased by an annualized 0.8 percent and the Gini increased by an annualized 1 percent.[27]

Inequality trends in hourly wages for our sample of women with at least one year of job tenure are even flatter than trends for our sample of women working full-time, full-year. Inequality in women's hourly wages increased at an annualized 0.4 percent rate in the 90-10 differential in log hourly wages in the 1980s and an annualized 0.7 percent rate in the 1990s. For the entire period, there was a slight decrease in the Gini coefficient.

Given these trends in female earnings inequality, we would expect the increased participation of women in the labour market to have a moderating effect on trends in family earnings inequality, somewhat offsetting the increases in men's earnings inequality, as suggested by Picot (1998). For the United Kingdom, Harkness et al. (1997) find that women's earnings indeed had a sizable equalizing impact on family earnings. This effect would explain the Canada-United States difference in patterns of family earnings inequality in the 1980s. The substantial increases in female earnings inequality in the mid to late 1980s in the United States were accompanied by slight increases in family earnings inequality, increases not found in Canada.

As discussed earlier, another factor contributing to increased family income inequality among families composed of married or cohabiting individuals is the trend to increased assortative mating. This phenomenon has been described by sociologists (Mare 1991) as an increasing correlation in the educational attainment of spouses. Schooling is thought to affect mate selection as well as the organization of marriage markets. Education levels increasingly define the strata into which individuals choose to marry and, with delayed age of first marriage, post-secondary educational institutions increasingly become an environment of choice for meeting prospective spouses. Since educational attainment is a main determinant of earnings, it is not surprising to find an increase in assortative mating being reflected in earnings. Table 11.3 presents cross-tabulations of the husbands' and wives' earnings deciles in 1982 and 1997 for couples without children – for whom the wives' labour market decisions are less constrained than couples with children. In this table, increases in the proportions of couples around the right diagonal (husbands and wives in the same earning decile) indicate increases in assortative mating.[28] For example, among married couples without children, wives in the three upper deciles were more likely in 1997 than in 1982 to have husbands whose earnings were in these upper deciles than in the first three lower deciles. In 1997, women in the lower three deciles of female earnings were less likely to be married to men in the three upper deciles than they were in 1982. Thus, a potentially important impact of increased assortative mating is to increase family earnings inequality.

Figures 11.5 to 11.9 present these trends in equivalent family earnings for all families and for our original four family types of Table 11.1. In equivalent family earnings for all families, displayed in Figure 11.5, there is a moderate increase of 9 percent in the median over the 1980s, followed by a general stagnation of earnings in the 1990s. For families of married couples in Figures 11.6 and 11.7, we find similar patterns of increases in median equivalent family earnings. For other families with kids (87 percent headed by women) in Figure 11.8, the measure of median equivalent family earnings is somewhat noisy but does not indicate a consistent pattern of increase. Similarly, for other families without kids (53 percent headed by men), median earnings have barely kept up with inflation, as shown in Figure 11.9. To the extent that these last two types of families have younger heads, these trends are similar to earnings trends for younger individuals described in Picot (1998) and Kapsalis et al. (1999), among others.[29]

Turning to inequality measures, we find that equivalent family earnings inequality increased for all families in the early 1980s, peaked in 1984, and then declined for the rest of the 1980s. From 1984 to 1989, the 90-10 differential in log equivalent family earnings declined by an annualized 1.1 percent, while the Gini declined at an annualized rate of 0.6 percent. By contrast, through the 1990s, earnings inequality among all families increased, with the 90-10 differential rising by an annualized 0.4 percent and the Gini by 0.4

TABLE 11.3

Assortative mating measures: proportion of married couples without children in the cross-tabulation of female and male earnings deciles

Male earning decile		Female earning decile										Total
		1	2	3	4	5	6	7	8	9	10	
1982	1	**0.74**	1.33	1.64	0.74	0.85	0.67	0.57	0.53	0.82	0.84	8.72
	2	0.97	**1.42**	1.26	1.39	1.25	1.01	0.96	0.89	0.85	0.45	10.46
	3	0.88	0.95	**1.05**	1.08	1.31	1.61	1.16	1.32	0.74	0.64	10.74
	4	1.10	0.90	1.30	**0.85**	1.67	1.56	1.21	1.29	0.56	0.59	11.03
	5	0.63	0.84	1.02	1.17	**0.76**	1.25	1.82	1.76	1.07	0.93	11.25
	6	0.76	0.65	0.74	1.06	1.25	**1.54**	1.34	1.16	1.47	0.92	10.87
	7	0.51	0.69	0.93	0.99	1.05	0.83	**1.10**	1.65	1.25	1.54	10.54
	8	0.66	0.78	0.99	1.01	0.78	0.92	1.30	**1.62**	1.00	0.79	9.85
	9	0.61	0.53	0.68	0.69	0.79	0.91	0.74	1.17	**1.25**	1.58	8.94
	10	0.58	0.59	0.63	0.66	0.74	0.83	0.50	0.62	0.87	**1.56**	7.59
	Total	7.44	8.69	10.26	9.64	10.43	11.12	10.70	12.00	9.89	9.83	100
1997	1	**1.46**	1.39	1.23	1.44	0.68	0.61	0.53	0.38	0.43	0.48	8.63
	2	0.98	**1.30**	1.32	1.69	1.21	0.87	0.54	0.76	0.75	0.38	9.80
	3	0.67	1.06	**1.20**	1.39	1.92	0.83	0.65	0.63	0.59	0.36	9.29
	4	0.72	1.46	1.23	**1.22**	1.27	1.48	1.77	1.23	0.83	0.48	11.68
	5	0.38	0.82	0.99	1.20	**0.93**	1.03	1.04	1.53	0.50	0.38	8.80
	6	0.59	1.02	1.31	0.95	1.29	**1.42**	1.10	1.27	0.96	0.61	10.51
	7	0.47	1.03	0.60	0.79	0.94	1.30	**1.46**	0.82	1.93	0.74	10.08
	8	0.52	0.65	0.83	1.28	0.79	1.15	1.00	**1.37**	1.51	1.54	10.65
	9	0.80	0.55	0.83	0.81	0.95	1.09	1.09	1.12	**1.25**	1.71	10.20
	10	0.85	0.89	0.51	0.65	0.74	0.62	1.00	1.21	1.26	**2.62**	10.35
	Total	7.45	10.17	10.04	11.43	10.72	10.39	10.17	10.31	10.01	9.31	100

NOTE: The degree of assortative mating can be characterized by the sum of the diagonal (in bold). The degree of assortative mating for couples without children was 11.89% in 1982 and 14.23% in 1997. The degree of assortative mating for couples without children was 11.64% in 1982 and 13.49% in 1997.
SOURCE: See note to Table 11.2

FIGURE 11.5

Summary measures for log equivalent family earnings (all families, 1982 = 100)

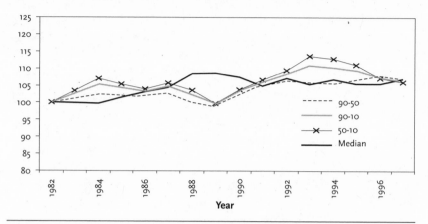

NOTE: Calculated using the SCF (Census Families) 1982, 1984, and 1986-97. The data points presented for 1983 and 1985 are averages of adjacent years. Sample restrictions are described in the text.

FIGURE 11.6

Summary measures for log equivalent family earnings (married, with kids, 1982 = 100)

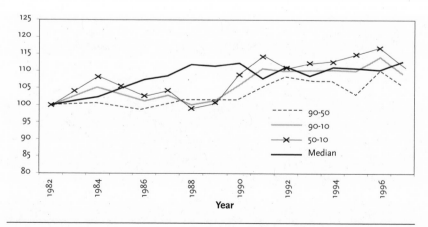

NOTE: Calculated using the SCF (Census Families) 1982, 1984, and 1986-97. The data points presented for 1983 and 1985 are averages of adjacent years. Sample restrictions are described in the text. Married individuals include those living common-law. A family with kids reports that there are children under the age of 18 in the census family.

FIGURE 11.7

Summary measures for log equivalent family earnings (married, no kids, 1982 = 100)

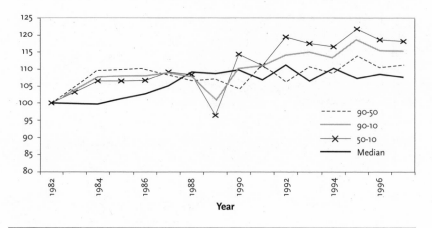

NOTE: See note to Figure 11.6.

FIGURE 11.8

Summary measures for log equivalent family earnings (other families with kids, 1982 = 100)

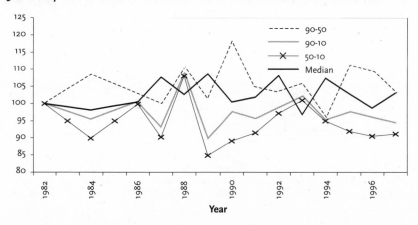

NOTE: See note to Figure 11.6. Other families include individuals who have never married and others who may be divorced, separated, or widowed.

FIGURE 11.9

Summary measures for log equivalent family earnings (other families, no kids, 1982 = 100)

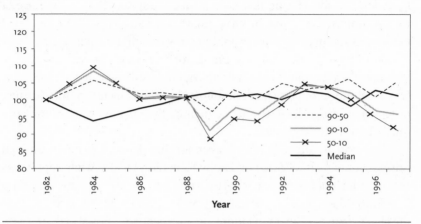

NOTE: See note to Figure 11.6. Other families include individuals who have never married and others who may be divorced, separated, or widowed.

percent. The increase in inequality among different types of families in the 1990s was most significant among married couples, which constitute roughly 55 to 60 percent of all families. It was most notable among married couples without children, who saw an annualized 0.7 percent increase in the 90-10 differential. In contrast, inequality among other families (with and without children) was either constant or declining over the 1980s and 1990s. Thus trends in equivalent family earnings inequality over the 1980s and 1990s appear to be dominated by trends among couples, with trends among singles producing smaller offsetting effects.

Accounting for Changes in the Distribution of Equivalent Family Earnings.

DECOMPOSITION METHODOLOGY

We begin with a description of the procedure used to decompose changes in the density of log equivalent family earnings in terms of the six factors identified earlier. This description generally follows the notation of DiNardo et al. (1996). In this decomposition, we construct counterfactual densities that represent the density of log equivalent family earnings that would have prevailed in 1997 had each of the six explanatory factors remained as in 1982. The decomposition is sequential in that, once the 1997 density has been adjusted for a factor, that factor remains adjusted in the next stage of the decomposition. Thus, in the primary-order decomposition described below and summarized later in Table 11.4, we begin by adjusting the 1997 density of log equivalent family earnings for changes in the structure of male earnings, then we adjust the resulting counterfactual density for changes to female labour force participation, followed by adjustments for the structure of female earnings, then assortative mating, then family composition, and finally family characteristics.

This primary order implicitly assumes that demand factors – through prices – come first, followed by family formation factors, while supply factors – through quantities – come last. This ordering is consistent with findings from other countries, where changes in male inequality accounted for the larger share of changes in family income inequality. It is also in line with the majority opinion in the American literature on inequality, which holds demand-side factors such as skill-biased technological change to be the primary explanatory factors. We also perform a reverse-order decomposition that places supply factors first.

Taking the logarithm of equation (1), we get

$$y_t \equiv \log(EFE_t) = \log(E_t) - 0.5\log(F_t),$$

where family earnings E_t is the sum of the male earnings, E_t^M, and female earnings, E_t^F, when applicable; then

$$E_t = E_t^M + E_t^F + v_t, \tag{2}$$

where

$$E_t^M = \exp(X_{Mt}\beta_{Mt} + \varepsilon_{Mt} + l_{Mt})$$
$$E_t^F = \exp(X_{Ft}\beta_{Ft} + \varepsilon_{Ft} + l_{Ft}),$$

where X_{Mt} is a vector of the male/husband characteristics, X_{Ft} is a vector of the female/wife characteristics, ε_{Mt} and ε_{Ft} represent the residual male and female earnings not explained by their characteristics, l_{Mt} and l_{Ft} represent the log of weeks worked by male/husband and female/wife, and v_t represents the residual equivalent family earnings that are not explained by the female or male characteristics, which may include children's earnings.[30]

To understand the decomposition procedure, it is useful to view each family observation as a vector (y, L, A, C, X, t) made up of the family's log equivalent family earnings (y), the female labour force participation choice (L), the degree of assortative mating in the family (A), family composition (C), the vector $X = [X_M, X_F]$ of family characteristics that may be partitioned as the male/husband characteristics (X_M) and the female/wife characteristics (X_F), and a date t.[31] Each family observation belongs to the joint distribution $F(y, L, A, C, X, t; \beta_{Mt}, \beta_{Ft})$ characterized by the population parameters describing the structure of men's earnings (β_{Mt}) and women's earnings (β_{Ft}). The joint distribution of log equivalent family earnings and characteristics at one point in time is the conditional distribution $F(y, L, A, C, X \mid t; \beta_{Mt}, \beta_{Ft})$. The density of log equivalent family earnings at one point in time, $f_t(y)$, can be written as the integral of the density of equivalent family earnings conditional on a set of family attributes, given the structure of male and female earnings $(\beta_{Mt}$ and $\beta_{Ft})$ at a date t:

$$
\begin{aligned}
f_t(y) = \iint \iint f \left(y \mid L, A, C, X; t_{\beta_M} = t, t_{\beta_F} = t \right) \\
dF \left(L \mid A, C, X, t_{L|A,C,X} = t \right) dF \left(A \mid C, X, t_{A|C,X} = t \right) \\
dF \left(C \mid X, t_{C|X} = t \right) dF \left(X \mid t_{X_M, X_F} = t \right) \\
= f_t \left(y ; t_{\beta_M} = t, t_{L|,A,C,X} = t, t_{\beta_F} = t, t_{A|C,X} = t, t_{C|X} = t, t_X = t \right).
\end{aligned} \tag{3}
$$

The estimation of counterfactual densities for the decomposition involves the combination of different "datings" for the different explanatory factors. The last line introduces the notation that accounts for these. For example,

$$
f_{97}(y; t_{\beta_M} = 97, t_{L|A,C,X} = 97, t_{\beta_F} = 97, t_{A|C,X} = 97, t_{C|X} = 97, t_X = 97)
$$

represents the actual density of equivalent family earnings in 1997.

We begin the primary order decomposition by adjusting the 1997 equivalent family earnings distribution for changes to men's wage structure. That is, we want to find the counterfactual density

$$
f_{97}(y; t_{\beta_M} = 82, t_{L|A,C,X} = 97, t_{\beta_F} = 97, t_{A|C,X} = 97, t_{C|X} = 97, t_X = 97). \tag{4}
$$

We first estimate male weekly earnings in 1982 and 1997. The econometric model used to describe male log weekly earnings, e_t^M, is

$$e_t^M = X_{Mt}\beta_{Mt} + \varepsilon_{Mt},\qquad(5)$$

where X_{Mt} is a vector of characteristics specific to the male head of the family. The vector of characteristics X_{Mt} includes a quadratic in age and dummy variables indicating province of residence, education level, and full-time or part-time job status.

Male log weekly earnings are adjusted for wage structure by applying the 1982 parameter estimates $(\hat{\beta}_{M82})$ to 1997 characteristics of men in the labour force and adding the residuals of the 1997 male log weekly earnings regression. That is,

$$e_{X97\beta82}^M = X_{M97}\beta_{M82} + \varepsilon_{M97}.\qquad(6)$$

These estimates are then used to adjust the equivalent family earnings of all families with a male head (in the labour force) present by replacing $E_{X97\beta82}^M = \exp(e_{X97\beta82}^M + l_{M97})$ in (2) with the adjusted value from (6).[32]

Next, we adjust the density of log equivalent family earnings for changes in female labour force participation. That is, we want to find

$$f_{97}\left(y;\ t_{\beta_M} = 82, t_{L|AC,X} = 82, t_{\beta_F} = 97, t_{A|C,X} = 97, t_{C|X} = 97, t_X = 97\right)$$
$$= \iint f_{97}\left(y\ |L, A, C, X; t_{\beta_M} = 82, t_{\beta_F} = 97\right)$$
$$\psi_{L|A,C,X}\left(L, A, C, X\right) dF\left(L\ |A, C, X, t_{L|A,C,X} = 97\right)\qquad(7)$$
$$dF\left(A, C, X\ |t_{A,C,X} = 97\right)$$

where

$$\psi_{L|A,C,X}(L,A,C,X) = \frac{dF(L|A,C,X,t_{L|A,C,X} = 82)}{dF(L|A,C,X,t_{L|A,C,X} = 97)}$$

is a reweighing function that represents the changes that have occurred between 1982 and 1997 in female labour force participation. Labour force status L takes on the values of 0 or 1; hence the reweighing function can be stated as

$$\psi_{L|A,C,X}(L,A,C,X) = L \frac{\Pr(L=1 \mid A,C,X,t_{L|A,C,X}=82)}{\Pr(L=1 \mid A,C,X,t_{L|A,C,X}=97)}$$
$$+ (1-L) \frac{\Pr(L=0 \mid A,C,X,t_{L|A,C,X}=82)}{\Pr(L=0 \mid A,C,X,t_{L|A,C,X}=97)} . \tag{8}$$

We estimate the above probabilities using a probit model in which the latent variable determining a woman's labour force participation is a function of age, education, and province of residence. The predicted reweighing function is then multiplied by the weights of each observation for which a female head/wife is present.[33]

Our third adjustment modifies this counterfactual density for changes to the wage structure of women. That is, we want to estimate

$$f_{97}(y; t_{\beta_M}=82, t_{L|A,C,X}=82, t_{\beta_F}=82, t_{A|C,X}=97, t_{C|X}=97, t_X=97). \tag{9}$$

The econometric model used to estimate female log weekly earnings is

$$e_t^F = X_{Ft}\beta_{Ft} + \varepsilon_{Ft}. \tag{10}$$

Here, X_{Ft} includes a quadratic in age and dummy variables indicating province of residence, education level, and full-time or part-time job status. The estimates of β_{F82} are applied to the 1997 female characteristics to adjust female log weekly earnings:

$$e_{X97\beta82}^F = X_{F97}\beta_{F82} + \varepsilon_{F97}. \tag{11}$$

In turn, these estimates are used to adjust the family's equivalent family earnings in (2).

The fourth step in the decomposition is to adjust the density of equivalent family earnings for the degree of assortative mating within families. That is, we want to estimate

$$f_{97}(y; t_{\beta_M}=82, t_{L|A,C,X}=82, t_{\beta_F}=82, t_{A|C,X}=82, t_{C|X}=97, t_X=97). \tag{12}$$

To obtain this density, we multiply the density represented by (9) by the reweighing function

$$\psi_{A|C,X}(A,C,X) = \frac{dF(A|C,X,t_{A|C,X} = 82)}{dF(A|C,X,t_{A|C,X} = 97)}.$$

This reweighing function represents the changes that have occurred between 1982 and 1997 in assortative mating and is similar in concept to the reweighing function for labour force participation. Assortative mating is described by the likelihood of a husband in the earnings decile i to be married to a wife in the earnings decile j ($i,j=1,2,...10$). The reweighing function can be written as

$$\psi_{A|C,X}(A,C,X) = S \sum_{m=1}^{10} I_m \sum_{n=1}^{10} I_n \frac{\Pr(i = m, j = n | C, X, t_{A|C,X} = 82, S = 1)}{\Pr(i = m, j = n | C, X, t_{A|C,X} = 97, S = 1)}$$
$$+ (1 - S) \sum_{m=1}^{10} I_m \sum_{n=1}^{10} I_n \frac{\Pr(i = m, j = n | C, X, t_{A|C,X} = 82, S = 0)}{\Pr(i = m, j = n | C, X, t_{A|C,X} = 97, S = 0)}, \quad (13)$$

where $S = 1$ if there are children present in the family and zero otherwise. I_m is an indicator function that takes on a value of 1 if $i = m$ and zero otherwise, and similarly for I_n. The probabilities used to estimate this reweighing function are simple cross-tabulations of the husbands' and wives' earnings deciles and are estimated for married couples with ($S = 1$) and without children ($S = 0$) separately to recognize different degrees of assortative mating among couples with children and couples without children.[34] The counterfactual density is found by multiplying this reweighing function by the weights on each observation.

In the fifth stage of the decomposition, we want to estimate the density

$$f_{97}(y; t_{\beta_M} = 82, t_{L|A,C,X} = 82, t_{\beta_F} = 82, t_{A|C,X} = 82, t_{C|X} = 82, t_X = 97), \quad (14)$$

which is found by multiplying the density represented by (12) by the reweighing function

$$\psi_{C|X}(C,X) = \frac{dF(C|X,t_{C|X} = 82)}{dF(C|X,t_{C|X} = 97)},$$

which represents the changes that have occurred between 1982 and 1997 in family composition. The reweighing function can be written as

$$\psi_{C|X}(C,X) = \sum_{s=1}^{4} I_s \frac{\Pr(C=s\,|\,X, t_{C|X}=82)}{\Pr(C=s\,|\,X, t_{C|X}=97)}, \tag{15}$$

where I_s is an indicator function taking on a value of 1 when $C = s$ and zero otherwise. Recall that four categories of family composition are used here (married with kids, married without kids, others with kids, and others without kids). The probabilities used to estimate $\psi_{C|X}(C,X)$ are found using a multinomial logit model, the equation for which is

$$\Pr(C=s\,|\,X, t_{C|X}=t) = \frac{\exp(X_{st}\beta_{st})}{1 + \sum_{j=1}^{4} \exp(X_{jt}\beta_{jt})}, \tag{16}$$

where X_{st} represents a subset of X for family type s, which includes the age of the family head, age squared, and dummy variables indicating province of residence.

Finally, the densities are reweighed to account for changes to family characteristics. That is, we want to estimate

$$f_{97}\left(y; t_{\beta_M} = 82,, t_{L|A,C,X} = 82, t_{\beta_F} = 82, t_{A|C,X} = 82, t_{C|X} = 82, t_X = 82\right)$$

$$= \iint \iint f\left(y\,|\,L, A, C, X; t_{\beta_M} = 82, t_{\beta_F} = 82\right)$$

$$\psi_{L|A,C,X}(L, A, C, X)\, dF\left(L\,|\,A, C, X, t_{L|AC, X} = 97\right)$$

$$\psi_{A|C,X}(A, C, X)\, dF\left(A\,|\,C, X, t_{A|C,X} = 97\right) \tag{17}$$

$$\psi_{C|X}(C, X)\, dF\left(C\,|\,X, t_{C|X} = 97\right) \psi_X(X)\, dF\left(X\,|\,t_{X_M, X_F} = 97\right),$$

where the reweighing function for family characteristics is

$$\psi_X(X) = \frac{dF(X, t_X = 82)}{dF(X, t_X = 97)}. \tag{18}$$

To estimate (18), we need to distinguish between married couples and families headed by single individuals. We therefore estimate the reweighing function as

$$\psi_X(X) = I_C \frac{\Pr(t_X = 97\,|\,I_C = 1)}{\Pr(t_X = 82\,|\,I_C = 1)} \frac{\Pr(t_X = 82\,|\,X, I_C = 1)}{\Pr(t_X = 97\,|\,X, I_C = 1)}$$

$$+ (1 - I_C) \frac{\Pr(t_X = 97\,|\,I_C = 0)}{\Pr(t_X = 82\,|\,I_C = 0)} \frac{\Pr(t_X = 82\,|\,X, I_C = 0)}{\Pr(t_X = 97\,|\,X, I_C = 0)}, \tag{19}$$

Table 11.4

Weights used in the decomposition

Primary-order decomposition		Reverse-order decomposition	
(1) Male wage structure	ψ	Female characteristics	$\psi\psi_{X_F}$
(2) Female labour force participation	$\psi\psi_L$	Male characteristics	$\psi\psi_{X_M}\psi_{X_F}$
(3) Female wage structure	$\psi\psi_L$	Family composition	$\psi\psi_{X_M}\psi_{X_F}\psi_C$
(4) Assortative mating	$\psi\psi_L\psi_A$	Assortative mating	$\psi\psi_{X_M}\psi_{X_F}\psi_C\psi_A$
(5) Family composition	$\psi\psi_L\psi_A\psi_C$	Female wage structure	$\psi\psi_{X_M}\psi_{X_F}\psi_C\psi_A$
(6) Male characteristics	$\psi\psi_L\psi_A\psi_C\psi_{X_M}$	Female labour force participation	$\psi\psi_{X_M}\psi_{X_F}\psi_C\psi_A\psi_L$
(7) Female characteristics	$\psi\psi_L\psi_A\psi_C\psi_{X_M}\psi_{X_F}$	Male wage structure	$\psi\psi_{X_M}\psi_{X_F}\psi_C\psi_A\psi_L$

NOTE: The functions ψ_L, ψ_A, ψ_C, ψ_{X_M}, ψ_{X_F} are the conditional reweighing functions defined by equations (7), (12), (14), and (18). ψ represents the original raw weights contained in the SCF microdata files. Notation for conditional weights has been simplified here for the sake of exposition.

where $I_C = 1$ if the family consists of a married couple and zero otherwise. Equation (19) can be found by applying Bayes' rule. The conditional probabilities $\Pr(t_X=t|X,I_C=1)$ and $\Pr(t_X=t|X,I_C=0)$ are obtained by pooling the 1982 and 1997 samples and then using a probit model with the year as a binary dependent variable to estimate the probability of each observation's falling into the 1997 sample, based on the characteristics X and given marital status. The unconditional probabilities $\Pr(t_x = t)$ are the weighted shares of the 1982 and 1997 samples in the pooled sample.

Implementation of the reverse-order decomposition involves reversing the order in which the weights are estimated and applied. Table 11.4 summarizes the weights used in each stage of the primary and reverse-order decomposition.

Results

An overview of the results is presented in a series of figures, followed by a step-by-step discussion.

In Figure 11.10, we plot the estimated counterfactual densities that result from the sequential decomposition. The raw densities are presented as a solid line in Panel A (1997) and a dashed line in Panel F (1982). These densities

FIGURE 11.10

1997 densities of log equivalent family earnings adjusted in steps for the indicated factors (1992 dollars)

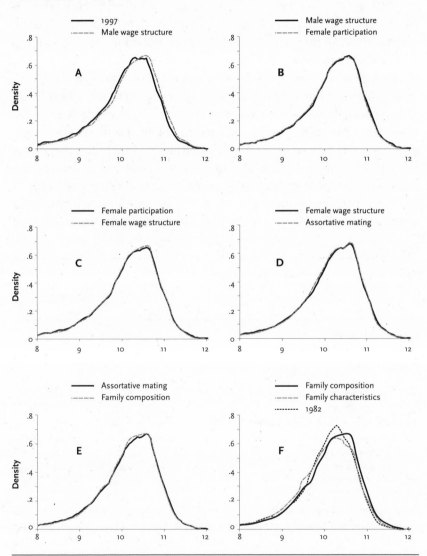

NOTE: The densities presented are the counterfactual densities that result from the sequential decomposition. The 1997 density of log equivalent family earnings is adjusted for changes in the male wage structure since 1982, then female labour force participation, female wage structure, assortative mating, family composition, and finally family characteristics. The last adjusted density can then be compared to the 1982 density of log equivalent family earnings.

exhibit the widening of the distribution of family earnings over this period. Comparing these densities, there is a rightward shift of the upper tail of the family earnings distribution while a substantial portion of the lower tail of the 1997 distribution remains pinned at the 1982 density levels. There is also a substantial reduction in mass around the mode (10) of the distribution by 1997. We turn now to consider the contributions of each factor to these overall changes.

Each panel in Figure 11.10 represents counterfactual densities of the 1997 density of log equivalent family earnings, holding each factor at 1982 levels. In each panel, the adjustment is shown as a dashed line, which becomes the solid line to be adjusted in the next panel. The inequality statistics corresponding to each density are presented in Panel B of Table 11.5. Panel A of Table 11.6 evaluates the effects of the counterfactual experiments on the changes in the distribution of log equivalent family earnings from 1982 to 1997. The magnitude of the changes in the different inequality measures corresponds to 6 to 8 percent of the 1982 values. For the United States, Daly

TABLE 11.5

Decomposition results: inequality statistics

	90-10	90-50	50-10	Standard deviation	Gini
A. Initial estimates					
1982	1.751	0.644	1.106	0.806	0.322
1997	1.873	0.686	1.187	0.872	0.343
B. Primary-order decomposition					
Male wage structure	1.858	0.681	1.177	0.865	0.341
Female labour force participation	1.866	0.688	1.178	0.865	0.343
Female wage structure	1.834	0.680	1.154	0.851	0.340
Assortative mating	1.802	0.672	1.129	0.839	0.336
Family composition	1.744	0.660	1.084	0.817	0.330
Family characteristics	1.813	0.703	1.110	0.857	0.343
C. Reverse-order decomposition					
Family characteristics	1.959	0.726	1.233	0.931	0.358
Family composition	1.905	0.717	1.188	0.909	0.352
Assortative mating	1.856	0.709	1.147	0.895	0.346
Female wage structure	1.823	0.706	1.118	0.836	0.343
Female labour force participation	1.822	0.710	1.112	0.832	0.345
Male wage structure	1.805	0.706	1.099	0.831	0.343

NOTE: Calculated using the SCF (Census Families) 1982 and 1997. See text for details.

and Valletta (2000) report changes in the inequality measures ranging from 6 percent (for the 90-50) to 16 percent (for the 90-10).

As shown in Panel A of Figure 11.10, holding the male wage structure at its 1982 level leads to a substantial rightward shift of the 1997 family earnings distribution. This reflects the stagnation, if not the decline (Burbidge et al. 2002), in the returns to education for men over the 1990s, which actually cause the density to shift to the right.[35] That is, if the returns to education had remained as in 1982, there would have been more families in the upper end of the distribution. The rightward shift (decrease in the constant) is also consistent with evidence of declining wages for younger and less educated male workers (Picot 1998; Beaudry and Green 2000). The changes in inequality statistics in Table 11.6 indicate that changes to the male wage structure explain around 13 percent of the increase in family earnings inequality that is seen between 1982 and 1997. Interestingly, changes in the male wage structure account for similar increases in the 90-50 and 50-10 log earnings differentials, reflecting the fact that the widening male wage distribution occurred in both the upper and lower ends as indicated earlier. Using a different methodology, Burtless (1999) found that changes in the distribution of male earnings could account for 28 percent of the increase in the Gini coefficient in the United States between 1979 and 1996. Here we consider changes in the returns to the male individual characteristics separately from the changes in the characteristics themselves, which are considered last.

Second, it appears that the increase in female labour force participation has acted to reduce inequality among families between 1982 and 1997. By adjusting the 1997 density to hold female labour force participation at 1982 levels, the measures of inequality (generally) increase, indicating that inequality in 1997 would have been higher, had women not entered the labour force in greater numbers. This factor most strongly influences the 90-50 log differential (17 percent) and the Gini coefficient (12 percent), which suggests that changes in women's participation were most important for pulling up the middle of the earnings distribution.

The third factor of the decomposition, changes in the female wage structure, explains a substantial portion (up to 29 percent) of the increase in family earnings inequality between 1982 and 1997. Given that there were substantial increases in the returns to experience and education for women, it is not surprising that the effects of changes in the female wage structure on family inequality are greater than changes in the male wage structure.[36] Changes in the female wage structure on equivalent family earnings inequality

TABLE 11.6

Decomposition results: changes in inequality measures

	90-10	90-50	50-10	Standard deviation	Gini
Total change	0.122	0.042	0.080	0.067	0.021

A. Primary-order decomposition results

EFFECT OF:

	90-10	90-50	50-10	Standard deviation	Gini
Male wage structure	0.016	0.005	0.010	0.007	0.003
	(12.8)	(13.1)	(12.6)	(10.9)	(12.8)
Female labour force participation	−0.008	−0.007	−0.001	0.000	−0.003
	(−6.7)	(−16.6)	(−1.6)	(0.0)	(−12.0)
Female wage structure	0.032	0.008	0.024	0.014	0.003
	(26.2)	(19.9)	(29.4)	(21.2)	(13.9)
Assortative mating	0.032	0.007	0.025	0.012	0.004
	(26.2)	(16.9)	(31.1)	(17.9)	(19.5)
Family composition	0.058	0.012	0.046	0.022	0.007
	(47.3)	(29.2)	(56.7)	(33.2)	(31.3)
Family characteristics	−0.069	−0.043	−0.026	−0.040	−0.013
	(−56.3)	(−101.6)	(−32.7)	(−59.4)	(−63.1)
Unexplained	0.062	0.058	0.004	0.051	0.021
	(50.6)	(139.0)	(4.4)	(76.3)	(97.7)

B. Reverse-order decomposition results

EFFECT OF:

	90-10	90-50	50-10	Standard deviation	Gini
Family characteristics	−0.086	−0.039	−0.046	−0.059	−0.014
	(−70.0)	(−94.0)	(−57.5)	(−87.4)	(−66.9)
Family composition	0.054	0.009	0.046	0.022	0.005
	(44.4)	(20.9)	(56.6)	(33.5)	(25.9)
Assortative mating	0.049	0.008	0.041	0.014	0.006
	(39.8)	(18.8)	(50.7)	(20.7)	(26.3)
Female wage structure	0.033	0.003	0.029	0.058	0.003
	(26.6)	(7.9)	(36.3)	(87.2)	(15.3)
Female labour force participation	0.001	−0.004	0.006	0.005	−0.002
	(1.1)	(−10.4)	(7.1)	(6.9)	(−7.5)
Male wage structure	0.017	0.004	0.013	0.001	0.002
	(13.7)	(10.2)	(15.6)	(1.4)	(8.1)
Unexplained	0.054	0.061	−0.007	0.025	0.021
	(44.4)	(146.6)	(−8.9)	(37.8)	(98.8)

NOTE: Percentage of total variation explained in parentheses. "Unexplained" is the residual not accounted for by all other factors. The effect of an explanatory factor indicates how much of the difference between the 1997 and 1982 density is explained by replacing the 1997 density with the corresponding counterfactual density.

affect more importantly the 50-10 log earnings differential, consistent with our earlier observation that inequality for women increased more at the bottom of the wage distribution.[37] Furthermore, all of the inequality measures are substantially affected by this factor. This indicates that changes in the female wage structure were important for explaining changes in family earnings throughout the entire distribution, as found in the United Kingdom (Harkness et al. 1997).

Assortative mating proves to be an equally important factor for explaining the increase in family earnings inequality. The cross-tabulations of the husbands and wives earnings deciles, reported in Table 11.3, indicate a substantial increase in assortative mating from 1982 to 1997. Although barely indistinguishable in Panel D of Figure 11.10, the increased likelihood that husbands and wives have similar incomes has implied a hollowing out of the lower-middle portion of the family earnings distribution in favour of the upper and, more importantly, of the lower ends of the distribution. This is supported by the large changes (from 26 to 31 percent) in the 90-10 and 50-10 log differentials relative to the other measures of inequality.

As earlier studies concluded, changes in family composition are found to be the dominant factor accounting for increases in inequality among families. From Panel E of Figure 11.10, it is apparent that many families moved from the middle to the lower end of the family earnings distribution as a result of changes in family composition, reflecting in particular the significant increase in single parents.[38] More precisely, the changes to family composition account for 47 percent of the changes in the 90-10, for 29 percent of the changes in the 90-50, and for 57 percent of the changes in the 50-10 log earnings differentials. For the United States, Daly and Valletta (2000) find that changes in family structures are a factor explaining from 22 to 53 percent of the changes in measures in equivalent family income inequality from 1979 to 1989.

Finally, we adjust the 1997 family earnings distribution to account for changes in family characteristics. Since both male and female heads or spouses became older and more educated from 1982 to 1997, reverting these characteristics to the 1982 levels will naturally generate a substantial leftward shift of the density. This generates a lump around the 25th percentile of the log equivalent family earnings distribution, which actually leads to an increase in our measures of earnings inequality. Because we do not have information on union status, we cannot generate the mass present near the mode in 1982, which corresponds to a union lump. Fortin and Lemieux (2000) have shown that the decline in union density from 1995 to 1998 generates such a transfer of mass from the mode to the mid-lower part of the wage distribution.

Because we cannot account for changes in union density, our end results seem to have less explanatory power in terms of the inequality measures than they do in terms of the densities, if we visually transpose the counterfactual mass around the 25th percentile to the 50th percentile. In Panel F of Figure 11.10, we superimpose the last counterfactual density that accounts for all of the above six factors (i.e., ending with family composition) and the actual 1982 density. Discrepancies between the 1982 density and the counterfactual density reflect unexplained changes. Aside from the effect of unionization, our explanatory factors seem to account for most of the changes in the distribution of log equivalent family earnings, as shown by the 50-10 differential, for example.

ROBUSTNESS

In Panel C of Table 11.5 and Panel B of Table 11.6, we repeat the analysis in reverse order. We thus begin our sequential analysis with the effect of family characteristics, followed by the effects of family composition, assortative mating, the female wage structure, female labour force participation, and, finally, the male wage structure. The decomposition appears relatively robust to the order of the decomposition. Changing the order of the decomposition changes the impact (however small) of adjusting the 1997 density for female labour force participation in that the 90-10 and 50-10 differentials demonstrate that increasing female labour force participation has contributed to increasing family earnings inequality rather than offsetting the effects of other factors. While the magnitude of the changes attributable to each of the different factors changes somewhat, the ordering to their importance is relatively unchanged. Changes in family characteristics and composition remain the dominant factors, followed by assortative mating and changes in the female wage structure.

As with similar decomposition studies, all the different factors may not be fully independent; for example, female labour force participation has been significantly linked to marital status and thus to family composition. This may explain some amount of the "overexplaining" in our decomposition. The exercise remains instructive, however, with respect to the distributional consequences of the various explanations, even if the magnitude of the effects contains some margin of error.

Conclusion

Women made important economic progress in the last two decades of the twentieth century. In the 1980s, this progress was marked by large increases in female labour force participation. In the early 1990s, there was much progress in women's labour market earnings. Similarly, there was significant progress in the relative earnings of women, measured by the female/male earnings ratio. Thereafter, there are some concerns about the stagnation of female labour force participation since the early 1990s and about the levelling-off of female median earnings and of the female/male earnings ratio since the mid-1990s. This latter stabilization is shared by the United States (O'Neill 2003) and many OECD countries (Clarke 2001). The analysis of these troubling trends will be an important topic of research in the years to come. Early indications are that the 2000s have brought more favourable trends. Here, however, our focus is on the impact of the improvements of the 1980s and early 1990s in the labour market outcomes of women on the levels and dispersion of family earnings.

From 1982 to 1997, the increase in median log equivalent family earnings corresponds to a change of 6 percentage log points, while the increase in the 90-10 differential was 12 log points, with most of the increase (8 log points) occurring in the 50-10 differential. We find that changes in the wage structure dwarf socio-demographic factors in accounting for these changes in equivalent family earnings dispersion. Over that period, the workforce aged and reached substantially higher levels of educational attainment, which caused a substantial shift in the upper part of the equivalent family earnings distribution. Notwithstanding our exclusion of any union effect, these demographic changes explain most of the increase in the 90-50 differential. Another notable socio-demographic change over that period was the substantial decrease in the proportion of married (including cohabiting) couples among all families; this factor accounts for more than half of the increase in the 50-10 differential. We find that other gender-specific factors, such as the increase in female labour force participation and changes in the female wage structure, had very significant impacts on family-earnings inequality. The changes in female labour force participation to some extent offset the increase in the 50-10 differential, consistent with the idea that female sole heads of households are more likely to work than when a male earner is present. Changes in the female wage structure increased wage inequality more evenly across the family earnings distribution. With increased assortative mating, many married working women found themselves in the upper deciles of the family earnings distribution, but many married women in the lower deciles of the female earnings distribution found that their husbands' earnings had slipped into lower deciles of the male earnings distribution. Also, many more women in 1997 than in 1982 were finding themselves sole heads of households.

We thus find that the implications of women's economic progress for the welfare of families have been uneven over the past two decades. Women and their families in the upper deciles of the family earnings distribution have been enjoying rising incomes, while families in the middle of the family earnings distribution have seen their family earnings eroded by the stagnation of men's earnings in the 1990s. There has been relatively little change for those families at the bottom of the family earnings distribution.

NOTES

1 After 1976, these figures come from the CANSIM II Series – V2461672 for all women fifteen to sixty-four years of age and are computed from the Labour Force Survey (LFS). The participation rate of prime age women (twenty-five to fifty-four years of age) reached a plateau of about 75 percent in the early to mid-1990s. In the early 2000s, it climbed again to around 80 percent (CANSIM II Series – V2461670).

2 From 1980 to 2000, Heisz et al. (2002) report declines in the median real earnings of full-time male workers, except among those aged forty-five to sixty-four. By contrast, they report increases in the median real earnings of full-time female workers in all age groups except those aged eighteen to twenty-four.

3 The ratios are from the CANSIM II Series – V1542068. In the later 1990s, men's earnings began to climb again, eroding women's relative progress, and the ratio remained between 69 and 71 percent. Drolet (2002) finds a higher number for the raw hourly wage ratio of 80 percent in 1997, which increases to 89 percent when adjusting for a host of human capital, workplace, and other characteristics. We also find more favourable numbers from an hourly wage measure.

4 Wolfson and Murphy (2000) also report substantial increases in family market earnings inequality in Canada from 1985 to 1995.

5 Other studies have used tax-based data (Baker and Solon 2003). Further discussion of the different data sources is provided in Chapters 3 and 5.

6 The SCF employs a multi-stage stratified clustered probability sample. The weights are designed to reflect the sample design and differential response rates for households, among other things.

7   That is, we exclude individuals who report being in the labour force but who worked zero weeks, worked zero hours, or had zero annual earnings. We also exclude individuals who report not being in the labour force but whose main activity is work.

8   The CPI is from the CANSIM II Series – V737344. The questionnaire used in the survey asks the respondent "During the 12 months ending December 31, (year), what was your income from the following sources? 1. Wages and salaries before deductions, including military pay and allowances." For non-respondents, income is imputed by Statistics Canada on the basis of geographically nearest respondent records possessing similar characteristics.

9   An alternative to truncating the sample is to "winsorize" the data by, for example, setting the values of the observations in the bottom or top deciles equal to the value of the observation at the tenth or ninetieth percentile. This technique is more desirable than truncating if it is believed that the extreme values are exaggerated versions of the true values but that the true values lie in the tails. Truncating the sample is more desirable if the extremes are believed to be simply mistakes. See Angrist and Krueger (1999) for a thorough discussion of trimming techniques. Eliminating these extreme observations removes less than 1 percent of our sample.

10 Our trimming of the sample by hourly wages corresponds exactly to the trimming by annual earnings described earlier when assuming a person works forty hours a week for fifty weeks of the year.

11 For example, for our female sample of workers with more than one year of job tenure, allowing for extremely low or high wages will result in measured increases in inequality among women in the early 1980s, increases that our trimmed sample does not depict.

12 The SCF defines a census family as either a husband and wife (married or common-law) or one parent with unmarried children. A single individual living alone or with unrelated individuals is a one-person census family. The analysis of inequality in more encompassing measures of family income can be found in Chapter 3.

13 We also exclude families whose head had zero annual earnings but reports being in the labour force.

14 For example, setting $\sigma = 0$ assumes that infinite economies of scale are achieved by a family, while setting $\sigma = 1$ assumes that no economies of scale may be achieved. We find that using $\sigma = 0.5$ in our measure of equivalent family earnings produces the same general trends in earnings and inequality as measures using $\sigma = 0$ or $\sigma = 1$.

15 By contrast, Atkinson and Bourguignon (1987) suggest a two-stage procedure in which the household's original income is first adjusted to accommodate differences in needs and then further adjusted for family size.

16　After some experimentation with different equivalence scales, we find that our simplified measure of equivalent family earnings reproduces the same general trends in earnings and inequality as measures that adjust family income according to the age structure of the family (used by Statistics Canada and the OECD).

17　Yet, because they represent such a small proportion of families, this yields sample sizes too small to be considered separately in our decomposition analysis.

18　See Crossley and Curtis (2003) for a discussion of changes to provincial social assistance programs. As an example, using information provided by the National Council of Welfare (2004), there was a 25 percent real decrease in benefits to single parents (with one child) in Ontario between 1994 and 1997. Only in New Brunswick did real benefits to single parents increase (by 5 percent) over this period.

19　The difference between men's and women's working hours has remained fairly constant from 1981 to 1997. The male-female difference in hours for the sample of full-time, full-year workers ranges from a low of 3.09 hours/week in 1981 to a high of 3.81 hours/week in 1994, with an average male-female difference of 3.5 hours/week. The male-female difference in hours is also fairly constant across education groups, averaging 3.54 hours/week among high school dropouts, 3.66 hours/week among individuals with high school, and 3.11 hours among university graduates in the full-time, full-year sample. The male-female difference in hours for a sample of workers with more than one year job tenure ranges from 6.35 hours/week in 1989 to 7.14 hours/week in 1991.

20　Kesselman and Cheung in Chapter 12 provide a thorough discussion of inequality measures.

21　Calculated from Katz and Autor (1999, Table 1) for which they use a sample of males working full-time full-year between 1979 and 1987.

22　Annualized changes calculated from Katz and Autor (1999, Table 1) using a sample of males working full-time, full-year between 1987 and 1995.

23　Katz and Autor (1999, Table 4.b); the figure is from the CPS-MORG.

24　Using the sample of men with job tenure greater than one year, in 1985, the men with a university degree worked 1.4 hours a week more than men who were high school dropouts. This difference in weekly hours was 2.1 in 1990 and 3.2 in 1994.

25　Toward the end of the 1990s, we see a dramatic decline in the weekly hours worked among more-educated individuals. The source of that change is not clear. A reporting change is a possibility since there have been changes in the hours-of-work question series in the LFS questionnaire. Changes in Employment Insurance eligibility, which became hourly based, is another possibility.

26　Annualized changes calculated from Katz and Autor (1999, Table 1), using a sample of females working full-time, full-year during 1979-87.

27 Calculated from Katz and Autor (1999, Table 1), using a sample of women work-
    ing full-time, full-year between 1987 and 1995.
28 A similar table for married couples with children indicates similar increases in
    assortative mating, albeit a somewhat lower magnitude.
29 Forty-six percent of other families are headed by (single) individuals under the
    age of thirty-five, while 17 percent are headed by individuals under the age of
    twenty-five. This compares to only 25 percent of married couple families headed
    by individuals under thirty-five and 3 percent of married couples headed by indi-
    viduals under twenty-five.
30 Note that we add a measure of labour supply, l, in the above because we actually
    estimate the log weekly earnings of the head/spouse and then convert this back to
    log annual earnings.
31 As explained earlier, the empirical evaluation of residual wage inequality in the
    SCF may be difficult.
32 Note that we abstract from changes in labour supply by holding l_{M97} and l_{F97} con-
    stant and from changes in residual earnings inequality by holding ε_{M97} and ε_{F97}
    constant.
33 Note that the reweighing function $\psi_{L|A,C,X}(L,A,C,X)$ is set equal to 1 when a female
    head or wife is not present in the family.
34 Note that the reweighing function is set equal to 1 for single individuals.
35 In our regressions for men's log weekly earnings, the coefficients on indicator
    variables for high school, post-secondary education, and university degree were
    0.166, 0.222, and 0.425, respectively, in 1982 and 0.077, 0.176, and 0.414, re-
    spectively, in 1997. In these regressions, the constant was 4.070 in 1982 and 3.791
    in 1997.
36 In our regressions for women's log weekly earnings, the coefficients of the con-
    stant, age, age squared (/100) were 4.122, 0.042, -0.046, respectively, and the
    coefficients of the indicator variables for high school, post-secondary education,
    and university degree were 0.185, 0.366, and 0.652, respectively, in 1982. In 1997,
    the coefficients on the constant, age, and age squared (/100) were 3.502, 0.062, -
    0.066, and the coefficients of the education dummies 0.201, 0.314, and 0.678,
    respectively.
37 Burtless (1999) also considers the impact of changes to the distribution of female
    earnings in the United States and finds that 5 percent of the increase in the Gini
    coefficient could be attributed to changes in female earnings inequality.
38 Reweighing the 1997 density to reflect 1982 family composition reduced the pro-
    portion of single-parent families (as a proportion of all families with at least one
    head in the labour force) from 6.7 percent to 5.3 percent.

REFERENCES

Angrist, Josh D., and Alan B. Krueger. 1999. "Empirical Strategies in Labor Economics." In Orley Ashenfelter and David Card, eds., *Handbook of Labor Economics*. Vol. 3A, 1277-366. New York and Oxford: Elsevier Science, North-Holland.

Atkinson, A.B., and Francois Bourguignon. 1987. "Income Distribution and Differences in Needs." In George R. Feiwel, ed., *Arrow and the Foundations of the Theory of Economic Policy*, 350-70. New York: Macmillan.

Autor, David H., Lawrence F. Katz, and Alan B. Krueger. 1998. "Computing Inequality: Have Computers Changed the Labor Market?" *Quarterly Journal of Economics* 113(4): 1169-213.

Baker, Michael, and Gary Solon. 2003. "Earnings Dynamics and Inequality among Canadian Men, 1976-1992: Evidence from Longitudinal Income Tax Records." *Journal of Labor Economics* 21(2): 289-321.

Bar-Or, Yuval, John Burbidge, Lonnie Magee, and A. Leslie Robb. 1995. "The Wage Premium to a University Education in Canada: 1971-1991." *Journal of Labor Economics* 13(4): 762-94.

Beach, Charles M. 1989. "Dollars and Dreams: A Reduced Middle Class? Alternative Explanations." *Journal of Human Resources* 24(1): 162-93.

Beach, Charles M., and George A. Slotsve. 1994. "Polarization in the Canadian Labour Market." In Thomas J. Courchene, ed., *Stabilization, Growth and Distribution: Linkages in the Knowledge Era*, 299-347. Kingston, ON: Queen's University, John Deutsch Institute for the Study of Economic Policy.

Beaudry, Paul, and David A. Green. 2000. "Cohort Patterns in Canadian Earnings: Assessing the Role of Skill Premia in Inequality Trends." *Canadian Journal of Economics* 33(4): 907-36.

Beaudry, Paul, and Thomas Lemieux. 1999. "Evolution of the Female Labour Force Participation Rate in Canada, 1976-1994: A Cohort Analysis." *Canadian Business Economics* 7(2): 57-70.

Blackburn, McKinley L., and David E. Bloom. 1993. "The Distribution of Family Income: Measuring and Explaining Changes in the 1980s for Canada and the United States." In David Card and Richard B. Freeman, eds., *Small Differences That Matter: Labor Markets and Income Maintenance in Canada and the United States*. Chicago: University of Chicago Press.

Burbidge, John B., Lonnie Magee, and A. Leslie Robb. 1997. "Canadian Wage Inequality over the Last Two Decades." *Empirical Economics* 22(2): 181-203.

—. 2002. "The Education Premium in Canada and the United States." *Canadian Public Policy* 28: 203-17.

Burtless, Gary. 1999. "Effects of Growing Wage Disparities and Changing Family Composition on the U.S. Income Distribution." *European Economic Review* 43(4-6): 853-65.

Clarke, Steve. 2001. "Earnings of Men and Women in the EU: The Gap Is Narrowing but Only Slowly." *Statistics in Focus: Population and Social Conditions* 5 (May). Luxembourg: Eurostat.

Crossley, Thomas F., and Lori J. Curtis. 2003. "Child Poverty in Canada." Working Paper 2003-06. Hamilton, ON: McMaster University, Department of Economics.

Daly, Mary C., and Robert G. Valletta. 2000. "Inequality and Poverty in the United States: The Effects of Changing Family Behavior and Rising Wage Dispersion." Working Paper 2000-06. Federal Reserve Bank of San Francisco.

DiNardo, John, Nicole M. Fortin, and Thomas Lemieux. 1996. "Labor Market Institutions and the Distribution of Wages, 1973-1992: A Semiparametric Approach." *Econometrica* 64(5): 1001-44.

Donaldson, David, and Krishna Pendakur. 2004. "Equivalent Expenditure Functions and Expenditure-Dependent Equivalence Scales." *Journal of Public Economics* 88 (1-2): 175-208.

Drolet, Marie. 2002. "Can the Workplace Explain Canadian Gender Pay Differentials?" *Canadian Public Policy* 28(S1): S41-S63.

Ebert, Udo, and Patrick Moyes. 2003. "Equivalence Scales Reconsidered." *Econometrica* 71(1): 319-43.

Fortin, Nicole M., and Thomas Lemieux. 2000. "Income Redistribution in Canada: Minimum Wages versus Other Policy Instruments." In W. Craig Riddell and France St-Hilaire, eds., *Adapting Public Policy to a Labour Market in Transition*, 211-47. Montreal: Institute for Research on Public Policy.

Gao, Danielle. 2003. "Wage Analysis Computations." In Lawrence Mishel, Jared Bernstein, and Heather Boushey, eds., *The State of Working America 2002-03*, Appendix B. Ithaca, NY: Economic Policy Institute.

Harkness, Susan, Stephen Machin, and Jane Waldfogel. 1997. "Evaluating the Pin Money Hypothesis: The Relationship between Women's Labour Market Activity, Family Income and Poverty in Britain." *Journal of Population Economics* 10(2): 137-58.

Heisz, A., A. Jackson, and G. Picot. 2002. "Winners and Losers in the Labour Market of the 1990s." Statistics Canada, Business and Labour Market Analysis Division. Working Paper 184.

Henderson, D.W., and J.C. Rowley. 1977. "The Distribution and Evolution of Canadian Family Incomes, 1965-1973." Ottawa: Economic Council of Canada. Discussion Paper 91.

Hyslop, Dean R. 2001. "Rising U.S. Earnings Inequality and Family Labor Supply: The Covariance Structure of Intrafamily Earnings." *American Economic Review* 91(4): 755-77.

Juhn, Chinhui, and Kevin M. Murphy. 1997. "Wage Inequality and Family Labor Supply." *Journal of Labor Economics* 15(1): 72-97.

Kapsalis, C., Rene Morissette, and Garnett Picot. 1999. "The Returns to Education and the Increasing Wage Gap between Younger and Older Workers." Working Paper 131. Statistics Canada, Business and Labour Market Analysis Division.

Karoly, Lynn A. 1993. "The Trend in Inequality among Families, Individuals, and Workers in the United States: A Twenty-Five Year Perspective." In Sheldon H. Danziger and Peter Gottschalk, eds., *Uneven Tides: Rising Inequality in the 1980s*, 19-97. New York: Russell Sage Foundation.

Karoly, Lynn A., and Gary Burtless. 1995. "Demographic Change, Rising Earnings Inequality, and the Distribution of Personal Well-Being, 1959-1989." *Demography* 32(3): 379-405.

Katz, Lawrence F., and David H. Autor. 1999. "Changes in the Wage Structure and Earnings Inequality." In Orley Ashenfelter and David Card, eds., *Handbook of Labor Economics*. Vol. 3A, 1463-549. New York and Oxford: Elsevier Science, North-Holland.

Lemieux, Thomas. 2002. "Decomposing Changes in Wage Distributions: A Unified Approach." *Canadian Journal of Economics* 35(4): 646-88.

Machin, Stephen, and Jane Waldfogel. 1994. "The Decline of the Male Breadwinner: Changing Shares of Husbands' and Wives' Earnings in Family Income." Working Paper WSP/103. London School of Economics, Suntory-Toyota International Centre for Economics and Related Disciplines.

Mare, Robert D. 1991. "Five Decades of Educational Assortative Mating." *American Sociological Review* 56(1): 15-32.

Morissette, Rene, John Myles, and Garnett Picot. 1994. "Earnings Inequality and the Distribution of Working Time in Canada." *Canadian Business Economics* 2(3): 3-16.

—. 1995. "Earnings Polarization in Canada, 1969-1991." In Keith G. Banting and Charles M. Beach, eds. *Labour Market Polarization and Social Policy Reform*, 24-50. Kingston ON: Queen's University, School of Policy Studies.

National Council of Welfare. 2004. *Welfare Incomes 2003*. Vol. 121. Ottawa: The Council.

O'Neill, June. 2003. "The Gender Gap in Wages, Circa 2000." *American Economic Review Papers and Proceedings* 93(2): 309-14.

Picot, Garnett. 1997. "What Is Happening to Earnings Inequality in Canada in the 1990s?" *Canadian Business Economics* 6(1): 65-83.

—. 1998. "What Is Happening to Earnings Inequality and Youth Wages in the 1990s?" Working Paper 116. Statistics Canada, Business and Labour Market Analysis Division.

Wolfson, M., and B. Murphy. 2000. "Income Inequality in North America: Does the 49th Parallel Still Matter?" *Canadian Economic Observer* (August): 3.1-3.24. Statistics Canada, Cat. No. 11-010-XPP.

12
Taxation Impacts on Inequality in Canada: Methodologies and Findings

Jonathan R. Kesselman and Ron Cheung

The modern state plays an important role in moulding the distribution of income and well-being among its citizens and moderating the market economy's inequalities. It pursues these goals by setting the legal framework for business, regulating labour markets, supplying public goods and services, providing cash transfers, and collecting taxes to finance its activities. The contemporary welfare state takes as much as one-half of national income in taxes, and it often uses tax provisions such as credits and benefit clawbacks to redistribute income. Moreover, taxation and other policy interventions to moderate inequality exert their own influence on distributional outcomes through market responses. Thus, the distributional pattern of taxation is of paramount importance. Yet there remains much dispute over that pattern and the effects of taxes on inequality – issues at the core of public debate over the size and scope of the welfare state, how to finance its activities, and how to mitigate inequality.

Improved understanding of how tax burdens are distributed and how to measure their impacts is vital in formulating and assessing taxation policies. For example, does greater progressivity in the income tax rate schedule contribute to increases in *effective* progressivity and inequality reduction, and, if so, to what extent? Does the answer to this question differ depending upon whether the tax policy is at the national or the subnational level? How do indirect taxes on consumption affect distributional outcomes, and does the answer hinge on whether one takes an annual or a lifetime perspective? Similarly, what are the short-run and long-run distributional impacts of shifting the personal tax base away from income and toward consumption? And how should one assess the progressivity or inequality impacts of changes in various types of taxes or of shifts in the mix among these types? While tax economists tend to emphasize the efficiency and growth aspects of tax policies, politicians and the public are fixated on the distributional dimension.

A large body of research investigates the distribution of the tax burden, with some studies focusing on the inequality impacts and others on the progressivity of taxes. A key issue in all studies is how to deal with the economic incidence of each tax – how its burden is actually borne by different groups. This chapter critically assesses the state of knowledge about the distributional impacts of the tax system, reviewing both foreign and available Canadian research.[1] We gauge these impacts in terms of inequality and progressivity, and we review the relevant measures and their interrelations. An overarching theme of the studies is their approach to treating the incidence of various taxes. Previous work on tax incidence has sometimes been casual in describing the progressivity of taxes and in making comparisons. By bringing together the analysis of tax incidence with formal measurement of progressivity and inequality, we improve the rigour of the discussion. We examine these issues in a selective synopsis of research on the distributional impact of taxes, both in Canada and cross-nationally, along with the comparative impact of cash transfers. Finally, we offer suggestions about priorities for future research and thoughts about what tax policy inferences can be drawn from the current state of knowledge.

Types of Analytical Frameworks

Studies of the distributional impacts of taxation can be classified into three types based on their varying analytical frameworks and methodologies and, hence, in the social science and public policy questions they can address. We denote the three types as "inequality" (INEQ), "computable general equilibrium" (CGE), and "fiscal incidence" (FINC) studies. Each type of study has unique attributes (see Table 12.1) with associated advantages and weaknesses.

"Inequality" studies are an offshoot of recent research to track income inequality both in changes over time and differences across countries. These studies estimate the difference in inequality measures between gross (or market) income and net (or disposable) income of households. Typically, they make adjustments using family equivalence scales to gauge the well-being of individuals in households of differing sizes. Many INEQ studies do not distinguish between the impacts of taxes and those of cash-type transfers; they simply compare the pre-tax, pre-transfer (market income) distribution with the post-tax, post-transfer (disposable income) distribution. Identifying the taxation effects on inequality requires abstracting from the effects of the cash transfer system. Since they examine primarily the difference between gross and net incomes, INEQ studies usually consider only personal income taxes (PIT) and, in some cases, payroll taxes for social security programs. These types of taxes are assumed to fall fully on the individual, thus obviating any incidence analysis.

The principal advantage of INEQ studies is their use of datasets that allow tolerably consistent comparisons across countries both at a point in time and across years. They can also decompose households into individuals using family equivalence scales, and they can decompose inequality impacts into within-group and across-group effects. INEQ studies can help show how various components of a personal income tax affect inequality outcomes. They allow for variations in the inequality parameter in order to examine the effects of different degrees of inequality aversion. The principal drawback of INEQ studies is that they consider only direct personal taxes, thereby omitting the full range of indirect taxes and business taxes, and they assume that personal taxes are fully borne by taxpayers, thus missing any economic shifting of tax burdens and most likely overstating the redistributive effects of progressive personal taxes. INEQ studies are also limited to annual data and therefore do not capture the lifetime impacts, which, again, likely leads them to overstate the long-run inequality reduction from tax policy.

In "computable general equilibrium" studies, in contrast, the assumed structure and parameters of an economic model dictate incidence outcomes. CGE studies focus on the long-run distributional effects of taxation via its impacts on employment, wages, profits, prices, and economic growth. These studies can report distributional outcomes by both income class and summary inequality measures, and they compute outcomes in utility and net income terms. Typically, CGE studies are highly stylized in their treatment of individuals (as against households) and the range of taxes considered (often cast as labour income, capital income, and consumption), and they do not always distinguish between taxes imposed at the business level and at the individual level. Most CGE studies are geared to consider the lifetime as well as the transitional and intergenerational distributional impacts of taxes.[2]

CGE studies offer several advantages over other types of studies.[3] A dynamic CGE model can reveal the time path of the distribution of gains or losses from tax changes; static analysis ignores the impact of tax changes on future generations and on transitional generations during an economy's adjustment. A CGE model generates the incidence of all taxes in a logically consistent framework rather than making various tax incidence assumptions.

TABLE 12.1

Types of studies of the distributional impact of taxation

Type	Taxes covered	Tax incidence	Time horizon	Observation unit	Income measure	Distributional impact measure
INEQ	Only PIT and, in some studies, payroll tax	Assumed to fall fully on the individual	Annual	Individuals using family equivalence scale	Net income	Index of inequality
CGE	Stylized forms of major taxes	Generated by CGE model, structural and parameter assumptions	Static or dynamic over lifetime	Individual or stylized household	Net income or utility	Utility change by lifetime income groups
FINC	All taxes	Taken from other studies, sensitivity analyses	Annual or lifetime	Household	Pre-tax, pre-transfer income or broad income	ATRs by income groups or index of progressivity

NOTE: INEQ = inequality; CGE = computable general equilibrium; FINC = fiscal incidence.

The implied incidence of taxes can be related to key behavioural parameters in the model – the elasticities of substitution between capital and labour and between current and future consumption – where empirical evidence can be used. The CGE approach also can simultaneously assess the distributional and efficiency effects of taxes within the same model. In a policy context with competing goals, both of these effects are germane to decision-making; a more progressive tax system may entail greater inefficiencies. Finally, the lifetime view of individual well-being in this approach accords with empirical evidence about individuals' consumption behaviour, which is tied more closely to longer-term income flows than to current income. The lifetime view may also conform to ethical views about how society should gauge the impact of public policies.

Among their limitations, CGE models require specific functional forms, structural assumptions, and parameter values for which empirical estimates are uncertain.[4] Because they employ highly aggregated modelling and data, CGE models cannot capture the effects of detailed tax policy changes. Data for lifetime incomes and their composition between capital and labour sources are not directly available and must be simulated, with limited guidance from longitudinal datasets. CGE models use a common interest rate for borrowing and lending, which renders capital income irrelevant in computing lifetime income. However, a common interest rate is an empirically false assumption that ignores the borrowing constraints that many households face. An annual perspective may be more readily understood by policy makers than the lifetime perspective, given the reality of frequent changes to the tax system. The complexity of CGE modelling also means that its distributional findings will be less comprehensible to policy makers and politicians than those from other types of studies.

"Fiscal incidence" studies typically present their results by income classes of taxpayers, so that findings are reported in terms of progressivity (the pattern of average tax rates or ATRs) rather than inequality measures. They usually consider the household, not the individual, as the unit of observation, and most studies of this type use annual data. FINC studies can be pursued either with relatively aggregated data by income class (for the distributions of income receipts of various types and savings patterns) or with micro datasets.

FINC studies have notable strengths that account for their early and continued widespread use. They can include a large number of tax types, consider a wide range of assumptions about the incidence of each tax, and allow sensitivity analyses to explore alternative incidence assumptions. As they build on micro datasets that often contain details about particular tax provisions, some FINC studies can examine the distributional effects of those provisions. This class also includes studies that cover the distributional impacts of the expenditure side as well as the revenue side of public budgets. The methodology of FINC studies forms the framework for most distributional analyses undertaken by governments in Canada and elsewhere for marginal changes in tax policy.[5]

Several comparative weaknesses of FINC studies also warrant noting. Researchers diverge on the appropriate income base to use in computing ATRs, a choice that can significantly affect whether a tax appears progressive or regressive. Also, ATRs measure the departure of the tax system from proportionality, which does not directly reveal the extent of inequality reduction, unlike the use of inequality indices in INEQ studies. Moreover, ATRs are computed for households and expressed across household income groups, in some studies without adjustment for the numbers or ages of individuals in each household. In the Canadian context, one might question the use of households, since the single largest tax, the personal income tax, is normally applied on the basis of individual income, not family income. Finally, the unconstrained choice of shifting assumptions for each tax in FINC studies may lead to economic inconsistencies. In contrast, CGE studies, even though undertaken within a simplified and restrictive economic model, at least enforce consistency in the underlying economics of tax incidence.

Measures of Inequality and Progressivity

Comparing the results of various studies, as well as making sense of them individually, requires a clear understanding of inequality and progressivity indices.[6] Although the two kinds of measures can be related, they are also quite distinct. Inequality is defined over the entire income distribution, while progressivity is defined over the tax system as it applies at different income levels. Inequality measurement involves taking the distribution of incomes (whether pre-tax or post-tax) and transforming it into an index. As long as it satisfies some plausible properties, an inequality index is comparable across different income distributions. That is, we can say whether one income distribution is "more equal" than another and by how much. The present purpose is to compare either inequality pre-tax versus post-tax or inequality before and after specified tax changes. Inequality indices can also be used to compare the distributional impacts of taxes across countries, despite dramatic differences in their tax systems.

Progressivity measures, in contrast, focus on the relative average tax rates faced by various income groups. These measures can be either local – that is, showing the ATR for each of many such income groups – or global, an index summarizing the overall pattern of tax progressivity. Local progressivity measures allow for a more detailed view of the relative impacts of taxes on each of many income groups than a summary index. However, local measures of progressivity do not allow for easy comparability of tax policies across countries or over time for a given country. As will be shown, global progressivity measures can be constructed so that they correspond directly to counterpart inequality measures of the impact of taxes. We also consider measures of the horizontal inequity of taxes; this is closely related to both inequality and progressivity measures.

MEASURES OF INEQUALITY

The characteristic common to all inequality indices is that they measure the dispersion of income across the population. Inequality indices offer both benefits and challenges for assessing the distributional impacts of taxes. We must first clearly define what we want to measure and then find an appropriate index to measure it. The difficulty is that researchers do not agree about what constitutes an appropriate and informative measure. A second issue concerns the relationship between inequality measures and social welfare functions. Some analyses seek to determine the types of social welfare functions implied when income distributions are ranked in terms of a particular index of inequality (Blackorby and Donaldson 1978). Since an index summarizes an entire income distribution in one number, some judgment is required in formulating the index. This judgment, in turn, is based on how the observer values inequality, which is in effect the choice of the social welfare function. For example, should the index use equal weights for all households, or should lower-income households be given a greater weight? In order to obtain indices that satisfy some plausible criteria, the social welfare functions underlying them may have to be very restrictive. We review the principal methods used to measure inequality in studies of tax incidence and then briefly consider other indices. We also note the formulation, merits, and drawbacks of the various indices.

The Lorenz Curve and Gini Coefficient

A simple way of illustrating inequality is the Lorenz curve. It is not a numerical index as such, but it motivates how such indices are created. The Lorenz curve is drawn graphically in a square of length 1 (for 100 percent), as in Figure 12.1. The horizontal axis represents the proportion of the population, ordered by income from lowest to highest. The vertical axis plots the cumulative proportion of income held by that part of the population. In a completely equal society, where everybody has identical incomes, the Lorenz curve will be the straight line connecting the points along the diagonal labelled D. That is, the bottom 10 percent of the income distribution has 10 percent of the income, and so forth. If there is any inequality in the society, the Lorenz curve will lie below this diagonal because the poorer half of the population must have less than half of total income. This deviation from the 45-degree diagonal allows some income distributions to be ranked. If the Lorenz curve

FIGURE 12.1

Lorenz and tax concentration curves, Gini, and progressivity indices

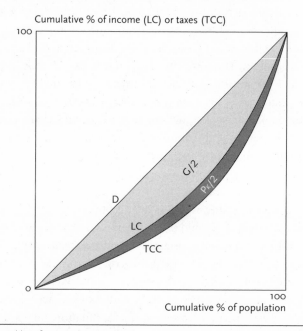

D = diagonal line for complete equality
LC = Lorenz curve for pre-tax incomes
TCC = tax concentration curve (shown for a progressive tax system)
G = Gini coefficient for pre-tax incomes (twice the shaded area between D and LC)
P_{κ} = Kakwani progressivity index (twice the shaded area between LC and TCC; shown for a progressive tax system)

of a distribution B lies entirely below that of distribution A, we say that distribution A "Lorenz-dominates" B, or that distribution A is more equal than B. In effect, this means that it is possible to go from distribution A to B (assuming their means to be equal) by transferring income from the poor to the rich. However, this ranking criterion is not complete. If the Lorenz curves of two income distributions cross, neither can be said to dominate the other, and hence further assumptions about how one values equality at various points in the income distribution are needed for ranking.

This incomplete ordering of income distributions using Lorenz curves motivates the Gini coefficient, a related inequality index that allows any two distributions to be compared (see Table 12.2 for the formula). For any income distribution, the Gini coefficient is twice the area between the diagonal and its Lorenz curve (see Figure 12.1). Since the Lorenz curve for a fully unequal distribution (one person has all the income) coincides with the bottom and the right edges of the box, the maximum value of the Gini coefficient is 1, twice the area of the triangle under the diagonal. The smallest value of the Gini is 0, which occurs with complete equality when the Lorenz curve coincides with the diagonal. The Gini coefficient has some desirable properties that make it the most commonly used inequality index (Myles 1995). The Gini is independent of scale, so that a proportional change in everyone's income will not alter its value. It satisfies the Pigou-Dalton principle of transfers, which states that any transfer from a poorer household to a richer household must increase inequality. The Gini coefficient also can be defined over negative income observations, which frequently occur in empirical data.

Generalized Entropy Class of Indices

A "generalized entropy" class of inequality indices based on information theory includes as special cases the often-used Theil, squared coefficient of variation, and mean log deviation indices. Formulas for the generalized entropy index and its subcases appear in Table 12.2. All members of this class of indices share several useful properties – scale independence, Lorenz domination, the principle of transfers, and decomposability (defined below). However, some forms of the index involve taking the natural logarithm of income and thus are not defined over zero or negative values of income. These indices assume values ranging from 0 (complete equality) to unboundedly large (extreme inequality). A major benefit of this class of indices is their ability to decompose overall inequality into within-group and

TABLE 12.2

Major inequality indices and their progressivity indices

Inequality index	Progressivity index
Gini	Kakwani $P_K = C(t) - G(x^g)$
$$G = \frac{1}{2n^2\bar{x}} \sum_{i=1}^{n} \sum_{j=1}^{n} \left| x_i - x_j \right|$$	Musgrave-Thin $P_{MT} = [1-G(x^n)]/[1- G(x^g)]$
	Reynolds-Smolensky $P_{RS} = G(x^g) - G(x^n)$
Generalized entropy (for $c \neq 0, 1$)	Zandvakili $P_E = E_c(x^g) - E_c(x^n)$
$$E_c = \left\{ \frac{1}{nc(c-1)} \right\} \sum_i \left[\left(\frac{x_i}{\bar{x}} \right)^c - 1 \right]$$	
Mean logarithmic deviation ($c = 0$)	
$$E_0 = \frac{1}{n} \sum_i \ln \frac{\bar{x}}{x_i}$$	
Theil ($c = 1$)	
$$E_1 = \frac{1}{n} \sum_i \frac{x_i}{\bar{x}} \ln \frac{x_i}{\bar{x}}$$	
Squared coefficient of variation ($c = 2$)	
$$E_2 \Rightarrow CV^2 = \frac{1}{n\bar{x}^2} \sum_i (x_i - \bar{x})^2$$	
Atkinson (for $0 < e \neq 1$)	Kiefer $P_i = I_e(x^g) - I_e(x^n)$
$$I_e = 1 - \left[\frac{1}{n} \sum_i \left(\frac{x_i}{\bar{x}} \right)^{1-e} \right]^{1/(1-e)}$$	Blackorby-Donaldson $$P_i^* = [I_e(x^g) - I_e(x^n)]/[1- I_e(x^g)]$$
Atkinson (for $e = 1$) yields mean logarithmic deviation (as with generalized entropy for $c = 0$)	

NOTE: There are n individuals; x_i = income of individual i; x^g = vector of pre-tax (gross) incomes; x^n = vector of post-tax (net) incomes; x_{EDE} = equally distributed equivalent income (see text); $C(t)$ = tax concentration coefficient; and $\bar{x} = \frac{1}{n} \sum_i x_i$.

cross-group inequality, which can be useful in assessing the effects of tax policies. For example, assume that we have defined subgroups of households with and without earners and, further, that an entropy index of before-tax incomes is stable but the index of after-tax incomes is falling over time, which indicates that net incomes are becoming more equal due to tax changes. We can then decompose this fall in the index into a between-groups component and a within-groups component to see how changes in the tax system have exercised their equalizing influence.

Generalized entropy indices contain a parameter, c, to reflect the weight assigned to distances between incomes at different parts of the distribution; this parameter can assume any real value. Choosing lower values for c make the index more sensitive to changes in the lower tail, while higher values for c make the index more sensitive to changes in the upper tail. Certain values of the parameter yield the special subcases of the index shown in the table. A value of $c = 0$ produces the mean logarithmic deviation, which weights by population shares, while a value of $c = 1$ produces the Theil index, which weights by income shares. The Theil index is more bottom-sensitive than the Gini, thus giving more weight to changes at the lower end of the income distribution. Choosing $c = 2$ yields another common measure of inequality, the squared coefficient of variation (CV^2), which is more sensitive to income changes at higher incomes.

Atkinson Index

Atkinson (1970) formulated an inequality index that stresses the linkage between statistical measures and social welfare. Its general expression, I_e, with inequality aversion parameter e, is given in Table 12.2. Higher values of e correspond to greater social valuation of equality. Atkinson inequality indices range from 0 (for no inequality) to 1, as does the Gini coefficient. This index shares the desirable properties of the generalized entropy indices; indeed, setting $c = 1 - e$ makes the generalized entropy class of indices ordinally equivalent to the Atkinson class, for $c < 1$. With $e = 1$, the Atkinson index yields the mean logarithmic deviation, just as does the generalized entropy index for $c = 0$.

The Atkinson index can also be expressed in the following form:

$$I = 1 - \frac{x_{EDE}}{\bar{x}},$$

where $\bar{x}$ is mean income and x_{EDE} is "equally distributed equivalent" income as follows:

$$\sum_{i=1}^{n} U(x_i) = nU(x_{EDE}).$$

In words, x_{EDE} is the level of income that, if given to every individual, would create the same level of social welfare (the sum of individual utility levels, U) as the actual income distribution. For example, with $I = 0.3$, if incomes were distributed equally, only 70 percent of present national income would be needed to achieve the current level of social welfare. Assuming concavity of the utility function, $x_{EDE} \leq \bar{x}$, which ensures that the Atkinson index will lie between 0 (complete equality) and 1 (complete inequality). Intuitively, as equality rises, a higher level of equally distributed income is needed to achieve the same level of welfare as the original distribution; hence the index I falls.

Other Measures of Inequality

Still other indices are used to measure inequality, and their advantages and disadvantages often hinge upon the researcher's focus. Three basic indices involve computing the ratio between incomes of certain individuals. The P_{10} and the P_{90} take the incomes of the individuals at the tenth and ninetieth percentiles of the distribution and divide each by the income of the median individual. These indicate the state of the poor and the rich relative to the median in the population. Dividing the P_{90} by the P_{10} yields the "decile ratio" or "social distance."[7] These three measures can serve as a quick standard of comparison in cross-country or time-based studies of inequality. However, because they do not make use of the entire income distribution, they lose much of the information present in the more complex indices discussed above. Some studies, such as Gottschalk and Smeeding (2000), report the P_{10}, P_{90}, and P_{90}/P_{10} alongside the Gini coefficient. Indeed, it is common for empirical studies of tax incidence to report more than one index of inequality. Jäntti (1997), for instance, works primarily with the CV^2 because he is interested in decomposing the between-group and within-group elements of inequality, but he also reports the Gini coefficient and the mean logarithmic deviation. Zandvakili (1994) computes inequality using both the generalized entropy and Atkinson indices, each for a range of parameter values.

Axiomatic View of Inequality Indices

Many authors have outlined axioms that an inequality index should meet; it is informative to check whether the measures cited above satisfy these axioms.[8] The Pigou-Dalton principle of transfers, noted earlier, is satisfied by the Gini, generalized entropy, and Atkinson indices. Scale independence is satisfied by most indices, with the exception of the variance. Anonymity or symmetry requires that the inequality measure not be affected by the order in which households are labelled; that is, inequality depends solely on the distribution of incomes, not on which individuals hold it. Again, the Gini, generalized entropy, and Atkinson indices satisfy this. Finally, decomposability is a desirable attribute for applying an index to study the channels of redistribution by the tax system.[9] As noted above, the Theil, squared coefficient of variation, and other entropy indices are decomposable, as is the Atkinson index using special methods. However, the Gini coefficient is decomposable only if the subgroups do not overlap in the income distribution.[10] Thus, our example above involving the inequality effects of taxes on households with and without earners could not be decomposed using the Gini coefficient because there is clearly overlap in incomes between these groups.

MEASURES OF TAX PROGRESSIVITY

Another way to gauge the distributional impacts of taxes is to assess their progressivity or regressivity, that is, the pattern of effective average tax rates across incomes. The ATR for an income group is computed as its tax liability divided by a relevant measure of its income (an issue discussed later). An ATR that rises over a range of income is said to be progressive in that range, an ATR that declines is regressive, and an ATR that is steady is proportional. Local indices of progressivity can rank a given type of tax or the total tax system over a given range of income, but, because progressivity can vary with income level, a global progressivity index is needed to characterize the tax or tax system across the entire income scale. Hence, a global index is usually needed to compare tax progressivity across time, countries, or policy changes. Global progressivity indices have been constructed to match corresponding inequality indices, such that a more progressive tax is associated with a more equal after-tax distribution (and vice versa). Local progressivity can be thought of as how much the tax system deviates from proportionality *at a specific point in the income distribution*. A tax or tax system can be progressive at the lower tail of the distribution but regressive at the upper tail, or vice versa. Local progressivity measures can reveal patterns of ATRs, such as an inverted-U, whereas global measures cannot. Thus, estimates of the pattern of local progressivity can add information to a global progressivity index.

Local Indices of Progressivity

The simplest way of displaying local tax progressivity is to chart the pattern of ATRs computed by income level, where income is shown either by dollar intervals or by groups such as percentiles or deciles. This approach was standard in early FINC studies and remains popular in recent studies of that type.[11] A closely related local index is called the "relative share adjustment" (RSA), developed in Baum (1987) and used in the empirical work of Ruggeri and Bluck (1990) and Ruggeri et al. (1994, 1996). It measures the local redistributional impact of a given tax compared with a proportional tax:

$$RSA_i = (1 - ATR_i)/(1 - ATR),$$

where ATR_i is the average tax rate paid by the ith income group, and ATR is the total tax collected divided by aggregate income. Clearly, if the ith income group's taxes were at the overall average rate, $RSA_i = 1$. An $RSA_i > 1$ indicates that this income group pays a locally progressive tax, and an $RSA_i < 1$ indicates a locally regressive tax. The RSA index can be used to calculate the gain or loss to a specific income group of switching to a fully proportional tax. For example, an RSA_i of 1.03 implies that the ith taxpayer would suffer an income loss of about 3 percent if the existing tax system were replaced by a proportional tax. Charting the RSA_i against income produces a virtual mirror image of the chart of ATRs by income, since the numerator of RSA_i is $1 - ATR_i$ and the denominator is constant across incomes.

This approach to characterizing the progressivity of a tax can also be implemented using other local measures. Jakobsson (1976) assesses four such measures: average rate progression (rate of change of the ATR), marginal rate progression (rate of change of the marginal tax rate), liability progression, and residual income progression. The last two measures were proposed by Musgrave and Thin (1948). Liability progression $(LP(x))$ is the elasticity of tax liability with respect to pre-tax income, and residual progression $(RP(x))$ is the elasticity of post-tax income to pre-tax income, each evaluated at a given pre-tax income level, x. Their formulas follow:

$$LP(x) = \frac{xMTR(x)}{T(x)} = \frac{MTR(x)}{ATR(x)} > 1 \text{ for progressivity}$$

$$RP(x) = \frac{x[1 - MTR(x)]}{x - T(x)} = \frac{1 - MTR(x)}{1 - ATR(x)} < 1 \text{ for progressivity,}$$

where $T(x)$ is the tax function, $MTR(x)$ the marginal tax rate, $ATR(x)$ the average tax rate $(= T(x)/x)$, and $MTR(x) > ATR(x)$ for all x for strict progression. Jakobsson proves that of these four indices, only residual progression satisfies the property that, if it is increased at every income level, then the Lorenz curve shifts upward. Graphically, this "Lorenz criterion" states that if the tax system is everywhere progressive, then the post-tax Lorenz curve should lie above the pre-tax Lorenz curve at all incomes and without crossing.

Global Indices of Progressivity

Global indices of progressivity offer a compact and informative way to measure the impacts of taxes on the distribution of incomes. They are especially useful in tracking progressivity over time or in comparing progressivity across countries. Note that global progressivity indices can be constructed so as to focus on departures from proportionality or on the redistributive effects of taxes. As articulated by Musgrave and Thin (1948, 510, emphasis in original): "effective progression ... measures the extent to which a given tax structure results in a *shift in the distribution of income toward equality*." Computing a global progressivity index requires knowledge of the income distribution to which a tax or tax system is applied. Hence, a change in the pre-tax income distribution will usually affect the measured global progressivity of an unchanged tax or tax system. The less equal is the pre-tax income distribution, the greater will be the equalizing effects and hence the global index of progressivity of a given progressive tax structure. Thus, comparisons of global tax progressivity measures across countries or over time for a given country may reflect changes or differences in pre-tax distributions along with changes or differences in the taxes under study.

One global index builds on the local index of relative share adjustment described above. The global index of redistribution is a weighted sum of the RSA_is taken over each income class (Cassady et al. 1996):

$$RSA_G = \sum_{i=1}^{n} w_i RSA_i ,$$

where

$$w_i = y_i \left(y_i + 2 \sum_{j=i+1}^{n} y_j \right),$$

and y_i is the ith taxpayer's share of post-fisc income (see later discussion). The index is designed to place greater weight on lower income classes. The interpretation of the index is similar to that for the local index: an $RSA_G > 1$ indicates that the overall tax system is progressive, $RSA_G = 1$ for proportional, and $RSA_G < 1$ for regressive. The value of the index ranges from 0 to 2.

Several global progressivity indices based on the Gini index of inequality have been proposed. The Kakwani (1977) progressivity index reflects the extent to which a tax system departs from proportionality and can be derived graphically. On the same axes used for the Lorenz curve, one plots the tax concentration curve, which is the cumulative proportion of taxes versus position in the pre-tax income distribution (see Figure 12.1). If the tax system is proportional, then the tax concentration curve coincides with the Lorenz curve for pre-tax incomes. A progressive system implies that the tax concentration curve lies outside the Lorenz curve, and conversely for a regressive tax. The Kakwani index is twice the difference in area between the Lorenz curve and the tax concentration curve, defined so that the index is positive if the tax is progressive, zero if proportional, and negative if regressive. Table 12.2 shows the Kakwani index, P_K, as the difference between the tax concentration coefficient (the Gini for taxes using the ranking by pre-tax incomes) and the Gini for pre-tax incomes (x^g).

Two other global tax progressivity indices based on the Gini inequality index focus on the redistributive effect rather than on departures from proportionality. An index attributed to Musgrave and Thin (1948) uses the Gini coefficients of the distributions of pre-tax and post-tax (x^n) incomes (see Table 12.2).[12] Another Gini-related progressivity index is that of Reynolds and Smolensky (1977), P_{RS}; it reduces to simply the difference between the Gini coefficients computed for the pre-tax and post-tax income distributions. A useful relationship between Kakwani's disproportionality index of progressivity and the Reynolds-Smolensky redistributive index of progressivity is:[13]

$$P_{RS} = \frac{g}{1-g} \, P_K,$$

where g is the aggregate average tax rate. Intuitively, a tax that is highly progressive (in the sense of departure from proportionality) can exert a large redistributive effect only to the extent that the tax system is applied heavily, with a high overall average tax rate.[14] A country with only moderate progressivity of rate schedules but a high average tax rate can redistribute more than another with rates that are more steeply graduated but much lower.

Global progressivity indices can also be constructed for the generalized entropy and Atkinson inequality indices. These measure the redistributive effect of taxes rather than departures from proportionality as such. For the generalized entropy indices, Zandvakili (1994) offers a progressivity index that is simply the difference between the entropy measure of pre-tax incomes and the entropy measure of post-tax incomes. A positive difference indicates a progressive tax, a negative difference a regressive tax, and equality a proportional tax. The decomposability of the generalized entropy index extends to the index of progressivity, so that one can analyze the progressivity of taxes between and within subgroups of the population. Two global progressivity measures have also been advanced for the Atkinson inequality index. Kiefer (1984) proposes the simple difference between the Atkinson index computed for pre-tax and post-tax incomes, while Blackorby and Donaldson (1984) suggest a progressivity index that is the proportional increase in equality relative to the initial level of equality (see Table 12.2).

MEASURES OF HORIZONTAL INEQUITY

Real-world tax systems not only redistribute incomes vertically but also inevitably apply different tax burdens to units with the same incomes. Traditionally this "unequal treatment of equals" has been called the horizontal inequity of the tax system. However, more recently, analysts have distinguished between the tax system's horizontal inequity and its "re-ranking" units from their pre-tax to their post-tax rankings even when their pre-tax incomes are unequal. The total redistributive effect (RE) of taxes can thus be decomposed into three components: vertical redistribution, V, if there were no differential tax treatment of equals; the loss of redistributive effect due to horizontal inequity, H; and the further loss due to re-ranking, R:[15]

$$RE = V - H - R = G(x^g) - G(x^n).$$

The total redistributive effect is measured as the difference between the pre-tax (and post-transfer) Gini coefficient, $G(x^g)$, and the post-tax Gini, $G(x^n)$.

The inequality reduction from the vertical redistribution component is $V = P_{RS}$, the Reynolds-Smolensky progressivity index; as defined earlier, this index is proportional to the Kakwani tax progressivity index (P_K) and the aggregate tax rate. As long as the income tax rate schedule is progressive, P_K

will be positive, and the total redistributive effect will have an inequality-reducing vertical component offset in part by the inequality-increasing effects of horizontal inequity and re-ranking.[16] Horizontal inequity, H, is measured as a weighted sum of the post-tax-income Gini coefficients of households with given pre-tax incomes; these Ginis are zero only with no differential tax treatment of equals. Re-ranking, R, is measured as the difference between the post-tax Gini coefficient and the post-tax concentration coefficient. Re-ranking can arise only with differential tax treatment, so that positive values of R imply positive values of H. However, horizontal inequity need not imply re-ranking.

The Measurement of Economic Well-Being

Unit of Observation: Individual or Household?

Studies of taxation impact are based on data for families and unattached persons (usually microdata), and, in INEQ and some CGE and FINC studies, they are converted into "equivalized" individuals (or adult equivalents) to reflect the scale economies of shared consumption.[17] This conversion can be done by using the equivalence scales implicit in poverty thresholds or those derived from budget studies, or by applying a formula for the number of adult equivalents in a household:

$$N = (A + aK)^b \quad 0 \le a \le 1, 0 \le b \le 1,$$

where the unit contains A adults and K children. Each child's needs can be counted as proportion a of an adult's needs, and scale economies are shown by b less than one. The family's total money income is deflated by the equivalence scale factor to obtain equivalized individual income, and applying a similar deflator to the family's total taxes obtains equivalized individual taxes. The equivalized data are then weighted by the number of adult equivalents in each family based on its composition. This procedure assumes that all persons in each family enjoy equal shares of the family's total income; it ignores the possible presence of differential shares by age or sex of the family members.

This research has used various equivalence scales. Jäntti (1997) uses the scales implied by the United States poverty line, where the factor for a family of four equals twice that of a single person; Fritzell (1993) uses the "OECD equivalence scale" (a factor of 1.0 for a one-person household, 0.7 for each other adult, and 0.5 for each child); and Wagstaff et al. (1999) use the formula given above with the parameters a and b both set equal to 0.5.[18] Another method is simply to take the square root of the total number of persons in the household; this is equivalent to setting a at 1 and b at 0.5.[19] Inequality measures – whether Lorenz curves, Gini coefficients, quintile distributions, decile distributions, or 90:10 decile ratios – are then based on the weighted equivalized individuals. A few INEQ studies (e.g. Zandvakili 1994) and most FINC studies do not convert their household income data into equivalized individuals.[20] This creates some confounding of larger households with higher incomes – since FINC studies present their results as ATRs in relation to household income levels – and a less accurate measure of the well-being of individuals. An exception is Ruggeri et al. (1994, 1996), who use the scales of Statistics Canada's low-income measure (1.0 for the first member, 0.4 for the second, and 0.3 per additional member). Fullerton and Rogers (1993) undertake a CGE study that ignores children as such and assigns half of the parents' combined income to each parent without accounting for scale economies.

Income Measure: Pre-fisc, Broad, or Post-fisc?

To assess the distributional impact of taxes – to rank individuals and determine groups' relative tax burdens – a measure of individual well-being is needed. Ideally this would be based on lifetime levels of utility, although measurement problems restrict most analyses to annual data and some form of income. The definition of income can be narrower or broader, reflecting either less or more of the impacts of public policies. The principal choices for the income measure are as follows:

- *actual market income,* often including imputations for in-kind forms such as employee fringe benefits and owner-occupied housing
- *money income,* including transfer payments along with actual market income
- *"pre-fisc income,"* based on what market income (plus any imputations) would be in the absence of taxes and public expenditures; this measure adds back the taxes that are assumed to be borne by lower gross payments to capital and labour
- *"broad income,"* which is pre-fisc income plus public transfer payments and cash-like subsidies (such as food stamps or rent subsidies) but not the benefits from publicly supplied goods and services

- *after-tax or disposable income,* which subtracts taxes from broad income and hence includes cash transfers but not the benefits from other public spending
- *"post-fisc income,"* which reflects the addition of benefits from publicly supplied goods and services as well as transfers and nets out the taxes borne, to obtain a measure of material well-being after all government fiscal actions.

FINC studies that examine only tax incidence often use broad income, whereas those that also examine the incidence of public expenditures typically use post-fisc income. In employing the post-fisc income measure, however, one has to allocate the benefits of publicly supplied goods and services across the population. This exercise entails arbitrary choices, which lend much uncertainty to the resulting income figures. A study that examines only tax incidence can sidestep these complexities and uncertainties by considering pre-fisc income or broad income, but such measures omit the benefits of certain public outlays. Moreover, broad income is sensitive to whether a particular benefit is delivered via cash transfers or in-kind services. Accordingly, some analysts argue that only pre-fisc or post-fisc income offers a consistent measure of fiscal incidence (Ruggeri et al. 1994, 422; Gillespie 1966, 6-11). In response, proponents of broad income argue that it avoids the vagaries of allocating non-cash public expenditures and that it also accords more closely with measuring taxes as a proportion of the income that individuals directly control, namely their market plus transfer receipts (Vermaeten et al. 1994, 353-54).

Regardless of which measure is chosen, a post-fisc income base, by adding equalizing program benefits to incomes, makes taxes look more progressive (or less regressive) than does a broad income base. A pre-fisc income base makes taxes appear most regressive for low-income households, since it excludes the cash transfers that make up a large part of their total resources.

CGE studies can most closely approximate a lifetime utility measure, as they are based on dynamic models that include individual utility functions. INEQ studies of tax incidence typically compare the distribution of disposable income with that of broad income. Because most such studies consider only the personal income tax and assume that its full incidence falls on the individual, they do not need to use a "pre-fisc" adjustment to find what market incomes would have been in the absence of the tax.[21] INEQ studies generally are not concerned with adjustments for the benefits of non-transfer public expenditures. One study found that adding the benefits of public spending for health care and education reduced income inequality in 1979-81 for most countries, especially in West Germany and Canada, but was slightly favourable for upper earners in Sweden (Smeeding et al. 1993). A tax incidence analysis that used this broader measure of income likely would find less redistributive effects of taxes since the pre-tax income distribution would already be more equalized.

Period of Observation: Annual or Lifetime?

Almost all income and tax data for studying distributional issues are available on an annual basis, and most personal tax systems use an annual accounting period for applying their progressive rates (though some allow for cross-year tax averaging). Nevertheless, it is an open question whether a year or a longer period, such as the individual's lifetime, is preferable for measuring inequality and the distributional pattern of taxes.[22]

Advocates of the lifetime perspective cite the high variability of annual income, both year to year and over an individual's life, and the much smoother pattern of annual consumption. They then infer that consumption levels are a better index of the individual's well-being and that lifetime-discounted income is superior to annual income. They also argue that the permanent income and life-cycle income theories demonstrate how transitory deviations from the individual's average income exaggerate the regressivity or progressivity of taxes when measured annually. It has been estimated that lifetime labour endowments display about one-third to one-half less inequality than annual labour endowments (Mincer 1974, 119; Blomquist 1981, 255). The lifetime perspective has been used in a couple of FINC studies, by simulating lifetime incomes, ranking individuals by their lifetime incomes, and assessing lifetime taxes on that basis. Most recent CGE studies are constructed to answer questions about the lifetime incidence of taxes, both in the transition following tax rate changes or reforms and in the economy's steady-state outcome.

Advocates of the annual perspective argue that simulating lifetime income series leads to much uncertainty. They query lifetime models' strong assumption of ready borrowing and lending at a common interest rate. And they assert that taxpayers and policy makers are interested in taxes over a much shorter period than a lifetime. They further cite the frequency of changes in tax policies as a reason to focus on annual incidence, as all INEQ studies and the great majority of FINC studies do.

The use of an annual period for assessing the inequality effects or progressivity of transfers and taxes combines two kinds of redistribution. Much public spending aims at smoothing year-to-year income variability (unemployment insurance, social assistance, workers' compensation) or smoothing incomes over different life stages (public pension plans, educational subsidies, public healthcare). This represents horizontal redistribution – the same individuals are receiving benefits in some years and paying for them through taxes in other years. Much of the high ATRs of "progressive" personal taxes for individuals with unusually high income in a given year or the high ATRs of "regressive" sales taxes for individuals with unusually low income in a given year would be smoothed away if they were observed over more years. A multi-year or lifetime perspective can much better distinguish the vertical component of redistribution.

Range of Tax Policies and Tax Incidence

Studies of distributional impact must draw a line between tax policy and transfer policy. Many countries use the tax system to deliver transfer-like programs, often via refundable tax credits, with Canada being a leader in such policies. These provisions make cross-country comparability difficult, since other countries deliver their benefits through direct cash transfers. They also complicate comparisons over time in Canada itself, as some benefits have been shifted from cash transfer programs to refundable tax credits. Many such provisions are intended as relief for those with lower incomes or in special circumstances, thus substituting for more explicit cash transfer programs. Further issues arise when the personal income tax is used to claw back cash transfer benefits from higher income earners; without any adjustment to the data, these clawbacks make the personal tax appear more progressive over certain income ranges, whereas in other times or countries, the income targeting is achieved within the benefit program. Careful choices must be made to maximize comparability over time or across countries, but an arbitrary element will inevitably remain.

The literature varies widely with respect to the range of taxes considered and the economic incidence assumed for each tax. INEQ studies consider only the difference between post-transfer, pre-tax incomes and post-transfer, post-tax incomes – essentially, the personal income tax and payroll taxes for social insurance. In practice, many of these studies ignore payroll taxes as well as the impact of indirect, property, and business taxes on both market incomes and on the real value of disposable incomes. All types of studies assume that the full burden of personal income taxes falls on the individual taxpayer. If, in fact, the tax is partially shifted forward into higher remuneration for the individual, then the measure of distributional impact will be distorted. Highly skilled, mobile, well-paid workers may be able to shift some personal tax increases to their employers or customers. In this case, the reported pre-tax distribution will not accurately measure the distribution of market incomes that would arise in the absence of the personal tax; market incomes of higher earners would be lower without the tax shifting. Hence, this method may overstate the efficacy of nominally progressive personal taxes in reducing inequality.

CGE and FINC studies consider a wider range of tax policies and some alternatives for the incidence of each tax.[23] CGE studies examine several stylized forms of tax that cover the great majority of total tax revenues but omit a few of the smaller taxes. Incidence in this framework is generated by the structure of the CGE model and by parameters that typically are chosen to generate equilibrium outcomes that benchmark aggregate measures for the economy. The widest range of tax types and shifting patterns for the various taxes is found in FINC studies, where the researcher must specify the incidence of each tax type, drawing on information from both theoretical and empirical studies. Alternative shifting assumptions are easily introduced to examine the effects on the distribution of the tax across income groups as well as the incidence of the total tax system. In our later review of FINC studies, we critically examine the standard incidence assumptions used for the personal income tax as well as for other taxes.

Primer on Tax and Expenditure Progressivity and Inequality

Taxes and the public expenditures they finance affect the inequality of incomes or economic resources of individuals. In assessing the effects of taxes on inequality, one must bear in mind the expenditure side of the equation. Public expenditures include both cash transfers and outlays for public goods and services, each of which has its distinct distributional pattern. Most studies of inequality, including almost all INEQ studies, count the impacts of cash transfers but completely neglect the distribution of benefits from in-kind benefits and general public services. For a given level and composition of public expenditures and a given total of tax revenues, the mix and structure of taxes will affect the inequality of after-tax incomes. Shifting the tax system toward greater progressivity will, by most measures, reduce the inequality of after-tax incomes. Moving the tax system to lesser progressivity or to regressivity, conversely, will increase the inequality of after-tax incomes. Changes in the tax system that increase progressivity (or reduce regressivity) in some income ranges while lowering progressivity (or raising regressivity) for other incomes will have a net impact on inequality that depends on the index employed and the inequality aversion parameter.

Many issues of public policy involve changing the scale of public spending along with total tax revenues. This perspective is also relevant when countries with public sectors of different sizes are compared; then, the net impact on inequality hinges on the progressivity of taxes (P_t) relative to the progressivity of expenditures (P_e).[24] We later show that cash transfers are highly progressive in Canada – they decline sharply as a percentage of money income as one moves up the income quintiles. The progressivity of total public expenditures – including in-kind benefits and general public outlays as well as cash transfers – has been addressed in several studies.[25] The benefits of non-cash programs can be distributed in various ways – lump sums per head, proportional to income, or rising as a percentage of income. Clearly, the type of program will affect its distributional pattern, with the benefits of health care being closer to per capita sums (and thus highly progressive) and those of public opera houses rising more than proportionally to income. Since cash transfers include some income-targeted programs, they are more progressive than overall public spending, but total public spending is still found to be significantly progressive.

For purposes of illustration, let us first assume that the entire tax system is strictly proportional. In itself, a proportional tax system does not affect the level of inequality; neither do changes in the proportional rate of tax, so long as the extra revenues are disregarded. But raising overall taxes finances larger public outlays, which with $P_e > P_t$ reduces measured inequality. By extension, even if the tax system is regressive, raising more taxes and spending them in a progressive way can also reduce economic inequality, so long as the progressive effects of spending outweigh the regressive effects of the taxes.[26] This inequality-reducing effect of larger government is even stronger under a proportional or progressive tax system, but tax progressivity is not required. Hence, the size of government may be even more important to reducing inequality than the progressivity of taxes as such.

Inequality Studies of Taxes

The inequality impacts of personal income taxes have been studied as an offshoot of research that measures trends in inequality for a given country

over time and differences in inequality across countries. The basic methodology of INEQ studies is simple: take the difference between the pre-tax and
post-tax measures of inequality (usually the Gini). Typically, only the personal income tax is considered, although payroll taxes for social insurance
are occasionally included as well. As noted above, the income tax is assumed
to be borne fully by the taxpayer, which likely overstates the efficacy of the
tax in reducing inequality. Moreover, in ignoring all other taxes, INEQ studies focus on the most redistributive element of the tax system and neglect
other major taxes that are much less progressive and often regressive. Consequently, they provide a misleading view if one is interested in the equalizing
effects of the tax system as a whole. Two studies of this type have gone a step
further by exploring components of the personal tax structure that contribute to the equalization of incomes.

TAXES, TRANSFERS, AND THE PATTERN OF INEQUALITY IN CANADA
To set the stage for the redistributive effects of personal income taxes, it is
useful to compare their magnitude with those of cash transfers for various
income groups.[27] Table 12.3 presents, by income quintile, the proportions of
total money income both received as cash transfers and paid in personal
income taxes (PIT) from 1971 to 2000. Several general patterns appear clearly.
First, the proportions of both rose fairly continually across all quintiles and
household types over the period. Second, cash transfers increased much more
for the lower quintiles than for the highest, while taxes increased much more
for the higher quintiles than for the lower. Hence, the redistributive tilt of
both cash transfers and personal taxes has increased over the period. Third,
transfer programs exerted a *proportionally* much larger impact in raising the
money incomes of the lowest two quintiles than did PIT in reducing the net
incomes of the top two quintiles. Fourth, the PIT was strongly progressive for
all household types and time periods. Finally, some disturbing departures
from these general trends emerged in the latter half of the 1990s: transfer
receipts fell significantly for the bottom two deciles, and personal taxes as a
share of incomes rose sharply for the bottom decile.[28] Thus, the redistributive efficacy of the tax-transfer system was diminished.

From Statistics Canada's annual Gini coefficients for income before transfers, total money income, and income after tax over the period,[29] one can
observe both patterns of inequality over time and the separate effects on
inequality of cash transfers and the PIT. This analysis, however, omits all
other taxes (which, on balance, are regressive in an annual view) as well as

Table 12.3

Transfers and income taxes as a percentage of money income, Canada, 1971-2000

Quintile		1	2	3	4	5	Total
Transfer receipts							
Unattached	1971-75	58.1	66.0	17.9	5.0	1.6	12.3
	1976-80	66.8	61.4	18.4	6.1	1.6	13.3
	1981-85	61.9	64.5	23.8	7.2	2.2	15.7
	1986-90	59.5	63.6	24.5	8.4	2.9	16.9
	1991-95	61.9	70.2	34.2	12.4	3.5	20.5
	1996-2000	58.3	65.1	32.9	12.3	3.6	19.3
Families	1971-75	43.8	11.6	6.0	4.1	2.5	7.2
	1976-80	47.6	13.4	6.9	4.4	2.7	8.0
	1981-85	52.1	18.9	9.3	5.5	2.8	9.8
	1986-90	53.2	20.0	9.6	5.7	2.8	10.1
	1991-95	60.0	26.7	13.0	7.1	3.4	12.4
	1996-2000	53.6	23.9	11.6	6.2	3.0	10.9
All units	1971-75	55.9	20.0	7.3	4.5	2.7	7.9
	1976-80	57.9	22.5	8.6	5.1	2.8	8.7
	1981-85	59.6	28.8	11.7	6.4	3.1	10.7
	1986-90	59.2	30.4	12.8	6.8	3.2	11.2
	1991-95	65.5	38.7	17.1	9.0	3.9	13.8
	1996-2000	61.4	34.3	16.1	8.1	3.5	12.3
Income taxes							
Unattached	1971-75	0.8	1.0	7.1	13.4	19.9	14.0
	1976-80	0.4	0.7	6.7	13.3	19.7	13.6
	1981-85	0.2	1.5	8.8	15.4	21.9	15.3
	1986-90	0.8	3.3	11.8	17.9	24.5	17.4
	1991-95	0.9	2.9	11.5	18.1	26.0	18.1
	1996-2000	3.5	3.7	11.4	18.0	26.2	18.5
Families	1971-75	2.6	9.0	13.0	15.5	20.1	15.2
	1976-80	2.1	9.0	13.3	15.7	19.8	15.2
	1981-85	2.1	9.1	13.9	16.8	20.7	15.9
	1986-90	3.2	11.6	16.6	19.7	24.0	18.8
	1991-95	2.8	11.0	16.8	20.4	25.6	19.6
	1996-2000	5.7	12.1	17.3	20.3	25.4	20.0
All units	1971-75	1.8	7.2	12.1	14.9	19.6	15.1
	1976-80	1.3	6.9	12.1	15.1	19.3	14.9
	1981-85	1.7	7.3	12.8	16.3	20.3	15.8
	1986-90	2.8	9.5	15.4	18.9	23.4	18.5
	1991-95	2.6	8.9	15.3	19.5	24.9	19.3
	1996-2000	5.5	10.1	15.9	19.6	24.8	19.7

SOURCE: Statistics Canada (1996, 1999, 2001, 2002) and authors' calculations; figures are averages of the annual figures for the specified periods.

in-kind transfer programs, such as public healthcare and education (which are progressive in the sense that they raise real incomes by larger proportions for lower-income individuals). Table 12.4 shows that, taking income before transfers, inequality was fairly constant over the period for unattached individuals but increased for families. The cash transfer and income tax systems taken together substantially lowered the after-tax income inequality of individuals; for families they served to neutralize significant increases in market income inequality. Again, the last half of the 1990s is seen to depart from the longer-run trends; inequality increased for unattached individuals and for families, reflecting the impacts of changes in both transfer receipts and personal tax payments as well as in the labour market.

TABLE 12.4

Gini coefficients for various income measures and attribution to transfers and taxes, Canada, 1971-2000

Family type		Gini coefficient for income			Reduction in Gini coefficient		
		Before transfers	Total money	After tax	Total %	% by transfers	% by inc. tax
Unattached	1971-75	0.556	0.449	0.414	25.5	75.4	24.6
	1976-80	0.544	0.428	0.390	28.2	75.6	24.4
	1981-85	0.545	0.411	0.367	32.6	75.5	24.5
	1986-90	0.533	0.391	0.343	35.7	74.8	25.2
	1991-95	0.565	0.392	0.338	40.1	76.3	23.7
	1996-2000	0.563	0.410	0.358	36.4	74.5	25.5
Families	1971-75	0.378	0.330	0.302	20.1	62.1	37.9
	1976-80	0.378	0.326	0.297	21.3	64.9	35.1
	1981-85	0.396	0.329	0.299	24.5	68.6	31.4
	1986-90	0.402	0.331	0.295	26.4	66.5	33.5
	1991-95	0.422	0.336	0.294	30.3	67.6	32.4
	1996-2000	0.430	0.352	0.310	27.9	65.3	34.7
All units	1971-75	0.446	0.394	0.367	17.7	66.4	33.6
	1976-80	0.448	0.390	0.363	18.9	68.9	31.1
	1981-85	0.459	0.386	0.357	22.3	71.8	28.2
	1986-90	0.467	0.389	0.355	24.0	69.8	30.2
	1991-95	0.492	0.395	0.356	27.6	71.5	28.5
	1996-97	0.497	0.402	0.363	27.0	70.5	29.5

SOURCE: Statistics Canada (1996, 1999, 2001, 2002) and authors' calculations; figures are averages of the annual figures for the specified periods. Statistics Canada stopped publishing Gini coefficients for "all units" after 1997.

Transfers and taxes have different effects on the total decline in inequality. Moving from the pre-tax, pre-transfer distribution to total money income reflects the impact of adding transfer receipts alone; moving from total money income to after-tax income reflects the impact of income taxes alone.[30] As the last two columns of Table 12.4 show, transfers account for about three times as much of the reduction in total inequality as income taxes do for unattached individuals and for nearly twice as much of the reduction for families.[31]

Duclos and Lambert's (2000) study of the distributional impacts of Canada's fiscal system focuses on the relative contributions of PIT and cash transfers to *horizontal* inequity. They propose an index that expresses the gain in per capita revenue that would arise from eliminating horizontal inequity in a welfare-neutral manner. Their index also measures the horizontal inequity's associated loss of vertical equity based on the Blackorby-Donaldson progressivity index (see Table 12.2). They apply their schema to assess Canadian income taxes and cash transfers between 1981 and 1994. They find that the largest source of horizontal inequity arises from old-age transfers for the bottom 60 to 85 percent of the income distribution and from income taxes for the top 15 to 40 percent. They also find a slight increase in the variability of income taxes between 1981 and 1990 (which bracket the 1987 tax reforms) for market incomes below the median but no change for persons in higher percentiles. Duclos and Lambert attribute the increased variability for incomes in the lower levels of the distribution to the growing differentiation of provincial tax policies over this period.

PERSONAL TAXES AND CROSS-COUNTRY INEQUALITY

Several INEQ studies examine the inequality impacts of personal taxes in a cross-country framework. These studies use the Luxembourg Income Study (LIS) dataset, which was designed for cross-country comparability over time, but many have deficiencies for assessing tax impacts.[32] Some studies (for example, Fritzell 1993; Atkinson 2004) do not distinguish the effects of taxes from those of transfers, that is, they compare pre-tax, *pre-transfer* inequality with post-tax, *post-transfer* inequality. Others (such as Ervik 1998) distinguish the separate effects of income taxes on inequality but omit Canada from their sample. Moreover, these studies' exclusion of indirect, property, and business taxes affects the measured impact of taxation on inequality and distorts cross-country comparisons. In concept, many of the excluded taxes could be incorporated into the analysis via tax effects on the consumer price index. However, as Pendakur (2002) shows, the relevant price indices may differ across income groups – a point especially relevant for indirect consumption taxes that use exempt or zero-rated classes of goods for distributional purposes.

A relatively simple research strategy is to test for Lorenz dominance of tax progression curves in comparing tax systems either over time or across countries. Bishop et al. (1995) pursue this method using the PITs and payroll taxes of six countries, including Canada, for two points in the late 1970s and the 1980s. These tax progression curves can be constructed based on either the residual or the liability progression concept. Those concepts apply at a given point in the tax schedule or distribution of pre-tax incomes, and a corresponding tax progression curve can be constructed like a Lorenz curve.[33] Then the tax progression curves can be compared across countries or over time to assess whether one curve "Lorenz dominates" the other (meaning the former is more progressive), whether the two are Lorenz-equivalent, or whether there is a "Lorenz crossing" (yielding no conclusive ranking). Using the liability progression concept, Bishop et al. (1995) find for systems around 1980 that Canadian direct taxes were more progressive than those in Sweden and the United Kingdom, less progressive than West Germany's, equivalent to Australia's, and Lorenz-crossing with American taxes. For observations around 1986 they find that Canadian direct taxes were more progressive than those of Australia, Sweden, the United Kingdom, and the United States and less progressive than those of West Germany. Between 1981 and 1987, Canadian direct taxes exhibited no change in liability progression.

Zandvakili (1994) assesses the impacts of PITs in nine countries including Canada using the LIS and inequality measures of the generalized entropy and Atkinson types. He computes two inequality measures, based on gross income, x^g, and net income, x^n, then compares the two to gauge the impact of income taxes. Income tax progressivity is gauged by the index P_E, which is the difference between pre-tax and post-tax generalized entropy measures of inequality. Table 12.5 presents Zandvakili's country rankings based on generalized entropy indices for a range of values of the parameter c. As shown, the choice of parameter c affects the ranking of countries. For high inequality aversion at lower incomes ($c = -1$), Canada ranked near the middle of the nine countries on pre- and post-tax income inequality and tax progressivity but last on percentage decline in inequality of pre-tax incomes. For lower inequality aversion (larger values of c), Canada's ranking worsened on tax progressivity but improved on percentage decline in inequality. Sweden ranked highly on pre-tax income equality but near the bottom on both measures of

TABLE 12.5

Ranking of nine countries' pre- and post-tax income distributions by generalized entropy inequality measures, 1979-83

Country/year		Generalized entropy parameter c =		
		-1	0	0.5
Australia/1981	$E_c(x^g)$	1.0835 [8]	0.2997 [7]	0.2605 [6]
	$E_c(x^n)$	0.8225 [8]	0.2323 [6]	0.2020 [6]
	P_E	0.2610 [2]	0.0674 [2]	0.0585 [2]
	% decline in $E_c(x^g)$	24.0% [3]	22.4% [2]	22.4% [3]
Canada/1981	$E_c(x^g)$	0.6840 [6]	0.2695 [5]	0.2324 [5]
	$E_c(x^n)$	0.5629 [6]	0.2293 [5]	0.1990 [5]
	P_E	0.1211 [4]	0.0402 [6]	0.0334 [7]
	% decline in $E_c(x^g)$	17.7% [9]	14.9% [7]	14.3% [6]
France/1979	$E_c(x^g)$	0.5927 [5]	0.3508 [9]	0.3514 [9]
	$E_c(x^n)$	0.4782 [5]	0.2737 [8]	0.2655 [9]
	P_E	0.1145 [5]	0.0771 [1]	0.0859 [1]
	% decline in $E_c(x^g)$	19.3% [6]	21.9% [4]	24.4% [1]
Germany/1981	$E_c(x^g)$	0.3262 [1]	0.2025 [3]	0.1831 [3]
	$E_c(x^n)$	0.2356 [2]	0.1574 [3]	0.1454 [3]
	P_E	0.0906 [7]	0.0451 [5]	0.0377 [5]
	% decline in $E_c(x^g)$	27.7% [2]	22.2% [3]	20.5% [4]
Netherlands/1983	$E_c(x^g)$	0.3306 [2]	0.1897 [2]	0.1719 [2]
	$E_c(x^n)$	0.2309 [1]	0.1439 [1]	0.1328 [1]
	P_E	0.0997 [6]	0.0458 [4]	0.0391 [4]
	% decline in $E_c(x^g)$	30.1% [1]	24.1% [1]	22.7% [2]
Sweden/1981	$E_c(x^g)$	0.3584 [3]	0.1854 [1]	0.1659 [1]
	$E_c(x^n)$	0.2927 [3]	0.1611 [2]	0.1436 [2]
	P_E	0.0657 [9]	0.0243 [9]	0.0223 [9]
	% decline in $E_c(x^g)$	18.3% [8]	13.1% [8]	13.4% [7]
Switzerland/1982	$E_c(x^g)$	0.7689 [7]	0.2875 [6]	0.2851 [7]
	$E_c(x^n)$	0.5996 [7]	0.2509 [7]	0.2497 [8]
	P_E	0.1693 [3]	0.0366 [8]	0.0354 [6]
	% decline in $E_c(x^g)$	22.0% [4]	12.7% [9]	12.4% [9]
United Kingdom/1979	$E_c((x^g)$	0.4207 [4]	0.2512 [4]	0.2259 [4]
	$E_c(x^n)$	0.3413 [4]	0.2135 [4]	0.1962 [4]
	P_E	0.0794 [8]	0.0377 [7]	0.0297 [8]
	% decline in $E_c(x^g)$	18.8% [7]	15.0% [6]	13.1% [8]
United States/1979	$E_c(x^g)$	1.5697 [9]	0.3427 [8]	0.2902 [8]
	$E_c(x^n)$	1.2495 [9]	0.2762 [9]	0.2331 [7]
	P_E	0.3202 [1]	0.0665 [3]	0.0571 [3]
	% decline in $E_c(x^g)$	20.3% [5]	19.4% [5]	19.6% [5]

NOTE: E_c is the generalized entropy index of inequality based on pre-tax income (x^g) and post-tax (x^n) income, respectively; P_E is the associated tax progressivity index (see Table 12.2); c is the inequality aversion parameter; figures in square brackets show ranking of countries for each measure (and same c value), where rank [1] denotes lowest inequality, highest tax progressivity, and largest percentage decline in E_c (x^g).

SOURCE: Zandvakili (1994, 482-83), with kind permission of Springer Science and Business Media©.

the equalizing effects of taxes. This outcome may reflect the dependence of this tax progressivity measure on the distribution of pre-tax incomes (see Lambert and Pfähler 1992). The Netherlands had nearly as much pre-tax income equality as Sweden, but its tax system performed much better in measured progressivity and inequality reduction.

Because the generalized entropy family of inequality measures is decomposable, it can be used to assess the relative contribution of income taxes to equality arising from within-group and cross-group effects. Very roughly speaking, this corresponds to the distinction between the horizontal and vertical equity effects of taxes. Zandvakili (1994) pursues this decomposition based on numbers of earners in the family (ranging from zero to three) and also by household size (ranging from one to five and over). With parameter $c = 0$, the largest share of redistribution arises within rather than between groups of households with different numbers of earners for most countries – 100 percent for France and Sweden, 76 percent for Switzerland, 71 percent for Canada, 69 percent for the Netherlands, and 65 percent for the United States. For two countries, most of the redistribution arises between groups – 99 percent for Germany and 60 percent for the United Kingdom. When the data are decomposed by household size, the great bulk of tax redistribution is found to arise within rather than between groups – 88 percent in Switzerland and the Netherlands and more than 90 percent in all other countries, except for 68 percent in Germany.

Jäntti (1997) distinguishes the equalizing contributions of personal income and payroll taxes as well as the separate effects of social insurance benefits and income-tested benefits for five countries including Canada. Income-tested transfers would be expected to contribute much more to equalization (in the vertical equity sense) than social insurance transfers (which aim more at horizontal redistribution). Social insurance programs could even raise inequality, insofar as their benefits are positively linked to earnings and many of the lowest income households have no earned income. However, with annual data, social insurance benefits could appear as equalizing in that they tend to buffer earnings during temporary dips such as joblessness or illness. These benefits are also typically capped in dollar terms even if they are earnings-linked, and those at the highest incomes have a higher proportion of unearned income.

Jäntti observes two years for each of the five countries in his sample (though none more recent than 1987) and finds that income taxes are most effective in reducing inequality in the United States and least effective in the

United Kingdom. Canada and the other countries are intermediate in this dimension. In their relative contribution to equality, income taxes are most equalizing in Sweden and the Netherlands; they become more important in relative terms for those countries because of their initially lower levels of market income inequality. Additionally, the relative contribution of income taxes to reducing inequality declined only in Sweden and the United States, the two countries that reduced rate progressivity between the two years. Payroll taxes also contribute significantly to reducing inequality in all the countries (excluding Canada, which lacks these data). The effect of means-tested transfers is quite small, while social insurance transfers are only slightly equalizing in the United Kingdom and Canada. The latter finding contrasts with the evidence for Canada given earlier in Table 12.4 and is perhaps explained by the fact that Jäntti's squared coefficient of variation is much less sensitive to lower-tail income levels than the Gini used in our tabulations.

Decomposing Personal Tax Policies and Cross-Country Inequality

Some research has attempted to distinguish among the redistributive dimensions of the personal income tax in a cross-country setting. Wagstaff et al. (1999) applies a methodology developed in Aronson and Lambert (1994) to pursue this issue for eleven European countries plus the United States. The study decomposes the redistributive effects into three components: vertical redistribution, V, horizontal inequity, H, and a re-ranking effect, R. Table 12.6 presents the results, with each component expressed as a percentage of the total redistributive effect in each country (so that $V - H - R = 100$ percent). Horizontal inequity is relatively small in all countries, and differential taxation manifested as re-ranking is substantial only in Denmark, France, and Switzerland.[34] The study finds personal tax to be most progressive in France, Ireland, and Spain and least progressive in Sweden and Denmark. Despite the rate-reducing reforms of the 1980s, British and American income taxes remain relatively progressive. The relatively low tax progressivity found in Scandinavian countries (in this study and in Jäntti) results from the combination of a progressive national tax combined with larger flat-rate income taxes applied by localities.

One study goes a step further in exploring how the *structure* of the personal income tax affects inequality in a cross-country comparison. Wagstaff and Van Doorslaer (2001) distinguish among allowances (personal exemptions in North American jargon), deductions (such as those for medical costs), non-refundable tax credits, and the statutory rate schedule. This is useful,

TABLE 12.6

Decomposition of tax systems' redistributive effects for twelve OECD countries

Country/year	$G(x^g)$	$G(x^n)$	RE	g	K_T	V	V (%)	H (%)	R (%)
Denmark/1987	0.3023	0.2703	0.0320	0.2966	0.0938	0.040	123.8	1.9	21.9
Finland/1990	0.2685	0.2253	0.0432	0.2188	0.1644	0.046	106.7	1.0	5.7
France/1989	0.3219	0.3065	0.0154	0.0620	0.2717	0.018	116.6	1.9	14.8
Germany/1988	0.2591	0.2312	0.0279	0.1108	0.2433	0.030	108.5	1.3	7.3
Ireland/1987	0.3870	0.3418	0.0452	0.1540	0.2685	0.049	108.2	1.0	7.3
Italy/1991	0.3248	0.3009	0.0239	0.1354	0.1554	0.024	102.0	0.4	1.6
Netherlands/1992	0.2846	0.2517	0.0329	0.1487	0.1977	0.035	104.9	0.7	4.2
Spain/1990	0.4083	0.3694	0.0389	0.1397	0.2545	0.041	106.1	0.4	5.7
Sweden/1990	0.3004	0.2608	0.0396	0.3270	0.0891	0.043	109.3	1.5	7.8
Switzerland/1992	0.2716	0.2541	0.0174	0.1210	0.1528	0.021	120.7	1.7	19.0
United Kingdom/1993	0.4121	0.3768	0.0352	0.1421	0.2278	0.038	107.1	0.9	6.3
United States/1987	0.4049	0.3673	0.0376	0.1370	0.2371	0.038	102.6	0.4	1.9

NOTE: $G(x^g)$ and $G(x^n)$ are pre-tax and post-tax Gini coefficients; RE is the redistributive effect, the difference between the two Ginis; g is the average income tax rate; K_T is Kakwani's index of progressivity computed on the assumption that all households face the same tax schedule; V, H, and R are the values of the vertical redistribution, horizontal inequity, and re-ranking effect, respectively, with $RE = V - H - R$ and each component expressed as percents of RE.

SOURCE: Reprinted from Wagstaff et al. (1999, 82), with permission from Elsevier©.

since the progressivity of net taxes overall depends on the mix of these components and the progressivity of each – for example, one country may allow deductions that decline as a percentage of income, while another may allow the most generous deductions at the highest incomes. The study has limitations, however. The year chosen for Canada, one of the fifteen OECD countries included, is 1986, which predates the 1988 reforms that converted personal exemptions and several tax deductions into non-refundable credits. Moreover, the study uses decile averages, excludes all non-taxfilers as well as, in some countries, subnational taxes, and uses as the unit of observation the taxable unit, the definition of which varies across countries. Furthermore, interpolation problems arising from the data cause the sum of the estimated contributions of the four components to depart in some cases from the total estimated progressivity. This divergence is particularly severe for the United States and Canada.

Keeping in mind these limitations, we note that Wagstaff and Van Doorslaer find net tax liabilities to be least progressive with respect to income subject to tax (before deductions and allowances) in the Scandinavian countries (because of their flat local income taxes) and most progressive in France, the Netherlands, Spain, Canada, and Australia. The tax credit's contribution to progressivity is relatively small, except in Denmark and Italy; in Australia and France tax credits *reduce* the progressivity of net tax liabilities. Deductions reduce progressivity in most countries but increase progressivity in Australia, Finland, France, and Germany. Tax progressivity is attributable almost entirely to the rate structure in Italy, the Netherlands, and Spain. In contrast, allowances account for almost all progressivity in Canada, Ireland, the United Kingdom, and the United States. It would be useful to undertake this analysis with a better dataset and for a more recent year, after Canada's 1988 personal tax reforms. Since various deductions were converted into credits at the bottom-bracket tax rate, this change should have increased effective progressivity. However, the 1988 Canadian reforms also flattened the tax rate schedule and lowered the top rate, thus offsetting the increase in progressivity (see Cloutier and Fortin 1989).

Computable General Equilibrium Studies of Taxes

Computable general equilibrium (CGE) models offer another approach to assessing the distributional impact of taxes and the tax system. Using a dynamic framework developed by Auerbach and Kotlikoff (1987), these analyses can evaluate both the efficiency and the distributional effects of taxes.

Because CGE models reflect the labour supply and savings responses to tax policies, the distributional impacts can be measured in terms of impacts on households' lifetime utilities (or the equivalent money sums). The Auerbach-Kotlikoff framework includes multiple overlapping generations but not multiple households in each generation, so that its distributional analysis is limited to intergenerational issues. Later analysts have extended the framework to encompass within-generation distributional impacts of taxes as well. Most of these studies assess the distributional impacts of tax reforms – such as changing the personal tax base to consumption or to comprehensive income or flattening the tax rate schedule – rather than the impacts of existing taxes.

Fullerton and Rogers (1993) present one of the few CGE studies to assess the distribution of the existing tax system and its components. While the study applies to the United States, the similarities of its economy and tax mix to those of Canada make the findings of interest. Table 12.7 summarizes the study's key findings. The upper part of the table displays the impacts of replacing each of the five main types of taxes with a proportional tax on each household's labour endowment. Households are arrayed by lifetime income decile, with the bottom and top deciles each further subdivided into the lowest and highest two percentiles and the balance. The impacts are stated in terms of a dollar measure of utility, equivalent variation,[35] EV, as a percentage of that income group's lifetime income. For example, replacing a tax might increase the net income while decreasing the leisure time of a particular group; because leisure affects utility, the net income impact alone would overstate the utility gain to that group. The figures in the upper part of the table reflect the EV gains as a percentage of lifetime income to the "steady-state" generation, which is the cohort after all economic adjustments to the tax change have taken place. For the steady-state generation, only the personal income tax is found to be strongly and consistently progressive; payroll tax is regressive; sales and excise taxes are regressive except slightly progressive for the top decile; corporate taxes display a shallow U-shaped incidence pattern; and property tax has a highly variable pattern with its heaviest incidence on the top and bottom two percentiles. All taxes taken together display a variable pattern, but the top decile bears the heaviest relative tax burden.[36]

In models of this kind, the steady-state utility gains of replacing a distorting tax with a non-distorting form are not pure efficiency gains. The gains to the steady-state generation omit the economic effects on transitional generations. When moving to non-distorting or less-distorting taxes, future

TABLE 12.7

Distribution of tax burden in equivalent variation for steady-state generations, US, 1984

Lifetime income decile or group	Equivalent variation as percentage of lifetime income for steady-state generations from the tax on:					
	Personal income	Sales + excises	Payrolls	Property	Corporate income	All taxes
1a (bottom 2%)	−4.31	2.69	1.24	0.84	1.16	−0.06
1b (next 8%)	−0.23	1.70	0.69	0.63	0.90	3.13
2	−0.92	1.35	0.59	0.21	0.79	1.41
3	0.35	1.19	0.55	0.29	0.81	2.37
4	1.99	1.09	0.56	0.01	0.77	3.58
5	0.03	0.90	0.48	0.08	0.76	1.39
6	1.64	0.89	0.44	0.50	0.85	3.46
7	1.60	0.74	0.45	−0.01	0.75	2.51
8	2.13	0.68	0.45	0.01	0.76	2.95
9	2.26	0.70	0.38	0.04	0.74	3.01
10a (next 8%)	3.92	0.91	0.24	0.76	0.83	5.55
10b (top 2%)	9.00	1.03	0.23	1.20	0.94	11.10
Total	2.02	0.94	0.44	0.30	0.80	3.52
Steady-state EV as % of revenue	9.83	7.29	5.93	7.27	240.03	6.48
Efficiency measure as % of:						
Lifetime income	0.68	0.28	0.10	0.20	0.26	1.29
Revenue	3.14	2.11	1.29	4.47	65.01	2.26

NOTE: "All taxes" do not equal the sum of the component taxes because of economic inter-actions among the taxes. Incidence is estimated relative to a proportional labour endowment tax; a positive gain from removal of a tax is interpreted as the burden of that tax.
SOURCE: Fullerton and Rogers (1993, 172-85), with permission from Brookings Institution Press©.

generations benefit at the expense of earlier generations, which bear the costs of the adjustment. For example, replacing the income tax with an endow-ment tax raises the burdens on older individuals who paid income taxes during their working years and are now retired and enjoying leisure. This additional revenue from those who are old at the time of the change means that less tax needs to be collected from the young and from future genera-tions. Since part of the gain to the steady-state generation reflects this form of redistribution, a true efficiency measure needs to sum the present value of EV impacts for all annual cohorts. The last two rows of Table 12.7 show the efficiency costs of the various taxes, with corporate (or capital) income taxes having the highest such costs and payroll taxes having the lowest.[37]

The very few CGE studies that have examined the Canadian tax system use static models that do not account for the tax system's lifetime effects on individuals. Moreover, the Canadian research has investigated the efficiency and distributional effects of switching the personal income tax to a flat tax rather than the effects of the existing set of taxes. One such study, Beauséjour et al. (1996),[38] finds that a simple flat tax would benefit two-earner couples and singles; adding a $500 credit to the scheme increases the gains for singles and also benefits seniors. The losers under these schemes are found to be single parents and one-earner families. Using an Atkinson index with a moderate degree of inequality aversion (parameter $e = 1.5$), Beauséjour et al. find that the simple flat tax would raise inequality of after-tax incomes by 10 percent; adding the credit reduces this increase in inequality to 6 percent. This adverse effect on inequality could be mitigated by, for example, providing large additional credits for single parents and for non-working spouses, as has been done under Alberta's provincial flat tax scheme.

Fiscal Incidence Studies of Taxes

Fiscal incidence studies are the earliest and still most popular method of assessing the distribution of the tax burden. They combine assumptions about the incidence of each type of tax with datasets on the distribution of incomes by sources and uses to derive the income profiles of average tax rates (ATRs). Typically, the analysis is performed on household units using annual data, though there are exceptions. This approach seeks to capture the effects of taxes, via demand and supply, on prices in the economy – chiefly the prices of factors of production (wage rates and the return to capital) and the prices of consumption goods at various times and of various types. When the tax impact falls on the prices of factors, it is said to operate on the "sources" side of households' incomes, which are decomposed into labour, capital, and transfer incomes. When the tax impact falls on prices of consumption goods, it is said to operate on the "uses" side of income, which is decomposed into consumption and savings and may distinguish between goods taxed at lower and higher rates. Assumptions about the incidence or "shifting" of each type of tax are taken from partial and general equilibrium models and empirical studies. A microdata set distributive series of each type of income source and use by household income can then be applied to each of the taxes, using a specified set of shifting assumptions, to compute the distributional burden of each tax and of total taxes.

FINC studies were pioneered in the United States by Musgrave et al. (1951) and by Pechman and associates (1974, 1985) at the Brookings Institution and in Canada by Goffman (1962) and by Gillespie's (1966) research for the Carter Commission and his later work (1980).[39] This method also underlies the distributional tables produced for tax policy changes in the budgets of Canada and many other countries. A series of periodically updated studies by the Fraser Institute, now in its fourteenth version (Veldhuis and Walker 2006), uses this method. We turn now to the findings of a few of the more recent Canadian studies of this type, including both annual and lifetime perspectives. We then examine the incidence or shifting assumptions that these studies employ for each type of tax and the related economic evidence.

Overview of Canadian Findings

We begin by noting an earlier study's analysis of the critical role of tax-shifting assumptions (Whalley 1984). Table 12.8 shows the pattern of estimated total ATRs by household income group for 1972 using Whalley's "central case" view of the most plausible shifting assumptions. Whalley finds that total taxes across income groups are moderately progressive, with ATRs ranging from 27.5 percent for the lowest income group to 43.0 percent for the highest. Combining the most progressive of shifting assumptions for the various taxes yields a pattern that is sharply more progressive, with ATRs ranging from 11.6 to 70.6 percent. Conversely, the assumption that capital income does not bear any tax burden and is construed to include all human capital yields a highly regressive pattern, with ATRs ranging from 83.5 percent at the lowest incomes to 22.2 percent at the highest. All these results use the same definition of the income measure, which includes transfer incomes and is gross of personal income taxes but net of all other taxes. Varying this definition alters the measured regressivity or progressivity of the tax system.

Two more recent studies of Canadian tax incidence offer contrasting findings and a useful backdrop to our subsequent discussion of the economics of tax shifting. Both studies use Statistics Canada's Social Policy Simulation Dataset/Model (SPSD/M). Vermaeten et al. (1994), whose results are summarized in Table 12.9, use data from 1988.[40] In this study's "standard-case" shifting assumptions, both the personal and corporate income taxes are sharply progressive; commodity taxes (including both excises and broad-based forms) and property taxes are highly regressive; and the ATRs for payroll taxes

TABLE 12.8

Average tax rates for alternative incidence assumptions and income bases, Canada, 1972 (percentages)

Households by income	(percentiles)	Tax incidence and income base assumptions		
		Central case	Most progressive	Most regressive
Bottom	16.6	27.5	11.6	83.5
	7.1	32.7	19.6	59.2
	6.9	35.4	23.0	53.5
	8.0	35.0	25.5	45.4
	8.9	36.1	27.5	40.8
	8.6	35.3	30.3	40.0
	8.5	35.6	32.0	38.4
	7.3	35.7	35.0	38.2
	5.6	37.8	38.3	35.8
	4.6	37.1	37.4	35.6
	9.3	37.4	44.4	34.5
Top	8.6	43.0	70.6	22.2

SOURCE: Whalley (1984, 660, 666, 670) with permission of *Canadian Journal of Economics*©; see original study for incidence and income base assumptions of each case.

display an inverted-U shape, with their heaviest relative burden at middle incomes. When taxes are grouped by level of government, federal taxes over-all are quite progressive, provincial taxes are roughly proportional, and local taxes are regressive. The table also presents variants of the Vermaeten et al. results for "progressive" and "regressive" shifting assumptions as well as the standard shifting case using a pre-fisc income base. The latter makes the overall tax system very regressive at low incomes and otherwise roughly proportional.

Ruggeri et al. (1994), applying a similar methodology to 1986 data, use a post-fisc income base. Table 12.10 shows their computed global relative share adjustment (RSA) indices both by type of tax and level of government. Like Vermaeten et al., Ruggeri et al. find personal income tax to be the most progressive tax; however, their different shifting assumptions cause them to find that the corporate income tax is much less progressive. For the same reason, Ruggeri et al. find general sales taxes (though not liquor and tobacco taxes) to be progressive. They find federal taxes to be the most progressive, but differ from Vermaeten et al. in also finding provincial taxes to be progres-sive and local taxes to be proportional rather than regressive. Table 12.11 presents the findings of Ruggeri et al. for effective ATRs by income group and

TABLE 12.9

Average tax rates by family broad income groups, Canada, 1988 (percentages)

Family income percentiles	Low 8.3	14.4	13.3	11.8	10.5	8.8	7.0	5.7	4.7	3.7	7.9	3.1	Top 0.8	All 100.0
Base case taxes														
PIT	0.7	4.4	7.6	9.9	11.5	12.9	13.7	14.0	14.2	14.7	15.5	16.2	14.5	13.1
CIT	0.3	0.5	0.6	0.6	0.7	0.8	0.8	0.9	1.0	1.1	1.3	3.8	12.3	2.2
Commodity	14.6	11.9	11.1	10.7	10.0	9.5	8.9	8.3	7.8	7.7	7.0	6.1	4.2	8.2
Payroll	2.2	3.6	5.1	6.1	6.3	6.5	6.3	6.0	5.8	5.5	4.8	3.0	0.8	4.9
Property	7.0	5.6	4.6	4.2	3.8	3.5	3.3	3.2	3.1	2.9	2.8	2.5	2.4	3.3
Other taxes	5.3	3.2	2.4	2.0	1.8	1.7	1.5	1.4	1.4	1.3	1.2	1.1	1.2	1.6
Total taxes	30.1	29.2	31.4	33.5	34.2	34.9	34.5	33.8	33.2	33.3	32.6	32.7	35.3	33.4
Federal taxes	8.7	10.9	13.8	15.8	16.6	17.4	17.5	17.3	17.2	17.3	17.2	17.8	19.0	16.8
Provincial taxes	13.9	12.3	12.7	13.3	13.5	13.8	13.5	13.2	12.7	12.9	12.4	12.2	13.8	13.0
Local taxes	7.5	5.9	4.9	4.4	4.1	3.7	3.5	3.3	3.3	3.1	3.0	2.6	2.5	3.5
Progressive case	19.6	22.1	25.3	27.4	28.6	29.3	29.5	29.1	28.6	29.2	29.4	32.7	42.3	30.2
Regressive case	42.2	37.4	36.9	37.7	37.4	37.0	36.3	35.2	35.0	33.9	33.8	33.4	33.0	35.5
Base case with pre-fisc income	89.3	41.6	39.7	38.6	38.1	37.4	36.1	35.3	34.4	34.1	33.3	33.1	35.5	36.4

NOTE: All results except for the last line use the broad income measure. For progressive, regressive, and pre-fisc income base cases, the income percentiles differ somewhat from the charted figures, though the underlying dollar income ranges are unchanged; see the original study for the incidence and income base assumptions of each case.

SOURCE: Vermaeten et al. (1994, 401, 414-15), with permission from the Canadian Tax Foundation©.

household type, with personal income tax shown separately from all other taxes. The income tax remains progressive with income for all household types, but all other taxes display ATR patterns across incomes that vary with household type.

Dyck (2003) has updated the general methodology used in the earlier studies to examine the Canadian "fiscal restructuring" of the latter 1990s. This was a period when governments at all levels were reining in large deficits by controlling public spending and initially raising taxes and then, in some cases, reducing taxes for lower-income and middle-income households. Dyck finds that overall fiscal redistribution (including expenditures as well as taxes) remained progressive in the period 1994 to 2000 and has increased slightly since the 1980s; the RSA index for total taxes was more than twice as large as for transfers and for non-transfer public expenditures. As in earlier periods, taxes were most redistributive at the federal level and least at the

TABLE 12.10

Redistributional impact of taxes by order of government and type of tax, Canada, 1986 (global relative share adjustment indices)

Tax entity	Base case	Progressive variant	Regressive variant
Order of government			
Federal	1.041	1.042	1.038
Provincial	1.024	1.025	1.022
Local	1.001	1.006	0.996
Type of tax			
Personal income tax	1.0567	1.0576	1.0562
Corporate taxes	1.0019	1.0021	0.9988
Payroll taxes	1.0018	1.0023	1.0013
General sales taxes	1.0018	1.0022	1.0014
Fuel taxes	1.0000	1.0001	1.0000
Liquor and tobacco	0.9985	0.9986	0.9983
Natural resources	1.0001	1.0001	1.0000
Real property tax	1.0009	1.0061	0.9967
Fees and charges	1.0000	1.0001	1.0000
Miscellaneous revenue	1.0017	1.0018	1.0016
Total	1.0853	1.0958	1.0728

SOURCE: Ruggeri et al. (1994, 431, 439), with permission from the Canadian Tax Foundation©; see text for definition of global RSA index; see original study for the incidence and income base assumptions of each case.

TABLE 12.11

Average tax rates by household type and income level, Canada, 1986 (percentages)

	Household type					
Income group	Non-elderly singles	Single parents	1-earner couples	2-earner couples	Seniors	Combined total
Poor	[27.9]	[48.6]	[17.1]	[4.5]	[35.6]	[21.6]
PIT	0.7	0.2	1.0	1.3	0.0	0.5
Other taxes	31.8	11.1	14.8	18.3	7.7	16.3
All taxes	32.5	11.3	15.7	19.7	7.7	16.8
Low income	[19.6]	[20.1]	[17.6]	[10.1]	[29.9]	[18.5]
PIT	6.8	3.7	5.9	6.1	1.0	4.5
Other taxes	29.8	16.8	20.1	21.3	6.8	17.9
All taxes	36.6	20.5	26.0	27.4	7.8	22.4
Lower-middle	[13.1]	[15.1]	[19.5]	[15.6]	[11.3]	[14.7]
PIT	11.8	8.2	10.1	10.4	4.1	9.4
Other taxes	32.7	23.2	23.1	24.0	9.7	22.6
All taxes	44.5	31.3	33.1	34.4	13.8	32.0
Upper-middle	[21.1]	[11.3]	[25.1]	[30.8]	[11.2]	[22.2]
PIT	14.9	12.2	13.7	15.2	8.0	13.9
Other taxes	33.1	23.8	23.7	24.2	10.0	24.0
All taxes	48.0	36.0	37.3	39.4	18.0	37.9
High income	[16.7]	[4.5]	[16.1]	[33.8]	[9.8]	[19.6]
PIT	19.1	15.3	17.5	20.6	12.8	18.9
Other taxes	29.0	24.0	21.8	22.9	12.9	22.6
All taxes	48.0	39.3	39.3	43.5	25.7	41.5
Rich	[1.7]	[0.3]	[4.6]	[5.2]	[2.2]	[3.3]
PIT	26.6	37.8	28.5	31.0	25.8	29.2
Other taxes	21.2	21.5	16.7	17.2	15.8	17.3
All taxes	47.8	59.3	45.2	48.3	41.6	46.5
All incomes	[100.0]	[100.0]	[100.0]	[100.0]	[100.0]	[100.0]
PIT	13.5	6.0	14.0	17.9	7.0	14.1
Other taxes	30.3	17.7	20.9	22.5	9.9	21.2
All taxes	43.9	23.7	34.9	40.3	17.0	35.3

SOURCE: Ruggeri et al. (1996, 24, 45) with permission of Queen's University School of Policy Studies and Caledon Institute of Social Policy©; figures in square brackets are the percentage of that household type in that income group.

municipal level, and the personal income tax remained by far the most progressive category. The estimated RSA index for total taxes of 1.100 in 1997
exceeded the 1.085 estimated by Ruggeri et al. for 1986, suggesting a significant increase in total tax progressivity. This change could be explained by a
series of tax increases from the latter 1980s until 1996 that were targeted
most heavily at upper incomes.

In an earlier, path-breaking study, Davies et al. (1984) applied FINC
methodology to examine the distribution of lifetime taxes over lifetime incomes. This required the micro-simulation of life-cycle savings and bequest
behaviour. Davies et al. generated lifetime distributive series on income, consumption, transfers, and taxes, each of which displayed much less dispersion
than annual data because it removed both year-to-year and life-cycle variations. This approach allowed for the comparison of lifetime and annual tax
incidence patterns using a common dataset, which they drew from Canadian data for 1970. Table 12.12 presents the study's findings by major type of
tax for both the annual and lifetime bases and for a couple of variants of tax
shifting. Both the annual and lifecycle views yield moderate progressivity in
total taxes across the household income deciles, though progressivity is reduced in the lifetime view (except for the bottom decile). While the personal
income tax is less progressive in the lifetime than in the annual view, this is
offset by the fact that most other taxes are less regressive. The lifetime incidence results are also much less sensitive to alternative tax-shifting assumptions than are the annual results, because of the lesser lifetime dispersion of
the underlying economic series.

INCIDENCE BY TYPE OF TAX

Personal Income Taxes and Labour Earnings

All FINC and INEQ distributional studies assume that the economic burden
of the personal income tax (PIT) falls fully on the individuals who nominally pay it. This is a critical assumption because of the relative size and
progressivity of the PIT. Indeed, the PIT is the largest single source of tax
revenue in Canada, accounting for 57 percent of federal and 37 percent of
provincial government tax revenues in 2000 (including social security contributions, the amounts are, respectively, 46 and 35 percent of tax revenues).[41]
Because of the PIT's dominance, the tax's effective progressivity is a key reason studies have found that the federal tax system is substantially progressive
and provincial tax systems are just somewhat progressive.

TABLE 12.12

Average tax rates for households by deciles, annual vs. lifetime views, Canada, 1970 (percentages)

Tax/Decile	1	2	3	4	5	6	7	8	9	10	All
Annual incidence (deciles ranked by annual income), central case											
Corporate income tax	1.0	1.3	1.6	1.6	1.2	1.4	1.2	1.7	2.7	9.8	4.2
Property tax	1.1	1.5	1.8	1.7	1.3	1.5	1.3	1.9	2.9	10.6	4.5
Sales and excises	27.2	20.3	15.8	14.6	14.0	13.4	13.5	13.2	12.8	8.5	12.4
Payroll tax	1.7	2.5	4.1	4.3	4.2	3.9	3.8	3.4	3.0	1.4	2.9
Personal income tax	4.3	2.8	6.8	9.8	11.9	13.4	13.8	14.8	15.4	15.7	13.5
All taxes	35.4	28.4	30.1	31.9	32.6	33.7	33.6	35.0	36.8	46.0	37.5
Lifetime incidence (deciles ranked by lifetime resources), central case											
Corporate income tax	2.2	2.9	2.6	3.0	2.9	3.3	3.3	4.1	3.4	5.1	3.6
Property tax	2.4	3.1	2.8	3.3	3.2	3.6	3.6	4.5	3.7	5.6	3.9
Sales and excises	15.0	14.3	14.1	13.9	13.8	13.5	13.6	13.3	13.2	12.4	13.5
Payroll tax	3.9	4.0	3.9	4.0	3.8	3.8	3.6	3.6	3.4	2.8	3.6
Personal income tax	7.3	11.3	12.5	13.5	14.5	15.1	15.7	16.7	17.7	20.5	15.8
All taxes	30.9	35.5	35.9	37.7	38.1	39.3	39.8	42.2	41.3	46.5	40.2
Lifetime incidence (deciles ranked by lifetime resources), "noncompetitive" case (other taxes as in central case)											
Corporate income tax	3.1	3.3	3.2	3.4	3.3	3.4	3.4	3.8	3.4	4.2	3.6
Property tax	3.4	3.6	3.4	3.6	3.9	3.7	3.7	4.2	3.7	4.6	3.9
All taxes	32.8	36.4	37.1	38.4	39.2	39.5	40.1	41.6	41.4	44.6	40.2
Lifetime incidence (deciles ranked by lifetime resources), "Browning-Johnson" case (other taxes as in central case)											
Sales and excises	12.0	12.7	13.1	13.3	13.3	13.6	13.5	13.7	13.8	13.9	13.5
All taxes	27.9	34.0	34.9	37.0	37.6	39.4	39.8	42.6	41.8	48.0	40.2

SOURCE: Davies et al. (1984, 641, 644) with permission of the American Economic Association©; see original study for the incidence and income base assumptions of each case.

Evidence exists, however, that individual taxpayers do not bear the full incidence of the PIT. More worrisome for the validity of results from existing studies is evidence of a distributional twist in the incidence of the PIT that reduces effective progressivity. Block and Shillington (1994, 37) note that "at the upper end of the income distribution, after-tax income is the basis for negotiations on remuneration," which suggests some shifting of the PIT by higher earners. A similar result arises with the "tax equalization" provisions offered by many multinational corporations when they relocate top managers to Canada. Their salaries are increased to offset the amount by which their Canadian income taxes exceed those in their home countryies. By a process of emulation or competition, similar salary premiums may spread to top managers of domestic origin. Thus, the shifting of PIT works to undo at least part of its progressivity.

This result is also common to long-run models of human capital formation and occupational choices. If one uses the pure "schooling" variant of the human capital model and assumes no ability or quality differences across individuals, tax progressivity will be completely undone in the long run by occupational choices and related schooling investments (Montmarquette 1974). Individuals will choose their schooling to maximize lifetime earnings net of tax, which makes tax progressivity useless for reducing inequality of net incomes; the PIT progressivity is simply shifted into correspondingly higher gross wages.[42] In a more realistic model with ability differences across individuals, the effective progressivity of a PIT would still be reduced but not eliminated.

An intriguing analysis by Lockwood and Manning (1993) relates the progressivity of the PIT and other labour taxes to wage formation via a bargaining model.[43] They suggest that their model extends beyond unionized workers to include the bargaining power that high earners may exercise over their employers through their firm-specific skills. In a fairly general model of wage setting, they reach several conclusions when the firm's profit and union utility functions are iso-elastic.[44] First, increasing the marginal tax rate (MTR), while holding constant the ATR, will decrease the pre-tax real wage rate. Second, increasing the ATR, while holding constant the MTR, will raise the pre-tax real wage by more than the tax increase – hence backward shifting more than 100 percent. Third, it is the ratio of the ATR to the MTR that affects the wage rate. As a result, the number of tax brackets affects the pre-tax income distribution; a strongly progressive PIT, with many rising MTRs, yields the flattest pattern of pre-tax wages and the most progressive distribution of net incomes. And a linear tax system would worsen the distribution of *pre-tax* labour incomes. The authors find that their model can explain the increase in gross wages of high earners in the United Kingdom in the 1980s following large cuts in their MTRs, and this outcome has nothing to do with improved incentives for hard work. Their empirical tests provide support for the role of the wedge between average and marginal tax rates as a determinant of pressure on gross wages.

Additional evidence stems from research that relates PIT rates to labour supply or migration responses that affect gross wages, particularly for skilled workers. Bingley and Lanot (2002) examine the impact of income taxes on labour supply and gross wages simultaneously. If the tax reduces the amount of labour supplied at a given wage, it will raise the equilibrium pre-tax wage rate, thus shifting part of the burden onto employers. They find that more of the adjustment is in gross wages than hours, which is consistent with a model where aggregate labour supply is more elastic than labour demand.[45] Bingley and Lanot do not, however, distinguish between tax shifting for high-wage versus low-wage labour and thus do not directly address the progressivity issue. Feldstein and Wrobel (1998) attack this problem by examining differential progressivity across American states to see whether state taxes can redistribute income. They conclude that state taxes cannot do so, that interstate migration in response to tax rate differentials causes gross wages to adjust so that net-of-tax wages are equalized across states. This wage adjustment, with full incidence falling on employers rather than individuals paying the PIT, means that a more progressive state tax system raises the cost to firms of hiring more highly skilled workers.[46] The adjustment, which occurs within just a few years, does not require extensive migration; rather, there simply needs to be enough movement of more heavily taxed workers to raise their marginal product relative to that of less heavily taxed workers to offset the tax rate differential. Day and Winer (1994) suggest that this process is at least partially operative in Canada.

Also relevant is empirical research on international migration, principally the asserted "brain drain" from Canada to the United States. The fact that emigration from Canada has been concentrated in a few highly paid occupational categories has been cited as evidence that Canada's tax rates are too high and too progressive (see Finnie 2001, for a review of such studies). The economic adjustment process here would be similar to that across subnational jurisdictions with differing degrees of progressivity. That is, within the limits of allowed immigration, the outflow would continue until the gross wage differentials across countries offset the tax rate differentials. That would constrain the ability of Canada to implement greater PIT progressivity than the United States.[47] However, while Canadian PIT rates overall are higher than those in the United States, they are less progressive at the federal level, with higher bottom and lower top rates and the top rate arising at lower incomes (Kesselman 2000, 2004). For that reason, any tax-motivated emigration from Canada might better be ascribed to the level rather than the progressivity of Canadian taxes.[48] Most likely, non-tax factors such as higher gross wage rates (unrelated to tax factors) and unique work opportunities in the United States are the predominant explanation.

Payroll Taxes

The most common incidence assumption for payroll taxes in FINC (and INEQ) tax distribution studies is that the full burden of both employer and employee portions falls on employees via lower gross wages and salaries. However, variations in the assumed incidence of payroll taxes, particularly of the employer share, are used for sensitivity analysis in a number of FINC studies. For example, Vermaeten et al. (1994, 368-69) adopt the standard payroll incidence view as consistent with a small open economy model where capital is more mobile than labour, and product markets are highly competitive. In a "progressive" variant, they consider a small open economy with less capital mobility than in their standard model, full mobility of consumer outlays, and labour market imperfections that inhibit the backward-shifting of business taxes (such as unions bargaining on an after-tax basis with respect to payroll taxes). In that case they assume that the employer portion of payroll taxes is borne by capital, while the employee portion is borne by labour. In a "regressive" variant, Vermaeten et al. consider an economy with fully mobile capital but imperfectly competitive product markets with oligopolistic elements that allow for forward-shifting of taxes to consumers. In that case, they assume that the employer portion of payroll taxes is shifted onto consumers via higher product prices, while the employee portion remains a burden on labour.

One needs to distinguish between benefit-linked payroll taxes and "general" payroll taxes whose revenues go into the consolidated budget or are not linked to workers' benefit entitlements. A benefit-linked payroll tax is more like a user charge for a publicly supplied service, where the tax reflects the value of associated benefits. Rather than the "wedge" imposed between the buyer's and seller's price by a conventional tax, the labour supply curve is shifted down by the prospective benefits just as the labour demand curve is shifted down by the payroll tax. If a worker values the benefits at their full cost, these shifts are equal, and the full incidence of the tax will fall on the employee without any decline in equilibrium work hours (Summers 1989). Yet one might ask whether benefit-linked payroll taxes should even be included in tax incidence studies, any more than are the charges for publicly-supplied water or electricity.[49] Tax distribution studies for Canada and the United States typically find that payroll taxes are progressive from low to middle incomes and regressive over higher income ranges. However, this reflects the dominance of benefit-linked forms of payroll tax and their use of annual ceilings on taxed earnings of each worker; it neglects the fact that the associated benefit entitlements are similarly capped by maximum levels.

The incidence of general payroll taxes, sometimes not distinguished from benefit-linked payroll taxes, has been subject to intensive research, as have their employment effects (see Kesselman 1997, 55-81, for a review). When a general payroll tax is applied to all employment income across a national economy, the incidence is determined by the interplay of aggregate labour demand and labour supply curves. While there is some divergence of estimates, most research finds that a general payroll tax on employees is fully and immediately borne by workers and that a tax on employers is shifted fully or almost fully to workers via lower wages and salaries over several years. Hence, the standard assumption used for payroll taxes in most tax incidence studies appears to be supported for both benefit-linked and general payroll taxes of broad application. It is well-established in tax economics that the ultimate incidence of a tax does not depend on whether the tax is nominally levied on buyers and sellers if markets are competitive, and this result is upheld for payroll taxes after an adjustment period.

The employer payroll levies of four Canadian provinces have no linkage between payments (all by employers) and individual worker health care benefits, for which they are nominally applied, so they are entirely general payroll taxes. In addition, all provinces apply employer payroll taxes to finance schemes of workers' compensation, with the rates often varying by industry and at times by firms (so-called experience rating). General payroll taxes applied at differential rates across provinces, industries, and/or firms raise further questions about economic incidence. To the extent that a payroll tax is applied at a differentially high rate on certain firms, they will bear the burden (reducing the return to owners or capital), while the base rate of tax applying to all firms will be borne by labour (Vaillancourt and Marceau

1990).[50] If the tax is applied at a differentially high rate on a particular industry, it is likely to be shifted to output prices and thereby borne by consumers of that industry's product. A provincially differentiated payroll tax rate, such as those applied by four provinces, should have incidence similar to that of subnational PITs, discussed earlier. This outcome is contrary to the assumptions commonly used in tax incidence studies.

Taxes on Goods and Services

Indirect taxes on goods and services are the second largest source of tax revenues for the Canadian federal and most provincial governments. These take the form of a multi-stage goods and services tax (GST) for the federal and four provincial governments; single-stage retail sales taxes for five provinces; excise taxes on alcohol, gasoline, and tobacco products at both levels; and federal import duties. While the various indirect taxes have differences that can affect their incidence, the key issue in tax distribution studies is whether the burdens should be allocated based on the "uses" or the "sources" side of households' budgets.

The traditional view was that indirect taxes are borne by households in proportion to their outlays on taxable items. That is, consumers who pay the tax also bear its full economic incidence. Intuitively, when one goes from an income tax to a consumption tax, the prices of the taxed consumer goods increase relative to untaxed capital goods. There is no change in relative factor prices, so the price increase falls on consumers and not savers. Because in annual data the savings rate rises with household incomes, the traditional view implies that indirect taxes are very regressive.[51] The higher proportion of outlays on the highly taxed excise products by lower-income households accentuates the regressive pattern. The traditional incidence assumption is adopted as the standard case in Vermaeten et al. When Davies et al. use this incidence assumption and move from an annual to a lifetime view, sales and excise taxes change from highly regressive to only slightly regressive ("central case" in Table 12.12).

An alternative view, proposed by Browning (1978; see also Browning and Johnson 1979), asserts that the burden of indirect taxes should be distributed by the sources side, or factor incomes, rather than by the uses of income.[52] Browning observes that the traditional incidence view was based on only two types of income – labour and capital – and ignored transfer incomes. Transfer payments make up a larger proportion of lower household incomes (as in Table 12.3) and are often indexed for changes in the price level. Hence, when an indirect tax rate is raised, the recipients of transfer income are insulated from the price level impact via an adjustment of their transfer payments. To the extent that transfer recipients are compensated for the impact, the indirect taxes can be borne only by the recipients of market incomes and, in particular, labour incomes. In this view, indirect taxes are progressive from low to middle incomes, proportional for upper-middle incomes, and regressive for high incomes. Combining Browning's assumption with lifetime income measures, Davies et al. (1984) find that indirect taxes have a slightly progressive distributional pattern across all incomes. Yet Browning's view can be critiqued on several grounds.[53] For example, transfer benefits are not the only source of income that is partially indexed; many wage contracts are indexed (as are some pensions), and interest incomes also respond to higher inflation rates induced by indirect tax rate hikes. Moreover, even though some transfer benefits (such as CPP, GIS, and Old Age Security) are indexed, benefit levels are subject to periodic legislative review, and any discretionary raises are likely to be diminished if there is indexation.

Another issue relates to indirect taxes, such as provincial retail sales taxes (RST) and fuel excises, which apply to business intermediate inputs and capital goods. Indeed, more than one-third of the total revenue from RSTs is estimated to arise from such business inputs. Unlike value-added taxes, which are designed to apply solely to households' final consumption, RSTs and some excises on business are typically assigned to factors of production, on the assumption that both exporters and import-competing firms are price takers at world prices (see Ruggeri and Bluck 1990). Some analysts, such as Ruggeri et al. (1994), split the burden of these taxes equally between labour and capital; others, such as Vermaeten et al. (1994), take a more regressive view by assigning the indirect taxes paid by business to labour, the more immobile factor.

A final issue for the incidence of indirect taxes is how to treat any associated compensation provisions for lower-income households. Indirect taxes are commonly structured to offer relief for such households via differential rates on various goods and services; for example, RSTs typically exempt items such as groceries and residential rents, while the GST offers zero-rating for groceries and exempts residential rents. These provisions are fully recognized in standard tax distribution studies by allocating the actual indirect taxes paid by income class. However, additional compensation for indirect tax burdens is provided by federal GST refundable tax credits for lower-income households (and credits for the preceding federal sales tax) and by the sales tax credits of some provinces. The question is whether such provisions should be treated as transfer payments – and therefore ignored in tax distribution studies – or counted as offsets to indirect taxes paid by households receiving the credits. Statistics Canada classifies such tax credits as part of the transfer system rather than the tax system (as in our Tables 12.3 and 12.4). In their study of the distribution of taxes and public benefits, Ruggeri et al. (1994) also classify the federal and provincial sales tax credits as transfers. In contrast, Vermaeten et al. (1994) net out federal and provincial tax credits for sales tax from the indirect tax burdens of the beneficiaries; they similarly net out provincial property tax credits against the property tax liabilities of the credit recipients. This approach seems preferable, as the relief for lower-income payers of a tax can be provided through either an income-targeted tax credit or a relieving provision in the tax.

Property Taxes

Property taxes, the largest source of tax revenues for municipal governments, are levied on land and structural improvements of both the household and business sectors. In tax distribution studies, it is generally agreed that landowners should bear the property tax on land, owing to its immobility. There is, however, disagreement about where the burden of property taxes on structures should fall, since structures are a form of capital and are thus subject to behavioural responses.[54]

In the traditional view, the property tax has "excise" effects that shift the tax burden from the owners of structures to the consumers of the structures' services. The combined assumptions of a small open economy, internationally mobile capital, and immobile renters and consumers means that this part of the property tax operates like an excise tax on structures. The tax on structures is then borne by owner-occupants and owner-operators as well as renters of housing; this part of the tax for commercial and industrial properties is passed forward to consumers via higher product prices. Thus, the traditional view yields a relatively regressive pattern of property tax incidence, a view adopted in the standard case of Vermaeten et al. (1994) and the "regressive" variant of Ruggeri et al. (1994).

In the "new" view of property tax incidence, the tax on structures falls entirely on the profits of capital owners. The underlying model for this view assumes that labour and consumers are more mobile than structural capital, so property tax changes are reflected in changes in the value of capital. Hence, the property tax on structures is borne by the owners and falls on capital income. Because capital ownership is correlated with household income, this view implies that the property tax is progressive rather than regressive, as in the traditional view. However, the "factor return" effects of the new view can also be considered jointly with the excise effects of the traditional view, with the latter applying to tax rate differentials in nearby municipalities. The new view is adopted for property tax incidence in the "progressive" variants of Vermaeten et al. and Ruggeri et al. as well as the standard case of Davies et al. In addition, the base case of Ruggeri et al. and a "regressive" variant of Davies et al. use shifting assumptions intermediate between the new and traditional views; the tax on structures is borne half by renters and consumers and half by capital owners.

Corporate and Capital Income Taxes

Taxes on capital income can be distinguished by who pays the bill: corporate income tax (CIT), paid directly by corporations, or PIT, paid by individuals on their capital incomes, including dividends, interest, rents, capital gains, and profits from unincorporated business.[55] However, studies of tax incidence tend to make the same incidence assumptions about both kinds of tax. Most analyses of capital income tax incidence for Canada use a small open economy model in which capital moves freely between countries. Hence, some of the tax can be shifted from the owners of capital to more immobile taxpayers and factors of production. In contrast, for the much larger American economy, the US Congressional Budget Office (2001) assumes that the CIT (like the PIT) falls entirely on households, allocated in proportion to their income from interest, dividends, rents, and capital gains.

For Canada, the portion of the CIT that cannot be shifted is the common world capital tax rate, which Vermaeten et al. (1994) assume is the American tax rate; this portion is fully borne by owners of corporate income. Vermaeten et al. argue that the burden of the rest of the CIT is shifted either to immobile factors, such as labour, or forward to consumers. They suggest that effective tax rates and average corporate tax burdens are similar for both Canada and the United States, so that the differentially shifted portion is zero. Thus Vermaeten et al. assume that the entire CIT is borne by owners of capital income, which makes the tax look progressive overall because of the income pattern of capital income receipts. In contrast, Ruggeri et al. (1994) employ a less progressive approach, assuming that half of the CIT and PIT on capital income is borne by owners of capital, while the other half gets shifted forward to consumers. In both of these studies, the portion of capital that is held by foreign households is deducted from the income base; this accounts for 31 percent of the CIT. Ruggeri et al. also deduct the foreign tax credit from the domestic tax on capital.

One complication arising for CIT incidence is the degree of integration between the CIT and the personal tax system. Vermaeten et al. argue that unless the CIT is fully integrated with the PIT – resulting in all earnings generated through corporations being taxed at the PIT rate of the individual shareholder – the theoretical shifting assumptions may be incorrect. Under a fully integrated CIT, a change in the CIT (and hence PIT) rate will not cause movement of capital between the corporate and unincorporated sectors; this means that the capital tax will be fully borne by capital owners, the standard assumption. However, if the CIT is not fully integrated, then a rise in the CIT rate will drive capital from the corporate to the unincorporated sector. The unincorporated sector will see its after-tax rate of return fall, thus bearing some of the CIT burden. The Canadian PIT and CIT are less than fully integrated, with dividend tax credits that are inadequate to offset the CIT except for small Canadian-controlled corporations. Vermaeten et al. note that this differential is more than offset by PIT provisions such as preferential tax on capital gains, resulting in a slight advantage for the corporate sector vis-à-vis the unincorporated sector. Indeed, the authors assume the difference to be zero in their incidence analysis, which could be a small potential source of error in their study.

The difference between annual and lifetime incidence calculations also affects the treatment of corporate and capital income taxes. Davies et al. (1984) note that capital income, while important in annual incidence calculations, is not part of a household's discounted lifetime income since it simply reflects a choice between consuming now and consuming later in life. How, then, does the researcher assign the burden of capital income taxes? Rather than focusing on capital-owning households, Davies et al. assign the burden of these taxes to families that defer consumption – namely, savers – and distribute the taxes via the discounted value of all investment income received over the lifetime. Their justification is that capital taxes have a uses-side impact and a sources-side impact. On the uses side, capital taxes reduce the net interest rate to savers, which increases the price of future consumption. The taxes thus hurt savers and benefit consumers. On the sources side, the lower after-tax interest rate lowers the relative discounted incomes of those who receive income later in life, again hurting savers. (In contrast, annual incidence calculations assume only a sources-side impact of capital taxes.) Because the amount of consumption that a family forgoes as a result of capital taxes equals the reduction in current investment income, discounted lifetime investment income is the appropriate distributive series. Estimates of lifetime incidence of the CIT show less progressivity than annual calculations, which is consistent with Davies et al.'s other findings.

Additional Issues and Research Priorities

From our review of studies on the distributional impacts of taxes, we can suggest directions for future research. For one thing, almost all studies of the Canadian tax system are now quite dated. Few capture the major PIT reforms of 1988, the adoption of the GST in 1991, or the increasing use of payroll taxes since 1990. None captures the move of provincial PITs to a "tax on income" basis and the associated flattening of rate schedules, beginning in 2001, or more recent federal and provincial PIT and CIT rate cuts. Because these changes alter the tax mix and the bases and rate structures of component taxes, they would likely produce quite different findings, even using the same research methodology. Moreover, future research needs to incorporate changes in our understanding of the economic incidence of some taxes, such as the PIT and indirect taxes, and the possible change in incidence of taxes for the Canadian economy. We examine these and other issues in this section.

THEORETICAL AND EMPIRICAL ANALYSIS OF TAX SHIFTING

The shifting or incidence of component taxes is a crucial underpinning of INEQ and FINC studies. Even if we assume a closed national economy, the incidences of a national PIT, subnational PITs, and payroll taxes are not fully resolved. Given the relative magnitude of the PIT and its role as the leading progressive component of the revenue system, the distributional burden of this tax warrants high priority for further theoretical and empirical research. So do the distributional effects of subnational taxes, study of which is limited for the United States and absent for Canada. One might expect that linguistic and cultural barriers to internal migration would enter the analysis, as Quebec traditionally has had the highest provincial tax burden, and the Atlantic provinces, the highest sales and income tax rates. Moreover, the shift by the provinces to a "tax on income" approach has greatly relieved the constraints for provincial tax progressivity to mirror federal progressivity. Some provinces have flattened their tax rate schedules, Alberta's single-rate tax being the polar case. Based on the analysis in Feldstein and Wrobel (1998), it is *differences* in subnational tax progressivity (not the degree of rate progressivity in itself) that undermine effective progressivity of taxes applied at that level.

Recognizing that Canada is a small open economy with international mobility that is high for capital, significant for highly skilled labour, and limited for most occupations adds further insights to the incidence analysis. The effective progressivity of the PIT may be attenuated for Canada, especially with respect to the highest earnings brackets, in a way that does not arise for a larger economy. While this issue has been addressed in a few studies on Canada-United States migration and the determinants of the "brain drain," it is still unknown how far this process undermines the effective progressivity of Canada's federal PIT. The numbers of people migrating to the United States are quite moderate, but, as noted before in the provincial tax context, it may not require large-scale movement of workers to induce significant tax shifting. Nevertheless, informal observations of relative gross pay for professional, skilled, and managerial workers in the two countries suggests that any diminution of effective progressivity of the Canadian PIT has been limited. Moreover, the incidence of taxes on corporate and capital incomes will be affected by provisions for foreign tax credits, bilateral tax treaties, the definitions of tax residence, and mobility of capital owners as well as legal structures for moving assets outside their country of tax residence. Studies of the integrating European economies and theoretical analyses of the impacts on redistributive tax and transfer policies of factor mobility across borders (Wildasin 2000, and sources therein) may provide useful insights for Canada.

Another neglected aspect of tax incidence research relates to the highest earners, who pay a disproportional share of personal and (likely) corporate income taxes. A sound economic analysis of the behaviour of this group is a prerequisite for assessing the shifting of their taxes. Many top earners derive their income as successful proprietors, owners, and entrepreneurs, thus combining their labour, abilities, and financial capital. Standard economic analysis of this phenomenon divides their returns into capital and labour components; the analysis relates capital-based taxes to the capital component and labour-based taxes to the implicit labour return. However, a thriving business involves the application of labour-like skills to give capital a rate of return above the normal rate. While excess returns could be attributed entirely to the labour component, without access to financial capital, labour alone would not generate high returns.

ANNUAL VERSUS LIFETIME MEASURES AND DATA NEEDS

Lifetime measures of tax incidence offer advantages over annual measures by avoiding the confounding effects of life-cycle and annual income fluctuations. However, the simulation of lifetime incomes and taxes in CGE and some FINC studies has significant limitations in terms of the underlying models. One way to avoid such hazards would be to disaggregate groups by life-cycle cohorts, then adjust the aggregate data to reflect each cohort's characteristic savings and spending patterns. Another method would be to minimize the impact of year-to-year variations in individual incomes by taking multi-year averages. The recent development of a Canadian longitudinal dataset from the Survey of Labour and Income Dynamics should facilitate this exercise. Each panel of respondents is included in the survey for six years, a period sufficiently long to smooth the effects of temporary shocks to labour, business, and investment incomes.[56] Hence, a measure of the tax unit's permanent income can be obtained for use in the tax incidence analysis. It might also be feasible to combine the two methods sketched here, so as to remove the effects of both inter-year and life-cycle income variations.

HORIZONTAL EQUITY, DIFFERENTIAL TAX TREATMENT, AND INEQUALITY

Existing tax distribution studies use a measure of market, pre-fisc, broad, or post-fisc income, in some cases with various imputations, as the index of well-being for individuals or households. Thus, tax provisions that differentiate the tax liabilities for units with the same measured level of taxpaying ability typically reduce the estimated equalizing effects of the tax system. A few studies (such as Wagstaff et al. 1999) attempt separate estimates of such horizontal inequity and re-ranking effects to see how they offset the vertical redistribution effects of taxes. However, many tax provisions that apply differential treatment for units with the same measured taxpaying ability actually work to *improve* the horizontally equitable treatment of taxpayers.[57] These provisions recognize characteristics of taxpayers – such as disabilities, medical costs, high living costs in remote locales, moving costs, age, or dependants – that affect well-being or taxpaying ability *for a given level of measured income*. In these studies, however, they are measured as *muting* the vertical redistribution of the tax system – indeed, in some, as creating horizontal *inequities*.

Tax Policy Inferences

The research literature on the distributional effects of taxes is large and diverse, but inconclusive in many ways. Accordingly, one can draw from it only highly qualified inferences for the direction of Canadian tax policies.[58] It is clear that, although the personal income tax plays a key role in the progressivity of the overall tax system, at best the tax is less progressive than the naïve assumption of no shifting, and this reduction in effective progressivity is likely more pronounced for provincial than for federal taxes. Given this finding, those who desire more inequality reduction, regardless of any attendant economic costs, would want to steepen personal tax rate schedules or expand the tax base progressively. Those more concerned about economic efficiency and growth would counsel moderating the steepness of rate schedules, since society is achieving less effective tax progressivity for a given economic cost than was once thought.

Tax economists commonly call for shifting the tax system away from income bases and toward consumption-type bases. This change, they argue, would improve the economy's efficiency and growth rate by making the tax system more neutral vis-à-vis savings, investment, and capital. For those who are concerned about the distributional dimension, however, such a change would have further policy implications because it would tend to reduce the tax burdens on wealthier, high-income individuals.[59] Careful tax design can moderate these disequalizing effects. First, any further move toward a consumption base should be pursued through changing the personal tax base, since progressive rates can be applied in the personal tax, rather than by shifting the tax mix toward greater reliance on indirect consumption taxes. The evidence is that indirect taxes are regressive, albeit more so in an annual than in a lifetime perspective. Second, in reforming the personal tax toward a consumption base, it is important to use transitional methods that do not provide a windfall for holders of savings and wealth at the time of the change. Rather, the goal should be to shelter incremental savings generated from labour earnings after the change.[60] Regardless, a shift of the tax base toward consumption would carry some unavoidable reduction in effective tax progressivity, even in a lifetime view, unless rate schedules were steepened.

A related question is how tax policies that shift the base toward consumption to promote economic growth would affect the distribution of *pre-tax* earnings. Conventional economic findings (e.g., Murphy et al. 1998) suggest that increasing the economy's capital stock tends to increase inequalities between skilled and unskilled labour, either through the complementarity between capital and skilled labour or through skill-biased technology embodied in new capital. Thus, increased inequality of market incomes would compound the reduced equalization of a reformed tax system and increase the inequality of net incomes. However, one model (Beaudry and Green 1998, 2003) suggests a very different conclusion. If increasing the capital stock affects industry's choice of techniques, capital might be pushed disproportionally into sectors that intensively employ less-skilled labour. This would raise labour productivity and wages in both sectors, but more favourably for unskilled labour, which would reduce the inequality of market earnings. Consequently, shifting toward consumption-based taxes could, in the long run, reduce pre-tax earnings inequality, perhaps sufficiently to offset any initial loss of tax progressivity. It might also mitigate inequality by reducing the long-run returns to capital owners, though this effect would be muted for Canada, given its open economy and the highly mobile nature of international capital.

The tax distribution literature also suggests the need to differentiate between federal and provincial tax policies. Because of labour's much greater inter-regional than international mobility, one would expect redistributive policies to be weakened much more at the provincial level than at the federal level. Provinces with more progressive tax policies will lose some higher earners to other jurisdictions, thereby pushing up the gross wages of skilled labour. Thus, the effective burden of those higher taxes gets shifted to the industries that employ them, in turn shrinking the high-value-added sectors of the provinces seeking more progressive policies. These observations apply with respect to both the progressivity of personal taxes and the overall tax burden (including payroll, sales, and property taxes) relative to the value of public services supplied. In the Canadian context, this effect may be restrained by factors – such as Quebec's linguistic distinctness, Ontario's economic rents for top earners in certain industries, and Atlantic Canada's regional preferences – that inhibit the mobility of skilled labour even when heavily taxed. Nevertheless, any remaining restraint on redistribution at the provincial level may warrant more progressive tax and expenditure policies at the federal level.

Taxes on business are popular because the public believes they are paid by the owners of capital. Economists, in fact, dispute the incidence of these taxes. Some assign their burden entirely to capital owners, others split it between capital and consumption, and still others see a part of it shifted to labour. Given the environment in which Canadian business operates, one can reasonably assume that business taxes at rates that equal foreign rates will be borne by capital, but that any higher rates will be shifted onto relatively immobile factors such as workers and consumers. Corporate and business taxes thus are better utilized as instruments for promoting growth of the economy, productivity, jobs, and real wages than as direct instruments for inequality reduction. Moreover, for many small and medium-sized businesses, corporate income taxes bear on both capital incomes and labour earnings of owner-proprietors who do not take their returns in the form of salaries. Hence, tax provisions that favour smaller businesses, including lower corporate tax rates and the lifetime capital gains exemption, may exert significantly regressive effects on some high earners.

A final important implication of the research findings is that the size of the tax bite matters as much as its progressivity. Even if the tax system reflects a pattern of tax rates that is only moderately progressive, it can be substantially redistributive if the overall tax level is high. Moreover, the larger the tax revenues, the more potential this offers for redistributive policies on the expenditure side of public budgets. We found that cash transfers are more important than personal income taxes in enhancing equality for most groups other than the highest earners. Public spending through in-kind goods and services can also play a major redistributive role, especially in areas such as health care and education. One can point to the experience of northern European countries with tax systems of modest progressivity but high overall tax rates that finance generous and highly redistributive social programs. Any assessment of the potential for using tax policy to mitigate inequality in Canada must take a similarly holistic view of the problem.

ACKNOWLEDGMENTS

This chapter is a condensed and revised version of Jonathan R. Kesselman and Ron Cheung, "Tax Incidence, Progressivity, and Inequality in Canada" (2004) *Canadian Tax Journal* 42(3): 709-89, and is published with permission of the Canadian Tax Foundation. The authors thank the following for useful comments: Charles Beach, David Bradford, Bev Dahlby, Jim Davies, Don Fullerton, Peter Lambert, Alan Macnaughton, Kevin Milligan, Finn Poschmann, Jim Poterba, Joe Ruggeri, Andrew Sharpe, and Mike Veall. Responsibility for views and any errors in this chapter lies fully with the authors.

NOTES

1 The last comprehensive survey of Canadian tax incidence and inequality impacts is now quite dated, and much research has appeared subsequently; see Dahlby's (1985) study for the Macdonald Commission. A similarly dated survey of the technical economics of tax incidence was provided in Kotlikoff and Summers (1987) and updated in Fullerton and Metcalf (2002).

2   Earlier-generation CGE tax models were static and did not incorporate dynamic or intertemporal effects; see Shoven and Whalley (1984).

3   This discussion draws heavily on Fullerton and Rogers (1993).

4   This discussion draws heavily on Gale et al. (1996) and Block and Shillington (1994).

5   These can use either "static" or "dynamic" assumptions about behavioural responses (see the studies in Bradford 1995) but still do not attempt to capture the deadweight efficiency costs of taxes.

6   This section draws heavily on the comprehensive analysis by Lambert (2001) and the compact exposition by Litchfield (1999). For analysis of the relations between local and global progressivity measures and inequality reduction, see Podder (1997) and Duclos (1997).

7   The P_{90}/P_{10} is sometimes called the 90:10 ratio or the 90-10 differential; for example, see Phipps and Lethbridge in Chapter 8 and Fortin and Schirle in Chapter 11.

8   See, for example, Myles (1995) and Litchfield (1999).

9   Litchfield (1999) offers a summary of decomposition techniques for assessing the sources of inequality. Fortin and Schirle in Chapter 11 employ a different decomposition method for explaining changes in inequality.

10   If the subgroups do have overlapping incomes, there is a "residual" that measures overlap and has been used in tax studies to capture re-ranking (see Aronson et al. 1994, and Wagstaff et al. 1999).

11   A CGE study could also chart the pattern of lifetime ATRs with respect to lifetime incomes, but the typical approach is to focus on the pattern of gains and losses to lifetime utility by lifetime incomes.

12   This formulation was suggested by Blackorby and Donaldson (1984, 688), but it is consistent with the Musgrave and Thin (1948, 510) assertion that effective progression can be expressed as the ratios of the coefficients of equality of distributions of post-tax to pre-tax incomes.

13   If the ranking of units by pre-tax incomes differs from their ranking by taxes, a correction term for re-ranking needs to be introduced to the relationship. See Kakwani (1984).

14   This point was also recognized by Musgrave and Thin (1948, 510): "effective progression depends upon the general level of rates as well as upon the steepness of the rate structure as such."

15   See Wagstaff et al. (1999) or Aronson and Lambert (1994) for more detailed discussion of this decomposition.

16   This approach *assumes* that pre-tax incomes are a good measure of "ability to pay" and hence define "equals" among taxpayers. Yet many special provisions of the personal income tax are intended to refine the measure of ability to pay (such as recognizing medical care costs as different from ordinary consumption), so that one need not agree with the measures of H or R.

17 US Congressional Budget Office (2001, 19-20) discusses the relative merits of using the household or family as the unit of analysis and opts for the household.

18 Aronson et al. (1994) found that these parameter values minimized the measure of horizontal inequity for the United Kingdom's personal income tax.

19 See for example Atkinson et al. (1995) and the US Congressional Budget Office (2001, 24). On occasion, this has been called the OECD method.

20 The US Congressional Budget Office (2001) undertakes FINC estimates of ATRs using equivalized incomes for ranking of households by percentile groups, but it presents its results based on total household incomes unadjusted by household size (ibid., 24, 30, 36).

21 One INEQ study that includes payroll taxes does make such an adjustment by adding the employer's portion of the tax to market incomes, which then enters broad income (Jäntti 1997).

22 For proponents of the lifetime view, see Davies et al. (1984) and Fullerton and Rogers (1993, 17-21); for proponents of the annual view, see Goode (1980) and Vermaeten et al. (1994, 355).

23 Devarajan et al. (1980) compare earlier forms of studies of the CGE and FINC types and find patterns of incidence that are generally similar but substantially different in magnitude; the early CGE studies assumed fixed supplies of capital and labour.

24 Here we address the general conceptual issue, not exact definitions of progressivity. We assume simply that progressivity for both taxes and expenditures is measured with respect to the same money income base. Moreover, we apply the term "progressive" to expenditures that decline as a proportion of income with higher incomes; some studies call this pattern "regressive" for parallelism with the term's use for taxes (for example, Dahlby 1985, 116; Lambert 2001, 269).

25 For example, see Dodge (1975), Gillespie (1980), and Ruggeri et al. (1996).

26 Exactly this outcome was reported in a study of Quebec for 1981. Taxes were found to be regressive, while transfers and government spending on goods and services were progressive, yielding a slightly progressive net outcome. See Payette and Vaillancourt (1986).

27 For a somewhat similar analysis for the period 1971-92, see Beach and Slotsve (1996, 98-108).

28 Declining transfer receipts at the bottom of the income distribution likely reflected a combination of an improving economy and discretionary policy cuts to social assistance and employment insurance benefits. The notable jump in personal tax burdens likely resulted from both rising nominal incomes and a deficiently indexed tax system.

29 Frenette, Green, and Picot in Chapter 3 report that the surveys that underlie these Gini coefficients (the Survey of Consumer Finances to 1996 and thereafter the Survey of Labour and Income Dynamics) may understate levels and trends in inequality. They base this view on comparative analysis with more comprehensive

tax-based and census datasets and suggest that the survey coverage may be missing growing numbers of the lowest-income households.

30   An important caveat is needed here. The order in which the two "programs" (transfers and taxes) are considered can affect the relative equalizing effect attributed to
each, since the first program applied will naturally have the largest opportunity to
reduce inequalities in market incomes (unless the two programs are orthogonal).
Hence, the discussion in the text should be read as indicating the general trends
over time and across household types. Also, it is natural to consider cash transfer
programs first, since income taxes apply to total incomes including many of the
transfers. Ervik (1998) proposed this approach.

31   Wolfson and Murphy (2000) find that, for both Canada and the United States,
income transfers had significantly stronger equalizing effects than income taxes
and that during 1985-97 income transfers had a stronger equalizing effect in
Canada than in the United States.

32   Some problems of comparability for the LIS are discussed in Gottschalk and
Smeeding (2000).

33   The residual progression curve is constructed by adding values of $LC(x^n) - LC(x^g)$
at each quantile point to the ordinate of the 45-degree line, where LC is the Lorenz
curve of post-tax or pre-tax income distributions. Similarly, the liability progression curve is constructed based on $LC(t) - LC(x^g)$, where $LC(t)$ is the Lorenz curve
of taxes paid.

34   The authors concede that the division between H and R is sensitive to the size of
the income groups used to define "equals," so that a more reliable approach may
be to view the sum of H and R as the differential tax treatment.

35   EV, a standard measure of efficiency costs, is the maximum amount of income
that an individual would pay to forgo the tax or tax change.

36   All of the tabulated impacts are relative to a proportional tax on lifetime labour
endowments, which rise with the wage rate of each lifetime income group. This is
an example of "differential tax incidence" analysis, which avoids the problems of
assuming an unbalanced budget when removing taxes, but it yields results that
are sensitive to the choice of tax that is assumed to replace the lost revenues.

37   This ranking of taxes by their efficiency costs accords roughly with that found in
several other economic studies. For a review of this literature, see Kesselman (1997,
42-49).

38   This study is unpublished, but a detailed account of it, as well as another unpublished Canadian CGE study that focuses more on methodological issues, is provided in Ruggeri and Vincent (1998, Chapter 5).

39   For reviews of these and other FINC studies, see Dahlby (1985), Vermaeten et al.
(1994, 348-55), and Ruggeri et al. (1996, 6-11).

40 The same authors also provide findings from a useful extension of this analysis to show changes in tax incidence in Canada over the period 1951 to 1988 (Vermaeten et al. 1995).

41 Authors' calculations from OECD (2002, Tables 45, 142). Federal social security funds include all contributions to CPP and EI; provincial social security funds include all contributions to QPP and hospital insurance premiums; provincial payroll taxes are classified along with tax revenues.

42 The extreme regressive findings illustrated by Whalley (1984), as shown in the right-hand column of our Table 12.8, reflect a similar economic assumption that human capital does not bear any of the tax burden.

43 If this kind of bargaining power exists, it would undermine the validity of the perfect competition assumptions that underlie the models of CGE studies.

44 Their analytical result on the tax determinants of wage pressure involve the coefficient of residual progression, $RP(x)$ as defined earlier, and hence the ATR and MTR are relevant factors.

45 See Bingley and Lanot (2002, 174-75) for a review of recent literature on PIT shifting.

46 Hence, it is the *differential* progressivity of subnational PIT systems that gives rise to the migration. If all states had the same degree of progressivity, there would be no migration, and the taxes would remain effectively progressive with full incidence of the higher rates falling on the workers.

47 The overall process is somewhat more complex, as individuals consider the public services and civic values that they enjoy in each country as well as the taxes they pay, and those taxes in turn influence the level of public services and civic values; see Kesselman (2001).

48 The sole empirical study of the relationship between Canada-United States tax differentials and migration, by Wagner (2000), found that only about 10 to 15 percent of flows to the United States could be explained by taxes.

49 A payroll tax for social insurance is a mandatory payment, unlike a user charge for a public utility, but it does have an associated benefit. This, along with political reasons, may explain why governments, and the OECD, often describe social security contributions as something other than taxes. Also see Kesselman (1997, 38-39) for discussion of the economic distinctions between benefit-linked and general payroll taxes.

50 Yet another consideration is that, if the premiums are experience-rated by firm, they may reflect benefits that are valued by firms at the same rate. For example, workers' compensation relieves firms of legal liability for civil suits related to worker injuries, so they may have no change in their demand curve for labour as a result of the combined premiums and benefits.

51   Note that the regressivity of indirect taxes is accentuated by the progressivity of the PIT, as households can spend only out of their after-PIT incomes, which are eroded by proportionally larger amounts of PIT at higher incomes.

52   Browning (1985) later applies differential tax incidence to argue that indirect taxes should be assigned to factor incomes and not transfer incomes, even abstracting from any indexation of transfer payments. This result follows from the standard assumption in differential analysis that transfers and other public outlays should be held constant in real terms when assessing the substitution of a sales tax for some other tax.

53   For further critique, see Dahlby (1985, 137), Vermaeten et al. (1994, 365), and Davies (1992, 180).

54   For analysis of the alternative views on property tax incidence, see Mieszkowksi (1972), Aaron (1975), and Kitchen (1992).

55   Property taxes also impinge on capital incomes from structures, plant, and equipment, but their incidence analysis is treated separately.

56   To the extent that the samples under-represent households with very low or temporarily very low incomes, there may be hazards in using the SLID dataset, as suggested by Frenette, Green, and Picot in Chapter 3.

57   Lerman and Yitzhaki (1995) recognize that re-ranking may improve equity by unscrambling an "unfair" pre-tax ranking of households to reflect other characteristics relevant to well-being. For the analytics of dealing with differences in characteristics and measuring horizontal inequities, see Lambert (2001, 183-86), Aronson and Lambert (1994), and Aronson et al. (1994). See Le Grand (1987) for careful discussion of the broader issues around the horizontal equity concept.

58   The discussion in this section mirrors some of the policy prescriptions in Kesselman (2004).

59   The great majority of Canadian taxpayers are already treated on a consumption basis by the personal tax due to provisions for registered savings and the non-taxation of capital gains on homes.

60   This design issue is discussed in Kesselman (2004) and Kesselman and Poschmann (2001).

REFERENCES

Aaron, Henry J. 1975. *Who Pays the Property Tax? A New View.* Washington, DC: Brookings Institution.

Aronson, J. Richard, and Peter J. Lambert. 1994. "Decomposing the Gini Coefficient to Reveal the Vertical, Horizontal, and Reranking Effects of Income Taxation." *National Tax Journal* 47(2): 273-94.

Aronson, J. Richard, Paul Johnson, and Peter J. Lambert. 1994. "Redistributive Effects and Unequal Income Tax Treatment." *Economic Journal* 104(423): 262-70.

Atkinson, A.B. 1970. "On the Measurement of Inequality." *Journal of Economic Theory* 2(3): 244-63.

—. 2004. "Increased Income Inequality in OECD Countries and the Redistributive Impact of the Government Budget." In Giovanni Andrea Cornia, ed., *Inequality, Growth, and Poverty in an Era of Liberalization and Globalization*, 221-48. Oxford: Oxford University Press.

Atkinson, A.B., Lee Rainwater, and Timothy Smeeding. 1995. *Income Distribution in OECD Countries: Evidence from the Luxembourg Income Study.* Social Policy Studies No. 18. Paris: OECD.

Auerbach, Alan J., and Laurence J. Kotlikoff. 1987. *Dynamic Fiscal Policy.* New York: Cambridge University Press.

Baum, Sandra R. 1987. "On the Measurement of Tax Progressivity: Relative Share Adjustment." *Public Finance Quarterly* 15(2): 166-87.

Beach, Charles M., and George A. Slotsve. 1996. *Are We Becoming Two Societies? Income Polarization and the Myth of the Declining Middle Class in Canada.* The Social Policy Challenge No. 12. Toronto: C.D. Howe Institute.

Beaudry, Paul, and David A. Green. 1998. *What Is Driving U.S. and Canadian Wages: Exogenous Technical Change or Endogenous Choice of Technique?* NBER Working Paper No. W6853. Cambridge, MA: National Bureau of Economic Research.

—. 2003. "Wages and Employment in the United States and Germany: What Explains the Differences?" *American Economic Review* 93(3): 573-602.

Beauséjour, Louis, G.C. Ruggeri, and Baxter Williams. 1996. "Efficiency and Distributional Effects of Flat Tax Proposals." Paper presented at 1996 conference of the Canadian Economic Association. Ottawa: Department of Finance.

Bingley, Paul, and Gauthier Lanot. 2002. "The Incidence of Income Tax on Wages and Labour Supply." *Journal of Public Economics* 83(2): 173-94.

Bishop, John A., K. Victor Chow, and John P. Formby. 1995. "The Redistributive Effect of Direct Taxes: A Comparison of Six Luxembourg Income Study Countries." *Journal of Income Distribution* 5(1): 65-90.

Blackorby, Charles, and David Donaldson. 1978. "Measures of Relative Inequality and Their Meaning in Terms of Social Welfare." *Journal of Economic Theory* 18(1): 59-80.

—. 1984. "Ethical Social Index Numbers and the Measurement of Effective Tax/Benefit Progressivity." *Canadian Journal of Economics* 17(4): 683-94.

Block, Sheila, and Richard Shillington. 1994. "Incidence of Taxes in Ontario in 1991." In Allan M. Maslove, ed., *Taxation and the Distribution of Income*, 3-39. Research Studies of the Fair Tax Commission of Ontario. Toronto: University of Toronto Press.

Blomquist, Nils S. 1981. "A Comparison of Distributions of Annual and Lifetime Income: Sweden around 1970." *Review of Income and Wealth* 27(3): 243-64.

Bradford, David F., ed., 1995. *Distributional Analysis of Tax Policy.* Washington, DC: The AEI Press.

Browning, Edgar K. 1978. "The Burden of Taxation." *Journal of Political Economy* 86(4): 649-71.

—. 1985. "Tax Incidence, Indirect Taxes, and Transfers." *National Tax Journal* 38(4): 525-33.

Browning, Edgar K., and William R. Johnson. 1979. *The Distribution of the Tax Burden.* Washington, DC: American Enterprise Institute.

Cassady, K., G.C. Ruggeri, and D. Van Wart. 1996. "On the Classification and Interpretation of Global Progressivity Measures." *Public Finance* 51(1): 1-22.

Cloutier, A. Pierre, and Bernard Fortin. 1989. "Converting Exemptions and Deductions into Credits: An Economic Assessment." In Jack Mintz and John Whalley, eds., *The Economic Impacts of Tax Reform*, 45-73. Toronto: Canadian Tax Foundation.

Dahlby, B.G. 1985. "The Incidence of Government Expenditures and Taxes in Canada: A Survey." In François Vaillancourt, ed., *Income Distribution and Economic Security in Canada*, 111-51. Research Studies of the Royal Commission on the Economic Union and Development Prospects for Canada. Toronto: University of Toronto Press.

Davies, James B. 1992. "Tax Incidence: Annual and Lifetime Perspectives in the United States and Canada." In John B. Shoven and John Whalley, eds., *Canada-U.S. Tax Comparisons*, 151-88. Chicago: University of Chicago Press.

Davies, James B., France St-Hilaire, and John Whalley. 1984. "Some Calculations of Lifetime Tax Incidence." *American Economic Review* 74(4): 633-49.

Day, Kathleen M., and Stanley L. Winer. 1994. "Internal Migration and Public Policy: An Introduction to the Issues and a Review of Empirical Research on Canada." In Allan M. Maslove, ed., *Issues in the Taxation of Individuals*, 3-61. Research Studies of the Fair Tax Commission of Ontario. Toronto: University of Toronto Press.

Devarajan, Shantayanan, Don Fullerton, and Richard A. Musgrave. 1980. "Estimating the Distribution of Tax Burdens: A Comparison of Different Approaches." *Journal of Public Economics* 13(2): 155-82.

Dodge, David A. 1975. "Impact of Tax, Transfer, and Expenditure Policies of Government on the Distribution of Personal Income in Canada." *Review of Income and Wealth* 21(1): 1-52.

Duclos, Jean-Yves. 1997. "Measuring Progressivity and Inequality." *Research on Economic Inequality* 7: 19-37.

Duclos, Jean-Yves, and Peter J. Lambert. 2000. "A Normative and Statistical Approach to Measuring Classical Horizontal Inequity." *Canadian Journal of Economics* 33(1): 87-113.

Dyck, Dagmar. 2003. *Fiscal Redistribution in Canada, 1994-2000.* Working Paper 2003-22. Ottawa: Department of Finance.

Ervik, Rune. 1998. *The Redistributive Aim of Social Policy: A Comparative Analysis of Taxes, Tax Expenditure Transfers and Direct Transfers in Eight Countries.* Working Paper 184, Luxembourg Income Studies. Syracuse, NY: Syracuse University, Maxwell School of Citizenship and Public Affairs.

Feldstein, Martin, and Marian Vaillant Wrobel. 1998. "Can State Taxes Redistribute Income?" *Journal of Public Economics* 68(3): 369-96.

Finnie, Ross. 2001. "The Brain Drain: Myth and Reality." *Choices* 7(6). Montreal: Institute for Research on Public Policy.

Fritzell, Johan. 1993. "Income Inequality Trends in the 1980's: A Five-Country Comparison." *Acta Sociologica* 36(1): 47-62.

Fullerton, Don, and Diane Lim Rogers. 1993. *Who Bears the Lifetime Tax Burden?* Washington, DC: Brookings Institution.

Fullerton, Don, and Gilbert E. Metcalf. 2002. "Tax Incidence." In Alan J. Auerbach and Martin Feldstein, eds., *Handbook of Public Economics*. Vol. 4, 1787-872. Amsterdam: North Holland.

Gale, William G., Scott Houser, and John Karl Scholz. 1996. "Distributional Effects of Fundamental Tax Reform." In Henry J. Aaron and William G. Gale, eds., *Economic Effects of Fundamental Tax Reform*, 281-320. Washington, DC: Brookings Institution.

Gillespie, W. Irwin. 1966. *The Incidence of Taxes and Public Expenditures in the Canadian Economy*. Studies of the Royal Commission on Taxation, No. 2. Ottawa: Queen's Printer.

—. 1980. *The Redistribution of Income in Canada*. Agincourt, ON: Gage Publishing, and Carleton University, Institute of Canadian Studies.

Goffman, Irving Jay. 1962. *The Burden of Canadian Taxation: Allocation of Federal, Provincial, and Local Taxes among Income Classes*. Toronto: Canadian Tax Foundation.

Goode, Richard. 1980. "The Superiority of the Income Tax." In Joseph A. Pechman, ed., *What Should Be Taxed: Income or Expenditure?* 49-73. Washington, DC: Brookings Institution.

Gottschalk, Peter, and Timothy M. Smeeding. 2000. "Empirical Evidence on Income Inequality in Industrialized Countries." In Anthony B. Atkinson and François Bourguignon, eds., *Handbook of Income Distribution*. Vol. 1, 261-307. New York and Oxford: Elsevier Science, North-Holland.

Gravelle, Jane G. 2001. "Economic Issues Affecting Across-the-Board Tax Cuts." *Tax Notes* 90 (January 15): 367-82.

Jakobsson, Ulf. 1976. "On the Measurement of the Degree of Progression." *Journal of Public Economics* 5(1-2): 161-68.

Jäntti, Markus. 1997. "Inequality in Five Countries in the 1980s: The Role of Demographic Shifts, Markets and Government Policies." *Economica* 64(255): 415-40.

Kakwani, Nanak C. 1977. "Measurement of Tax Progressivity: An International Comparison." *Economic Journal* 87(345): 71-80.

—. 1984. "On the Measurement of Tax Progressivity and Redistributive Effect of Taxes with Applications to Horizontal and Vertical Equity." *Advances in Econometrics* 3: 149-68.

Kesselman, Jonathan R. 1997. *General Payroll Taxes: Economics, Politics, and Design*. Toronto: Canadian Tax Foundation.

—. 2000. "Flat Taxes, Dual Taxes, Smart Taxes: Making the Best Choices." *Policy Matters* 1(7). Montreal: Institute for Research on Public Policy.

—. 2001. "Policies to Stem the Brain Drain – Without Americanizing Canada." *Canadian Public Policy* 27(1): 77-93.

—. 2004. "Tax Design for a Northern Tiger." *Choices* 10(1). Montreal: Institute for Research on Public Policy.

Kesselman, Jonathan R., and Finn Poschmann. 2001. "Expanding the Recognition of Personal Savings in the Canadian Tax System." *Canadian Tax Journal* 49(1): 40-101.

Kiefer, Donald W. 1984. "Distributional Tax Progressivity Indexes." *National Tax Journal* 37(4): 497-513.

Kitchen, Harry M. 1992. *Property Taxation in Canada.* Toronto: Canadian Tax Foundation.

Kotlikoff, Laurence J., and Lawrence H. Summers. 1987. "Tax Incidence." In Alan J. Auerbach and Martin Feldstein, eds., *Handbook of Public Economics.* Vol. 2, 1043-92. Amsterdam: North Holland.

Lambert, Peter J. 2001. *The Distribution and Redistribution of Income.* 3rd ed. Manchester: Manchester University Press.

Lambert, Peter J., and Wilhelm Pfähler. 1992. "Income Tax Progression and Redistributive Effect: The Influence of Changes in the Pre-Tax Income Distribution." *Public Finance* 47(1): 1-16.

Le Grand, Julian. 1987. "Equity, Well-Being, and Economic Choice." *Journal of Human Resources* 22(3): 429-40.

Lerman, Robert I., and Shlomo Yitzhaki. 1995. "Changing Ranks and the Inequality Impacts of Taxes and Transfers." *National Tax Journal* 48(1): 45-59.

Litchfield, Julie A. 1999. "Inequality: Methods and Tools." At the World Bank's PovertyNet website on Inequality, Poverty, and Socio-economic Performance: http://www1.worldbank.org/prem/poverty/inequal/methods/litchfie.pdf.

Lockwood, Ben, and Alan Manning. 1993. "Wage Setting and the Tax System: Theory and Evidence for the United Kingdom." *Journal of Public Economics* 52(1): 1-29.

Mieszkowski, Peter. 1972. "The Property Tax: An Excise Tax or a Profits Tax?" *Journal of Public Economics* 1(1): 73-96.

Mincer, Jacob. 1974. *Schooling, Experience and Earnings.* New York: Columbia University Press.

Montmarquette, Claude. 1974. "A Note on Income (Labor) Inequality: Income Tax Systems and Human Capital Theory." *Journal of Political Economy* 82(3): 620-25.

Murphy, Kevin M., W. Craig Riddell, and Paul M. Romer. 1998. "Wages, Skills, and Technology in the United States and Canada." In Elhanan Helpman, ed., *General Purpose Technologies and Economic Growth,* 283-309. Cambridge, MA: MIT Press.

Musgrave, R.A., and Tun Thin. 1948. "Income Tax Progression, 1929-48." *Journal of Political Economy* 56(6): 498-514.

Musgrave, R.A., J.J. Carroll, L.D. Cook, and L. Frane. 1951. "Distribution of Tax Payments by Income Groups: A Case Study for 1948." *National Tax Journal* 4(1): 1-53.

Myles, Gareth D. 1995. *Public Economics*. Cambridge: Cambridge University Press.

OECD (Organisation for Economic Co-operation and Development). 2002. *Revenue Statistics, 1965-2001*. Paris: OECD.

Payette, Micheline, and François Vaillancourt. 1986. "L'incidence des recettes et dépenses gouvernementales au Québec en 1981." *L'Actualité Économique* 62(3): 409-41.

Pechman, Joseph A. 1985. *Who Paid the Taxes, 1966-85?* Washington, DC: Brookings Institution.

Pechman, Joseph A., and Benjamin A. Okner. 1974. *Who Bears the Tax Burden?* Washington, DC: Brookings Institution.

Pendakur, Krishna. 2002. "Taking Prices Seriously in the Measurement of Inequality." *Journal of Public Economics* 86(1): 47-69.

Podder, Nripesh. 1997. "Tax Elasticity, Income Redistribution and the Measurement of Tax Progressivity." *Research on Economic Inequality* 7: 39-60.

Reynolds, Morgan O., and Eugene Smolensky. 1977. *Public Expenditures, Taxes, and the Distribution of Income: The United States, 1950, 1961, 1970*. New York: Academic Press.

Ruggeri, G.C., and K. Bluck. 1990. "On the Incidence of the Manufacturers' Sales Tax and the Goods and Services Tax." *Canadian Public Policy* 16(4): 359-73.

Ruggeri, G.C., R. Howard, and D. Van Wart. 1996. *The Government as Robin Hood: Exploring the Myth*. Kingston, ON: Queen's University, School of Policy Studies; Ottawa: Caledon Institute of Social Policy.

Ruggeri, G.C., D. Van Wart, and R. Howard. 1994. "The Redistributional Impact of Taxation in Canada." *Canadian Tax Journal* 42(2): 417-51.

Ruggeri, G.C., and Carole Vincent. 1998. *An Economic Analysis of Income Tax Reforms*. Aldershot, UK: Ashgate.

Shoven, John B., and John Whalley. 1984. "Applied General-Equilibrium Models of Taxation and International Trade: An Introduction and Survey." *Journal of Economic Literature* 22(3): 1007-51.

Smeeding, Timothy M., et al. (8 co-authors) 1993. "Poverty, Inequality, and Family Living Standards Impacts across Seven Nations: The Effect of Noncash Subsidies for Health, Education and Housing." *Review of Income and Wealth* 39(3): 229-56.

Statistics Canada. 1996, 1999. *Income after Tax, Distributions by Size in Canada*. Catalogue no. 13-210-XPB. Ottawa: Statistics Canada, Income Statistics Division.

—. 2001, 2002. *Income in Canada, 1999, and 2000*. Catalogue no. 75-202-XPE. Ottawa: Statistics Canada, Income Statistics Division.

Summers, Lawrence A. 1989. "Some Simple Economics of Mandated Benefits." *American Economic Review* 79(2): 177-83.

US Congressional Budget Office. 2001. *Effective Federal Tax Rates, 1979-1997*. Washington, DC: Congress of the United States.

Vaillancourt, François, and Nicolas Marceau. 1990. "Do General and Firm-Specific Employer Payroll Taxes Have the Same Incidence?" *Economics Letters* 34(2): 175-81.

Veldhuis, Niels, and Michael Walker. 2006. *Tax Facts 14*. Vancouver, BC: Fraser Institute.

Vermaeten, Arndt, W. Irwin Gillespie, and Frank Vermaeten. 1995. "Who Paid the Taxes in Canada, 1951-1988?" *Canadian Public Policy* 21(3): 317-43.

Vermaeten, Frank, W. Irwin Gillespie, and Arndt Vermaeten. 1994. "Tax Incidence in Canada." *Canadian Tax Journal* 42(2): 348-416.

Wagner, Donald Mark. 2000. "Do Tax Differences Contribute toward the Brain Drain from Canada to the U.S.?" Chapter 3 in "Essays on the Mobility of Goods and People." PhD thesis. Vancouver, BC, University of British Columbia, Faculty of Commerce and Business Administration, 77-112.

Wagstaff, Adam, et al. (25 co-authors) 1999. "Redistributive Effect, Progressivity and Differential Tax Treatment: Personal Income Taxes in Twelve OECD Countries." *Journal of Public Economics* 72(1): 73-98.

Wagstaff, Adam, and Eddy Van Doorslaer. 2001. "What Makes the Personal Income Tax Progressive? A Comparative Analysis of Fifteen OECD Countries." *International Tax and Public Finance* 8(3): 299-315.

Whalley, John. 1984. "Regression or Progression: The Taxing Question of Incidence Analysis." *Canadian Journal of Economics* 17(4): 654-82.

Wildasin, David E. 2000. "Factor Mobility and Fiscal Policy in the EU: Issues and Analytical Approaches." *Economic Policy* 15(31): 337-78.

Wolfson, M., and B. Murphy. 2000. "Income Inequality in North America: Does the 49th Parallel Still Matter?" *Canadian Economic Observer* (August), 3.1-3.24. Ottawa: Statistics Canada.

Zandvakili, Sourushe. 1994. "Income Distribution and Redistribution through Taxation: An International Comparison." *Empirical Economics* 19(3): 473-91.

13
Dis-embedding Liberalism? The New Social Policy Paradigm in Canada

Keith G. Banting

> If you don't know where you are going, you may end up
> somewhere else.
>
> – YOGI BERRA

A new paradigm has come to dominate social policy debates in Canada. As in many western nations, the understandings that underpinned the postwar welfare state have given way to new ideas about the social problems facing us in a global era and the appropriate responses to them. The postwar strategy has been described as "embedded liberalism," because it combined liberalization of the economy with the expansion of social security programs designed to provide economic security for the population as a whole. The new paradigm embraces further waves of economic liberalization but advocates a different approach to economic security. Rather than trying to protect individuals from economic disruptions through a variety of instruments, especially income transfer programs, the new social policy places greater emphasis on providing citizens with the knowledge and skills required to prosper in a knowledge-based, global economy. Wherever possible, we are told, the primary goal of policy reform should be investing in human capital rather than redistributing income.

The pervasiveness of these core ideas in policy-making circles in OECD countries is striking, and Canada has embraced the new discourse with particular enthusiasm. The analysis, assumptions, and priorities of the approach reverberate in policy documents and political speeches in federal and provincial capitals. Canadian social policy is seldom made in large, radical steps (Battle 2001), but the broad directions of incremental change in our social programs parallel this approach.

Whenever a set of ideas gains such predominance, it cries out for critical analysis. The essential question for those interested in such values as equality, security, and community concerns the impact of this new approach to social policy. Is this strategy simply a new means of pursuing traditional social goals, in effect re-embedding liberalism by deploying instruments better suited to the new economy? Or does this new paradigm dis-embed liberalism by retreating from the postwar commitment to social protection and economic security for the population as a whole?

This chapter argues that we are in real danger of dis-embedding liberalism. Our current strategy faces two weaknesses. The first weakness is one of execution. In practice, Canadian governments have proven readier to reduce income transfer protections than to reinforce their commitment to education and training, and they are shifting the burden of investing in human capital increasingly to private shoulders. Moreover, they have been guilty of the most common of political weaknesses – impatience. A serious strategy focused on enhancing the human capital of Canadians will take at least a generation, if not more, to bear fruit, and a transition from a redistributive to an investment strategy needs very long time horizons. Reducing transfers first has the historical sequence exactly backwards, and it exposes the unskilled of today, especially older workers, to a harsher world with weakened protection systems.

Even if these failures of execution were overcome, an investment strategy faces deeper challenges. Despite the complexity of some income support programs, people from all social backgrounds can generally access benefits to which they are entitled. In comparison, effective participation in human capital strategies is conditioned by the social context in which a child is born and matures. As much as we would like to believe otherwise, a child's life chances and educational attainment are strongly influenced by family background and social context. Education and other learning systems do not compensate fully for the problems of poverty and inequality, or for differences in the cultural capital that families bring to their children's development. Although levels of participation in education are rising among children of all social backgrounds, a stubborn gap persists between the relative educational attainments of children from advantaged and disadvantaged backgrounds. This education gap is not going away. As a result, a strategic shift from income redistribution to human capital involves a shift from an instrument readily accessible to all Canadians to one in which the accidents of birth and family background matter a lot. This is hardly a recipe for a fair society.

What follows from this? Clearly, investing in human capital is central to any viable conception of security in the economy of today, and there is a critical agenda here, especially in areas where Canada is an international laggard, such as early childhood education and adult retraining. But income transfers will also remain essential to any approach to economic security that responds to the needs of all Canadians. There is no escape from traditional concerns about poverty and the legitimate need for economic security among those who do not possess the magic keys to the modern economy. The chapter therefore concludes that a compelling challenge before us is to integrate investment and redistribution by designing a redistributive complement to a human capital strategy.

This argument unfolds as follows. We begin with a brief discussion of the postwar strategy of embedded liberalism and then highlight the distinctive features of the new paradigm. Next we examine the extent to which the new approach has been implemented in Canada, focusing first on income transfers and then on education and training. Finally we review the main threads of our recent experience and their implications for the patterns of equality, security, and community in the generations to come.

Then and Now: The Postwar Paradigm and the New Social Policy

The basic social and economic strategy of the postwar era has been described by John Ruggie (1983, 1994) as "embedded liberalism." On one side, governments encouraged the liberalization of the economy through deregulation and successive rounds of the GATT, slowly breaking down the regulatory regimes and barriers to trade that were put in place during the Depression and the Second World War. On the other side, the expansion of social programs compensated for the risks inherent in economic liberalization. In Ruggie's words: "governments asked their publics to embrace the change and dislocation that comes with liberalization in return for the promise of help in containing and socializing the adjustment costs" (Ruggie 1994, 4-5).[1] It is perhaps not surprising in this context that smaller countries with comparatively open economies tended to develop more expansive social programs as a means of cushioning workers and their domestic society more generally from economic shocks originating outside their borders (Cameron 1978; Katzenstein 1983, 1985; Rodrik 1997).

The builders of the postwar welfare state used a full set of tools. The foundation stone for Keynes, Beveridge, Marsh, and the Swedish social democrats alike was full employment, or "high and stable levels of employment," to use the more cautious language of the federal government's 1945 white paper on employment and income (Canada 1945). An impressive set of social programs was built on this foundation. A rapidly growing education system would expand equality of opportunity, and comprehensive health insurance would spread the benefits of health care to the population as a whole. And a full range of income transfer programs – unemployment insurance, workers' compensation, disability benefits, old age pensions, survivors' benefits, children's allowances, and social assistance – would protect citizens from the economic risks associated with modern life.

The fundamental purpose of this postwar social contract was *economic security*. The touchstone for the builders of the welfare state was the Depression of the 1930s, with its mass dislocation and widespread economic insecurity; and their aim was to protect citizens from what they saw as the universal risks associated with a market economy. This quest for security pervaded the Marsh Report, which laid the intellectual foundations for the welfare state in Canada. Writing at the height of a world war, Marsh summed up the case for the welfare state as follows: "The general sense of security which would result from such programs would provide a better life for the great mass of people and a potent antidote to the fears and worries and uncertainties of the times. The post-war world would not have to be anticipated with fear and trepidation" (Marsh 1943, 17).

The risks, it is important to note, were considered to confront virtually the entire population, not just a specific group labelled "the poor." As a result, security became associated with the concepts of social rights and universality, and it was embodied in programs such as demogrants and social insurance for health care and income stabilization. The priority was predictability and security for the population as a whole. In contrast, vertical redistribution from the rich to the poor was a secondary goal. Indeed, if anything, the postwar paradigm represented a shift away from vertical redistribution as the primary goal of social policy. Whatever else one might say about the social programs of the interwar years, such as the 1927 Old Age Pension Act, Mothers' Allowances, and local relief, their primary goal was to redistribute money toward groups of the poor seen as morally worthy. They provided selective, means-tested benefits that were financed from general revenues. In contrast, the universal programs put in place from the 1940s to the 1970s shifted redistribution primarily in a horizontal direction: from the employed to the unemployed, from the healthy to the sick, from the young to the elderly, from the childless to families with children, and so on. As a secondary feature, universal programs financed through progressive taxation did have a mildly redistributive impact between the rich and poor. However, that was not the primary aim.

By international standards, the Canadian version of the postwar welfare state was a modest enterprise. As Table 13.1 indicates, social expenditures in 1980 represented a smaller proportion of GDP than in other affluent democracies generally, and levels of child poverty and inequality in Canada remained comparatively high. In terms of the typology developed by Gøsta Esping-Andersen (1990), Canada clustered with other "liberal" welfare states, such as Australia, the United Kingdom, and the United States, a group that stood in striking contrast to the more expansive "corporatist" and "social-democratic" welfare states of continental Europe. Nevertheless, the postwar welfare state in Canada did represent an effort to balance economic liberalization and economic security, one that contributed to a relatively broad political consensus underpinning the role of the state for almost half a century.

TABLE 13.1

The postwar welfare state, Canada in comparative perspective, 1980 or near year

Country	Social expenditures (% of GDP)	Child poverty rate (%)	Inequality (Gini)
Australia	11.3	13.8	0.281
Austria	23.3	4.8	0.227
Belgium	24.2	4.0	0.227
Canada	13.3	14.8	0.284
Denmark	29.1	4.7	0.254
Finland	18.5	2.8	0.209
France	21.1	7.2	0.288
Germany	20.3	2.8	0.244
Netherlands	27.3	2.7	0.260
Norway	18.6	4.8	0.223
Sweden	29.0	4.8	0.197
United Kingdom	18.2	9.0	0.270
United States	13.1	20.4	0.318
Average	20.6	7.4	0.251

NOTE: The poverty rate is set at 50 per cent of median adjusted disposable income for all persons. The inequality measure is based on household disposable income.
SOURCE: Data on public social expenditures are from OECD SocX data set (http://www.oecd.org); data on child poverty and inequality are from the Luxembourg Income Study (http://www.lisproject.org).

Fast forward to the contemporary period. Beginning in the 1980s and gathering momentum in the 1990s, a new social policy discourse has come to dominate policy debates in western nations. This intellectual transition has been driven by the major economic and political forces of our time. During this period, governments of all persuasions found it increasingly difficult to sustain full employment, and the focus of labour market strategies increasingly shifted from the demand side to the supply side. This trend was reinforced by economic globalization, technological change, and the emergence of a knowledge-based economy, factors which place a premium on flexibility in labour markets and effective adjustment to new forms of production. And at the level of political ideas, neoliberal doctrines called for further deregulation of economic relationships from regulatory constraints and celebrated a culture of greater individual responsibility for meeting social needs.

At its heart, the new paradigm represents a different conception of the sources of security in an insecure world. In policy circles, security no longer means protection from disruption inherent in the market. Such security as is available in the contemporary world is seen as flowing from the capacity to participate in the market and to adapt to a changing global economy. At the level of ideas, the transition is from security as protection *from* change, to security as the capacity *to* change; and at the level of policy design, the challenge is to transform social policy into an instrument of change by trimming historic protections, strengthening incentives to adjust, and equipping citizens to cope more effectively with economic transitions.

This paradigm points to a rebalancing of the social policy instruments created in the postwar era, with a reduction in reliance on income transfers and increased investment in human capital. On the first side, the new approach argues that social programs should be employment-friendly, encouraging engagement in the labour force. Restrictive labour legislation and practices should be relaxed; the tax and transfer system should be restructured to reduce welfare dependency; incentives to engage in employment should be strengthened to "make work pay"; support for the unemployed should move from "passive" transfers to "active" programs that encourage re-engagement in the labour force; and in some versions of the argument, family support systems such as child care should also be strengthened to help people, especially women, enter the labour market.

On the second side, this approach insists that education and training are the real source of security in a technological economy. Knowledge workers are likely to enjoy rising incomes, challenging work, mobility on an international level, and a secure future; low-skill workers are likely to face declining real incomes, precarious employment, and an uncertain future. As a result, a country's learning systems are critical to both economic competitiveness and social equity. Policy attention, according to this approach, should focus in particular on children, to ensure that they have a rich learning environment, especially in the early childhood years. In addition, young people should be educated to higher levels than in the past, and learning should become a life-long process. Citizens should continually upgrade their skills, and training programs should re-equip older workers who have been displaced by the forces of "creative destruction" inherent in economic growth.

In this new world, traditional concerns with greater equality of outcomes give way to a discourse focused on social inclusion. Even in its centre-left versions, the new paradigm places less emphasis on a more equal distribution of income as such. As Saint-Martin (2000, 43) points out, the dichotomy that orients the new discourse is not equality/inequality, but social inclusion/exclusion; and Giddens (1998, 102) agrees that "the new politics defines equality as inclusion and inequality as exclusion." The spotlight is thus trained on special barriers confronting vulnerable groups such as single parents, immigrants who have arrived in recent years, Aboriginal peoples, and disabled Canadians. It is important to underscore, however, that the new paradigm assumes that inclusion is achieved through movement into the paid labour force, and that growing inequality among paid workers is of secondary interest.[2]

As noted earlier, the pervasiveness of these ideas in social policy discourse is striking. At the international level, this approach was led by the OECD, especially through its *Jobs Study* and the stream of successor documents (OECD 1994a, 1994b, 1994c, 1995, 1996, 1999a). The shift is also central to the politics of the "third way," the redefinition of the political left in Britain and several other European countries. Authors such as Giddens have articulated a social-democratic version of the argument, suggesting that welfare expenditures should remain at European rather than American levels, but should be switched as far as possible from income redistribution to investment in human capital, replacing the traditional welfare state with a "social investment state" (Giddens 1998, 2000, 2001).

The same themes pervade Canadian policy discourse. In the words of a leading policy economist, "we are presented with a historically unprecedented societal window, since a commitment to a human capital future is emerging as the principal avenue by which to succeed on both the economic competitiveness and social cohesion fronts" (Courchene 2001, 154;

see also Courchene 2002 and Hicks 2002). Government planning documents articulate similar views. In 1994, the federal government launched a major review of income security programs arguing that "the tumultuous social and economic changes of the past decade and a half have left us with a system that is out of date and in need of reform. The system is geared to help people where change was the exception, not the rule, so it does too little to help people to adjust to change" (Human Resources Development Canada 1994, 21). Almost a decade later, the federal innovation strategy placed the spotlight squarely on knowledge and skills development as the key to the economic future for citizens and the country as a whole (Human Resources Development Canada 2002; see also Advisory Council on Science and Technology 2000). At the provincial level, advisory bodies similarly advocate a "human capital society" (Ontario 2004; also Ontario 1990). At the political level, the federal finance minister argued in 1999 that "providing security and opportunity for Canadians in the future means investing in their skills, in their knowledge and their capacity to learn ... In a real sense, good skills are an essential part of the social safety net of the future" (Martin 1999).

Einstein once observed that "everything has changed except our ideas." In the case of social policy, it is clear that at least some of our ideas have changed. The question is whether our actions have also changed. To what extent has the new approach influenced social programs since the early 1980s? And what have been the results? The next sections pursue these questions by examining the restructuring of income transfer programs and then developments in education and training.

Income Transfers

Canada has emerged as a poster child for the new social policy in the field of income transfers.[3] While pension programs for the elderly have changed little, virtually every program with more direct implications for labour market performance has been restructured in important ways, reducing the levels of economic security provided to beneficiaries. Within this process, the biggest changes were felt in unemployment insurance and social assistance.

In many ways, unemployment insurance was the bellwether program, providing the earliest evidence that the tide of history was turning. A limited unemployment insurance program had originally been introduced in 1940 and then expanded in a long series of incremental steps in the decades that followed, with a particularly significant enrichment coming in 1971. This last step turned out to be one of the last major social policy reforms of the postwar era. The expanded program quickly came under intense criticism from policy analysts and conservative political voices, who argued that the benefits increased the structural rate of unemployment, especially in poorer regions of the country. Slowly at the beginning and then with increasing force, the expansion of 1971 was rolled back. Cuts in benefit levels proceeded slice by slice, reducing the replacement rate from the high of 66 percent of previous earnings set in 1971 to 60 percent in 1978, 57 percent in 1993, 55 percent for some workers in 1994, and 50 percent for repeat beneficiaries in 1996 (although offset for some recipients by an increased family supplement). In addition, changes in the 1990s tightened eligibility requirements, reduced the duration of benefits, introduced limited experience rating for repeat beneficiaries, and deepened the clawback of benefits through the tax system from beneficiaries with annual incomes above a certain threshold. Some critics were disappointed that the changes did not go further in eliminating the regional differences in the program that created a more generous benefit structure in regions of high unemployment. Nevertheless, the OECD judged these to be "impressive reforms," which dealt with "nearly all of the concerns expressed by the *Jobs Strategy*" (OECD 1999b, 57). As Figure 13.1

FIGURE 13.1

Recipients of unemployment insurance benefits as a proportion of unemployed persons, Canada and the US, 1985-99

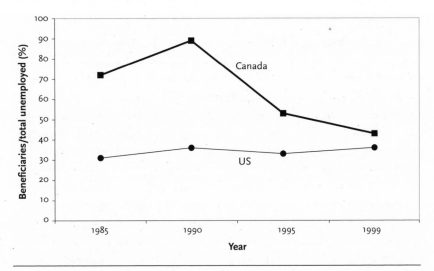

SOURCE: Data kindly supplied by Gerard Boychuk.

FIGURE 13.2

Unemployment insurance generosity index, Canadian provinces and US states, 1995 and 1999

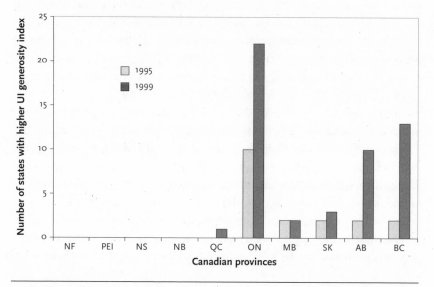

NOTE: The generosity index multiplies the beneficiary rate (beneficiaries as a proportion of total unemployed) by the replacement rate (average weekly benefits as a proportion of average weekly wages).

SOURCE: Boychuk and Banting (2003).

indicates, the changes contributed to a sharp drop in the portion of the unemployed who receive unemployment benefits, producing a massive convergence on norms in the United States.[4] Indeed, given the regional variation in the Canadian program, this overall convergence understates the change in Canada west of the Ottawa River. As Figure 13.2 confirms, by the late 1990s the Canadian unemployment insurance program in those provinces was less generous than were the programs operating in many American states.

Social assistance programs also underwent considerable retrenchment. In most provinces, benefit levels were relatively stable in the second half of the 1980s, and, in the case of Ontario, successive Liberal and NDP governments significantly raised benefits and relaxed eligibility requirements in the in the early 1990s (Courchene with Telmer 1998). The rest of the decade and the early 2000s, however, witnessed serious retrenchment. The intensity of the changes varied across the provinces, with the steepest and sharpest reductions

coming in Ontario when a new Conservative government reversed the increases of its predecessors. Nevertheless, the direction of change was consistent across the country. The real value of benefits fell, in many instances by
large amounts. In addition, eligibility rules were tightened in most provinces, especially for new entrants; and administrative procedures were tough-
ened with the employment of additional monitors and the opening of "snitch"
lines (Finnie et al. 2004a; National Council of Welfare 2000).

Nor did social assistance recipients benefit from the only significant enrichment in the transfer system during the 1990s. As federal finances came
back into balance late in the decade, the government ramped up the Canada
Child Tax Benefit, an income-tested payment delivered each month to low-
income and middle-income families. The primary goal of the increases was
to reduce poverty among working-poor families. In the case of welfare families, however, the increases were largely offset by the provinces as part of a
joint federal-provincial strategy to "make work pay." As noted earlier, making work pay is an integral component of the new social policy paradigm

FIGURE 13.3

**Average welfare income, single parents and one child (2003 constant dollars),
1986-2003**

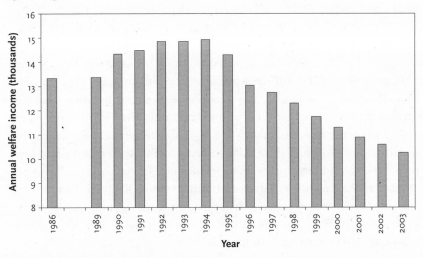

NOTE: Welfare income includes social assistance and child benefits. Average welfare
income is the average of provincial welfare incomes weighted by provincial populations.
SOURCE: Data on welfare incomes are from National Council of Welfare (2004). Data
on provincial populations are from Statistics Canada, Table 051-00011,2.

FIGURE 13.4

Average welfare income for single employables (2003 constant dollars), 1986-2003

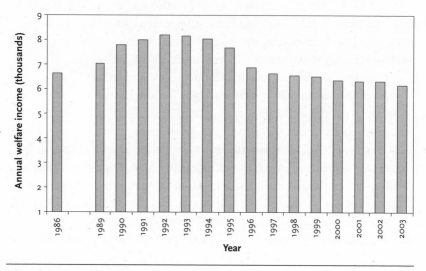

NOTE: See note to Figure 13.3.
SOURCE: See source for Figure 13.3.

(Myles and Pierson 1997; Battle and Mendelson 2001; Myles and Quadagno 2000). The basic federal-provincial strategy was simple. As the federal Child Tax Benefit was increased, most provincial governments reduced the child component of their social assistance benefits by the same amount, leaving welfare families in the same net position. The long-term goal was to "take kids off welfare" completely, and provinces agreed to reinvest the resulting savings in child-related services, such as child care. This restructuring represented an improvement in many ways. It would ensure that social assistance recipients do not lose all their child-related benefits when moving into low-paid work; it would reduce the financial incentive for low-wage workers with children to leave work for welfare; and families would hopefully benefit from enhanced child-related services. What the restructuring could not do, however, was cushion the decline in the income of social assistance recipients relative to that of the wider community.

The decline was dramatic for some welfare recipients. Figure 13.3 tracks the evolution of the average income (social assistance and child benefits) for a single parent with one child. The national average rose in the early 1990s, reflecting the enrichment of the program in Ontario, but then declined

FIGURE 13.5

Average welfare income as a proportion of average family income, 1989-2002

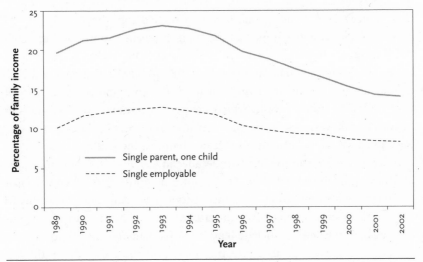

NOTE: See note to Figure 13.3. Average provincial family income is for economic families of two or more.
SOURCE: Data on average welfare incomes are from National Council of Welfare (2003). Data on average provincial family incomes are from Statistics Canada, CANSIM, table 202-0403.

precipitously, falling well below the level prevailing in the mid-1980s. Admittedly, not all categories saw such a dramatic decline. Figure 13.4 provides the same tracking for single employables; here the decline was less pronounced, presumably because support was already very low, representing about $500 a month in 2003 dollars. Figure 13.5 makes the point in another way, showing average welfare incomes for these two groups as a proportion of the average income enjoyed by families generally. By the dawn of the new century, Canada was providing less than in earlier times to those dependent on social assistance.

Other programs were restructured as well. Workers' compensation and disability benefits were changed to reduce the possibility that they would become a *de facto* early retirement program, especially for older, low-skilled workers displaced by technological or other economic shocks. Eligibility for disability benefits under the federal Canada Pension Plan and provincial social assistance programs was tightened to reflect more narrowly defined medical criteria and to de-emphasize the use of socioeconomic factors in allowing benefits (OECD 1999b, 58).

Clearly, the restructuring of income transfers has been pervasive. Indeed, when the OECD assessed the extent to which member countries had embraced their strategy, Canada stood among those who had gone the furthest (OECD 1999a). The cumulative impact of the changes has been a weakening of the redistributive role of the Canadian state. Figure 13.6 tracks the level of inequality among Canadian families from 1980 to 2002 for three definitions of income: market income, which includes earnings and other sources of private income; total income, which includes government income transfer payments; and disposable income, which reflects the impact of both taxes and transfers. As in virtually all western nations, inequality in market incomes has grown over the last two decades in Canada. The Canadian state offset this growth in market inequality until the mid-1990s, when the most significant reductions in income transfers took place. After that, inequality in disposable income began to drift upwards. Moreover, the measure of inequality used here, the Gini coefficient, tends to be particularly sensitive to changes around the mean, and other measures that focus more directly on the top

FIGURE 13.6

Inequality among families, three measures of income, 1980-2002

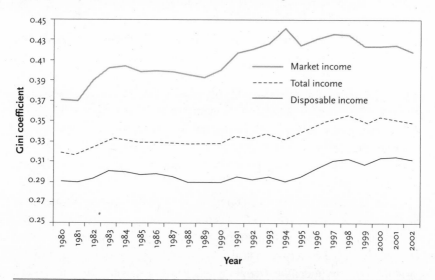

SOURCE: Statistics Canada (2004).

and bottom of the income scale point to a greater widening in the gap between rich and poor (Atkinson 2003). The growth in inequality in Canada may not have been as dramatic as it has been in countries such as the United States and the United Kingdom. But the direction of change was the same.

As noted earlier, however, the primary goal of the postwar welfare state was less redistribution from rich to poor than economic security for the population as a whole. The issue from this perspective is therefore whether income security programs continue to protect Canadians from economic reverses resulting from important risks inherent in modern life, such as unemployment, ill health, retirement, and so on. One answer to this question can be derived from the index of economic security developed by Osberg and Sharpe (2002). This measure is based on four specific risks: unemployment, illness, single-female parenthood, and old age. A sub-index is calculated for each of these risks on the basis of both the proportion of the population affected by the risk and the extent to which government transfers offset income losses associated with the risk. For example, the economic risk associated with unemployment is calculated as the product of the risk of unemployment and the extent to which people are protected from income losses during jobless spells by unemployment benefits. The four sub-indices are then integrated into an overall index of economic security. Figure 13.7 tracks changes in the index of economic security between 1989 and 2003, comparing it with changes in two other measures of economic performance, overall consumption and the level of wealth, in the same period. As one can see, in an era in which overall consumption and wealth were growing in Canada, economic security was eroding.[5]

Thus, Canadian policy-makers have embraced the new discourse in income security programs. The commitment to economic security through income transfers has weakened, and Canadians face the future with a more limited version of the income security system developed by the postwar generation. They will increasingly have to look elsewhere for the well-springs of economic security in an uncertain world. Is investment in human capital filling the gap?

Investing in Human Capital

Education and training are hardly new components of the welfare state. Historically, liberal welfare states saw the expansion of educational systems as enhancing equality of opportunity and supplying the well-educated workforce needed for economic growth. Social-democratic welfare states of northern

FIGURE 13.7

Trend in economic security, 1989-2003

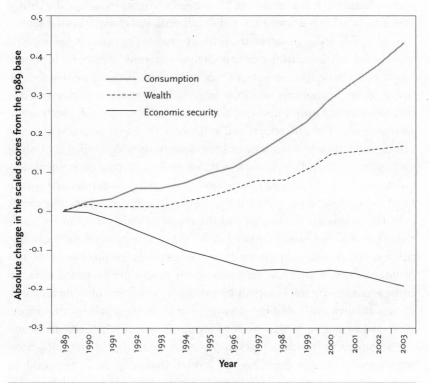

NOTE: Absolute change in scaled scores from 1989 base.
SOURCE: Data kindly supplied by the Centre for the Study of Living Standards.

Europe went further, seeing educational reform as a pathway to greater equality of condition; raising the skill levels of the bottom third of the labour force increased their productivity, employment opportunities, and wages relative to those of the better educated (Esping-Andersen 1990).

Canada invested heavily in advanced education during the postwar era. The university sector grew rapidly, and participation rates rose dramatically, primarily because of the movement of young women into universities. In addition, Canada created a system of vocationally oriented community colleges, significantly increasing postsecondary educational opportunities for those not bound for university. In this period, Canada became an international leader in educational expenditures. In the mid-1990s, the country was devoting approximately 7 percent of GDP to education, the highest among the G7 countries and the fourth highest in the OECD, exceeded only by three Scandinavian countries (OECD 2000).

As a result, Canada might seem to be an exemplar of the new social model. Almost half of Canadians have completed a university degree or college program, and Canada leads OECD countries in the number of years of tertiary education that seventeen-year-old women and men complete. Yet, closer inspection does reveal weaknesses. We have a surprisingly large number of students who do not complete high school. Additionally, our impressive completion rates at the tertiary level reflect the size of the college sector rather than university completion, which is closer to the OECD average and significantly below that of the United States.[6] Nevertheless, Canadians perform strongly on direct measures of adult skills. In the International Adult Literacy Survey, conducted in twelve OECD member countries, Canadians, especially young Canadians, performed comparatively well (OECD 1998a, Figure 2.3). In the words of one Canadian study, "by commonly employed measures, recent cohorts of young adults are among the most highly educated in the world" (Riddell and Sweetman 2001, 85). The OECD concurs: "Canada has one of the most highly-educated populations among industrial countries" (OECD 1999b, 60).

Moreover, advanced education does seem to produce greater economic security for those who receive the training. Studies of the returns to education have explored the incomes and employment patterns of skilled and unskilled labour in industrial nations. In general, skilled workers enjoy stronger employment prospects, and in some countries, especially the United States, the wage premium enjoyed by highly educated workers has been rising steadily during the last two decades. In Canada, a significant expansion in the supply of educated workers has meant that the earnings differential between more-educated and less-educated workers has changed only modestly (Riddell and Sweetman 2001; Sweetman 2002). In the longer term, however, the premium to skills seems likely to grow in Canada, as it has elsewhere.

Does this mean that education and training instruments represent a functional equivalent to income transfers in providing economic security for the population as a whole? Are education and training fulfilling the expectations that swirl around them in the current policy debates? Here the difficulties begin to emerge. Although Canada may rank among educational leaders in the OECD, close to half of all young Canadians still do not complete post-secondary education, leaving them facing the future without the keys to the new economy and with diminished protection from transfer programs. If a human capital strategy is to be meaningful, it must go a lot further. But two types of constraints limit movement forward: weaknesses of execution and weaknesses intrinsic to the strategy itself. Both deserve closer attention.

EXECUTION: THE PUBLIC/PRIVATE BALANCE

Despite the rhetoric of a knowledge-based society, Canada has not been reinforcing its collective investment in education and training. Financial support for advanced educational institutions weakened on a per student basis during the 1990s. But the real hallmark of the decade was an emphasis on private rather than collective responsibility for the development of human capital. This pattern can be glimpsed from several rungs of the educational ladder.

The pattern starts in the pre-school years. Contemporary research emphasizes the importance of childhood learning as a key to the long-term success of a human-capital strategy. Yet, in the euphemistic words of an OECD review team, Canadian policy on early childhood education is still "in its initial stages" (OECD 2004, 6). Deeply held assumptions define the education and care of young children primarily as a private responsibility of individual families rather than a collective task demanding strong public support. As a result, parents contribute a comparatively high portion of the total costs, perhaps twice the European average. In addition, the "education" and "care" of young children have developed separately. Child care tends to be seen as a means of freeing up parents to work in the paid labour force, and early childhood education is underdeveloped.[7] As Table 13.2 indicates, both the proportion of children in pre-primary education and the level of expenditure on such education are low not only by general international standards but even by the pattern prevailing in the United States. Canada seems a long way from the key policy strategies advanced by the OECD, which emphasize a universal approach to access and substantial public investment (OECD 2001, 2002). Canadian researchers have been in the forefront of research on the importance of early childhood development, but Canadian governments have been laggards in developing appropriate policy responses.

Similarly, post-secondary education has been marked by growing emphasis on private responsibilities. In most provinces (Quebec remains an exception), tuition fees rose significantly during the 1990s. The average increase for an undergraduate arts degree over the decade was about 85 percent, with larger increases in other fields of study, especially in professional

Table 13.2

Pre-primary education in selected OECD countries, 2000

	Net enrolment rate (%)		Expenditure
	Three-year-olds	Four-year-olds	% of GDP
Australia	16.4	50.1	0.09
Austria	39.3	79.6	0.53
Belgium	98.2	99.2	0.48
Canada	0	39.9	0.25
Denmark	71.8	90.6	0.78
Finland	33.9	41.9	0.40
France	100.0	100.0	0.68
Germany	54.8	81.4	0.57
Italy	97.6	97.3	0.43
Japan	59.8	94.9	0.18
Netherlands	0.1	99.5	0.36
New Zealand	80.5	93.1	0.19
Norway	70.9	78.1	0.80
Sweden	68.0	72.8	0.58
United Kingdom	53.9	100.0	0.42
United States	36.0	63.6	0.39

NOTE: Expenditure data are for 1999 and refer to direct and indirect public and private expenditure on educational institutions.
SOURCE: OECD (2002, 34).

programs such as medicine, law, and business, where tuition increases often induced sticker shock in even the most stoic of middle-class families. In addition, financial aid to students shifted dramatically from grants to loans in the early 1990s. This trend was led by the federal government's Canada Student Loans Program, which raised loan limits and required participating provincial governments to provide much larger loans to students. Most provincial governments responded by scaling back or eliminating their grants programs. The combination of higher tuition fees, higher loan limits, and less grant assistance has had a significant impact on the average debt of students who have borrowed over the course of their degree programs (Canadian Millennium Scholarship Foundation 2002; Finnie and Usher 2005).

This emphasis on private rather than collective responsibility is even more evident in adult training. The rhetoric of an "active" labour market policy has not led to the investment of a larger portion of our national resources in active labour market programs; indeed, as Figure 13.8 indicates, Canada's committment to this type of programming is lower than the OECD average. Moreover, active programs in Canada focus less on basic training and remedial education than on employment readiness and job search. As a result, most serious adult training is employer-sponsored. While these developments may ensure that adult training is more directly relevant to the workplace, they accentuate the polarization of training opportunities. The self-employed and other workers who do not have a long-term attachment to a major employer are increasingly responsible for investing in their own human capital. Moreover, individuals who already possess high levels of human capital get a disproportional amount of training while those with low levels of human capital are under-represented. Canadian experience in this regard is consistent with experience across many OECD countries (de Broucker 1997; OECD 1998b, 209-10; Larsen and Istace 2001). Betcherman and his colleagues spell out the implications: "One segment of the labour force – largely composed of those who already have substantial human capital – is well served by the current state of affairs. This group finds itself in a

FIGURE 13.8

Expenditures on active labour market programs as a percentage of GDP, 1980-2001

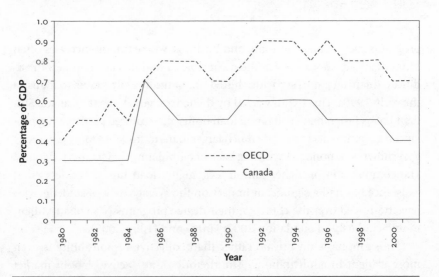

SOURCE: OECD (2004), Social Expenditure Database, 1980-2001.

virtuous circle of a strong skills base, challenging job requirements, and additional human capital investments. However, too many Canadians, including many young people, are in a more *vicious circle* of skills deficit, underinvestment, and declining employability. If Canada is to avoid creating an underclass of poorly educated people, it will have to give more serious attention to the distribution of training" (Betcherman et al. 1998, 5).

Clearly, the evolving public/private balance raises questions about Canada's commitment to investing in the human capital of the population as a whole. The contrast with the approach of the postwar generation is striking. That generation sought to establish a *social right* to security, as they understood it. Our generation is not establishing a comparable right to the sources of security, as we are coming to understand them. The logic of the new paradigm would seem to point to a set of *educational rights*. However, consolidating such rights in practice, as opposed to rhetoric, would represent a major change in current directions in Canada.

EXECUTION: TIMING AND SEQUENCE

Failures of timing and sequence have also weakened our commitment to economic security. Whereas the postwar approach to transfers responded directly to disruptions in income, in effect promising security now, human capital strategies hold out the promise of security in the future. Social investment requires long time horizons. As noted earlier, current research suggests that the largest payoffs come from concentrating efforts on early childhood development, and the full benefits of new strategies will therefore take at least a generation to emerge, even if we make the right design choices now. However, assuming we will get it right immediately seems heroic. We are not sure about what works here, and we are still experimenting with different types and levels of intervention. Getting it right is likely to take time. In effect, the transition to a human capital strategy requires that most elusive of commitments, patient capital, on the part of normally impatient governments.

In the meantime, the problems of low-skilled workers remain. It might be argued that cutting transfers now will sharpen the incentives to undertake the painful process of retraining. However, such an argument assumes that the primary barrier to the retraining is the motivation of workers. As we have just seen, however, Canadian governments do not provide serious remedial education for adults, and there are real questions about the effectiveness of the type of training that is provided. Poor evaluation results of many programs have generated considerable skepticism about the potential for human-capital policies to benefit poorly educated adult workers. (Heckman and Lochner 2000; Heckman et al. 1999; Lefebvre and Merrigan 2003). Retraining, certainly as currently conceived in Canada, seems a slender reed on which to build economic security for older, low-skilled workers in this generation, and income-protection strategies will remain essential in even the most committed of human-capital societies.

In effect, a transition to a social investment strategy that also keeps faith with the commitment to economic security will be a long-term process. If the strategy works, income transfers will decline naturally, as future workers face less unemployment and enjoy stronger earnings. During the transition period, however, we face a "double-funding" problem: the need to invest in future workers but to continue to provide economic security for the low-skilled workers of today and tomorrow.[8] To cut income transfers before investments in human capital come to fruition is a recipe for lower levels of economic security among low-skilled workers in this generation and perhaps several to come. Yet that is precisely the pattern Canada has followed.

INTRINSIC LIMITS: THE SOCIAL DETERMINANTS OF EDUCATIONAL ATTAINMENT
Problems of implementation are not inevitable. A society might well decide to commit the patient capital needed to make the transition to the new social policy in a meaningful way. But there are also more deeply rooted challenges to a human-capital strategy. Most important is the inescapable fact that the educational attainments and life chances of children are shaped by the social and family context into which they are born. While overall participation rates continue to climb among young people from all social backgrounds, a stubborn gap persists in the relative educational success of children from advantaged and disadvantaged backgrounds.

The gap between rich and poor has always mattered in the educational world. During the twentieth century, Western countries went through remarkable transformations, moving from agricultural to industrial then to post-industrial social structures. In the same period, they dramatically expanded their educational systems, with rising proportions of the population participating at all levels of education. However, when attention shifts to the *relative* educational attainments of people from different social strata, the picture is one of stability. A recent survey completed for the OECD concluded that "overall the expansion of tertiary education in the OECD appears to have had little impact on the *relative* prospects of young people from less advantaged backgrounds" (Blöndal et al. 2002, 45). A more in-depth analysis of the experience of thirteen industrial countries over the course of the entire twentieth century concluded that, despite major expansions and reforms of educational systems, there was no general decline in the impact of social background on relative educational achievement (Shavit and Blossfeld 1993; Ambler and Neathery 1999).

The exceptions to this pattern are revealing. The two countries in which the link between social background and educational attainment loosened over time were Sweden and the Netherlands, a fact that led analysts to specu-late that a long-term commitment to socioeconomic equality is important to achieving educational equality as well (Shavit and Blossfeld 1993, 19; also Jonsson et al. 1996). More recent evidence from the International Adult Lit-eracy Survey points in the same direction (OECD and Statistics Canada 2000). Figure 13.9 confirms that there is a relationship between the level of in-come equality in a country and the extent of inequality in literacy among

FIGURE 13.9

Economic inequality and literacy inequality

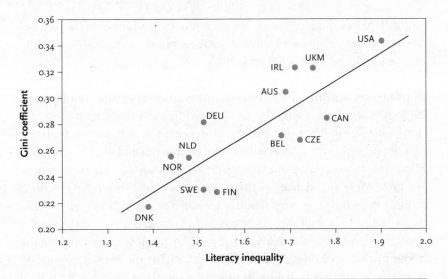

NOTE: Economic inequality is the inequality in the distribution of income within countries, as measured by Gini coefficients. Literacy inequality is the inequality in the distribution of literacy scores (prose scale, 1994-98) within countries, as measured by the ratio of the ninth decile to the first decile.

SOURCE: OECD and Statistics Canada (2000).

its adult population: societies with high levels of income inequality tend to have high levels of dispersion in literacy levels.[9] The causal relationships between educational equality and income equality likely flow in both directions. Increasing the educational levels of the bottom third of the labour force raises their productivity and income prospects. But reducing the levels of poverty and economic inequality undoubtedly also contributes to equality in educational attainment.

Canadian experience is consistent with the international pattern. Although our record is better than those of many western countries, social factors still matter for educational outcomes. The National Longitudinal Survey of Children and Youth indicates that by the time children enter kindergarten, a significant socioeconomic gradient has emerged in readiness for school, as measured by vocabulary development and other capacities (Ross and Roberts 1999; Duncan et al. 1998). Although the educational system reduces the gradients as children move from level to level (Wanner 1999), differences in participation levels persist right through to the university sector. There is evidence that the gap in university participation rates narrowed during the postwar decades, in contrast to the pattern across OECD countries more generally (Christophides et al. 2001). Nonetheless, significant differences remain, and Table 13.3 provides a hint that the gap between families of low and middle socioeconomic status (SES) actually widened again between 1986 and 1994.

While there is widespread agreement that the SES of families is important, "the mechanism is the subject of intense, heated debate" (Finnie et al. 2005, 300; see also Ma and Klinger 2000; Willms 1999). Economic status is clearly one factor. Poverty in childhood is associated with lack of readiness for primary school, problems with school attendance and marks, anti-social behaviour, and dropping-out. The relationship persists to the post-secondary level. While attendance at college is not associated with family income, children from higher-income families are much more likely to go to university, as Table 13.4 indicates. As one group of analysts asks: "Are particular institutions and particular fields of study – perhaps those more valued in the labour market – the domain of students with higher income backgrounds?" (Corak et al. 2005, 259). This quiet process of social sorting is exacerbated by the urban/rural divide. Increased distance to university is associated with lower attendance and a greater tendency to go to a local community college (Frenette 2004).

TABLE 13.3

University participation of persons aged 18-21 by family socioeconomic status (SES), 1986-94

Family SES	1986	1994	Change
Highest	32.9	40.3	7.4
Middle	14.5	25.3	10.8
Lowest	13.7	18.3	4.6
Total	18.4	26.4	8.0

NOTE: University participation rate: people aged 18-21 with at least some university education as a percentage of all persons aged 18-21. Family socioeconomic status is defined as the Blishen socioeconomic index for father's occupation when respondents were 15 years old.
SOURCE: Bouchard and Zhao (2000).

TABLE 13.4

Participation in post-secondary education (PSE) of persons aged 18-21, by family income, 1998

PSE participation (highest level)	Family income		
	Lowest quartile	Middle half	Highest quartile
All PSE	56.1	62.2	69.7
University	18.8	27.5	38.7
College	28.8	28.8	28.3

NOTE: Family income is family income at the time the student was aged 16.
SOURCE: Statistics Canada (2001).

If the social determinants of educational attainment were purely economic, the policy challenges would be simpler. In reality, however, the factors at work go beyond money. The cultural capital that different families bring to their children's development is key. Many studies from a number of countries confirm that children's educational attainment and literacy levels are more strongly associated with their parents' level of education than their parents' income. Families are critical to cognitive stimulus in early childhood, to the aspirations that are nurtured as children grow, and to the life choices that are supported at critical transition points. By the high school years, the influence of family background can be detected in such things as grades, attitudes toward higher schooling, the number of hours devoted to part-time jobs, and so on. The cumulative effects over a child's lifetime are substantial: de Broucker and Underwood (1998) found that Canadians with highly educated parents are 2.4 times more likely to obtain a post-secondary credential than are those whose parents have not completed high school, and that this polarization of educational achievement appeared to be growing over time, a finding confirmed more recently by Finnie et al. (2004b).[10]

Unfortunately, political debates about educational inequality have focused almost exclusively on the impact of rising tuition fees on access to post-secondary education. While the jury is still out on this issue, the most recent evidence suggests that, although the association between family income and university participation did get stronger in the early 1990s, when tuition fees first experienced substantial increases, it eased again later in the decade when borrowing limits were raised and other forms of financial assistance were increased. As a result, the relationship was no stronger in 1997 than it had been at the beginning of the decade (Corak et al. 2005). However, such debates distract from the core issues. While it is reassuring that tuition policy in the 1990s may not have actually made things worse, unequal participation at the university level was problematic well before the run-up in fees. Moreover, the focus on the post-secondary level misses the real action. The cumulative impact of social background emerges over the entire life cycle, and the toll exacted by social disadvantage begins much earlier.

Compensating for subtle social influences in the lives of children and young people is a difficult task. As Esping-Andersen observes, "we cannot pass laws that force parents to read to their children," but we can seek to compensate through a major expansion of early childhood education, giving priority to children from vulnerable families (Esping-Andersen 2002, 49). As we have seen, Canada has a long way to go in this field. But we also need to have realistic expectations. There has been a long history of compensatory intervention through Head Start in the United States and parallel programs elsewhere, and evaluations of such interventions have been decidedly mixed (Currie 2001). We have even less evidence about what works at later stages of the educational progress. A variety of programs have emerged in different countries to provide information, counselling, and financial incentives designed to encourage young people to stay in school and go on to post-secondary education. But such programs tend to be experimental in nature, and evaluations of them have been difficult and controversial. We are still finding our way here.

The bottom line is clear. The accident of birth still matters in the educational world, and a social policy premised on investment in human capital raises the policy salience of the education gap exponentially. Undoubtedly, enriched learning systems can help; equal access to high-quality early childhood education is an obvious place to start. However, effective action to reduce the socioeconomic gradient in educational attainment will require a wider range of policy instruments than purely educational ones. The cross-national relationship between economic and educational inequality suggests that a successful strategy of investing in human capital cannot be divorced from a continuing concern about inequality and poverty, especially child poverty. Here, Canada made no real progress in the last two decades of the twentieth century. The country's child poverty rate in 2000, as measured by the Luxembourg Income Study, was 14.9 percent, virtually identical to the rate in 1980 (Table 13.1).

INTRINSIC LIMITS: THE NARROWNESS OF HUMAN CAPITAL INSTRUMENTS

Finally, it seems obvious but still important to note that strategies premised on the development of human capital miss many of the social needs of vulnerable groups who face a concentration of disadvantages that limit their participation in the mainstream of society. Single mothers and their children, recently arrived immigrants, people with disabilities, many homeless people with serious problems of substance abuse: these and others face a complex set of hurdles and require services and supports that go well beyond education and training. Most challenging of all, Aboriginal people face a unique set of cultural and economic challenges that are only partially met through educational strategies. An agenda of social inclusion of these marginalized groups will need to lean heavily on diverse sets of strategies and policy instruments.

In sum, the new paradigm in social policy faces formidable constraints. In practice, the transition to a new social policy is weakened by an uncertain collective commitment to human capital and problems of timing and sequence. Moreover, advocates of the new approach pay inadequate attention to the policy implications of the socioeconomic gradient in educational attainment and to the wide range of social problems that lie well beyond the reach of education and training.

Are We Dis-embedding Liberalism?

It is time to return to the questions with which we began. Canada has embraced the new social policy with enthusiasm. Income transfer programs have been restructured, and investment in human capital has been given pride of

place in policy rhetoric, if not in actual budgetary allocations. Is Canada up-
dating its conception of social protection to accord with new economic realities? Or are we retreating from a collective commitment to economic security for the population as a whole? Are we re-embedding or dis-embedding
liberalism?

On balance, it is difficult to avoid the conclusion that we have weakened
the collective mechanisms of economic security. We have not fashioned adequate replacements, with the result that we are socializing fewer of the costs
of adjustment to economic change. Canadian governments have embraced
the first side of the new social policy paradigm, cutting and restructuring
income-security programs in ways that reduce the levels of economic security assured to working-age Canadians. They have also been guilty of the sin
of impatience, cutting transfers long before social investment strategies could
possibly bear fruit. But a large question mark lingers over the second side of
the contemporary social policy paradigm. Governments have proven readier
to reduce income-security protections than to reinforce their commitment to
education and training. Despite the heady rhetoric about a human capital
society, our commitment to public investment in human capital is faltering,
and the responsibility for investing in learning has been shifted in part to
private shoulders. While the postwar generation sought to establish a right to
economic security, as they understood that concept, our generation is moving away from the idea of a right to the sources of economic security as we
have come to understand that concept in our time.

Even if the transition to a social investment strategy was well designed
and governments were prepared to be patient investors, deeper problems
remain. In contrast to the transfer programs, successful participation in educational and training systems is conditioned by complex social forces. A
human-capital strategy is more accessible to families richly endowed with
economic and cultural capital, and its advocates need to come to grips with
the policy implications of the socioeconomic gradient in educational attainment. Education and training systems on their own cannot compensate fully
for poverty, inequality, and the differences in cultural capital that parents
bring to their children's upbringing. On their own, education and training
do not represent a pathway to economic security that is equally accessible to
all Canadians. On their own, they do not represent the basis of a fair society.
Cynics might conclude that the primary role of the new discourse on social
policy has been to provide political cover for a stealthy retreat from the aspirations that underpinned Canadian social policy for generations. To dispel

this danger, Canadians need to engage in a much more critical reassessment of where we are going. It is time for a mid-course correction.

Learning remains central to the new economy, and an important agenda remains, especially in early childhood development and adult retraining. But learning is being asked to carry too much weight in the new social discourse. A social policy premised on human capital is likely to fail, even in its own terms, if growing economic inequality is followed by growing educational inequality. We are led inevitably back to a debate about redistribution. A successful strategy of investing in human capital cannot be divorced from a continuing concern for child poverty and inequality, and a coherent social agenda will depend on the integration of income redistribution and invest-ment in human capital.[11] The key challenge is one that is largely being ig-nored: to design a redistributive complement to a human-capital strategy, one that makes meaningful the promise of education as an instrument of economic security and compensates for its limitations.

In our current trajectory, Canadians are being asked to embrace new waves of economic openness without a coherent, collective approach to the issues of economic security. The transition is far from complete, and the eventual outcome remains contested. But one thing is clear: we're not quite sure where we're going. Yogi Berra would have understood.

ACKNOWLEDGMENTS
Earlier versions of this chapter were presented at meetings of the International Political Science Association, the Roundtable on Globalization, Governance, and Social Policy sponsored by Human Resources Development Canada, and the workshop of the Equal-ity, Security and Community Project held at the University of British Columbia. I would like to thank participants in those seminars, as well as Ken Battle, Jane Jenson, Jonathan Kesselman, John Myles, John Richards, and Arthur Sweetman for their comments and insights. In addition, I wish to thank Ian Cummins, Erich Hartmann, and Suzanne Ma for excellent research assistance. A condensed version of this chapter appeared in De-cember 2005 as Keith G. Banting, "Do We Know Where We Are Going? The New Social Policy in Canada," *Canadian Public Policy* 31(4): 421-30.

NOTES
1   In developing his concept of "embedded liberalism," Ruggie drew directly on Karl Polanyi's analysis of the "great transformation" in relations between market and society in the postwar era. Polanyi argued that society sought to protect itself from the insecurities inherent in the market through a "double movement" represented

by two organizing principles: "The one was the principle of economic liberalism, aiming at the establishment of a self-regulating market ... [and] the other was the principle of social protection aiming at the conservation of man and nature" (Polanyi 1944, 131).

2   See Levitas (1996) for a critique of "social exclusion" as a much narrower concept than inequality. Concern over inequality more generally does creep into some versions of the new discourse in the form of a concern with "social cohesion," and a fear that growing economic inequality will exacerbate major fault-lines in society and generate higher levels of conflict and instability. As Finlayson (1999, 276-77) argues, the ethics of equality in "third way" theory are not derived from concern with equality as a key principle, but, rather, with concern that high levels of inequality might erode the basis for a cohesive society.

3   In contrast to Europe, the new discourse in Canada has focused more on income transfers than employment legislation. According to the OECD, Canadian employment protection – both in the level of protection provided by law and in the prospects of having legal provisions actually enforced – is relatively close to the American pattern (OECD 1994b, 73). While this analysis may understate the importance of legislated notice requirements at the provincial level and consultative requirements that apply in cases of mass dismissals, Canadian employment protection laws are undoubtedly much less demanding than those in a number of European countries (Kuhn 1997). Considerable controversy did surround employment equity legislation during the 1990s, especially in Ontario and a number of other provinces (Bakan and Kobayashi 2000). With this exception, however, the primary political action was in the field of income transfers.

4   The decline in the proportion of unemployed receiving benefits also reflected changes in forms of employment, which decrease eligibility for the program. See Human Resources Development Canada (1998).

5   For a critique of the measure as overly sensitive to changes in unemployment, see Hicks (2002).

6   See Riddell (2001) for a useful summary of the evidence. On the particular problem of the high levels of non-completion of high school in Canada, see Parent (2001).

7   In the words of an OECD official, "Canada seemed to be more focused on child care rather than early development and learning ... It was some place for the children to go while the parents work rather than focusing on the children themselves and what do these children need" (quoted in Philp 2004).

8   I am especially indebted to comments from Jane Jenson and John Myles on the issues of sequence and timing.

9   Remarkably similar findings emerge from comparative studies that focus on the level of social mobility in industrial nations (Erikson and Goldthorpe 1992).

10   There is a large literature pointing to similar conclusions. See also Drolet 2005;
      Knighton and Mirza (2002); Finnie and Meng (2002); OECD and Statistics Canada
      (2000); Butlin (1999, 2000); Ryan and Adams (1999); and de Broucker and Lavallée
      (1998).
11   Gøsta Esping-Andersen advances a similar argument that "there is a tendency to
      rely too much on activation, make-work-pay and lifelong learning" and that a
      combined strategy of investment and redistribution is essential (2002, 66; also
      Esping-Andersen 2004). See also Scott (2005, 29-31).

REFERENCES

Advisory Council on Science and Technology. 2000. *Stepping Up: Skills and Opportunities in
    the Knowledge Economy – Report of the Expert Panel on Skills.* Ottawa: Industry Canada.
Ambler, John S., and Jody Neathery. 1999. "Education Policy and Equality: Some Evi-
    dence from Europe." *Social Science Quarterly* 80(3): 437-56.
Atkinson, Sir Anthony. 2003. "Globalization and the Welfare State." The Douglas Gibson
    Distinguished Lecture. Queen's University, School of Policy Studies.
Bakan, Abigail, and Audrey Kobayashi. 2000. *Employment Equity Policy in Canada: An
    Interprovincial Comparison.* Ottawa: Status of Women Canada.
Battle, Ken. 2001. "Relentless Incrementalism: Deconstructing and Reconstructing
    Canadian Income Security Policy." In Keith Banting, Andrew Sharpe, and France
    St-Hilaire, eds., *The Review of Economic Performance and Social Progress: The Longest
    Decade – Canada in the 1990s,* 183-229. Montreal: Institute for Research on Public
    Policy; Ottawa: Centre for the Study of Living Standards.
Battle, Ken, and Michael Mendelson, eds. 2001. *Benefits for Children: A Four Country
    Study.* Ottawa: Caledon Institute of Social Policy.
Betcherman, Gordon, Karen McMullen, and Katherine Davidman. 1998. *Training for the
    New Economy: A Synthesis Report.* Ottawa: Canadian Policy Research Networks.
Blöndal, S., S. Field, and N. Girouard. 2002. "Investment in Human Capital through
    Post-Compulsory Education and Training: Selected Efficiency and Equity Aspects."
    Economics Department Working Paper 330. Paris: OECD.
Bouchard, Brigitte, and John Zhao. 2000. "University Education: Recent Trends in Par-
    ticipation, Accessibility and Returns." *Education Quarterly Review* 6(4): 24-32.
Boychuk, Gerard W., and Keith G. Banting. 2003. "The Paradox of Convergence: Na-
    tional versus Sub-National Patterns of Convergence in Canadian and American
    Income Maintenance Programs." In Richard Harris, ed., *North American Linkages:
    Challenges and Opportunities,* 533-72. Calgary: University of Calgary Press.
Butlin, George. 1999. "Determinants of Postsecondary Participation." *Education Quar-
    terly Review* 5(3): 9-35.
—. 2000. "Determinants of University and Community College Leaving." *Education
    Quarterly Review* 6(4): 8-23. Ottawa: Statistics Canada.

Cameron, David R. 1978. "The Expansion of the Public Economy: A Comparative Analysis." *American Political Science Review* 72: 1242-61.

Canada. 1945. *White Paper on Employment and Income.* Ottawa: Department of Reconstruction.

Canada Millennium Scholarship Foundation. 2002. *The Price of Knowledge: Access and Student Finance in Canada.* Montreal.

Christophides, Louis N., Jim Cirello, and Michael Hoy. 2001. "Family Income and Postsecondary Education in Canada." *Canadian Journal of Higher Education Research* 31(1): 177-208.

Corak, Miles, Garth Lipps, and John Zhao. 2005. "Family Income and Participation in Postsecondary Education." In Charles Beach, Robin Boadway, and Marvin McInnes, eds., *Higher Education in Canada,* 255-94. Kingston, ON: John Deutsch Institute; Montreal: McGill-Queen's University Press.

Courchene, Thomas. 2001. *A State of Minds: Towards a Human Capital Future for Canadians.* Montreal: Institute for Research on Public Policy.

—. 2002. "Embedding Liberalism: A Human Capital Perspective." *Policy Matters* 3(4). Montreal: Institute for Research on Public Policy.

Courchene, Thomas, with Colin Telmer. 1998. *From Heartland to North American Region State: The Social, Fiscal and Federal Evolution of Ontario.* Toronto: University of Toronto, Faculty of Management.

Currie, Janet. 2001. "Early Childhood Education Programs." *Journal of Economic Perspectives* 15(2): 213-38.

de Broucker, Patrice. 1997. "Job-Related Training: Who Has Access?" *Education Quarterly Review* 4: 10-31.

de Broucker, Patrice, and Laval Lavallée. 1998. "Intergenerational Aspects of Education and Literacy Skills Acquisition." In Miles Corak, ed., *Labour Markets, Social Institutions and the Future of Canada's Children,* 129-43. Ottawa: Statistics Canada.

de Broucker, Patrice, and Kristen Underwood. 1998. "Intergenerational Education Mobility: An International Comparison with a Focus on Parental Education." *Education Quarterly Review* 5(2): 30-51.

Drolet, Marie. 2005. "Participation in Post-secondary Education in Canada: Has the Role of Parental Income and Education Changed over the 1990s?" Analytical Studies Branch Research Paper Series. Ottawa: Statistics Canada.

Duncan, Greg J., Jean Yeung, Jeanne Brooks-Gunn, and Judith R. Smith. 1998. "How Much Does Childhood Poverty Affect the Life Chances of Children?" *American Sociological Review* 63(3): 406-23.

Erikson, Robert, and John Goldthorpe. 1992. *The Constant Flux: A Study of Class Mobility in Industrial Societies.* Oxford: Clarendon Press.

Esping-Andersen, Gøsta. 1990. *The Three Worlds of Welfare Capitalism.* Princeton, NJ: Princeton University Press.

—. 2002. "A Child-Centred Social Investment Strategy." in Gøsta Esping-Andersen, with Duncan Gallie, Anton Hemerjick, and John Myles, eds., *Why We Need a New Welfare State*, 26-67. Oxford: Oxford University Press.

—. 2004. "Untying the Gordian Knot of Social Inheritance." In Arne L. Kalleberg, Stephen Morgan, John Myles, and Rachel Rosenfeld, eds., *Inequality: Structures, Dynamics and Mechanisms – Essays in Honour of Aage B. Sorenson.* Oxford: Elsevier Ltd.

Finlayson, Alan. 1999. "Third Way Theory." *Political Quarterly* 70: 271-79.

Finnie, Ross, Ian Irvine, and Roger Sceviour. 2004a. "Social Assistance Use in Canada: National and Provincial Trends in Incidence, Entry and Exit." *Canadian Journal of Regional Science* 27(2): 207-22.

Finnie, Ross, Christine Laporte, and Eric Lascelles. 2004b. "Family Background and Access to Post-Secondary Education: What Happened over the 1990s?" Analytical Studies Research Branch Research Paper Series. Ottawa: Statistics Canada.

Finnie, Ross, Eric Lascelles, and Arthur Sweetman. 2005. "Who Goes? The Direct and Indirect Effects of Family Background on Access to Post-Secondary Education." In Charles Beach, Robin Boadway, and Marvin McInnes, eds., *Higher Education in Canada*, 295-338. Kingston, ON: John Deutsch Institute; Montreal: McGill-Queen's University Press.

Finnie, Ross, and Ronald Meng. 2002. "A Recursive Income Model for Canadians: The Direct and Indirect Effects of Family Background." Working Paper 28. Kingston, ON: Queen's University, School of Policy Studies.

Finnie, Ross, and Alex Usher. 2005. "The Canadian Experiment in Cost-Sharing and its Effect on Access to Higher Education, 1990-2002." Discussion Paper 39. Kingston, ON: Queen's University, School of Policy Studies.

Frenette, Marc. 2004. "Access to College and University: Does Distance to School Matter?" *Canadian Public Policy* 30(4): 427-43.

Giddens, Anthony. 1998. *The Third Way: The Renewal of Social Democracy*. Cambridge: Polity Press.

—. 2000. *The Third Way and Its Critics*. Cambridge: Polity Press.

—, ed. 2001. *The Global Third Way Debate*. Cambridge: Polity Press.

Haveman, Robert, and Barbara Wolfe. 1995. "The Determinants of Children's Attainments: A Review of Methods and Findings." *Journal of Economic Literature* 33(4): 1829-78.

Heckman, James, Robert Lalonde, and Jeffrey Smith. 1999. "The Economics and Econometrics of Active Labor Market Programs." In Orley Ashenfelter and David Card, eds., *Handbook of Labor Economics*. Vol. 3A. New York: North-Holland Elsevier.

Heckman, James, and Lance Lochner. 2000. "Rethinking Education and Training Policy." In Sheldon Danziger and Jane Waldvogel, eds., *Securing the Future: Investing in Children from Birth to College*, 47-86. New York: Russell Sage.

Hicks, Peter. 2002. "Preparing for Tomorrow's Social Policy Agenda." Working Paper Series 02-04. Ottawa: Social Research and Demonstration Corporation.

Human Resources Development Canada. 1994. *Improving Social Security in Canada: A Discussion Paper*. Ottawa: Supply and Services Canada.

—. 1998. *An Analysis of Employment Insurance Benefit Coverage*. Ottawa: Applied Research Branch.

—. 2002. *Knowledge Matters: Skills and Learning for Canadians*. Ottawa.

Jonsson, Jan, Colin Mills, and Walter Müller. 1996. "A Half Century of Increasing Educational Openness? Social Class and Educational Attainment in Sweden, Germany and Britain." In Robert Erikson and J. Jonsson, eds., *Can Education Be Equalized? The Swedish Case in Comparative Perspective*. Boulder, CO: Westview Press.

Katzenstein, Peter. 1983. "The Small European States in the International Economy: Economic Dependence and Corporatist Politics." In John Gerard Ruggie, ed., *The Antinomies of Interdependence: National Welfare and the International Division of Labor*. New York: Columbia University Press.

—. 1985. *Small States in World Markets: Industrial Policy in Europe*. Ithaca, NY: Cornell University Press.

Knighton, Tamara, and Sheba Mirza. 2002. "Postsecondary Participation: The Effects of Parents' Education and Household Income." *Education Quarterly Review* 8(3): 25-32.

Kuhn, Peter. 1997. "Canada and the 'OECD Hypothesis': Does Labor Market Inflexibility Explain Canada's High Level of Unemployment?" In W. Craig Riddell and France St-Hilaire, eds., *Adapting Public Policy to a Labour Market in Transition*, 177-209. Montreal: Institute for Research on Public Policy.

Larsen, Kurt, and David Istace. 2001. "Lifelong Learning for All." *OECD Observer* 225 (March): 21-23.

Lefebvre, Pierre, and Philip Merrigan. 2003. "Assessing Family Policy in Canada: A New Deal for Families and Children." *Choices* 9(5). Montreal: Institute for Research on Public Policy.

Levitas, Ruth. 1996. "The Concept of Social Exclusion and the New Durkheimian Hegemony." *Critical Social Policy* 46: 5-20.

Ma, Xin, and Don A. Klinger. 2000. "Hierarchical Linear Modelling of Student and School Effects on Academic Achievement." *Canadian Journal of Education* 25(1): 41-55.

Marsh, Leonard. 1943. *Report on Social Security for Canada*. Toronto: University of Toronto Press (reprinted 1975).

Martin, Paul. 1999. "A Presentation to the House of Commons Standing Committee on Finance." November 2. Available at http://www.fin.gc.ca/update99/speeche.html.

Myles, John, and Paul Pierson. 1997. "Friedman's Revenge: The Reform of Liberal Welfare States in Canada and the United States." *Politics and Society* 25: 443-72.

Myles, John, and Jill Quadagno. 2000. "Envisioning a *Third Way*: The Welfare State in the Twentieth Century." *Contemporary Sociology* 29(1): 156-67.

National Council of Welfare. 2000. *Welfare Incomes 1999*. Ottawa: National Council of Welfare.

—. 2003. *Welfare Incomes 2002*. Ottawa: National Council of Welfare.

—. 2004. *Welfare Incomes 2003*. Ottawa: National Council of Welfare.

OECD. 1994a. *The OECD Jobs Study: Facts, Analysis, Strategies*. Paris.

—. 1994b. *The OECD Jobs Study: Evidence and Explanations, Part I: Labour Market Trends and Underlying Forces of Change*. Paris.

—. 1994c. *The OECD Jobs Study: Evidence and Explanations, Part II: The Adjustment Potential of the Labour Market*. Paris.

—. 1995. *The OECD Jobs Study: Implementing the Strategy*. Paris.

—. 1996. *The OECD Jobs Strategy: Pushing Ahead with the Strategy*. Paris.

—. 1998a. *Human Capital Investment: An International Comparison*. Paris.

—. 1998b. *Education at a Glance: OECD Indicators*. Paris.

—. 1999a. *Implementing the OECD Jobs Strategy: Assessing Performance and Policy*. Paris.

—. 1999b. *OECD Economic Surveys 1998-99: Canada*. Paris.

—. 2000. *Education at a Glance: OECD Indicators*. Paris.

—. 2001. *Starting Strong: Early Childhood Education and Care*. Paris.

—. 2002. "Strengthening Early Childhood Programmes: A Policy Framework." *Education Policy Analysis 2002*. Paris.

—. 2004. *Early Childhood Education and Care Policy. Canada Country Note*. Directorate for Education. Paris.

OECD and Statistics Canada. 2000. *Literacy in the Information Age: Final Report of the International Adult Literacy Survey*. Paris: OECD; Ottawa: Industry Canada.

Ontario. 1990. *People and Skills in the New Global Economy*. Toronto: Ontario Premier's Council.

—. 2004. Panel on the Role of Government. *Investing in People: Creating a Human Capital Society for Ontario*. Toronto: Queen's Printer for Ontario.

Osberg, Lars, and Andrew Sharpe. 2002. "An Index of Economic Well-Being for Selected OECD Countries." *Review of Income and Wealth* Series 48(3): 291-316.

Pal, Les. 1988. *State, Class and Bureaucracy: Canadian Unemployment Insurance and Public Policy*. Montreal: McGill-Queen's University Press.

Parent, Daniel. 2001. "Return to a High School Diploma and the Decision to Drop Out: New Evidence from Canada." Série scientifique. Montréal: CIRANO.

Philp, Margaret. 2004. "Canada's Child Care Is Failing, OECD Says." *Globe and Mail*, 25 October, A1.

Polanyi, Karl. 1944. *The Great Transformation: The Political and Economic Origins of Our Times*. Boston: Beacon Press.

Riddell, Craig. 2001. "Education and Skills: An Assessment of Recent Canadian Experience." In Patrick Grady and Andrew Sharpe, eds., *The State of Economics in Canada: Festschrift in Honour of David Slater*, 485-517. Kingston, ON: Queen's University, School of Policy Studies; Montreal: McGill-Queen's University Press.

Riddell, Craig, and Arthur Sweetman. 2001. "Human Capital Formation in a Period of Change." In Craig Riddell and France St-Hilaire, eds., *Adapting Public Policy to a Labour Market in Transition*. Montreal: Institute for Research on Public Policy.

Rodrik, Dani. 1997. *Has Globalization Gone Too Far?* Washington, DC: Institute for International Economics.

Ross, David, and Paul Roberts. 1999. *Income and Child Well-Being: A New Perspective on the Poverty Debate*. Ottawa: Canadian Council on Social Development.

Ruggie, John G. 1983. "International Regimes, Transactions and Change: Embedded Liberalism in the Postwar Order." In Stephen Krasner, ed., *International Regimes*, 195-231. Ithaca, NY: Cornell University Press.

—. 1994. "Trade Protection and the Future of Welfare Capitalism." *Journal of International Affairs* 48:1-12.

Ryan, Bruce, and Gerald Adams. 1999. "How Do Families Affect Children's Success in School?" *Education Quarterly Review* 6(1): 30-43.

Saint-Martin, Denis. 2000. "De l'État-providence à l'État d'investissement social: un nouveau paradigme pour *enfant-er* l'économie du savoir?" In Les Pal, ed., *How Ottawa Spends 2000-01: Past Imperfect, Future Tense*, 33-57. Don Mills, ON: Oxford University Press.

Scott, Katherine. 2005. *The World We Have: Towards a New Social Architecture*. Ottawa: Canadian Council on Social Development.

Shavit, Yossi, and Hans-Peter Blossfeld. 1993. *Persistent Inequality: Changing Educational Attainment in Thirteen Countries*. Boulder, CO: Westview Press.

Statistics Canada. Table 051-00011.2

Statistics Canada. 2004. *Income Trends in Canada 1980-2003*. Cat. 13F0022XIE.

Steering Group on Prosperity. 1992. *Inventing Our Future: An Action Plan for Canada's Prosperity*. Ottawa.

Sweetman, Arthur. 2002. "Working Smarter: Education and Productivity." In Andrew Sharpe, France St-Hilaire, and Keith Banting, eds., *The Review of Economic Performance and Social Progress: Towards a Social Understanding of Productivity*, 157-80. Montreal: Institute for Research on Public Policy; Ottawa: Centre for the Study of Living Standards.

Wanner, Richard A. 1999. "Expansion and Ascription: Trends in Educational Opportunity in Canada, 1920-1994." *Canadian Review of Sociology and Anthropology* 36(3): 409-42.

Willms, Douglas. 1999. *Inequalities in Literacy Skills among Youth in Canada and the United States*. Ottawa: Statistics Canada.

—. 2003. *Ready or Not: Literacy Skills and Postsecondary Education*. Montreal: Canada Millennium Scholarship Foundation.

Contributors

KEITH G. BANTING is a professor in the School of Policy Studies and the Department of Political Studies at Queen's University and holds the Queen's Research Chair in Public Policy. He was director of the School of Policy Studies from 1992 until July 2003. His research interests focus on the politics of social policy in Canada and other western nations. He is the author of *Poverty, Politics and Policy* and *The Welfare State and Canadian Federalism*. He is also the editor of another dozen books, most recently *Federalism and Health Policy: A Comparative Perspective on Multi-Level Governance*. His current research focuses on ethnic diversity, multiculturalism, and the welfare state.

CHARLES M. BEACH is a professor of economics at Queen's University and is currently director of the John Deutsch Institute for the Study of Economic Policy at Queen's. He is a past editor of *Canadian Public Policy*. His principal areas of research and publication are income distribution, empirical labour market analysis, immigration policy, and post-secondary education in Canada.

BRAHIM BOUDARBAT is an assistant professor in the School of Industrial Relations at the Université de Montréal. He earned his PhD in Economics from the Université de Montréal and was a post-doctoral and teaching fellow in the Department of Economics at the University of British Columbia from July 2003 to July 2004. His fields of interest are labour economics, applied econometrics, and the economics of immigration.

RON CHEUNG is an assistant professor of economics at Florida State University. He earned his PhD in Economics at the University of British Columbia in 2005. His primary fields of research are urban economics and public finance. His recent work focuses on the growing trend of homeowners' associations in housing developments – in particular, he is interested in how this form of service privatization affects local public finance. Other topics of interest include local expenditures and taxation, land use, and housing markets.

THOMAS F. CROSSLEY is an associate professor in the Department of Economics at McMaster University. His research interests focus on household behaviour, financial security, and living standards. This includes research on consumption, savings, and labour supply; life-cycle models; financial circumstances as well as living standards more broadly defined; inequality; and social insurance and other public policies directed toward household welfare. He also has interests in micro-econometrics and the analysis of survey data.

Prior to his death on 27 May 2005, **JAMES ENSIGN CURTIS** was a distinguished professor of sociology at the University of Waterloo, his home for thirty-five years. Jim was widely recognized for his peerless scholarship, his incomparable abilities as a teacher and sponsor of young social scientists, and his outstanding service to the discipline. Jim's publication record includes twenty monographs or edited collections, some hundred articles, and close to forty chapters in books. He was perhaps best known for his research in the areas of social inequality, the social significance of sport, comparative social structure, and voluntary association activity. He was editor of the *Canadian Review of Sociology and Anthropology* and an associate editor for the *Review*, the *Canadian Journal of Sociology*, and other journals. He also served as vice-president of the Canadian Sociology and Anthropology Association. In recognition of these and other accomplishments, Jim received the Award for Outstanding Contributions to Canadian Sociology from the CSAA in 2000. He was honoured with the University of Waterloo's Outstanding Performance Award in 2004 for his exceptional contributions to teaching and research. In 2004, Jim was admitted as a Fellow of the Royal Society of Canada.

AVIGAIL EISENBERG is an associate professor of political science and a faculty associate of indigenous governance at the University of Victoria. She is interested in Canadian politics and political theory related to minority rights, feminism, identity, and cultural politics. Her current research focuses on developing a guide for the assessment of claims made by minority groups for the protection of their identities. Her numerous publications include *Reconstructing Political Pluralism*, and she recently co-edited a collection of essays entitled *Minorities within Minorities*. She has held visiting fellowships at the Rockefeller Center in Bellagio Italy and at the Centre de recherche en éthique at the Université de Montréal.

NICOLE M. FORTIN is a professor of economics at the University of British Columbia. Her research revolves around two themes: labour market institutions, public policies, and wage inequality; and gender-equality policies and the economic progress of women. Her more influential work has examined the impact of minimum wages and unionization on US wage inequality, for which her 1996 *Econometrica* article won the Minnesota Award. Her other innovative research has focused on the ineffectiveness of the Ontario pay equity legislation at reducing the gender pay gap and on the impact of funding cutbacks on university enrolment rates in Canada.

MARC FRENETTE has been a research economist with the Business and Labour Market Analysis Division at Statistics Canada since 1997. His primary areas of interest include the economics of education and income inequality. His work in education has focused on the acquisition of human capital, with particular emphasis on its many barriers (e.g., distance to school, rapidly rising tuition fees in professional programs). His current and forthcoming work in income inequality focuses primarily on measurement issues. Other areas of interest include analysis of residential spells in low-income neighbourhoods and of immigrant earnings assimilation.

ELLEN MARGARET THOMAS GEE was a professor of sociology and former chair of the Department of Sociology and Anthropology at Simon Fraser University, her academic home for over twenty years. Her untimely passing in November 2002 has left a deep void in Canadian sociology and gerontology, as her contributions to both disciplines was immense. Over her career, Ellen served as the social sciences editor of the *Canadian Journal on Aging*, managing editor of the *Canadian Review of Sociology and Anthropology*, associate editor of *Canadian Public Policy*, and editorial board member of numerous journals. Her publication record includes six monographs, books, and edited collections and over one hundred articles and chapters in the areas of Canadian demography, sociology of aging, and sociology of the family. Ellen's prolific career as a researcher was also evidenced through her participation in many projects funded by SSHRCC and by Health and Welfare Canada, research that explored the intersections among ethnicity, immigrant status, class, gender, work, and health. As a teacher and mentor of emerging social scientists, Ellen's reputation was stellar; her warmth, compassion, commitment, and integrity invoked the "very best" in her students, many of whom pursued successful careers in academia and public service. Ellen's achievements were recognized by the Canadian Sociology and Anthropology Association's Outstanding Contribution Award in 2001 and posthumously by the International Research Promotion Council's Eminent Scientist of the Year 2004 Award.

EDWARD GRABB is a professor of sociology at the University of Western Ontario. His research focuses on the study of social inequality and comparative sociology, especially comparisons of Canada and the United States. Apart from many articles in top scholarly journals, his publications include *Regions Apart: The Four Societies of Canada and the United States* (2005), co-authored with James Curtis, and *Theories of Social Inequality: Classical and Contemporary Perspectives* (2002). He is also co-editor, with James Curtis and Neil Guppy, of *Social Inequality in Canada: Patterns, Problems, Policies* (2004). He has served as associate or consulting editor for both the *Canadian Review of Sociology and Anthropology* and the *Canadian Journal of Sociology*.

DAVID A. GREEN is a professor in the Department of Economics at the University of British Columbia. His recent research includes work with Paul Beaudry investigating the impact of technological change on labour markets ("The Changing Structure of Wages in the US and Germany: What Explains the Difference?" *American Economic Review* 93 [2003]). He has received a UBC Killam Research Prize and twice won the Harry Johnson Prize for best article in the *Canadian Journal of Economics* in a year. His current research focuses on links between redistributive policies and labour market outcomes.

JONATHAN R. KESSELMAN is a professor in the Graduate Public Policy Program at Simon Fraser University Vancouver and holds the Canada Research Chair in Public Finance. He was a professor of economics at the University of British Columbia (1972-2003), director of the UBC Centre for Research on Economic and Social Policy (1994-2003), and principal investigator of the Equality, Security, and Community project (1998-2004). His work has been recognized by the Reserve Bank of Australia's Professorial Fellowship in Economic Policy, the Doug Purvis Memorial Prize for Canadian economic policy research, and the Canadian Tax Foundation's Douglas Sherbaniuk Award for tax policy research. His research ranges widely over theoretical and policy aspects of taxation, income security, social insurance, and the tax-transfer interface.

KAREN M. KOBAYASHI is an assistant professor in the Department of Sociology and a research affiliate at the Centre on Aging at the University of Victoria. Her research interests focus on intergenerational relationships in visible minority and immigrant families over the life course, the "healthy immigrant effect" in mid-to-later life, and the social and cultural determinants of health and aging, in particular, the relationship between social networks, social support, and health services utilization in older adult populations.

THOMAS LEMIEUX is a professor of economics and a Distinguished University Scholar at the University of British Columbia. He is a research associate at the

National Bureau of Economic Research and the director of the Team for Advanced Research on Globalization, Education, and Technology at UBC. His research awards include the Canadian Economics Association's Rae Prize, UBC's Killam Senior Research Prize, and the Minnesota Award. He has published forty articles and two books on topics that include the underground economy, the impact of collective bargaining, the determination of ethnic and gender wage differentials, and the estimation of sectoral choice models. His recent research focuses on the determinants of the structure of wages in industrialized economies and on the causes and consequences of secular changes in educational attainment.

LYNN LETHBRIDGE has been a researcher with the Department of Economics at Dalhousie University for more than ten years. Her research interests include child health and well-being, poverty and inequality, and gender-related issues. Recently she has started work at Dalhousie University's Department of Medicine measuring quality of care indicators for women with breast cancer.

COLIN M. MACLEOD is an associate professor in the Faculty of Law and the Department of Philosophy at the University of Victoria. His research focuses on issues in contemporary moral, political, and legal theory with a special focus on distributive justice and equality; children, families, and justice; and democratic ethics. He is the author of *Liberalism, Justice, and Markets: A Critique of Liberal Equality* (Oxford University Press, 1998) and co-editor with David Archard of *The Moral and Political Status of Children* (Oxford University Press, 2002).

LARS OSBERG is McCulloch Professor of Economics at Dalhousie University. He attended Queen's University, the London School of Economics, and Yale University and served as a CUSO volunteer in Tanzania. The most recent of his ten books is *The Economic Implications of Social Cohesion* (edited 2003). He is also the author of numerous refereed articles, reports, and book chapters. His major research interests have been the extent and causes of poverty and economic inequality, with particular emphasis on social policy, social cohesion, and the implications of working time, unemployment, and structural change in labour markets. He was president of the Canadian Economics Association in 1999-2000 and is currently review editor for the *Review of Income and Wealth*. Recent papers can be found at http://myweb.dal.ca/osberg/.

KRISHNA PENDAKUR is an associate professor in the Department of Economics at Simon Fraser University. His research interests include economic inequality, poverty, and discrimination. He currently serves as an associate editor for the *Journal of*

Business and Economic Statistics and as co-organizer of the Applied Welfare Economics Study Group in Verona, Italy. His papers are available at http://www.sfu.ca/~pendakur.

THOMAS PERKS is an assistant professor in the Department of Sociology at the University of Lethbridge. His areas of research interest include social capital, social inequality, sport, and research methodology. His research includes collaboration with Jim Curtis and colleagues on trends in voluntary association activity over recent decades in Quebec and English Canada, and on patterns of public protest. He is co-author of a chapter on gender and community participation in Fiona Kay and Richard Johnston, eds., *Social Capital, Diversity, and the Welfare State* (2006).

SHELLEY PHIPPS is a professor and holder of the Maxwell Chair in the Department of Economics at Dalhousie University. She received degrees from the University of Victoria and the University of British Columbia. She has served as president of the Canadian Women Economists' Network and as academic director of the Atlantic Research Data Centre. Past research has focused on the health and well-being of Canadian children, the implications of women's paid and unpaid work for women's health, international comparisons of social policy, poverty, and inequality, and decision-making within families. Current interests include the economic vulnerability of Canadian families with children in terms of time as well as money and the implications of child disability for parental health and labour market participation.

GARNETT PICOT is director-general of the Socio-Economic and Business Analysis Branch of Statistics Canada. His research interests include topics such as earnings inequality, poverty, job stability, economic outcomes in cities and neighbourhoods, immigrant economic assimilation, worker displacement, job creation and destruction, and firm behaviour. He has written over thirty papers on these and other topics. He also has a strong interest in data development and has worked on the development of longitudinal surveys such as the Survey of Labour and Income Dynamics and the Workplace and Employee Survey. He has held positions at the University of British Columbia, the Department of Trade and Commerce in the BC Government, the federal Secretary of State, and Canadian General Electric. He holds degrees in Electrical Engineering and Economics.

STEVEN G. PRUS is an associate professor in the Department of Sociology and Anthropology at Carleton University. He has published several articles on economic and health inequalities over the life course. His current research looks at how various social factors, especially age and socioeconomic status, interact to shape the health of Canadians.

W. CRAIG RIDDELL is a Royal Bank Faculty Research Professor in the Economics Department at the University of British Columbia. His research interests are in labour economics, labour relations, and public policy. His current research is focused on skill formation, education and training, unemployment and labour market dynamics, experimental and non-experimental approaches to social program evaluation, unionization and collective bargaining, and unemployment insurance and social assistance. In addition to numerous publications in books and academic journals, he is co-author of the leading labour economics textbook, *Labour Market Economics: Theory, Evidence and Policy in Canada*. He is former head of the Department of Economics at the University of British Columbia, former academic co-chair of the Canadian Employment Research Forum, and past president of the Canadian Economics Association.

TAMMY SCHIRLE is an assistant professor in the Department of Economics at Wilfrid Laurier University. She earned her PhD in Economics at the University of British Columbia in 2006. Her research interests include the economics of the elderly, income inequality, social policy, and the economics of gender. Her recent research has focused on the labour market behaviour of older individuals, with an emphasis on the joint labour supply decisions of older couples and the effects of health and pensions on retirement behaviour.

Index

labour force participation, 21, 314
unpaid labour, and distributive
    equality, 49-50, 52-53, 54-55
wage gains, comparison with men,
    315-316, 315(f)
wage structure, 329, 332(t), 333(f),
    334(t), 335, 336(t)
wage inequality
    and education, 284-85, 284(f),
        285(f), 294(t)-295(t)
    by age, 287, 287(f)
    by education-experience, 289(f),
        291, 291(f), 292(f), 293, 297,
        297(f), 299(f), 300(f), 301-2
well-being and earnings mobility, 8-9,
    120-21, 122
work hours. *See* hours of work; working
    time

working time
    cross-country comparison, 155, 159-
        60, 162(t), 167
    labour/leisure choice model, 11, 12,
        158-60
    measurement issues, 179-82
    "time culture" of countries and social
        values, 163-64
    and well-being, 155-56
    women's work in home, 164-67
    working hours per household and
        income distribution, 177-79
    See also employment; hours of work
World Values Survey (WVS), 165, 190,
    199-205

Zandvakili progressivity index, 356(t),
    363

Printed and bound in Canada by Friesens

Set in Giovanni and Scala Sans by Artegraphica Design

Text design: Irma Rodriguez

Copy editor: Larry MacDonald

Proofreader: Dianne Tiefensee

Indexer: Annette Lorek